The Case Approach to Financial Planning

Bridging the Gap between Theory and Practice, Third Edition

John E. Grable, Ph.D., CFP

National Underwriter Academic Series

ISBN 978-1-945424-02-1

THE NATIONAL UNDERWRITER COMPANY

Copyright © 2008, 2013, 2016
The National Underwriter Company
a division of ALM Media, LLC
4157 Olympic Blvd., Suite 225
Erlanger, KY 41018

Third Edition

Printed in the United States of America

ABOUT THE AUTHOR

JOHN E. GRABLE, Ph.D., CFP®

Professor and Athletic Association Endowed Professor of Financial Planning at the University of Georgia

John Grable received his undergraduate degree in economics and business from the University of Nevada, an MBA from Clarkson University, and a Ph.D. from Virginia Tech. He teaches and conducts research in the CFP Board of Standards Inc. undergraduate and graduate program at the University of Georgia. Prior to entering the academic profession he worked as a pension/benefits administrator and later as a Registered Investment Advisor in an asset management firm. Dr. Grable served as the founding editor for the *Journal of Personal Finance*, a rigorous peer-reviewed research journal. He served as the founding co-editor of the *Journal of Financial Therapy* and as the academic editor of the *Journal of Financial Planning* from 2013 through 2015. His research interests include financial risk-tolerance assessment, financial planning help-seeking behavior, behavioral financial planning, and financial therapy/counseling. He is the Director of the Financial Planning Performance Lab a The University of Georgia. He has been the recipient of several research and publication awards and grants, and he is active in promoting the link between research and financial planning practice where he has published numerous refereed papers, co-authored two financial planning textbooks, and co-edited a financial planning and counseling scales book. In 2015, he was recognized as one of the five most published authors in the field of financial planning. Dr. Grable has served on the Board of Directors of the International Association of Registered Financial Consultants (IARFC), as Treasurer and President for the American Council on Consumer Interests (ACCI), and as Board member and Treasurer for the Financial Therapy Association. He currently serves on the financial planning advisory board at Berkeley College. He also served on the Research Advisory Council of the Take Charge America Institute (TCAI) for Consumer Education and Research at the University of Arizona. He is the recipient of the prestigious Cato Award for Distinguished Journalism in the Field of Financial Services, the IARFC Founders Award, the Dawley-Scholer Award for Faculty Excellence in Student Development, and the ACCI Mid-Career Award.

ABOUT THE AUTHOR

JOHN E. CRABBE Ph.D. CPP

ACKNOWLEDGMENTS

Creating a book of this magnitude is not without challenges. Several individuals have been instrumental in keeping the project on task. First and foremost, I will always be grateful for the help of Dr. Ruth Lytton and Derek Klock of Virginia Tech. I am also indebted to my editor at *The National Underwriter Company*—Jason Gilbert. Jason showed unwavering confidence in this casebook concept. Without his editorial leadership this edition of the book would never have come to fruition. His encouragement, patience, and editing skills made this revision come together. Thanks also goes to Gerry Centrowitz and Jay Caslow for fully supporting this book from revision to publication. The anonymous reviewers who spent countless hours evaluating chapters prior to publication also deserve sincere thanks.

I am also thankful for the opportunity to have worked with undergraduate, graduate, and certificate financial planning students over the past decade. The idea of this case book was formulated through this daily work with students. I am immensely thankful for what each student has taught me. Although students do not generally know this, the reality is that to teach is to learn again. Each student I have had in class has challenged me to strive for better ways to explain and teach financial planning.

Additionally, I am very grateful to all of my colleagues around the country (and world) who have adopted this book and stuck with me through these revisions. I am honored to be a part of each instructor's class. Finally, I would also like to say a special "thank you" to my family. Without your support this revision of the book would never have been completed.

PREFACE

The profession of financial planning has expanded quickly since its inception in 1969. During the 1960s and 1970s, financial planning consisted of little more than a small consortium of financial service professionals interested in offering clients something in addition to insurance and mutual fund products. Since those early days financial planning has grown into a dynamic, growing, and respected profession. The importance of financial planning, as a career, is captured in broad but dynamic statements such as "financial planners and wealth managers help individuals plan their financial futures."[1] Financial planning is perennially ranked as one of the top five fastest growing and most prestigious careers. It is not surprising that the Bureau of Labor Statistics has predicted that employment opportunities for personal financial advisers will continue to grow much faster than average. The Bureau projects more than a 32 percent growth in employment through 2020, which is more than twice the average growth rate for all other occupations.[2]

One outcome associated with the growth of the financial planning profession is that the study of financial planning has taken root as an academic discipline on college campuses. It is possible today to obtain an undergraduate and graduate education in financial planning. The need for a case study methodology to help educate future financial planners has been ongoing since the first financial planning courses were developed. The 2012 requirement that a financial plan development course be included in the curriculum for all students undertaking a CFP Board of Standards, Inc., registered program cemented this need. With the growing demand for well-educated financial planners, the demand for cases today is more apparent than ever. *A Case Approach to Financial Planning: Bridging the Gap between Theory and Practice, Third Edition* was written to meet the need for a comprehensive case study methodology textbook.

This text was not designed to be simply another casebook, nor was it conceptualized as an advanced financial planning book or a CFP® certification exam preparation book—although some have noted that, to some extent, it is a combination of all three. As a casebook, this text includes a comprehensive teaching case, fifteen cases, and numerous computational examples and practice problems. As an advanced financial planning book, it provides a review of basic—and in some chapters, more advanced—content, particularly as applied to strategy development. Finally, as a CFP® certification exam preparation book, it attempts to provide a review of relevant content matched to many of the nearly all of the CFP Board topical areas. *A Case Approach to Financial Planning, Third Edition* is the first and only book of its kind where the advanced concepts of developing an integrated financial plan are presented from the foundation of a client situational analysis leading to actionable recommendations that can be critiqued and combined into a comprehensive financial plan.

PURPOSE

This book was written to illustrate how the financial planning process can be used to help clients achieve multiple financial goals and objectives through a financial plan. A second purpose of the book was to provide quality case studies to practice the case study methodology and help students gain confidence in identifying, applying, and integrating synergistic personal financial planning strategies into plans. Several objectives guided the development of the book:

- A review of the steps necessary to complete a current situation analysis in the core content areas of financial planning;

- Summarized reviews of commonly used financial planning product and procedural strategies;

- A review of the unique challenges of each core content area as applied to a special population or more narrowly defined financial planning audience;

- A continuous case that can be used to practice current situation analyses and to write a comprehensive financial plan;

- Computational questions and client-centered case studies that illustrate the use of specific strategies to meet client needs;

- End-of-chapter analytical practice problems that apply core content planning knowledge from each chapter; and

- Several targeted financial planning cases that address and, in some situations, integrate specific financial planning knowledge.

UNDERLYING ASSUMPTIONS

When first conceptualized, *A Case Approach to Financial Planning* was unlike any other casebook of its kind. Little has changed today except that the demand for a case study methodology for developing a plan, cases for applying knowledge and practicing skills, and models for integrated, actionable financial planning recommendations continues to grow. This third edition has been refined to better meet the needs of students and instructors. Because of its unique focus, it is very important that readers fully understand the core assumptions of the book before reading chapters or completing case assignments. The following points comprise key underlying assumptions:

- This book assumes that readers already have a foundation in the understanding and applying the process of financial planning; thus, only a limited review of the process is provided in Chapter 1.

- This text is intended for use in mid-level or capstone courses in financial planning programs at colleges, universities, and certificate programs. It is appropriate for use at the undergraduate, graduate, and certificate levels. When used at the undergraduate level, it is assumed that the book will be used in the final course of a student's last year of study. Although a review of key financial planning assumptions is provided in each core content chapter, this book is not—nor should it be considered—a replacement for a financial planning textbook in each core content area. *A Case Approach to Financial Planning, Third Edition,* as the name implies, is primarily a case book that illustrates a case methodology in the context of the financial planning process.

- To successfully complete case assignments and questions, students are assumed to have already completed or be enrolled in classes in the six core areas of financial planning: Financial Situation Analysis, Tax Planning,

Insurance (Risk Management) Planning, Investment Planning, Retirement Planning, and Estate Planning. This text offers a review of important concepts and strategies, but in no way are the core content chapters intended to provide a comprehensive overview of each financial planning topic.

- This book is not intended for use solely as a CFP® examination study guide. The comprehensive case, the end-of-chapter materials, and the mini-cases were designed to help faculty and students assess minimum financial planning competencies. The cases can certainly help those who wish to sit for the comprehensive CFP® certification examination, but they are not intended for that purpose exclusively.

- *A Case Approach to Financial Planning, Third Edition* is intended to present timely and accurate information; however, the strategies, tools, and techniques presented are designed for educational purposes only. Although the author and outside reviewers have reviewed the information, data analysis methods, recommendations, strategies, and other material, some material presented in the text could be affected by changes in tax law, court findings, or future interpretations of rules and regulations. Therefore, the accuracy and completeness of the information, data, and opinions in the book are in no way guaranteed. The author specifically disclaim any personal, joint, or corporate (profit and nonprofit) liability for loss or risk incurred as a consequence of the content of the book.

FEATURES

Underlying the development of this text and the various student learning experiences is Bloom's taxonomy of cognitive skills.[3] For example, *knowledge* and *comprehension* are covered through the traditional presentation and testing of financial planning concepts. *Application* and *analysis* are fostered through discussions of planning strategies, where students are challenged to evaluate the advantages and disadvantages of each relative to the needs of the individual client situation. The book excels at building skills in *synthesis* and *evaluation*. Designing an integrated, actionable plan matched to a client's situational factors and resources requires competency across Bloom's taxonomy of cognitive skills. Furthermore, faculty and peer review of the potential efficacy of a plan and its presentation to clients present additional opportunities to use the taxonomy of cognitive skills to foster identification of best practices and professional judgment.

Readers will find this book unique in focus and approach. Several educational strategies to promote student focus, retention, and research are repeated in each chapter, including the following:

- Learning objectives that summarize important financial planning concepts;

- Lists of key terms, shown in bold font and defined in the text;

- An updated index at the end of the book;

- A review of computational skills related to each content area;

- A presentation of important financial planning skills for each content area;

- A review of product and procedural strategies commonly used by financial planners for each content area;

- An expanded list of supplementary Chapter Resources and Notes to promote self-study or additional research, including books, journal articles, and internet information;

- A summary of important computations and formulas at the beginning of each content chapter, when appropriate, is new to the third edition; and

- The text and the website have been updated with several important pedagogical features to enhance student learning, as discussed below.

Chapter Overview

The book includes a review of the financial planning process (Chapters 1 and 14), personal finance math computations (Chapter 2), and a review of core financial planning content domains in Chapters 3 through 13. These chapters also include an explanation of several product and procedural strategies unique to each core content planning area.

One of the purposes of a financial planning case course is to provide a forum for students to develop and critique financial planning strategies matched to a client's needs. For many students, the capstone course is the only place in a college or university curriculum where all core content planning areas are reviewed and integrated in the context of a specific client situation. This book provides a variety of commonly used financial planning strategies matched to each core content planning area for classroom review and discussion. In addition, an assortment of computational examples and end-of-chapter problems are presented in each chapter. The major parts of the book and the content in each part include:

Part I—Review of the Process and Computational Skills for Developing a Financial Plan

1. *The Financial Planning Process*. This chapter describes the general financial planning process and outline of the book. The financial planning process, the basis of the case methodology, is also presented. The comprehensive Bedo financial planning case is introduced in an appendix to this chapter.

2. *Computations for Financial Planning*. This chapter provides a comprehensive review of key concepts related to time value of money and general personal finance calculations.

Part II—Analyzing and Evaluating a Client's Financial Status to Plan for Client Earnings

3. *Cash Flow and Net Worth Planning*. This chapter examines the process of analyzing and evaluating a client's current financial situation. It offers common planning strategies that financial planners regularly use to improve a client's cash flow and net worth position.

4. *Income Tax Planning.* The purpose of this chapter is to review the basic steps involved in analyzing and evaluating a client's current tax planning situation. In addition, the chapter provides a review of several widely used tax planning strategies.

Part III—Analyzing and Evaluating a Client's Financial Status to Plan for Client Risk Protection

5. *Life Insurance Planning.* This chapter reviews the basic steps involved in a financial planner's analysis and evaluation of a client's current life insurance situation. It also presents popular life insurance planning strategies.

6. *Health Insurance Planning.* This chapter reviews the fundamental steps of a financial planner's analysis of a client's current health insurance situation. Common health insurance strategies are presented.

7. *Disability Insurance Planning.* This chapter reviews the steps involved in conducting a disability insurance planning analysis, including several disability insurance planning strategies that can be adapted to meet client needs.

8. *Long-Term Care Insurance Planning.* This chapter examines the process underlying a financial planner's analysis and evaluation of a client's long-term care insurance situation. The chapter also presents common product and procedural strategies.

9. *Property and Liability Insurance Planning.* This chapter considers issues related to maximizing a client's plan for protecting property and minimizing liability exposure. The chapter reviews the fundamental steps in the analysis and evaluation of a client's current property and liability situation and presents examples of commonly used strategies used to protect client assets.

Part IV—Analyzing and Evaluating a Client's Financial Status to Plan for the Growth and Distribution of Assets

10. *Investment Planning.* In this chapter, important issues surrounding the analysis of a client's investment situation are explored. The investment planning process is reviewed and examples of how to develop strategies to meet client needs are provided. How investment strategies can influence a client's financial goals is explained.

11. *Education Planning.* The steps typically followed when analyzing and evaluating a client's current educational funding situation are reviewed. A selection of education funding strategies demonstrating how some financial planners strategize when planning for a client's education situation is presented.

12. *Retirement Planning.* This chapter describes the analysis and evaluation of a client's current situation and reviews common retirement planning strategies that can be used to meet retirement objectives. Strategies to develop recommendations for retirement planning across the life cycle are also provided.

13. *Estate Planning.* Essential steps for conducting an estate planning analysis are reviewed. A brief outline of how financial planners estimate a client's gross and taxable estate is provided. Other important issues are presented, such as transferring assets, providing for survivors or other legacy needs, and planning for incapacitation and other end-of-life decisions. The chapter ends with a review of how certain estate planning strategies can be used in the financial planning process.

Part V—Review of the Process

14. *Moving from Strategies to Plan Development.* This chapter reviews important concepts related to recommendation development, plan implementation, and monitoring. Important considerations in ranking, integrating, and funding recommendations in the development of a comprehensive plan are explained and illustrated using financial planning forms.

Part VI—Financial Planning Case Studies

Fifteen multiple-choice cases appear in Part VI. Although these cases are not as comprehensive as the continuous Bedo family case that appears in Chapters 3 through 13, the mini-cases help develop a student's ability to quickly evaluate a client's current financial situation, arrive at correct outputs from analysis and calculations, and then choose from appropriate financial planning strategies to develop actionable recommendations for a financial plan. A financial planning ethics case is also presented in the unique format of dialogue in a play. The ethic's case is designed to test students' knowledge of securities rules and financial planning practice standards.

Planning for Special Populations

Revised for the third edition of this text, Chapters 3 through 13 each include one or two features called *Planning for Special Populations*. These features reflect the CFP Board of Standards, Inc. focus on planning for clients with special circumstances. These features also illustrate an important takeaway from the book; namely, the process can and should be applied consistently, regardless of differing planning situations or clients. Each chapter features a different special population to illustrate that planning needs likely differ based on each client's unique needs and complexities.

Case Studies and Quantitative/Analytical Mini-Case Problems

Although successfully developing a financial plan for a client situation is rewarding, the downside to conducting a case analysis is that the process can sometimes seem far removed from reality. This book attempts to bridge the gap between theory and practice by providing short cases and computational problems at the end of chapters 3 through 14. These chapter case studies illustrate how financial planning strategies can be developed and shaped into tools and matched to a client's situational factors to meet specific financial planning goals and objectives.

End-of-chapter quantitative and analytical problems challenge students to practice calculation and critical thinking procedures. These skills are essential to the application, synthesis, and evaluation needed to artfully analyze a client's situation, identify and match workable strategies to the client's situation, and then to integrate these strategies into actionable recommendations for implementation.

All of the cases, as well as the continuous Bedo case, are designed to remind students that despite the focus on analytical skills and detailed factual knowledge, clients—real people—and their financial goals and dreams are truly the reason for financial planning. As noted earlier, financial planners help clients, people with whom planners may develop relationships that span decades and often even generations, *plan* their financial futures.

Comprehensive Bedo Case

A significant feature of the book is the inclusion of the Tyler and Mia Bedo comprehensive case, which was designed to test a student's ability to evaluate a client's current financial situation, review strategies, develop recommendations, and integrate these recommendations into a comprehensive financial plan. Questions related specifically to the Bedo case are included at the end of Chapters 1 and 3 through 14. Questions can be answered using a time value of money calculator or self-developed Excel sheets. After answering the questions for each chapter, it will be possible to write a comprehensive financial plan for the Bedo family. New to the third edition is an added focus on oral, written, and graphic presentations in each core content chapter.

Two objectives guided the development of the Bedo case narrative. The first was to be as comprehensive as possible, meaning that it is difficult, if not impossible, to develop client alternatives for one section of the case without influencing other case sections. Second, the narrative was developed to support both simple and complex strategies and recommendations. This latter aspect of the case enables instructors to adapt the expectations to challenge students along the spectrum of financial planning knowledge and experience to provide unique client solutions.

Fillable Forms

The financial planning process promotes the repeated use of planning forms and procedures to guide and document the planning process. Some financial planners, instructors, and students find tools and techniques useful for framing a protocol to "attack" the issues presented by a client's situation. All of the forms presented in the book are available on the book's accompanying website at: http://pro.nuco.com/booksupplements/NUCollege-CaseBook3e.aspx as fillable forms for students and instructors to download and complete.

Instructor's Resources

A number of resources are available on the book's companion website for instructors. PowerPoint presentations are provided for each chapter. Answers to select end-of-chapter questions and the 15 mini-case questions are provided in a separate Instructor's Manual, which provides insight into possible case answers while showing solutions using the Financial Facilitator spreadsheet when applicable. Also, to keep the Bedo case fresh for use in different classes, suggestions are presented regarding how to make changes to the case to reduce student sharing of information without having to identify a new case each time the class is taught.

Tips for Case/Plan Development Success

The case study methodology presented in this book was developed and tested by the instructors at several universities over the past decade. The outcomes associated with these methods have been successful. During a fifteen-year period, teams of undergraduate students taught by the author have used the tools and techniques presented in this book to compete in and win several national collegiate financial planning championships. A team mentored by the author has competed in every Financial Planning Invitational championship since 2000. Many students who have used these tools in their plan writing course, using the case methodology, have gone on to pursue successful careers in the fields of financial planning and financial services.

Four aspects of student success are tied directly to how well students do when working on the development of financial planning strategies. First, successful students tend to have a strong proficiency in the use of personal finance calculators. Second, the best students have an interest in working with computer spreadsheets and confirming calculations obtained on their calculator with spreadsheets. Third, successful students do extremely well at applying critical thinking skills. Exploring issues, looking for the integration of concepts, and willingness to research and use reference materials are all indicators of success for those engaged in the case study method. Finally, the most successful students understand that developing a plan in response to a case situation—especially a comprehensive case—takes time. A commitment to taking the time to analyze a situation, develop strategies, craft workable client-centered recommendations, and work on ways to implement and monitor recommendations is critical to plan writing success.

Summary

It is my sincere hope that you find this revised edition of the *A Case Approach to Financial Planning* to be helpful in applying the financial planning process to the completion of case studies and when developing financial plans for clients. All of the changes, which are significant, in this edition have come about because of reader comments and suggestions. Please feel free to contact me if you have a suggestion for the next edition. My email is: grable@uga.edu.

Notes

1. Careers-in-Finance, *Careers in Financial Planning and Wealth Management*. Available at: www.careers-in-finance.com/fp.htm.

2. Bureau of Labor Statistics, *Occupational Outlook Handbook, Personal Financial Advisors*. Available at: www.bls.gov/ooh/business-and-financial/personal-financial-advisors.htm.

3. B. S. Bloom, *Taxonomy of Educational Objectives, Handbook I: The Cognitive Domain* (New York: David McKay, 1956)

ABBREVIATIONS COMMONLY USED IN FINANCIAL PLANNING

Alternative Minimum Tax—AMT

Assets Under Management—AUM

Accredited Investment Fiduciary®— AIF®

Certificate of Deposit—CD

Certified Financial Planner Board of Standards, Inc.—CFP Board

Certified Financial Planner® Certification Examination—CFP® exam

Certified Investment Management Analyst—CIMA

Certified Investment Management Consultant— CIMC (No longer awarded)

Certified Life Underwriter—CLU

Charitable Remainder Annuity Trust—CRAT

Charitable Remainder Unitrust—CRUT

Chartered Financial Analyst—CFA

Chartered Financial Consultant—ChFC

Chartered Investment Counselor—CIC

Chartered Life Underwriter—CLU

Consolidated Omnibus Budget Reconciliation Act of 1986—COBRA

Coverdell Education Savings Account—Coverdell ESA or CESA

Discretionary Cash Flow—DCF

Employee Retirement Income Security Act of 1974—ERISA

Enrolled Agent—EA

Errors and Omissions— E&O

Exchange Traded Fund—ETF

Financial Industry Regulatory Authority—FINRA

Financial Planning Association—FPA

Flexible Spending Account—FSA

Grantor Retained Annuity Trust—GRAT

Grantor Retained Unitrust—GRUT

Guaranteed Auto Protection Insurance—GAP Insurance

Health Insurance Portability and Accountability Act of 1996—HIPAA

Health Savings Account—HSA

High Deductible Health Plan—HDHP

Homeowners Policy—HO Policy

Incentive Stock Option—ISO

Individual Retirement Arrangement—IRA

Investment Advisor Representative—IAR

Investment Advisor Registration Depository —IARD

Investment Policy Statement—IPS

Internal Revenue Code—IRC

Internal Revenue Code Section 529—529 Plan

Internal Revenue Service—IRS

Irrevocable Life Insurance Trust—ILIT

Joint Tenancy with the Right of Survivorship—JTWROS

Long Term Care—LTC

Million Dollar Round Table—MDRT

National Association of Insurance Commissioners— NAIC

National Association of Personal Financial Advisors—NAPFA

North American Securities Administrators Association—NASAA

Payable on Death—POD

Personal Automobile Policy—PAP

Personal Financial Specialist—PFS

Qualified Personal Residence Trust— QPRT

Qualified Terminable Interest Property Trust—QTIP Trust

Real Estate Investment Trust—REIT

Registered Investment Advisor—RIA

Securities Investor Protection Corporation—SIPC

Self-Regulatory Organization—SRO

Transferable on Death—TOD

Uniform Gift to Minors Act Account—UGMA Account

Uniform Prudent Investor Act—UPIA

Uniform Transfers to Minors Act Account—UTMA Account

U.S. Securities and Exchange Commission—SEC

Variable Universal Life—VUL

SUMMARY TABLE OF CONTENTS

Part I: Review of the Process and Computational Skills
for Developing a Financial Plan

Part II: Analyzing and Evaluating a Client's Financial Status
to Plan for Client Earnings

Part III: Analyzing and Evaluating a Client's Financial Status
to Plan for Client Risk Protection

Part IV: Analyzing and Evaluating a Client's Financial Status to
Plan for the Growth and Distribution of Assets

Part V: Review of the Process

Part VI: Financial Planning—Case Studies

The fillable forms needed to complete text activities can be found on the student website at: http://pro.nuco.com/booksupplements/NUCollege-CaseBook3e.

DETAILED TABLE OF CONTENTS

Part I: Review of the Process and Computational Skills
for Developing a Financial Plan

PART I: Review of the Process and Computational Skills for Developing a Financial Plan

Chapter 1

A Review of the Financial Planning Process

Learning Objectives

1. The financial planning process, as defined by the Certified Financial Planner Board of Standards, Inc. (CFP Board), serves as a framework for guiding financial planners when providing services to client. CFP Board defines financial planning, the six steps that comprise the planning process, and the seven content areas typically included in the scope of financial planning. Financial planning typically includes, but is not limited to, seven content areas: (a) financial statement preparation and analysis (including cash flow analysis/planning and budgeting); (b) insurance planning and risk management; (c) employee benefits planning; (d) investment planning; (e) income tax planning; (f) retirement planning; and (g) estate planning.

2. Financial planners who hold the CFP® certification and those who are studying financial planning in a CFP Board registered program must follow *Financial Planning Practice Standards*, a *Code of Ethics*, and *Rules of Conduct* as promulgated by CFP Board.[1]

3. The financial planning process promotes the repeated use of planning forms and protocols to guide and document planning procedures and outcomes. Because of its organized, consistent methodology, this approach facilitates the organization and analysis of client data into a manageable format by focusing attention on critical planning needs. The process helps financial planners identify needs where additional client information or assistance from other professionals may be warranted, and discern routine and creative strategies that help clients meet household financial and personal goals. Perhaps most importantly, consistent use of the financial planning process can foster confidence that relevant issues have not been overlooked and planning for client needs has been done thoroughly and competently.

4. The breadth and depth of client information sought by a financial planner will vary with the scope of financial planning services provided. Qualitative data include information

Learning Objectives

on a client's temperament, personality, attitudes, beliefs and behaviors, all of which influence financial decisions and help the financial planner better understand the client, the client's map of reality, and the client's money scripts. Examples of quantitative data are socioeconomic descriptors, economic information, and other factual financial data. A client's financial knowledge and experience may reflect the interaction of both qualitative and quantitative information. Data are collected from original source documents (e.g., an income tax form), data intake forms or other questionnaires completed by the client, and focused interviews and other discovery meetings conducted by the financial planner.

5. This chapter introduces the entire financial planning process. Chapters 3 through 13 focus on Step 3 of the process—Analyze and Evaluate the Client's Financial Status—by reviewing analytical procedures and widely used financial planning strategies. Chapter 14 reviews issues related to recommendation development, plan writing, implementation, and monitoring of recommendations.

Key Terms

Actionable Recommendation

Analytical Skills

Analyzing and Evaluating a Client's
Financial Situation

Assumptions

Attitudes

Behaviors

Beliefs

Business Cycle

Certified Financial Planner

Certified Financial Planner (CFP) Board
of Standards, Inc.

CFP Board Rules of Conduct

Client Intake Form

Client Interviews

Client-Based Recommendations

Client-Centered Financial Planning

Client-Planner Interviews

Code of Ethics

Coincident Economic Indicators

Collaboration

Compensation Arrangements

Complementary Good

Conflicting Goals

Conflicts of Interest

Consumer Price Index (CPI)

Continuing Case

Cost of Recommendations

Credit Markets

Current Financial Situation

Data Gathering

Demographic Profile

Develop Client-Based Recommendations

Disclosure

Discount Rate

Discovery

Document Tracking Form

Economic Indicators

Empathy

Experiential Map

Federal Funds Rate

Federal Open Market Committee (FOMC)

Federal Reserve

Fiduciary

Financial Experience

Financial Knowledge

Financial Life Planning

Financial Planning

Financial Planning Practice Standards

Financial Planning Process

Financial Risk Tolerance

Key Terms

Financial Therapy

Financial Well-Being

Fiscal policy

Focused Interview

Form ADV

Framing Goals and Objectives

Gather Data and Frame Goals and Objectives

Government Spending

Grable and Lytton Risk-Tolerance Scale

Gross Domestic Product (GDP)

Heuristics

IAPD Website

Identification

Implementation Questions

Inflation

Intermediate-Term Goal

Lagging Economic Indicators

Law of Supply and Demand

Leading Economic Indicators

Life Cycle Events

Life Transition

Lifestyle Factors

Liquidity

Long-Term Goal

Macroeconomic Concepts

Microeconomic Concepts

Modular Financial Plan

Monetary Policy

Money Disorders

Money Scripts

Money Talk

Multiple-Choice Mini-Cases

Objectivity

Open-Ended Questions

Opportunity Costs

Opt-Out Procedures

Personal Goal Hierarchy

Planning Recommendation Form

Price Elasticity

Privacy Statement

Problematic Money Behaviors

Procedural Strategy

Producer Price Index (PPI)

Product Knowledge

Product Strategy

Professional Judgment

Professional Misconduct

Qualitative Data

Quantify

Key Terms

Quantitative Data

Registered Investment Advisor (RIA)

Reserve Requirements

Review Prospective Planning Strategies

Risk Capacity

Risk Tolerance

Robo-Advisors

Rules of Conduct

Securities and Exchange Commission (SEC)

Short-Term Goal

Situational Factors

Social Status

Socioeconomic Descriptors

Source Documents

Standardized Interview

Standards of Professional Conduct

Substitute Good

Suitability

Supporting Documents

Financial Planning Process

Targeted Financial Plan

Temperament

Time Horizon

Transformation

Uniform Application for Investment Advisor Registration

Yield Curve

Yield to Maturity (YTM)

CFP® Student-Centered Learning Objectives

A.1. CFP Board's Code of Ethics and Professional Responsibility and Rules of Conduct

A.2. CFP Board's Financial Planning Practice Standards

A.3. CFP Board's Disciplinary Rules and Procedures

B.8. Financial Planning Process

B.12 Economic Concepts

B.14. Client and Planner Attitudes, Values, Biases, and Behavioral Finance

B.15. Principles of Communication and Counseling

DEFINING THE FINANCIAL PLANNING PROCESS: DETERMINING THE NEED

Disciplinary Rules

Only CFP® practitioners and students enrolled in a CFP Board registered academic program are required to abide by the CFP Board Code of Ethics and follow all CFP Board rules and regulations.

Practice Principles

The CFP Board Code of Ethics and Professional Responsibility is premised on the following seven principles:

1. Integrity
2. Objectivity
3. Competence
4. Fairness
5. Confidentiality
6. Professionalism
7. Diligence

The growth of financial planning, both as a recognized profession and as an important behavioral change force in the lives of individuals and families, has been remarkable. Starting with fewer than fifty Certified Financial Planner (CFP®) certificants in the early 1970s, the number of CFP® certificants had grown to over 70,000 by 2016. Worldwide growth is outpacing growth in the United States. As the profession has expanded in recent years, the number of students studying financial planning has also grown.

Professional organizations and leading members of the financial planning community have defined financial planning in a variety of ways. The most recognized definition, offered by the **Certified Financial Planner Board of Standards, Inc. (CFP Board)**, defines financial planning as a process. According to CFP Board, **"Financial planning** denotes the process of determining whether and how an individual can meet life goals through the proper management of financial resources. Financial planning integrates the financial planning process with the financial planning subject areas."[2] In its *Standards of Professional Conduct*, CFP Board further explains the **financial planning process** as involving the following six steps:

1.   Establishing and defining the client-planner relationship;

2.   Gathering client data, including goals;

3.   Analyzing and evaluating the client's financial status;

4. Developing and presenting financial planning recommendations and/or alternatives;

5. Implementing the financial planning recommendations; and

6. Monitoring the financial planning recommendations.[3]

CFP Board identified the subject areas of the financial planning process as typically including, but not limited to, the following: financial statement preparation and analysis (including cash flow analysis/planning and budgeting); insurance planning and risk management; employee benefits planning; investment planning; income tax planning; retirement planning; and estate planning.

CFP Board has also developed and promulgated the *Financial Planning Practice Standards*, a *Code of Ethics*, and *Rules of Conduct*—all of which have evolved with the profession to guide professional actions and benefit consumers. Specifically, the CFP Board noted that the Practice Standards are intended to:

- Assure that the practice of financial planning by CFP professionals is based on established norms of practice;

- Advance professionalism in financial planning; and

- Enhance the value of the financial planning process.[4]

Figure 1.1 CFP Board's Financial Planning Process, Content Areas, and Practice Principles

Steps in the Financial Planning Process:	Financial Planning Content Areas:	Practice Principles:
1. Establishing and defining the client-planner relationship;	1. Financial statement preparation and analysis	1. Integrity
2. Gathering client data, including goals;	2. Insurance planning and risk management	2. Objectivity
3. Analyzing and evaluating the client's financial status;	3. Employee benefits planning	3. Competence
4. Developing and presenting financial planning recommendations and/or alternatives;	4. Investment planning	4. Fairness
5. Implementing the financial planning recommendations; and	5. Income tax planning	5. Confidentiality
6. Monitoring the financial planning recommendations	6. Retirement planning	6. Professionalism
	7. Estate planning	7. Diligence

Whether a financial planner (1) produces a comprehensive plan, (2) works on a per-project basis focusing on analysis and advice, (3) writes a targeted or modular plan, (4) provides financial planning analysis—but no plan—as a means to provide products, or (5) develops a plan as a means to establish product needs he or she should the **financial planning process**. The constant in these situations is the fundamental process used to direct planning efforts. Use of the financial planning process not only helps guide the analytic work of a financial planner, the process also help define the presentation, implementation, and monitoring of a financial planning plan.

The financial planning process approach can also aid financial planners develop the methods to effectively collect and utilize appropriate client information. Although the financial planning process is intended for use by comprehensive financial planners, the process is equally applicable for those who want to conduct a defensible analysis of client investment or investment-based insurance product suitability. Financial planners who follow the process will have greater confidence that:

1. a client's personal and financial objectives will be incorporated into the planning process;

2. client goals and objectives are being met in an effective, efficient, and defensible way; and

3. the process can be easily documented.

It is important to identify accepted and effective methods for conducting work at Step 3—**Analyze and Evaluate the Client's Financial Status**—if norms of practice are to gain widespread acceptance. The focus of this book is on the core content planning areas that CFP Board refers to as "financial planning subject areas." Chapters 3 through 13 provide a review of the key strategies often used by financial planners when assessing a client's financial situation through risk cash flow and net worth management, tax evaluation, insurance management, investment planning, education planning, retirement planning, and estate planning.

Because financial planners must go beyond comprehension of isolated analytical methods to the application, analysis, synthesis, and evaluation levels of knowledge and skill to craft an integrated comprehensive financial plan, the case study methodology is an ideal way to practice. Consequently, the need for financial planning cases has increased. To that end, a comprehensive client case, the *Bedo household*, is introduced as an appendix to this chapter. This **continuing case** provides practice in analyzing and evaluating the Bedos' financial situation in each of the core financial planning content areas in Chapters 3 through 13. The end-of-chapter Bedo Case Analysis Questions lead the reader through the planning process. Product and procedural strategies at the end of each core content planning chapter can be used to answer case questions and help students build an arsenal of strategies for future use.

Finally, Chapter 14 provides an overview of Steps 4, 5, and 6 of the financial planning process. Chapter 14 describes the method by which client specific recommendations are integrated and prioritized for formulation into a comprehensive financial plan that can then be implemented and monitored in response to a client's goals. Thus, this chapter offers the opportunity to integrate the Bedos' situation and financial planning needs in a comprehensive manner. Throughout the book the concept is emphasized that planning is a process, and a decision made in one core content area of a client's plan will undoubtedly influence other planning areas. The continuing Bedo case is designed to enhance communication skills, decision-making skills, and critical thinking skills, as well as problem structuring and problem-solving abilities—all of which must be demonstrated throughout the planning process, but which are particularly relevant in the last three steps of the financial planning process.

Several **multiple-choice mini-cases** are provided in Part VI: Additional Financial Planning Case Studies. Each case is targeted to one or a few core financial planning content areas. Sometimes a client's objectives can be met most effectively through a **targeted financial plan** or **modular financial plan** in which recommendations are focused on one or a few specific client goals. These cases provide opportunities to practice the planning process and explore some of the complexities involved when conducting modular planning.

Whether a financial planner writes a comprehensive or targeted financial plan independently or with the help of a professional software package, the craft of (1) analyzing a client's situation, (2) identifying strategies, and (3) developing recommendations can be improved by applying the case study approach. Becoming a proficient financial planner entails adequate time devoted to understanding and practicing the process of planning. In the end, there is only one way to truly become more proficient at analyzing financial cases, fictional or real, and developing financial plans. The secret is deceptively simple: practice and apply the tools and techniques learned in the classroom to client situations. Over time, the process will become so routine that it is followed reflexively, and the goals of establishing norms of practice, advancing professionalism, and promoting the value of the financial planning process will be achieved. Accomplishing these goals will benefit students and professionals individually, benefit the profession globally and—most importantly—ensure that clients are well served.

Financial Planning Process Skills

It is quite common for novice financial planners to search diligently for a single correct answer when addressing a client's questions. While a written financial planning cases study will generally have one right answer, real life financial planning does not always lend itself to a single correct response. As acknowledged by CFP Board, there may be multiple solutions that enable a client to reach a goal. These answers flow from subjective **professional judgment**. Client situations can be addressed in multiple ways by different financial planners. Some recommendations might be equally effective and others dismissed as less likely to result in successful goal attainment or simply ill-conceived. Some strategies, although generally valid and workable, might not match a client's values or personality. It is important for students and practitioners to thoroughly review the methodology used to guide the progression from strategies and recommendations to a final plan.

This approach to financial planning promotes the repeated use of planning forms and protocols to guide and document the planning process. Some financial planners will find tools and techniques useful for framing a protocol to "attack" the issues presented by a client's situation. Others will conclude that such tools limit creativity and are cumbersome or repetitive. Overall, however, because the approach is methodical and organized, planning tools can help financial planners:

- Organize what may initially appear to be an overwhelming mass of data and analysis into a manageable format,

- Focus attention on critical planning needs,

- Focus attention on problems or issues that might require research or consultation with other professionals,

- Focus attention on issues or questions that require additional input from the client,

- Recognize the need for creative alternatives to meet the client's goals, and

- Feel confident that relevant issues have not been overlooked.

Finally, it is important to note that the conceptualization of the process as distinct and sequential steps is a conceptual representation of the reality of planning. In actual client work, and when done in the context of different business planning models, some activities might not occur exactly as described. Because of the recursive nature of the financial planning process, several steps can be ongoing and overlapping as the client progresses through the process on different goals and objectives. Also, as a result of monitoring the plan for changes needed in response to the client's situation; the success of the products or strategies recommended; or the current economic, market, or tax environment, it may be necessary to start the process over for some goals or objectives.

Planning Skill 1: Mastering the Process of Establishing and Defining the Relationship[5]

The financial planning process begins by **establishing and defining the financial planner-client relationship**. This step is complicated by the need to combine professional, disclosure, and contractual responsibilities with initiating a trusting and personal yet professional financial planner-client relationship. At this stage of the process a planner initiates the relationship with potential clients (by referral or marketing strategies), meets with prospective clients to discuss potential products and services, and formalizes the scope of the client-planner engagement. The relationship should begin by outlining the responsibilities of both planner and client and the extent of the contractual arrangement. Specifically, **conflicts of interest, compensation arrangements**, the length of the agreement period, and the products or services to be provided should be fully disclosed and agreed on. In short, Step 1 of the planning process encompasses the regulatory, contractual, and professional expectations of the client-planner relationship.

Professional practice expectations and regulatory agencies determine the objectives of this step. For example, the **Securities and Exchange Commission (SEC)** and state regulatory agencies require that a **registered investment advisor (RIA)** distribute Part 2 of **Form ADV**—the **Uniform Application for Investment Advisor Registration**—to prospective clients before or at the time an agreement is executed. Similarly, a **privacy statement** and **opt-out procedures** for sharing information with nonaffiliated third parties must be provided before the agreement is executed. The privacy statement must be provided annually, and clients must be informed of material changes in ADV Part 2 and offered a copy annually. The most recent copy of an investment adviser's Form ADV is available at the Investment Financial planner Public Disclosure Web site (typically referred to as the *IAPD Website*), for either state- or SEC-registered financial planners.

Planning Skill 2: Mastering the Process of Gathering Data and Faming Goals and Objectives

The second step in the financial planning process involves **collecting information and identifying client goals**. Client information can be obtained through **data collection questionnaires** (completed by the client independently or in conjunction with the financial planner), client-planner **interviews**, and original source documents provided by the client. Regardless of the method(s) utilized, however, the primary objective is for the financial planner to gather vital financial and personal information— quantitative and qualitative—that encourages discussion. Best planning practices suggest that clients should be encouraged to complete basic data forms independently, via hard copy or secure encrypted electronic access, whenever possible. This frees up financial planner-client meeting time to review the **quantitative data** to ensure full understanding by both parties, and it allows more time to explore the client's values, goals, dreams, attitudes, and beliefs.

The importance attributed to attitudes, beliefs, and values—all forms of **qualitative data**— in shaping both the client's relationship with money and the client's goals has expanded this aspect of the **data-gathering** or **discovery process**, with clients.

Klontz, Kahler, and Klontz noted that **money scripts**, which they defined as "unconscious beliefs people hold about money, often unexplored and only partially true [that] are formed in childhood,"[6] can have a significant influence on adult money behaviors. They offered exercises for exploring money scripts as well as issues related to **money disorders** (e.g., compulsive spending or hoarding)

Who is a Client?

CFP Board defines a client as, "a person, persons, or entity who engages a certificant and for whom professional services are rendered. Where the services of the certificant are provided to an entity (corporation, trust, partnership, estate, etc.), the client is the entity acting through its legally authorized representative.

CFP Board further requires that financial planning services be accompanied by a written agreement that identifies:

1. the parties to the agreement;

2. the date of the agreement and its duration;

3. the procedure and terms for terminating the agreement; and

4. a description of the services to be provided as part of the agreement.

and **problematic money behaviors** (e.g., overspending or underspending).

Financial life planning is an offshoot of traditional planning methodologies that is most closely aligned with the use of qualitative data. The definition and scope of **financial life planning** as actually practiced by financial advisers varies; however, the focus of financial life planning has tended to be grounded in a client's past, present, and future life. Financial life planning integrates financial planning and **financial therapy**. Exploring a client's attitudes, beliefs, and values can encompass the emotional, experiential, and spiritual issues that influence not only the use of money, but also the goals that frame a meaningful life for the client. Because of the scope of the questions and methods that might be employed in this holistic exploration, this portion of the data collection process has come to be called *discovery* or referred to as **discovery meetings**.

There are two very important outcomes associated with discovery meetings: (1) the establishment of **trust** between the parties and (2) the exploration and collection of information to help the financial planner understand the client and the client's financial situation. Because of the significance of this step, and the variety of approaches utilized in practice, the following discussion focuses on the abstract and practical implications of four fundamental questions:

1.   What client data are collected?

2.   How does the planner use the data?

3.   How are the data collected?

4.   What does it mean to frame goals and objectives?

Planning Skill 3: Determine What Data Are Collected?

Financial planners are challenged daily to gain enough information to fully understand a client, assess the client's situation, and generate a workable plan that is acceptable to the client, and to do so effectively and efficiently. As if this was not sufficiently challenging, it is important to remember that most people find talking about money to be difficult. **Money talk** is generally culturally unacceptable. For many individuals, any talk of money is laden with emotional undertones that may reflect explicit memories (good or bad) or an implicit uneasiness that defies explanation. It is not hard to understand why many financial planners prefer the safety of products to the psyche of the client, but increasingly planners are considering both.

There are four **situational factors** that characterize clients and influence their money scripts. The first three factors also characterize financial planners—as both individuals and professionals. These factors are:

1. *Temperament and Personality.* **Temperament** is commonly explained by inherited cross-cultural traits that characterize mood or disposition. Behavioral, emotional, and attitudinal tendencies comprise **personality**. Together, these dimensions profile individuals and offer insight into their relationships with others and with money. An extroverted client who is talkative, full of life, and spontaneous will likely have a very different view of retirement than the introvert who is organized, disciplined, and enjoys a quiet home life. A moody, anxious client who lacks organization and persistence might be easily distracted from financial goals; such clients could require more planner and staff time to collect needed data or need more motivation to implement recommendations.

> ### Self-Test 2
>
> Lionel is preparing for a meeting with a prospective client. Under CFP Board rule, all of the following must be disclosed to the client, EXCEPT:
>
> a. Lionel's marital status.
>
> b. Lionel's fee schedule.
>
> c. Any conflicts of interest.
>
> d. Only b and c.

2. *Attitudes, Beliefs, and Behaviors.* Attitudes, beliefs, and **behaviors** are interrelated concepts in that attitudes and beliefs are thought to affect behavior. **Attitudes** may reflect an individual's views, opinions, desires, choices, purposes, or values. Although the concept of belief connotes different meanings, in psychology **beliefs** are recognized as a type of attitude because the belief reflects an interpretation, expectation, or claim about some aspect of life. Values represent strongly held attitudes. Beliefs indicate an individual's perception of what is right or desirable. **Values** are said to reflect an individual's fundamental meaning or interpretation of life and as such are a significant influence on personal goals and choices.

Although other attitudes related to *financial well-being*, economic trends, or market returns can be assessed, a client's financial risk tolerance is the attitude most frequently considered. **Financial risk tolerance** is defined as the maximum amount of risk a client is willing to take when faced with a choice that entails the possibility of a financial loss. This attitude affects a wide range of financial decisions beyond the obvious applications of investments, retirement planning, or investment-based insurance, where questions of **suitability** are typical and assessment of risk tolerance is required. There is a need to understand the client for the purposes of **client-centered financial planning** as well as a need to document the client's risk tolerance for regulatory compliance. To accomplish this, some financial planners use scales included in financial planning software or provided by their broker-dealer or custodian, while others purchase psychometric tests from independent firms, such as FinaMetrica, RiskAlyze, Pocket Risk, and Oxford Risk. Still other firms rely on publically available risk scales, such as the popular **Grable and Lytton Risk-Tolerance Scale**.[7]

Considered in the context of portfolio management, *risk tolerance* centers on a client's reactions to, or level of comfort with, losses in investment value. A client's risk tolerance can also influence decisions concerning the type of mortgage, debt level, emergency fund, choice of insurance coverage, tax preparation approach, or estate tools. A client with a high level of risk tolerance can be expected to take greater risks and act with less information than less risk-tolerant individuals who require that more certainty be associated with financial decisions.

3. *Financial Knowledge and Experience.* **Financial knowledge** and **financial experience** sometimes represent the most extreme difference between financial planner and client; both parties bring different levels of knowledge and experience to the planning engagement. Some clients lack knowledge, while others may have the knowledge but lack confidence and want a financial planner to confirm that their "financial situation is okay." Professional responsibility and **CFP Board Rules of Conduct** constrain CFP practitioners to offering services within the purview of their acknowledged expertise that is suitable based on a client's knowledge, experience, and **risk capacity** (i.e., the financial ability of a client to withstand a potential financial loss). Some recommendations will almost certainly include products or services about which a client lacks experience or knowledge. In such cases, it becomes even more important to educate clients about the risks and benefits of the product or service.

4. *Socioeconomic Descriptors.* **Socioeconomic descriptors** represent a broad range of factual or quantitative characteristics to describe clients. Categories of information include the **demographic profile** of a client's household, including relevant medical history or other factors that can influence client goals, financial data (income, assets, liabilities, insurance coverage, etc.), and a description of the client's lifestyle (or what might be referred to as **social status** or position). **Lifestyle factors** can include travel, hobbies, collectibles, leisure activities, personal property, or real estate that supports the client's lifestyle.

Gathering client data needed for a thorough and defensible evaluation of a client's situation—whether for a single issue analysis, to support a product sale, or to complete a comprehensive plan—may appear intrusive, but in fact these data provide a foundation for the client's financial future. Throughout the planning process, the financial planner or planning team must demonstrate to the client genuine **empathy**, balanced with rigorous **analytical skills** and **product knowledge**.

Planning Skill 4: Understand How a Financial Planner Uses Collected Data?

A client and financial planner enter the planning relationship with unique characteristics of temperament, personality, attitudes, beliefs, financial knowledge, and experience that shape the planning process. Without specific training, or the input of a trained professional such as a psychologist or a financial therapist as a part of the planning team, a financial planner's experience may be the best guide when working with the range of temperaments, personalities, attitudes, knowledge, and experience that a client may exhibit. The more a financial planner knows about a client, the greater the likelihood of developing a plan that will accommodate the client's unique situation. A financial planner's role is to collect and objectively process client data. However, three limitations must be acknowledged.

First, regardless of all efforts to function as objective, independent professionals, financial planners are constrained to some extent by their own personal temperament, personality, attitudes, beliefs, values, and financial knowledge and experience. These "filters" directly and indirectly influence the planning process. Although this may be equally true of other professionals, it is more apparent in financial planning because of the need to divulge extremely private information to craft a plan matched to a client's unique situation. Care must be taken to minimize the impact of personal feelings, interpretative judgments, subjective inferences, and opinions; all interpretations should be confirmed with the client.

Second, a financial planner is privy only to the information that a client is willing to share. Clients may knowingly withhold information from lack of trust or unknowingly because the information is thought to be irrelevant or was overlooked. Without a client's full disclosure, a financial planner will not be able to suggest optimal solutions. It is incumbent on financial planners to make every attempt to encourage clients to divulge as much relevant information as can be useful to the planning engagement.

Third, as professionals, financial planners must fully acknowledge their own limitations of expertise, **conflicts of interest**, or other paradigms could adversely influence or bias the client-planner relationship. Steps should be taken to compensate for or overcome such issues in the professional relationship. Typically, providing services a **fiduciary**—someone who places the client's needs above their own at all times—and providing full **disclosure** of conflicts of interest provide a way to deal with this issue.

Planning Skill 5: Establish a Procedure for Collecting Data

Several methods can be used to collect client data, initially at Step 2 of the financial planning process, and during ongoing financial planner-client meetings. Accuracy and security are primary concerns. As noted earlier, financial planners must strive for professional **objectivity** and extreme accuracy when collecting and recording client data. Care also must be taken to ensure, to the extent possible, that the client is candid and forthright as a way to counteract the tendency to not want to disclose information or to provide answers that are more socially acceptable or "what the planner expects." Financial planners should develop a secure system for collecting, organizing, and managing data throughout the planning process, as well as safeguarding these data for the future. Three data collection methods are considered below:

1. *Supporting Documents.* Original **source documents** can be used to verify information already provided by the client, while other documents can provide technical information beyond the scope of a client's knowledge. Clients can also authorize a financial planner to obtain data from other financial service professionals. For example, it may be appropriate to request tax form from a client's CPA or legal documents from the client's attorney. Care must be taken to safeguard these documents and the client's privacy and to return original documents quickly after electronic scanning or copying.

   Financial planners and clients can use a **Document Tracking Form** such as the one shown in Figure 1.2. This form can be used to trace the flow of original documents between parties. The supporting documents column can also be duplicated and modified to verify or acknowledge the receipt—or later, the return—of documents. These forms can include a line for the signatures of planning staff or the client, respectively, to verify transfers. This from can be completed for the household. Individual lines can be added in each category, as applicable, for spouses or partners, or a single form can be completed for each individual.

Figure 1.2 Client Supporting Document Tracking Form

Date Requested from Client	Date Received from Client	Date Returned to Client	Supporting Document (for Client 1, Client 2, and joint accounts, as applicable) Latest bank statement(s)
			Latest investment account statement(s)
			Loan statement(s) (e.g., real estate 1, real estate 2, car 1, car 2, boat/ motorcycle/ATV/R, student loan(s), etc.)
			Real estate deed, deed of trust, and HUD-1: summary of closing costs
			Latest credit card and/ or department store credit statement(s)
			Federal and state tax returns for the last three years
			All insurance policies (e.g., life, disability, health, homeowners, automobile, umbrella, etc.)
			Any current budget or record of spending
			Most recent paycheck stub(s)
			Employee benefit statement(s)
			Employee retirement plan statement(s)
			Other retirement plan statement(s)
			Summary of the retirement plan description
			Wills, trusts, or other estate planning documents
			Other:
			Other:

2. *The Client Intake Form.* Although not all financial planners use a formalized **client intake form** or **data collection questionnaire**, such forms provide several benefits. First, because data gathering can be somewhat subjective, it is a good policy to complete an objective data collection questionnaire with every client. To the extent it is completed with accuracy and candor, a well-designed form or questionnaire can capture a client's quantitative and, to a more limited extent, qualitative information. Second, a form can reduce professional liability claims from clients, family members, or legal entities. Financial planners who document client responses objectively and definitively are usually better prepared to defend themselves against claims of **professional misconduct**. Third, the consistent use of a standard form can help a planner pinpoint a client's financial strengths and weaknesses as well as attitudes or expectations that could affect the client-planner relationship. In summary, the use of a client data-gathering questionnaire provides a framework for summarizing a client's goals, attitudes, and financial profile, all of which are needed to write a comprehensive plan. More importantly, it opens up discussion of other issues, fears, or concerns beyond the obvious data collected on the form.

The client intake form discussed here is available on the website for this text. The form provides an example of the range of client information collected. Some financial planners use specialized data collection forms for targeted client situations, such as small business owners or retirement plan participants, whereas others use forms associated with professional software to facilitate data entry. Finally, for financial planners affiliated with product providers, a proprietary client data form may be required to ensure regulatory compliance.

3. *Guided Client-Planner Interviews.* The meaningful exploration of a client's financial situation and its many nuances does not typically occur solely through conversation. Financial planners who work with clients to jointly complete or review a client intake form have a purpose: to collect accurate, factual data. However, in order to expand that preliminary exchange into the realm of goals, attitudes, values, dreams, concerns, fears surrounding money, or the role of money in a client's life could necessitate entering into a conversation with a purpose—an interview. A **focused interview** is an excellent way to explore another person's feelings, experiences, perceptions, attitudes, views, or knowledge. The concept of a semi-standardized, or focused interview, is borrowed from social science research, where a set of questions guides the interview, but the order of the questions, their wording, and the follow-up probes and interviewer responses can be adapted by the interviewer. The interview is focused on learning about the client's **experiential map**, as defined by feelings, experiences, views, or knowledge that define the individual, whereas a **standardized interview** would be formally structured, like the client intake form, to collect specific quantitative data.

Approaching a **client meeting** as an interview should not inadvertently change the tone or formality of the meeting, but it does take preparation. An issue oriented, topical list or set of questions must be carefully planned to guide the interview. However, a financial planner's questions and approach should still allow for adaptations regarding the level of language, word choice, or order of questioning to best match the client and the situation. **Open-ended questions** that are nonjudgmental and respect the sensitivity of the topic are most effective. Questions beginning with *why* should be avoided because they can cause defensiveness. The objective is to encourage a client too openly and freely share information, feelings, perceptions, or observations. Follow-up questions and verbal or nonverbal reinforcements should be used as necessary to encourage clients to elaborate.

Where do financial planners obtain targeted questions for discovery meetings? Specialized approaches, such as those promoted by George Kinder,[8] Mitch Anthony,[9] Roy Diliberto,[10] and Carol Anderson,[11] for example, offer financial planners training, as well as interview questions and other assessment tools, to help clients increase their understanding of financial and life planning issues. Kinder, one of the founders of life planning movement, is recognized for introducing the following questions (asked in this order) to help clients explore what he calls "a life worth living":

1. "If you had all the money you needed, what would you do with your life?"

2. "If you had only five to ten years to live, but would be in good health the entire time, what would your life look like?"

3. "If you knew you were going to die tomorrow, what did you miss? What did you not get to do? Who did you not get to be?" [12]

Although some planners argue that these global questions are beyond the scope of financial planning, other financial planners are embracing the integration of financial planning and life planning. Developing a focused interview matched to a financial planner's business model can: (1) increase the planner's confidence, (2) encourage more in-depth understanding of the topic and the client's perspectives and motives, and (3) build a trust-based client-planner relationship. The shift from a client relationship based on one or more separate *transactions* to one based on complete *transformation* could have a significant impact on the practice of financial planning.

Planning Skill 6: Determine What It Means to Frame Goals and Objectives

Framing goals and objectives requires a financial planner, in consultation with a client, to identify results or accomplishments that should flow from the planning process. Broadly defined, **goals** should give meaning to a client's life and motivate the client to pursue the financial planning process. Depending on the issue considered, a goal can range from the abstract to the concrete. A *goal* is a more global statement of a client's personal or financial purpose, while an **objective** is a more discrete financial target that supports a goal. For example, a client may set the goal of a "comfortable retirement,"

Recording Client Goals

Recording a client's goals and objectives is a good way to develop a checklist for further discussion. Furthermore, realistically framing, articulating, and ranking goals can occur only as the client's "dreams" are brought into perspective by the data-gathering and analytical skills of the planner. A thoughtful and honest interchange between client and planner is necessary to arrive at final goals for the plan—and everyone must realize that both goals and plan are subject to changing circumstances and the vagaries of the future.

Self-Test 4

Lanny is an accomplished golfer. He intends to join the senior tour when he retires from his position as a senior executive with a large firm. He tells his financial planner that he would like to have a home in Florida, California, and Wisconsin so that he has a "home base" while playing golf around the country. Lanny's desire can best be described as a:

a. Need

b. Want

c. Necessity

d. Goal Hierarchy

but only through further discussions and clarification can a financial planner discern a definite objective, based on the client's proposed retirement lifestyle, of accumulating, say, $2.65 million by age fifty-five.

Although clients' goals can be framed or defined in limitless ways, goals basically emanate from:

- wants and needs

- life cycle events

- life transitions

Wants and needs are differentiated by their significance in sustaining life, while **life cycle events** represent typical biological, socioeconomic, or sociocultural events that occur over a lifetime. Anthony defined goals as what the client would like to "have, do, or be" during life, whereas a **life transition** represents a "change or transition" currently faced or expected to occur in the near future.[13] Clients can identify a new goal, modify existing goals, or change the hierarchy of goals as the result of a perceived want or need, life cycle event, or life transition. These categories are not mutually exclusive. Divorce, for example, may result from an unfulfilled personal need or be viewed as a life cycle event or a life transition.

Often, through the discovery process, a financial planner will uncover a goal that the client was either uncomfortable listing, thought was beyond accomplishment, or simply could not fully articulate. The communication required to fully identify and frame goals can sometimes be challenging. Such insights increase a financial planner's understanding of a client and help the client and financial planner identify nuances and subtle priorities among the goals. Recognizing and examining these relationships provides a deeper understanding of the client's situation, and the outcomes attained are essential to preparing feasible, actionable, client-centered recommendations. Goals and recommendations may be subject to further refinement based on the planner's own financial planning knowledge and experience as well as other descriptive factors.

Financial planners and clients should not look at a goal in isolation. Goals can be independent, interrelated, or interdependent. The best solution for one goal may have a deleterious effect on achieving another goal. For interrelated goals, the first goal might have to be fulfilled as a prerequisite to fulfilling the second goal. Goals are typically categorized by a **time horizon** for accomplishment. **Short-term** goals can be accomplished in less than two years, while it may require two to ten years to accomplish an **intermediate-term** goal. **Long-term** goals, such as preparing for retirement, take more than ten years and could actually require effort over several decades.

The idea of a **personal goal hierarchy** or ranking is commonly accepted, and some clients can easily prioritize their goals. But in cases where a client has several equally important but somewhat **conflicting goals,** ranking becomes significantly more problematic. Of course, the ranking of goals may not be an issue if sufficient funding is available; however, this is rarely the case. Because goals can be ranked does not necessarily mean that the highest-ranking goal should be dealt with first. Client goals and objectives and the corresponding recommendations developed can be moderated by a financial planner's professional judgment and knowledge of a client's situational factors.

Planning Skill 7: Master the Tools and Techniques Involved in Analyzing and Evaluating a Client's Financial Status

Many financial planning practitioners view the step of **analyzing and evaluating a client's financial situation** as the essence of financial planning. The realities of a client's income and expenses, net worth, financial products owned, and financial strategies employed to date are scrutinized during this step in the financial planning process. From the narrowest viewpoint, this step is fact based and solution oriented. But central to this step in the process is a perspective that goes beyond the present factual situation, to a larger and perhaps more multifaceted view of the client, as characterized by the situational factors and the client's financial future.

It might take years of study and practice to fully comprehend the nuances and complexities of conducting a thorough analysis and evaluation of a client's situation. Mastering this skill is a financial planning challenge built on known facts about the client, inferences gleaned from the client-planner relationship, and assumptions that should be mutually agreed on by the financial planner and client. Too often at this step, the "solution-focused" planner overemphasizes quantitative analysis to the detriment of the person for whom the plan is designed. It is instead essential that a financial planner consider a client's goals and related planning assumptions when conducting an analysis. Only by knowing a client's specific goals and using the assumptions agreed on with the client can a financial planner anticipate, determine, and quantify planning needs. Then, in conjunction with the client, a course of action that offers the best risk-adjusted probability of success can be identified.

As illustrated in Figure 1.1 above, Step 3 of the financial planning process is a multi-layered stage comprising three steps:

1. Analyze the current situation.

2. Review prospective planning strategies.

3. Develop client-based recommendations.

These steps can be summarized as: know your client, consider the universe of strategies for meeting the client's needs, and match the two to formulate the client specific recommendations most likely to meet the client's goals. Each step is explained in further detail below.

Planning Skill 8: Develop an Expertise in Analyzing a Client's Current Situation

Analysis of a client's **current financial situation** requires a financial planner to review and distill all of the information collected about a client's situation in the context of the marketplace, including the tax, economic, political, and legal or regulatory environment. This analysis is designed to answer four questions in the context of each core financial planning content area:

1. *What is the client's planning need?* Financial planning needs can range from a discrete financial question or issue involving one core content planning area to an extensive review of all of a client's financial matters. The determination, or **identification**, of the planning need is based on a financial planner's professional judgment and familiarity with the client's situation. Both quantitative and qualitative data are considered to identify both known and unknown needs. For example, currently known or identified financial needs might cross several different core content planning areas. The review can also reveal other unknown or unrecognized needs that could affect the client now or in the future. For example, a forty-five-year-old client might be strongly committed to purchasing a long-term care insurance policy—now or in the future—because of a foreseen need created by a family history of Alzheimer's disease. Planning needs may be identified by the client or the financial planner.

2. *What assumptions are relevant to the client's planning need?* **Assumptions** are inferences based on premises, reasoned conclusions, facts, or circumstantial evidence that affect a client's planning need and the quantification of that need. For example, historical stock market returns, recent inflationary increases in the cost of higher education, and average skilled nursing home costs are supported by factual data and can be included in the quantification of a client's need. These assumptions and many others reflect the current or projected marketplace, such as the tax, economic, political, and regulatory environments. Other assumptions reflect a client's personal situation (e.g., the assumed need for long-term care insurance, the likelihood of a child receiving college scholarships or fellowships, or life span projections). Assumptions must be fully disclosed, mutually agreed upon, and realistic.

3. *Can the client's planning need be quantified?* Technical expertise, computations, and other analytical tools should be used (where applicable) to objectively analyze and *quantify* a client's need. For some core content planning areas, such as estimating life insurance needs, several recognized approaches are available and supported by software applications. The quantification of other needs (e.g., the need for long-term care insurance protection) can be far harder to calculate and defend because of multiple seemingly unrelated factors, such as the client's projected net worth or the daily benefit amount for future medical care.

4. *How is the planning need currently being met?* A financial planner must document planning efforts currently in place to meet identified needs or the absence of any efforts on the part of the client to address them. Then, a thorough and objective assessment of the products and strategies currently in use must be completed to project the likelihood of achieving the goal. Results of this evaluation can reveal needed changes or validate the client's approach and show that no changes are warranted.

Although these four questions must be applied to each core content planning area, sources of data considered and the analytics used to evaluate a client's situation can be quite different. Because of its importance and complexity, the step called **Analyze the Current Situation** should be applied individually and systematically within each of the core content planning areas.

At this juncture in the financial planning process, based on data gathered and analysis of the client's current situation, a financial planner should have an arsenal of useful information to incorporate into planning models, as outlined below:

> ### Recommendation and Implementation Questions
>
> When developing and presenting recommendations it is important to address seven implementation questions:
>
> Who should implement?
>
> What should be done?
>
> When should the recommendation be implemented?
>
> Where should implementation take place?
>
> Why should the client implement?
>
> How should implementation occur?
>
> How much is needed and/or how much will implementation cost?

- Insights into the client's temperament, personality, motivations, risk tolerance, financial knowledge, experience, and perceived level of financial success to this point. The financial planner can begin to answer the key strategy, recommendation, and implementation questions of *who* and *why* as well as the questions *for whom*, *what*, and *how*.

- Clear, mutually agreed-upon definitions of client goals, planning objectives, and the desired outcomes of the planning process. The financial planner can begin to answer the questions of *why*, *what*, *when*, and *for whom*.

- For each of the core content planning areas—cash flow and net worth management, income taxes, risk management (e.g., life, health, disability, long-term care, property, and liability), investments, education or other special needs planning, retirement planning, and estate planning—the financial planner can begin to answer *why*, *what*, *when*, *where*, *how*, and *how much* questions based on the following results:

    a. Quantitative data analyses built on mutually agreed upon personal and economic assumptions and conducted independently and systematically for each of the core content planning areas;

b. Qualitative and household needs assessments to identify potential individual, lifestyle, life event, or other factors that could affect the client in any of the core content planning areas;

c. The financial planner's knowledge and professional insights regarding factors that might influence the client in any of the core content areas, including issues, problems, or concerns beyond the client's awareness;

d. The financial planner's and/or client's scan of the legislative, tax, political, economic, and regulatory environmental factors that could have an impact on the implementation of the plan, immediately or in the future; and

e. The financial planner's consultation or collaboration with other professionals.

Planning Skill 9: Understand How Economic Concepts Influence the Financial Planning Process

Financial planners, by the very nature of their training and education, tend to bring a multidisciplinary perspective to their practice. This is one reason financial planners need to understand and eventually master economic concepts as an element of the financial planning process. Issues related to macroeconomic events, the money supply, and interest rates all play an important role in shaping the types of strategies and recommendations used to help clients reach their financial goals. This brief discussion highlights some of the most important economic concepts underlying many financial planning strategies.

Microeconomic Concepts

One of the building blocks of economic theory is the **law of supply and demand**. This law states that there is a direct positive relationship between prices and supply and an inverse relationship between demand and prices. Application of this law can be seen in the marketplace when prices increase for a product or service. Demand usually drops with other products and services acting as a **substitute good** for the original item. For example, as fees on mutual funds increased from the 1970s through the 1990s, investors substituted other products with lower fees, such as exchange traded funds. This had an overall effect of decreasing fees across all investment products. Sometimes an item acts as a **complementary good**. This can be seen in the life insurance marketplace. The

> ### Self-Test 5
>
> John is a stamp collector. He really enjoys finding, sorting, and price stamps. He spends several thousand dollars each year on his hobby. His financial planner thinks buying stamps is a bad investment. The planner recently pointed out that John's rate of return on his stamp purchases was about 3 percent, whereas the stock market, during the same time period, returned 9 percent. The 6 percent difference is known as John's:
>
> a. Substitution effect cost.
>
> b. Opportunity cost.
>
> c. Complementary good cost.
>
> d. Discount rate.

demand for life insurance generally increases as wealth increases, even though the effect should be the other way around.

The law of supply and demand helped introduce the notion of **opportunity costs**, which are the explicit or implicit costs associated with forgoing one choice in favor of another option. For instance, assume a client elects to save for college expenses using a Section 529 plan. There is an opportunity cost associated with this choice; namely, the forgone opportunity to save for retirement or another goal using a different product. Another important microeconomic concept is the degree to which products and services exhibit **price elasticity**. Price elasticity refers to the degree demand for a product or service drops as the result of a price increase. Something is considered to be relatively **price inelastic** if demand drops slightly or not at all when prices move up. Some have argued that financial planning services are relatively price inelastic; however, the introduction of **Robo-advisors** is putting this assertion to the test. Robo-advisors provide automated financial planning services at a very low cost. If successful, robo-advisory firms should grow as more consumer shift from higher priced traditional firms to these lower cost structure service providers.

> **Self-Test 6**
>
> All of the following are Assumptions, EXCEPT:
>
> a. The annualized rate of return that can be earned on retirement assets.
>
> b. The life expectancy of a client.
>
> c. The future cost of living in a large city.
>
> d. The date when a client can claim Medicare.

Macroeconomic Concepts

Fiscal policy tends to be a topic of great importance among financial planners. **Fiscal policy** refers to the government's tax and spending policies. As one of the four components of **gross domestic product (GDP)**, **government spending**—a direct element of fiscal policy—plays a role in shaping economic growth and **inflation** (i.e., a phenomenon marked by generally increasing prices).

The financial planning community also pays close attention to actions taken and forecast to be taken by the **Federal Reserve (the Fed)** through **monetary policy**. Monetary policy encompasses the Fed's control of the **credit markets** and establishment of **reserve requirements**. Historically, the Fed, as an independent federal agency, has been tasked with the dual objective of maintaining high national employment and relatively low inflation. The Fed attempts to meet these seemingly contradictory objectives by establishing the **discount rate** at which the Fed charges depository institutions, such as banks and credit unions, for short-term loans. If the Fed is attempting to increase employment, the Fed will decrease the discount rate to spur lending.

> **Self-Test 7**
>
> The Fed controls:
>
> a. The federal funds rate.
>
> b. The CPI.
>
> c. The discount rate.
>
> d. All of the above.

The Fed also intervenes in the bond market via the **Federal Open Market Committee (FOMC)**. The FOMC is based out of the Federal Reserve Bank of New York. The purpose of the FOMC is to engage in open market buying and selling of U.S. Treasury securities. The FOMC can increase **liquidity** in the markets—thus stimulating demand and increasing inflation and GDP—by purchasing bonds. Although not used often, the Fed can also change reserve requirements for depository institutions. Since the Great Recession, reserve requirements—the percent of total deposits a depository institution must keep in reserve—has been near historical low levels. The Fed has other tools but these are typically used infrequently (e.g., *term auction facilities*, *money market investor funding facilities*, *commercial paper funding facilities*, etc.).

Financial planners tend to also be interested in tracking the overall health of the economy. This fascination stems from the need to project current events into planning assumptions for future analyses. For example, a financial planner might reasonably ask if she should continue to project very low interest rates into long-term retirement distributions scenarios. One way to answer this question involves tracking **economic indicators**. Some of the most important indicators include:

- **Consumer Price Index (CPI)**: This measure of inflation represents a market basket of household goods. An alternative is the **CPI-U**, which represents inflation in urban markets.

- **Producer Price Index (PPI)**: Producer prices tend to be a leading indicator—a precursor to something that will happen in the future—of inflation. This measure is watched by those in the financial planning community to anticipate future changes in the price of goods and services.

- **Gross Domestic Product (GDP)**: The state of the economic environment can be measured by GDP, which is comprised of government spending, business investment, consumer expenditures (consumption), and net exports.

- **Business Cycle**: A country's stage of growth can be defined by the business cycle, which itself is an indication of GDP. Figure 1.3 illustrates the two stages of the business cycle: contraction and recovery/expansion. As shown, the contraction phase is marked by a peak and decline in GDP to a trough, whereas the expansion phase is represented by an increase in GDP from trough to peak.

Figure 1.3 The Business Cycle

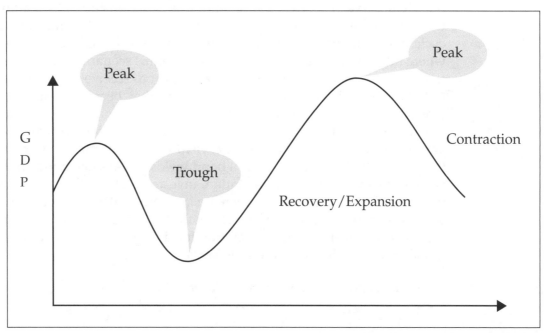

In addition to these economic indicators, financial planners often group economic data as being a leading, coincident, or lagging indicator. The following economic data points are considered to be **leading economic indicators** of future expansion or contraction: unemployment claims, manufacturing new orders, product delivery times, new orders for capital (non-defense) goods, building permits, stock prices, money supply growth, the spread between the **federal funds rate** (i.e., the rate at which depository institutions lend money to other depository institutions) and ten-year U.S. Treasury bonds, and consumer expectations. Four indicators are thought to be indicative of current market conditions or **coincident economic indicators**: industrial production, personal income less transfer payments (e.g., Social Security), manufacturing sales, and nonagricultural payrolls. The following indicators are considered to be **lagging economic indicators** of economic growth: loans outstanding, duration of unemployment, change in labor cost per unit of output, the level of installment credit to personal income, the ratio of inventories to sales, the prime interest rate, and the CPI for services.

Self-Test 8

Tabatha inherited a 20-year A+ rated bond from her uncle two years ago. Yesterday she found out the Fed had raised interest rates. She does not know whether to be happy or sad about this event. What will happen to the value of Tabatha's bond now that rates have increased?

a. Nothing, the bond value will remain unchanged.

b. The value of the bond will increase.

c. The value of the bond will decrease.

d. The value of the bond will first increase, then decrease, and finally emerge unchanged.

Financial planners also place a great deal of emphasis on tracking and predicting the **yield curve**. The yield curve shows the relationship between bond yields and bond durations. The yield curve can be used to describe and predict the business cycle and inflation. Figure 1.4 illustrates a typical positively sloping yield curve where rates increase as maturity increases. In this scenario, investors expect inflation to increase over time, and as such, they expect to receive a higher **yield to maturity (YTM)** on their fixed-income investments. Further, because the risks associated with longer maturity bonds tend to be higher than short maturity bonds due to liquidity, reinvestment, and default risks, investors typically expect to receive a higher return on their investment. Sometimes the yield curve will invert, with yields on short-term bonds higher than long-term bond yields. This is generally an indication of an economic slowdown. In this situation, investors believe that the economy is near a peak, which should prompt an increase in interest rates. When and if an interest rate increase occurs, bond values will fall, with the longest maturity bonds dropping by the greatest percentage. In preparation for this potentiality, investors flock to short-term bonds, which inverts the yield curve.

Figure 1.4 A Positive Sloping Yield Curve

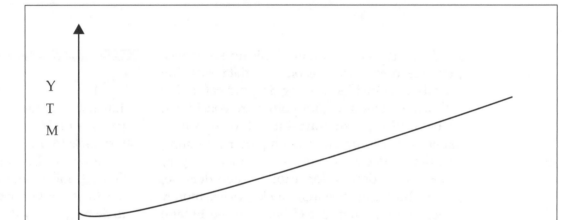

Short [Time to Maturity] Long

Planning Skill 10: Master the Process of Reviewing Prospective Planning Strategies

Once an analysis of a client's financial situation is complete, the financial planner should have a clear understanding of the issues to be addressed and thus be ready to proceed to the next step in the financial planning process—**Review Prospective Planning Strategies**. This step in the process of analyzing a client's situation focuses on the identification of possible strategies or alternatives available to meet the client's needs and goals. With the results of the quantitative and qualitative analysis complete, a financial planner can begin to fully answer the strategy, recommendation, and implementation questions of *why*, *when*, *where*, *how much*, *how*, and *by whom*.

Strategies reflect a financial planner's technical competence and the universe of solutions that could apply to a client's situation. Strategies represent a financial planner's toolkit of tools, techniques, solutions, and answers that can be applied to help a client reach their financial goal(s). Strategies can be categorized as product or procedural. A **product strategy** reflects the use of a specific type of product or product feature to meet a planning goal or need. A **procedural strategy** emphasizes a process, service, or type of ownership rather than a product. Product and procedural strategies are identified for each of the core content planning areas discussed in Chapters 3 through 13.

Professional judgment, ethics, and practice standards constrain planners to offer services within the purview of their acknowledged expertise, to seek the collaboration of other professionals, or to refer clients to other professionals. Financial planners can become accustomed to using certain strategies or products or focusing on particular patterns of information. This practice can sometimes result in problematic client outcomes. Sometimes strategies become dated or inappropriate. At other times, new products enter the marketplace. These products can make an older strategy obsolete. Whenever a financial planner turns to the use of **heuristics**, or favored solutions, when working with a client, an opportunity to miss something new emerges. The biggest problem associated with continually using the same solution with multiply clients is that a financial planner may become entangled in needing to defend a recommendation that is later deemed not suitable for a client.

Although commonly used strategies or products can increase a financial planner's efficiency and promote an increased depth of knowledge in a diverse universe of products, the used of some strategies may or may not yield the best client outcome. Professional judgment and ethical practice standards suggest that financial planners acknowledge any limitations, prejudices, or other relationships that could adversely affect or bias the client-planner relationship. Furthermore, financial planners are encouraged to continually apply professional skepticism to compensate for or override such issues.

Planning Skill 11: Master the Development of Client-Based Recommendations

With strategies identified, a financial planner can make **recommendations** matched to the client. These client-centered or **client-based strategies** might need to be altered or combined as the financial planner weighs the advantages and disadvantages of each potential recommendation and considers the probable outcomes and effects on a client's situation. As the financial planner attempts to align recommendations with a client's goal(s), the total cost of the recommendations must be compared to the available cash flow or other assets available to fund the recommendations.

Consider the example of an investment recommendation to fund a future goal (e.g., retirement, education, a vacation home, etc.) based on a product strategy recommendation of an actively managed mutual fund. Facts and assumptions are an issue as the financial planner considers increasing the anticipated rate of return (an assumption) in an attempt to limit or reduce the present value cost (a fact). Another relevant assumption, the client's risk tolerance for the goal, must be incorporated into the analysis. This planning input influences portfolio allocation decisions and projected return assumptions, as well as the client's potential comfort with, and commitment to, the recommendation if risk tolerance is exceeded.

Self-Test 9

Which of the following recommendations is closest to be an actionable recommendation?

a. Refinance your mortgage as soon as possible.

b. Purchase a stock mutual fund in the next 30 days.

c. Save $300 per month into EE Savings Bonds using Treasury Direct.

d. All of the above.

The process of separating, distilling, and integrating client situational factors, planner factors, and strategies often results in the development of one or more **client-based recommendations** that define the scope of the planning engagement. This is true whether a financial planner is developing a comprehensive plan or a modular plan that targets a single issue. Recommendations should offer the client cost-effective, adaptable alternatives. Contingent on the scope of the engagement, and the degree of specificity implied in that arrangement, recommendations should address the following **implementation questions**:

- Who should implement the recommendation?

- What should be done?

- When should the recommendation be implemented?

- Where should the client (or other party) implement the recommendation?

- Why should the recommendation be implemented? Why is it important to the client's financial future?

- How should implementation take place?

- How much should be purchased, saved, or invested to implement the recommendation? Specifically, what is the cost of the recommendation?

The significance of considering each of these questions when developing recommendations should not be overlooked. The questions may seem too simplistic to be meaningful, or answering all seven may seem unnecessary. However, experience shows that the routine use of this simple rubric for framing recommendations can be a powerful tool for two reasons. First, careful consideration of these questions helps a financial planner reconsider the logic of each recommendation and its consistency with the client's goals and situation. Second, the rubric helps financial planners meticulously consider and articulate funding and other implementation issues critical to sound plan development and motivated client action.

Figure 1.5, illustrates **The Planning Recommendation Form**, which is discussed in more detail in Chapter 14. This form can help financial planners focus on the essential issues to include in an **actionable recommendation**. This useful planning tool, recommended in the planning process, summarizes the answers to the seven critical recommendation questions of *who, what, when, where, why, how,* and *how much* into one simple format. When initially identifying possible recommendations, the form is useful for summarizing and projecting the costs and benefits of recommendations. As the plan develops, it may be necessary to combine, sort, and rank recommendations from other core content planning areas, and the forms can quickly be revised for each recommendation. Once finalized, the forms can be used to document information for planning staff or to communicate information to the client. Possibly one of the most beneficial uses of the form is to document the titling of assets and beneficiary designations.

Figure 1.5 Planning Recommendation Form

Financial Planning Content Area					
Client Goal					
Recommendation No.		**Priority (1-6)** lowest to highest:			
Projected/Target Value ($)					
Product Profile					
Type					
Duration					
Provider					
Funding Cost per Period ($)					
Maintenance Cost per Period ($)					
Current Income Tax Status		Tax-qualified		Taxable	
Projected Rate of Return					
Major Policy Provisions					
Procedural Factors					
Implementation by Whom		Planner		Client	
Implementation Date or Time Frame					
Implementation Procedure					
Ownership Factors					
Owner(s)					
Form of Ownership					
Insured(s)					
Custodial Account		Yes		No	
Custodian					
In Trust For (ITF)		Yes		No	
Transfer on Death (TOD)		Yes		No	
Beneficiary(ies)					
Contingent Beneficiary(ies)					
Proposed Benefit					

Planning Skill 12: Master the Financial Planning Process by Practicing Case Studies

Introducing the Comprehensive Case: Tyler and Mia Bedo

A running case is provided in each of the chapters in this book. The case features Tyler and Mia Bedo and their family (see the Appendix 1A for more information about the Bedo family). The Bedos, a hypothetical household, are meant to represent the type of clients that might seek the help of a financial planner just starting out in the profession. The Bedos earn more income than the average American family and significantly more than the typical family living in Springfield, Missouri, where they reside.

Some may ask, "Does the fact that the Bedos earn more than other young families make the case too easy?" Having high relative income does not necessarily make the case any easier—it merely provides different planning strategies and alternatives for use by those working on the case. Additionally, having more income to work with provides greater opportunities to meet a client's long-term goals by allowing the development of more creative solutions. As a client's income increases, so does the range and complexity of solutions. This means that in terms of pure simplicity, it can sometimes be easier to work with clients who are aspiring to wealth because suggestions and alternatives tend, by default, to be constrained by available cash flow. Because higher-income clients may not be as income constrained, potential solutions are often riddled with the complexities inherent in multiple, interrelated options.

Furthermore, income and lifestyle are relative measures. Certainly, the Bedos earn a respectable amount of money for a young couple living in southwest Missouri. On the other hand, their income may be quite modest in relation to the cost of living and different lifestyle demands of a similar household in cities like Los Angeles, San Francisco, New York, Washington, or Boston. But the fact that a client earns a relatively high income in no way means that all goals and objectives can be met. Clients tend to "live up" to their level of income regardless of how much they earn. In other words, high-income clients tend to spend much of their income, just as moderate-income clients tend to spend most of their income.

The Bedo case narrative was developed with two aims in mind. One goal was to make the case as comprehensive as possible, meaning that it is impossible to resolve issues in one core content planning area without influencing the Bedos' other issues and goals. When faced with developing strategies and recommendations, financial planners will encounter several interrelated issues and constraints, all of which influence each other. These interacting issues make the case relatively difficult to analyze, yet not too difficult to develop a plan to improve the Bedos' financial situation—both now and in the future. The second goal was to allow the Bedos' needs to be resolved using both simple and complex solutions. This aspect of the case approach provides greater opportunities to offer unique client proposals that may vary by financial planner but still offer a viable option for meeting the Bedos' goals and objectives.

The Bedos are introduced in Appendix 1A. Specific questions to guide the analysis and development of appropriate strategies and recommendations are provided at the end of Chapters 3–14 as well as this chapter. By following the chapter structure and the financial planning process, it is possible to analyze the case and write a financial plan.

Quantitative/Analytical Mini-Case Problems

Later chapters include quantitative or analytical problems that challenge readers to practice the skills from specific core financial planning content areas—usually in the context of a short case situation. Although software applications can perform these functions in the typical financial planning office, it is important that planners have the skill to understand and test the assumptions and results provided.

Comprehensive Bedo Case—Analysis Questions

The Bedo case is an integral part of learning and applying the financial planning process. This case and the other cases found throughout the book present clinical studies of real-life situations that financial planners might face. They are meant to confront—but also confine—the complexity and ambiguity of the practical world by focusing on the questions to ask, the assumptions to use, and the calculations to complete when analyzing a situation.

There should be a logical progression from the analysis of each of the core content areas to the identification of strategies consistent with the Bedos' client situational factors. Through integrative analysis of the client's situation and identification of potential strategies, client specific recommendations and a plan will emerge. The identification of implementation and monitoring plans completes the financial planning process.

1. Complete the Client Intake Form, available in the companion book, *The Process of Financial Planning, Second Edition,* and on the Web site for this book, for Tyler and Mia Bedo. For any client situational factor information that is not provided, make a defensible assumption to guide the planning process. For information that is unavailable, note how it would have been collected from the Bedos.

2. As part of Step 1: Establish and Define the Relationship, develop a thorough but brief description of the financial planning process to help the Bedos understand the services to be provided. Prepare this description (narrative, outline, etc.) for inclusion in the financial plan *or* for presentation to the client with or without the aid of PowerPoint slides or handouts.

3. Within the scope of Step 1, what documents would have been presented to the Bedos? Why are they included in this step of the process? What purpose do the documents serve? For additional information, see the companion book, *The Process of Financial Planning, Second Edition,* or *CFP Board's Standards of Professional Conduct.*

4. Develop a preliminary list of five to ten financial strengths, weaknesses, opportunities, and threats (typically referred to as a SWOT analysis) for the Bedo household. During which step(s) of the financial planning process might these be identified—in general or through more in-depth analysis?

5. Why is a goal stated as "to live life with a relatively high level of financial satisfaction" not very useful in terms of a practical financial planning analysis?

6. List and prioritize the Bedos' financial goals. Classify each as emanating from needs or wants, a life cycle event, or a life transition. Classify each as short-, intermediate-, or long-term.

7. What needs, wants, life cycle events, or life transitions might influence the Bedos' financial plans over the next five years? The next fifteen years? Why is it important to consider these issues, either independently as a planner or in discussion with the Bedos?

8. What other information would be helpful to obtain from the Bedos as you move forward with developing a comprehensive financial plan?

9. Make a list of additional information or original source documents that you would request from the Bedos. Be sure to review the Client Intake Form and the Client Supporting Document Tracking Form for ideas. What explanation would you provide regarding why the documents are needed?

10. Prepare and organize a list of general or critical core content planning area-specific assumptions for use when working on the case.

11. Answers to questions 6–10 may emerge from the Client Intake Form or an initial conversation with the Bedos regarding their reason(s) to seek financial planning. However, other questions, as part of a focused interview or the discovery meetings, will likely be necessary to gain a broader understanding of the Bedos. Generate a list of questions based on a review of the financial planning literature or interviews with financial planners. (Note: This may be assigned as a small group or class project.)

12. Given the initial review of the Bedos' situation, what other professionals might be needed to help the planner develop the Bedos' plan? How are these decisions guided by CFP Board for CFP® certificants?

13. If you were to rewrite the case narrative, given the current state of the economy, how would you change the rate-of-return assumptions presented in the case? What other assumptions should be changed or updated?

14. Complete the following for the introductory sections of the Bedos' financial plan:

    a. Draft the introductory cover letter to the client.

    b. Prepare the client profile and draft a summary of goals and general or specific assumptions that will guide the planning process. (Note: The list of goals and assumptions will be reviewed and revised in each core content planning area for final inclusion in the plan.)

Chapter Resources

Anthony, M. *Your Clients for Life: The Definitive Guide to Becoming a Successful Financial Planner*. Chicago, IL: Dearborn Financial Publishing, 2002.

Assessing Your Financial Risk Tolerance (njaes.rutgers.edu:8080/money/riskquiz/).

Certified Financial Planner Board of Standards, Inc. (www.cfp.net).

Diliberto, R. T. Financial Planning—The Next Step: A Practical Approach to Merging Your Clients' Money with Their Lives. Denver, CO: FPA Press, 2006.

Financial Industry Regulatory Authority (FINRA) (www.finra.org).

FinaMetrica® (www.finametrica.com).

Financial Therapy Association (financialtherapyassociation.org/).

Investment Financial planner Registration Depository (www.iard.com/).

Investment Financial Planner Public Disclosure Web site (www.adviserinfo.sec.gov/ (S(l2wrhvakmfteghqc1qtt0v5m))/IAPD/Content/IapdMain/iapd_SiteMap.aspx).

Kinder, G. *Seven Stages of Money Maturity: Understanding the Spirit and Value of Money in your Life*. New York: Dell Publishing, 2000.

Kinder, G., and S. Galvan. *Lighting the Torch: The Kinder Method™of Life Planning*. Denver, CO: FPA Press, 2006.

Klontz, B., R. Kahler, and T. Klontz. *Facilitating Financial Health: Tools for Financial Planners, Coaches, and Therapists; Second Edition)*. Cincinnati, OH: National Underwriter Company, 2015.

Klontz, B., and T. Klontz. Mind over Money: *Overcoming the Money Disorders That Threaten Our Financial Health*. New York: Crown Business, 2009.

Lytton, R., J. Grable, and D. Klock. *The Process of Financial Planning: Developing a Financial Plan*, 2nd Ed. Erlanger, KY: National Underwriter, 2012.

Money Quotient® Putting Money in the Context of Life™ (moneyquotient.org/).

The Kinder Institute of Life Planning (www.kinderinstitute.com/index.html).

The Financial Life Planning Institute (www.flpinc.com/.

U.S. Securities and Exchange Commission (www.sec.gov).

Your Mental Wealth™ (www.yourmentalwealth.com/)

Self-Test Answers

1: b, 2: a, 3: c, 4: b, 5: b, 6: d, 7: c, 8: c, 9: c

Endnotes

1. For more information see CFP Board's Standards of Professional Conduct, available at: www.cfp.net/Downloads/2010Standards.pdf.

2. Certified Financial Planner Board of Standards, Inc., *CFP Board's Standards of Professional Conduct.* Available at www.cfp.net/Downloads/2010Standards.pdf, p. 4.

3. CFP Board, *Standards of Professional Conduct*, p. 5.

4. CFP Board, *Standards of Professional Conduct*, p. 14.

5. This section of the chapter was summarized from the companion text by Lytton, Grable, & Klock, *The Process of Financial Planning: Developing a Financial Plan* (Cincinnati, OH: National Underwriter, 2012).

6. B. Klontz, R. Kahler, and T. Klontz, *Facilitating Financial Health* (Erlanger, KY: National Underwriter, 2008): 14.

7. Available at: njaes.rutgers.edu:8080/money/riskquiz/.

8. G. Kinder, *Seven Stages of Money Maturity: Understanding the Spirit and Value of Money in Your Life* (New York: Dell, 1999).

9. M. Anthony, *Your Clients for Life: The Definitive Guide to Becoming a Successful Financial Planner* (Chicago: Dearborn Financial Publishing, 2002).

10. R. D. Diliberto, *Financial Planning—The Next Step, A Practical Guide to Merging Your Clients' Money with Their Lives* (Denver, CO: Financial Planning Association Press, 2006).

11. Carol Anderson, *MoneyQuotient® Putting Money into the Context of Life.* For more information see moneyquotient.org/.

12. "Interview: George Kinder & Life Planning," *NAPFA Advisor* (August 2003): 7–13.

13. M. Anthony, *Life Transitions Profile, Financial Life Planning Institute.* Available at www.financialifeplanning.com.

Appendix 1A

Meet Your Clients

INTRODUCING THE BEDO CASE STUDY

The purpose of this narrative is to provide you with the information needed to write a comprehensive financial plan for your clients, Tyler and Mia Bedo. By studying this case, you should have a relatively solid understanding of the types of personal and financial information that a planner needs to write a comprehensive financial plan. It will become increasingly important for you to have a clear understanding of the case facts.

As you read through the case, you should make a concerted effort to highlight and note any special assumptions presented. Strive to be inquisitive and to anticipate how certain case facts and assumptions might influence your choice of strategies, the development of interrelated recommendations, the implementation of recommendations, and future monitoring actions. Train yourself to identify the client's financial strengths and weaknesses. This list will help ensure that the Bedos' stated—and even unrecognized—financial goals and objectives have been addressed.

By the end of the planning process, you should be able to collaborate with the Bedos to prioritize their goals and objectives, determine the net impact of strategies on cash flow and net worth, and develop a clearly delineated implementation plan that will enable them to accomplish their primary financial aspirations. And in doing so, you will chart a course that could change the Bedos' financial lives and establish the foundation of a long-term client-planner relationship.

THE BEDO FAMILY PROFILE

Recently, Tyler and Mia Bedo took time to start thinking about financial planning issues. They were prompted to do so by two events. First, Mia's close high school friend Brenda died of a heart attack. Brenda left a grieving husband and three children. She had no life insurance, and from what Mia could learn, Brenda's husband was having a hard time financially. This event was followed by an advertisement by a major financial planning firm that caught their attention. The advertisement encouraged viewers to start planning today for the future.

These two events started the Bedos thinking about the need for financial planning. As a result, they made a new year's resolution to seek the counsel and advice of a competent financial planner in January.

Today is the day the Bedos have come to see you, armed with a large amount of financial and personal information. The following narrative provides more detail about the Bedos' financial life.

Personal and Family Information

Tyler Bedo	**Mia Bedo**
Age: 42	Age: 42
State of residence: Missouri	State of residence: Missouri
Citizen: U.S.	Citizen: U.S.
Health status: No known health issues	Health status: No known health issues
SS#: 555-55-5555	SS#: 555-55-4444

Dependent Children

Becky Bedo
Age: 5
Health status: No known health issues

Home Address

727 Success Lane
Springfield, MO

Employment

Tyler's:	**Mia's:**
Golden Tee Golf Association, Inc.	The Family and Career Institute
6282 Star Drive	5600 Cedar Lane Road, Suite #150
Springfield, MO	Springfield, MO
Occupation: Sales consultant	Occupation: Career counselor
Years employed: 12	Years employed: 3

Overview of Family History

Tyler and Mia Bedo met during their undergraduate days at the University of Nevada in Reno. After graduation, they were married at a Lake Tahoe chapel. Shortly thereafter, they moved to Springfield, Missouri, so that Tyler could begin his career as a golf course sales consultant. The Bedos love Springfield and have no plans to leave the area.

This is Tyler and Mia's first marriage and, from what you've learned, they are happily married. Their first child, Becky, was born five years ago. At this point, they do not anticipate having any more children.

Becky is a bright and enthusiastic child. She is actively involved in sports. She particularly likes youth basketball and soccer. She and her mom are taking golf lessons together. She is currently taking piano lessons. Becky's future is one reason the Bedos were prompted to seek your financial advice. By talking with their friends and co-workers, they have learned that college can be expensive.

Because one of their goals is to fund as much of Becky's college as possible, they thought now could be the time to work through some college funding numbers with a professional. The good news is that the Bedos have already investigated some college costs. They have determined that four years of in-state tuition to a good public university today would cost about $10,000 per semester, including room and board.

Mia is the youngest child of a very large family. She has four brothers and three sisters. Her mother Jenny passed away when Mia was age thirty. Her father Terrance passed away three years later. Both died of cancer. Mia's parents donated the majority of their estate to a church in California. Mia received a few items from the estate, including a gold nugget ring, three signed collector paintings, an antique china cabinet with a full eight-piece set of collector's china, and her mother's harp.

Tyler's child life was significantly different from Mia's. Tyler is the only child in his family. His parents, both ages sixty-five, are healthy and living in Springfield. His parents' wills currently list him as the sole beneficiary of their combined assets. However, the Bedos are not expecting an inheritance anytime soon, and they do not want to plan on receiving assets from Tyler's parents.

Neither Tyler nor Mia has had much experience working with other professional advisors. They have used the services of an enrolled agent at tax time. They are pleased with the service provided. They do not have a relationship with an attorney or any other financial planning professional. Until this point, they have relied on advice from friends and family regarding their financial situation.

CASH FLOW PLANNING

Income Discussion

Mia enjoys her job as a career counselor. She received her undergraduate degree in Family Studies but, because she was unable to find a job right after college, she decided to pursue a graduate degree in Family Counseling. Her first job as a counselor was with a small private practice in Springfield. She worked for the firm for four years before resigning to spend time with Becky.

When Becky was older, Mia took a part-time job with her current employer, The Family and Career Institute of Missouri. She is paid a monthly salary and anticipates receiving a 3.0 percent salary increase each year in the future.

Currently, Becky is enrolled in kindergarten on a half-day basis. Her grandmother picks her up from school and takes care of Becky until the early afternoon. They have no regular child care expenses. As soon as Becky begins school, Mia plans to devote more time to volunteer activities in the community.

Tyler is highly valued by his employer. He has a degree in golf course management and a Masters in Business Administration. Tyler works for Golden Tee Golf Association, Inc., a relatively small (twenty-nine employees) golf course management consulting firm.

Tyler's job requires him to travel monthly to golf courses associated with his firm and conduct onsite management and consulting services. He is also responsible for soliciting new golf course management contracts. He is very successful in his career and plans to stay with his current employer until he retires.

Tyler is currently paid a salary and bonus. He conservatively estimates that his salary will increase by 3.0 percent each year. His bonus—50 percent of his salary paid out semiannually—is very generous, and also very consistent.

Before meeting with you, the Bedos summarized their current yearly income in Figure 1A.1.

Figure 1A.1 Income (Gross)

Client	Client	Amount	Frequency
Salary	Tyler	$2,633.33	Biweekly
Salary	Mia	$2,708.00	Monthly
Salary	Tyler	$17,116.65	Semiannually

Expense Summary

Unlike many clients, the Bedos have always kept a close eye on their income and expenses. The majority of their annual expenses are detailed in Figures 1A.2–1A.5.

Figure 1A.2 Income and Payroll Taxes

	Amount	Frequency
Tyler		
Federal income tax withholding	$ 718.00	Biweekly
State and local income tax withholding	$ 187.00	Biweekly
FFICA (Social Security and Medicare) tax withholding	$ 300.00	Biweekly
Mia		
Federal income tax withholding	$ 292.50	Monthly
State and local income tax withholding	$117.00	Monthly
FICA (Social Security and Medicare) tax withholding	$207.17	Monthly

Note: Late last year, the Golden Tee Golf Association, Inc. had a computer payroll problem. The firm responsible for tracking FICA withholding miscalculated the maximum cap on the Social Security portion of FICA. Tyler believes that the amount withheld for FICA may be incorrect.

Both Tyler and Mia are allowed to invest in a limited number of mutual funds within their 401(k) plans. These mutual funds are the same ones that your financial planning firm tracks on a regular basis. For a complete listing of the funds, refer to the rates-of-return section presented later in the case. Figure 1A.3 lists the funds that Tyler and Mia are currently using to fund their retirement objectives.

Figure 1A.3 Retirement Plan Contributions

	Contribution Amount	Notes	Employer Contribution
Tyler's Investment Choices			
Consumer Fund	3% of base salary	401(k) plan deductions are not taken from bonus payments (the employer does not match bonus payments)	0%
Graham Fund	3% of base salary		3% (100% match on the first 3%)
Mia's Investment Choices			
Rocket Fund	10% of salary	For future planning, 401(k) plan deductions are not taken from bonus payments (the employer does not match bonus payments)	3% (50% match on the first 6%)

The Bedos are diligent savers. Figure 1A.4 shows how much they save each month. Note that at the current time, only annuity and money market account savings are allocated to a goal. Additional regular expenses are shown in Figure 1A.5.

Figure 1A.4 Systematic Savings Outside of Qualified Retirement Plans

Description	Amount	Frequency	Savings Purpose
Sagebrush Fund	$250	Monthly	Any purpose
Haley G&I Fund	$250	Monthly	Any purpose
Ruth Fund	$250	Monthly	Any purpose
Individual conservative fixed-annuity contract	$250	Monthly	Mia's retirement
Money market account	$150	Monthly	Cash reserves

Figure 1A.5 Expenses

Housing	Periodic Amount	Frequency
Real estate taxes	$1,675	Annually
Homeowners insurance	$700	Annually
Utilities (e.g., electric, fuel, water, sewer)	$350	Monthly
Other household (e.g., yard service, trash)	$100	Quarterly
Food/Clothing/Transportation		
Food/groceries	$425	Monthly
Clothing	$700	Quarterly
Auto maintenance (e.g., oil, fuel)	$125	Monthly
Auto insurance premiums	$1,000	Semiannually
Missouri vehicle plate/tag tax	$450	Annually
Loan Payments		
Mortgage loan payments	$1,088	Monthly
Auto loan payments	$451	Monthly
Charge account and credit card payments	$425	Monthly
Other Committed Expenses		
Medical costs (copay)	$20	Monthly
Prescriptions	$20	Monthly
Dental and eye care expenses	$50	Monthly
Life insurance premiums	$172	Monthly
Medical (health) insurance premiums (pretax through a § 125 plan)	$300	Monthly
Umbrella insurance premiums	$175	Annually
Disability insurance premiums	$25	Monthly
Other misc. insurance premiums	$25	Monthly
Telephone (land line and cell)	$125	Monthly
Bank charges	$10	Monthly
Personal care (e.g., hair, dry cleaning)	$100	Monthly

Figure 1A.5 Expenses (*cont'd*)

	Periodic Amount	Frequency
Discretionary Expenses		
Entertainment (e.g., movies, plays, shows)	$225	Monthly
Satellite TV	$50	Monthly
Dining out	$275	Monthly
Recreation (e.g., boating, hiking)	$225	Monthly
Travel (e.g., trips to Branson)	$3,000	Annually
Savings for art and art gallery	$150	Monthly
Gifts to charities:		
University alumni fund	$1,000	Annually
Church	$350	Monthly
United Way	$50	Monthly
Holiday giving	$1,800	Annually
Home improvements	$150	Monthly
Dues (e.g., organizations, golf course, health clubs)	$150	Monthly
Subscriptions (e.g., Time, Money)	$80	Monthly
Housekeeping service	$80	Monthly
Pet care expenses	$35	Monthly
Tax preparation fees	$400	Annually
Note: Some expenses may not be accounted for in this table.		

Asset and Liability Summary

The Bedos live in a split-level, 2,250-square-foot home on a ¾-acre lot. It has a brick veneer on the first level and vinyl siding over the upper floor. It has a formal living room, dining room, and kitchen on the main floor; three bedrooms and two full baths on the upper floor; and a family room, laundry area, and a half-bath on the ground floor along with a two-car attached garage. Their home features a gas fireplace, a vaulted ceiling in the living and dining rooms, and a standing-seam metal roof. The metal roof is fairly new and was recommended to them because of the wind associated with violent spring thunderstorms that frequently develop tornadoes.

The Bedos have also provided you with a list of their assets and liabilities, with current market values. They have attempted to calculate all of their liabilities, but in a few cases they were unable to determine a pay-off value. They are hoping you can help them determine some of these key account balances. Assets and liabilities are shown in Tables 1A.6–1A.10

Figure 1A.6 Personal and Real Assets

Description	Owner/Title	Current Value
Home	Joint	$250,000
Furnishings	Joint	$45,000
Four-door sedan (3 years old, Ford Taurus)	Joint	$20,000
Minivan (5 years old, Nissan Quest)	Joint	$15,500
Yard equipment (John Deere x500, plus other small equipment)	Joint	$8,000
Jewelry and collectibles (Mia's ring, paintings, china cabinet w/china, and harp)	Joint	$10,000
Phil Mickelson-signed Calloway Driver golf club	Joint	$5,000
Golf clubs/other sporting equipment	Joint	$2,500
Golf artwork (Linda Hartough reproductions, set of 5 lithographs)	Joint	$5,000
Aluminum boat (2001 Alumacraft V16 Lunker LTD; w/ 50hp Mercury motor)	Joint	$5,800

Figure 1A.7 Monetary Assets

Description/Purpose	Owner	Market Value	Current Yeild
Savings account (cash reserve)	Joint	$10,000	3.00%
Checking account (cash reserve)	Joint	$3,500	0.00%
Money market account (cash reserve)	Joint	$10,000	3.00%
Checking account II (savings: art gallery/collection)	Joint	$5,000	0.00%

Figure 1A.8 Investment Assets (Nonretirement)

Description	Owner	Market Value	Current Yeild
Miscellaneous EE bonds*	Joint	$25,000	3.50% Deferred
Haley G&I Fund**	Joint	$69,000	3.20%
Konza Fund**	Joint	$43,000	1.75%
Ruth Fund**	Joint	$13,000	4.00%
Sagebrush Fund**	Joint	$8,000	0.50%

* The EE bonds were purchased 12 years ago by Tyler's parents as a gift for Tyler and Mia. The bonds will earn interest for the next 18 years and reach their $30,000 face value in another 5 years, as guaranteed by the U.S. Treasury.

**The Bedos' basis in these assets is equal to 50 percent of the assets' value.

Figure 1A.9 Retirement Assets

Description	Owner	Market Value	Rate of Return
Tyler's 401(k)	Tyler		
Consumer Fund		$69,000	8.75%
Graham Fund		$134,000	4.10%
Tyler's traditional IRA certificate of deposit	Tyler	$52,000	3.50%
Mia's 401(k) Rocket Fund	Mia	$15,250	14.00%
Mia's Rollover IRA Ruth Fund	Mia	$32,500	4.80%
Mia's traditional IRA certificate of deposit	Mia	$52,000	3.50%
Conservative annuity Potsdam Fixed Annuity	Mia	$125,000	5.00%

Figure 1A.10 Other Liabilities

	Liability 1	Liability 2	Liability 3	Liability 4
Description	Mortgage	Sedan car loan	Visa credit card	MasterCard credit card
Loan detail	Springfield National Bank (joint liability)	Ford Motor credit (joint liability)	Springfield National Bank (joint liability)	University Bank (joint liability)
Loan type	Installment	Installment	Revolving	Revolving
Interest rate (APR)	7.875%	3.90%	18.25%	16.75%
Minimum payment calculation	Amortization	Amortization	Greater of 4% of monthly balance or $50	Greater of monthly interest charge + 1.5% of balance or $50
Minimum payment	$1,087.60	$451.00	$140.00	$60.00
Payment frequency	Monthly	Monthly	Monthly	Monthly
Original balance	$150,000* *The Bedos purchased this home with a special 100% financing loan option.	$24,549	$3,500 (current balance)	$2,000 (current balance)
Number of payments made	124	36	NA	NA
Original term (months)	360	60	NA	NA

INSURANCE PLANNING

Tyler and Mia are also concerned about the negative outcomes associated with dramatic events like death or disability. Over the past several years, they have taken steps to purchase insurance to meet different life, health, and property contingencies. They are still uncertain whether these policies are best suited to their needs. Details about their insurance policies are presented below.

Health Insurance Policies

Health insurance is provided for the entire family by a group health insurance policy offered through Tyler's work. The health provider, Peacock & Peacock, is a health maintenance organization. Tyler pays $300 a month in premiums for this coverage through his company's § 125 plan. The plan allows for pretax premium payments.

The policy has an annual deductible of $450 and a stop-loss of $3,000. Under the policy, doctors' visits cost $20 per appointment to the primary care physician and $40 per visit to specialists, and for emergency treatment a $100 copayment is required. Monthly prescriptions are $10 for generic brands and $25 for other brands. There is no copayment for hospitalization in semiprivate accommodations, and private rooms are provided when medically necessary. The original lifetime ceiling for services, per family member, was $2 million; however, with the passage of the Patient Protection and Affordable Care Act limits have been removed.

Over the past several years the Bedos have averaged about $50 per month in dental and eye care expenses, which they pay out of discretionary cash flow. A flexible spending account for health costs is available through Tyler's employer. They have not funded this account in the past because of uncertainty related to "use it or lose it" rules.

Disability Policies

The Bedos are automatically covered for disability by their employers. Mia also pays for additional long-term disability coverage through her employer. Information about each policy is presented in Figure 1A.11.

Figure 1A.11 Disability Policies

	Policy 1	Policy 2	Policy 3	Policy 4
Type of Policy	Group	Group	Group	Group
Insurance company	Mid-America Disability Assurance Corporation	All-World Life and Disability Company	Mid-America Disability Assurance Corporation	All-World Life and Disability Company
Rating	A.M. Best: A	A.M. Best: A	A.M. Best: A	A.M. Best: A-
Person insured	Tyler	Mia	Tyler	Mia
Wait periods (days)	0 days	0 days	90 days	90 days
Benefit period	90 days	90 days	To age 65	To age 65
Disability benefit	100% of salary and bonus	100% of salary and bonus	60% of salary and bonus	70% of salary and bonus
Definition	Own occupation	Own occupation	Own occupation	Modified own occupation
Benefit frequency	Biweekly	Monthly	Biweekly	Monthly
Premium amount	Company paid	Company paid	Company paid	$25 monthly (purchased through employer with pretax dollars)
Premium payment frequency	NA	NA	NA	Monthly

Life Insurance Policies

The Bedos currently have life insurance through their employers and through private policies. Their private policies were purchased several years ago from a friend who was selling life insurance. Information about their policies is shown in Figure 1A.12.

Figure 1A.12 Life Insurance Policies

	Policy 1	Policy 2	Policy 3	Policy 4
Type of Policy	Whole-life*	Whole-life*	Group term	Group term
Insurance company	Manhattan Insurance Company	Manhattan Insurance Company	Great Plains Assurance and Protection Corporation	Virginia Highland Life Insurance Company
Rating	A.M. Best: A	A.M. Best: A	A.M. Best: A	A.M. Best: A
Equivalent after-tax rate of return	5.50%	5.50%	0%	0%
Death benefit	$100,000	$100,000	1 x salary (not including bonus)	4 x salary (not including bonus)
Person insured	Tyler	Mia	Tyler	Mia
Owner	Tyler	Mia	Tyler	Mia
Beneficiary	Mia	Tyler	Mia	Tyler
Cash value	$8,750	$8,350	$0	$0
Premium amount	$92	$80	Company paid	Company paid
Payment frequency	Monthly	Monthly	NA	NA

*At the beginning of last year, the cash value of their whole-life policies equaled $7,850 for Tyler and $7,500 for Mia. They both received a dividend in the policy equal to $250.

Automobile Insurance

Tyler and Mia have split-limit coverage of 100/300/50 on both of their cars, in addition to $100,000 of uninsured/underinsured motorist coverage. Automobile insurance is provided by Missouri Valley Insurance Corporation (A.M. Best Rating: A). Deductibles are $500 for comprehensive coverage and $500 for collision coverage. This insurance includes medical payments, car rental coverage, and towing.

Homeowners Insurance

The Bedos currently have an HO-3 policy with a $100,000 liability limit that provides replacement value on contents through an endorsement underwritten by Missouri National Insurance (A.M. Best rating: A). Their home is currently insured for $225,000. They do not know if their policy has an inflation endorsement. The deductible is $500. The premium is $700 per year.

Three years ago, their insurance agent recommended that they purchase a $500,000 umbrella insurance policy. The premium for the policy is $175 per year.

INVESTMENT PLANNING

Before meeting with you, Tyler and Mia completed a confidential risk tolerance questionnaire downloaded from an Internet Web site. The results from the risk quiz suggested that both Tyler and Mia have a moderate to lower level of financial risk tolerance.

Tyler and Mia are interested in ideas that could improve their current returns without taking excessive risk. However, Tyler has made it very clear that he is extremely apprehensive about investing and feels that he tends to be risk averse. Mia, on the other hand, feels comfortable taking additional risks if she is confident that she can earn higher returns.

RETIREMENT PLANNING

Tyler and Mia have expressed a strong desire to retire at age 62. They both feel that they have other talents and dreams that they would like to pursue during retirement. Tyler loves golfing, gardening, and traveling. His dream is to teach aspiring young golfers on a volunteer basis during retirement.

Mia loves to paint, attend art shows, and occasionally golf. With the demands of her job, motherhood, and volunteer activities, she has had little time for any of these activities. Her plan in retirement is to build a small addition to their home and fill it with art. If built today, the addition would cost $20,000.

Mia would then like to open a small art gallery in downtown Springfield. She estimates that the cost of the gallery would be $80,000 if opened today. If she is successful as an art gallery owner, she plans to donate any net revenue from the art gallery to local youth groups to enhance creative learning.

In addition, Mia would like to improve her golf game so that Tyler would enjoy playing more golf with her.

Neither Tyler nor Mia has a strong desire to travel in retirement. Tyler travels enough now, and he would prefer to enjoy life in southwest Missouri during retirement. They do, however, plan on taking an occasional trip, especially to go and see their daughter if she is not living in Springfield.

Tyler and Mia feel that with these occasional trips, they will need approximately 85 percent of their current earned before-tax income (in today's dollars) when they retire. They believe they will receive Social Security benefits, and they want to take their benefits at the earliest opportunity. Also, they have a strong desire to leave an estate as large as possible for Becky's benefit at their death. Therefore, they would very much like to minimize the depletion of their retirement assets.

ESTATE PLANNING

Tyler and Mia have wills that they created when Becky was two years old. They used a will kit purchased at an office supply store because they did not have much time—they were about to begin a fourteen-day vacation in Europe when it occurred to them that they should have a will. They have not looked at their wills since.

In their wills, Mia's oldest sister Barbara—who is single and living in Oregon—was named Becky's guardian. The Bedos' wills leave all assets to each other in case of death.

Tyler and Mia want to make sure that they do not pay unnecessary estate taxes. They have also been reading magazine articles about probate. Mia is particularly concerned about maintaining privacy and making Becky's life less complicated in the event that she or Tyler was to die.

ADDITIONAL INFORMATION AND ASSUMPTIONS

Working Assumptions

Your firm has established expected rate-of-return and portfolio risk objectives for all investment portfolios and has concluded that these rate-of-return expectations (shown in Figure 1A.13) represent the maximum returns that should be used in financial planning models.

Figure 1A.13 Expected Rates of Return

	Expected Before-tax Total Rate of Return*	Estimated Target After-tax Total Rate of Return**	Beta (indexed to S&P 500)	Standard Deviation
Conservative	5.25%	3.7%	< 0.40	< 7.0
Moderately conservative	7.75%	5.4%	< 0.80	< 9.0
Moderately aggressive	10.00%	7.0%	0.80 < 1.00	< 13.0
Aggressive	12.14%	8.5%	> 1.00	> 13.0
*Note that these returns include capital appreciation, dividends, and interest received.				
** Assumes a combined federal and state tax rate of 30 percent.				

Your financial planning firm uses a screening technique to select and track mutual funds that can be used in client portfolios. Your firm currently uses eleven equity funds, six bond funds, one money market fund, and one variable-annuity product. Tyler and Mia, after consulting with you, have agreed to use these investments, as you recommend, to meet their financial planning goals and objectives. (These are the same investments available in their 401(k) plans.) Detailed information on each investment product is presented in Tables 1A.14 and 1A.15.

Figure 1A.14 Equity Funds

Fund	Investment Style	Before-tax Rate of Return	Standard Deviation	Correlation with Equity Market	Yield
Value Fund	Large cap	9.00%	12.00%	0.95	3.00%
Growth Fund	Large cap	10.20%	15.00%	0.90	2.00%
Eastside Fund	Mid-cap	8.40%	10.00%	0.92	2.00%
Konza Fund	Mid-cap	9.20%	13.00%	0.91	1.75%
Sagebrush Fund	Small cap	11.20%	21.00%	0.80	0.50%
Rocket Fund	Small cap	14.00%	22.00%	0.75	0.00%
Consumer Fund	Small cap	8.75%	11.00%	0.99	2.50%
Acquisitions Fund	Mid-cap	7.50%	5.20%	0.20	4.00%
International Fund	International (EAFE Index)	10.00%	11.20%	0.50	2.00%
Haley G&I Fund	Large cap	8.00%	10.00%	0.90	3.20%
Graham Fund	Real Estate and Precious Metals	4.10%	12.00%	0.10	2.00%

Figure 1A.15 Bond Funds

Fund	Investment Style	Before-tax Rate of Return	Standard Deviation	Correlation with Bond Market	Yield
Ruth Fund	Government bond	4.80%	4.90%	0.85	4.00%
Cardinal Fund	Corporate bond	5.20%	5.10%	0.90	4.80%
Clock Fund	Corporate bond	6.00%	6.20%	0.98	5.40%
Ely Fund	Government bond	6.10%	6.05%	0.92	6.00%
Companion Fund	High yield	7.00%	13.00%	0.80	6.10%
States Fund	Government bond	5.70%	6.00%	0.75	4.00%
Barrister Fund	Money market	3.00%	0.00%	0.00	3.00%

Other investments available for use when working with the Bedos include:

- The Potsdam Fixed Annuity (current guaranteed yield of 5.0 percent). Contract was purchased eight years ago and the guaranteed yield period will expire in two years.

- The Bostonian Variable Annuity includes a guaranteed investment contract that currently yields 5.0 percent and allows investments in all of the funds listed in the preceding tables. The cash and cash equivalent assets listed in the following table are also available.

Additionally, your financial planning firm finds it useful to create custom benchmarks by which to measure the performance of each client's portfolio. General information about the various segments of the market are shown in Tables 1A.16 and 1A.17

Figure 1A.16 Market Indexes

Index	Before-Tax Rate of Return*	Standard Deviation	Yeild*
Treasury bills	3.00%	5.00%	3.00%
Treasury coupon bonds	5.00%	6.00%	5.50%
Treasury zero-coupon bond "strips"	6.00%	6.50%	0.00%
Investment-grade corporate coupon bonds	7.00%	7.00%	7.00%
Investment-grade corp. zero-coupon bonds	7.50%	8.00%	0.00%
High-yield corporate bonds	9.00%	12.00%	9.00%
International bonds	10.00%	15.00%	10.00%
U.S. large-cap equity	10.00%	18.00%	2.25%
U.S. small-cap equity	12.00%	+20.00%	<1.00%
Developed international equity	15.00%	+25.00%	≈0.00%

* More representative of long-term averages than current market conditions.

Figure 1A.17 Cash and Cash Equivalents

Asset	Yeild*
Savings accounts	2.00%
Money market accounts	3.00%
Money market mutual funds	3.00%
Missouri municipal money market account	2.30%
One-year certificates of deposit	3.50%

* More representative of long-term averages than current market conditions.

Universal Assumptions

- The universal inflation rate is expected to average 3.0 percent per annum.

- The prime interest rate is currently 3.25 percent, but is expected to increase in the future.

- Life expectancy for Tyler and Mia is age ninety-five.

- They would like to assume a 30.0 percent combined state and federal tax bracket until retirement and a 25.0 percent combined state and federal marginal tax bracket during retirement.

SPECIFIC GOALS AND OBJECTIVES

Tyler and Mia's primary goal is to live life with a relatively high level of financial satisfaction. They want to be self-sufficient in retirement. As such, their primary objective is to retire at age sixty-two, if possible. Their secondary objective is to provide 100 percent of Becky's college education.

As suggested earlier, Mia would like to turn her love of collecting art into a small business during retirement by renting a retail outlet and selling art supplies and collectibles. They are also interested in maintaining the privacy of their financial affairs. Finally, they would like to ensure Becky's financial welfare if they die.

ISSUES

Cash Reserve Issues

- Their cash reserve goal is six months of total dedicated and discretionary expenses, not including taxes paid. In case of an emergency, Mia is willing to use her accumulated art gallery savings as long as the money remains in a bank, checking, or money market account. They would like to achieve this goal within two years.

- They are comfortable assuming a yield of 3.0 percent before taxes on their savings and money market accounts. Their checking accounts do not earn interest.

- The Bedos are comfortable assuming that their EE savings bonds will grow at a 3.50 percent tax-deferred rate and not mature for at least another 10 years.

- For simplified tax-planning purposes, dividends are considered nonqualified and do not qualify for reduced tax rates.

- The Bedos do not want to pay off their car loan at this time. They anticipate always having some form of auto loan in the future.

- Any mortgage refinancing will incur 3.0 percent of the mortgage as a closing cost. The Bedos would like to see an analysis showing the impact of both including closing costs in the mortgage and paying closing costs from assets.

- Their home is expected to appreciate by approximately 4.0 percent annually over the long-term.

- The Bedos would also like to assume that any interest earned from savings is reinvested rather than spent on household expenses, and that all dividends and capital gains from other investment assets are also reinvested.

Tax Issues

- The Bedos spent several hours the previous day calculating their state income tax liability. They believe that the amount of state tax withholding closely matches their estimated state tax due for the year, but they would like you to double-check their figures.

- For the purposes of this case, the Bedos are in the 5.0 percent Missouri tax bracket; they qualify for one state deduction worth $1,000 and two state exemptions valued at $900 each. The state calculation is based on federal adjusted gross income.

Disability Insurance Coverage Issues

After careful thought, the Bedos are willing to assume the following:

- They will receive no Social Security disability benefits.

- They plan to continue to save for other financial planning goals in the event of a disability.

- Any cash settlements received will be invested using a moderately conservative asset allocation approach.

Long-term Care Issues

The following assumptions should be used only to address long-term care insurance planning issues.

- For planning purposes the Bedos would like to assume that annual nursing home expenses in in their area are currently $49,000.

- The average age for entering as assisted living facility is 75, with an assumed average length of stay of 2.5 years.

- The average age for those entering a nursing home is 83, with an assumed average stay of 1.5 years.

- Long-term care expenses have been increasing at 5.0 percent per year.

- In the event that either client enters a nursing home, household expenses are expected to be approximately $115,000 per year (in today's dollars).

- Assets for use in funding long-term care expenses will grow at a modest 5.5 percent after-tax rate of return.

Asset Management Issues

- Mia's annuity is invested 100 percent in the Potsdam Fixed Annuity earning 5 percent (no other investment alternatives are available within the annuity). She originally purchased the annuity when she was twenty-seven years of age. The annuity has a ten-year declining withdrawal penalty.

- Both traditional IRAs are in one-year certificates of deposit maturing in a few months. The CDs yield 3.50 percent annually. The renewable rate is also 3.5 percent.

- Mia's rollover IRA is currently invested in the Ruth Fund.

- Tyler's 401(k) has a 100 percent employer match, up to 3 percent of the amount he contributes. The entire match is going to the Graham fund.

- Mia is contributing 10 percent to the Rocket Fund in her 401(k) plan. Her employer is matching 50 percent of her contributions, up to 6 percent of contributions.

- In the event that an investment asset is sold, the Bedos would prefer to assume (for tax purposes) that their basis in all after-tax investments is equal to 50 percent of the fair market value of these assets, and that all investment gains are subject to ordinary income tax rates.

- The Bedos would also like to assume that any interest earned from savings is reinvested rather than spent on household expenses, and that all dividends and capital gains from other investment assets are also reinvested.

Education Issues

The following assumptions should be used only to address education planning issues.

- In-state tuition at a good private university for four years will cost $10,000 per semester, including room and board (in today's dollars).

- Tuition costs are increasing at 5.0 percent per year.

- Tyler and Mia are willing to invest in a moderately aggressive portfolio for this goal, before Becky begins college and during her college years.

- The Bedos want all college savings to be accumulated before Becky begins college and therefore plan to stop saving for college expenses once Becky begins college.

- No assets are currently targeted for college savings needs.

- They would prefer to invest in a tax-advantaged investment to pay for college, if possible.

Premature Death Issues

The following assumptions should be used only to address life insurance planning issues.

- Assets available at Tyler's death include his IRA and 401(k) plan.

- Assets available at Mia's death include her IRA, her 401(k) plan, the annuity, and her IRA rollover account.

- The clients will need $115,000 in before-tax yearly income to fund total household expenses at the death of either Tyler or Mia.

- The Bedos are willing to allocate $100,000 of their nonretirement investment assets toward survivor needs.

- In case of death, the surviving spouse will invest any cash settlements in a moderately conservative portfolio before and after retirement; the Bedos want this assumption to supersede all other rate-of-return assumptions used in other calculations.

- Tyler and Mia would like to prefund their retirement and education objectives, even if one of them dies.

- For insurance planning purposes, the surviving spouse will need approximately $115,000 per year (in today's dollars) when the spouse retires.

- They feel that the following allocations will meet their final expense needs: $20,000 for final debts (e.g., credit card, auto loans, etc., but not the mortgage); $1,500 for final illness costs; $9,000 for funerals; $13,500 for estate administration costs; $10,000 for other short-term needs; and $25,000 for a spousal adjustment period.

- In the event that either Tyler or Mia dies prematurely, each would like all liabilities, including the home mortgage, to be paid off.

- Social Security benefits, in the event of Tyler's death, are as follows:

  - $23,448 yearly to Mia after age sixty-seven

  - $17,580 additional yearly to Mia until Becky turns age eighteen

  - $17,580 yearly to Becky until age eighteen

  - $16,765 yearly to Mia from age sixty to age sixty-seven (This is a 28.5 percent reduction in benefits based on age-sixty-seven survivor benefits.)

- Social Security benefits, in the event of Mia's death, are as follows:

  - $26,400 yearly to Tyler after age sixty-seven

  - $9,552 additional yearly to Tyler until Becky turns age eighteen

- $9,552 yearly to Becky until age eighteen

- $0 to Tyler from age sixty to sixty-seven

- In the event of either spouse's death, the other spouse plans to stop working at age sixty and begin taking early retirement survivor benefits (if available).

- For conservative planning purposes, the Bedos do not plan to use interest or dividends as an income source when planning insurance needs.

- The capital retention replacement ratio is assumed to be 100 percent.

Retirement Issues

The following assumptions should be used only to address retirement planning issues.

- Mia would like to build a small addition to their home and fill it with art. If built today, the addition would cost $20,000.

- Mia would then also like to open a small art gallery. She estimates the cost of the gallery would be $80,000 if opened today.

- The Bedos are willing to invest in a moderately aggressive portfolio to fund the art gallery and house addition. Currently, assets and savings for these goals are invested very conservatively in a bank account.

- They will need approximately 85 percent of their current earned before-tax income (in today's dollars) when they retire.

- They are willing to reallocate retirement assets and savings to earn a before-tax moderately conservative rate of return prior to retirement. The Bedos are willing to increase their rate of return through a reallocation of their retirement assets to meet these return assumptions. At the current time, however, the Bedos are earning less, given the allocation of their current portfolio. It is necessary to calculate their current rate of return to determine their retirement income need.

- Once retired, the Bedos would like to assume a before-tax conservative rate of return.

- The Bedos would like to assume a 25 percent federal marginal tax bracket while in retirement.

- Normal retirement age is age sixty-seven for Tyler and Mia.

- The Bedos want to retire at age sixty-two, but it is more important that they do not deplete their assets over their lifetime.

- They are unwilling to reduce their projected life expectancy unless absolutely required to achieve their age-at-retirement objective.

- They are willing to reallocate assets and savings to meet their retirement objective.

- They believe that their incomes will increase at the rate of inflation into the future.

- The Bedos plan to increase contributions to their retirement accounts by 3.0 percent each year.

- The primary insurance amount in today's dollars at age sixty-seven for Tyler is $2,200 and $1,300 for Mia.

Estate Planning Issues

The following assumptions should be used only to address estate planning issues.

- The assumed appreciation rate on their gross estate, debt, loans, and other financial position items is 4.0 percent.

- Funeral and administration expenses are assumed to be $9,000 for each person. These expenses will grow 4.0 percent annually. Executor fees are anticipated to be approximately $13,500 each.

Computations for Financial Planning

1. The purpose of this chapter is to provide a review of some of the most important computations used by financial planners on a daily basis. The chapter begins by examining holding-period returns. A holding-period return, or the total return for a defined period of time, is typically calculated as a ratio of how much money was earned from an investment to the original investment amount. The ratio is normally the total change in value divided by the amount invested. Also considered total returns are (1) dollar-weighted returns that adjust for the timing of intermediate cash flows so returns are more accurately represented by the total dollars invested over time, and (2) time-weighted returns that do not consider whether more or less money was invested, but instead consider the length of time the investment lasted.

2. Average annual returns can be computed using a linear series average. The outcome can be either an arithmetic average or a geometric series average, which is known as a geometric average. As noted in the chapter, both are accurate representations of past performance, but they should not be used without consideration for the purposes of projecting future value. Because of the variability of returns over time, the geometric average is more accurate for projecting long-term values. A weighted-average return calculation can be used in the same manner to determine the return for a multi-asset portfolio. The weight is determined based on the relative amount of the asset owned compared to the total value of the portfolio.

4. This chapter highlights the many ways interest rates can be calculated. Interest rates show a relative measure of output given a certain input; however, the output may need to be adjusted for one or more of several factors. Most frequently, interest rates are adjusted for inflation or taxes. Inflation-adjusted (real) or growth-adjusted (serial) interest rates consider losses or gains in purchasing power. The result of this adjustment is a measure of purchasing

Learning Objectives

power parity. Tax-adjusted interest rates are useful because various investments have different tax treatments. To be comparable on a tax-neutral basis, an adjustment must be made to compare tax-exempt to taxable investment returns.

5. This chapter discusses ways in which risk shapes rate of return assumptions. Typically, there is some uncertainty about the outcome, or future value, of an investment. The amount of return that is required by a potential investor is in no small part based on the level of uncertainty. Although investors are willing to invest money at a risk-free rate if they are only delaying consumption without accepting any risk, they need and want to be compensation for risk in the form of a higher return. Types of risk for which an investor would seek compensation include, but are not limited to, inflation risk, interest rate risk, and default risk.

6. Time value of money (TVM) concepts represent one of the foundational computational skills that must be mastered by a financial planner. TVM calculations are predicated on the idea the people would rather consume today than postpone consumption. Put another way, a dollar spent (or received) today is assumed to be more valuable than it is tomorrow. To determine how much more (or less) valuable a monetary asset is depends on the rate of return required by an investor and the length of time until the asset is needed or realized. Proper use of the TVM formulas allows for an accurate comparison of money spent (or received) at different points in time by aligning the two dollar amounts.

7. The future or present value of a single sum formula is most often applied when a direct comparison needs to be made about a single exchange—one inflow and one outflow. An example of this includes making a single investment in a certificate of deposit. The future value formula tells an investor how much the certificate will be worth when it matures, whereas the present value formula can be used to determine how much the client needs to invest today to achieve a particular goal upon maturity. In the former case, value today is known, and in the latter, the goal is known.

8. The future or present value of an annuity formula can be used to determine the future or present value, respectively, of a stream of equal payments, projecting the value into the future or discounting the stream of payments back to a current time period. An example of this includes making a series of payments into an individual retirement account. The future value formula tells an investor how much the account will be worth at some future date. In contrast, if an investor were promised a series of payments in the future, such as from a fixed annuity, the present value of an annuity formula can be used to determine how much the promised series of payments is actually worth today. Accuracy depends on determining the correct number of compounding periods by adjusting the calculation to reflect whether payments occur at the beginning or end of the year (i.e., an annuity due or an ordinary annuity).

Learning Objectives

9. The future or present value of a geometrically varying or "growing" annuity formula is used to determine the future or present value, respectively, of a stream of annually increasing payments, projecting the value into the future or discounting the stream of payments back to a current time period. An example of this would be making a series of payments to a 529 college savings plan where the investor plans to increase the payment amount by 5 percent annually. The future value of an annuity formula, adapted for the annual "growth" of the payment, tells the investor how much will be available to fund college at a future date. Alternatively, if the investor wants to provide the future college student a series of allowance payments that increases by 4 percent annually, the present value of a geometrically varying or "growing" annuity formula may be used to determine how much the investor needs to have available when the student begins college. Accuracy depends on determining the correct number of compounding periods by adjusting the calculation to reflect whether payments occur at the beginning or end of the year (i.e., an annuity due or an ordinary annuity).

10. This chapter introduces the notion of nominal rates and effective rates. Effective rates adjust for non-annual compounding periods. Most interest rates are stated in nominal terms without reference to the underlying compounding period. Effective rates are actual (or realized) rates of return after an adjustment for non-annual compounding. Although effective rates can be stated in any compounding frequency (e.g., monthly, semiannually, etc.), most often effective rates are converted into an expected annual return (EAR) form because it is the most intuitive method for stating rates.

11. A trial-and-error method for determining the internal rate of return (IRR) of an investment can easily be eliminated by using a TVM calculator to solve for the IRR of even cash flows (i.e., an annuity) or by using a calculator cash flow functions (registers) for uneven cash flows. A spreadsheet may be the easiest approach to quickly display how changes in interest rates or the term of a loan influence other loan information. The present value of an annuity formula can quickly provide the outstanding loan balance, which can then be calculated for different points in time and compared to the sum of the total payments to determine the total interest paid over the loan period. This chapter provides information on how to use both a calculator and a spreadsheet.

Key Terms

Accrued Annual Interest Rate

After-Tax Returns

Amortization Schedule

Annual Percentage Rate (APR)

Annuity

Annuity Due

Annuity Equations

Arithmetic Mean

Asset Control

Average Annual Returns

Average Return

Bias

Capital Gains

Cash Flow

Cash Flow Functions

Compound Annualized Growth
    Rate (CAGR)

Compound Interest

Compounding

Continuously Compounded

Default Risk

Deterministic Modeling

Discount Rate

Dollar-Weighted Return

Double Discounting

Downward Bias

Effective Annual Rate (EAR)

Effective Periodic Rate (EPR)

Exchange Rate Risk

Financial Calculator

Fisher Equation

Fixed, Constant-Dollar Annuity

Frequency of The Cash Flow

Future Value (FV)

Future Value of a Growing Annuity

Future Value of a Lump Sum

Future Value of an Annuity

Future Value of an Annuity Due

Geomean

Geometric Average

Geometrical Annuity

Geometrically Varying Annuity

Graduated Annuity

Gross Return

Growing Annuity

Growth Rate (G)

Growing Annuity

Holding-Period Return (HPR)

Income

Key Terms

Inflation	Rate of Return
Inflation Rate (I/Y)	Reinvestment Risk
Inflation Risk	Required Rate of Return
Interest Rate	Risk-Free Rate
Interest Rate Risk	Rule of 72
Internal Rate of Return (IRR)	Semimonthly
Investment	Serial Interest Rate
Level-Payment Annuity	Standard Deviation
Lump Sum	State Income Taxes
Marginal Tax Bracket	State Tax Rate
Mixed Sum	Tax Impact
Number of Payments in an Annuity (N)	Taxable Equivalent Yield (TEY)
Net Present Value (NPV)	Taxable Rate of Return
Nominal Return	Tax-Adjusted Returns
Nominal Value	Tax-Exempt Rate of Return
Payment (PMT)	Tax-Free Investment
Political Risk	Texas Instruments Baii Plus
Present Value (PV)	Time Value of Money (TVM)
Present Value of a Growing Annuity	Time-Weighted Return
Present Value of a Lump Sum	Total Return
Present Value of an Annuity	Upward Bias
Present Value of an Annuity Due	Varying Annuity
Present Value of Perpetuity (PVP)	Variance Drag
Present Value Of Growing Perpetuity	Weighted Average
Purchasing Power	

CFP® Principal Knowledge Topics

B.13. Time Value of Money Concepts and Calculations

E.36. Measures of Investment Returns

Chapter Equations

Fundamentals:

Equation 2.1: Average (Time-weighted) Return (AR) = $\dfrac{\Sigma r}{n}$

Equation 2.2: Geometric Mean = $[(1 + i_1) \times (1 + i_2) \times \ldots \times (1 + i_n) \times]^{1/n} - 1$

Calculating Return and Yield:

Equation 2.3:
Holding Period Return (HPR) = $\dfrac{\text{Income} + (\text{End Value} - \text{Beg. Value}) - \text{Costs}}{\text{Beg. Value}}$

Equation 2.4:
Tax Adjusted HPR = $\dfrac{(\text{Income} - [\text{End Value} - \text{Beg. Value} + \text{Deposits} - \text{Withdrawals}] - \text{Costs}}{\text{Beg. Value}}$

Equation 2.5: Dollar-Weighted Return =

$$\dfrac{\text{Income} + \text{End Value} - (\text{Beg. Value} + \text{Deposits} - \text{Withdrawals}) - \text{Costs}}{\text{Beg. Value} + \text{Time-Weighted Deposits} - \text{Time-Weighted Withdrawals}}$$

Equation 2.6: Porfolio Return = $\Sigma W \times r$

Equation 2.7: Real Return = $\left(\dfrac{1+\text{Nominal Return}}{1+\text{Inflation Rate}}\right) - 1$

Equation 2.8: After Tax Return = Nominal Return × (1 – Applicable Tax Rate)

Equation 2.9: Taxable Equivalent Yield (TEY) = $\dfrac{\text{Nominal Yield}}{(1 - \text{FMTB})}$

Time Value of Money (TVM):

Equation 2.10: Effective Annual Rate = $\left(1+\dfrac{\text{APR}}{m}\right)^m - 1$

Equation 2.11: Effective Periodic Rate (EPR) = $\dfrac{\text{APR}}{m}$

Equation 2.12: Future Value $(\text{FV}_n) = \text{PV}_0\,(1+i)^n$

Equation 2.13: Present Value $(\text{PV}_0) = \dfrac{\text{FV}_n}{(1+i)^n}$

Equation 2.14: Future Value of an Annuity $(\text{FVA}_n) = \dfrac{\text{PMT}}{i}\,[(1+i)^n - 1]$

Equation 2.15: Present Value of an Annuity $(\text{PVA}_0) = \dfrac{\text{PMT}}{i}\left[1-\dfrac{1}{(1+i)^n}\right]$

Equation 2.16: Present Value of a Delayed Annuity $(\text{PVA}_d) = \dfrac{\dfrac{\text{PMT}}{i}\left[1-\dfrac{1}{(1+i)^n}\right]}{(1+i)^d}$

Equation 2.17:
Future Value of a Growing Annuity $(\text{FVGA}_n) = \dfrac{\text{PMT}_1}{i-g}\,[(1+i)^n - (1+g)^n]$

Equation 2.18: Present Value of a Growing Annuity $(\text{PVGA}_0) = \dfrac{\text{PMT}_1}{(i-g)}\left[1-\dfrac{(1+g)^n}{(1+i)^n}\right]$

FINANCIAL COMPUTATIONS: DETERMING THE NEED

Almost all aspects of personal financial planning involve mathematical calculations. The good news is that the math is not extremely complex. Furthermore, sophisticated calculators and software programs are available to do most of the work. The most important caveat when attempting to complete financial planning computation is that outputs depend entirely upon the quality of inputs.

The formulas needed for the majority of the calculations are relatively easy to memorize. Applying the correct formula and related inputs within a calculation usually causes the most difficulty. More important than the formulas themselves is a fundamental understanding of the logic, or reasoning, required to identify the correct mathematical formula for a particular purpose.

Once the logic has been established, there may be multiple ways to derive the correct solution to a financial planning question. For example, one financial planner may choose to adjust a future value calculation for taxes at the end of period, while another may wish to adjust a savings need at the beginning to account for taxes. Both financial planners should arrive at the same answer. This can sometimes be confusing to those who are new to the logic of time value of money computations.

What is important, then, is for financial planners to choose a method that they are comfortable with and practice that method until the process becomes second nature. Then, it is equally important to ensure accuracy—in both the input of the data and the supporting assumptions on which a calculation is based.

The purpose of this chapter is to briefly review some of the most important calculations made during the personal financial planning process. After reading this chapter, readers should understand rates of return and time value of money formulas and how to set up equations for later use in a spreadsheet application or financial calculator. It is assumed that much of the content of this chapter is a review.

FINANCIAL COMPUTATION PLANNING SKILLS

Planning Skill 1: Understand How Investors Earn a Rate of Return

One of the most elementary of all personal finance calculations is determining the **total return** earned on an investment. Financial planners use this calculation to determine how much profit has been earned on an investment during a certain period of time. **Rate of return** describes the relationship between profit or loss relative to the amount saved or invested. For example, assume an investor deposits $1,000 into an account, the account has a stated rate of return of 6 percent, and the investor leaves the deposit in the account for one year. What will be the account balance at the end of the investment period? How much of the account balance is principal and how much is interest? How much will the account be worth in real terms if **inflation**—the general increase in the price of goods and services over time—averages 4 percent over the same time period? How much money will be available after paying taxes on the earnings? All of these questions are answered by using various rate of return calculations.

To calculate that rate of return on an investment, all sources of income must be identified. The two most common sources of return are **income** and **capital gains**. In general, income is derived from periodic payments received by an investor, either in cash or as deposits to an account during the investment period. Examples include stock dividends, bond interest payments, mutual fund dividends, or savings account interest payments. Capital gains (or losses), on the other hand, are generally received or realized when an investment period ends and the investment is sold, liquidates, or matures. If the security is sold for more (or less) than the purchase price, the investor will realize a capital gain (or loss).

These two sources of cash inflow serve as the basis for the nominal return on investment. A **nominal value**, in its simplest form, means an unadjusted value. A nominal value can be thought of as the **gross return**. The most common adjustment made to a nominal value is an inflation adjustment; however, nominal values can be adjusted for many other reasons. Later in the chapter, nominal values will be the basis of adjustments for inflation (real returns), taxes (after-tax returns), compounding frequencies (effective returns), and others. When calculating total returns or future values, it is as important to understand the interrelationship between the nominal and adjusted rate as it is to be able to accurately calculate the nominal rate of return.

Planning Skill 2: Master Average Annual Return Calculations

Average annual returns are some of the most quoted statistics in finance. These returns are easy to calculate, relatively simple to interpret, and —for the most part—intuitive. However, the most common usage for these statistics is to incorporate them into models to predict future investment results. It is important to keep in mind that most calculations of historic returns tend to have a **bias** or partial perspective when used to project future or terminal values. A **downward bias** means that the average used to project the future value tends to underestimate the actual outcome. An **upward bias** results in overestimation. Such bias occurs because cumulative return is a nonlinear function of average return.

The following discussion of arithmetic averages and geometric averages not only presents the calculation of the two statistics but also addresses two issues inherent in using either average as a means to project future results: standard deviation and time horizon. Both of these factors play a role in the bias created when projecting terminal values.

Arithmetic and Geometric Means—Calculation and Deterministic Forecasting

Although holding-period based returns are very simple to use and calculate, most returns are quoted on an average annual basis because annual returns are more intuitive for investors to understand and are often required by regulators. A financial planner can use a number of different methods to measure average rates of return. The simplest method is to calculate the **arithmetic mean**, which is a linear interpretation of past performance.

Equation 2.1: Average Return (AR) = $\dfrac{r_1 + r_2 + r_3 + \dots r_1}{n}$

Where:

r = return for period

n = number of periods

Example: Consider a client who makes 8 percent, 2 percent, and -5 percent in each of three years, respectively. The average of these returns is 1.67 percent.

$$AR = \frac{8\% + 2\% - 5\%}{3} = 1.67\%$$

The arithmetic mean, although quick to calculate and easy to explain, is often a poor representation of actual performance due to the variability (measured by *standard deviation*) of returns. Therefore, it can be said that the higher the standard deviation of returns, even over a short time period, the greater the potential upward bias of the projection. The resultant overestimation of future values is even more problematic when short-term arithmetic averages are used for long-term forecasting.

For longer forecasting periods, or for forecasting using a more highly varied return, a **geometric average** is more appropriate because this mean estimate is computed using a geometric series. A geometric mean takes on more of the characteristics found in long-term averages and corrects for any upward bias. In other words, future values, by their very nature, are the result of a geometric series of returns rather than linear series. The rule is that, unless the variation of returns (standard deviation) is zero, the geometric average will always be lower than the arithmetic return. How much less depends on the variation of returns. **Standard deviation** is the average difference between an individual outcome (in this case the investment return) and the average, or expected, outcome for the applicable group. Standard deviation will be discussed in more depth later in the chapter

Consider a $100 stock that rises 50 percent in one year and falls 50 percent the next. The arithmetic mean return is zero. However, when the return is tracked, it is apparent that in the first year the final price was $150. Then the 50 percent drop results in a final value of $75. The total return is obviously less than zero—it is a negative 25 percent total return. It is also a negative 13.4 percent geometric return. For this reason, the geometric mean is recommended for forecasting future values. The geometric mean is often referred to as "geomean," "annualized return," or the "compound annualized growth rate" (CAGR). The formula for calculating a geometric average is as follows:

Equation 2.1: Geometric Mean

$$GeoMean = [1 + i_1) * (1 + i_2) * \ldots * (1 + i_n)]^{1/n} - 1$$

Where:

   i = return for period

   n = number of periods

Example: Tonya purchased an investment seven years ago. According to the annual report, the investment earned the rates of return shown in the table below. She wants to know what return she could project for the next seven years by calculating the annualized return.

Year	Rate of Return
1	9%
2	-8%
3	2%
4	12%
5	18%
6	-7%
7	4%

$$GeoMean = [1.09 * 0.92 * 1.02 * 1.12 * 1.18 * 0.93 * 1.04]^{1/7} - 1 = 0.039 \; or \; 3.90\%$$

Now compare this result to the simple linear average.

$$\text{Arithmetic Mean (Average)} = \frac{\Sigma\, i}{n}$$

$$\text{Average} = \frac{0.09 - 0.08 + 0.02 + 0.12 + 0.18 - 0.07 + 0.04}{7}$$

Clearly, the arithmetic average overstates expected return with an upward bias. For example, seven years ago a client might have asked for the future value of $500,000 in seven years. Using the arithmetic average of 4.29 percent would have resulted in a projected value of $670,916.82; however, the account actually only grew to $653,550.03. Using the arithmetic average to project the future value would have resulted in an overstatement of the actual account value by $17,366.79. This may seem like an insignificant amount given the very fluid nature of financial markets and the subjective nature of projections. But what if the client had $2,000,000 and asked for a 25-year projection? In this case, the difference between the arithmetic projection and the geometric projection would have been more than half a million dollars, which would have most likely undermined the client-planner relationship.

Self-Test 1

A _____ would typically induce a downwards bias on near-term future values, whereas a _____ might induce an upward bias on long-term future values.

a) geometric, arithmetic

b) arithmetic, geometric

c) geometric, geometric

d) arithmetic, arithmetic

Using a geometric average will result in a more precise measure of the client's true return when projecting account values into the future. The arithmetic mean can be useful in certain circumstances or for a quick estimate, but for actual reporting and forecasting, the geometric mean is generally preferred. However, this method too is not without flaws. A future value calculated using a geometric average is likely to have a slight downward bias. This means that the actual future value achieved is likely to be slightly greater than the future value projected using the geometric average. The amount of underestimation will depend on the ratio of the sampled estimation period compared to the forecasted period. The closer the ratio is to one, the less likely the downward bias.

The following rules generally hold true:

- When forecasting periods that are much shorter than the sample period from which the averages were calculated, the true average tends to be closer to the arithmetic mean.

- For forecasting periods that are much closer in length to the sample period, the true average will be closer to the geometric mean.

Arithmetic vs. Geometric: Margin for Error

When comparing the arithmetic mean and the geometric mean, it is interesting to note that as the standard deviation of the returns approaches zero, the difference between the arithmetic mean and the geometric mean also approaches zero. This is because the arithmetic mean and the geometric mean are equal if the return is fixed, meaning that the exact same outcome (return) occurs in each period, which results in a standard deviation of zero. However, the inverse is also true. As the standard deviation of outcomes increases, the difference between the arithmetic mean and the geometric mean also increases.

Consider the S&P 500 total returns in Figure 2.1. The difference between the two means is quite large, 1.90 percent (10.10 percent – 8.20 percent), because the standard deviation is nearly 20 percent. As this example illustrates, the relationship between the two statistics becomes quite apparent and very important.

Figure 2.1 Investment Market Returns

Year	Annual Return	Year	Annual Return
Year 1	-3.10%	Year 11	-9.10%
Year 2	30.46%	Year 12	-11.89%
Year 3	7.62%	Year 13	-22.10%
Year 4	10.08%	Year 14	28.68%
Year 5	1.32%	Year 15	10.88%
Year 6	37.58%	Year 16	4.91%
Year 7	22.96%	Year 17	15.80%
Year 8	33.36%	Year 18	5.49%
Year 9	28.58%	Year 19	-37.00%
Year 10	21.04%	Year 20	26.46%
Arithmetic Average	10.10%	Geometric Average	8.21%
Variance	3.89%	Standard Deviation	19.73%

Example: A client has an account balance of $50,000. The client assumes that since the average annual return of the stock market has been 10 percent over the last 20 years, the next 20 years should result in the same return. Even if history were to repeat itself, the client still should not use the 10.1 percent average annual return but should instead use the 8.2 percent geometric average return. By using the incorrect average return for projecting the value of the account in 20 years, the client will likely overstate the account balance by nearly $95,000. Using the incorrect 10 percent return results in an account balance of $336,375.00; using the more accurate 8.2 percent return results in an account balance of $241,832.81.

One of the most significant issues associated with calculating geometric averages is that individual periodic returns are needed to construct the geometric series; however, the literature and internet sites typically provide only multi-period average returns (e.g., 3-year, 5-year, 10-year). However, if the standard deviation is also available for a corresponding period, then the geomean can be estimated. Referring back to the inset discussing variance drag, the following formula can be used to back into the geomean if a return series is unavailable:

> Geometric Mean = Arithmetic Mean – ½ Variance

Using the preceding example where the arithmetic average was 10.10 percent and the variance was 3.89 percent, the geomean can quickly be estimated as:

> Geometric Mean = 10.10% – ½ * 3.89% = 8.155%

Variance Drag

The difference between the arithmetic average of a series of returns and the geometric average of the same series is known as Variance Drag. The variance drag can estimated as one-half of the variance of the returns. For example, the long-term standard deviation of annual returns for the equity markets has been about 17.3%; therefore the variance is 0.03. Taking one-half of this value results in a variance drag of 1.5%. A more in depth example is provided on the following pages.

Planning Skill 3: Master Calculating Holding-Period Return Calculations

Holding-Period Return

A simple method of calculating **nominal returns** involves determining an investor's **holding-period return (HPR)**. The formula considers a beginning and ending value for the investment, income earned during the holding period, and transaction costs. The income received could be dividends from an equity (or stock) investment, or the income could be coupon "interest" payments from a debt (or bond) investment. The formula is as follows:

Equation 2.3: Holding Period Return HPR =

$$\frac{\text{Income} + (\text{Ending Value} - \text{Beginning Value}) - \text{Transaction Costs}}{\text{Beginning Value}}$$

Example: Bob purchased one share of stock for $45 per share, received two dividend payments of $1 each that were not reinvested, and paid a transaction fee of $5. Bob then sold the stock for $55. What was Bob's holding-period return?

$$\text{HPR} = \frac{\sum \text{Div} + (\text{End} - \text{Beg}) - \text{Costs}}{\text{Beg}}$$

$$\text{HPR} = \frac{(1 + 1) + (55 - 45) - 5}{45} = \frac{2 + 10 - 5}{45} = 15.6\%$$

A common modification to nominal rates of return is an adjustment for taxes paid at the state and federal levels. However, calculating **tax-adjusted returns** can be complex. First, a financial planner needs to know what type of income was generated as a result of the return. Second, the financial planner must know what tax rate applies to each type of return. For example, interest income, dividends (qualified or nonqualified), and capital gains may be taxed at different rates. The rates may also vary depending on the holding period for the investment (e.g., short-term or long-term capital gains).

To accurately calculate the tax-adjusted rate of return, the HPR must be offset by any tax liability generated as a result of owning the investment. The following adjustment can be used for historical return calculations:

Equation 2.4: Tax Adjusted HPR =
$$\frac{(\text{Income} - \text{IncomeTax}) + (\text{CapitalGains} - \text{CapGainsTax}) - (\text{Costs adjusted for Taxes})}{\text{BeginningValue}}$$

Obviously, this equation can be used only for historical calculations because the actual amount of tax liability must be determined prior to calculating the return. However, to estimate the after-tax rate of return for projection purposes, where taxation occurs annually, a financial planner can also use the following equation:

$$r_t = R \times (1 - t)$$

Where:

r_t = tax-adjusted return

R = nominal return

t = investor's marginal tax bracket

Example: Expanding on the previous example, assume Bob owned the stock in a non-tax-qualified account and dividends and capital gains are taxed at a short-term tax rate of 15 percent. His after-tax rate of return would be 13.26 percent, as shown below:

$$r_t = 15.6\% \times (1 - 0.15) = 13.26\%$$

Dollar-Weighted Return

The problem with using a holding-period return is that the formula does not account for the timing of subsequent cash flows into or out of an account. A very basic formula that corrects for the timing of subsequent cash flows is the dollar-weighted return formula, shown below:

Equation 2.5: Dollar-Weighted Return

$$\text{Dollar-Weighted HPR} = \frac{\text{Inc} + [\text{End} - (\text{Beg.} + D - W)] - \text{Costs}}{\text{Beg.} + D_t - W_t}$$

Where:

Inc = income

End = ending value

Beg = beginning value

D = deposit amount

W = withdrawal amount

Costs = transaction costs

Dt = D × (1 - timing of deposit)

Wt = W × (1 - timing of withdrawal)

Example: Altering the preceding example, assume that one year after Bob made his initial one share purchase he bought an additional two shares of stock at $48 ($48 × 2 = $96). Further, assume that he sold one share at $45 at the end of the second year and liquidated the account after three years at $50 per share ($50 × 2 = $100). He will still receive semiannual dividends of $1 per share ($12 total); the total transaction cost is still $5. What is Bob's dollar-weighted rate of return?

$$\text{Dollar-Weighted HPR} = \frac{\$12 + [\$100 - (\$45 + \$96 - \$45)] - \$5}{\$45 + \left[\$96\left(1 - \frac{12}{36}\right)\right] - \left[\$45\left(1 - \frac{24}{36}\right)\right]}$$

$$= \frac{\$12 + \$4 - \$5}{\$45 + \$64 - \$15} = 11.7\%$$

Time-Weighted Return

An alternative to dollar-weighted returns is a **time-weighted return**. This method of calculation ignores the actual value of the investment during each time period.

Example: Using Bob's situation, it is known that the stock was initially purchased for $45 per share and was valued as follows:

End of Year 1 = $48

End of Year 2 = $45

End of Year 3 = $50

Using the holding-period return formula results in the following annual rates of return:

$$\text{Year 1} = \frac{\$2 + (\$48 - \$45)}{\$45} = 11.1\%$$

$$\text{Year 2} = \frac{\$2 + (\$45 - \$48)}{\$48} = -2.1\%$$

$$\text{Year 3} = \frac{\$2 + (\$50 - \$45)}{\$45} = 15.6\%$$

$$\text{Average} = \frac{11.1\% - 2.1\% + 15.6\%}{3} = 8.2\%$$

#Remember

A series of time-weighted returns can be converted to a geometric mean only if every period of time is the same length (e.g., annual, quarterly, etc.)

Thus, the average of the three annual returns results in a time-weighted return of 8.2 percent. Note that the dividend was the same for all three periods because the time-weighted return ignores the number of shares (dollar amount) owned in each period.

Which measure is superior? It depends on asset control. Investors who control their own investments (both the timing and amount of purchases) will want to use the dollar-weighted average. In this case, the more money invested when a stock is performing well, the more money the investor will have in the end. However, a person who does not control the timing and amount of the investment, such as a portfolio manager, would want to measure performance using the time-weighted measure. It would be inappropriate to examine a manager's success or failure based on a measure over which the manager does not have complete control.

Planning Skill 4: Master-Weighted Average Return Calculations

Multi-Asset Portfolio Returns

Sometimes it is necessary to calculate a weighted average return for different assets or values. A **weighted average** is calculated by multiplying an investment return by the proportion of the investment, stated as a percentage of the total portfolio, and then summing the total for all of the investments.

Equation 2.6: Portfolio Return

$$\text{Portfolio Return} = \sum W \times r$$

Where:

W = weight of each asset in the portfolio

r = return of each asset in the portfolio

For example, Figure 2.2 provides rate of return data from seven mutual funds. The amount invested in each fund is also provided. These data were used to determine that this portfolio has a weighted average rate of return of 5.64 percent.

Figure 2.2 Hypothetical Portfolio Values and Returns

Fund	Objective	Value (A)	Percent of Portfolio (B)	RoR (C)	Weighted Return (D)
	Calculation		(A/E)		(BxC)
Fund A	Moderately Aggressive	$75,000	15.79%	8.00%	1.26%
Fund B	Moderately Conservative	$100,000	21.05%	9.00%	1.89%
Fund C	CD	$94,000	19.79%	3.00%	0.59%
Fund D	Aggressive	$14,000	2.95%	10.00%	0.29%
Fund E	Conservative	$35,000	7.37%	3.00%	0.22%
Fund F	CD	$45,000	9.47%	2.00%	0.19%
Fund G	Conservative	$112,000	23.58%	5.00%	1.18%
Total: (E)		**$475,000**	**100.00%**		**5.64%**

Scenario-Based Return Forecasting

Nearly all financial planning forecasts are based on the notion that the future will closely resemble the past. This is, obviously, a tenuous assumption. **Deterministic modeling** based on historical averages can sometimes be highly misrepresentative of the near-term future. It is sometimes better to account for multiple potential outcomes, where each outcome is assigned a probability of occurrence. Using the same methodology to determine a weighted average return, where the weights each represent a percentage of the entire portfolio, a financial planner can reassign the weights to the probability of occurrence, as shown in Figure 2.3. Then each outcome can be assigned a corresponding potential return.

Figure 2.3 Scenario-Based Potential Returns

Potential Economic Outcome	Probability of Occurrence (A)	Corresponding Return (B)	Weighted Return (AxB)
Super-normal growth	15.0%	20.00%	3.00%
Normal growth	55.0%	12.00%	6.60%
Stagnation	5.0%	3.00%	0.15%
Recession	20.0%	-8.00%	-1.60%
Depression	5.0%	-25.00%	-1.25%
	100.00%		6.90%

Planning Skill 5: Understand the Types and Forms of Interest Rates

Real vs. Nominal Rates

Nearly all interest rates quoted online, in magazines, and in annual reports are **nominal rates**, meaning that the rate has not been adjusted to account for inflation. Nominal rates are used when the actual dollar amount of an investment is important. By contrast, the **real rate of return** is the return "left over" after adjusting for inflation. This return provides a more accurate representation of **purchasing power**, which is an important consideration for long-term investments. A client may be interested in having a portfolio value of $1 million when she turns 65, but she needs to recognize that the purchasing power of such a portfolio will be far less than what $1 million provides today. This is why adjusting returns to account for inflation is of paramount importance.

Two equations are used to account for the effects of inflation: one if the nominal rate of return is continuously compounded and another if the nominal rate is discretely or not continuously compounded. If the nominal rate of return is **continuously compounded**, it is appropriate to subtract the inflation rate from the nominal rate to determine an approximation of the real rate.

#Remember

The "risk-free" rate only compensates an investor for waiting and should be very close to the inflation rate.

$$R^* = R - I$$

Where:

R* = real rate

R = nominal rate

I = inflation rate

Example: The nominal annual rate of return on Mary's portfolio is 9 percent and the annual inflation rate is 4 percent. In this case, the nominal rate of return is continuously compounded. What is her real rate of return?

$$R^* = 0.09 - 0.04 = 0.05 \ or \ 5.0\%$$

Self-Test 2

True or False: The real return provides a better indication of a client's future purchasing power.

However, if the nominal rate is not continuously compounded, a different equation, often referred to as the **Fisher Equation**, should be used to take into account the effects of this compounding difference. The result of this calculation is sometimes referred to as a **serial interest rate**.

Equation 2.7: Real Return

$$R^* = \left(\frac{1 + R}{1 + I} \right) - 1$$

Where:

R*= real rate

R = nominal rate

I = inflation rate

Example: The nominal annual rate of return on Mary's portfolio is 9 percent and the annual inflation rate is 4 percent. In this case, the nominal rate of return is not continuously compounded. The real rate of return is no longer 5 percent, but slightly less than 5 percent.

$$R^* = \left(\frac{1.09}{1.04} \right) - 1 = 0.0481 \; or \; 4.81\%$$

This calculation should be used whenever a client faces *inflation risk* when making an investment. These are particularly important formulas when determining the present value of an inflation-adjusted dollar amount—as is the case anytime a financial planner or investor is calculating future values but stating the results in today's dollars.

Tax-exempt vs. Taxable Rates

In addition to the difference between nominal and real rates of return, financial planners need to account for differences between taxable and tax-exempt rates of return. In the earlier discussion of holding-period returns, the concept of **tax impact** was briefly introduced. For the most part, exact **after-tax returns** cannot be determined until the end of an investing period. However, applying a client's **marginal tax bracket** to a return calculation can at least offer a reasonable estimate of future tax impact on a projected return using Equation 2.8.

Equation 2.8: After-Tax Return

After Tax Return = Nominal Return × (1 – Applicable Tax Rate)

Example: A client is in the 25 percent marginal tax bracket and the expected return on an investment is 7 percent. By applying the following formula, a financial planner can determine how much of the return will actually benefit the client. In other words, how much of each dollar earned will be retained after taxes?

$$R' = R \times (1 - t)$$

Where:

R´ = after-tax rate

R = nominal rate

t = federal marginal tax rate

$$R' = 0.07 \times (1 - 0.25) = 0.0525 \; or \; 5.25\%$$

> **Taxable Equivalent Yield**
>
> A taxable equivalent yield is an investor's implied required rate of return on a taxable investment with identical risk/reward characteristics.

In this case, the investor's after-tax return will be 5.25 percent. If a client invested $1,000 in a taxable account and the account returned 7 percent per year, or $70, then the client would keep $52.50 of those dollars. The investor would pay $17.50 in taxes. This formula can also be expanded to include effect of state taxes on nominal returns.

In many states, **state income taxes** are levied against only gains that remain after the federal tax liability has been applied; in such states, the **state tax rate** cannot simply be added to the federal tax rate in the preceding formula. The state tax rate is, in essence, reduced by the client's federal tax bracket. This is accomplished by using the same formula as above, except that the nominal rate in the formula is replaced by the state tax rate.

$$S' = S \times (1 - t)$$

Where:

S' = applicable state tax rate

S = state tax rate

t = Federal tax rate

Now the combined after-tax rate can be determined by combining both of the preceding equations.

$$R' = R \times [1 - (t + (S \times (1 - t)))] \; or \; R \times [1 - (t + S')]$$

This may seem like a lot of manipulation for a fairly simple projection; however, this approach can be useful when determining the **taxable equivalent yield (TEY)**. If an investor could earn 6 percent on a tax-free investment, the TEY would need to be higher to compensate the investor equally on an after-tax basis. The formula to determine exactly how much higher is a variation of the preceding formulas.

The following formula can be used to determine the TEY on a taxable investment that can then be compared with a federal **tax-free investment** (e.g., an out-of-state municipal bond) using the *federal marginal tax bracket* (FMTB).

Equation 2.9: Taxable Equivalent Yield (TEY)

$$\text{Taxable Equivalent Yield (TEY)} = \frac{\text{Nominal Yield}}{1 - \text{FMTB}}$$

Where FMTB = the applicable federal marginal tax bracket rate.

Keep in mind that this formula accounts only for federal taxes and it applies only to certain situations, including:

- the purchase of out-of-state municipal bonds;

- the comparison of in-state municipal bonds to Treasury bonds when neither bond is subject to state taxes; and

- when a client's state of residence does not levy a state income tax.

Outside of these situations, the impact of both federal and state taxes should be considered. To include the impact of state taxes, the formula needs to be slightly altered to include the *state marginal tax bracket* (SMTB).

$$\text{Taxable Equivalent Yield (TEY)} = \frac{\text{Nominal Yield}}{1 - [\text{FMTB} + (\text{SMTB} \times (1 - \text{FMTB}))]}$$

Example: A client desires a fixed-income investment and has narrowed the list of choices to two bonds: (1) an in-state municipal bond with an annual coupon rate of 6 percent and (2) a corporate bond with an annual coupon rate of 8 percent. The investor is in the 25 percent federal tax bracket and the 5 percent state tax bracket. Which would be the better bond to purchase?

At first glance, it would seem that the corporate bond that pays $80 per $1,000 invested would be the better choice. However, the client would have to pay taxes on the $80, leaving the client with less than $80 after taxes. The other choice is the municipal bond that pays only $60, but the client would, under most circumstances, not owe any federal or state taxes on that amount.

By using the TEY formula, the client can determine the required yield on the taxable investment that would provide equal compensation. In other words, this is the yield that is required to net the client the same amount of spendable dollars after paying the tax liability on the earnings.

$$\text{TEY} = \frac{0.06}{1 - [0.25 + (0.05 \times (1 - 0.25))]} = \frac{0.06}{0.7125} = 0.0842 \text{ or } 8.42\%$$

Using the formula above, a financial planner can determine that the taxable return would have to be 8.42 percent for the client to maintain the same net return. Therefore, the client would be better off purchasing the in-state municipal bond.

Planning Skill 6: Identify Risk and Return Factors

Inflation risk, default risk, interest rate risk, reinvestment risk, political risk, exchange rate risk, and other factors must be analyzed and either removed, mitigated, or compensated for when making investment planning and rate of return assumptions. To be compensated for these risks (discussed in more detail in Chapter 10), an investor must receive a rate of return high enough to adjust for the risk. The outcome of this adjustment is an investor's **required rate of return**. This rate will nearly always be greater than the **risk-free rate** that simply compensates an investor for delaying consumption. An investor's required rate of return is universally used as the basis for time value of money calculations.

Planning Skill 7: Master Time Value of Money Calculations

Some have argued that a financial plan serves as the foundation of a client's financial future. If that is the case, then time value of money concepts are the cornerstone of that foundation. The **time value of money** (**TVM**) formulas can be used for two primary purposes: (1) to estimate how money can be moved around in time while accurately reflecting its true value or purchasing power; and (2) to solve for complex spending and savings scenarios, such as college or retirement funding. TVM formulas can be used to answer questions such as: What will be the value of a client's savings in ten years? How much does a client need to save today to fund something in the future? What will be the impact of inflation on a client's standard of living?

The underlying assumption behind all TVM calculations is that it is generally more beneficial to receive a dollar today than in the future. Someone who waits to receive a dollar, rather than taking it today, must be compensated for waiting. That person would be willing to spend less than a dollar today in order to receive a dollar in the future. The following discussion provides an overview of some of the cornerstone concepts underlying TVM calculations.

Effective and Nominal Rates of Return

Compound interest is premised on the idea that interest earned in a prior period is reinvested and therefore earns additional interest in subsequent periods. Referred to by Albert Einstein as the "eighth wonder of the world," this mechanism adds a level of complexity when calculating present or future values, which substantiates the less well-known component of his quote: "He who understands it, earns it…he who doesn't, pays it."

The simplest example is that if a $100 investment earns a simple 10 percent per year, then the account will pay the owner $10 the first year, the tenth year, and every year thereafter. If the same investor reinvests or compounds the interest, the account will earn more interest in each subsequent year. While the first year still returns $10, the tenth year will return $23.58 based on a prior year value of $235.79.

For TVM calculations, it is generally assumed that all accounts will compound interest earned; therefore, the **interest rate**, or the investor's required rate of return, is the variable that compounds or discounts the cash flows. **Compound interest** takes into account both principal and the interest earned on the principal. This is the variable that keeps values equal across time. When using TVM formulas, it is critical that the interest rate used be an **effective rate**—one that considers the effects of **compounding** when compounding occurs more than once a year. In other words, this is the actual **accrued annual interest rate**.

If the rate is not an effective rate, then it is a nominal rate, often referred to as an **annual percentage rate** (**APR,** sometimes written as I_{NOM}). The nominal rate may be used in a financial calculator because the calculator can, if set correctly, automatically adjust for the compounding period (normally the payment frequency). It generally may not be used in mathematical formulas unless adjustments are made to the formulas. The following formula is used to adjust a nominal rate to an effective rate:

Equation 2.10: Effective Annual Rate (EAR)

$$EAR = \left(1 + \frac{APR}{m}\right)^m - 1$$

Where:

APR = annual percentage rate, or the nominal rate

m = number of compounding periods per year

The **effective annual rate** (**EAR**) is the rate of return that, under annual compounding, will produce the same future value at the end of one year as produced by more frequent compounding. If compounding occurs on an annual basis, m = 1, making the effective annual rate and the nominal rate the same. If compounding occurs more frequently, the effective annual rate will always be greater than the nominal rate.

In addition to the effective annual rate, there is also an **effective periodic rate** (**EPR**). The EPR (or "i_{PER}" as compared to "i_{NOM}") is the rate charged by a lender or paid by a borrower each period. The EPR can be a semiannual, quarterly, monthly, or daily rate; in fact it can be any time interval, for example, every 10 years. If the compounding frequency and the payment frequency are the same (*m*) then the following formula may be used.

Equation 2.11: Effective Periodic Rate (EPR)

$$EPR = \frac{APR}{m}$$

However, if the compounding period is different from the payment period then the EPR must be found based on the EAR using the following formula where m is the payment frequency:

Effective Periodic Rate = $(1 + EAR)^{1/m} - 1$

Example: What is the EAR in a bank account that has an APR of 6 percent, but the interest is compounded quarterly?

$$EAR = \left(1 + \frac{0.06}{4}\right)^4 - 1 = 0.0614 \ or \ 6.14\%$$

Example: What is the effective monthly interest rate on a mortgage with a stated APR of 8 percent? This would be the rate necessary to determine the monthly interest charges on a simple-interest mortgage with a monthly payment.

$$EPR = \frac{0.08}{12} = 0.00667 \text{ or } 0.667\%$$

In the cases where the compounding frequency and the payment frequency are different the EAR formula and the EPR formula (for non-annual payments) would have a different m.

Example: In the previous example it is assumed that the payment frequency and the compounding frequency are both monthly. Now assume that the payment frequency is semi-monthly, but the compounding period is still monthly. In this case it is necessary to determine the effective annual rate, based on monthly compounding before the effective periodic, in this case semi-monthly, rate can be found. Therefore both of the preceding formulas must be used in sequence.

$$EPR = \left(1 + \frac{0.08}{12}\right)^{12} - 1 = 0.0830 \text{ or } 8.30\%$$

$$EPR = (1.0830)^{1/24} - 1 = 0.00\overline{3} \text{ or } 0.33\%$$

Figure 2.4 summarizes common variations of the equations used to adjust between nominal and effective interest rates.

Figure 2.4 Adjusting Between Nominal and Effective Interest Rates

Type of Interest Rate Known	Type of Interest Rate Desired	Formula Needed
EAR	EPR	$EPR = (1 + EAR)^{1/m} - 1$
EAR	APR	$APR = [(1 + EAR)^{1/m} - 1] *m$
EPR	EAR	$EPR = (1 + EPR)^{m} - 1$
EPR	APR	$APR = EPR \times m$
APR	EAR	$EAR = \left(1 + \frac{APR}{m}\right)^{m} - 1$
APR	EPR	$EAR = \frac{APR}{m}$
Note: In all cases, m is the number of compounding periods per year (i.e. 12 for monthly, 4 for quarterly).		

One of the most important concepts to understand when manipulating rates of return in TVM equations is that the compounding frequency of the effective rate must match the payment frequency. In other words, the rate used must match the compounding frequency of how often cash flows, or payments, occur. For example, if a payment is occurring monthly, then the effective rate needs to be adjusted so that it is also compounded monthly. This adjustment does not influence the actual interest earned; it simply adjusts how the rate is interpreted within the equation.

Payments are the periodic inflows or outflows that occur during a valuation period. Payments are used only with **annuity equations**. For a cash flow to be considered a *payment*, it must occur more than once and happen on a fixed periodic basis (e.g., monthly, semiannually, annually, etc.). Because the frequency of a payment and the interest rate must match, and the payment frequency is independent, the interest rate must be adjusted to match the payment frequency.

Self-Test 4

Which of the following is the correct combination of frequencies (m) to solve for the appropriate EPR if the payments are made on a quarterly basis but compounding happens daily?

a) 360,120

b) 4,360

c) 12,400

d) 360,400

Example: A client is planning to save for retirement by contributing to an employer-sponsored 401(k) plan on a semimonthly (twice per month) basis. However, the account reports and compounds at a monthly rate of 0.721 percent. For a TVM equation to be accurate, the rate must reflect the equivalent semimonthly compounding period. To make this conversion, two of effective rate equations must be used. First convert the monthly effective rate into an EAR.

$$EAR = (1.00721)^{12} - 1 = 0.090 \ or \ 9.00\%$$

Second, the EAR must be converted back into a semimonthly effective rate.

$$EPR = (1.090)^{1/24} - 1 = 0.0036 \ or \ 0.36\%$$

This new EPR can be used in the formula to determine what the required savings amount needs to be, the future value of the account, or whatever else the financial planner may be calculating.

Basic Time Value of Money Calculations

Every TVM calculation involves at least three of six possible variables, including.

1. **FV-** A single **cash flow** or series of cash flows (FVA) that occur at any point(s) in time after the present.

2. **PMT-** A series of equal* and uninterrupted cash flows that occur for multiple consecutive periods (*payments may not be equal, but related, in the case of growing annuities).

3. **PV-** The value today of a single cash flow or of a series of cash flows (PVA) that will occur in the future. It is important to note, however, that present values can exist at any point in time so long as the cash flows are being discounted.

4. **I/Y-** The rate of return required by an investor to forgo consumption in the current time period. This is often referred to as the **discount rate** and can be used interchangeably with *internal rate of return* (IRR) because this rate equates future benefits with current costs.

5. **N-** The number of periods (and payments, if an annuity) across which cash flows are being discounted or compounded. Typically, N is used to denote years and M is used to denote periods or payments per year, but often the variable N is used to represent the total number of periods regardless of the duration of the period.

6. **G-** The **growth rate** or **inflation rate** at which a payment increases or decreases over the annuity period. Growth rates apply only to annuities, which are often then referred to as *geometrically varying, graduated,* or *growing annuities.*

Understanding not only the definitions of each variable but the impact of changing each variable is paramount to truly understanding TVM computations. Figure 2.5 provides an overview of the assumptions imbedded in TVM formulas.

Figure 2.5 Relationships between Inputs and Outcomes in Time Value of Money Computations

Variable Change (All Others Constant)	Effect on			
	Present Value of a Lump Sum	Future Value of a Lump Sum	Present Value of Annuity	Future Value of Annuity
Increase I/Y	Decrease	Increase	Decrease	Increase
Decrease I/Y	Increase	Decrease	Increase	Decrease
Increase N	Decrease	Increase	Increase*	Increase
Decrease N	Increase	Decrease	Increase	Decrease
Increase PMT	N/A	N/A	Increase	Increase
Decrease PMT	N/A	N/A	Decrease	Decrease
Increase G	N/A	N/A	Increase	Increase
Decrease G	N/A	N/A	Decrease	Decrease

* This may counter intuition, but as the number of payments increase, total value increases.

Future Value of a Single Sum

One of the most common questions in all of finance is, "How much will a sum invested today be worth in the future?" To answer this question, a financial planner should use a basic **future value** formula. The **future value of a single sum** formula is as follows:

Equation 2.12: Future Value (FV_n)

$$FV_n = PV_0 (1 + i)^n$$

Where n is the number of time periods that the amount is "moving" through time.

Example: Assume that Jack made a $10,000 deposit into a three-year certificate of deposit that paid an annual interest rate of 5 percent. How much will Jack accumulate when the certificate of deposit matures? To answer this question, insert the facts into the formula as follows.

$$FV_3 = \$10,000 \ (1.05)^3 = \$11,576.25$$

A **financial calculator**, such as a *Texas Instruments BAII Plus*, can also be used to quickly derive the solution to this type of problem. The following inputs correspond to calculator key strokes that can be used to determine the future value of a lump sum.

Input	Keystroke	Result
0	[PMT]	PMT = 0.00
10000 [+/-]	[PV]	PV = -10,000.00
5	[I/Y]	I/Y = 5.00
3	[N]	N = 3.00
[CPT]	[FV]	FV = 11,576.25

Note: The PV is input as a negative because an investment is an assumed outflow.

Figure 2.6 shows the solution to the same client question assuming various compounding frequencies. It is interesting to note that a continued increase in compounding frequency decreases the marginal effect.

Figure 2.6 Effects of Compounding Frequency on Future Values

Compounding Frequently	Effective Periodic Rate	Effective Annual Rate	Formula	Future Value
Annual	0.05/1 = 0.0500	0.05000	10,000*(1.05003*1)	$11,576.25
Semiannual	0.05/2 = 0.0250	0.05063	10,000*(1.02503*2)	$11,596.93
Bimonthly	0.05/6 = 0.0083	0.05105	10,000*(1.00833*6)	$11,611.12
Monthly	0.05/12 = 0.0042	0.05116	10,000*(1.00423*12)	$11,614.72
Weekly	0.05/52 = 0.0010	0.05125	10,000*(1.00103*52)	$11,617.51

Note: EPRs and EARs are rounded for display but are not rounded for calculation.

Present Value of a Single Sum

A **present value** formula is used to determine the value of a future asset in today's dollars. The **present value of a single sum** formula follows:

Equation 2.13: Present Value (PV_0)

$$PV_0 = \frac{FV_n}{(1 + i)^n}$$

Example: Assume that Melissa needs to accumulate $50,000 in 10 years. She is confident that she can earn an annual effective rate of 8 percent per year in her portfolio. How much does Melissa need to deposit into the account today to achieve her goal? The present value of a single sum formula can be used to solve this question. The answer to Melissa's question is easily found by entering the known variables into the formula, as shown below:

$$PV_0 = \frac{\$50,000}{1.08^{10}} = \$23,159.67$$

Here are the keystrokes need to solve this problem using a financial calculator:

Input	Keystroke	Result
0	[PMT]	PMT = 0.00
50000 [+/-]	[FV]	FV = 50,000.00
8	[I/Y]	I/Y = 8.00
10	[N]	N = 10.00
[CPT]	[PV]	PV = -23,159.67

Note: In this case, the present value answer is given as a negative because this is the amount Melissa would have to part with today.

Both future value of a lump sum and present value of a lump sum calculations assume that a client is dealing with a single **lump sum** of money being invested or received. However, sometimes a client needs to know the future or present value of a series of equal payments rather than a lump sum. A series of equal payments or receipts is known as an **annuity**. For a series of payments to be considered an annuity, the series must adhere to three rules:

1. the payments must be equal in amount;

2. the payments must continue on a fixed frequency (e.g., monthly, annually, weekly, etc.); and

3. the required rate of return must remain constant over the entire period of the annuity payments.

The Rule of 72

A quick estimate for calculating the future value of a single sum is the rule of 72, which can be used whenever a client wishes to know approximately how long it will take to double an investment. To answer such a question, 72 is divided by the interest or discount rate earned. For example, it will take approximately eight years to double an investment that earns 9% annually ($72/9 = 8$).

If the series of payments adheres to these three rules, then the payments may be treated as an annuity.

The annuity equation is set up to perform two calculations simultaneously. First, it discounts (or compounds) each cash flow payment to a common point in time—most often the current time. Second, it summates the now discounted (or compounded) payments. The annuity equation is represented as either:

Equation 2.14: Future Value of an Annuity (FVA$_n$)

$$FVA_n = \sum_{n=1}^{t} CF_n (1 + i)^n$$

or

Equation 2.15: Present Value of an Annuity (PVA$_n$)

$$PVA_n = \sum_{n=1}^{t} \frac{CF_n}{(1 + i)^n}$$

These equations show how each payment will be discounted (or compounded). Once this is established, the sum of the number of payments to occur is totaled. A discussion of future and present value annuities follows.

Future Value of an Annuity

The **future value of an annuity** values a series of uninterrupted payments as of when the last payment occurs. That is, if an annuity pays 20 annual installments starting at time 1 and ending at time 20, then the future value formula will provide a value for the series of payments at time 20. The formula for the future value of an ordinary annuity follows:

$$\text{Future Value of an Annuity } (FVA_n) = \frac{PMT}{i}[(1+i)^n - 1]$$

Example: Thomas would like to know how much he will accumulate if he invests $5,000 per year in a Roth IRA for 20 years earning an annual 9 percent rate of return. As shown below, answering Thomas's question is easy using the future value of an ordinary annuity formula or a financial calculator.

$$FVA_{20} = \frac{\$5,000}{0.09}[(1.09^{20} - 1] = \$255,800.60$$

Input	Keystroke	Result
5000	[PMT]	PMT = -5000.00
0	[PV]	PV = 0.00
9	[I/Y]	I/Y = 9.00
20	[N]	N = 20.00
[CPT]	[FV]	FV = 255,800.60

Note: In this case, the payment is given as a negative because this is the amount that Thomas would have to pay each year.

Present Value of an Annuity

The **present value of an annuity** is used to determine the value of a series of equal, uninterrupted payments as of the beginning of a period in which the first payment occurs. If an annuity pays annual payments beginning at time 1 and lasting for four years, the present value equation will return a value at the beginning of period 1 or time 0. The present value of an ordinary annuity formula is as follows:

$$\text{Present Value of an Annuity } (PVA_n) = \frac{PMT}{i}\left[1 - \frac{1}{(1+i)^n}\right]$$

Example: Consider Erik and Erin, who want to make an immediate lump sum deposit into an account earning an annual rate of 5 percent to fund four years of college expenses beginning at the end of the current year. College costs are currently assumed to be $15,000 per year and are not expected to change. How much do they need in the account today? To gauge the true amount needed, the present value of an annuity formula should be used as follows:

$$PVA_n = \frac{\$15,000}{0.05}\left[1 - \frac{1}{1.05^4}\right] = \$53,189.26$$

The calculator keystrokes necessary to solve the problem are:

Input	Keystroke	Result
15000	[PMT]	PMT = 15,000.00
0	[FV]	FV = 0.00
5	[I/Y]	I/Y = 5.00
4	[N]	N = 4.00
[CPT]	[PV]	PVA = -53,189.26

Note: In this case, the present is given as a negative because this is the amount Erik and Erin would have to pay today.

In other words, Erik and Erin need to deposit $53,189.26 into an account today, earning 5 percent per year, to fund college costs of $15,000 per year for four years with the first payment occurring one year from today.

Using a Financial Calculator to Solve Annuity Problems with Non-Annual Payments

Using the formulas to solve annuities with non-annual payments is as simple as it is for lump sums. Simply change your interest rate into the corresponding EPR form and solve for the answer. However, using the financial calculator is a bit more involved in that you have to manually change some of the basic calculator settings.

To adjust your calculator for non-annual payments, you must press the [2nd] key, then press the [I/Y] key. This allows access to the payments-per-year setting. Once "P/Y = M" (where M is the number of payments per year) is displayed, you must type the number of payments desired (e.g., 12 for monthly payments) and then press [Enter.] You may now exit the settings by pressing the [2nd] key and then the [CPT] key.

Another result of changing this setting is that when you changed the payments per year the calculator also adjusted the compounding period per year to correspond. The benefit is that the calculator will now calculate the appropriate EPR behind the scenes; therefore, you can input the APR as usual.

Example: Reconsider Erik and Erin, who still want to make an immediate lump sum deposit into an account earning an annual rate of 5 percent to fund four years of college expenses beginning at the end of this year. However, now it is assumed that college costs are paid $7,500 per semester (six months apart) and are not expected to change. How much do they need in the account today?

First, it is necessary to calculate the appropriate EPR for semiannual payments.

$$\text{EPR} = \frac{\text{APR}}{m} = \frac{0.05}{2} = 0.025 \text{ or } 2.5\%$$

Now, using the EPR, it is possible to solve for the present value normally, as follows:

$$PVA_0 = \frac{\$7,500}{0.025}\left[1 - \frac{1}{1.025^8}\right] = \$53,776.03$$

The calculator keystrokes for this problem are as follows:

Input	Keystroke	Result
7500	[PMT]	PMT = 7,500.00
0	[FV]	FV = 0.00
5 (as APR)	[I/Y]	I/Y = 5.00*
4	[2nd] [N] [N]	N = 8.00
[CPT]	[PV]	PVA = -53,776.03

*After adjusting the m to two periods per year, the APR will still display on the calculator screen although the EPR is actually being used for the calculation.

Present Value of a Delayed Annuity

What happens when a financial planner needs to know the present value of an event in the future rather than today? For example, assume a financial planner need to estimate the cost of college on a child's fifth birthday, rather than simply at the beginning of college? Again, consider Erik and Erin, who are planning for future education expenses, perhaps for a younger child. In the previous example, it was assumed that the first tuition payment occurred at the end of the first year. What would happen if that tuition payment was not due until the end of the eleventh year?

#Remember

You can't simply divide the original annual payment into the number of non-annual periods because it doesn't account for the change in interest earned or paid.

The clients would need to know how much they need to save by the beginning of college, but they now have 10 years for an account to accumulate the required amount before the first tuition payment. The formula to solve for this type of equation is a combination of two of the previous formulas: the present value of an annuity and the present value of a single sum. The two equations are:

$$PVA_n = \frac{PMT}{i}\left[1 - \frac{1}{(1+i)^n}\right] \ and \ PV_0 = \frac{PVA_n}{(1+i)^n}$$

The solution to this situation begins in the same way as the previous example, by solving for the present value of the annuity for the four years of college. However, in the first example this answer was as of today (T_0); now, it is as of 10 years from today (T_{10}).[2] Therefore, the value would have to be discounted a second time—back to today. This is referred to as **double discounting** because the first equation discounts the four payments to the beginning of the payment period and the second equation discounts the result back to today. Functionally, the first answer, which was solved for as a present value, becomes a future value when solving for the second answer. These equations may be combined into one equation that handles both steps. The equation on the left is then substituted into the numerator of the equation on the right, as shown below:

Equation 2.16: Present Value of a Delayed Annuity (PVA_d)

$$PVA_n = \frac{PMT}{i}\left[1 - \frac{1}{(1+i)^n}\right] \rightarrow PV_0 = \frac{PVA_d}{(1+i)^d}$$

Where:

  n = number of payments

  d = number of periods the annuity is delayed

Completely combining the two equations results in the following:

$$PVA_0 = \frac{\dfrac{PMT}{i}\left[1 - \dfrac{1}{(1+i)^n}\right]}{(1+i)^d}$$

#Remember

An ordinary annuity assumes that the first payment comes at the end of the first period. So the present value is given as of the beginning of that period.

Example: To return once again to Eric and Erin, the financial planner would solve for the present value of the annuity at year 10, which is $53,189.26, and then discount that result back to today. The final need can then be determined as $32,653.59. The calculation is shown in the following equation.

$$PV_0 = \frac{\dfrac{\$15,000}{0.05}\left[1 - \dfrac{1}{1.05^4}\right]}{1.05^{10}} = \frac{\$53,189.26}{1.62889} = \$32,653.59$$

In essence, in the second discounting period (during periods 1–10), the equation backs out the interest earned between today (T_0) and the beginning of the year in which the first payment occurs (T_{10}).

This is also the first instance where it may be simpler to use the equations than to use TVM keys on a financial calculator. This is because the calculator cannot handle both steps of the equation simultaneously. Instead, it is a two-step solution, as shown below:

Step 1:

Input	Keystroke	Result
15000	[PMT]	PMT = 15,000.00
0	[FV]	FV = 0.00
5	[I/Y]	I/Y = 5.00
4	[N]	N = 4.00
[CPT]	[PV]	PVA10 = -53,189.26

Step 2:

Input	Keystroke	Result
0	[PMT]	PMT = 7,500.00
53,189.26	[FV]	FV = 53,189.26
5	[I/Y]	I/Y = 5.00*
10	[N]	N = 10.00
[CPT]	[PV]	PV0 = -32,653.59

*The present value of the annuity at time 10 in Step 1 becomes the future value of the lump sum in Step 2.

This type of combined equation can be used anytime a stream of payments begins after the first period. In such a case, it is appropriate to discount the cash flow twice: once to bring the stream back to the beginning of the year in which the first payment occurs, T_n; and once again to bring that result back to the present time, T_0.

Future Value of a Geometrically Varying Annuity (Growing Annuity)

Up to this point, the assumption has been that the dollar amount of each payment received or paid during an annuity is fixed. To differentiate, this assumption is sometimes referred to as a *fixed*, *constant-dollar*, or *level-payment annuity*. However, there is an alternative. Sometimes a client's payment will increase from year to year by a constant percentage. (Note: The rate of change must always be at a constant percentage amount and *not* a constant dollar amount.) This can occur based on a number of factors (e.g., changes in salary, changes in disposable income, etc.), but the most common reason for an increasing payment is inflation.

A **growing annuity** is actually very common. In fact, most payments (e.g., college, retirement, and Social Security) typically change over time by some rate of inflation. The issue is that rates of inflation are not constant, so to be able to treat a series of payments as an annuity one must make an assumption about what the average rate of change will be. For example, actual annual inflation is almost never constant, but this simplifying assumption is needed to make the formula work.

If a client wants a payment, either in or out of an annuity, to keep pace with inflation, then a growth rate must be applied. The growth rate may be positive or—though it apparently contradicts its name—negative, but it cannot be equal to the rate of return. If the growth rate is zero, then the fixed annuity equation should be used. Growing annuities apply to either present value or future value situations. The equation for the **future value of a growing annuity** follows:

> **Self-Test 6**
>
> True or False: If the first payment in an ordinary annuity stream occurs at time 15 then the appropriate number of discount periods (d) would be 14 because the annuity formula valued all of the payments as of the beginning of the year in which the first payment occurred – Time 14.

Equation 2.17: Future Value of a Growing Annuity ($FVGA_n$)

$$FVGA_n = \frac{PMT_1}{i-g} [(1+i)^n - (1+g)^n]$$

Where:

i = interest rate ($i \neq 0$)

g = growth rate of payment ($i \neq g$)

The growing annuity equation performs three calculations simultaneously. First, it changes the payment at a constant rate. Second, it compounds each payment to a common point in time. Third, it summates the now compounded payments. Breaking the annuity equation into its component parts looks like this:

g = growth rate of payment ($i \neq g$)

$$FVGA_n = PMT_1(1+g)^{n-n}(1+r)^{n-1} + PMT_1(1+g)^{n-(n-1)}(1+r)^{n-2} + \ldots + PMT_1(1+g)^{n-1}(1+r)^{n-n}$$

Consider a client who participates in a 401(k) or 403(b) plan. Usually, defined contribution plan salary reductions are based on a percentage of an employee's annual income. So, if the client's income increases by 3 percent annually it follows that the retirement plan contribution will also increase by the same percentage. A basic future value of annuity formula cannot account for this assumption. A *geometrically varying annuity* formula must be used to determine a future value whenever a payment is expected to increase at a fixed geometric rate.

Example: Assume that Jorge will make annual payments[3] into a 401(k) for 20 years, earning an effective annual rate of 9 percent. He will begin with a $3,000 contribution, which is 5 percent of his income. Every year thereafter, he will increase his deposit by 3 percent to reflect the expected increase in his salary. Using this assumption, how much will Jorge accumulate at the end of 20 years?

$$FVGA_n = \frac{\$3,000}{(0.09 - 0.03)} [1.09^{20} - 1.03^{20}] = \$50,000 * 3.7983 = \$189,914.98$$

In this case, the fact that Jorge's subsequent deposits into the 401(k) grow by 3 percent annually means that he will have approximately $189,915 in the account at the end of 20 years. When using growing annuities, it is often beneficial—or at least interesting—to compare the results of a growing annuity and a fixed annuity, keeping all of the variables besides the growth rate fixed.

Solving the previous example, but without growing the payment by 3 percent per year, can be done using the same formula and entering a zero for the growth rate, or it can be solved using the fixed annuity equation as shown below:

$$FVGA_n = \frac{\$3,000}{(0.09 - 0.00)} [1.09^{20} - 1.00^{20}] = \$33,333.33 * 4.6044 = \$153,480.36$$

By removing the growth rate, the value in Jorge's account at the end of 20 years is $36,435 ($189,915 - $153,480) less if he chooses not to increase his annual payment. As shown here, increasing payments over a long-term planning horizon can have a significant impact on meeting a client's financial goals.

It is also important to note that when using a growing annuity equation, the payment used in the calculation will be the first payment. Similarly, when using the equation to solve for the payment amount, the equation solves for the first payment (**PMT1**). It is important to understand that this distinction is relevant because the value increases or decreases across the series of payments in a growing annuity, whereas in a fixed annuity all of the payments are the same, so no differentiation is needed. All other payments must be derived by using PMT1 and then increasing payments by the growth rate. Therefore PMT2 equals PMT1*(1 + g)[1] and so on.

Present Value of a Geometrically Varying Annuity

An equation that is very similar in form and function to the present value of a fixed annuity equation is the one used to estimate a present value of a growing annuity. As was the case with the future value of a growing annuity, a growth rate must be assumed. For instance, a client may desire to know the amount that must be saved, or available, at the beginning of a withdrawal period if the desired withdrawal amount changes over time. This is a likely scenario because of the effects of inflation on purchasing power. In this situation, the client wants to know the **present value of a growing annuity**. The following formula can be used for this purpose:

Equation 2.18: Present Value of a Growing Annuity (PVGA$_0$)

$$PVGA_0 = \frac{PMT_1}{(i-g)} \left[1 - \frac{(1+g)^n}{(1+i)^n} \right]$$

The growing annuity equation does three calculations simultaneously. In this case, it (1) changes the payment at a constant rate, (2) discounts each payment to a common point in time, and (3) summates the now discounted payments. Breaking the present value of a growing annuity equation into its component parts looks like this:

$$PVGA_n = \frac{PMT_1(1+g)^{n-(n-0)}}{(1+r)^{n-(n-1)}} + \frac{PMT_1(1+g)^{n-(n-1)}}{(1+r)^{n-(n-2)}} + ... + \frac{PMT_1(1+g)^{n-1}}{(1+r)^{n-(n-n)}}$$

Example: Middle-aged clients, Joshua and Rebecca Rosenbaum, want to know how much they need to have saved by retirement to withdraw $80,000 in the first year and to have that amount increase by 4 percent per year. They assume that they can earn an EAR of 8.5 percent throughout their 25 years of retirement.

$$PVGA_0 = \frac{\$80,000}{(0.085 - 0.04)} \left[1 - \frac{1.04^{25}}{1.085^{25}} \right] = \$1,777,777.78 * 0.65319 = \$1,161,228.92$$

In this case, the Rosenbaums must save $1,161,228.92 by the time they retire to meet their withdrawal goal. However, similar to the previous comparison conducted with the future value of a growing annuity, they need to save only $818,735.26 if they choose not to increase their annual withdrawal by 4 percent. Note again that assuming the growth rate is zero allows the fixed payment annuity equation to be used.

$$PVGA_0 = \frac{\$80,000}{(0.085 - 0.00)} \left[1 - \frac{1.00^{25}}{1.085^{25}} \right] = \$941,176.47 * 0.8699 = \$818,735.26$$

Serial Interest Rates

Another method for solving growing annuity equations is to calculate the **serial interest rate**. In fact, if a financial calculator is to be used, the serial rate will be required. The serial rate is calculated using the same equation used to determine the real rate.

$$Serial\ Rate = \frac{(1+i)}{(1+g)} - 1$$

Where:

i = interest rate

g = growth rate of payment (could be the inflation rate)

Example: Consider the first step to the previous retirement savings example, where Joshua and Rebecca needed to determine how much to save by retirement to fund a growing stream of retirement payments. Using assumptions identical to those above, the problem may also be solved using the fixed annuity equation by substituting the serial rate for *i*. First, solve for the serial rate:

$$Serial\ Rate = \frac{1.085}{1.04} - 1 = 0.04327\ or\ 4.327\%$$

Second, the serial rate should then be inserted into the adjusted present value of a fixed annuity formula as follows:

$$PVA_n = \frac{PMT_1/(1+g)}{i}\left[1 - \frac{1}{(1+i)^n}\right]$$

$$PVA_n = \frac{\$80,000/1.04}{0.04327}\left[1 - \frac{1}{1.04327^{25}}\right] = \$1,777,746.17 * 0.65320 = \$1,161,219.63$$

The difference from the earlier calculation is caused by rounding. If the serial rate 4.327 percent were not rounded, the PVA_n would equal \$1,161,228.91.

It is worth noting the small adjustment that was made to the present value formula. Notice how the payment was adjusted down by the factor of $(1 + g)$. Why was this necessary? It was necessary because the serial rate cannot distinguish when the payment needs to grow (e.g., from time 1 to time 2) or when it does not grow (e.g., from time 0 to time 1). Refer again to the present value of a growing annuity formula, this time simplified with $N = 5$:

$$PVGA_n = \frac{PMT_1(1+g)^{5-(5-0)}}{(1+i)^{5-(5-1)}} + \frac{PMT_1(1+g)^{5-(5-1)}}{(1+i)^{5-(5-2)}} + ...+ \frac{PMT_1(1+g)^{5-1}}{(1+i)^{5-(5-5)}}$$

$$PVGA_n = \frac{PMT_1(1+g)^0}{(1+i)^1} + \frac{PMT_1(1+g)^1}{(1+r)^2} + ...+ \frac{PMT_1(1+g)^4}{(1+r)^5}$$

The calculation clearly shows that the relationship between the number of periods of growth and the number of periods of discounting is off by one period. This is because payment 1 is given in terms of time 1 and not time 0. Said another way, the first payment does not grow, but it is still discounted. The serial rate is constant for all time periods, so an adjustment must be made to allow the serial rate to both grow and discount the first payment; this adjustment is made by forcibly reducing the value of the first payment to its time 0 equivalent.

$$PMT_0 = \frac{PMT_1}{1+g}$$

The use of the serial rate is also required when using a financial calculator to solve growing annuity calculations. Keep in mind that a financial calculator does not provide a separate input for "G." The following keystrokes can be used to determine the amount the Rosenbaums' need to save for retirement:

Input	Keystroke	Result
80000/1.04	[PMT]	PMT = 76,923.08
0	[FV]	FV = 0.00
4.327	[I/Y]	I/Y = 4.327
25	[N]	N = 25.00
[CPT]	[PV]	PVA = -1,161,219.64

Note: The initial payment is adjusted by the factor of $(1 + g)$ to resolve the serial rate issue previously discussed.

Revisiting the prior problem, what if the Rosenbaums needed to determine the future value of their retirement annuity? (Not that this is a realistic issue, because knowing the future value of a prior payment stream at death is not very useful, but it serves for demonstration purposes). This situation presents an interesting challenge.

When calculating the serial rate, increases in G functionally serve to decrease I/Y. Therefore, the serial rate cannot be used to directly solve for future values of growing annuities. Instead, the serial rate is used to determine the present value of the growing annuity, and the second step is to calculate the future value of that lump sum using the original nominal interest rate.

#Remember

Figure 2.5, did you notice that, for the present value of an annuity, a change in G has the opposite effect as a change in I/Y? This explains why serial rate can't be used.

This now becomes a two-step solution.

Step 1:

Input	Keystroke	Result
80000/1.04	[PMT]	PMT = 76,923.08
0	[FV]	FV = 0.00
4.327	[I/Y]	I/Y = 4.327
25	[N]	N = 25.00
[CPT]	[PV]	PVA = -1,161,219.64

Step 2:

Input	Keystroke	Result
0	[PMT]	PMT = 0.00
-1,161,219.64	[PV]	PV = -1,161,219.64
8.5	[I/Y]	I/Y = 8.50*
25	[N]	N = 25.00
[CPT]	[FV]	FV = 8,926,019.42

*The nominal rate is used to determine the compound future rate.

Annuity Due Payments (Payments Occurring at the Beginning of Each Period)

So far, all of the examples presented in this chapter have assumed that each payment has occurred at the end of each time period or "in arrears." This is not always the case. For example, tuition is normally paid at the beginning of each semester, "in advance." The term **annuity due** is used whenever the present value of an "in advance" payment is needed. This obviously influences the value or cost of college in that each payment is now taken out six months earlier; meaning six months of interest will not be earned.

The only way to make up for this is to save more money. So it stands to reason that the present value of an annuity due will need to be greater than that of an ordinary annuity. How much greater? The answer will need to be approximately one period of interest greater for each payment because not only will the first payment be removed six months early, *every* payment will be removed six months early. Therefore, the present value of every payment will have to increase. The **present value of an annuity due** formula is presented below:

$$PVA_0 = \left[\frac{PMT_1}{(1+i)^1} + \frac{PMT_2}{(1+i)^2} +...+ \frac{PMT_n}{(1+i)^n} \right] or \frac{PMT_1}{i} \left[1 - \frac{1}{(1+i)^n} \right]$$

To account for the additional period of interest each payment earns because it was deposited at the beginning of the period an interest factor of $(1+i)$ is serially added to each payment.

$$PVAD_0 = \left[\frac{PMT_1(1+i)^1}{(1+i)^1} + \frac{PMT_1(1+i)^2}{(1+i)^2} +...+ \frac{PMT_1(1+i)^n}{(1+i)^n} \right]$$

Simplifying the numerator by factoring out the $(1+i)$ adjustment from each leaves:

$$PVAD_0 = \left[\frac{PMT_1}{(1+i)^1} + \frac{PMT_2}{(1+i)^2} +...+ \frac{PMT_n}{(1+i)^n} \right] (1+i) or \frac{PMT_1}{i} \left[1 - \frac{1}{(1+i)^n} \right] (1+i)$$

The difference in value between an ordinary annuity and an annuity due is simply a factor of (1 + i). Reworking the problem of Erik and Erin, who want to fund four years of college expenses starting at the *beginning* of this year, is as simple as this:

$$PVA_0 = \frac{\$15,000}{0.05} \left[1 - \frac{1}{1.05^4} \right] (1.05) = \$53,189.26 * 1.05 = \$55,848.72$$

This adjustment also works when calculating the future value of an annuity. Even if it is a growing annuity, the adjustment remains the same. The factor (1 + i) always works!

Present Value of a Growing Perpetuity

Although not very common, there are certain instances when a payment will either be made or received indefinitely. For example, this might occur in retirement planning scenarios when a client wants to be very conservative. The **present value of growing perpetuity** (**PVP** assumes that the principal of an investment is never liquidated and continues in "perpetuity."

$$Prevent\ Value\ of\ a\ Growing\ Perpetuity\ (PVGP_0) = \frac{PMT}{(i-g)}$$

Example: A client wants to make sure that he leaves a legacy for his wife and children, but he also wants to ensure a comfortable retirement while alive. He requires an annual rate of return of 7.0 percent. He wants an initial annual payment of $100,000 that will keep pace with expected inflation of 3.5 percent. How much does the client need to save by the beginning of the withdrawal period? The following formula can be used to answer the question:

$$PVGP_0 = \frac{\$100,000}{(0.070 - 0.035)} = \$2,857,142.86$$

In order for the client to ensure that he will not outlive his money, nor lose purchasing power to inflation, he needs to have nearly $2.9 million saved on the first day of retirement.

An interesting thing about perpetuities is that the present values are not significantly larger than traditionally estimated annuities. This is because the payments are being added to the end, so the further away they are the lower the present value of each subsequent payment. See Figure 2.7 for a summary of present values for different terms.

Figure 2.7 Comparison of Present Values by Term Length

Periodic Payment	Discount Rate	Years	Present Value
$1,000	7%	20	$10,594
$1,000	7%	35	$12,948
$1,000	7%	50	$13,801
$1,000	7%	65	$14,110
$1,000	7%	Infinite	$14,286

Mixed-Stream Calculations

A **net present value** (**NPV**) method of calculation can be used when a series of payments, either made by the client or received by the client, fluctuates on a per-period basis. The traditional present value of annuity calculation assumes that payments remain fixed, or if they do change, that the rate of growth is fixed. NPV is defined as the present value of a stream of earnings less the present value of contributions. The formula for NPV is:

NPV = PVA of Inflows – PVA of Costs

Where:

NPV = net present value

PV = present value

NPV compares benefits and costs. The rule for NPV is that if the present value of benefits *exceeds* the present value of costs (NPV > 0), then the investment should be accepted; if the present value of benefits *does not exceed* the present value of costs (NPV < 0), then the investment should be rejected. The following formula illustrates how a present value cost is subtracted from the discounted future value benefits of a particular investment opportunity:

$$NPV_0 = \frac{PMT_1}{(1 + i)^1} + \frac{PMT_2}{(1 + i)^2} + ... + \frac{PMT_n}{(1 + i)^n} + \frac{FV_n}{(1 + i)_n} - PV_{Costs}$$

A simple example can be used to illustrate the NPV method.

Example: Assume that a client is considering an investment of $5,000. Currently, the client is making 11 percent on the $5,000 in an alternative investment. The client anticipates that the investment will make payments back as shown below:

Year 1: $1,500

Year 2: $1,000

Year 3: $500

Year 4: $500

Year 5: $4,000

Should the client make the investment? A quick way to answer this question might be to compute NPV using the cash flow functions in a financial calculator (shown in the next section). However, the formula may also be used to find a solution.

$$NPV_0 = \frac{\$1,500}{1.11^1} + \frac{\$1,000}{1.11^2} + \frac{\$500}{1.11^3} + \frac{\$500}{1.11^4} + \frac{\$4,000}{1.11^5} - \$5,000$$

$$NPV_0 = \$1,351.35 + \$811.62 + \$365.60 + \$329.37 + \$2,373.81 - \$5,000 = \$231.75$$

When using the NPV method, it is critical to understand what the answer is saying. When the NPV is positive, it means that the internal rate of return (IRR) is greater than the required rate, and therefore, the investment should be accepted. If the NPV is negative, it means that the IRR is less than the required rate, and therefore, the investment should be rejected. If the IRR equals the required rate, then the investment should be accepted because the required rate is expected to be achieved. The NPV as a planning tool is generally constrained to investment scenarios where a known initial investment has or will be made. Additionally, NPV estimates assume that and investment generates an investment return.

Planning Skill 8: Master Internal Rate of Return Calculations

What if a financial planner knows both how much a client is willing to spend today (PV) and the values of the future cash flows (FV)? This raises an interesting and different question: what is the **internal rate of return (IRR)** on the investment? The IRR, and its close cousin NPV, are more sophisticated methods that determine whether or not an investment is expected to meet a client's required rate of return.

IRR Rules

Similar to NPV rules, as discussed previously, if the IRR of an investment exceeds the required rate of return, then accept the investment; if IRR does not exceed the required rate of return, reject the investment.

The IRR measures the discount rate at which the present value of cash inflows (returns or benefits) equals the present value of cash outflows (investments or costs). IRR takes into account the time value of money by considering the amount and timing of cash inflows and outflows over the life of an **investment**. Calculating the IRR can be done through a trial-and-error process. IRR can be calculated manually by completing multiple iterations of NPV estimates with different interest rates until the NPV is equal to zero. The trial-and-error calculation can also be automated by using the IRR function in a computer spreadsheet program or using the cash flow functions in a financial calculator.

As a reminder, an IRR measures the present value of a series of cash flows in relation to an initial (and possibly subsequent) investment amount. The formula for calculating IRR is used when both the value of each subsequent cash flow and the present value are known:

$$PV_0 = \frac{PMT_1}{(1 + IRR)^1} + \frac{PMT_2}{(1 + IRR)^2} + ... + \frac{PMT_n}{(1 + IRR)^n} + \frac{FV_n}{(1 + IRR)^n}$$

Where:

PV = present value

FV = future value

PMT = periodic payment

IRR = internal rate of return

As mentioned earlier, it would take multiple iterations to determine the rate that would result in the NPV being equal to zero. Using the formula for calculating IRR can be tiresome. Fortunately, IRRs can be determined relatively easily using a financial calculator. There are two main methods for determining the IRR: (1) using the TVM keys if future cash flows can be considered as an annuity or (2) using cash flow functions if the future cash flows are uneven; this is often called a **mixed sum**.

Using TVM Keystrokes to Solve for IRR

Using TVM keystrokes to solve for IRR is as simple as using a calculator to solve any other TVM problem. As long as at least three inputs are known, it is as simply as entering the known variables and solving for those remaining.

Example: Assume that Jesus invests $500 today in an investment that will pay him $50 per year for 10 years. At the end of the investment period, Jesus receives $1,000. What rate of return did he earn? Entering these data into a financial calculator, as shown below, results in an IRR equal to 14.94 percent.

Input	Keystroke	Result
100	[PMT]	PMT = 100.00
-1000	[PV]	PV = -1,000
10	[N]	N = 15.00
2000	[FV]	FV = 2000
[CPT]	[I/Y]	I/Y = 14.94%

Although the method for calculating IRR looks innocuous enough, its application can become quite tedious, especially when the periodic payments fluctuate every period. However, a financial calculator can also be used if the periodic cash flows are not fixed.

Using Cash Flow Functions to Solve for IRR

By using the built-in **cash flow functions** or registers, individual cash flows may be entered separately in a financial calculator. To enter the cash flow functions in the BA II Plus calculator, press the [CF] key. Always begin by clearing the register of any previous work by pressing the [2nd] key and then the [CLR WORK] key in succession. It is important to remember a major difference between using the TVM keys and the CF functions: in order to enter the value into the tables, the [enter] key must always be pressed after entering the desired value.

> *Example:* Assume that Shameka is considering an investment that requires a $5,000 payment today. The required rate of return, based on her next best investment choice, is 11 percent in a mutual fund. If she anticipates receiving the following payments, should she make the investment?
>
> Year 1: $1,500
>
> Year 2: $1,000
>
> Year 3: $500
>
> Year 4: $500
>
> Year 5: $4,000

Calculating the IRR of these individual cash flows is possible using the following formula; however, it would require a great deal of time and some more difficult algebra.

$$\$5,000 = \frac{\$1,500}{(1 + IRR)^1} + \frac{\$1,000}{(1 + IRR)^2} + \frac{\$500}{(1 + IRR)^3} + \frac{\$500}{(1 + IRR)^4} + \frac{\$4,000}{(1 + IRR)^5}$$

Instead, it is much easier to let a financial calculator handle the algebra and use the cash flow functions as demonstrated below. There are always two sets of entries when using cash flow functions: the amount of each cash flow and the number of consecutive times the cash flow happens, which is known as the **frequency of the cash flow**. Once all of the cash flows have been entered into the cash flow table, IRR can be computed by pressing the [IRR] key and then pressing the [CPT] key, as shown below:

Input	Keystroke	Result
	[CF]	Turn-on functions
[2nd]	[CLR WORK]	Clear register
–5000	[ENTER]	CF0 = -5,000,00
[↓] 1500	[ENTER]	CF1 = 1,500.00
[↓] 1*	[ENTER]	F01 = 1.00
[↓] 1000	[ENTER]	CF2 = 1,000.00
[↓] 1	[ENTER]	F02 = 1.00
[↓] 500	[ENTER]	CF3 = 500.00
[↓] 2	[ENTER]	F03 = 2.00
[↓] 4000	[ENTER]	CF4 = 4,000.00
[↓] 1	[ENTER]	F04 = 1.00
[IRR]	[CPT]	IRR = 12.55%
*One is the default entry for the frequency of the cash flow.		

In this case, the IRR is 12.55 percent, which is greater than her next best alternative of 11 percent. Therefore, applying the decision rule previously discussed, she would accept this investment alternative.

To solve for NPV, however, an estimated rate of return must be entered. After the [NPV] key is pressed, the calculator will ask for the required rate of return—in this case, 11 percent. Once the return is entered, pressing the down arrow key again will display the NPV, which will be computed when the [CPT] key is pressed. For this example, the NPV is $231.74. The keystrokes required to arrive at this conclusion are:

Input	Keystroke	Result
[NPV] 7	[CLR WORK]	I/Y = 11.00%
[↓]	[CPT]	NPV = $231.74
Note: One is the default entry for the frequency of the cash flow.		

Basically, this means that if Shameka's required return is 11 percent, she should be willing to pay up to $231.74 more ($5,231.74) for the agreed upon cash flows. Both the IRR and NPV methods of computing the value of cash flows produce the same decision conclusion—accept the investment.

Planning Skill 9: Master Loan and Amortization Schedules

One of the most common uses for TVM formulas occurs when a client or financial planner is working with an amortized loan, which is a liability where the payment is normally fixed and set to repay the obligation over a fixed period of time. Every payment for a loan is composed of principal and interest and, as the loan is paid back, the percentage of each payment attributable to interest declines. This happens because a simple interest loan (which represents the majority of loan structures to individuals) recalculates the interest expense each period based on the remaining outstanding balance. Therefore, as the outstanding balance declines, so does the periodic interest expense. This also means that lenders receive more interest at the beginning of a loan repayment period than at the end of the period.

> **#Remember**
>
> Since the compounding frequency and the payment frequency are the same the EPR is simply APR/m.

A widely used method of presenting this information to a client is with an amortization table. An **amortization schedule** can be created for any loan that has a fixed rate of interest and a known number of payment periods. Although an outstanding loan balance can be calculated using a financial calculator or present value of an annuity formula, it is sometimes more helpful to create an amortization schedule using a computer spreadsheet.

Figure 2.8 Partial Amortization Spreadsheet with Formulas

| Inputs | Interest Rate Present Value Term | | 7% APR (0.583% monthly EPR) $100,000 30 years (360 months) | | |
A Month	B Beginning Balance	C Total Montly Payment	D Monthly Interest Payment	E Montly Principal Payment	F Ending Balance
			(B * EPR)	(C - D)	(B - E)
1	$100,000.00	$665.30	$583.33	$81.97	$99,918.03
2	$99,918.03	$665.30	$582.85	$82.45	$99,835.58
...					
359	$1,319.05	$665.30	$7.69	$657.61	$661.44
360	$661.44	$665.30	$3.86	$661.44	$0.00

A spreadsheet can more easily display different loan payoff amounts at different times. It can also be used to illustrate how a change in interest rates or duration can change a client's cash flow situation. Figure 2.8 provides an example of how an amortization schedule can be created in a computer spreadsheet.

Example: Recall the sample loan from Figure 2.8. The table illustrates how the loan is amortized, but in this example it does not show the outstanding balance at all points in time. If a client wanted to pay off this loan after the 120th payment (in conjunction with the 121st payment), the client would need to know the outstanding balance at that time. To provide the client with the necessary information, the financial planner would solve for the PVA with the PMT equaling $665.30, the periodic interest rate equaling 0.583 percent, and the number of payments remaining equal to 240 (360 total payments - 120 payments previously paid). The formula is shown below:

$$\text{Balance} = \text{PVA}_t = \frac{\text{PMT}}{i} \left[1 - \frac{1}{(1 + i)^{n-t}} \right]$$

$$\text{PVA}_{120} = \frac{\$665.30}{0.00583} \left[1 - \frac{1}{1.00583^{360-120}} \right] = \$114,116.64 * 0.75220 = \$85,838.54$$

Calculator vs. Tables

Another method can also be useful, and much faster, when trying to calculate the outstanding balance of a loan. It uses the previously discussed present value of an annuity (PVA) formula. The key is to change the n (number) in the equation to reflect the number of payments remaining.

Although it hardly seems to make sense that more than 85 percent of the loan remains outstanding, this is a common occurrence because the progression of a geometric function is not linear over time. In other words, the loan balance does not decline in a straight line.

Another useful application based on the TVM formulas is to determine how much money has already been paid on a loan. This is necessary information when determining the total amount of interest paid because the difference between the total amount of payments and the change in the outstanding balance is the total interest paid to date. The following formula is used to determine the total amount paid to date on a loan:

Total of Payments = PMT Amount * Number of PMTs

Example: Revising the previous example, it was already been determined that the client had reduced the outstanding balance of the loan by $14,161.46 ($100,000 - $85,838.54); however, this does not indicate how much the client has paid in total. Nor does it tell how much interest the client has paid over the first 10 years of the loan. To determine the total amount paid, the monthly payment should be multiplied by the number of payments made, as shown below:

Total of Payments = $665.30 * 120 = $79,836.00

Note: The change in balance outstanding is simply the original balance (or the balance at the beginning of the analyzed period) minus the balance at the end of the analyzed period.

Change in Balance = $100,000.00 – $85,838.54 = $14,161.46

To determine the total amount of interest paid, the change in outstanding balance should be subtracted from the total amount of payments. In this example, the total interest paid to date is $65,674.54.

Total Interest = Total of Payments – Change in Balance

Total Interest = $79,836.00 – $14,161.46 = $65,674.54

Quantitative/Analytical Mini-Case Problems

1. Holding-Period Returns

    a. Last year Marla purchased 100 shares of stock for $8 per share. She paid a flat $75 to purchase the shares. Since making her purchase, she has received $200 in dividends. Marla is concerned that the stock price will fall below its current FMV of $7. Calculate her holding-period return if she sells today and pays a $75 commission.

    b. Swarn bought 200 shares of a stock for $36 per share. He paid $245 in trading commissions. He has received dividends in the amounts of $98, $156, and $300 over the last three years, respectively. Assuming that Swarn is in the 15 percent marginal tax bracket for capital gains and dividends, what is his holding-period return if he sells all of the shares at $40 each with a $245 trading commission? What is Swarn's tax-adjusted holding period rate of return?

2. Dollar-Weighted Returns

    a. Brad purchased 10 shares of stock for $10 per share. He paid a $5 commission. One year later, he purchased another 10 shares at $9 per share. Again, he paid a $5 commission. In the second year, his disappoint got the best of him and he sold 10 shares at $7 per share, paying another $5 commission. At the end of third year, Brad liquidated his holdings, paying $5 in commissions at $8 per share. What was his dollar-weighted rate of return?

    b. Buckley purchased a collectible stamp for $600. He was thrilled to learn that the stamp price had moved up, so one year later he purchased another stamp for $700. At the end of the second year, he sold one of the stamps for $800. He held his original stamp for the third year. Buckley then sold his stamp at the end of the fourth year for $1,000. What was Buckley's dollar-weighted rate of return?

3. Time-Weighted Returns

    a. Camerin purchased one ounce of gold for $1,400. The following year, the price of gold shot up to $1,800, but in the third year prices fell back to $1,500. What was Camerin's time-weighted return?

    b. Marybeth purchased one share of stock for $92. At the end of year 1, the stock was worth $95. At the end of year 2, the stock was worth $100; and at the end of year 3, the stock was worth $92. What was Marybeth's time-weighted return? How does this compare to her holding period rate of return?

4.   Mean Returns

   a.   Maurice purchased a coin collection several years ago. Each year he has had the collection appraised by a reputable coin dealer. Maurice has calculated the yearly percentage gain or loss based on the appraisal, as shown below:

Year	Return
1	10%
2	5%
3	9%
4	-5%
5	2%
6	-3%
7	12%

   What is the average (mean) return of the coin collection over the seven-year period?

   Use the rate of return data provided by Maurice to calculate the geometric mean return. How does this compare to the mean return?

5.   Weighted Average Returns

   a.   Sherman is a novice investor. The following table shows his portfolio holdings and market values for each holding. Please calculate Sherman's weighted average return for his portfolio.

	Market Value	Rate of Return
Junk Bond Fund	$13,000.00	7.50%
Gold Fund	$19,500.00	12.00%
Small Cap Fund	$36,000.00	3.40%
Index Fund	$9,800.00	6.20%
CD	$41,000.00	1.00%

   b.   Sonya and Josh own several pieces of expensive jewelry. The following table summarizes their most important gem assets:

	Market Value	Rate of Return
Diamond Ring	$12,000.00	$7,250.00
Sapphire Necklace	$23,000.00	$18,875.00
Emerald Pendant	$19,500.00	$19,000.00
Ruby Brooch	$21,200.00	$23,000.00
TOTAL	$75,700.00	$68,125.00

   Use this information to calculate the holding-period return.

6. Real and Nominal Rates

   a. Consumer prices have been averaging 3.50 percent in South Korea. If So-Hyun can earn a nominal rate of return on her investment portfolio of 10.25 percent, what is her real rate of return, assuming continuous compounding?

   b. Farrell wants to retire in six years. To have sufficient assets to fund retirement, Farrell needs to accumulate an additional $400,000 between today and retirement. As his planner, you assume that inflation will average 5 percent. You are also confident that you can build a portfolio that will generate an 8 percent compounded annual after-tax return. What serial payment should Farrell invest at the end of the first year to fund this goal?

7. Tax-Exempt and Taxable Rates

   a. Thomas Jones is in the 25 percent marginal federal tax bracket, the 4 percent marginal state tax bracket, and the 2 percent marginal city tax bracket. If he earns 9.25 percent on his portfolio, what is his after-tax rate of return?

   b. Stephanie is considering purchasing a fixed-income investment. She has narrowed her list of bond choice to two AAA-rated investments. The first is a corporate bond that matures in seven years. The bond yields 6.35 percent. The second bond also matures in seven years; however, this bond is a municipal bond issued by the state in which Stephanie resides. The bond has a current coupon rate at 4.79 percent. Stephanie is in the 25 percent marginal federal tax bracket and the 3.50 percent marginal state tax bracket. Which bond should she invest in to maximize her after-tax rate of return?

8. Effective Rate Conversion Problems

   a. A client was earning an EAR of 7 percent. The client was contributing to the account on a monthly basis. What would be the appropriate EPR?

   b. A client wants to compute the estimated future value of a bank account. The account pays a semiannual rate of 4 percent (EPR). The client is investing in the account on a biweekly basis. What is the appropriate EPR to be able to solve for an estimated future value for the client?

9. Future Value Problems

   a. Ted has $1,000. He can earn an annual effective rate of 5 percent. How much will he have in 10 years?

   b. Lanisha currently earns $45,000 per year. She expects her salary to increase by 3.5 percent per year. She plans to work for another 20 years. How much will she earn in her final year of work?

10. Present Value Problems

   a. Tammy has determined that she will need $3 million when she retires in 45 years. The current interest rate is 7 percent (EAR). How much does she need today to fully fund this goal at that rate?

b.   David and Iantha expect their 10-year-old daughter to get married someday. They estimate that her wedding would cost $30,000 today. Wedding costs will increase by 3 percent per year, and she will marry in 15 years. David and Iantha earn a pre-tax annual rate of 5 percent. They are in the 20 percent marginal tax bracket. What amount do they need to set aside today for their daughter's wedding?

11.   Future Value of Annuity Problems

a.   Sue wants to save $1,000,000 in 20 years. She estimates she can earn 8.5 percent on savings. She intends to make deposits at the beginning of every year in a series of equal payments starting today. How much does she need to save each year to reach her goal?

b.   Merita has been offered a choice of either receiving $100,000 in 10 years or receiving $7,000 per year (at the end of each year) for the next 10 years. Which is the better option if her required annual rate of return is 7 percent?

12.   Present Value of Annuity Problems

a.   Mike needs to receive $40,000 per year (at the beginning of each year) from his investments for the next 30 years. His opportunity cost of money is 5 percent. How much does he need in an account today to generate this level of income if he fully depletes the account?

b.   Roshanna has just won the lottery. Her required rate of return is 6 percent. Should she take the annual annuity payment of $125,000 for the next 20 years or an immediate lump-sum payout of $1.5 million?

13.   Future Value of Growing Annuity Problems

a.   Martha wants to start saving for college. She estimates that she will need $50,000 when she starts college four years from now. She plans to save $9,500 this year and increase deposits by 5 percent annually (payments at the end of each year). She can earn 7 percent on her savings. Will she meet her savings goal of $50,000 for college four years from now?

b.   Todd is saving $3,000 annually into an account (payments at the end of each year). He plans to increase the annual level of savings by 5 percent each year. He can earn 9 percent annually. How much will he have in the account at the end of 20 years?

14.   Present Value of Growing Annuity Problems

a.   Mike wants to receive $40,000 per year pretax from his investments for the next 30 years. He is concerned about inflation, which he expects to average 3 percent. He can earn a pretax rate of 6 percent on his money. How much does he need in an account to generate $40,000 in annual inflation-adjusted income (payments at the end of each year)?

b.   A client is doing some investment/retirement planning. She is attempting to determine how much of her estate she needs to set aside today to fully fund her retirement. She desires annual beginning-of-period withdrawals for the next 25 years. She would like inflation-adjusted withdrawals that start at $50,000 per year. Assume an annual post-tax rate of return of 7.5 percent and that inflation will increase at an annual effective rate of 3.5 percent. What amount does she need to dedicate to this goal?

15. Present Value of Delayed Annuity Problems

   a. Jonas desires fixed annual income of $85,000 beginning 20 years from now and lasting for 20 years. He plans to deplete the account. His annual required return is 9.5 percent. How much does he need to invest today to achieve his goal?

   b. An investor has two options: (1) $50,000 received at the end of this year, or (2) $10,000 received each year for 10 years but beginning 10 years from now. Assume the rate of return is 7 percent. Which option has the higher present value?

16. Present Value of Perpetuity Problems

   a. An investment would provide end-of-year annual income of $2,000. The client's required rate of return is 12.5 percent. What price should the client be willing to pay for the investment?

   b. Jose Marie and his wife, Ayna, want to ensure that they do not outlive their money. They want to make end-of-year withdrawals that start at $80,000 after tax and increase by 4 percent per year. They can earn an annual effective rate of 7.2 percent after tax. How much do they need to have invested to make withdrawals that last forever?

17. Internal Rate of Return

   a. Ruth invested $16,000 in an exchange-traded fund six years ago. Dividends and earnings were automatically reinvested in new shares. Although Ruth considers herself to be a buy-and-hold investor, she nonetheless made a few trades during the time period, as follows:

   $3,025 redemption at the end of the second year

   $1,825 redemption at the end of the third year

   $4,200 additional investment into the fund at the end of the fifth year

   $19,885 received at the end of the sixth year, when Ruth redeemed the shares.

   What was Ruth's internal rate of return on the investment?

   b. Lawrence Block is considering investing in a gold coin. The coin costs $47,500. He anticipates spending $1,000 to have the coin's value reevaluated by experts at the end of the first year. Lawrence believes that he can receive $3,500 in exhibitor fees by allowing a major museum to showcase his coin during the second year of ownership. He would like to sell the coin, but he will need to market and promote it first. He anticipates spending $2,000 by the end of the third year on the process. If he can receive $50,000 at the end of the fourth year, should Lawrence make this investment if he needs to earn 4.50 percent on it?

18. Net Present Value

   a. Derek invested $12,000 in a mutual fund five years ago. He received a dividend check for $1,000 after the first year. He received $750 after the second year. At the end of the third year, he received a check for $1,500. After the fourth year, he collected $750. His final dividend check of $1,000 was received at the end of the fifth year. Assume that Derek sold the mutual fund at the end of the fifth year for $18,000. What was Derek's internal rate of return on this investment?

b. Kristy purchased shares of a mutual fund five years ago. She has since made the following additional transactions:

End of year 2, invested additional $2,500 in the fund

End of year 3, invested additional $9,000 in the fund

End of year 5, redeemed all of her shares in the fund, receiving $16,000

Kristy just told you she achieved an annual return of 9 percent in this investment. If Kristy is correct, what was her initial investment in the fund?

19. Loan Amortization Problems

a. Willy and Ursha have just purchased a new car for $38,000. They financed $35,000 for five years at 6.75 percent (APR). What is the monthly payment and total interest expense?

b. Assume an initial loan amount of $150,000, an APR of 6.5 percent, fixed monthly payments, and an amortization period of 20 years. What is the outstanding balance on the loan after 60 payments have been paid?

20. Kristin and Dan Peterson

Kristin and Dan Peterson wonder how much they will need to save to fully fund four years of college for their daughter, Samantha, who is 12 years old today. She plans to attend college at age 18. They know that their first choice of college currently costs $13,000 per year. College costs are increasing 5 percent annually. They feel that it is possible to earn an effective annual rate of 8.3 percent (8 percent compounded monthly), both before and during college.

a. How much will Samantha's first year of college cost?

b. How much do the Peterson's need to fully fund college costs when Samantha begins college?

c. How much do Kristin and Dan need to deposit in an account today to fully fund four years of expenses?

d. How much will they need to save on a monthly basis starting at the end of this month to fully fund four years of expenses?

21. Tony Mitchell

Tony Mitchell has been eyeing a new car. Last weekend, he went to the dealership and noted that his dream car would cost $23,000 if purchased today. Tony currently has $9,000 saved. He does not want to go into debt to buy the car, so he has decided to save toward the purchase for three years. Tony estimates that inflation will average 4.5 percent per year. He earns 7 percent (EAR) on his savings.

a. How much will the car cost in exactly three years?

b. How much must he save per year (at end of each year) to purchase the car in three years?

22. John Johnson

John Johnson is an avid stamp collector. He has been noting the rapid rise in prices for stamps printed in the nineteenth century. Some of the best stamps from that time period have been increasing in value by 12 percent per year. John has the rare opportunity to purchase several impressive stamps from a reputable dealer.

The dealer has offered to sell the stamps to John for $65,000 today. As an alternative, John can put down $10,000 toward the purchase today and buy the stamps outright for an additional $89,500 in four years. Assume an annual discount rate of 12 percent. Assuming John has the cash for either deal, which should he take?

Comprehensive Bedo Case—Analysis Questions

There are no Bedo case questions for this chapter. The preceding quantitative/analytical mini-case problems can serve as a good review. TVM concepts will be applied to the Bedo case in many other chapters to quantify needs and funding.

Chapter Resources

Texas Instruments BAII Plus Reference Manual (education.ti.com/guidebooks/financial/baiiplus/BAIIPLUSGuidebook_EN.pdf).

The *Financial Facilitator* and all fillable forms needed to complete text activities can be found on the student website at: pro.nuco.com/booksupplements/NUCollege-CaseBook3e.

Self-Test Answers

1: b, 2: True, 3: b, 4: d, 5: a, 6: True

Endnotes

1. E. Jacquire, A. Kane, and A. Marcus, "Geometric or Arithmetic Mean: A Reconsideration," *Financial Analyst Journal* 59, no. 6 (2003): 46–53.

2. T_0 is always the present time, "today." Future points in time are then counted, with the first period (T_1) being one period in the future. For example, 10 periods in the future would be designated as T_{10}. The period could be years, months, or any other definable period.

3. Annual payments are assumed because the growth rate is annual. Semimonthly or biweekly payments would be expected. However, the growing annuity equation assumes that the payment change frequency caused by applying the growth rate is the same as the payment frequency.

PART II: Analyzing and Evaluating a Client's Financial Status to Plan for Client Earnings

Chapter 3

Cash Flow and Net Worth Planning

Learning Objectives

1. Cash flow and net worth planning serves as the foundation of the financial planning process and provides a window into a client's financial situation. Calculation of the cash flow statement and the net worth statement provide insights into a client's efforts to manage income in support of short-, intermediate-, and long-term financial goals. Financial ratios offer additional insights into strengths and weaknesses that may not be immediately evident from the financial situation documents. This analysis of the client's financial situation, serves as the foundation of the planning process and the identification of strategies that can improve management, increase earnings, or reduce the cost of debt.

2. A client's temperament, personality, attitudes, beliefs, financial knowledge, and experience are reflected in a client's financial statements. For example, a client's values and attitudes are often apparent from spending patterns, whereas risk tolerance, financial knowledge, and experience may be inferred from a client's net worth statement. A client's emotional reaction to spending patterns or other financial decisions can offer additional useful insights during the discovery process. As noted in this chapter, care should be taken to explore qualitative situational factors fully in an effort to better explain a client's cash flow and net worth planning intentions, and to provide necessary insights from which to approach the client about any recommended changes.

3. Care must be taken to thoroughly and accurately identify all dedicated and discretionary expenses to construct a cash flow statement. Dedicated expenses are controlled (1) by contract or other similarly binding agreement or (2) by the client's commitment to protect (through insurance) and accumulate (through saving and investing) assets. On the other hand, within reason, the client has control over the amount of income attributed to individual discretionary expenses. If a client is over committing income to savings, debt

Learning Objectives

repayment, or uncontrolled spending, then the cash flow statement will reveal a negative level of cash flow, which indicates an over commitment of future income to repay current expenses. Conversely, excess positive cash flow means income is available to support other goals or objectives.

4. This chapter describes how a cash flow statement summarizes income and expenses for a predetermined period of time, typically one year. The resulting positive or negative position of cash flows indicates an opportunity or a challenge for the client and financial planner. A balance sheet summarizes assets owned and liabilities owed to reveal a client's net worth on the date of the assessment. Similarly, solvency or insolvency indicates an opportunity or a challenge for the client and the planner.

5. Nine financial ratios are discussed in this chapter. These ratios can be used to diagnose a client's liquidity (income adequate to cover expenses) and solvency (assets adequate to cover liabilities). Approximate benchmarks are provided for use in interpreting the ratios. Care must also be taken to clearly delineate the determination of the income, expenses, assets and liabilities used in the ratio calculations because precise definitions must be matched to the client situation. Such standards ensure that accurate ratio calculations occur across time for the same client. However, variations in definitions can make it more difficult to compare ratios across clients.

6. Whereas there is agreement that most clients should have some assets designated as an emergency fund, there is widespread disagreement on the number of months of expenses that should be protected and possible funding sources. Liquidity is the key to an emergency fund, but large sums committed to low-yielding savings alternatives are generally considered imprudent. Likewise, the unplanned selling of assets to cover an emergency situation could yield price and tax consequences. The amount and combination of assets designated for emergency situations will vary with a client's risk tolerance, the number of household earners, the use of credit, employment and income security, and other factors. A combination of "funded" and "unfunded" substitutes may be the best solution for many clients.

7   Consumer debt, secured and unsecured, can enable a client to more quickly attain a desired lifestyle. The costs of borrowing, and the associated emotional stress, can be problematic for those who cannot manage excessive debt. Financial planners—and in extreme situations, financial counselors—can help clients analyze debt loads and determine the best strategies for paying off, reducing, or consolidating debt. Central to this is the reduction and elimination of the costs of borrowing as well as an understanding of the factors that contributed to the excessive dependence on debt. Available assets, client attitudes, and client asset preferences must be balanced against the mathematical logic of interest earned and interest paid.

Learning Objectives

8. The variety of mortgage alternatives available at any given time varies with the economic climate. This chapter presents two basic considerations that are important when standardizing the process of matching a mortgage product, for a purchase or refinance, to a client's situation. First, how long does the client anticipate remaining in the property, and what are the client's attitudes about and risk tolerance for the debt? Second, given the client's net worth and income situation, which mortgage product provides the best financial return, considering interest and tax implications? Mortgage debt is yet another situation where available assets, client attitudes, and client asset preferences must be balanced against the mathematical logic of interest earned and interest paid.

9. As illustrated in this chapter, there are numerous strategies that can be used to enhance a client's financial situation. Although recommendations will differ based on each client's unique situation, the fundamentals of cash flow and net worth planning apply to all clients. As such, a thorough analysis of client specific qualitative and quantitative situational factors is necessary to ensure that appropriate and reasonable recommendations are identified and adopted by the client. As the foundation of the financial planning process, cash flow and net worth management allows a financial planner to use the current financial situation to more fully understand the past and to establish financial management strategies that will foster future success in reaching a client's goals.

Key Terms

§79 Plans

2/6 Rate Restriction

28 Percent Rule

36 Percent Rule

529 Plan Account

529 Plan Accounts

Adjustable Rate Mortgage

Annual Cash Flow Statement

Arm

Back-End Mortgage Qualification Ratio

Balance Due

Balance Sheet

Break-Even Period

Budget

Buy Down

Cash Flow Statement

Cash-Out Refinance

Certificates Of Deposit (CDs)

Closing Costs

Collateral

Consumer Credit Repayment

Coverdell Savings Account

Credit Card Debt

Credit Score

Credit Usage Ratio

Current Bills

Current Liabilities

Current Ratio

Debt Limit Ratios

Debt Ratio

Debt Repayment Ratio

Debts

Debt-To-Income Ratio

Dedicated Expense

Dedicated Expenses

Discount Point

Discount Points

Discretionary Cash Flow

Discretionary Expenses

Effective After-Tax Rate

Emergency Fund

Emergency Fund Expenses

Emergency Fund Ratio

Expenses

Fair Market Value

Fico Credit Score

Financial Assets

Financial Benchmark

Financial Counselor

Financial Flexibility

Key Terms

Financial Health	Long-Term Liabilities
Financial Ratio	Marginal Tax Bracket
Financial Therapist	Monetary Assets
Fringe Benefits	Month's Living Expenses Covered Ratio
Front-End Mortgage Qualification Ratio	Monthly Cash Flow Statement
Fundamental Living Expenses	Monthly Living Expenses
Group Term Life Insurance	Mortgage Debt Service Ratio
HELOC	Mortgage Duration
High-Net-Worth Client	Mortgage Qualification Ratios
Home Equity Line Of Credit	Mortgage Refinancing
Imputed Income	Net Worth
Income	Net Worth Statement
Income And Expense Statement	Nontaxable Income
Income Shifting Strategy	Payment Caps
Interest-Only Mortgage	Personal Property
Internal Revenue Code §79 Income	Physical Asset
Investment Assets	PITI
Liabilities	Policy Loan
Life Insurance Cash Value	Primary Residence
Lifestyle Assets	Principal, Interest, Taxes, And Insurance
Liquidity	Qualified Mortgages
Loan Payments	Rate Cap Restrictions
Loan-To-Value	Real Asset
Long-Term Debt Coverage Ratio	Refinancing Risks
Long-Term Debt Payments	Rental Expense Ratio

Key Terms

Retirement Assets

Retirement Contributions

Rolling Closing Costs Into The Mortgage

Savings Ratio

Section 79 Taxable Income

Seven-Year Balloon

Solvency

Special Needs Assets

Take Home Pay

Taxable Income

Tax-Advantaged Savings For Education

Tax-Efficient Debt

Ultra-High-Net-Worth Client

Unsecured Debt

Unsecured Non-Tax-Deductible Debt

Use Assets

Variable Expense

Wealth

CFP® Principal Knowledge Topics

B.9. Financial Statements

B.10. Cash Flow Management

B.11. Financing Strategies

B.14. Client and Planner Attitudes, Values, Biases and Behavioral Finance

B.16. Debt Management

Chapter Equations

Equation 3.1:

$$= \S\,79 \text{ Taxable Income} \quad \frac{\text{Insurance in excess of } \$50,000}{\$1,000} \times \text{Table Factor} \times 12$$

Equation 3.2:

$$\text{After tax Rate of Return} = \text{Nominal Rate} \times (1 - \text{Marginal Tax bracket})$$

Equation 3.1 (two versions):

Refinance Benefit

$$= \frac{\text{Old PMT - New PMT}}{i}\left[1 - \frac{1}{(1+i)^n}\right] +/- \frac{\dfrac{\text{Longer PMT}}{i}\left[1 - \dfrac{1}{(1+i)^{n'-n}}\right]}{(1+i)^n} - \text{Costs}$$

Refinance Benefit

$$= \frac{\text{PMT}_1 - \text{PMT}_2}{i}$$

$$- \left[\frac{1}{(1+i)^n}\right] +/- \frac{\dfrac{\text{PMT}_1}{i_1}\left[1 - \dfrac{1}{(1+i_1)^{n'-n}}\right] - \dfrac{\text{PMT}_2}{i_2}\left[1 - \dfrac{1}{(1+i_2)^{n'-n}}\right]}{(1+i_3)^n} - \text{Costs}$$

CASH FLOW AND NET WORTH PLANNING: DETERMINING THE NEED

Helping clients achieve their lifetime financial goals starts with an assessment of their current financial situation. The calculation of a client's annual cash flow and current net worth situation, coupled with diagnostic financial ratios, provides the foundation for evaluating a client's financial strengths and weaknesses. The process of evaluation begins with an analysis of a client's income and expense situation.

Income is typically divided in one of two ways: (1) based on source—earned or unearned (passive); or (2) based on tax consequence—taxable or nontaxable.

Expenses, on the other hand, can be divided in many ways: (1) fixed or non-discretionary versus variable or discretionary, (2) short-term versus long-term, and (3) one-time versus recurring.

In this book, however, the following terminology will be used to describe expenses: dedicated and discretionary. **Dedicated expenses** are cash flows required by contract or other similarly binding agreement. It is important to remember that such a narrow definition may not be appropriate all the time. A more flexible definition for this category expenses includes additional client defined life and goal "essential" items (e.g., insurance and savings). **Discretionary expenses**, on the other hand, are cash flows that a client completely controls and can change as necessary to meet other objectives.

From a financial planner's perspective, **discretionary cash flow** measures how much income remains at the end of the period after accounting for all expenses. Discretionary cash flow is defined as follows:

Discretionary Cash Flow = Total Income – Dedicated Expenses – Discretionary Expenses

A negative discretionary cash flow indicates that a client is spending more than is earned on a periodic basis. A positive discretionary cash flow suggests that a client has unallocated income that can be used to meet other goals and objectives. Without positive cash flow, or the potential to generate positive cash flow—possibly via reductions in dedicated expenses or reallocation of discretionary expenses—it is difficult for clients to fund their financial goals.

A thorough cash flow and net worth analysis should be conducted for every client seeking comprehensive financial planning services. Goal achievement cannot be achieved unless a client has the capacity to fund most of, or at least the most important of, a financial planner's recommendations. Although reducing spending, increasing saving, or restructuring liabilities could meet some needs, nearly all long-term financial goals are met through the planned allocation of discretionary cash flow and savings, a reallocation of other assets, or a reduction in liabilities.

The process begins with the identification of a client's income and expense situation. This is done using an **income and expense statement** or what is called a **cash flow statement** in this text. A cash flow statement differs from a budget or spending plan. A **budget** is a written projection of how much a client thinks they will earn and spend in any given period, whereas a cash flow statement reflects actual consumption. Although it is important for most clients to have a budget, when it comes time for serious planning, a complete cash flow statement should be used to generate recommendations. The amount of detail in the cash flow statement can vary with the financial complexity of the client.

It is equally important to understand the balance of assets owned and debt owed, because these factors play a role in increasing or decreasing a client's annual cash flow. A **net worth statement**, also commonly referred to as a **balance sheet**, provides a one-time picture of a client's asset (i.e., what a client owns) and liability situation (what a client owes). A balance sheet provides an estimate of a client's cumulative financial progress. As shown in the following formula, the result of subtracting liabilities from assets is **net worth**, or **wealth**.

> **§79 Income and Expenses**
>
> To accurately calculate discretionary cash flow, all §79 income should also be shown as an expense on the Dedicated Expense sheet. If this offsetting expense is not recorded, discretionary cash flow will be overestimated. §79 imputed income, although taxable, is not available for clients to spend.

Net Worth = Total assets – Total liabilities

Before beginning the analysis of a client's financial situation, a financial planner must determine a starting and ending date for the data collection period. An **annual cash flow statement** is typically recommended because annualized statements limit confusion about the timing of income and expenses. If a **monthly cash flow statement** is used, for example, it becomes difficult to account for income earned on a biweekly basis or expenses incurred on a non-monthly basis. Using income and expenses from the prior month or two and then extrapolating to an annual basis is a viable alternative, but this technique can lead to serious inaccuracies, depending on a client's recordkeeping. Annualized statements, on the other hand, provide a broad view of a client's asset and liability situation, which can be used to determine a client's financial position.

In general, one of two annual statement alternatives can be used. First, and perhaps the easiest, is to reproduce a calendar year twelve-month period. In this case, the cash flow and net worth statement would show a start date of January 1 and an end date of December 31. A second method is to reflect the twelve months preceding the month closest to the date of a client engagement. If a client were to engage financial planning services on May 8th, for example, the easiest approach would be to develop the cash flow statement from May 1st of the previous year through April 30th of the current year. The important thing to remember is that accuracy and consistency really count. Finally, because the net worth statement reflects a point in time, and not a period of time, a financial planner can choose any reasonable date close to the initiation of the planning process.

Calculating a Cash Flow Statement

Developing a cash flow statement for a client is relatively straightforward, although again there are several different approaches to categorizing income and expenses. The approach presented here is both mechanically and philosophically different from some other approaches in that cash flows committed to client goals are identified as dedicated expenses. A more traditional approach, as mentioned at the beginning of the chapter, limits dedicated expenses to what are traditionally defined as contractual obligations. Granted, clients do have the discretion to stop allocations to short-term savings and long-term investments at any time and, in the process of working with a financial planner, may choose to do so in lieu of other financial goals. However, identifying these savings and investment expenses as equally important to debt service or insurance protection can change the way they a client views them.

As shown in Figure 3.1, an annual cash flow statement provides an easy way to summarize a client's earned, unearned, and nontaxable income. Income should be reported on an annual before-tax basis. Total potentially **taxable income** includes all sources of income that could be subject to federal and state taxation (e.g., wages, salaries, tips, bonuses, group benefit income, interest, dividends, tax refunds, and pensions). It is also important to include all sources of **nontaxable income** (e.g., gift, child support, qualified distributions for a Roth plan) to provide a complete accounting of all income sources available to the household.

The term **dedicated expense** refers to everyday expenditures that a client has little control over, either because of a contractual commitment or a dedicated personal commitment to fund a goal. Primary categories of dedicated expenses include *income tax*, *debt service*, *insurance premiums*, and *savings and investments*. Note also that total potentially taxable income is reduced by pretax employer deductions, such as employer-sponsored health and disability insurance, as well as deductions for other pretax benefits and funded retirement plans. Care should be taken to determine whether disability insurance is, in fact, a pretax deduction; if so, any benefits subsequently received are then taxable. Mortgage, auto, and education **loan payments** as well as **retirement contributions** generally occur on a regular basis. Often, an employer or creditor may deduct these obligations electronically.

Discretionary expenses, as compared to dedicated expenses, are variable outlays that a client can control more directly, either by the choice to spend or the amount to spend. Major categories of discretionary expenses include *communication*, *entertainment*, *education*, *food*, *housing operation*, *household and personal care*, *medical*, *transportation*, *banking and investment*, and *miscellaneous*. Discretionary, or daily living, expenses are variable and as such can vary month-to-month and year-to-year. Unlike a mortgage payment, for instance, expenses such as entertainment and dining, home improvements, and telephone expenses tend to fluctuate from one period to the next. Separating dedicated expenses from discretionary expenses is necessary to better understand where a client's income is being spent.

The term *discretionary expense* is interchangeable with **variable expense**, which is an expression used to describe everyday living expenses that clients can more easily control. It is important to note that not everyone will agree that the expenses shown in Figure 3.1 are truly discretionary. In many respects, the choice to call an expense *dedicated* (fixed) or *discretionary* (variable) is something a financial planner must make in consultation with the client to best represent the client's perception of the individual expense. For example, tuition expenses for a child to attend private or parochial school or the adjacent public school district are discretionary expenses that may not be necessary given the availability of a local free public school. However, parents who choose to pay the education expenses, for whatever personal reason, would likely assert that the expense is not discretionary. What is really important is to account for all of a client's expenses, regardless of whether the expense is deemed dedicated or discretionary.

Self-Test 1

All of the following are examples of dedicated (fixed) expenses, EXCEPT:

a. Mortgage Payment

b. Utility Payment

c. Student Loan

d. 401(k) Contribution

Figure 3.1 Annual Cash Flow Statement

Taxable Income	Amount	Non-Taxable Income	Amount
Earned Income		Allowances	
Wages, Salaries, Tips		Child Support	
Bonuses & Commission		Gifts	
Other		Qualified Roth Distributions	
		Grants/Loans/Scholarships	
Unearned Income			
Taxable Interest			
Ordinary Dividends			
Tax Refunds and Credits			
Business Income			
Alimony			
Realized Capital gains			
IRA/Pension Distributions			
Rental/Royalty/Trust Income			
Other Imputed Income (§79)			
TOTAL-INCOME			

Figure 3.1 Annual Cash Flow Statement (*cont'd*)

Dedicated Expenses	Amount		Amount
Salary Reduction		*Debt Services*	
Health Care Premiums		Housing Payment(s)	
Section 125 Plan Contributions		Home Equity Payment(s)	
Pretax Benefit Contributions		Auto Payment(s)/Lease(s)	
Retirement Plan Contributions		Student Loan Payment(s)	
Social Security Contributions		Secured Consumer Debt Payment(s)	
FICA Contributions		Unsecured Credit Payment(s)	
Federal Income Tax Withholding		Credit Card Payments(s)	
State Income Tax Withholding		Other Payment(s)	
Imputed Income Expenses			
Insurance Premiums		*Savings/Investments*	
Auto		Emergency Fund	
Homeowner's (if not included in mortgage)		Short-Term Goals	
Life		Intermediate-Term Goals	
Disability		Long-Term Goals	
Health		Optional Retirement/IRA	
Long-Term Care		Education Goals	
Other		Special Needs Goals	
		Other Goals	
		Reinvestment of Dividends,	
		Capital Gains, and Interest	
TOTAL-DEDICATED EXPENSES			

Figure 3.1 Annual Cash Flow Statement (*cont'd*)

Discretionary Expenses	Amount		Amount
Communication		*Entertainment*	
Subscriptions		Media Networks	
Telephone(s)		Hobbies	
Alarm System		Recreation	
		Club Dues	
Education		*Housing & Utilities*	
Lessons		Household Maintenance	
College		& Repair	
Tuition		Lawn/Yard Maintenance	
Room & Board		Utilities	
Books & Fees			
Travel		*Food*	
Professional		Groceries	
		Away from Home	
Household & Personal Care		*Medical*	
Clothing and Accessories		Health Deductibles/Co-Pays	
Laundry/Dry-cleaning		Prescriptions	
Personal Care & Grooming		Unreimbursed Expenses	
Furnishing		*Transportation & Gas*	
Equipment		Maintenance	
Allowances		Licenses & Registration	
Child/Elder Care		Parking & Tolls	
Domestic Help		Public/Personal Property Tax	
Pet Care			
Banking & Investment		*Miscellaneous*	
User Fees		Contributions	
Bank Fees		Travel	
IRA Fees		Vacations	
Commissions		Business	
Legal/Accounting Fees		Tobacco/Gambling/Alcohol	
		Child Support	
		Alimony	
		Pet Care & Supplies	
		Postage	
		Gifts	
		Others	
Total–Discretionary Expenses			
Total–Income			
Total–Expenses			
Total–Discretionary Cash Flow			

When calculating a client's cash flow situation it is important to account for **imputed**—taxable but not spendable—income. **Internal Revenue Code §79 income** is an often overlooked, but commonly available, source of unearned income. Certain employer-provided benefits, such as **group term life insurance** plans, can cause gross taxable income to be greater than salary or wages. Employer related term insurance plans are sometimes known as §79 plans. The first $50,000 in employer-funded group term life insurance coverage is generally tax free to all participants; premiums paid by the employer for the benefit of the employee on amounts over $50,000 are subject to federal income tax. (Note that a key employee in a discriminatory plan cannot exclude the first $50,000 of coverage and is required to use the actual cost if it is higher than the imputed income based on Figure 3.2.) The taxable amount of the premium is calculated based on each participant's age and amount of insurance above $50,000 (if excludible) as shown in Figure 3.2. The figures in Figure 3.2 are used to calculate the amount of taxable income that must be added to income and reported on a Form W-2.

Figure 3.2 IRS Table I: Employer's Tax Guide to Fringe Benefits

Age	Cost per Month per $1,000 of Term Insurance Coverage	Cost per Year per $1,000 of Term Insurance Coverage
Under 25	$0.05	$0.60
25–29	0.06	0.72
30–34	0.08	0.96
35–39	0.09	1.08
40–44	0.10	1.20
45–49	0.15	1.80
50–54	0.23	2.76
55–59	0.43	5.16
60–64	0.66	7.92
65–69	1.27	15.24
70 and above	2.06	24.72

Source: IRS Employer's Tax Guide to Fringe Benefits, Publication 15-B, p. 14.

Example. Assume that a client, age forty-two, earns $80,000 per year, and is insured for twice her annual salary ($80,000 × 2 = $160,000). The client may receive $50,000 in coverage tax-free, but premiums paid by the employer for the remaining $110,000 of the policy are subject to tax. Therefore the client's reported taxable income will increase by $132 for the year, as shown below.

Equation 3.1:

$$\S\,79 \text{ Taxable Income} = \frac{\text{Insurance in excess of } \$50,000}{\$1,000} \times \text{Table Factor} \times 12$$

$$\S\,79 \text{ Taxable Income} = \frac{\$160,000 - \$50,000}{\$1,000} \times 0.10 \times 12 = \$132.00$$

This calculation was completed using the IRS Table I rates shown in Figure 3.2. Taxes on the premium cannot be avoided by assigning the policy to another individual.

Calculating Net Worth

A client's net worth is calculated by subtracting liabilities from assets using a balance sheet. Assets are typically recorded on a balance sheet in a hierarchical manner based on liquidity.

Use an Amortization Schedule to Estimate the Remaining Debt on a Mortgage

Use an amortization schedule to determine the monthly mortgage payment on a loan or the remaining balance on a mortgage. Revisit Chapter 2 for more information.

There are two broad asset categories: financial assets and use assets. Loosely defined, **financial assets** can be spent or invested. **Use assets** support a client's lifestyle and could necessitate property or liability insurance protection. Although exceptions occur when a use asset might also be a financial asset (e.g., art work, collectibles), these terms provide an easy preliminary method for categorization. Aside from these conventions, the categorization of assets may vary. An example of a balance sheet is illustrated in Figure 3.3 such as cash, checking accounts, money market mutual funds, and short-term certificates of deposit are summed to calculate total **monetary assets**—defined as financial assets that can be easily and quickly converted to cash (e.g., cash, checking or savings accounts, certificates of deposit, or money market mutual funds)—available to the client. While **investment assets** can include some of the same financial products as monetary assets, investments are designated for longer-term goals, rather than the day-to-day operation of the household. Additional investment assets include stocks, bonds, or mutual funds.

Retirement assets, which are typically delineated by special tax or ownership status, can include some of the same financial products as the preceding categories. However, separating these assets facilitates financial planning analyses.

Another category of assets includes **tax-advantaged savings for education**, such as **529 Plan accounts**, **Coverdell savings accounts**, and other assets specifically devoted to funding education expenses. In cases where a client has special goals (e.g., funding a house addition or improvement, funding a vacation) or special needs (e.g., accumulating funds for long-term support of a dependent with special needs), these assets should also be clearly identified. Other **special needs assets** might include annuities or legal settlements. Because of special tax treatment and government regulations, **life insurance cash value** is also included as a separate category.

A client's **primary residence** is an example of a **real asset**, which is defined as a **physical asset**, as compared to a financial asset. Other real assets include a second home, ownership interests in vacation property, and other direct real estate holdings. If a client owns collectibles, art, antiques, and other assets, these as well as other **personal property**, such as vehicles, motorcycles, or boats (which are subject to personal

Self-Test 2

Michelle has three credit cards. Two of the cards she pays off each month, but she revolves a balance on the third card each month. She just received statements from each card company. The 1ˢᵗ card has a balance of $500. The 2ⁿᵈ card has a balance of $3,500. The third card (the one she revolves month-to-month) has a balance of $900. How much should Michelle record as a liability on her net worth statements?

a. $900

b. $1,400

c. $4,000

d. $4,900

property tax in many states) should be listed as personal/collectible assets. Finally, furniture, appliances, electronics, and all other assets that support daily life are listed as use assets or **lifestyle assets**. Carefully listing use assets can help a financial planner spot property and liability insurance needs that may be necessary to fully protect the client. A classification system that is systematically used can also help reduce the work associated with calculating a client's estate tax liability.

Liabilities, or **debts**, are also listed in hierarchal order the balance sheet. **Current liabilities** include debts due within the month or other accounts that can be paid in full within the next twelve months. Although **credit card debt** is technically a liability, given the nature of revolving credit, credit cards may or may not be considered **current bills**. Clients who pay their credit card bills in full every month would have no outstanding credit card liability. This is true even if the bill has not been paid, because the actual expenses (e.g., restaurant bills, shopping charges, entertainment expenses) on the credit card statement are accounted for on the cash flow statement as routine expenses. As long as the bill is, or will be, paid monthly, it would be inappropriate to count the expenses as debt. In this case, the credit card is simply used as a cash management tool for easy payment.

Once all current liabilities have been recorded, **long-term liabilities** must be identified. Examples include *mortgage debt*, *home equity debt*, *automobile loans*, *boat and recreational vehicle debt*, *education loans*, *life insurance loans*, *retirement plan loans*, and other types of *installment loans* with durations of more than one year.

When calculating a client's net worth always use the **fair market value** of each asset and the full, or outstanding, **balance due** for each liability. The subtraction of total liabilities from total assets yields net worth.

Figure 3.3 Balance Sheet

Assets	Amount	Liabilities	Amount
Monetary Assets		*Current*	
Cash		Credit Card 1	
Checking		Credit Card 2	
Saving		Credit Card 3	
Money Market Funds		Short-Term Installment	
Certificate of Deposit			
Other			
Investment Assets		*Long-Term*	
Stocks		First Mortgage	
Bonds		Second Mortgage	
Mutual Funds/ETFs		Auto 1	
Brokerage Accounts		Auto 2	
Annuities		Auto 3	
Other		Consumer Loan(s)	
		Other Debt	
Retirement		**TOTAL LIABILITIES**	
IRAs			
401(k), 403(b), etc.			
Annuities			
Other			
Insurance			
Policy Cash Value			
Other			
Education			
529 Plan			
Other			

Figure 3.3 Balance Sheet (*cont'd*)

Assets	Amount	Liabilities	Amount
Real Assets			
Primary Residence			
Secondary residence			
Vacation Home			
Other			
Personal/Collectibles			
Auto 1			
Auto 2			
Watercraft			
Other			
Use/Lifestyle			
Furniture			
Electronics			
Other			
TOTAL ASSETS			
ASSETS LIABILITIES NET WORTH			

Cash Flow and Net Worth Planning Skills

Conducting a financial situation analysis, at the outset of a financial engagement, identifies the financial strengths and weaknesses a client brings to the planning relationship. Model clients have the cash flow, net worth and motivation to fully take advantage of available financial planning strategies and products. Other clients' attitudes and willingness to work with a planner collaboratively to achieve financial goals and follow sound financial advice may impede progress. Regardless of how the client-planner relationship evolves, it is important initially to communicate to clients that they are managing some of their financial affairs well and to compliment these successes, even if they are doing other things imprudently. Exploring the clients' values and attitudes can offer needed insights to the client and planner.

Planning Skill 1: Evaluate Income, Expenses, and Net Worth

Some financial planners initially consider where or how a client spends money. Others unquestionably accept spending patterns reported by a client. Certain benchmarks, usually developed in-house by a financial planner, which are based on regional or national spending data, can be used to suggest that the client might be overspending or not effectively managing cash flow. Some financial planners—and clients—are reluctant to engage in a discussion of the client's lifestyle and spending patterns. Depending on the client-planner relationship, and the amounts of income and discretionary cash flow available, the discussion may or may not be necessary.

For some clients with sufficient income to fund living expenses and identified goals, the discussion may be moot, regardless of the amount of income or net worth. Other clients, again regardless of the amount of income or net worth, may be over spenders who will resist a financial planner's efforts to address the topic. For these reasons, a review of spending may be perilous to the client-planner working relationship. Asking a client to reduce expenditures may be paramount to asking a chocoholic to give up chocolate. It might be the right thing to do, but it still may be met with resistance.

On the other hand, engaging a client in this discussion can lead to increased client motivation to seriously review and weigh the benefits of their current lifestyle against the benefits of accomplishing other short- or long-term goals. Discussing income and expense relationships can also be a simple and effective way to communicate a very important message; a financial planner can be a knowledgeable coach, but not a financial magician. Although a review of spending patterns may or may not yield a sufficient increase in discretionary cash flow for funding all the planning needs identified, it can be a simple, beneficial, and insightful exercise for the client.

The goal of maximizing earnings while maintaining access to monetary assets can also be addressed in a review of income, expenses, and net worth. An appraisal of account types and balances, as well as rates of returns being earned, can offer options not previously considered by a client. For example, it may be wise to move large balances in highly liquid low yielding accounts to other types of investments as a way to increase cash flow or earnings. Alternatively, such funds could be repositioned and used for funding goals or reducing debt without compromising the need for current spending or sufficient cash reserves.

In summary, whether a financial planner chooses to confront or ignore a client's spending patterns, the information gained from a thorough review of the supporting financial documents can offer valuable insights that can be used when crafting financial planning recommendations. Increased discretionary cash flow is the goal at this stage of the financial planning process. Any information gained while reviewing a client's cash flow and net worth situation can serve as a foundation in helping the client meet their financial goals and objectives.

Planning Skill 2: Use Financial Ratios to Assess Financial Wellness

Once a client's cash flow and net worth statements have been completed, it is time to interpret the findings. Simply looking at the numbers on a statement generally tells a limited story. **Financial ratios** help a financial planner better understand a client's current financial position by providing a quantitative measure of **financial health** that can be compared to a **financial benchmark**. As such, ratios are used to diagnose problems or identify issues not immediately evident from the basic financial statements.

Financial ratios have long been used as measures of financial health in corporate finance, and although the earliest household applications reference the 1960s, it was not until the 1980s and 1990s when work was applied to studying the applicability of financial ratios at the household level. Although there is still some disagreement about which are the most reliable ratios for predicting future economic health, it has become commonplace to apply a variety of ratios dealing with **liquidity** (having adequate income to cover expenses) and **solvency** (having adequate assets to cover liabilities) to household finance issues.[1]

A number of financial ratios are recognized as appropriate for establishing baseline information about clients. Care should be taken to interpret ratios within the broader context of a client's financial situation and not in isolation. These ratios are summarized in figure 3.4 and later described in more detail.

Figure 3.4 Commonly Used Financial Ratios

Ratio	Formula	Benchmark
Current ratio	$\dfrac{\text{Monetary assets}}{\text{Current liabilities}}$	> 1
Emergency fund ratio	$\dfrac{\text{Monetary assets}}{\text{Monthly living expenses}}$	3–6+ months
Savings ratio	$\dfrac{\text{Personal savings and employer contributions}}{\text{Annual gross income}}$	> 10%
Debt ratio	$\dfrac{\text{Total liabilities}}{\text{Total assets}}$	< 40%
Long-term debt coverage ratio	$\dfrac{\text{Annual gross income}}{\text{Total annual long-term debt payments}}$	> 2.5
Debt-to-income ratio	$\dfrac{\text{Annual consumer credit payment}}{\text{Annual take home pay}}$	< 15%
Credit usage ratio	$\dfrac{\text{Total credit used}}{\text{Total credit available}}$	< 30%
"Front-end" mortgage qualification ratio	$\dfrac{\text{Annual mortgage (PITI) payment}}{\text{Annual gross income}}$	< 28% to 30%
"Back-end" mortgage qualification ratio	$\dfrac{\text{Annual mortgage (PITI) and credit payment}}{\text{Annual gross income}}$	< 36 to 43%
Rental expense ratio	$\dfrac{\text{Annual rent and renter's insurance premium}}{\text{Annual gross income}}$	< 25%

The **current ratio** is a measure of client liquidity. This ratio indicates whether sufficient current monetary assets are available to pay off all outstanding short-term debts. The recommended benchmark for the current ratio is a number greater than one, which means that if all current liabilities were paid the client would still retain some monetary assets.

The **emergency fund ratio**, sometimes called the **month's living expenses covered ratio**, is very important because it indicates how long a client could live in a crisis situation without liquidating nonmonetary assets or being forced into an unfavorable employment situation. A minimum benchmark of three to six months, of expenses is the standard benchmark, although a range of nine to twelve months is often recommended, depending on the client situation and employment situation. The rationale for having a range rather than a single value is based on a number of factors. In addition to general economic conditions, including job and income stability, the number of household earners and the relative economic contribution of each, types and amount of available credit, the current credit usage ratio, and the current savings ratio all play a role in shaping the appropriate dollar amount.

> ### Self-Test 3
>
> All of the following are examples of emergency fund expenses, EXCEPT:
>
> a. Home Mortgage
>
> b. Automobile Lease Payment
>
> c. Electric Bill
>
> d. Entertainment

An alternative approach for calculating the emergency fund ratio uses monetary assets divided by monthly **emergency fund expenses**, rather than **monthly living expenses**. However, defining emergency fund expenses can be problematic. For example, this number can be computed by taking gross living expenses and subtracting federal, state, and FICA taxes paid, dedicated savings, and other expenses that are not essential to the maintenance of a household, assuming that the emergency is caused by unemployment, disability, or a similar event.

Another approach focuses on **fundamental living expenses** that clients must continue regardless of employment status, such as auto and home loans, insurance premiums, utilities, and other variable expenses (e.g., grocery costs, utilities, home repairs). Regardless of what is or is not included, emergency fund expenses represent the bare minimum level of expense a household must pay in case of a financial crisis.

One of the most important questions clients ask financial planners is, "Am I saving as much as I should?" The **savings ratio** can be used to answer this question. This ratio sums a client's personal and retirement savings and employer contributions to retirement plans, and divides by the client's annual gross income. A benchmark of 10 percent or more is recommended. In other words, at least 10% of gross earnings should be saved annually. (Note: This ratio is very subjective and should not be blindly applied. Rather, great care should be taken to match clients' total savings need to their total goal-funding need.)

Clients often wonder whether they have too much debt. The **debt ratio** provides guideline to help answer this question. In effect, this ratio shows the percentage of total assets financed by borrowing. A benchmark of 40 percent is typically used for this ratio. That is, the typical client should strive to have no more than four dollars in liabilities for every ten dollars in assets.

As is the case with most financial ratios, the interpretation of this benchmark is flexible, depending on a client's unique circumstances and stage in the life cycle. For example, clients in the early stage of their careers may not have much choice except to exceed the optimal percentage because of car loans, education loans, revolving credit accounts (for furniture and appliance purchases), and other household formation costs. Older clients, and those with few debts, may easily meet the ratio benchmark.

The **long-term debt coverage ratio** tells how many times a client can make debt payments, based on current income. This formula can be calculated in several ways. A common method involves dividing annual gross income by total annual **long-term debt payments**. Another method uses **take home pay** (gross income less all taxes, deductions and deferrals) after-tax income as the numerator.

Examples of long-term debt payments include *mortgage payments*, *automobile loan payments*, *student loan payments*, and other debts that take more than one year to repay. If a client's monthly *credit card payment* is large enough that servicing the debt could take more than one year, this amount can also be included in the denominator of the formula.

A long-term debt coverage ratio of at least 2.5 is recommended. The inverse of this formula tells an interesting story. The inverse of a long-term debt coverage ratio of 2.5 is 0.40. This means that a client should allocate no more than 40 percent of income to cover long-term debt payments.

Related to the long-term debt coverage ratio is the **debt-to-income ratio,** which measures the percentage of take home pay committed to **consumer credit repayment**, defined as all revolving and installment nonmortgage debts. A ratio of less than 10 percent of take home, or disposable, income is optimal, although up to 15 percent is considered safe. Between 15 percent and 20 percent is considered a questionable practice, while consumer debt repayments in excess of 20% of take home pay are usually considered a serious problem. Because automatic payments, optional salary deferral retirement plans, and other employee benefits can further reduce after-tax income, it is important that financial planners use care when calculating this ratio. However the interpretation is rather clear: when clients commit 15 percent to 20 percent (or more) of disposable, or take home, pay to consumer debt repayment, usually little is left for meeting all other financial obligations.

The **credit usage ratio** is not only a factor used to determine the adequacy of the emergency fund ratio, but it is also one of the key factors in determining a **credit score**. High credit usage, such as balances above 50 percent of the credit limit, is usually considered negative. This is because creditors may think more credit is being used than can be repaid. (Note: For clients with very high credit scores, as little as 20 percent credit usage can have a minor negative impact on the credit score.)

Self-Test 4

Nathan has the following assets, liabilities, and income:

- Saving Account: $5,000

- Stocks: $8,000

- Income: $39,000

- Unpaid Credit Cards: $2,000

- 3 Year Auto Loan: $9,000

What is Nathan's current ratio today?

0.15

0.40

0.85

2.50

Lenders also use mortgage qualification ratios to measure repayment ability for mortgage qualification. Variations of debt-to-income ratios, in this case referred to as **mortgage qualification ratios,** are used to determine how much of a client's annual income would be used to pay for proposed monthly mortgage and existing nonmortgage, or consumer, debt payments. Two **debt limit ratios** are widely used.

The first is called the **28 percent rule,** or what some refer to as the **front-end mortgage qualification ratio** or the **mortgage debt service ratio.** This ratio results from a comparison of the projected total mortgage payment for **principal, interest, taxes, and insurance (PITI)** to gross household income. To pass this ratio, PITI generally cannot exceed 28 percent of gross annual income, although with increasing real estate prices, 30 percent has become a common lender standard.[2]

The second qualification ratio is called the **36 percent rule**, the **back-end mortgage qualification ratio,** or the **debt repayment ratio.** This rule states that a client should pay no more than 36 percent of gross income on the projected mortgage PITI plus other regular monthly consumer debt payments (e.g., credit card, student loan, and auto). However, a Consumer Financial Protection Bureau rule that took effect in 2014 established a back-end ratio of less than or equal to 43 percent based on the highest payment during the first five years of the loan as an underwriting criteria for qualified mortgages.[3]

These qualification ratios are currently applied throughout the mortgage industry for conventional loans, although the range may vary slightly by lender. Special loan programs or government-subsidized loan programs allow for more relaxed ratios. Clients whose ratios exceed these benchmarks may not qualify for a mortgage or refinance option. If allowed, a lender may require a higher rate of interest or suggest using other available assets to reduce debt. One final but important note: for a client to qualify for a maximum mortgage, these two ratios implicitly limit other consumer debt payments to 8 percent of gross income. This corresponds closely to the original debt-to-income ratio that recommends a consumer credit payment limit of 10 percent of take home income.

The **rental expense ratio** compares the cost of rent and renter's insurance to annual income. Renter's expenses are not too different from homeowner's expenses in that the rental income likely subsidizes principal, interest, taxes, and property insurance for the landlord, who also benefits from the equity in the property. Given this analogy to PITI, it is prudent to apply a slightly stricter benchmark to the rental expense ratio (< 25% to < 28% of gross income) similar to the front-end mortgage ratio. Although the cost of rent in major urban areas could make this benchmark unachievable, offsetting reductions in other expenses that are not part of the urban lifestyle can balance the increased housing costs.

Planning Skill 3: Identify the Elements of an Emergency Savings Fund

The establishment of a client **emergency fund** equivalent to three to twelve months of expenses is an important objective. Factors that can affect the number of months of needed expenses include job security and consistency of income (e.g., salary vs. commission), number of household earners, and availability of unused credit capacity.

The most common approach used to build an emergency fund involves increasing monetary assets. However, this is not the only option. In a low interest-rate environment, it may be better to designate other assets as available for emergency income if needed, and instead invest some of the monetary assets more aggressively to earn a higher rate of return. If a client does not have sufficient monetary assets or chooses to reduce monetary assets, other assets or income sources should be designated.

As might be expected, one source can be designated as, or a combination of sources can be combined to create, an emergency savings fund, contingent on the individual client situation. The key factor is that the asset or source of emergency income be designated and the ramifications of this decision fully considered.

If a financial planner and client believe that some or all of the assets should be readily available to meet emergencies, highly liquid short-term savings alternatives typically are recommended. Monetary assets that pay the highest rate of interest should be chosen, all other factors held constant. Possible accounts include money *market deposit accounts*, *money market mutual funds*, *Treasury bills*, *savings bonds*, and other liquid assets.

Certificates of deposit (CDs) and other assets with a distribution penalty (e.g., EE and I Savings Bonds have a penalty during the first five years) can offer safety of principal and competitive returns, but they could lack needed liquidity unless a laddered approach is used. An example of a ladder includes holding at least one month of living expenses in a highly liquid account. Assets equivalent to two to three months of expenses could then be held in other liquid assets, such as Treasury bills. Three-month CDs could then be used for the remaining assets. As the Treasury bills and CDs mature, the ladder would be restructured so that funds equal to at least three months of expenses are always available.

Some financial planners scoff at the idea of holding three to six months' living expenses in low-yielding assets. These risk-tolerant planners argue that certain types of bonds, stocks, or mutual funds can be used for emergency fund purposes. It should be noted, however, that this is a minority opinion. Should investment assets experience a loss in value when needed for an emergency expense, an untimely sale, without the flexibility of waiting for the value to rebound, could offset the possibility of a higher rate of return. Short-term bonds and bond mutual funds might be used as a compromise position, offering a safer alternative than stocks or equity mutual funds and, perhaps, a slightly higher yield than traditional monetary assets.

Other financial planners assert that although an emergency fund is essential and some level of monetary assets should be maintained, the choice of assets designated can be flexible. In other words, the emergency account can be funded, as explained above, or the account can be "unfunded," such as with a credit source. For example, **life insurance cash values** or other investment assets can be designated as a source of emergency income. Credit cards and a home equity line of credit can also be used as substitutes for, or supplements to, traditional monetary assets within an emergency fund. For clients who pay their credit cards in full each month, a credit line available might be thought of as an emergency fund.

Of more relevance for emergencies is a **home equity line of credit**. These open lines of credit are pre-established with a lending institution, but the client is under no obligation to use the loan. In fact, many institutions stipulate no costs to maintain an open, unused line of credit, so establishing one to ensure that funds available when needed can be an easy emergency fund solution. When the credit line is accessed, a payment schedule, similar to that for credit cards, is used to determine monthly debt payments.

There are potential disadvantages associated with this method of creating an emergency fund. First, the client's home is the **collateral** for the line of credit. Without careful use and repayment, this could put the home at risk. Second, this strategy might not work unless the line of credit is established prior to a financial emergency. This may not be an impediment if the home has adequate equity and the client's credit score and income support a quick establishment of the credit line. If this is a recommended strategy within a comprehensive financial plan, the client should be encouraged to implement the strategy sooner rather than later.

Planning Skill 4: Help Clients Restructure Unsecured and Secured Consumer Debt

One of the best places to look to increase a client's level of discretionary cash flow is on the liability side of the net worth statement. A review of a client's type of debt, as well as the available and outstanding balances, may reveal the need for better debt management. Two options for restructuring consumer credit to optimize cash flow include:

1. paying off **unsecured debt** with assets paying little or no after-tax return; and

2. replacing **unsecured non-tax-deductible debt** with **tax-efficient debt**.

In almost all cases, efforts should be made to pay off high interest non-tax-deductible debt using monetary assets earning low interest. The interest rate paid on credit card or other unsecured debt almost always exceeds interest earned on monetary assets. If a client still has short-term debt after reducing the balance with monetary assets, other short-term investment assets should be considered. The choice of which asset to use is contingent on the rate of return generated, although client preferences also must be considered. An EE Savings Bond, for instance, earning less than 3 percent compounded semiannually may be an appropriate asset to pay off a credit card charging 15 percent compounded monthly. The cost of the high interest debt, compared to the after-tax rate of interest earned, offsets the advantage of holding monetary assets.

Sometimes clients will be apprehensive about liquidating savings because they will feel worse off, temporarily. Unless there is an immediate need for monetary assets and no alternatives can be identified, using these assets to reduce debt is typically a good idea. When viewed from a strict financial ratio perspective, liquidating assets could cause a client to fall below emergency fund benchmark levels. However, paying off short-term debt leads to an instant increase in monthly discretionary cash flow that can be used to fund other goals or to rebuild monetary assets, assuming a client makes a commitment to avoid incurring revolving debt.

In some instances, restructuring assets and liabilities is not feasible or possible. Some monetary or investment assets could have particular significance or family value that excludes them from consideration in cash flow management planning. The client might prefer another alternative, regardless of the mathematical rationale. For clients who cannot manage cash flow to pay credit cards in full monthly, it may be necessary to consider other remedial debt management strategies.

Clients also might have a marginal loss of income from reduced interest on investment earnings. But in most cases, this trade-off is an attractive one. There is no change in net worth because, although an asset was used, there was an offsetting reduction in a liability, leaving a net zero change. In sum, using low-yielding assets to repay debt can have a major impact on the financial situation, countered by a modest impact on a client's tax plan.

The costs and benefits of liquidating longer-term investment assets to pay off non-tax-deductible debt must be carefully considered. This strategy subjects a client to the verities of market conditions. A client who sells an investment at a depressed price will be less satisfied than a client who uses monetary assets, if available. A break-even sale, or one with a gain, can offer the client fiscal benefits as well as psychological benefits from the elimination of the debt.

However, it is important to consider the cost to the goal the assets supported, as well as the after-tax return on the assets compared to the interest rate on the non-tax-deductible debt. Selling an investment to pay off debt could cause an unexpected tax liability, as well as commissions. However, liquidating an investment asset to pay off debt may be prudent when the sale can generate a needed capital loss.

Planning Skill 5: Understand How Mortgage Debt and a Home Equity Line of Credit (HELOC) Influence Borrowing Decisions

If credit cards and other high interest debts cannot be eliminated with monetary assets, it could be appropriate to analyze the costs and benefits of replacing these liabilities with tax-efficient debt. Using a home equity loan or line of credit is one way to increase discretionary cash flow and obtain an itemized tax deduction, if applicable, and the client is not subject to the Alternative Minimum Tax. It might also be wise to use a client's home equity to pay off automobile debt or to make a future purchase.

It could, however, be more appropriate for a client to finance certain purchases (e.g., furniture, appliances, automobiles) using manufacturer low- or zero-percent financing. Although the interest may not be tax deductible, the after-tax cost of the loan may be lower than that offered by a home equity line of credit or loan. Multiple types of credit also help to increase a client's **FICO credit score**, which can influence interest rates on all types of borrowing.

Example: A client plans to purchase a new car that costs $30,000. The car manufacturer is offering 0 percent financing for three years or $3,000 cash back. If the client is in the 28 percent marginal tax bracket, can borrow on a home equity loan at 5 percent, and has a required rate of return of 6 percent for investments, how should the client make the purchase?

At first glance, the 0 percent financing option looks attractive. However, two additional factors must be analyzed. One is that the client is comparing a tax-advantaged financing option (assuming the client is not subject to the Alternative Minimum Tax) to another that does not offer the same tax advantage. To make the two options similar, the client must determine the **effective after-tax rate** for the home equity loan using the following formula, where FMTB is the client's federal marginal tax bracket rate:

Equation 3.2:

After-tax Rate of Return = Nominal Rate x (1 - FMTB)

After-tax Rate of Return = 0.05 x (1 – 0.28) = 0.036 or 3.6 %

Now that the two loans are using equivalent interest rates, the monthly payments should be calculated. With the dealer financed option, if the initial loan amount is $30,000, the monthly payment is $833.33 ($30,000 ÷ 36 months).

With the home equity loan option, where the initial amount financed is $27,000 ($30,000 - $3,000 cash back), the monthly payment is effectively only $792.35 when using the after-tax home equity loan rate of 3.6 percent. However, it is really not quite that simple.

First, the actual monthly payment must be calculated, because this is the payment that the bank is going to expect to receive.

$$EPR = \frac{APR}{12} = \frac{0.05}{12} = 0.00417 \; or \; 0.417\%$$

$$\$27{,}000 = \frac{PMT}{0.00417}\left[1 - \frac{1}{1.00417^{36}}\right]$$

$$PMT = \$809.21$$

Next, the "effective rate" and "effective payment" can be compared to the original.

$$EPR = \frac{APR}{12} = \frac{0.036}{12} = 0.003$$

$$\$27{,}000 = \frac{PMT}{0.003}\left[1 - \frac{1}{1.003^{36}}\right]$$

$$PMT = \$792.35$$

The difference of $16.86 is really received in the form of a lower tax liability at the end of the year, or maybe as part of or an enhancement to a tax refund. In essence there are two differences to consider (1) the actual payment difference of $24.12 ($833.33 - $809.21) and (2) the $16.86 tax benefit. This may seem to be splitting hairs, but the bank won't think so when you send in the wrong payment.

However, assume that the whole difference of $40.98 ($24.12 + $16.86) is investable at some point in another account earning a monthly EPR of 0.5 percent as the required rate of return. By calculating the present value of a thirty-six-month annuity where the payments is $40.98 it is possible to determine that using the home equity loan results in a $1,347.05 lower present value cost.

$$PVA = \frac{\$40.98}{0.005} \left[1 - \frac{1}{1.005^{36}} \right] = \$1,347.05$$

Planning Skill 6: Determine the Cost Effectiveness of a Mortgage Refinance

Gone are the days of 100 percent financing and no-documentation loans where homeowners could use their home equity like a piggy bank. In the aftermath of the Great Recession, lenders have returned to more stringent underwriting standards. To consider a real estate loan, a lender will in most cases require a homeowner to have at least 20 percent initial or remaining equity in the home, have sufficient income to meet the qualification ratios previously discussed, be able to substantiate all sources of income claimed on the loan application, and have a high credit score. For qualified homeowners, however, the resulting low interest-rate environment has created a great opportunity.

Whenever mortgage rates are declining, clients should consider **mortgage refinancing** alternatives. Generally, refinancing makes sense for a client whenever the available mortgage rate is at least 1 percent to 2 percent less than the client's current mortgage rate. Depending on the client situation and the costs to refinance, savings could be worthwhile with as little as a 0.5 percent to 0.75 percent reduction in annual interest rate. In addition to rate and refinance costs, other factors to consider are estimated time in the house (i.e., the life of the loan), credit history, current income, and the current **loan-to-value** of the home.

Refinancing can offer valuable benefits matched to an individual client's financial situation. There are three primary reasons to refinance mortgage debt: (1) to reduce the payment amount, (2) to reduce the total amount of interest paid over the remaining life of a loan, and (3) to take available equity out of the house. Nearly all clients consider refinancing when interest rates have fallen sufficiently to make it cost effective. A reduction in the mortgage interest rate can reduce payments (depending on the loan term) and the total interest cost of the loan. Other clients could benefit from the option to increase the amount of the mortgage and to use the proceeds for other needs, such as paying off non-tax-advantaged debt. Refinancing can even benefit clients who can afford to pay off their mortgage but choose to retain financing or perhaps even extend the payoff period to allow other assets to remain invested, thereby targeting a higher rate of return than the cost of borrowing. Creativity with the balance, term, and interest rate of a mortgage can help a client retain or increase financial flexibility and improve overall cash flow management.

Refinancing is typically not cost free, because it involves paying all **closing costs** (commonly estimated between 1 percent and 3 percent of the value of the mortgage to cover legal fees, bank fees, title search fees, and appraisal work) and any **discount points** associated with the new mortgage. (A point is equivalent to 1 percent of the borrowed amount.) However, many homeowners choose to borrow an extra amount to cover these costs, provided the value of the home allows this option. This is called **rolling closing costs into the mortgage**. This alternative, used by many who refinance, marginally increases the monthly mortgage payment but allows the client to avoid funding closing costs from monetary assets or current income.

Assuming a client can meet the mortgage qualification ratios, another option is to increase the balance of the new mortgage above the payoff on the existing mortgage. Known as a **cash-out refinance**, this option can be used to consolidate other debts into the new mortgage balance (e.g., car loans or credit card liabilities) or to generate funds for other goals or needs. Consolidating other debt can decrease the monthly total payment relative to the multiple payments and offer the benefit of converting non-tax-advantaged debt to tax-deductible debt, assuming the client is not subject to the Alternative Minimum Tax.

However, this strategy effectively extends the repayment for the consumer debt over the life of the mortgage—a disadvantage not to be overlooked—unless the mortgage rate is substantially lower than that of the consumer debt. Nevertheless, the consumer debt is refinanced over the life of the mortgage, typically fifteen to thirty years, far beyond the useful life of most consumer durables or nondurables.

Central to the refinance decision is the choice of **mortgage duration** that best corresponds with a client's overall financial goals. For instance, if a client would like to retire in twenty years, it might be wise to choose a twenty-year mortgage, although the monthly payment will be higher than for a comparable thirty-year mortgage. Conversely, the thirty-year mortgage without a prepayment penalty could be a better alternative. The lower monthly mortgage payments associated with a thirty-year mortgage allow greater **financial flexibility** now and the payments could, over the course of the loan, become relatively minor in inflation-adjusted terms. Those who favor a longer-maturity loan argue that a client can usually prepay a thirty-year simple interest mortgage to, in effect, make it a shorter-term loan without sacrificing itemized interest deductions or financial flexibility.

An aversion to housing debt could make a long-term refinance option unattractive to some clients. They would prefer to make higher monthly mortgage payments to eliminate the debt in fifteen years. Other financial planners and clients argue that using a fifteen-year mortgage does not take advantage of time value of money principles. Although interest rates with a fifteen-year mortgage are typically lower than for a longer-term loan, which means lower total interest costs, the impact of the higher monthly payments on cash flow management should not be overlooked. Once the debt is repaid, reallocating the mortgage payment for other goals could be an attractive benefit to some clients.

Arguments for the optimal mortgage term are open for debate when the original mortgage has a remaining term of more than twenty to twenty-five years. In most cases, it is best to refinance mortgages with a term of twenty years or less remaining with a similar maturity loan. The reason for this recommendation is that clients with fifteen years or less remaining on a thirty-year mortgage could also be closer to retirement. These clients may not be able, or willing, to make a mortgage payment, albeit a small one, in retirement. However, it may be prudent to recommend a thirty-year mortgage regardless of a client's age, if (1) this is consistent with other financial plans (e.g., to live in the house for only a limited time prior to sale or relocation), and (2) the mortgage allows for prepayment.

One of the most fundamental analysis, but also one of the more complex, is doing the calculations around the mortgage refinance decision. The same fundamental methods that are used to determine the break-even analysis for paying discount points can be applied to the decision to refinance a mortgage. The simplest approach is to calculate the break-even period relative the number of months it will take to recoup the refinance closing costs:

$$\text{Breakeven months} = \frac{\text{Total Cost of Refinance}}{\text{Original PMT - New Payment}}$$

As with the discount points discussion above this method completely ignores the time value of money.

There are really two factors to consider when making a refinance recommendation (1) how long does the client plan to be in the home and (2) does the client need to free-up present or future cash flow. The second factor gets at the fundamental question of "are they wanting to lower the monthly payment or payoff the home as soon as possible?" Secondary to this is how much interest is potentially saved.

The simpler of the approaches assumes that in either case the client is going to remain in the home indefinitely. Under this assumption compare the monthly payment difference for the entirely of the longer term loan, use a reasonable rate of return expectation, and solve for the present value difference in total cash flows. It is easiest if the equation is broken into two steps.

Step one, solve for the present value difference of the monthly payment. (Note: The "common" period is defined as the length of time during which a loan payment would be made in either case.)

$$\text{PVA of difference during common period} = \frac{\text{Old PMT - PMT}}{i} \left[1 - \frac{1}{(1+i)^n} \right]$$

Where:

   n = the length of the shorter mortgage option

   i = the monthly required rate of return

The answer to this part of the analysis will be negative if the new monthly payment is higher and will be positive if the new monthly payment is lower. This addresses the present cash flow consideration. Step two, solve for the difference in the length of the loans. This is important because the client is either going to save money by having the loan paid-off more quickly or spend additional money if the loan continues for a longer time. And this addresses the future cash flow consideration.

$$\text{PVA of longer payment for remaining period} = \frac{\dfrac{\text{Longer PMT}}{i}\left[1 - \dfrac{1}{(1 + i)^{n'-n}}\right]}{(1 + i)^n}$$

Where:

       n = the length of the shorter mortgage option

       n′ = the length of the longer mortgage option

       i = the monthly required rate of return

If the "longer" payment is the old loan payment this answer should be added to the first answer, as having a new shorter payment is a benefit. If the "longer" payment is the new loan payment this answer should be subtracted from the first answer, as having a longer payment is a cost.

#Remember

Since the annuity of the remaining payment is "deferred" over the "common" period that an additional discounting factor must be applied.

The last step is to consider the closing costs of the refinance. This cost must be subtracted from the total of the above two steps. Finally, an answer. If the net total is positive, do the refinance, if not, do not.

The second method assumes that the client will not be in the home indefinitely so a "break-even point" must be calculated. This is the case because under most situations closing costs will be incurred and must be recouped to make the refinance worthwhile.

This second scenario also considers two sets of cash flows: a near-term and long-term. The near-term cash flow is the difference in monthly payment and assumes that the difference could be invested. The long-term cash flow is the difference in outstanding balance on the mortgage at the break-even point.

Step one, solve for the present value difference in the monthly payments for the period of time until the estimated "break even".

$$\text{PVA} = \frac{\text{PMT}_1 - \text{New PMT}_2}{i}\left[1 - \frac{1}{(1 + i)^n}\right]$$

Where:

       PMT_1 = the monthly payment on the original loan

       PMT_2 = the monthly payment on the alternative loan n   = the length of time until the "break-even" point.

i   = the monthly required rate of return for the alternative investment

The answer to this part of the analysis will be negative if the new monthly payment is higher and will be positive if the new monthly payment is lower. Step two, solve for the difference in the outstanding balances at the estimated break-even point. This is important as two loans with different interest rates, terms, and/or payments will have different balances every month during the amortization period.

$$PV = \frac{\frac{PMT_1}{i_1}\left[1 - \frac{1}{(1 + i_1)^{n'-n}}\right] - \frac{PMT_2}{i_2}\left[1 - \frac{1}{(1 + i_2)^{n''-n}}\right]}{(1 + i_3)^n}$$

Where:

n   = the length of time until the "break-even" point.

n'   = the remaining term of the old loan

n''   = the term of the new loan

i_1 = the interest rate on the old loan

i_2 = the interest rate on the new loan

i_3 = the monthly required rate of return for the alternative investment

---

Self-Test 6

Which of the following mortgage loans will have the smallest monthly payment on a $200,000 loan?

a. 15 year 4.0% loan.

b. 20 year 5.0% loan.

c. 25 year 5.5% loan.

d. 30 year 6.0% loan.

The answer to this part of the analysis will be negative if the new monthly payment has a higher remaining balance and will be positive if it has a lower remaining balance. Again, the last step is to consider the closing costs of the refinance. This cost must be subtracted from the total of the above two steps. If the net total is positive, do the refinance, if not, do not.

If the estimates from these models is attractive, and depending on a client's other goals and objectives, refinancing can offer benefits. One of those benefits is the ability to leverage cash flow. If a client has numerous other good investment opportunities (good meaning that the expected rate of return exceeds the interest rate on the mortgage over the life of the mortgage), then choosing the option with the lowest monthly payment and leveraging the additional discretionary cash flow could have benefits.

Planning Skill 7: Use Adjustable Rate Mortgages Prudently

Sometimes a simple thirty- or fifteen-year mortgage option will not work for a client. The monthly principal and interest payment associated with these traditional loans could exceed a client's budget or severely restrict discretionary cash flow for meeting other goals. Perhaps the client does not plan to live in the house for more than five to seven years but would prefer to have lower fixed payments during that time.

These and other situations often call for the use of an adjustable rate mortgage or some other form of mortgage loan. An **adjustable rate mortgage** (**ARM**) is one in which the initial interest rate is typically lower than that on a traditional fixed rate mortgage. Depending on the ARM contract, however, the interest rate on the loan can fluctuate in the future. Although adjustable rate mortgages typically offer an initial rate that is lower than the comparable fixed rate alternative, this is not always the case. In times of interest rate uncertainty or a rising rate environment, an ARM might have a higher initial rate, although that certainly decreases the favorability of the option.

Although certainly not as prevalent as during the height of the 2003–2007 real estate bubble, adjustable rate mortgages continue to offer flexibility to prospective homeowners who don't mind trading the risk of a variable interest for an initially lower rate. Although financial institutions structure ARM products differently, it is important to note that all rate increases are subject to the restrictions established in the mortgage agreement. Although restrictions can vary, a **2/6 rate restriction** is common with many lenders. This means that the rate can increase a maximum of 2 percent per year and no more than 6 percent over the life of the loan. **Rate cap restrictions** are always preferable to **payment caps**, which can result in negative amortization with significant rate increases. Some of the most popular forms of ARM products are described below.

- *10/1, 7/1, 5/1, or 3/1-year ARM:* The interest rate and monthly payment remain fixed for ten, seven, five, or three years, respectively. Beginning the subsequent year, the interest rate is adjusted annually for the remainder of the term, typically either twenty or thirty years. Because of the combination of fixed and adjustable rates, these loans are called hybrid mortgages.

- *5/5, 3/3, or one-year ARM:* The interest rate and monthly payment remain fixed for five, three, or one year(s), respectively. There are subsequent interest rate adjustments for each five-, three-, or one-year period, respectively, until the loan is repaid.

- *7/23 or 5/25-year ARM:* The interest rate and monthly payment remain fixed for seven or five years, respectively. In the next year, the interest rate adjusts based on the prevailing rates and remained fixed for the life of the loan.

- *5-year or more Balloon:* The interest rate and monthly payment remain fixed for five or more years. At the end of the term, the loan is due in full. Usually, the client must refinance at the prevailing rate and pay all closing costs for the new mortgage. A Consumer Financial Protection Bureau rule that took effect in 2014 limited the criteria for a balloon mortgage to be considered a qualified mortgage, thus restricting the use of balloon mortgages.[4]

Self-Test 7

What is the maximum possible interest rate on a 2/7 rate restriction loan?

a. 2%

b. 7%

c. 9%

d. 27%

Clients who choose an ARM over a fixed rate loan are, in some cases, speculating on the future. Some anticipate that increasing salary levels will offset potential mortgage payment increases. Others plan to refinance to lock in a lower rate if rates start to increase. Others reason that interest rates at the predetermined time of interest rate adjustment will be equal to or lower than when the loan originated.

When long-term rates begin to increase, clients should consider the benefits of a fixed rate mortgage relative to their ARM. This is especially true if a client plans to live in the house for a long time. Finally, it is important that clients fully understand the short-term benefits and potentially long-term implications of an ARM on cash flow management. For clients who do not anticipate living in the house for many years, an ARM could be the best option.

Planning Skill 8: Master the Intricacies of Buying Down a Mortgage Interest Rate

At times, refinancing a client's mortgage can offer one of the best ways to generate additional discretionary cash flow. There are three primary reasons to refinance mortgage debt: (1) to reduce the payment amount and thereby increase discretionary cash flow, (2) to reduce the total amount of interest paid over the remaining life of the loan, and (3) to take available equity out of the property. Adjusting the balance, term, and interest rate of the mortgage offers a financial planner and client a number of options for creating financial flexibility and improved overall cash flow management—whether for an initial purchase or a refinance.

For clients with available monetary assets, the option to pay loan discount points is another consideration. A **discount point** is 1 percent of the amount borrowed. A point is treated as prepaid interest on the loan. Mortgage lenders often allow a client to **buy down** the stated interest rate for a mortgage by paying *points*. The choice of prepaying interest with discount points should be based on a review of the following factors:

1. *The **break-even period** relative to an assumption about how long the client expects to live in the house.* The break-even period can be calculated in a number of ways.

   a. The first and most common method determines the number of months required to recover the cost of paying points and closing costs by dividing these costs by the difference in monthly principal and interest payments. However, this method ignores the time value of money, in that it assumes that the value of a lower payment paid today and the value of that same lower payment made in five years are equal; of course they are not.

   b. The second, more accurate, method considers the present value of the future stream of savings resulting from the difference in loan payments over the time period required to recoup the cost of the discount points and closing costs. It also considers the loan balance remaining at the end of the projection period. Note that this break-even approach does not address whether a client will save money on total interest paid over the course of the loan. This calculation simply shows how long it will take to recoup total closing costs if a loan is refinanced.

c. The third break-even method takes the present value of the future stream of savings resulting from the difference in interest expense over the time period required to recoup the cost of the discount points and closing costs. This method could be preferable over the standard break-even method if the term of the loan is shortened, thus increasing the payment amount. An increased payment, while lessening the total interest cost, can increase the break-even period. In some cases, if the new payment is higher than the old payment, a traditional break-even point will never be reached. However, this method is the most cumbersome because the difference in interest payments is neither constant nor variable at a fixed rate. Therefore, the present value of the interest payment difference cannot be solved for using a present value of annuity or present value of a geometric series; it must be solved for using a summation formula in a spreadsheet.

With all of these methods, the shorter the time period the client anticipates living in the house, the less attractive paying points and closing costs becomes. Financing closing expenses as part of the mortgage will exacerbate this by increasing the monthly payment and extending the break-even period.

2. *The future value of the after-tax earnings on the monetary assets used to pay points relative to the future value of the interest savings between the two mortgages.* Stated another way, paying points and closing costs out of pocket is not cost effective if the after-tax rate of return on the investment exceeds the mortgage rate. In essence, this would be leveraging in reverse. Typically, a client would want to keep money in whichever asset was earning more (i.e., cost less).

3. *The appropriate income tax treatment of any discount points paid as an itemized deduction on the client's income tax, which can vary from full deductibility for the current year to partial deductibility over the life of the mortgage.* Care must be taken to ensure the proper tax treatment of the points, but in almost all situations the points qualify as an itemized deduction and will potentially reduce taxable income, thus reducing tax liability.

Planning Skill 9: Determine When Renting May be Appropriate as a Cash Flow Management Tool

For nearly eighty years, home ownership has been the linchpin of the American Dream; however, following the Great Recession homeownership in the United States fell to its lowest level in years—approximately 65 percent in 2012. Changes in home ownership expectations have brought greater attention to the benefits of renting.

Although renting has advantages, including a low or no down payment, no market risk for the occupant, and possibly greater near-term affordability, many have historically believed that the disadvantages outweigh the advantages—so much so that renting was almost relegated to a mere after thought among those who wanted to accumulate wealth. Even young singles and families wanted their own home in which to live their lives. This all began to change in the mid-2000s. With the specter of negative equity, increasing payments due to adjustable rate mortgages, and potential foreclosure, many prospective homeowners decided that renting was not only a viable but an attractive alternative.

This housing choice presents several additional opportunities for financial planning discussions. From a cash flow perspective, renting moves the housing expense from a fixed expense to one that will vary over time. A renter should expect to experience a change in rent every contract period; sometimes this adjustment can reduce the cost, but in most cases rent prices increase. In some cases, these increases can be dramatic. Although it is easiest to consider the financial aspects of the housing decision, a financial planner should also recognize that it is also a lifestyle choice. Clients who have always lived in densely populated areas (e.g., New York City), or even clients who may originally be from another country (e.g., Japan, India, most of Europe), may be accustomed to and potentially prefer renting.

Cash Flow and Net Worth Planning Product & Procedural Strategies

Once a client's core financial strengths and weaknesses have been identified, the financial planning process turns to a review of the strategies available to improve management of the financial situation. Any number of financial planning techniques can be used to increase discretionary cash flow, increase assets, or reduce and possibly eliminate non-tax-efficient liabilities. The choice of strategies will depend entirely on the situation being addressed. Although this is true of all planning decisions, the fundamental connection between cash flow and net worth management and a client's lifestyle cannot be overlooked. The following product and procedural strategies represent just a few approaches that could be used when working with clients.

Product Strategy 1: Refinance Mortgage with a Fixed Rate, Fixed-Term Loan

This strategy offers clients one of the best ways to decrease expenditures for housing while increasing annual discretionary cash flow, assuming the term of the new loan is equal to or greater than the loan being replaced. A break-even analysis comparing monthly savings to total refinancing costs will indicate how long it will take to break even on a refinance decision. Disadvantages include the expenses associated with closing and the possibility that replacing a mortgage with a mortgage of a shorter duration will increase annual expenses. Interest for itemized deductions could decrease, resulting in a marginal increase in tax liability. A complete break-even analysis should be completed to determine the payback period and cost effectiveness of any refinance strategy.

Product Strategy 2: Obtain, or Refinance with, an Adjustable Rate Mortgage (ARM)

This strategy is effective when a client must significantly reduce housing expenses to increase annual discretionary cash flow. The strategy works best in a declining interest rate environment, unless the adjustable rate mortgage offers conversion to a fixed rate. The strategy can also work well if the sale of a client's house is planned during the initial fixed rate period of the ARM. Keep in mind, however, that using an adjustable rate mortgage could subject a client to fluctuations in interest rates in the future. If rates increase, a client's annual housing expenses will likely increase as the mortgage payment rises. This strategy also presents clients with **refinancing risks**—if rates do increase, a client could be forced to lock in a new mortgage with a higher interest rate.

Product Strategy 3: Use an Interest-Only Mortgage

Interest-only (IO) mortgages, as the name implies, allow a client to make monthly mortgage payments consisting entirely of interest for a predetermined number of years, after which the payments include both principal and interest. This strategy reduces a monthly mortgage payment when compared to a conventional mortgage. This is an effective strategy for clients who need to decrease housing expenditures to increase discretionary cash flow, or who anticipate an increase in income before the IO period ends. It is also a potentially effective strategy for the disciplined client who believes earnings on the money invested elsewhere will exceed the mortgage interest rate. IO mortgages are also attractive for those who know that they will live in the house for only a short period of time, and will sell the home before the IO period ends and the payments increase. In some high-priced housing markets, an IO mortgage can be an effective way to finance a house that would be unaffordable with a traditional mortgage.

This strategy is based on the notion that future housing prices will steadily appreciate, which, is not always the case. Clients who use this approach are assuming that the future home value will be substantially greater than the mortgage amount, so that future equity will be sufficient to reduce the outstanding mortgage. If housing prices do not increase as predicted, an IO mortgage can leave a client with a large outstanding balance, even after paying mortgage payments for many years. Also, should the client remain in the home, the payments will increase to amortize the balance over the remaining shorter period of the loan. This could work for a client whose income increases before the IO period ends, but otherwise could significantly strain cash flow.

Product Strategy 4: Consolidate Debts with a Home Equity Loan

This strategy offers the benefit of converting non-tax-advantaged consumer debt into a home equity loan with a lower interest rate and tax-deductible interest (assuming that a client is not subject to the alternative minimum tax), and that the non-acquisition based debt does not exceed $100,000). Another reason to consider this strategy is that total loan payments could be lower than payments made individually on unconsolidated debt. This is true because, generally, home equity loans carry a longer duration and a lower interest rate than open ended loans and collateralized loans typically used to purchase assets such as automobiles. It is worth noting that although this strategy can result in increased levels of discretionary cash flow, using a home equity loan to consolidate debt places the client's home at risk in case of default.

Product Strategy 5: Establish a Home Equity Line of Credit as a Source of Emergency Funds

This strategy is useful whenever assets designated for emergency savings are depleted for another purpose, or when a client's monetary assets are insufficient to meet the minimum of three to six months of emergency expenses. Essentially, the line of credit substitutes for actual assets. A home equity line of credit can typically be obtained with little or no closing costs, and there is no requirement that it be

#Remember

Some qualified defined contribution plans (e.g., 401(k) and 403(b)) allow participants to borrow up to $50,000 or 50% of their account balance, whichever is smaller. But, there is an opportunity cost, in that the borrowed money will not be earning market rates of return.

used. It is important to note that anything purchased using a line of credit subjects the client's home equity to risk. However, this option offers several benefits over other types of consumer credit or lending sources. Spending of equity should be restricted to true emergency situations. Failure to meet qualification standards could restrict the use of this strategy or increase the associated costs.

Procedural Strategy 1: Pay off Unsecured Debt with Assets Earning Lower Rates of Return

This strategy is most appropriate for clients who currently have a revolving balance on their credit cards or other unsecured debt. Implementing this strategy decreases annual interest expenses, thereby increasing annual discretionary cash flow for funding other financial goals or objectives. In the event of an emergency where assets are needed immediately, the client could re-incur debt, if necessary, to cover expenses. This strategy applies to a wide range of client situations. Two potential disadvantages are associated with this strategy. First, some clients find it psychologically difficult to reduce the level of cash or cash equivalents in their portfolio. Suggesting this strategy could cause stress for a client struggling with the thought of being "cash poor" until the liquidated assets can be restored. Second, for clients who fail to control spending, paying off debt could lead to the accumulation of more debt and a further reduction in net worth.

Procedural Strategy 2: Identify Client Expenses That Can Be Reduced

This strategy could uncover hidden or excessive lifestyle expenses that a client does not consciously consider on a daily basis. The importance of other goals or objectives could override the short-term benefits of these expenses and encourage the client to curtail or eliminate these costs. This is a very sensitive discussion that must balance a financial planner's knowledge of expense categories relative to household income with a sincere appreciation of a client's values and spending motives. However, this strategy can effectively increase discretionary cash flow without the cost of incurring liabilities or selling assets. Keep in mind that typically clients are committed to their lifestyle and the associated expenses. Asking a client to reduce or eliminate select expenses could cause a negative reaction. Nevertheless, a financial planner must clearly communicate the benefits (short- or long-term) of this strategy and give the client responsibility for the identification of acceptable spending changes.

Procedural Strategy 3: Use the Cash Value of Life Insurance as an Emergency Source of Income

The cash value portion of a life insurance policy can be designated and, if necessary, used as a source of emergency income. The cost of the loan is relatively inexpensive, and no qualification standards must be met. Taking a **policy loan** generally reduces the death benefit and the cash surrender value while the loan is outstanding. The loan also incurs an interest expense. (For an example of the loan amount available, see the discussion on nonforfeiture options in Chapter 4.) Depending on the policy, the return on the cash value could be reduced until the loan is fully repaid. Loans against the policy value reduce the amount of assets available for earnings used to offset future premium payments. Further, loans that go un-serviced for too long (i.e., no regular payments being submitted) can cause a policy to lapse, which can create a taxable event that could generate a substantial embedded tax liability.

Procedural Strategy 4: Use Financial Assets to Reduce Mortgage Debt

Using financial assets to reduce the outstanding balance lowers the loan-to-value (LTV) ratio of the mortgage and could increase the options available for refinancing. Banks are more willing to finance real estate that has an LTV ratio of less than 80 percent. This means a homeowner could have a wider choice of mortgage options, including a shorter loan term, a fixed versus variable rate, and a lower interest rate. Using assets that have a lower expected rate of return than the after-tax interest rate on the mortgage would also optimize overall investment returns. It is important to note that using financial assets to pay down mortgage debt can reduce financial flexibility in the event of an emergency. This can also have unintended consequences on the achievement of other financial goals. Additionally, using tax-sheltered assets would most likely trigger income tax and a tax penalty. Another consequence is that a lower mortgage balance would reduce the interest paid and therefore reduce itemized deductions.

Procedural Strategy 5: Borrow from 401(k) as an Emergency Source of Income or to Pay off High Interest Debt

Despite the consistent warnings that retirement savings should be maintained at all costs, in extreme dire circumstances, and with full awareness of the disadvantages, a qualified defined contribution plan (e.g., 401(k) and 403(b)) loan could be available at a relatively low rate of interest with no qualification standards, credit checks, or high fees. Terms of the loan will vary with the plan, and not all plans allow loans. The amount available to borrow is limited to the lesser of: $50,000 or one-half of the account balance. Regulations require repayment within five years (unless for a home purchase), although most do not have a prepayment penalty. Rates are typically based on the prime rate plus a margin, which could be significantly lower than other loans. However, the benefit is also the cost as earnings on the borrowed amount equal the interest rate, instead of higher market rate typically earned.

This opportunity cost can be high, and must be considered. The loss of compound earnings on the borrowed funds is another cost that must be considered. The opportunity cost is even greater if the plan prohibits contributions to the 401(k) plan during the term of the loan, which has the added disadvantage of increasing annual income taxes. Also, the loan amount will be subject to income taxes twice; once, when the loan is repaid with after-tax dollars and again when the 401(k) plan account (including the interest paid on the loan) is distributed as retirement income. Although a 401(k) plan loan may seem like a good deal, these factors as well as job stability must be considered.

Finally, the full loan balance must be repaid within sixty days of being laid off or leaving the job. The loan balance is considered a distribution subject to state and federal income taxes and, if applicable, penalties for early withdrawal. But with a secure job, the 401(k) loan is still a better option than a distribution from the plan, unless the client situation would qualify for a hardship withdrawal.

Procedural Strategy 6: Implement an Income Shifting Strategy When Appropriate

This strategy is designed to leverage the use of client monetary assets in a tax efficient manner. Consider the following case scenario. A client, age fifty-five, works for a college and has saved a substantial ($100,000) emergency fund that is earning 1 percent annually. Also assume that the client's primary goal is to accumulate enough savings to reach retirement in twelve years. The client's secondary goal is to reduce taxes paid on her $90,000 salary.

Here is how an income shifting strategy could work. First, the client would immediately maximize contributions to all available defined contribution plans at work. Because she is employed by a college, she is eligible for both a 403(b) and 457 retirement plan. Each has a contribution limit of $18,000 in 2016, plus a $6,000 catch-up provision because she is older than age fifty. She can effectively defer $48,000 in salary this year, which leaves taxable income equal to $42,000 ($90,000 - $48,000). While the client may like the fact that the contributions move her from the 25 percent marginal tax bracket to the 15 percent bracket, she will be concerned about a lack of cash flow to meet daily living expenses. This is where the income shift occurs. She should then supplement her income with savings. Given the balance of her account, she can shift income for two years.

The downside to this strategy is that her emergency savings fund will be depleted. However, should she need an emergency source of funds she could rely on other sources of credit, including credit cards and possibly a loan from the 403(b) account. In the case of a severe emergency, she could take distributions from the retirement accounts. Depending on her age and the purpose of the distribution, this may or may not trigger a penalty. It is worth noting that this type of strategy may also be effective for families who want to minimize their adjusted gross income in order to qualify for college and university grants, aid, and scholarships.

CASH FLOW AND NET WORTH PLANNING FOR SPECIAL POPULATIONS

Cash Management for Recent Widows and Widowers

Regardless of age or the circumstances surrounding the death of a spouse or partner, addressing cash flow management issues can be both psychologically and financially empowering. Grieving spouses should be cautioned not to make major financial or lifestyle decisions too quickly. But an important first step is to assist them in developing a new cash flow statement and balance sheet. This strategy can encourage independence and responsibility in the new situation; help the survivor avoid financial problems by addressing necessary changes in spending, employment, or lifestyle; and most importantly, provide needed peace of mind. Whether this is a new or ongoing professional relationship will determine the amount of effort required to build trust and collect information, but the following are three important considerations:

3. Identifying other professionals (e.g., estate planning attorney, accountant or tax professional, investment managers, insurance providers, bankers, creditors) who are, or should be, working in collaboration with the planner and the client. A valued family friend or child can also be involved.

4. Identifying all cash flows that could occur over a specified time period, for example, a year. Some of these may be glaringly obvious, while others could be overlooked if the financial planner does not systematically help the client identify income sources and expense needs. A comprehensive assessment can help discover (a) benefits (i.e., Social Security, COBRA coverage, retirement or life insurance benefits, or other services) that might be available, (b) service providers or additional expenses that need to be identified (e.g., a lawn service), and (c) changes that must occur to ensure financial stability for the selected time period.

5. Identifying all assets and liabilities for the new net worth statement will establish the financial position. Retitling inherited or jointly held assets may be necessary, debts may have to be restructured, or assets may need to be liquidated. These decisions cannot be made without an accurate assessment of cash flows and net worth.

Helping to stabilize the situation of widows and widowers by developing a new spending plan and net worth statement can increase the grieving spouse's feelings of control and reduce pressure to make major life changes.

Cash Management for the "Suddenly Wealthy"

It would be inaccurate to assume that all **high-net-worth** (HNW) and **ultra-high-net-worth** (UHNW) clients lack the need for cash flow planning. It would be easy to say that these clients must already have the skills in place to manage their day-to-day financial situation. This might perhaps be true if the person was self-made, but generally, high net worth individuals are rarely different than others—they have absolutely no idea how to manage cash flow effectively.

When windfall money is mentioned many think of lottery winnings, but much more often financial windfalls come from an inheritance or the sale of a business or the signing of a professional sports contract. (Although to the untrained such events could seem wonderful, financial planners must recognize that some windfalls come as the result of a loss—and in some cases, they create loss.) Advising a client who has just received a life altering sum of money about cash flow management can be incredibly difficult. After all, who goes broke after receiving millions of dollars?

> **Self-Test 8**
>
> Which of the following professionals is more likely to spend time learning about a client's situational factors, fears about money, and money scripts?
>
> a. Certified Public Accountant
>
> b. Stock Broker
>
> c. Financial Planner
>
> d. Financial Therapist

The internet is filled with stories of sudden millionaires who go from ignorance to bliss to broke in only a few years—and unsound financial advice or no financial advice is usually to blame. Building a simple cash flow statement and then using it as a platform for a reasonable budget can go a long way in helping those who have suddenly come into wealth preserve their financial situation. Cash flow planning, although normally thought of as the basis for becoming wealthy, is also a cornerstone for remaining wealthy.

Susan Bradley, who wrote a book on sudden wealth, suggests that a person who receives sudden wealth actually delay making any financial or other important decisions until after he or she feels comfortable and grounded in the new situation. This pause allows time for people to truly contemplate how they want their life to change rather than simply letting their life change. Life altering sums of money are just that—life changing, not merely lifestyle shifting. People have strange emotional reactions to receiving an over-sized amount of money at one time. Anxiety, guilt, resentment, fear, and isolation can all be emotional responses. So, it may be that a financial planner must first play the role of **financial counselor** or **financial therapist** before working as a planner-technician. Although many resources may be available about what to do with a financial windfall, precious few deal with how to cope with one.

Quantitative/Analytical Mini-Case Problems

Emily and Joel Schumaker

1. Emily and Joel Schumaker are married clients have just been approved for a twenty-year, $150,000 mortgage. They have been given a choice of two loans. One loan has an annual percentage rate (APR) of 8 percent and does not carry a fee, and the other has an APR of 7.5 percent but carries a discount fee of 2 percent of the initial loan amount. The fee for the second mortgage is payable in cash at loan inception and cannot be financed with the loan.

    From a present value cost perspective, which loan is the better deal, assuming they sell their home immediately after paying the 120th payment and require a 9 percent effective annual rate of return? In other words, which option has the lower cost?

    Assume all required payments are made at the end of each month and that interest is compounded monthly. Remember to consider the difference in loan payment, the difference in remaining balance at the time of sale, and the present value of the discount points on an after-tax basis assuming the points are fully deductible. The clients are in the 25 percent marginal tax bracket. (Hint: You can solve this problem at either T_0 or T_{120}.)

Bev Mickelson

2. Suppose a Bev Mickelson is in the market for a car. Bev can afford to spend $500 per month, but she decides it is best to buy a cheap car now and use what is left of the $500 to save for a really nice one later. These savings will earn an effective annual rate of 9 percent interest. Suppose she decides to borrow $15,000 to buy a used car. The loan is for forty-eight months at a 7.8 percent APR. Three years later she sells this car for $4,500.

    How much money will the client have for her new car after paying off the old one assuming that all payments and compounding occurred on a monthly basis? (Do not consider sales or income taxes in the calculations.)

Nina and Rafael Ruiz

3. Nina and Rafael Ruiz are married clients have just been approved for a thirty-year, $150,000 mortgage, with an APR of 7 percent. However, they know that they do not want to make only the regular payment and that they do not want to take the entire thirty years to pay off the balance. So they have suggested two options they would like analyzed. Option 1 requires a fixed monthly payment of $1,200. Option 2 requires that they start with the regular payment but then increase that amount by an effective monthly rate of 0.35 percent.

    They want to know the answers to the following questions.

    a. Which payment method will result in a faster payoff?

    b. What is the difference in total interest payments between the two alternative payment methods? Hint: The total of payment for Option 2 involves using the formula for the partial sum of a geometric series.

    c. Which repayment method results in higher home equity (the lower loan balance) after fourteen years?

Puneet and Theresa Chatterjee

4. Puneet and Theresa Chatterjee are both twenty-eight years old and have a two-year old child, Edward. They have asked you to construct financial statements based on the information provided. In addition, you are to analyze their current financial situation by calculating and explaining the results of their financial ratios. How would you generally describe the financial situation of this family?

    Income and expense information:

    *   **Income:** Puneet and Theresa earned $95,000 in salary. Puneet earned $50,000 as a data analyst, and Theresa made $45,000 as a nursing supervisor. Puneet and Theresa also received $35 in interest from their money market account, which they reinvested.

    *   **Taxes:** Their W-2 tax statements indicate that they paid $7,267 in FICA taxes, $10,500 in federal income tax, and $2,900 in state income taxes. Real estate taxes on their home were $1,800. Personal property taxes on the two vehicles they own equal $360.

    *   **Insurance:** Medical insurance is provided by their respective employers; however, they have to pay a portion of the premium, which amounted to $1,400. Their personal automobile policy premiums totaled $1,600. Homeowner's insurance premiums for the year were $1,200. Puneet and Theresa own term life insurance policies, and they paid $500 in premiums for both policies.

    *   **Loan payments:** Mortgage payments amounted to $20,253. Auto loan repayment for their two vehicles totaled $6,600. Student loan payments for Theresa's student loans when she was working toward her master's degree in nursing equal $4,500 for the year, and the boat payments for the year equal $3,112.

- **Savings payments:** Puneet and Theresa contributed $4,000 to their retirement accounts, $1,200 to an education fund for their child, and $1,200 to their money market account, and the $35 in interest that they reinvested in the money market account.

- **Daily living expenses:** Puneet and Theresa estimate, based on checking account records and credit card statements, that they spent approximately $4,000 on food at home. Clothing expenditures were estimated to be $1,800; laundry and dry cleaning expenses were $300; and personal care expenses were $1,000. Day care for Edward was $6,000. Expenses for gas and maintenance for their vehicles were $2,000. This year there were no auto repair costs.

- **Variable expenses:** They estimate that they spent $1,600 on entertainment, which includes dining out and admission charges for plays, movies, and sporting events. Puneet and Theresa also spent $1,500 on recreation and travel, which is how they categorize vacation expenses. Charitable contributions for the year totaled $2,000. Hobby expenses were $360 for the year. Gifts for family and friends throughout the year were $2,000.

- **Utilities:** Utilities for the year cost $4,000, which included $1,840 for gas and electricity, $720 for water, and $1,440 for telephone, internet access, and cable television.

- **Home maintenance and improvements:** They spent $1,200 annually in this category.

- **Miscellaneous expenses:** Unreimbursed medical expenses amounted to $300.

Asset and liability information:

- **Assets:** They have $2,000 in their checking account, $11,000 in their money market account, $6,000 in a mutual fund investment account, $5,500 in the education savings account for Edward, and $20,000 in their retirement accounts. Their home has a fair market value of $185,000, and the blue book value of their vehicles is $7,000 for Vehicle 1 and $5,500 for Vehicle 2. Their furniture and household goods have an estimated value of $20,000; they have sporting equipment estimated at $2,500, and a boat valued at $12,500.

- **Liabilities:** Theresa's and Puneet's current unpaid bills equal $500 and they owe $700 on their Visa credit card but will pay the entire balance off before the due date. They routinely charge during the month, but *always* pay the balance in full each month. The balance on their home mortgage is $182,510; their auto loan balance for Vehicle 1 is $8,500, and $2,000 for Vehicle 2. The balance on the loan for the fishing boat is $11,855, and Theresa's student loan balance is $5,700.

5. Using the Butterfield case in Part VI of the text, calculate and interpret the ratios. All needed information is provided, except for the total credit available, which is $10,000 on the Visa and $11,500 on the MasterCard. Then, answer the following questions based on your findings.

   a.   How would you rate the Butterfields' overall liquidity?

   b.   How would you rate the Butterfields' overall solvency?

   c.   Does their periodic savings rate meet the minimum suggested threshold?

   d.   Are they spending too much on housing?

Be sure to frame your answers as if you are speaking to or presenting them to the client.

Comprehensive Bedo Case—Analysis Questions

Several key pieces of information are needed to conduct an analysis of the cash flow and net worth situation for the Bedo household. Careful and accurate calculation of their gross income, expenses, and discretionary cash flow will establish the foundation of the financial plan. Earnings on the Bedos' monetary and investment assets must be calculated using the rates of return provided. Although insignificant in dollar terms, any §79 benefit income should be included in the statement of cash flows. To calculate the Bedos' net worth, it will be necessary to determine the outstanding mortgage and automobile loans. Finally, it is advisable to review the planning assumptions and specific client goals.

1. Develop a goal or goals for the Bedos' financial situation. When conceptualizing the goal or goals, consider the following.

    a. Is the goal developed in agreement with any or all goals and objectives that the clients have identified as important to their financial planning?

    b. What situational factors might influence their financial situation goals? Are these factors explicit, implied, or assumed? Is additional information required from the Bedos?

    c. What is the desired outcome for the clients?

2. Develop a list of globally accepted, client-specific, or planner-generated planning assumptions that will structure the financial situation analysis.

3. As part of the analysis of the Bedos' current financial situation, develop a cash flow (income and expense) statement and a net worth statement. Be sure to calculate the following:

    a. The amount of interest, capital gains, and other investment income earned by the Bedo household during the year.

    b. Any additional income obtained by the Bedos, including § 79 plan employee benefit income.

    c. Total income and expenses for the year.

    d. The amount of discretionary cash flow available to the Bedos.

    e. The amount of discretionary cash flow plus unallocated savings available to the household. Be sure to account for reinvested earnings and the § 79 plan employee benefit income.

    f. The net worth of the Bedo household.

4. As part of the current financial situation analysis, calculate the following diagnostic financial ratios for the Bedo household:

    a. The current ratio.

    b. The emergency fund ratio.

    c. The savings ratio.

d.   The debt ratio.

e.   The long-term debt coverage ratio.

f.   The debt-to-income ratio.

g.   The credit usage ratio.

h.   The front-end mortgage qualification ratio.

i.   The back-end mortgage qualification ratio.

5.   Calculate the following refinancing alternatives:

a.   The monthly payment on a fifteen-, twenty-, or thirty-year refinance alternative, assuming closing costs are paid from available monetary assets.

b.   The monthly payment on a fifteen-, twenty-, or thirty-year refinance alternative, assuming closing costs are included in the new mortgage balance.

6.   Summarize your observations about the Bedos' current financial situation, paying special attention to opportunities to reduce spending, optimize emergency fund balances, maximize earnings on monetary assets, and maximize tax and cash flow efficiency of debt.

7.   Based on the goals originally identified and the completed analysis, what product or procedural strategies might be most useful to improve the Bedos' cash flow and net worth situation? When reviewing the strategies, be careful to consider an approximate cost or savings, if applicable, as well as the most likely outcome(s) associated with each strategy.

8.   Write at least one primary and one alternative recommendation from selected strategies in response to each identified planning need. More than one recommendation may be needed to address all of the planning needs. Include specific, defensible answers to the who, what, when, where, why, how, and how much implementation questions for each recommendation.

a.   It is suggested that each recommendation be summarized in a Recommendation Form.

b.   Assign a priority to each recommendation based on the likelihood of meeting client goals and desired outcomes. This priority will be important when recommendations from other core planning content areas are considered relative to the available discretionary funds for subsidizing all recommendations.

c.   Comment briefly on the outcomes associated with each recommendation.

9.   Complete the following for the Financial Situation Planning section of the Bedos' financial plan.

a.   Outline the content to be included in this section of the plan. Given the preceding segments written, which segments are missing?

b.   Write the introduction to this section of the plan (no more than one to two paragraphs). Be sure to include an explanation of the purpose of the financial situation analysis and define any terms used.

c. Given the emphasis on financial statements, ratios, and other numerical data in this section of the plan, how might this information be most effectively presented to the client? What interpretation or explanation of the data would be necessary? What data might be graphically summarized? Develop an example for the Bedos' plan, including the financial statement, the interpretation of the statement, and one graphic representation of the data. The latter should help the client interpret the data.

d. For one other issue discussed in this chapter (e.g., cash flow analysis and spending; debt restructuring or mortgage refinance; emergency fund or funding sources; or ratios), complete the analysis, write the interpretation, and graphically present the findings for inclusion in the Bedo plan.

10. Prepare a ten- to fifteen-minute presentation for the Bedos of your observations and/or recommendation(s) regarding their cash flow planning. Be sure to include visual aids or handouts.

Chapter Resources

Bradley, Susan, and Mary Martin. *Sudden Money: Managing a Financial Windfall*. New York: John Wiley & Sons, 2000.

Home Affordable Refinance Program (HARP) (www.makinghomeaffordable.gov).

Leimberg, Stephan R., Martin J. Satinsky, Robert J. Doyle, Jr., and Michael S. Jackson. *The Tools & Techniques of Financial Planning*, 11th Ed. Cincinnati, OH: National Underwriter Company, 2015.

The *Financial Facilitator* and all fillable forms needed to complete text activities can be found on the student website at: pro.nuco.com/booksupplements/NUCollege-CaseBook3e.

Self-Test Answers

1: b, 2: a, 3: d, 4: d, 5: a, 6: d, 7: b, 8: d

Endnotes

1.   For additional information see:

Griffith, R. "Personal Financial Statement Analysis: A Modest Beginning." In *Proceedings of the 3rd Annual Conference of the Association for Financial Counseling and Planning Education, 3* (1985), 123–31.

Prather, C. G. "The Ratio Analysis Technique Applied to Personal Financial Statements: Development of Household Norms." *Financial Counseling and Planning,* 1 (1990): 53–69.

Lytton, R. H., E. T. Garman, and N. M. Porter. "How to Use Financial Ratios when Advising Clients." *Financial Counseling and Planning* 2 (1991): 3–23.

2.   Credit Infocenter. "Underwriting Guidelines for Mortgage Loans - Loan Requirements, Credit Review, Qualify for a Loan," Available at www.creditinfocenter.com/mortgage/guidelines.shtml.

3.   Consumer Financial Protection Bureau. "Summary of the Ability-to-Repay and Qualified Mortgage Rule and the Concurrent Proposal," Available at: files.consumerfinance.gov/f/201301_cfpb_ability-to-repay-summary.pdf.

4.   Consumer Financial Protection Bureau. "Summary of the Ability-to-Repay and Qualified Mortgage Rule and the Concurrent Proposal," Available at: files.consumerfinance.gov/f/201301_cfpb_ability-to-repay-summary.pdf.

Chapter 4

Income Tax Planning

Learning Objectives

1. Nearly every tax planning decision and strategy can have an impact on a client's cash flow and net worth situation. This is the primary reason tax planning occurs early in the financial planning process. Specifically, it is important to know how much discretionary cash flow exists after taxes have been calculated before additional planning recommendations are made. Additionally, tax planning can serve either to increase or decrease a client's cash flow and net worth position.

2. A review of a client's current tax situation starts by evaluating client situational factors related to the tax planning process. Competent financial planners understand not only their client's tax planning goals, but their temperament, personality, attitudes, beliefs and values, financial knowledge and experience, and socioeconomic descriptors that influence tax planning decisions. Understanding the emotional, personal, and nonfinancial aspects of a client's situation is as important as calculating a client's tax liability.

Additionally, a strong desire to minimize taxes paid to the government, or a willingness to pay "my fair share" of the tax burden, or even a simple desire to avoid being audited by the IRS can seriously shape a client's tax planning motivations.

3. Generally, federal income tax liability is calculated using a ten-step process that first determines total income, then the amount of income subject to taxation after applying all deductions and exemptions. Next, total tax liability is calculated, and finally the net tax liability is determined after all tax credits for which the tax filer is eligible have been applied. Specifically, the ten-step tax determination process includes: (1) recording potential gross income, (2) excluding nontaxable income and pretax items, (3) calculating grossing income, (4) reducing AGI by using above the-line-deductions, (5) reducing taxable income by either the standard deduction or itemized deductions, (6) reducing taxable income through personal exemptions, (7) calculating the

Learning Objectives

tax liability, (8) reducing tax liabilities by means of tax credits, (9) adding other tax liabilities, and (10) determining the amount owed or amount to be refunded.

4. A client's adjusted gross income plays an important role in shaping financial planning recommendations. AGI is important to clients because it is used to determine their eligibility for certain retirement contributions, deduction limits, and tax credits, among other things. Examples of above-the-line deductions include health care savings account contributions, the deductible portion of self-employment taxes, small business qualified plan contributions, alimony, traditional IRA contributions, and student loan interest. Examples of below-the-line deductions include the standard deduction or mortgage interest, state income tax, real estate taxes, unreimbursed medical expenses (limits apply), qualifying job-related expenses, and tax preparation fees.

5. Congress created the alternative minimum tax (AMT) to prevent wealthy taxpayers from taking advantage of preferential deductions and paying little or no income tax. Whereas the regular tax law gives preferential treatment to certain income and allows special deductions and credits for certain expenses, the AMT removes many of these special allowances, thus resulting in a greater tax liability. Common adjustments and tax preference items that can be affected by the AMT include personal exemptions, the standard deduction, miscellaneous itemized deductions, state and local taxes, accelerated depreciation of certain property, incentive stock options, and certain tax-exempt interest.

6. Tax planning is always important, but possibly never more so than in the context of retirement planning. All distributions from qualified retirement accounts are monitored by the IRS for potential tax implications. In fact, the IRS not only monitors but actually mandates action. For example, in most situations, if a client takes a qualified plan distribution before age 59½, the IRS will impose a penalty for accessing retirement money too early; if a client fails to withdraw money *after* age 70½ the IRS may also collect a penalty. Additionally, there are special situations that call for a tax-savvy solution, such as disposition of incentive stock options. In this case, depending on exactly how and when clients take a distribution from their employee benefit company-stock account, clients might pay (1) income tax on the entire amount immediately, (2) income tax on the basis immediately and the capital gains later, or (3) income tax on the entire amount later.

7. Although some financial planners outsource the calculation and filing of client tax returns to other professionals, it is nonetheless important for all financial planners to use a client's tax return to identify other planning opportunities. For example, clients are seldom in a position to determine whether owning municipal bonds compared to taxable corporate fixed-income securities makes sense from a tax perspective. Information from a client's tax return can help answer this question. Other areas of financial planning that can benefit from a tax planning review include cash flow planning, retirement planning, investment planning, education funding, insurance needs analysis, and estate planning.

Key Terms

Accident and Health Benefits

Average Cost Election

Complex Trust

Corporation (C Corp)

Custodial Accounts

De Minimis (Without Consequence) Benefits

Dependent Care Assistance

Disqualifying Disposition

Educational Assistance

Employee Discounts

Exclusion Ratio

Exercise Price

Fair Market Value

First In, First Out (FIFO)

Form 1065

Form 1120

Fringe Benefit

Group-Term Life

Health Savings Accounts

High Cost Election

Incentive Stock Option (ISO) Plan

Income in Respect of a Decedent (IRD)

Investment Income

Last In, Last Out (LIFO)

Like-kind Exchange

Limited Liability Company (L.L.C.)

Limited Liability Partnership (L.L.P.)

Loss/Gain Utilization

Low Cost Election

Marginal Tax Bracket (Federal and State)

Moving Expense Reimbursements

No-Additional-Cost Services

Nonstatutory Stock Option

Partnership

Retirement Planning

S Corporation (S Corp)

Sale of a Primary Residence

Sole Proprietorship

Specific Lot Identification

Statutory Stock Options

Taxable Equivalent Yield

Transportation (Commuting) Benefits

Unearned Income

Volunteer Firefighter And Emergency Responder Benefits

Working Condition Benefits

CFP® Principal Knowledge Topics

F.42. Fundamental Tax Law

F.43. Income Tax Fundamentals and Calculations

F.44. Characteristics and Income Taxation of Business Entities

F.45. Income Taxation of Trusts and Estates

F.46. Alternative Minimum Tax (AMT)

F.47. Tax Reduction/Management Techniques

F.48. Tax Consequences of Property Transactions

F.49. Passive Activity and At-Risk Rules

F.50. Tax Implications of Special Circumstances

F.51. Charitable/Philanthropic Contributions and Deductions

Chapter Equations

Equation 4.1:
$$\text{Exclusion Ratio} = \frac{\text{Total after-tax contribution}}{\text{Total expected distribution}}$$

Equation 4.2:
$$\text{Taxable Equivalent Yield (Federal Tax-exempt)} = \frac{\text{Tax-exempt bond yield}}{(1 - \text{FMTB})}$$

Equation 4.3:
$$\text{Taxable Equivalent Yield (State Tax-exempt)} = \frac{\text{Tax-exempt bond yield}}{(1 - \text{SMTB})}$$

Equation 4.4:
$$\text{Taxable Equivalent Yield (Fully Tax-exempt)} = \frac{\text{Tax-exempt bond yield}}{[1 - (\text{FMTB} + (\text{SMTB} \times (1 - \text{FMTB})))]}$$

Equation 4.5:
After-tax yield = Taxable rate $\times (1 - (\text{FMTB} + (\text{SMTB} \times (1 - \text{FMTB}))))$

TAX PLANNING: DETERMINING THE NEED

Several desirable outcomes are associated with income tax planning as part of comprehensive plan development. First, from a client's perspective, the assessment provides a roadmap for implementing strategies that can both reduce future tax liability and increase discretionary cash flow. Second, from a financial planner's point of view, a tax plan can serve as a valuable client-education tool. In addition to providing clients with background terms, definitions, and calculations, a tax plan can be used as a mechanism to facilitate client-planner discussions regarding retirement funding, insurance needs, college planning, and other client goals and expenses that can benefit from the use of tax-advantaged strategies.

Tax policy in the United States tends to be either progressive or regressive. With **progressive taxes**, the percentage of tax increases as taxable income increases. The tax rate burden in a progressive system falls disproportionately on higher-income earners. The federal income tax and the Alternative Minimum Tax (AMT) are progressive. With **regressive taxes**, the tax rate decreases proportionately as a person's taxable income decreases. The burden of tax, in a regressive system, falls on low-income earners. Self-employment and **sales taxes** are examples of regressive taxes. A 5 percent tax rate on food, for example, is proportionately more burdensome on someone earning $20,000 per year than on a person earning $100,000 annually, assuming that both eat the same amount and quality of food.

It makes sense for financial planners who do not consider themselves tax experts to establish working relationships with tax professionals such as **certified public accountants (CPAs), tax attorneys,** or **enrolled agents (EAs)**. The IRS recognizes these professionals as qualified to represent clients in tax disputes. A financial planner should also take the time to understand a client's knowledge of taxes and determine whether any previously undisclosed tax issues are present in the client situation. Referring a client to a CPA, attorney, or EA for complex tax help is often prudent, but such referrals do not remove the basic fact finding obligations associated with comprehensive financial planning. For instance, a client might not initially disclose an outstanding tax debt with the IRS or state taxing agency. Calculating tax liabilities and making recommendations without such information could cause serious tax and legal problems for the client. In this situation, information about the client issue would be essential to making a referral decision.

However, simply relying on the help of a CPA, attorney, or EA is not enough. It is essential that a financial planner have a solid understanding of current tax laws and rules. This is true because almost every aspect of financial planning is either influenced by or directly affects a client's tax situation. Consider a recommendation to increase contributions to a 401(k) retirement plan. This recommendation may appear to have only retirement planning implications, but it also influences a client's cash flow and tax situation. Contributions to a qualified retirement plan help reduce the amount of income reportable for income tax purposes. This, in turn, helps reduce a client's annual withholding requirement, which can increase **discretionary cash flow** during the year. Conversely, by not reducing the withholding requirement, the client could avoid or reduce additional tax payments for investment earnings. The combined tax ramifications of this simple recommendation can be significant.

Self-Test 1

A couple, who file their taxes as married filing jointly, originally purchased their home for $200,000 but because of escalating real estate prices over the 20 years they have lived there, it should sell for $1 million. How much should the Smiths project for capital gains taxes?

a. $0, they satisfy the holding period requirement

b. 15% on $800,000 or $120,000

c. 15% on $500,000 or $75,000

d. 15% on $300,000 or $45,000

A review of a client's current tax situation starts by evaluating client situational factors related to the tax planning process. This is just another way of saying that a planner ought to know the client's tax planning goals as well as temperament and personality, attitudes, beliefs and values, financial knowledge and experience, and socioeconomic descriptors that could influence tax planning decisions. Understanding the emotional, personal, and nonfinancial aspects of a client's situation is as important as determining the client's tax liability.

Every client is unique, and qualitative values and attitudes in addition to quantitative client data make each planning situation distinctive. Some clients have a strongly held desire to shelter as much income from taxes as possible, whereas this may be less of a concern for others. Certain clients, for example, may wish to push the limits of the tax law, and others will be unwilling to risk a potential tax audit. This is one reason it is important to assess a client's risk tolerance as part of the data-gathering phase of the planning process. The following list illustrates some of the viewpoints a client might have regarding taxes:

- A strong desire to minimize taxes paid to the government

- A willingness to pay "my fair share" of the tax burden

- A wish to make charitable contributions for tax advantages and the benefit of society

- A desire to avoid being audited by the IRS

The data-gathering phase of the financial planning process provides a very important context for tax planning. Recent or upcoming changes in a client's household situation can affect filing status, the number of personal exemptions claimed, or the availability of adjustments, itemized deductions, or credits. Common examples of important client situational issues include changes in marital status, reaching significant ages for taxpayers or dependents, an inheritance, a change in employment, a salary increase or decrease, the addition of a dependent (such as the birth of a child or taking on expenses for a relative), the purchase of a second home, or the sale of a primary residence or second home. These examples of life cycle events and life transitions represent both important milestones in a client's life and potential tax planning issues.

The purchase, sale, or refinancing of a personal residence provides an example of how client actions can trigger tax issues that call for advance planning. A married couple can exclude up to $500,000 ($250,000 for a single taxpayer) in gains on the *sale of a primary residence*. But to receive this exclusion, the client must have owned and used the home as a personal residence for two of the past five years—typically referred to as the **holding period requirement**. Any gains exceeding the excluded amount are generally taxed at the capital gains tax rate, currently a flat 15 percent. The itemized deduction for home mortgage interest is often cited as a tax benefit, but the deduction applies only to interest paid on the **primary mortgage initial acquisition debt**. Furthermore, the deduction applies only to the interest paid on the first $1 million spent to acquire, build, or improve a residence. Home equity lines of credit or loans are often recommended as sources of funding emergency needs, college costs, or meeting other short-term cash flow needs.

Typically, lower interest costs and tax-deductible interest are recognized benefits of **home equity debt**, despite concerns about leveraging the home for other goals. Home equity debt interest is deductible only if the loan is the lesser of $100,000 or the fair market value of the home, less the first mortgage debt. For AMT purposes, any refinanced indebtedness on which interest is deductible is limited to the amount of indebtedness prior to refinancing. Many clients understand some mortgage-related tax issues, but few remember all of the details. A proactive financial planner anticipates a client's need for this type of information.

While maintaining a perspective on the client's tax planning situation, the financial planner must also consider these changes in light of any upcoming changes in the tax code. Tax planning involves taking actions that maximize each client's situation in anticipation of household and/or tax code changes. It is imperative that a client's wishes and concerns as well as potential changes in the tax situation be taken into account when developing planning strategies and recommendations. In some situations, the timing of an action can have a significant impact on taxes due.

Determine Income Tax Liability

The estimation of a client's tax liability is based on identifying all sources of income. Two approaches can be used to determine a client's tax liability; both approaches occur as part of the current situation analysis. The first approach uses actual IRS tax forms, such as **IRS Form 1040** and IRS Schedules A, B, C, and D. The second approach, which may be slightly less accurate but more efficient, involves using some form of tax calculator or estimator. Either approach should lead to the same conclusion: the client will receive a refund, owe nothing, or owe additional tax.

Following is a basic ten-step income tax calculation that serves as a guide to calculating a client's tax liability, the overall tax planning process, and as an important client education tool.

Step 1- Record potential gross income.

Step 2- Exclude nontaxable income and pretax items.

Step 3- Calculate gross income.

Step 4- Subtract expenses for adjusted gross income (AGI) "above-the-line" deductions.

Step 5- Reduce taxable income by either the standard deduction or by the itemized deduction amount "below-the-line" deductions.

Step 6- Reduce taxable income by personal exemption amounts.

Step 7- Calculate tax liability.

Step 8- Reduce tax liability through the use of credits.

Step 9- Add in other tax liabilities.

Step 10- Determine the additional tax liability or the amount of the tax refund.

Following this simple ten-step approach to tax calculations ensures that all income is appropriately accounted for, expenses are recorded, and all tax-reduction tools and techniques are utilized. Of the ten steps, Steps 2, 4, 5, and 8 are areas where a financial planner can add the most value. At Step 2, a financial planner can help the client plan increase pretax expenses; at Steps 4 and 5, a planner can help the client maximize "above-the-line" and "below-the-line" deductions, or adjustments to income that occur before the determination of adjusted gross income or itemized deductions that occur after the determination of adjusted gross income. Although the number of the "line" may change from year to year, the term refers to the line that identifies adjusted gross income. At Step 8, the planner can help clients maximize available tax credits. Because of their importance, each of these steps is discussed in greater detail below.

At Step 2, a financial planner can help clients maximize income from sources that are not subject to taxation. **Municipal bonds** and tax-free money market accounts can be used to reduce a client's reported income, because the interest earned from these accounts, although reflected on IRS Form 1040, is generally not included in the total income calculation.

At Step 4, several different tax planning strategies are available to help clients manage tax liabilities. It is important to remember, however, that many of the benefits available in the tax code are subject to income limits. The limit most often imposed is based on **adjusted gross income (AGI)** or **modified adjusted gross income (MAGI)**. The actual definition or calculation of MAGI can vary with the tax issues in question. There are two methods for reducing AGI. One is to reduce the amount of income reported, as explained above, and the other is to increase negative adjustments to income.

Self-Test 2

Above-the-line deductions:

a. are also known as adjustments to gross income.

b. may be reduced based on AGI or MAGI.

c. include student loan interest, alimony paid, and some IRA contributions.

d. all of the statements are true about above-the-line deductions.

A financial planner can help clients maximize their **above-the-line deductions**, which are also referred to as **adjustments to gross income**. Examples of expenses that can be used to reduce gross income include *educator expenses, student loan interest, tuition fees, moving expenses, IRA early withdrawal penalties,* and *alimony paid*. Other examples include making deductible contributions to a traditional IRA (phase-out thresholds based on income for qualified plan participation could apply) or contributing to a *healthcare savings account* (HSA). For those who are self-employed, paying one-half of *self-employment taxes,* contributing to a self-employed retirement plan (e.g., a *Keogh* or *SIMPLE plan*), or purchasing health insurance are additional options that can be used to reduce gross income.

Adjustments to AGI often provide a marginal benefit for clients. For instance, if a client is in the 25 percent marginal tax bracket, a $1,000 deduction for AGI will generally result in approximately $250 in tax savings. All clients, subject to certain income phase-out restrictions, are eligible to deduct the preceding expenses.

Clients who are close to triggering the AMT could consider deferring expenses that result in a lower AGI.

At Step 5, a financial planner can help clients maximize below-the-line deductions. If above-the-line adjustments are either unavailable or exhausted, attention should turn to **below-the-line taxable-income reduction** by scrutinizing **itemized deductions**. Three areas where many clients can increase deductions and thereby reduce taxable income (assuming the client is not subject to the AMT) include converting non-tax-advantaged interest paid to *deductible mortgage interest*, increasing or accelerating taxes paid in a year, and increasing *gifts to charitable organizations*. A combination of any or all of these solutions can work to decrease taxable income. Charitable contributions are one expense that a client can influence directly compared to mortgage interest, *real estate taxes*, *property taxes*, or *state and local income taxes*. As a reminder, state and local income taxes and real property taxes are added back into taxable income to determine the AMT.

At Step 8, the financial planner can help the client maximize available **tax credits**—a dollar for dollar reduction in tax liability. A few of the most commonly used tax credits include the *child and dependent care credit*, the *Lifetime Learning education credit*, and the *saver's tax credit*. Maximizing available tax credits does not reduce a client's taxable income, but it does reduce tax liability. However, the availability of credits may depend on a client's AGI or MAGI meeting various qualification thresholds and on potential changes in the tax code.

Figure 4.1 highlights some of the most common solutions available to reduce AGI either by maximizing above-the-line deductions or to reduce taxable income by maximizing below-the-line deductions and tax credits. The process of choosing a strategy or finding an area to concentrate on for a client starts by determining whether the client is losing some benefits available in the tax code because AGI is too high.[1] For example, if AGI is above certain thresholds, the client may lose the benefits of deducting a traditional IRA contribution, making a Roth IRA contribution, deducting qualified education expenses, or claiming several tax credits.

Whether a financial planner is directly involved in the preparation of a client's income tax forms or indirectly involved in the analysis of the client's tax situation as part of a comprehensive planning engagement, the planner may be responsible for implementing the changes necessary to increase the client's tax efficiency. The benefits for clients who use some or all of these tax liability reduction methods can be mitigated or enhanced by other planning considerations. Investment and planning strategies that minimize tax liability should always be considered as part of the process. However, tax planning strategies should not be considered in isolation; they should be considered in conjunction with each client's other overriding planning needs. For example, increasing a client's municipal bond allocation could be a viable strategy to reduce taxable income. However, if the tax-free rate on the bonds does not exceed the after-tax return on another form of fixed-income investment, the client could be better off paying the taxes. To make matters even more confusing, high levels of tax-exempt interest could trigger the AMT, thus effectively reducing the availability of several deductions, including home equity interest.

Figure 4.1 Tax Planning Product and Solution Decision Tree

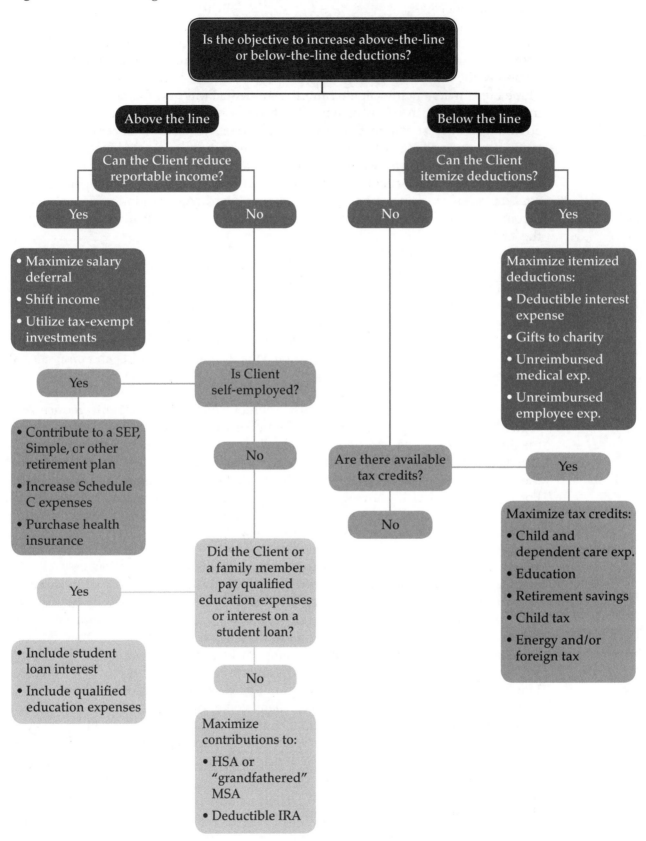

* Because of income-based phase-out or other reasons, not all of these options will be available to all clients.

Tax Planning Skills

Tax planning integrates with almost every other core content planning area. A planner can start by obtaining a client's tax returns from at least the previous two years. Analysis of previous returns provides trends in deductions, exemptions, and credits taken. Past tax returns can also indicate discrepancies in cash flow and net worth numbers. Previous returns also provide planners with needed tax loss carry-forward information. Once a thorough review of prior years' returns has been completed, a client's current-year tax liability can be estimated. Projections for up to five years of returns may also be appropriate, depending on the nature of the client's planning and tax situation. Projections are an excellent way to inform a client of the interrelationships and tax implications of other core content planning recommendations.

> **Self-Test 3**
>
> True or False: Tax credits, such as the Lifetime Learning education credit or the residential energy credit, reduce the tax liability dollar for dollar, while above-the-line and below-the line adjustments result in a tax savings of approximately the amount of the deduction multiplied by the marginal tax rate.

However, unless a financial planner is also a CPA or an EA, it is prudent to include a tax planning disclaimer when presenting any tax calculations, estimates, or recommendations. A statement such as, "Before implementing the advice provided, please confirm these suggestions with your tax professional" provides some liability protection for advisors and helps promote collaboration with the client's other financial professionals. Another part of the tax planning process is for the advisor to educate clients regarding the advisor's needs to review tax forms or collaborate with the client's tax professional to discuss a broad range of tax planning issues.

Planning Skill 1: Identify Sources of Income

When reviewing a client's cash flow and financial situation, it often becomes apparent that many clients have income from any number of sources, which can have a ripple effect on other core content planning areas. From solely a tax planning perspective, one of the major objectives of tax planning is to minimize a client's **average tax rate**—the average amount of each dollar earned that is paid in taxes. For tax planning purposes, income can be categorized in four ways:

1. income subject to the client's **marginal tax rate** (i.e., the tax rate at which the last dollar earned is taxed);

2. income subject to a potentially lower-than-marginal tax rate;

3. income subject to a potentially higher-than-marginal tax rate; and

4. income not subject to tax.

The fourth category is often referred to as "**tax-exempt income**." Examples include interest on municipal bonds, gifts, and inheritance, and several forms of government provided payments, such as governmental transfers and veterans' benefits.

To achieve the goal of reducing a client's total tax liability, a financial planner often starts with a focus on the client's **taxable income**, loosely defined as income that is usually subject to income tax. Examples of taxable income include *salaries, pensions, royalties, rent, dividends, interest, capital gains, gambling winnings, hobby income, commissions, tips, "Section 79" income,* and *business income.* Within this list, salary, pensions, non-qualified dividends, interest income, gambling winnings (net of gambling losses), hobby income, commissions, tips, and Section 79 income are subject to a client's marginal tax rate. *Royalty payments* and other business income are subject to a rate potentially higher than a client's marginal tax bracket because the client will most likely owe self-employment tax on the earnings. Under the current tax code, investment income, such as long-term capital gains and qualified dividends, are taxed at a rate that is likely to be lower than the client's marginal tax bracket. The following discussion reviews the most common source of income.

Earned income. As typically reported on a client's IRS **W-2 Form**, income earned from salaries, wages, tips, and commissions is relatively easy to document. The best and easiest way to reduce wage based income is to increase **elective deferrals** into retirement plans, health plans, or other tax favored employer provided benefits. In addition to the tax-deferral available through participation in an employer sponsored qualified retirement plan, an employee might also be able to purchase life, medical, dental, disability, and long-term care insurance. Contributions to a **Section 125 cafeteria plan**, if available, can also serve to reduce reported income. Some benefit plans also allow for payment of *unreimbursed medical expenses, child care expenses,* or even select *transportation costs.* However it is important to carefully monitor and account for how employer provided fringe benefits affect a client's tax situation. Internal Revenue Code (IRC) guidelines state that any fringe benefit provided to an employee by an employer is taxable unless specifically excluded in the IRC. Figure 4.2 summarizes the tax status of many popular **fringe benefits**. More information about various employer provided benefits is provided in applicable chapters throughout this book.

Figure 4.2 Special Rules for Determining the Tax Status of Select Fringe Benefits[2]

Type of Fringe Benefit	Treatment under Employment Taxes		
	Income Tax Withholding	*Social Security and Medicare*	*Federal Unemployment (FUTA)*
Accident and health benefits (including disability)	Exempt[1,2,] except for long-term care benefits provided through a flexible spending or similar arrangement	Exempt, except for certain payments to S-corporation employees who are 2% shareholders	Exempt
Achievement awards	Exempt[1] up to $1,600 for qualified plan awards ($400 for nonqualified awards)		
Adoption assistance	Exempt[1,3]	Taxable	Taxable
Athletic facilities	Exempt if substantially all use during the calendar year is by employees, their spouses, and their dependent children and the facility is operated by the employer on premises owned or leased by the employer		
De minimis (without consequence) benefits	Exempt	Exempt	Exempt
Dependent care assistance	Exempt[3] up to a maximum exemption of $5,000 of dependent care assistance benefits each year ($2,500 for married employees filing separate returns)		
Educational assistance	Exempt up to $5,250 of benefits each year		
Employee discounts	Exempt[3] up to certain limits		
Group-term life insurance coverage	Exempt	Exempt[1,4] up to cost of $50,000 of coverage. (Special rules apply to former employees)	Exempt
Health savings accounts (HSAs)	Exempt for qualified individuals up to HSA contribution limits		
Lodging on your business premises	Exempt[1] if furnished for your convenience as a condition of employment		
Meals	Exempt if furnished on your business premises for your convenience.		
	Exempt if *de minimis*.		
Moving expense reimbursements	Exempt[1] if expenses would be deductible if the employee had paid them		
No-additional-cost services	Exempt[3]	Exempt[3]	Exempt[3]
Retirement planning services	Exempt[5]	Exempt[5]	Exempt[5]
Transportation (commuting) benefits	Exempt[1] up to certain limits if for rides in a commuter highway vehicle and/or transit passes ($255), qualified parking ($255), or qualified bicycle commuting reimbursement6 ($20).		
	Exempt if *de minimis*.		

Figure 4.2 Special Rules for Determining the Tax Status of Select Fringe Benefits[2] (*cont'd*)

Type of Fringe Benefit	Treatment under Employment Taxes		
	Income Tax Withholding	Social Security and Medicare	Federal Unemployment (FUTA)
Tuition reduction	Exempt[3] if for undergraduate education (or graduate education if the employee performs teaching or research activities)		
Volunteer firefighter and emergency responder benefits	Exempt	Exempt	Exempt
Working condition benefits	Exempt	Exempt	Exempt

[1] Exemption does not apply to S corporation employees who are 2% shareholders.

[2] Exemption does not apply to certain highly compensated employees under a self-insured plan that favors those employees.

[3] Exemption does not apply to certain highly compensated employees under a program that favors those employees.

[4] Exemption does not apply to certain key employees under a plan that favors those employees.

[5] Exemption does not apply to services for tax preparation, accounting, legal, or brokerage services.

[6] If the employee receives a qualified bicycle commuting reimbursement in a qualified bicycle commuting month, the employee cannot receive commuter highway vehicle, transit pass, or qualified parking benefits in that same month.

If the benefits received from an employer exceed the limits described in the table, or the benefits are deemed to be nonexempt, the client's taxable income will increase. Without adjustment, a client could find that tax withholding is insufficient to cover the tax liability. It is important to account for fringe benefits whenever conducting a tax analysis. Finally, to reduce the amount of income reported, a client who is self-employed can attempt to transition personal expenses to deductible business expenses as reported on IRS Schedule C. This has the effect of reducing the amount of income reported, thereby reducing total income.

Business income. Two questions arise when identifying a client's business income. First, was the client engaged in a business or simply a hobby? Second, if it is in fact a business, then was client's engagement active or passive? The first question helps determine the output of the activity—was there the intent to make a profit? The second question looks more at input—what is the level of involvement in the activity?

A financial planner might have a client who engages in activities where it is difficult to distinguish between a **hobby** and a business. Such situations should be monitored for tax planning opportunities. Modifying or racing cars, writing travel books, photography, and small-scale farming are examples of activities that some clients feel are more business than hobby. To address this issue, the IRS has developed several rules to help determine when an activity is a hobby and when it is a business. The IRS asks whether the activity is run like a business, how much time a person spends on the activity, and whether the activity is engaged in for profit. This last hurdle is crossed if the activity results in a **profit** (income exceeds expenses resulting in a taxable gain) in three of the last five years, including the most recent year.[3]

If income is generated as the result of a hobby then the income is reported on the IRS Form 1040, and expenses associated with that hobby are deductible on IRS **Schedule A**. However, if income is generated as the result of a solely owned business, then the income and business-related expenses are reported on IRS **Schedule C**.

IRS Publication 925 provides a definitional framework for passive and at-risk "active" activities. Both terms are used to describe a client's role in the decision and management process when making an investment. The key to determining whether an activity is a **passive activity** is whether there is **material participation** in the operation. In other words, does the client work on a regular, continuous, and substantial basis in operations, including most rental income (although there are a few exceptions)?

> ### Self-Test 4
>
> All of the following are true about business income, except:
>
> a. the taxpayer spends time on the endeavor and attempts to operate it as a business, not just a hobby.
>
> b. the endeavor generates a profit (i.e. income is greater than expenses) in the most recent year and 5 of the last 7 years.
>
> c. the income and business-related expenses are reported on IRS Schedule C.
>
> d. restrictions apply on carrying forward passive activity losses and at-risk losses as it applies to offsetting future passive and non-passive income.

If a taxpayer does not materially participate, losses are passive. A **passive activity loss** is limited by the amount of **passive income** reported by the taxpayer. If a loss exceeds the income generated, the amount can be carried forward only to offset future passive income.[4]

On the other hand, **at-risk loss** is limited to the invested amount. If a loss exceeds the tax basis of the invested capital or property, then the remaining loss can be carried forward into subsequent years and used against non-passive income.[5]

Unearned income or investment income. Because a financial planner has a limited number of options to help clients reduce earned income, managing unearned or investment income, such as dividends and capital gains, becomes particularly important. For example, following the stock market meltdown of 2008, many investors sold securities at significant losses. Some justified the sale of stocks and other investments by assuming that they would be able to take large tax deductions. Unfortunately, some investors found that, because they did not have any capital gains to offset by the capital losses, they were effectively limited to the $3,000 maximum that can be annually deducted from regular income taxes. Although excess losses can be indefinitely carried forward, it is important for planners to help clients match losses against gains in particular years rather than having clients make investment and other financial decisions based on the client's assumptions about the tax code.

Planning Skill 2: Correctly Calculate the Cost Basis of an Investment

The Emergency Economic Stabilization Act of 2008 made a significant change to the way investors report the cost basis of mutual fund holdings. The IRS defines **cost basis** as the total cost, including transaction charges, of all shares held in an account or investment (e.g., mutual fund, exchange traded fund, individual securities). This initial cost basis is then adjusted for dividends, stock splits, distributions, depreciation, and other tax allowances. A client's basis is the amount invested, which is used to determine the amount of gain or loss (realized and/or recognized) reported by a client when an asset is sold or exchanged. In this way, under most circumstances, the higher the basis the lower the tax liability upon the subsequent sale.

#Remember

The cost basis reporting method can be changed, but only prospectively, not after a sale has occurred.

Although cost basis is typically evaluated and determined by the dollar amount paid for an asset, basis can be transferred to others when a gift or exchange is made. When an asset is inherited, under current tax code, the cost basis is determined either on the decedent's date of death, or the earlier of the *alternative valuation date* (see Chapter 13 for more information) or the date of transfer. In most cases this change in basis results in a "step-up". However, for gifts given prior to the donor's death, the donee does not receive the same step up in basis. Rather they receive the original basis for gifts of appreciated assets, and a "split" basis for assets that have depreciated. This means that the depreciated asset has two basis valuations, the higher one used for subsequent sale gains, and the lower for subsequent sale losses.

For investment purpose, new cost basis reporting rules require investment companies to maintain cost basis information for all shares purchased on or after January 1, 2012. The IRS classifies mutual fund shares acquired before January 1, 2012, as **non-covered shares**, meaning that mutual fund companies are not required to track or report the cost basis. According to the IRS code, investors may elect one of three cost basis calculation methods:

1. specific lot identification;

2. first in, first out (FIFO); and

3. average cost (which is only available if the shares are identical to each other).[6]

However, on many investment company websites it is common to find a list of seven different selections. But in actuality four of the seven are just automatic instructions given by the owner of the account to the investment company based on the ability to sell specific lots. These four other common "elections" are:

1. last in, last out (LIFO);

2. low cost;

3. high cost; and

4. loss/gain utilization

The **average cost method** is the default choice made by mutual fund companies if an investor does not make another election. This method of reporting, as illustrated in Figure 4.3, requires an investor to track the average cost of shares acquired over a period of time.

Figure 4.3 Average Cost Method Example

Date of Purchase	Purchase Amount	Number of Shares Purchased	Calculation	Average Price Per Share
1/10/15	$2,000	50	$2,000/50	$40.00
5/15/15	$100	2	$100/2	$50.00
12/12/15	$1,500	45	$1,500/45	$33.33
Total:	$3,600	97	$3,600/97	$37.11

The FIFO (and LIFO) methods of reporting assume that shares are depleted based on the date of acquisition; with either the first (or last) shares sold first, the 1/10/15 (or 12/12/15) shares.

The **specific lot identification method** requires an investor to indicate specifically which shares were sold. This approach allows for a secondary cost basis when shares cannot be identified. For many investors, this cost basis reporting method is the most time-intensive approach to share identification. Again, the following methods are just predetermined versions of specific lot identification.

The low-cost approach exhausts the lowest price shares first. (In the table, the shares purchased on 12/12/15 at $33.33 would be reported as first sold.) The high-cost approach assumes the highest price shares, the ones purchased on 5/15/15, are sold first – this method of reporting initially subjects the investor to smaller taxable gains (or maximum losses) while postponing larger taxable gains (or smaller losses) into the future.

The final choice is the loss/gain utilization approach (LGUT) and is somewhat more complex. Basically the instructions tell the mutual fund company to sell the shares in the following order:

1. Shares with a short-term loss (in descending order of largest loss to smallest)

2. Shares with a long-term loss (again, in descending order)

3. Shares held less than one year (i.e., short-term) with no loss or gain

4. Shares held more than one year (i.e., long-term) with no loss or gain

5. Shares with a long-term gain (in ascending order of smallest gain to largest) ; and

6. Shares with a short-term gain (again, in ascending order)

WARNING: If the shares have an unknown cost basis–such as (potentially) those purchased prior to January 1, 2012–then those shares will be sold on a FIFO ordering with smallest share lots sold first.

This approach to cost basis accounting typically assumes that shares with losses are depleted before shares with gains. But it is imperative to keep in mind that the investment company, custodian, or brokerage firm will only have access to the cost basis information for shares held with them. Therefore, while they would sell the assets held with them in a seemingly tax-efficient manner, it might not be the best for the client because of asset shares held elsewhere. This means that a financial planner who suggests the LGUT method needs to have the entire asset and cost basis information for the client.

For more information concerning cost basis reporting, see IRS Publication 550.

Planning Skill 3: Incorporate Alternative Minimum Tax Estimates in Tax Plans

Self-Test 5

If an investor does not elect a cost basis calculation method from the seven reporting methods, _____ is the default choice.

a. Specific lot identification

b. Average cost

c. First in, first out (FIFO)

d. Last in, last out (LIFO)

Congress enacted the **Alternative Minimum Tax (AMT)** to prevent wealthy taxpayers from taking advantage of preferential deductions and paying little or no tax, whereas the regular tax law gives preferential treatment to some kinds of income and allows special deductions and credits for particular kinds of expenses. Clients who have high incomes and benefit from preferential provisions for regular tax purposes may have to pay the AMT. Although this law was originally written with only the wealthy in mind, in recent years more individuals have found themselves liable for these alternative taxes which, in all cases, are higher than regular taxes.

To determine whether a taxpayer is subject to the AMT, a taxpayer's taxable income is altered for AMT adjustments and preferences to calculate the **alternative minimum taxable income (AMTI)**. Common adjustments and **tax preference items** that can trigger the AMT include those related to *personal exemptions*, the *standard deduction, miscellaneous itemized deductions, state and local tax, accelerated depreciation of certain property, incentive stock options, depletion allowances, intangible drilling costs*, and certain forms of *tax-exempt interest*. Taxpayers with high enough incomes and substantial preference items in any given year might trigger the AMT. The AMT has two tax rates: 26 percent on the taxable excess of tentative minimum taxable income over an exemption amount, and 28 percent on the taxable excess above that amount. The taxpayer's regular tax liability is subtracted from the tentative minimum tax to determine the AMT.

A few strategies can be used to mitigate the impact of the AMT if it appears that a client might be subject to the tax. First, preference deductions should be reviewed and reduced, if possible. For example, it may be appropriate to exercise incentive stock options over time rather than all at once. Another strategy includes exercising incentive stock options in a year when other AMT preference items are minimal. Clients with significant depreciation expenses could consider shifting from accelerated to straight-line depreciation. Another strategy involves accelerating current year income to help offset preference deductions. An increased bonus or salary advance could be used to increase income.

Planning Skill 4: Understand the Interplay between Tax and Retirement Planning

A client's plan to take a distribution from a **qualified retirement plan** could result in a 10 percent early withdrawal penalty tax, in addition to regular income tax, on the taxable portion of the distribution received before age 59½. Under most circumstances, clients under the age of 59½ pay a 10 percent penalty on distributions (25 percent from a SIMPLE plan during the first two years of plan participation) in addition to income taxes due.[7] However, the 10 percent penalty may be waived under certain exceptions. There are exemptions for distributions caused by death or disability, to pay for higher education expenses, and sometimes distributions for a first-time home purchase. A similar 10 percent penalty also applies to distributions from annuities, IRAs, and other tax-deferred investments.

> **#Remember**
>
> *NEVER* consider a client's current tax situation or a recommendation in isolation. A financial planning strategy that might, at first glance, appear to benefit a client's situation could have underlying tax consequences that must be fully considered for implications for other core content planning areas OR for implications over a longer time horizon.

Required minimum distributions (**RMDs**) are another area of tax law that affects decisions about retirement planning. Clients who have assets in traditional, SIMPLE, or SEP IRAs, and those with assets in a qualified defined contribution plan (excluding Roth plans), must begin taking RMDs by April 1 of the year following age 70½. IRS Publication 590 provides a set of Uniform Lifetime Tables that are used to determine minimum distributions. The IRS penalty for failure to take the prescribed RMD is 50 percent of the amount that should have been withdrawn.

Although the core RMD rule is straightforward, there are several interesting twists to the statute that are important to understand. Some of these include: (a) options for "stretch" IRAs that reduce the RMD and extend tax-deferred growth over a longer time period; (b) the alternative calculations of RMDs for inherited spousal and non-spousal IRAs and for surviving spouses who are more than ten years younger than the decedent; and (c) the option to utilize a tax-free RMD distribution to a charity.

Many clients accumulate **employer stock** in their employer sponsored retirement plans (e.g., 401k plan). Although other financial planning issues are related to the decision to include company stock in a retirement plan, distributions from such plans could be eligible for special tax treatment. First, it is important to remember that for taxation purposes the amount of a withdrawal from such a plan is considered in two parts: the cost basis and the accumulated value, or appreciation. The original cost basis of a withdrawal is taxed as ordinary income and therefore at the client's marginal tax rate. Any withdrawal above the cost basis amount is taxed at capital gains tax rates.

Second, it is important to consider that there are two options for withdrawing accumulated company stock—each resulting in different tax outcomes, the better of which may not be intuitively obvious. Clients who anticipate being in a higher marginal tax bracket in the future should consider taking company stock distributions directly rather than rolling assets into an IRA. The reason for this is that if the stock is rolled into a traditional IRA the entire withdrawal amount, basis and gain, is subject to taxation at ordinary rates upon final distribution from the IRA.

By taking an **in-kind, lump-sum distribution** from a qualified retirement plan and placing the assets in a **nonqualified account**, a client's stock assets become eligible for **net unrealized appreciation** (NUA) tax treatment. In this case, the distribution is immediately taxable at ordinary income rates, but only the cost basis of the distributed amount of stock is subject to income tax, not the appreciation portion of the account. In addition, a 10 percent tax penalty may also be applicable if the client is under age 59½. This is almost the reverse of other plans, where the basis is not taxable but the gains are; the choice of a qualified account is typically a better option than a nonqualified account. With the NUA tax treatment a client recognizes the income rather than the gain.

Because the stock was in a qualified retirement plan, the deferred income or employee benefit dollars used to purchase the stock originally were never taxed, so income tax is owed at the time of distribution. When the client subsequently sells the stock, taxes will be due at the long-term capital gains rate on any NUA and the applicable capital gains rate (i.e., short- or long-term) on any additional appreciation. With careful planning, it may be a better option to pay income tax on the basis and capital gains tax on the appreciation later than to pay income taxes on the entire value later when using a qualified IRA account.

These examples illustrate that it is not enough simply to know how to calculate tax liabilities; rather, it is important to integrate tax calculation estimates with client situational factors. These examples, some of which are discussed in greater detail in Chapter 12, also demonstrate how understanding a client's current situation and the tax code can directly influence tax planning. Furthermore, tax planning can significantly alter a client's goals and decisions across the life cycle.

Planning Skill 5: Understand the Filing Requirements for Trusts and Estates

For tax purposes, irrevocable trusts and the estate of a decedent is considered a separate tax entity. The trust may be liable for income taxes for any income that is accumulated within the trust—a complex trust. Form 1041 must be filed if a trust or estate has taxable income greater than $600, or if the estate has gross income in excess of $600, or any beneficiary of the trust or estate is a non-resident alien. Beneficiaries are taxed as if they received the income directly. For example, if an asset was sold in a trust for a long-term taxable gain, the distribution will be taxable to the beneficiary as a long-term gain.

Issues related to income in respect of a decedent (IRD) often come up in financial planning work. Beneficiaries of an estate are allowed to take an itemized deduction on Schedule A for the amount of estate taxes paid by the decedent's gross estate. For example, assume a client inherits an IRA worth $1 million. If the decedent paid $450,000 in estate taxes attributable to this asset, the client can deduct 45 percent of all distributions from the IRA.

Planning Skill 6: Develop a Basic Understanding of How to Challenge an IRS Decision

The IRS could impose penalties and enforce other deficiency actions when a client fails to pay the correct income, estate, or payroll tax. Although the IRS tends to be aggressive when enforcing deficiency notices, individual taxpayers can disagree and challenge the agency's findings. This is known as placing a ruling in IRS **dispute**. In most cases, the first step when disputing a deficiency involves filing an appeal with the administrative appeals office of the IRS. Once the appeal has been received, the appeals office will schedule a phone or in-person conference to discuss the case. Nearly all individual cases are settled at this level.

If not settled, the next step involves challenging the IRS decision by bypassing the appeals process and going directly to the courts. American citizens can take their claims to the United States Tax Court, the United States Court of Federal Claims, or the District Court where they reside. These courts are independent and not affiliated with the IRS; however, it is important to remember that a frivolous filing penalty of up to $25,000 can be imposed if a case is found to purposely cause a delay in collection. There are time limits and required paperwork for both courses of action, and as such, financial planners who are not attorneys, CPAs, or EAs should refer client deficiency cases to one of these professionals. However, planners should have a fundamental knowledge of the process of challenging an IRS decision. A number of IRS resources are available.[8]

Tax Planning Product & Procedural Strategies

The following strategies represent a cross section of tax planning strategies used by financial planners. It is important to note that these tools represent only a sampling of commonly used product and procedural strategies. When in doubt about which strategy to recommend, consult with a CPA, EA, or other tax professional, or collaborate with the client's tax professional.

Product Strategy 1: Convert Taxable Interest to Tax-Exempt Interest

This strategy helps reduce the amount of income reported on IRS Form 1040 by reducing the amount of interest income subject to tax. It is most appropriate for clients in the highest marginal tax bracket. This strategy can also be beneficial for clients in lower brackets whenever the return on a tax-exempt investment exceeds the after-tax return on taxable investments. Three potential drawbacks are associated with this strategy. First, municipal securities tend to trade less frequently and in smaller markets. Investors who use this strategy with individual securities could subject themselves to a higher degree of illiquidity and marketability than investors who purchase individual taxable securities. Second, the difference between a taxable and tax-free rate is not stable. In some instances, tax-free rates exceed after-tax rates of return. In other cases, a fully taxable security will provide a better return, even for high-marginal-tax-bracket clients. Third, certain tax-free interest can trigger the AMT. Clients with large amounts of tax-free interest should be aware that they may end up paying a higher tax rate if they trigger the AMT.

Product Strategy 2: Replace Consumer Debt with Tax-advantaged Debt

If a client has outstanding credit card bills or other short-term liabilities, one recommendation involves obtaining a **home equity loan** or **home equity line of credit** and using the proceeds to pay off short-term debt. This strategy should have two immediate results. First, it is likely that the client's monthly discretionary cash flow will increase. Home equity loans and lines of credit typically carry interest rates substantially below those paid for other open lines of credit. The reduction in interest paid should reduce monthly expenditures for debt payment.

Second, any interest paid on home equity loans and interest on expended lines of credit could be tax deductible if the client itemizes deductions. However, it is important to remember that there are several limitations to this strategy. First, home equity debt interest is deductible only if the loan is the lesser of (1) $100,000 or (2) the fair market value of the home, less first mortgage debt. Second, for AMT purposes, any refinanced indebtedness on which interest is deductible is limited to the amount of indebtedness prior to refinancing. Finally, initial acquisition debt interest is deductible for federal income taxes on only the first $1 million used to acquire, build, or improve a residence.

It is important to note that this strategy places a client's home equity at risk by converting short-term consumption debt into a long-term liability. This strategy should probably not be used if a client has a habitual spending problem or problems managing credit. Furthermore, this strategy may be limited or unavailable to clients subject to the AMT because interest deductions for refinanced property can be denied under certain circumstances.

Product Strategy 3: Consider Investing in a Roth rather than a Traditional IRA

A **traditional IRA**, with deductible contributions and tax deferral, provides a good way to reduce taxable income while saving for retirement. Another strategy may be to make nondeductible contributions to a **Roth IRA**. Qualified distributions from a Roth IRA can be received tax free. This tax-free distribution of income from a Roth IRA in the future can, under certain circumstances, provide greater after-tax benefits than the immediate tax deduction and tax deferral of a traditional IRA. This strategy subjects a client to two risks. First, Congress may someday repeal the tax-free status of Roth IRAs. Second, if marginal tax rates are lower when a client retires, the traditional IRA with its tax deduction could be preferable. Also, income restrictions apply that prohibit Roth IRA contributions for some clients. See Chapter 12 for more information on tax planning issues for Traditional and Roth IRA accounts.

Product Strategy 4: Compare 529 Plans, UGMAs, and UTMAs to Save Taxes and Plan for College

"**Section 529**" **plans** have gained popularity among financial planners and clients for two reasons. First, contributions are often given special state tax incentives. Second, withdrawals from such plans, if used in accordance with the rules, are tax free. Furthermore, in 2016, the annual gift exclusion of $14,000 applies to contributions per child; however, a special five-year provision can be elected that allows up to $67,000 to be contributed in one year to a Section 529 plan per beneficiary without triggering a tax liability. For more information on Section 529 plans see Chapter 11.

UGMA (Uniform Gifts to Minors Act) or **UTMA** (Uniform Transfer to Minors Act) accounts can also be used to save for college. Effective tax planning is needed at the outset and throughout the planning process to make this recommendation work. The only way to entirely avoid long-term capital gain taxes on custodial accounts is to make sure that asset sales do not push the child beneficiary into a marginal income tax rate higher than 15 percent. Also, to obtain the low capital gains rate, asset sales in an account must generally occur after the child turns age nineteen (age twenty-four if a full-time student). Asset sales prior to age nineteen (age twenty-four if a full-time student) could result in distributions being taxed at the parents' marginal tax rate.

Maybe the most important disadvantage financial planners and clients must understand is that funding educational expenses with custodial accounts does not guarantee that assets will be used for this purpose. With *custodial accounts*, parents lose control of the assets. Legally, assets are the property of the child, and at the age of majority, age eighteen or twenty-one in most states, the child controls the use of those assets. See Chapter 11 for more information on how to effectively use UGMA/UTMA assets for education expenses.

Procedural Strategy 1: Match Withholdings to a Client's Tax Liability

In the majority of cases, a client will be in the position of either over- or under-withholding taxes. In situations where a client is over-withholding taxes, it is a financial planner's responsibility to show how matching liabilities to withholding can enhance a client's financial situation. If the client can reduce withholding, the client can invest the increased cash flow immediately instead of waiting for a tax refund early the next year. For most clients, the amount earned on the accelerated cash flow is minimal. In cases where a client owes more than was withheld, it is important to show both how the tax liability can be paid and how tax liabilities and withholding can be matched in future years. Failure to withhold enough or to make estimated payments, if required, can result in the taxpayer having to pay interest and penalties. Keep in mind that matching tax withholding to tax liabilities does not work well for clients who need a measure of forced savings. By reducing monthly withholding, discretionary cash flow will increase. Clients who tend to spend rather than save may find that this strategy reduces their net worth while actually decreasing their annual level of discretionary cash flow.

Procedural Strategy 2: Maximize Deductions for Adjusted Gross Income

This strategy provides clients who are not subject to a phase-out for deductions or personal exemptions based on the amount of the client's income one of the best ways to decrease taxable income. Examples of deductions for AGI include educator expenses, contributions to traditional IRAs, student loan interest, tuition fees, moving expenses, one-half of self-employment taxes, self-employed qualified plan contributions, IRA early withdrawal penalties, and alimony paid. It may be possible to prepay some of these expenses in high-income years, thus reducing income for tax purposes. The primary disadvantage associated with this strategy is that many of the deductions for AGI are applicable to only certain taxpayers (e.g., some deductions apply only to the self-employed). Also, many deductions from AGI can be subject to a phase-out based on income. In that case, a deduction for AGI, which reduces AGI, can have the effect of reducing a deduction from AGI. Similarly, personal exemptions also may be subject to phase-out based on AGI.

Procedural Strategy 3: Increase Tax Credit Items

A tax credit decreases tax liability dollar for dollar. Some of the most common tax credits are the:

- foreign tax credit;

- credit for child and dependent care expenses;

- credit for the elderly or the disabled;

- education credits;

- retirement savings contributions credit;

- child tax credit; and

- adoption credit.

Paying for the educational expenses of the taxpayer or other dependents is a way to take advantage of education tax credits. For example, the use of the American Opportunity Tax Credit can reduce a client's tax liability by up to $2,500 in any given year, assuming the client meets AGI income limits. One disadvantage of this strategy is that the approach may not work for higher-income clients. Some of the most common tax credits are subject to income phase-out restrictions, making them out of reach for high-income clients. Another potential disadvantage is that some of the credits are intended to help younger taxpayers and families and may not be available or of use to others.

Procedural Strategy 4: Maximize Pretax Retirement Plan and Benefit Contributions

One of the best ways to minimize taxes is to legally reduce the amount of income reported for tax purposes. Maximizing pretax retirement plan and benefit contributions is one method to reduce reportable taxable income. Contributing more to a qualified retirement plan, such as a 401(k) or 403(b) plan, is one strategy that reduces current taxes while increasing savings for retirement.

> **Self-Test 7**
>
> True or False: The wide range of credits available (i.e., child and dependent care; elderly and disabled; education; retirement savings; adoption) offer a tax reduction for almost every taxpayer.

Other contribution alternatives include taking full advantage of employer provided health benefits, including medical, dental, eye, and disability insurance. Deductions for employer sponsored insurance typically reduce taxable income because the employee premium payments are not subject to income or FICA taxes. This tax-reduction strategy, in effect, reduces the overall cost of policy premiums, making group benefits more affordable in many cases.

Section 125 plans, also known as cafeteria plans or flexible benefit plans, allow employers to offer employees a choice between cash and a variety of nontaxable benefits. The benefits are typically paid for with pretax dollars from employee salary reductions or employer "credits." Pretax salary reduction plans are also available to fund a high deductible health plan and health savings account, as well flexible spending accounts for health care and dependent care expenses. Although restrictions apply, all of these benefit options offer the potential for significant tax savings. For more information on Section 125 plans, see Chapter 6.

Like many of the procedural strategies presented in this chapter, the tactic of reducing taxable income is not available to all clients. A client who currently maximizes qualified retirement plan contributions has fully realized the benefit. Furthermore, the types of group benefits provided by an employer may be limited. Additionally, when clients purchase group term life insurance it is likely they will incur a **Section 79 imputed income** tax liability (see Chapter 3 for more information on how to calculate Section 79 income).

Procedural Strategy 5: Maximize Qualified Dividends while Reducing Interest Received

Qualified dividends, generally, are (1) not taxed for taxpayers in the 10 and 15 percent tax rate brackets, (2) taxed at 15 percent for taxpayers with income in the 25, 28, 33, and 38 percent marginal tax brackets, and (3) taxed at 20 percent for taxpayers with income levels that place them in the 39.6 percent marginal tax bracket. This means that income received in the form of qualified dividends will typically be taxed at a lower rate than ordinary interest income. Although dividends are currently taxed at a low rate compared to regular interest, implementing this strategy for any reason other than to increase the rate of return on long-term savings or to supplement a fixed-income portfolio can be risky. For example, using dividend paying stocks as the basis of an emergency fund could create a liquidity risk for a client. Further, tax laws are constantly in flux. It is possible that the federal tax-advantaged nature of dividends will be repealed in the future. State income taxes may also apply.

Procedural Strategy 6: Show Preference for Long-term Capital Gains

Investment property sold for a **long-term capital gain** (which requires that the asset was held for one year or longer) is taxed the same rates as qualified dividends (as described above). State income taxes may also apply. Investment property that is held for less than one year generates **short-term capital gain**, which is taxed at the same rate as ordinary income. Because the tax rates for long-term capital gain are lower than the ordinary income rates for all taxpayers, holding capital assets for more than one year can reduce a client's tax liability. However, employing this strategy imposes an opportunity cost on clients by creating an incentive to hold an asset longer than might otherwise be prudent. For instance, a gain can quickly turn to a loss over a relatively short period of time. It is sometimes better to capture a short-term gain than to risk a loss to ensure a lower capital gain rate. As with all tax law, it is possible that the tax advantage associated with long-term capital gains will be repealed in the future.

Procedural Strategy 7: Donate Appreciated Investments to Charity

This can be one of the best strategies to reduce current taxable income and eliminate assets from a client's gross estate. If an appreciated asset, such as a stock or mutual fund, is sold first and the proceeds donated to charity, the client will have to pay a capital gains tax on the sale. Even though the long-term capital gains tax rate is relatively low, selling first reduces the amount of the total donation to the charity by up to 20 percent, in addition to any applicable state tax. Instead, clients should generally donate property and securities rather than selling them. The charity can then sell the property on a tax-free basis. In this way, the total amount of capital gains can be excluded from income. This strategy also maximizes the total amount of the charitable donation. This strategy is beneficial only if the property donated provides a long-term gain. Short-term gain property donated to a **qualified charity** is deductible only up to the client's basis in the property. In such cases, the client loses the capital appreciation amount as a potential donation.

Procedural Strategy 8: Shift Medical Expenses to a Lower Income Year

It can be difficult for clients to treat unreimbursed medical expenses as an itemized deduction because the IRS imposes a **10 percent medical deduction AGI** rule. Only those medical expenses that exceed 10 percent of a client's AGI may be itemized on Schedule A. (The AGI restriction is 7.5 percent for those age sixty-five or older). One strategy that can work for clients who do have large medical bills is to shift these expenses into years when household income is lower. For example, if a client knows that he or she will terminate employment or retire, it may be helpful to postpone major medical expenses until that year, if possible. The primary disadvantage associated with this strategy is that it may be difficult, if not impossible, to postpone certain medical expenses. In many cases, medical bills and related expenses are the result of an emergency or unplanned event, and as such, a client may have little control over the timing of care and payment of expenses.

Procedural Strategy 9: Maximize the Number of Dependents, or Exemptions, Claimed

If a client is paying the majority of expenses for a child, parent, sibling, or other qualifying person (e.g., a parent), efforts should be made to determine whether the person can be claimed as a **dependent**. The benefit of this strategy is that additional **exemptions for dependents** can be claimed in any given year, in addition to the **personal exemption** for the taxpayer and for the spouse, if applicable. This can result in a reduced tax liability. The IRS prescribes tests to determine if a dependent is a "qualifying child," or "qualifying relative," and thus eligible to be included as an exemption.

It is worth noting that whenever a child becomes semi-independent, a dilemma is created. It may be beneficial for a child who is in college, for instance, to claim that he or she is not a dependent of another person. This might result in increased levels of financial aid and other benefits, but *only* if the student meets the qualifications as an independent student for financial aid purposes. (For more information on the requirements, see Chapter 11.) *Tax status and federal financial aid status are not the same.* Furthermore, doing so reduces the number of dependents claimed by a parent, which could increase the tax liability for the parent.

Procedural Strategy 10: Consider Establishing a Business

All of the strategies provided up to this point have been general in nature and applicable to almost any client situation. This strategy, on the other hand, should be considered whenever a client's income exceeds phase-out limits for certain deductions and credits. Several forms of business ownership are available. Figure 4.4 shows each option and the resulting tax implication for a business owner.

Establishing a business can be a good way to convert non-tax-deductible expenses into income tax-reducing deductions. For example, someone who opens a consulting practice could begin to deduct some expenses related to travel, entertainment, and marketing. Other potential deductions include home office expenses, cell phone charges, and computer equipment. Furthermore, a business owner can deduct contributions to certain types of retirement plans.

Figure 4.4 Forms of Business Ownership

Type of Business	Does Business Entity Provide Liability Protection?	Tax Implications
Sole Proprietorship	No	All income passes directly to the business owner; income reported on Schedule C.
Partnership	No	The proportional share of business income flows through to the owner; income reported on Form 1065 and shown on Form 1040.
Limited Liability Company	Yes	The proportion share of business income flows through to the owner; income reported on Form 1065, 1120S or Schedule C depending on entity.
Corporation	Yes	Income taxed at corporate marginal rate; dividends from corporation taxed at owner's marginal tax rate; taxes filed on Form 1120.
S Corporation	Yes	Income flows through to owner; taxes filed on Form 1120S.

Keep in mind that tax law requires that a business show an operating profit in at least three out of five years, or at least on honest attempt to generate a profit. Some clients who attempt to implement this recommendation run afoul of hobby loss rules, which define which expenses are deductible when an activity is not classified as a profit-making endeavor. The IRS looks very critically at a commercial enterprise that may really be a hobby rather than a legitimate business.

Procedural Strategy 11: Use Like-Kind Exchange Strategies Appropriately

While the IRC addresses a dozen or more non-taxable exchanges, the two most common deal with investment property (Section 1031) and insurance policies (Section 1035).

U.S. Code Section 1031 features a provision for owners of investment property to exchange property without incurring immediate taxation. For this to be an effective tax-postponing strategy, a client must exchange his or her property for a similar kind or class of asset. For example, a business can be exchanged for another business, or an investment property (e.g., an apartment building) can be exchanged for another investment property (e.g., a rental house). **Boot**, defined as the receipt of non-like-kind property, can trigger taxation. Sometimes clients attempt to exchange investment securities or personal use property. The IRS will not allow such transfers. Furthermore, real estate can be exchanged only for real estate, which is defined as improved or unimproved land, buildings, warehouses, etc. For example, exchanging a mortgage for a piece of land would not be permitted under Section 1031. Keep in mind that the amount *realized* for tax purposes is often different from the amount *recognized* for tax purposes; in general, investors need only recognize for tax purposes the value of the boot received even though they may have realized an amount greater than reported for tax purposes.

U.S. Code Section 1035 provides for a tax-free insurance product exchange for owners of a life insurance policy, an endowment, or an annuity. Restrictions apply, but eligible product exchanges allow the taxpayer to avoid taxes due on the sale or redemption of the insurance product. Otherwise, the two-step process of the sale or redemption, minus the taxes owed, would result in a smaller amount for the subsequent insurance product purchase. For a more complete discussion, see Chapter 5.

Procedural Strategy 12: Understand the Implications of Realized and Unrealized Gains

A **realized gain** (or **realized loss**) is calculated by subtracting the adjusted basis in property from the sale price of the property. Realized gains (or losses) are reported on a client's Form 1040. Sometimes a gain (or loss) is realized but not immediately recognized (i.e., reported on Form 1040). In these situations, the gain (or loss) is *unrecognized*. Examples of situations that might result in an unrecognized gain (or loss) include completing a Section 1031 like-kind exchange, the sale of personal use assets, and some gains on the sale of a personal residence (e.g., a $250,000 gain for a single taxpayer). Understanding when a gain or loss must be reported can be an effective tool to help clients maximize cash flow by managing and minimizing tax liabilities. Misinterpretation of gains rules can result in tax penalties. For example, selling personal property for a loss is not an eligible tax deduction strategy; however, selling personal property (e.g., sales at a garage sale) that results in a gain is technically taxable. Care must be taken whenever a like-kind exchange strategy is employed.

Procedural Strategy 13: Calculate the Exclusion Ratio to Reduce the Tax on Annuity Distributions

Careful attention should be paid to situations where a client is taking distributions from an annuity, IRA, or qualified plan. If any contribution was made using after-tax dollars, or if any of the contribution was taxed previously, a portion of the total distribution will be considered a tax-free distribution. Calculating the exclusion ratio can reduce the probability that a client will pay unnecessary taxes. The exclusion ratio formula is as follows:

Equation 4.1:

$$\text{Exclusion Ratio} = \frac{\text{Total after-tax contribution}}{\text{Total expected distribution}}$$

Where the "total expected distributions" is calculated by multiplying the monthly distribution by the number of expected distributions (i.e. twelve per year).

Example, assume a client expects to receive $2,000 per month over a twenty-year period. If the client originally invested $300,000 on an after-tax basis, the exclusion ratio would indicate that 62.5 percent of each distribution would be received tax free; that is, 37.5 percent of each distribution will be taxable.

It is possible that distributions will last longer than the expected duration used in the formula. In these situations, all of the after-tax contributions are accounted for. This will result in all future distributions being fully taxable. Clients who fail to track cumulative distributions could incur tax penalties at some point in the future.

Procedural Strategy 14: Compare Taxable and Tax-free Interest on a Taxable Equivalent Yield Basis

Recall from Chapter 2 that financial planners should be adept at calculating **taxable equivalent yields** as a means of comparing taxable and tax-free fixed-income investments as it is not uncommon to find municipal bonds in a client's portfolio. An analysis may be required to determine whether municipal securities are in fact appropriate for a client. Some bonds are exempt from federal income tax, some are exempt from state income tax, and some are "fully exempt," meaning they incur neither federal nor state income tax liability. The following formulas should be used as a means of determining the yield needed for a taxable fixed-income investment to match that of a state and/or federally tax-free fixed income investment:

Equation 4.2: Taxable Equivalent Yield (Federal Tax-exempt)

$$\text{TEY (Federal Tax-exempt)} = \frac{\text{Tax-exempt bond yield}}{(1 - \text{FMTB})}$$

Equation 4.3: Taxable Equivalent Yield (State Tax-exempt)

$$\text{TEY (State Tax-exempt)} = \frac{\text{Tax-exempt bond yield}}{(1 - \text{SMTB})}$$

Equation 4.4: Taxable Equivalent Yield (Fully Tax-exempt)

$$\text{TEY (Fully Tax-exempt)} = \frac{\text{Tax-exempt bond yield}}{[1 - (\text{FMTB} + (\text{SMTB} \times (1 - \text{FMTB})))]}$$

Where:

TEY = Taxable Equivalent Yield

FMTB = Federal Marginal Tax Bracket

SMTB = State Marginal Tax Bracket

For example, if a client lives in a state with a 5 percent marginal rate and is in the 25 percent federal marginal tax bracket, it is possible to compare to two bonds—a fully taxable 8.25 percent corporate bond and a 6.0 percent municipal bond. The TEY on the municipal bond would be is 8.42 percent if the bond was issued from a municipality in the same state as the client's state of residence. In other words, a fully taxable bond would need to have an annual yield of 8.42 percent or greater to be the better investment. Therefore, the client would be better off purchasing the municipal bond. However, if the client purchased a municipal bond from another state, the interest would not be state tax exempt, so the TEY would be only 8.00 percent. In this case, the client should purchase the corporate bond and pay the tax.

Another, similar formula is for **after-tax yield** (or equivalent tax-free rate of return), which can be calculated using the following formula:

Equation 4.5: After-tax Yield

After - tax yield = Taxable rate x (1 – (FMTB + (SMTB x (1 – FMTB))))

Several assumptions are associated with the use of the preceding formulas. It is possible and likely that over time the marginal tax rates in a particular state will change. When this happens it is important to rerun the analysis. Also, bond rates change on a regular basis. What is an attractive tax-free rate today may be a less appealing rate tomorrow. Again, the use of this formula is not a one-time calculation; financial planners are encouraged to conduct yield analyses on an ongoing basis. Finally, it is important to remember that the tax-exempt status of municipal bonds does not extend to all instances of the AMT calculation.

Procedural Strategy 15: Understand When a Client Should Itemize Deductions

According to the IRS, financial planning clients should itemize deductions if their allowable itemized deductions are more than the **standard deduction**. Some clients itemize deductions because they do not qualify for the standard deduction. **Schedule A** is used to itemize the following deductions:

- Medical and dental expenses (subject to an AGI threshold);

- Deductible taxes (e.g., state income and local property taxes);

- Home mortgage points;

- Interest expenses (e.g., interest on home mortgages);

- Contributions;

- Casualty and theft losses (subject to an AGI threshold);

- Miscellaneous expenses (subject to an AGI threshold);

- Business use of home and car;

- Business travel and entertainment expenses;

- Educational expenses;

- Employee business expenses; and

- Casualty, disaster, and theft losses (subject to an AGI threshold).

There are many rules and limitations applicable to itemizing deductions, but whenever clients have eligible expenses that exceed the standard deduction, they should claim the higher itemized amount. However, this in turn can create additional income reporting confusion for the subsequent year. For example, clients who claim the *state income tax* as an itemized deduction are required to report any refund of state tax overpayment as income on the federal income tax form the following year. Forgetting to claim the state tax refund as income can result in fines and penalties. For clients who live in an income-tax-free state, Schedule A should be completed using IRS guidelines for the **sales tax deduction**, in lieu of the income tax deduction.

Procedural Strategy 16: Review Cost Basis Rules when Advising Clients about Gifts

Basis When Gift Taxes Were Paid

When a donor pays a gift tax on a gift, the donee's basis is equivalent to the donor's basis plus the amount of the gift tax attributable to the appreciation of the gift above the donor's adjusted basis. The following formula can be used to determine the new basis:

New Basis = Donor's Basis + ((Unrealized Appreciation of Gift/Taxable gift) x Gift Tax Paid).

For example, assume your client receives a stock worth $1,014,000 and the donor's adjusted basis was $764,000. Also assume the donor was subject to a 40% gift tax rate and that the gift tax exclusion is $14,000. Given this information, your client's new cost basis is: $848,619, after accounting for the excluded portion of the gift.

Solution: $750,000 + (($1,014,000 - $764,000)/$1,014,000) x (($1,014,000 - $14,000) x 0.40) = $848,619

Sometimes clients get confused when calculating the tax gain or loss on an investment asset received as a **gift**. The rules relating to **non-cash investment gifts** can be found in IRS Publication 550. A summary of these rules follows:

- The holding period of the asset is transferred to the giftee.

- If the asset is sold for less than its fair market value on the date of the gift, the basis is the date-of-gift fair market value.

- If the asset is sold for more than the original basis of the asset (i.e., the amount paid when the asset was originally purchased), the original basis is used.

- If the asset is sold for less than the original basis but more than the date-of-gift fair market value, no gain or loss is recognized.

Example: Your client's father purchases bonds for $20,000. The father gifts the bonds to your client. At the time of the gift the bonds are worth $10,000. If the bonds are sold for $9,000, the client records a $1,000 loss. If the bonds are sold for $25,000, the client records a $5,000 gain. If the bonds are sold for $15,000, no gain or loss is recorded.

It is worth noting to clients that whenever they give or receive a gift that could be deemed an investment they should record and retain information related to the date of the gift, its original basis, and the fair market value of the asset on the gift date. Without this information the IRS could limit claims of loss or maximize a sale gain if the client is audited. It is also worth noting that in cases where the current value of the asset is less than the original basis but more than the date-of-gift fair market value, the donee should be advised to sell the asset, capture the tax loss, and then transfer the assets to the giftee.

Figure 4.5 Decision Tree for Developing Tax Planning Recommendations

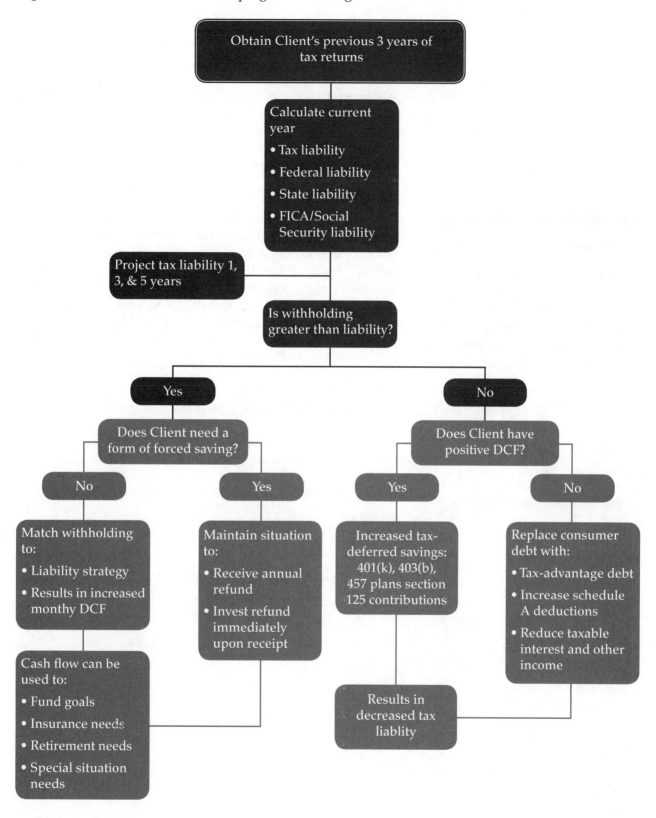

Procedural Strategy 17: Apply a Systematic Approach when Developing Tax Planning Recommendations

Tax planning is integrative to the extent that tax recommendations are incorporated into other parts of a client's financial plan. Effective tax planning can provide insights into ways to increase monthly discretionary cash flow. Tax planning can also be used to prompt deeper planner-client discussions regarding retirement, investment, insurance, and education planning. Figure 4.5 illustrates one process that can potentially be used to narrow strategies down into one or more client recommendations. Note that this process is premised on the notion that, regardless of the approach chosen, the recommendation or recommendations match the client's tax planning goals and objectives.

Finally, before making tax planning recommendations or recommendations in other core content planning areas, several issues should always be reviewed. This practice will can help novice financial planners gain confidence that their recommendations reflect current and proposed tax code rules, as well as the important and integrative role of taxes throughout the financial planning process. These issues include:

- possible AMT triggers;

- contribution levels to employer provided tax-advantaged benefit plans;

- allocations among pretax, taxable, and tax-free investment assets;

- present and future business ownership interests;

- non-tax-advantaged debt compared to home equity debt; and

- where applicable, the ability to meet tax adjustment, deduction, and credit income limits.

Self-Test 8

Roger gave his grandson bonds with a fair market value of $5,000. Roger originally paid $2,000 for the bonds. What is grandson's new basis in the bonds?

a. $2,000

b. $3,000

c. $2,500

d. $5,000

#Remember

Refundable tax credits provide a payment to the taxpayer. In other words, the amount of the credit that exceeds the full payment of the taxes is "refunded" to the taxpayer. To quickly identify refundable credits, check the payment box on the tax form.

TAX PLANNING FOR SPECIAL POPULATIONS

Tax Planning for Families with Children

In 2014, the U.S. Department of Agriculture estimated that the cost of raising a child born in 2013 to a middle income family from birth through age seventeen was more than $245,000.[9] The cost includes seven major budgetary categories, excluding the cost of prenatal care. In addition, many families have a goal to provide at least a minimum level of funding for post-secondary education. Although exact costs vary widely, an in-state, public college cost more than $19,500 for tuition, fees, room, and board for academic year 2015-16.[10] Between basic care and education, costs associated with raising a child can easily exceed $300,000. The IRS provides two very important tax credits to those who have qualifying expenses and meet the income limitations: the **Child and Dependent Care Tax Credit** and the **Child Tax Credit**.

The tax credit for child care and dependent care applies to the cost of care for qualified children under the age of thirteen or to adult relatives who live with the taxpayer but are physically or mentally incapable of providing for their own well-being. The current Child and Dependent Care Tax Credit allows for a maximum tax credit of 35 percent of qualifying expenses. Eligible families with one qualifying dependent can claim up to $1,050 (35 percent of $3,000) as a credit against their federal tax liability, and eligible families with two or more qualifying dependents can claim up to $2,100 (35 percent of $6,000) against their federal tax liability.[11] The federal credit can be used only to offset actual federal tax liability; any excess credit amount is lost. Unlike the **Earned Income Tax Credit (EITC)** and the Child Tax Credit, the Child and Dependent Care Tax Credit is **nonrefundable**. This means that if a family does not earn enough money to owe federal income taxes, it cannot benefit from the credit. Finally, taxpayers who file "married filing separately" are ineligible to claim this credit.

The Child Tax Credit provides a maximum credit of $1,000 for each qualifying child under age seventeen. Income limits apply, and for married taxpayers filing jointly the phase-out begins at $110,000 of AGI. For married taxpayers filing separate returns, it begins at $55,000 of AGI, and for all others the income phase-out begins at $75,000 of AGI.[12] There are seven tests to determine whether a child qualifies:

1. *Relation test:* the taxpayer's son, daughter, stepchild, foster child, brother, sister, stepbrother, stepsister, or descendant of any of them (for example, the taxpayer's grandchild, niece, or nephew).

2. *Age test:* was under the age of seventeen at the end of the calendar year.

3. *Support test:* did not provide more than half of his or her own support for the previous calendar year.

4. *Residence test:* lived with the taxpayer for more than half of the year (some exceptions do apply).

5. *Dependent test:* is claimed as a dependent on the taxpayer's return.

6. *Joint return test:* did not file a joint return for the year.

7. *Citizenship test:* was a U.S. citizen, a U.S. national, or a U.S. resident alien.[13]

In addition to the basic tax credit, there is an **Additional Child Tax Credit** that can be claimed by taxpayers who do not receive the full benefit of the basic credit because they pay too little tax. This provision makes this a **refundable credit**.

Tax Planning for Business Owners

As discussed earlier in the chapter, financial planners need to be familiar with different forms of business ownership, including:

*   sole proprietorships

*   partnerships

*   limited liability companies (LLCs)

*   S Corporations (S-Corps)

*   C-Corporations (C-Corps)

A **sole proprietorship** is a single-person business that provides the owner with the least liability protection but the easiest form of income taxation. In effect, the company and individual are the same entity.

A **partnership**, as the name implies, is a business owned by two or more individuals. Each partner is jointly responsible for the financial obligations of the company.

A **limited liability corporation LLC** provides greater liability protection than either a sole proprietorship or partnership while still allowing income to be taxed at the individual level. That is, earnings from the company are passed through to shareholders. Individuals, partnerships, trusts, and foreign investors can be shareholders. LLCs are inexpensive and easy to establish.

A **limited liability partnership (LLP)** is a type of LLC that combines elements of a corporation and a partnership. LLPs avoid double taxation by allocating profits among partners; however, unlike traditional partnerships, one LLP partner is not liable for another partner's misconduct or negligence.

S-Corps and **C-Corps** have many similarities. Shareholders with each entity have limited liability. Both must have an elected board of directors and officers. The primary difference between the two involves the number of shareholders and the taxation of profits. S-Corps limit the number of shareholders. More importantly, it is possible for C-Corps to incur double taxation, meaning profits can be taxed at the corporate level first and then taxed again as dividends at the individual level. In the case of an S-Corp, earnings pass directly through to shareholders, who are responsible for paying income tax directly, thus avoiding double taxation.

Tax Planning for Executives with Incentive Stock Options (ISOs)

Incentive stock option (ISO) plans are a fairly common but very complex financial planning issue for planners who counsel corporate executives. If an employer grants a client an option to buy stock, there are three potential tax-triggering events. Clients may have to realize income for tax purposes when they (1) receive the option, (2) exercise the option, or (3) sell or transfer either the option prior to exercise or the stock after exercise.

There are two types of stock options: **statutory stock options** and **nonstatutory stock options**. A statutory plan includes a plan document outlining the conditions of the plan and the number of options to be granted to each employee. Typically, stock options granted under an ISO plan are statutory stock options. ISO plans have two potentially important advantages in comparison to nonstatutory stock options.

First, exercising the ISO option does not trigger any recognition of income or gain. Only the sale of the stock creates a taxable event, and tax is then due only on the difference between the market price at exercise and the sales price.[14] Conversely, with nonstatutory options, income tax must be paid on the difference in the exercise price and the market price in the year the option is exercised.

Second, if the stock is held until at least one year after the date of exercise, or two years from the option grant date, whichever is later, all of the gains on the sale of the stock will be at capital gains rates rather than ordinary income rates. However, if the stock is sold or transferred before the expiration of that holding period—called a **disqualifying disposition**—then all income or gains derived are considered ordinary income.[15]

Although the exercise of an ISO does not trigger a taxable event under the regular tax system, it could under the AMT system. For AMT purposes, the aforementioned tax treatment does not apply to the transfer of stock acquired as a result of the exercise of an incentive stock option.[16] Therefore, for AMT purposes, the difference in the *fair market value* of the stock and the *exercise price* of the ISO is treated as taxable income as soon as the executive vests in the right to exercise. In other words, once a client can exercise the option even the unrealized gain on the implied value, considered an AMT adjustment, is taxable in the current year at ordinary income tax rates.

This AMT adjustment has two effects: (1) the adjustment amount may become subject to the AMT and the tax may have to be paid if the filer is subject to AMT and (2) the tax basis in the stock becomes the fair market value on the date the AMT adjustment occurred. Unfortunately, the tax basis of the stock is different for AMT purposes and for regular income tax purposes; hence, the subsequent sale of the stock could generate a gain for regular income tax purposes, whereas it might not generate gain for AMT purposes.

Mini-Case Problems

Liama MacDonald

1. Liama MacDonald is a thirty-two-year-old single female. She has gross wages of $95,000 (before deferrals) and $18,000 withholding for federal income tax. Given the information below, will she likely have too much or too little withheld for the current tax year, assuming the following facts? How much? For simplicity, do not consider AMT.

    - She estimates total itemized deductions of $9,450.

    - The standard deduction for a single person is $5,450.

    - The personal exemption for a single person is $3,500.

    - She will not have any interest or dividend income or capital gains.

    - She will not contribute to an IRA.

    - She will defer 5 percent of her gross salary into the qualified retirement plan.

Randy Cross

2. Randy Cross, a new financial planning client, makes a tax-deductible contribution of $4,000 to a traditional IRA. The client is in the 25 percent marginal tax bracket. How much are the approximate tax savings?

Frank and Louisa Beamer

3. Frank Beamer and his wife Louisa have owned and lived in their personal residence for ten years. They purchased the home for $300,000. They sell the home for $900,000. How much of the gain is taxable?

Luke Heckman

4. Luke Heckman has asked you to analyze the following investment alternatives for the highest after-tax rate of return under the assumption that the client is subject to a 28 percent marginal federal income tax and a 5 percent state income tax.

    - A corporate bond with a 7 percent pretax return

    - An out-of-state municipal bond with a 5.75 percent pretax return

    - An in-state municipal bond with a 5.5 percent pretax return

Anabell Snyder

5. A financial planner has just completed an analysis of Anabell Snyder's fixed-income holdings. She has determined each of Anabell's after-tax yields, but is cautioning Anabell that the tax implications of her holdings could change if Congress alters marginal tax rates. Based on the following after-tax yields, which of these bonds would offer the greatest after-tax return if Anabell's federal marginal tax bracket increased from 25 to 30 percent, while her state marginal bracket remained 4.5 percent?

    - A corporate bond with a 5.1 percent after-tax return

    - An out-of-state municipal bond with a 5.0 percent after-tax return

    - An in-state municipal bond with a 4.8 percent after-tax return

Comprehensive Bedo Case—Tax Planning Analysis Questions

Before beginning the tax analysis for the Bedo family, it is important to review assumptions and data related to income, including wages and salaries, dividends, interest, capital gains, bonus income, and income attributable to employer provided group benefits. When working with the data it will also be important to determine whether any phase-out limits based on income apply.

When reviewing their current situation, it will be helpful to formulate strategies that both increase discretionary cash flow and reduce tax liabilities. Recommendations should be as precise as possible.

For example, it is not enough to state that Tyler and Mia should match their tax withholdings to their tax liabilities. Exactly how should they do this? As their planner, it is acceptable to encourage both Tyler and Mia to complete a new IRS Form W-4 with their employer. It is also appropriate to indicate exactly how many exemptions they should claim on their W-4. Withholding tables can be found on the IRS Web site (www.irs.gov).

Use the following questions to guide you through the tax planning process.

1. Develop a tax planning goal for the Bedos. When conceptualizing this goal, consider the following.

a.   Is the goal developed in agreement with any or all goals and objectives that the clients have identified? What other goals have tax implications for the Bedos' financial plan?

b.   What situational factors might influence their tax planning goal? Are these factors explicit, implied, or assumed? Is additional information required from the Bedos, and if so, what?

c.   What is the desired tax planning outcome for the clients?

2.   Are there globally accepted, client-specific, or planner-generated planning assumptions that will influence the income tax planning situation analysis? List these assumptions as they might affect income tax planning?

3.   Make a list of specific federal income tax issues that should be evaluated as part of the documentation and evaluation of the Bedos' tax planning efforts.

4.   Conduct a current income tax situation analysis for the Bedos. Be sure to calculate the following:

a.   the Bedos' gross income before adjustments and exclusions;

b.   their gross taxable income (Hint: this amount is arrived at after subtracting all pretax payroll contributions and deductions and other exclusion items.);

c.   the Bedos' adjusted gross income;

d.   the amount of interest paid on their principal residence for the tax year;

e.   the amount that should be claimed for their annual deduction (standard or itemized);

f.   their taxable income for the year; and

g.   the estimated amount of federal tax owed or the amount of refund they can expect, after applying tax credits.

5.   Calculate the amount of FICA taxes withheld compared to the Bedos' actual FICA liability.

6.   Summarize your observations about the Bedos' current tax situation as they might appear in a client letter or plan.

7.   Based on the goals originally identified and the completed analysis, what product or procedural strategies might be most useful to satisfy the Bedos' tax planning needs? Where applicable, calculate an approximate annual tax savings, as well as the most likely outcome(s) associated with each strategy.

8.   Write at least one primary and one alternative recommendation from the strategies selected in response to each planning need identified. More than one recommendation may be needed to address all of the planning needs. Include specific, defensible answers to the *who, what, when, where, why, how*, and *how much* implementation questions for each recommendation.

a.   It is suggested that each recommendation be summarized in a Recommendation Form.

b.   Assign a priority to each recommendation based on the likelihood of meeting client goals and desired outcomes. This priority will be important when recommendations from other core planning content areas are considered relative to the available discretionary funds for subsidizing all recommendations.

c. Comment briefly on the outcomes associated with each recommendation.

9. Complete the following for the Income Tax Planning section of the Bedos' financial plan.

a. Outline the information to be included in this section of the plan. Assume the financial advisor is not a CPA, attorney, or EA, does not provide income tax preparation services, and limits income tax work to a review of tax forms and a projection of changes in response to other planning recommendations. What content might be included in this section to inform the client? What disclaimers, if any, might be included?

b. Draft an introduction to this section of the plan (no more than one paragraph).

c. Define five key terms that would be included in the plan or glossary to assist the client with tax education or client interpretation of the plan.

10. Prepare a ten- to fifteen-minute presentation for the Bedos of your observations and/or recommendation(s) for meeting their life insurance needs. Be sure to include visual aids, Excel handouts, and other materials that will make the recommendations more meaningful to the clients.

Chapter Resources

Internal Revenue Service (www.irs.gov).

Leimberg, S. R.; J. Katz; R. Keebler; J. Scroggins; M. Jackson. *The Tools & Techniques of Income Tax Planning*, 5th Ed. Cincinnati, OH: National Underwriter Company, 2016.

Tax Facts on Insurance & Employee Benefits 2016. Erlanger, KY: National Underwriter Company.

Tax Facts on Investments 2016. Erlanger, KY: National Underwriter Company.

The *Financial Facilitator* and all fillable forms needed to complete text activities can be found on the student website at: pro.nuco.com/booksupplements/NUCollege-CaseBook3e.

Self-Test Answers

1: d, 2: d, 3: True, 4: b, 5: b, 6: d, 7: False, 8: a

Endnotes

1. For the majority of taxpayers, adjusted gross income (AGI) and modified adjusted gross income (MAGI) are often the same for many purposes. Therefore, the terms are used interchangeably in this discussion. However, for some clients, or in certain situations, there will be a difference.

2. Source: IRS. Employer's Tax Guide to Fringe Benefits, p. 6 (www.irs.gov/pub/irs-pdf/p15b.pdf).

3. *IRS Publication 535: Business Expenses*, p. 5. Available at www.irs.gov/pub/irs-pdf/p535.pdf.

4. "Chapter 4—Material Participation," *IRS Passive Activity Loss ATG*. Available at www.irs.gov/businesses/small/article/0,,id=146335,00.html.

5. "At-risk limits," *IRS Publication 925*. Available at www.irs.gov/publications/p925/ar02.html#en_US_2010_publink1000104672.

6. *IRS Publication 550, Investment Income and Expenses*. Available at: www.irs.gov/uac/about-publication-550.

7. IRS Retirement Topics—Tax on Early Distributions. Available at www.irs.gov/retirement/participant/article/0,,id=211440,00.html.

8. For additional information, see the following sources: *Appeals…Resolving Tax Disputes*. Available at www.irs.gov/Individuals/Appeals-Resolving-Tax-Disputes. *IRS Publication 5: Your Appeal Rights and How to Prepare a Protest if You Don't Agree*. Available at www.irs.gov/pub/irs-pdf/p5.pdf. *IRS Publication 1: Your Rights as a Taxpayer.* Available at www.irs.gov/pub/irs-pdf/p1.pdf. And *IRS Publication 556: Examination of Returns, Appeal Rights, and Claims for Refund*, "Appeal Rights." Available at www.irs.gov/publications/p556/ar02.html#d0e976.

9. USDA, *Expenditures on Children by Families, 2013*, p. 21. Available at www.cnpp.usda.gov/sites/default/files/expenditures_on_children_by_families/crc2013.pdf.

10. The College Board, *College Pricing 2015*, p. 23. Available at trends.collegeboard.org/sites/default/files/trends-college-pricing-web-final-508-2.pdf.

11. *IRS Publication 503: Child and Dependent Care Expenses*, pp. 12–13. Available at www.irs.gov/pub/irs-pdf/p503.pdf.

12. *IRS Publication 972: Child Tax Credit*, p. 3. Available at www.irs.gov/pub/irs-pdf/p972.pdf.

13. *IRS Publication 972: Child Tax Credit*, p. 2.

14. I.R.C. §421(a).

15. I.R.C. §421(b).

16. I.R.C. §56(b).

PART III: Analyzing and Evaluating a Client's Financial Status to Plan for Client Risk Protection

Chapter 5

Life Insurance Planning

Learning Objectives

1. Life insurance planning plays an important role in a model of comprehensive financial planning. A client's life insurance need is normally evaluated early in the planning process to determine the fiscal and emotional costs associated with the client's premature death. Without proper levels of insurance in place—and funded—a client's entire financial plan could potentially collapse in the event of premature death, resulting in liquidity constraints and unfunded tax liabilities. In essence, life insurance is a cornerstone of a client's **risk capacity**—their financial ability to withstand a financial loss.

2. An essential first step in the life insurance planning process involves identifying common risk classification factors used in the life insurance underwriting process. Client lifestyle characteristics, such as using tobacco, alcohol, or drugs; a history of reckless driving; participating in sensation-seeking activities; and exhibiting low financial risk tolerance are all indicators of potential underwriting problems. These factors also are associated with high premiums and the possibility of limited coverage. As noted in this chapter, other factors that might indicate that a client is a substandard risk include working in a hazardous profession, piloting aircraft, being overweight, or having a family history of medical problems.

3. Five quantitative approaches commonly used to identify a client's need for life insurance are presented in this chapter. Financial planners must be familiar with the use and application of each of the following methods: (1) needs-based analysis, (2) human life value, (3) capital retention, (4) income retention, and (5) simple income multiplier approach. Rather than relying on one or two of these measures, it is often a good idea to triangulate results into an average need.

4. Although each insurance company in the marketplace has distinct names for its life insurance products, most policy types can be classified into one

Learning Objectives

of the following six groups: (1) term; (2) return of premium term; (3) whole; (4) universal; (5) variable; and (6) variable universal life. Competent financial planners, even those who do not deal daily with life insurance planning issues, should be able to identify each type of policy and match the appropriate policy to a client's needs.

5. Many financial planners regularly conduct policy replacement analyses for clients. This chapter presents the yearly price per thousand method formula to estimate the approximate cost of a cash value life insurance policy. Benchmarks developed by Joseph Belth are provided that can be used to determine whether a client should hold or replace a currently in-force policy.

6. Nonforfeiture techniques are presented in this chapter as a way for clients who own cash value policies to consider when thinking about the termination of an in-force policy. Nonforfeiture options include surrendering the policy for the cash value, using the cash value to purchase a paid-up cash value policy, or using the cash value to buy a fully paid term policy. Sometimes, however, it makes better financial sense to exchange a policy for another type of insurance product to avoid taxes. This chapter discusses five alternatives available with a Section 1035 exchange: (1) exchange a current life policy for a newly issued life policy; (2) exchange an endowment contract for another endowment contract; (3) exchange a current life insurance policy for an annuity contract; (4) exchange an annuity contract for a new annuity contract; or (5) exchange an annuity contract for a long-term care contract.

7. This chapter provides a broad overview of annuities, as used in the life insurance planning process. Annuities can be categorized in one of two ways: deferred and immediate income. Deferred annuities provide a tax-advantaged means for accumulating assets for future goals. Immediate annuities represent a way for clients to convert current financial assets into income-generating sources of income. Within any annuity product, clients can choose to invest in either a fixed-income or variable-income contract. Annuity products are gaining in usage among aging clients. Thus, it is essential that financial planners have a strong working knowledge of the types and uses of annuity products. Furthermore, a working familiarity with key annuity terms and features, such as joint-and-survivor payout alternatives, payout schedules, and early distribution penalties, is a characteristic that distinguishes the most competent financial planners.

8. The decision to recommend either a term or cash value policy is more complicated than simply implementing a "buy term and invest the difference" strategy. Information in this chapter suggests that every insurance recommendation should be based on a client's need for a policy. Permanent cash value policies might be more appropriate when a client has a long-term enduring financial need. In situations where the financial need is short and temporary, term insurance may be more appropriate. Other factors to consider when drafting life insurance recommendations include understanding the medical history of the client and his or her family.

Learning Objectives

Clients who could face underwriting challenges in the future should consider purchasing permanent life insurance today. Additionally, the aspect of forced savings can be important for some clients, resulting in a recommendation to purchase a cash value policy. Regardless of the final recommendation, financial planners must consider issues related to triggering the seven-pay test, which could limit the attractiveness of a policy recommendation.

9. There are a multitude of life insurance planning recommendations, both product and procedural, that can be used to help a client reach his or her financial goals. An important aspect of the financial planning process involves identifying and recommending prospective life insurance planning strategies that can be used to meet a client's unique financial situation and life goals. Financial planners who become experts at identifying the needs of current and prospective clients in relation to life insurance planning topics will find that the client-planner relationship greatly improves over time. Recommending life insurance strategies focused on helping clients reach their financial goals provides an excellent pathway for developing and strengthening relationships.

Key Terms

A.M. Best

Accelerated Death Benefit

Activities of Daily Living

Annuities

Annuity Due

Beginning-of-Period Payments

Beneficiary

Business Succession Plan

Buy Term And Invest The Difference

Buy/Sell Agreement

Capital Retention Approach

Cash Surrender Value

Cash Value Insurance

Chronic Illness

Contingent Beneficiary

Contract

Conversion Provision

Cost-Of-Living Rider

Cross-Purchase Plan

Death Benefit

Decedent

Declining Balance Term Insurance

Deferred Annuity

Demotech

Disability Waiver Provision

Discount Rate

Divorce

Early Distribution Penalities

Employer-Provided Group Coverage

Entity Purchase Plan

Face Amount of the Policy

Face Value Break Points

Family Member Support Ratio

Federal Gift Tax

Financial Planning Process

Fitch Ratings

Fixed Annuity

Forced Savings

Fully Paid Term Policy

Group Term Policy

Growing Annuity

Guaranteed Payout Schedule

Guaranteed Renewable

Human Life Value (HLV) Approach

Immediate Income Annuities

Immediate Variable Annuity

Incidents of Ownership

Income Multiplier Approach

Income Retention Approach

Insurable Interest

Key Terms

Insurance Bands

Insurance Company Rating Agency

Insured

Interest-Adjusted Net Cost Method

Internal Rate of Return Yield Method

Irrevocable Life Insurance Trust (ILIT)

Key Employee

Key Person Insurance

Lapse

Life Insurance Policy Replacement

Life Settlement

Modified Endowment Contract (MEC)

Moody's

Needs-Based Analysis Approach

Net Life Insurance Need

Nonforfeiture Provision

Paid-Up Cash Value Policy

Paid-Up Policy

Partnership

Per Diem

Perpetuity

Policy Loan

Policy Owner

Policy Replacement Analysis

Premature Death

Primary Beneficiary

Proof of Insurability

Replacement Ratio

Return of Premium

Return-of-Premium Term Insurance

Risk Capacity

Risk Classification Factors

Risk of Mortality

Section 79 Imputed Income

Section 1035 Exchange

Seven-Pay Test

Single-Premium Variable Universal Life Policy

Standard & Poor's

Substandard Risk Classification

Substandard Risks

Surrender Charge

Term Life Insurance

Terminal Illness

Traditional Net Cost Method

Transferring Life Insurance Policy Ownership

Triangulation

Unholy Trinity

Universal Life Insurance

Universal Policy

Key Terms

Variable Annuity

Variable Life Insurance

Variable Universal Life (VUL) Insurance

Viatical Settlement

Waiver of Premium for Unemployment

Weiss Ratings

Whole Life Insurance

Yearly Price per Thousand Method

Yearly Rate of Return Method

CFP® Principal Knowledge Topics

D.22. Principles of Risk and Insurance

D.23. Analysis and Evaluation of Risk Exposures

D.27. Annuities

D.28. Life Insurance (Individual)

D.29. Business Uses of Insurance

D.30. Insurance Needs Analysis

D.31. Insurance Policy and Company Selection

G.62. Business Succession Planning

Chapter Equations

Equation 5.1:

Present Value of an Annuity (PVA) = $\dfrac{PMT}{i}\left[1 - \dfrac{1}{(1+i)^n}\right]$

Equation 5.2:

Present Value of a Growing Annuity Due (PVGA) = $\dfrac{PMT_1}{(i-g)}\left[1 - \dfrac{(1+g)^n}{(1+i)^n}\right](1+i)$

Equation 5.3:

Present Value of Perpetuity (PVP) = $\dfrac{PMT}{i}$

Equation 5.4:

Present Value of an Annuity (PVA) = $\dfrac{PMT}{i}\left[1 - \dfrac{1}{(1+i)^n}\right]$

Equation 5.5:

Yearly Price per Thousand of Coverage (YPT) = $\left[\dfrac{(PMT + CV_0) \times (1+i) - (CV_1 + Div)}{(DB - CV_1) \times (0.001)}\right]$

LIFE INSURANCE PLANNING: DETERMINING THE NEED

The origins of personal financial planning can be traced back to insurance professionals' attempts to streamline the process of integrating insurance into the overall financial life of clients. This began in the late 1960s. Before this time, financial planning as a profession, or even a codified process, did not exist. It is not surprising that the insurance industry had such a strong impact on the financial planning profession from the beginning. Life insurance is, after all, a major component of every comprehensive financial plan. Protecting a client's current assets and lifestyle should be a leading goal of every financial planner. Without first protecting a client's current financial situation, all other suggestions, goals, strategies, and recommendations could be undone by a simple twist of fate.

A client's life insurance need is typically assessed early in the *financial planning process*. The logic for the placement of analysis within the financial planning process is simple: clients must be adequately insured to cover the fiscal and psychological costs of **premature death**. This is especially true if a client is married and/or has dependents, a significant life partner, a business, or other financial obligations that carry forward after the client's death, such as a substantial interest in a private firm.

Central to the analysis of a client's current life insurance situation—and all aspects of the financial planning process—is a thorough knowledge of the client. To complete a comprehensive assessment, this knowledge must encompass an understanding of:

1. the financial goals and objectives to be met by the insurance coverage in the event of premature death;

2. a broad range of personal characteristics that could affect the need for insurance;

3. appropriate product recommendations; and

4. documentation and review of any coverage currently available to the client.

Life insurance strategies and recommendations must be evaluated against certain client **risk classification factors**, which determine the availability and cost of insurance. Although financial planners might not be expected to be familiar with specific company underwriting methods, a general knowledge of the factors considered is critical to effective planning. When reviewing a client's hazards and risk characteristics, financial planners should consider the following factors:

- Lifestyle

    o Using tobacco, alcohol, or drugs

    o Convictions for reckless driving, driving under the influence of alcohol or drugs, or receiving multiple speeding tickets

    o Participating in sensation-seeking activities, including ultralight flying, scuba diving, or mountain climbing

    o Personal character or household financial situation

- Occupation

    o Working in a hazardous profession or occupation

    o Piloting commercial, private, or military aircraft

- Medical condition or history

    o Gender, age, height, and weight

    o Family medical history

Individuals who, because of any of these factors, have a higher than standard **risk of mortality** are considered **substandard risks**. Depending on the company and the underwriting and reinsurance standards, client insurability factors could result in:

- a denial of the policy application;

- increased policy costs because of the risk factors; or

- the inclusion of riders that exclude certain causes of death or reduce the benefits to the premiums paid, policy reserve accumulations, or the greater of the two.

Life insurance planning, in particular, exemplifies the need for a broad based exploration of a client's lifestyle, personal, and demographic profile. Additionally, a financial planner must collect the quantitative and qualitative data necessary to conduct a realistic needs assessment that will provide the coverage necessary to fulfill the client's goals. Throughout the life insurance planning process, the planner or planning team must demonstrate genuine client empathy, balanced with rigorous analytical skills.

The loss of a family member or a person who provides financial support to another is obviously a devastating emotional loss that cannot be overcome solely by insurance. However, such a loss could be compounded if the survivor(s) does not have adequate funds to (1) pay for the final expenses of the decedent or (2) maintain the same standard of living enjoyed prior to the death of the decedent. The need for life insurance is predicated on three basic notions:

1. People earn money during their working lives.

2. The money that they earn supports a desired standard of living.

3. A client's desired standard of living should not have to change because of the death of an earner.

The first step in the process of analyzing a client's current situation involves determining whether a client needs life insurance, and if so, the amount of coverage needed. Figure 5.1 provides a summary of questions needed to determine financial responsibility, net worth, charitable giving, and insurability factors to consider when deciding whether a client has a current need for life insurance.

Figure 5.1 Decision Tree for Determining a Client's Need for Life Insurance

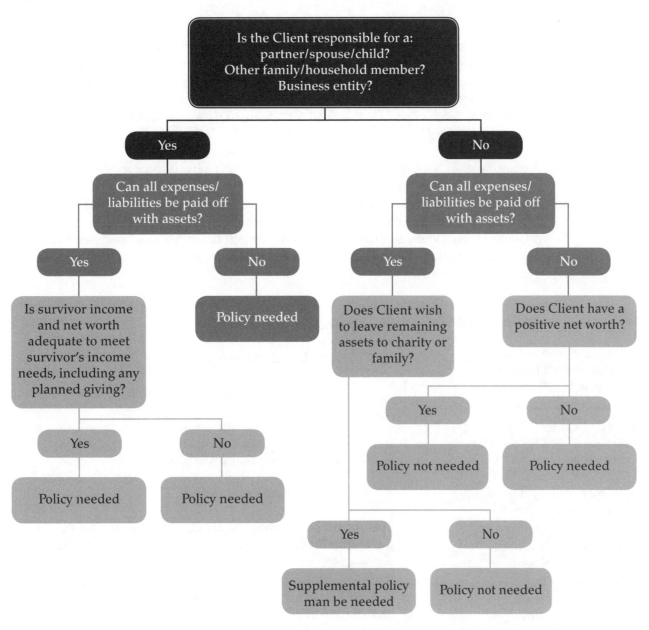

Of primary concern is whether the client is responsible for the financial welfare of another person (e.g., a spouse, partner, child, or parent) or business entity. If the answer is no, the financial planner should determine whether the client's net worth is large enough to meet all final expenses (e.g., medical, burial, tax, and other needs). If net worth is sufficient, then no coverage may be needed unless there are reasons to justify putting a policy in place to ensure future access to coverage. Furthermore, if the client is projected to have a net worth in excess of final expenses, the issue of charitable donations should be considered. Similarly, if the client would like to be a benefactor to another person or organization, then life insurance coverage could be warranted. However, if the answer to all these questions is negative, a life insurance purchase could probably be delayed. If this is the case, the financial planner should continue to regularly monitor future circumstances to determine whether and when the need might arise.

The same issues must be considered if the client has financial dependents. In this situation, net worth must be sufficient to meet final expenses, the survivor's future income needs, and if relevant, any planned inheritance or charitable gifts. Otherwise, life insurance protection may be needed. Finally, in the event assets are sufficient to satisfy all of these expenses, the need for life insurance as an estate tax planning tool must be considered.

Assuming that a client needs life insurance, the analysis proceeds to answer the following question: "How much life insurance does this client need?" It is likely that the typical financial planning client already has one or more forms of life insurance. The majority of clients have some **employer-provided group coverage**, unless they are self-employed. When analyzing the current situation, the financial planner's role is to determine whether the amount of coverage is sufficient to meet the client's financial goals and objectives.

#Remember

Anyone who is fully insured under Social Security is eligible to have his or her surviving spouse, and sometimes children, receive a lump sum death benefit of $255. Obviously, this lump sum payment is insufficient to pay for most final expenses; however, this is the maximum benefit available to those without a private insurance policy.

Five commonly used methods for determining a client's gross life insurance include the:

1. needs-based analysis approach;

2. simple income multiplier approach

3. human life value approach;

4. capital retention approach; and

5. income retention approach.

The most challenging, and arguably the most accurate of the methods for determining a client's insurance need, is the needs-based analysis approach. The easiest method, but also the most arbitrary, is the income multiplier approach. The human life value approach, the capital retention approach, and the income retention approach all rely on time value of money formulas that were discussed in Chapter 2.

One reason multiple methods are used to estimate life insurance needs is that financial planners cannot agree on the inputs or the best method. Additionally, each client's circumstances can make one approach superior to another at any given time – and the inputs for that are constantly changing. This points to several observations; namely, it is very important to understand that each calculation method is, in some way, flawed and the calculations should be periodically updated. Furthermore, understanding the flaws and adjustments for each method is crucial for preparing a thorough and defensible life insurance needs assessment. Each method for estimating life insurance needs is described below.

Needs-Based Analysis Approach

Of the five methods commonly used to estimate a client's life insurance need, the **needs-based analysis approach** is the most complicated but arguably the most accurate. Given the inherent complexity associated with the procedure, none of the certification examinations in the domain of financial planning test the use the technique; however, in practice, financial planners regularly use some type of needs-based analysis approach.

It is important to note that there is no standard formula or set of formulas that are used when conducting a needs-based analysis. Every financial planner either uses a firm approved methodology or an approach that has been personally developed with experience. A needs-based analysis should be designed to provide an estimate of the amounts needed for the following:

- Final expenses (e.g., medical bills and funeral expenses);

- Estate settlement expenses, including federal and state estate taxes and other settlement expenses (e.g., publication and mailing, administration, income taxes);

- Debt reduction (e.g., mortgage, credit card, auto, or other consumer debt);

- Transitional expenses (e.g., education or retraining for the survivor, child care or homemaker services, or other transitional needs);

- Special needs funding (e.g., education of the children, gifts or donations);

- Household expenses to maintain or readjust standard of living goals for the survivor, while the children are at home, if applicable;

- Household expenses to maintain or readjust standard of living goals for the survivor after the children leave home, if applicable;

- Funding to supplement the survivor's needs from age sixty to full retirement age, if needed;

- Funding to supplement or provide for the survivor's retirement.

Use of the life insurance needs-based analysis is predicated on a thorough investigation of a client's life objectives and an earnest attempt to quantify client goals and desires over the life cycle. Furthermore, a reasonable attempt should be made to project the exact cost of all future goals and the probable rate of return and effects of inflation.

Given the number of time value of money calculations involved in the analysis, care should be taken when projecting the future cost of a client's goals. Additionally, caution should be used when projecting which goals to fund (e.g., college costs, donations, etc.). It may be unwise to suggest funding certain goals through insurance proceeds (e.g., total mortgage payoff or excessive college expense funding) that in all likelihood would not have been available absent the death of the spouse, partner, or child. Furthermore, a prudent financial planner should consider how a client's feelings of grief, guilt, or other emotional distress might affect how life insurance proceeds will be used.

Income Multiplier Approach

The **income multiplier approach** is one of the most widely used methods because of its speed in assessing life insurance need. Financial planners who use this technique multiply the insured's current income by a multiplication factor arrive at an insurance need. Virtually any number from five to twenty-five could be used. For most situations, multiples between five and fifteen are typical; but, a planner could even justify a twenty-five as it would result in policy proceeds that would provide gross salary replacement income for life – assuming the 4 percent payout rule. The exact number is usually determined by evaluating a number of issues, including age (or years until retirement) of the insured, number and ages of financial dependents, amount and types of debt, percentage of household income lost, and availability and continuity of a survivor's income. The more factors that increase the need, the higher the multiplier used.

For example, a client with several dependent children or other ongoing financial demands could require a multiplier of twelve. A multiplier of seven might be appropriate for an individual with few or no dependents and a low level of debt and final expenses. However, even a multiple of fifteen could be inadequate for clients who are living well beyond their financial means or have a desire to leave a large legacy to children or charity. The choice of multiple is very subjective and almost always based on a financial planner's past experience in similar situations. The formula for this method is:

Current Need = Insured's Current Gross Income × Chosen Multiplier

Although gross income typically is used with this approach, net income can also be easily substituted. In either case, care must be taken when applying this formula as the only means of determining life insurance coverage needs. Because of the extremely general nature of this approach, even after years of experience, financial planners rarely use this as the sole measure. However, as mentioned earlier, this type of assessment can provide a quick, ballpark estimate before completing a more in-depth analysis.

Human Life Value Approach

The **human life value (HLV) approach** is used to determine the amount of income expected to be provided by the insured and therefore would need to be replaced upon the death of the insured. This approach bases the continuing stream of income from the life insurance benefits on two factors: (1) the current income of the insured and (2) the years remaining until the expected retirement of the insured. This projected income level can then be fine-tuned for self-maintenance costs, taxes, associated life insurance costs, other assets, or really any other reasonable adjustment. The calculation involves solving for the present value of the lost income stream using a present value of annuity calculation, where:

Equation 5.1: Present Value of an Annuity (PVA)

$$PVA = \frac{PMT}{i} \left[1 - \frac{1}{(1 + i)^n} \right]$$

PVA = present value of an annuity

PMT = insured's current income

i = projected after-tax rate of return on investment assets

n = insured's remaining work-life = (projected retirement age – current age)

This equation should be used to calculate each client's life insurance needs, and it should be recalculated annually or whenever a major career or lifestyle event occurs (e.g., career change, promotion, raise, loss of job) that results in a change in income. Recalculation is needed because the basic form of the HLV approach suffers from a major shortcoming; namely, the insured's income is assumed to remain static for the life of the survivor. However, it is possible to automatically adjust for this weakness by using the growing annuity formula and an estimation of the insured expected annual salary growth rate.

#Remember

Life insurance benefits are most likely to be received income tax free. So while either gross income or net income could be used for this and many other estimations of insurance need, so using grow income would overstate the amount of income actually received.

Equation 5.2: Present Value of a Growing Annuity Due

$$PVGA = \frac{PMT_1}{(i - g)} \left[1 - \frac{(1 + g)^n}{(1 + i)^n} \right]$$

While this adjustment is considered in greater detail a bit later in the chapter; there are two other flaws associated with the HLV approach. One, it does not consider other sources of income, and two it does not consider to what extent a decedent's income supported the family. Although normally associated with the income-retention approach, using a **replacement ratio** (also known as **family member support ratio**) to determine annual income need for the survivor(s) is one method that can be used to adjust for any possible overstatement in required income. Although little data exists on best practices, financial planners often use replacement ratios ranging from a high of 100 percent to a low of 70 percent. Commonly used standards of practice suggest that within a two-person household, the death of one adult reduces expenses by 30 percent. As household size increases, the percentage reduction in total living expenses declines. For example, for a surviving family of two, three, or four members, the expected reduction in expenses is 26, 22, and 20 percent, respectively. Expenses are generally reduced by only 2 percent with each additional surviving family member.

In addition to household size, other important factors in the choice of a replacement ratio include the survivor's earnings potential, the projected rate of return that can be earned on insurance proceeds, and other family issues, such as the need to eliminate debt or save for future goals. In effect, the more favorable the future looks for the survivor, the lower the replacement ratio that can be selected.

If the goal is merely to replace income until retirement, recalculation or the purchase of a **declining balance term insurance** policy could be appropriate because, as time goes by, there are fewer years until retirement. As the name implies, a declining balance term insurance policy is one where the annual premium remains constant, but the face value of the policy declines yearly. These policies are typically associated with mortgage products.

Capital Retention Approach

Similar to the HLV method, the **capital retention approach** bases the continuing stream of income from the life insurance benefits on the current income of the decedent. But unlike the HLV approach, the CR approach uses a **perpetuity** (i.e., an annuity payable forever) to determine the need. This method assumes that the survivor does not want to liquidate investment assets for current income. In other words, the capital is "retained." This income or payment level can be adjusted for self-maintenance costs, taxes, associated life insurance costs, or any other reasonable adjustment. Once the desired payment is determined, the resulting net income need is then divided by the projected rate of return of an investment portfolio, as shown in the following formula:

Equation 5.3 Present Value of Perpetuity (PVP)

$$PVP = \frac{PMT}{i}$$

PMT = insured's current gross income

i = projected rate of return on investment assets

The flaw associated with the capital retention approach is that it considers the income stream to continue in perpetuity. This is obviously not the case, because people do not live forever. Income will obviously not continue in perpetuity. Therefore, this equation can overestimate the required amount of insurance coverage needed. This flaw is compounded if an unreasonable discount rate is used. If the **discount rate** (i.e., what the client is projected to earn on any investments) is overestimated, the formula will understate the coverage need.

Because the CR approach assumes that a client's income needs continue forever, this calculation method normally results in the highest estimate of life insurance need. However, this approach also virtually guarantees that the survivor will not outlive the available capital. It is also the best approach for ensuring that future generations will receive an inheritance. Therefore, if providing for multiple generations is the goal, this life insurance estimation approach is worthy of consideration.

> *Self-Test 2*
>
> Pam, age 50, earns $165,000 per year. She plans to retire at age 67. If she can earn an annual rate of return equal to 8% how much life insurance does she need today using the HLV approach (rounded)?
>
> a. $750,000
>
> b. $1,000,000
>
> c. $1,500,000
>
> d. $2,500,000

Income Retention Approach

Unlike the previous two approaches, the **income retention approach** bases the continuing stream of income from the life insurance benefits on the expected income needs of the survivor. As such, this estimation procedure accounts for income earned or received by the survivor between the death of the decedent and the retirement of the survivor. Beginning with the gross income of the decedent, reductions can be made for:

1. any continuous income earned by the survivor;

2. the income taxes associated with the decedent's income;

3. any preretirement benefits received from Social Security or pensions; and

4. other reasonable adjustments (e.g., annuity payments, interest, or dividend income).

In other words, the amount of insurance purchased is assumed to cover only the net amount of income lost. As such, this life insurance estimation approach often yields the lowest approximation of required insurance coverage.

Equation 5.4: Present Value of an Annuity

$$PVA = \frac{PMT}{i} \left[1 - \frac{1}{(1 + i)^n} \right]$$

PVA = present value of an annuity

PMT = survivor's net income need after considering all sources of continuing income)

i = projected after-tax rate of return on investment assets

n = survivor's remaining work-life = (projected retirement age – current age)

Although the formula for this approach is the same as for the HLV method, a planner who uses this methodology must first complete an assessment of current annual income need (i.e., total annual expenses and savings). Once the amount for a single year has been determined, the financial advisor must use the present value of an annuity formula to calculate the required amount of current coverage that would provide adequate supplementary income over the survivor's future working lifetime. If there is a high probability that the survivor will remarry, and thus would not be overly dependent on insurance proceeds to maintain a standard of living, the income retention approach might be the most appropriate method to consider, despite the estimation of the lowest insurance coverage need.

Common Adjustments to the Annuity Calculations

Self-Test 3

Abed is 40 years old and is married to Sonya, also age 40. Abed earns $290,000 per year, whereas Sonya earns $100,000 annually. If they plan to retire at age 67 and can earn 7% on their investment assets, how much is Abed's life insurance need using the income retention approach (rounded)?

a. $1,200,000

b. $2,300,000

c. $3,000,000

d. $3,500,000

Although each of the life insurance calculation approaches discussed thus far uses one or more forms of present value equations, there are subtle differences among the methodologies, primarily in how the payment is determined. With the human life value and capital retention approaches, the payment (PMT) in the time value of money formula is based simply on the insured's gross or net income. In the income retention approach, the PMT is based on current required replacement income (i.e., gross income reduced by any sources of continuing cash flow available to the survivor). Another major difference between the income retention approach and the human life value approach is that the number of years for the projection period (n) is based on the *survivor's* remaining working life, rather than the insured's remaining working life. The distinguishing characteristic of the methods discussed thus far is that each can be manipulated to consider additional client specific information. All of the preceding calculations can be altered in several ways by changing how the variables are defined.

One of the most common adjustments is to change each formula to account for **beginning-of-period payments** rather than the typical end-of-year convention. Adding a (1 + i) to the basic form of the appropriate formula adjusts for this change. Making this adjustment increases the present value outcome by exactly one year of interest to account for the funds being withdrawn before expenses, instead of at the end of the year *after* the expenses. When using the beginning-of-period convention, it is customary to refer to the equation as an **annuity due** rather than as an ordinary annuity.

Another common adjustment involves applying a growth rate to the formula, thus becoming a **growing annuity**. All of the other variables remain the same as in the previous equations, but there is an additional variable to take into account (i.e., that the decedent's income would have continued to increase). This affects the present value need by assuming that the income would have increased at a fixed rate over the projected time period. The growth variable "g" should be a reasonable estimate of the average annual increase. This adjustment will always result in a higher present value need and, therefore, is a more conservative approach to life insurance needs analysis planning. The following growth-adjusted formula can be used to estimate this conservative approach:

$$PVGAD = \frac{PMT_1}{(i - g)} \left[1 - \frac{(1 + g)^n}{(1 + i)^n} \right] (1 + i)$$

This growth-adjusted formula can provide a more realistic measure of a client's life insurance need by assuming that the client's income will increase over time. By assuming a salary growth rate, the insured's life insurance need increases. However, it is more likely that the assets provided from the life insurance settlement will be sufficient to provide the surviving household or partner an increasing stream of income over the survivor's life.

> ### Using Living or Income Expenses in a Needs Analysis
>
> In some cases, financial planners substitute a household's current living expenses less the survivor's earnings for current income. The decision to make this choice will depend on a client's unique situation. The use of current living expenses will likely increase the amount of insurance needed. An alternative consideration involves whether current living expenses will be defined to include or exclude savings. Including current savings for the cost of education, for example, would increase, and potentially over-estimate, the insurance need.

For example, assume a client:

- earns a current annual income of $75,000;

- expects a 7 percent average after-tax return;

- anticipates a salary growth rate of 4 percent; and

- desires to work another twenty years.

With these assumptions, the amount of suggested life insurance coverage increases from about $850,000 to about $1,160,000 just by including a salary growth rate. Including a growth rate is prudent if salary is assumed to increase over the life cycle. However, because of this assumption, the total amount of insurance needed will initially be greater and may lessen the need to purchase additional life insurance in the future.

Determining the Additional Amount of Insurance a Client Should Purchase

Each of the estimation methods described above can be used to determine a client's gross life insurance need. To answer the question of how much life insurance a client needs (i.e., **net life insurance need**), currently available life insurance coverage(s) and selected assets should be subtracted from the gross need amount. First, the additional insurance need is calculated by subtracting the current face value of all in-force life insurance policies from the gross need, as shown below:

Additional insurance need = Gross estimated insurance need − Face value of in-force policies

Second, in some cases, a client's retirement assets, other investments, or additional assets can also be used to reduce the gross amount of insurance required. For example, a client may wish, after consulting with a financial planner, to use the equity in a principal residence to reduce the gross life insurance need. Another client, on the other hand, could determine, after consulting with her financial planner, that a conservative estimate of gross need less current insurance is most appropriate. Whatever the case or client, it is the financial planner's responsibility to help clients consider the complexities involved in determining which assets to use in case of death. Furthermore, the true emotional and financial impact of tapping the equity established in a principal residence must be carefully considered. This could mean selling the family home, which is a very significant lifestyle change following the loss of a loved one.

Ideally, a client's financial situation will be modeled using each of the preceding life insurance estimation approaches to determine the amount of insurance needed. In practice, however, few planners use more than one or two of these methods. A good approach involves triangulating results from at least three of the calculation methods. Figure 5.2 shows a hypothetical range of results from the different calculation methods that can be averaged into one dollar amount. **Triangulation** would take, for instance, the human life value ($555,323), the capital retention ($1,449,160), and the needs-based analysis approach results ($106,968), add them, and divide the sum by three. The average result, in this case $703,817, would flatten out the significant variances of each method alone. Triangulation can provide a more realistic indication of insurance needs. Note that the triangulation result of the three approaches mentioned is somewhere in the middle. In this regard, it is similar to the average need of $521,000 shown in Figure 5.2, which is the average of all five methods. However, taking an average can have its own drawbacks, because the different methods all measure different aspects of a client's financial situation.

Figure 5.2 Client's Net Life Insurance Need Based on Different Analysis Methods

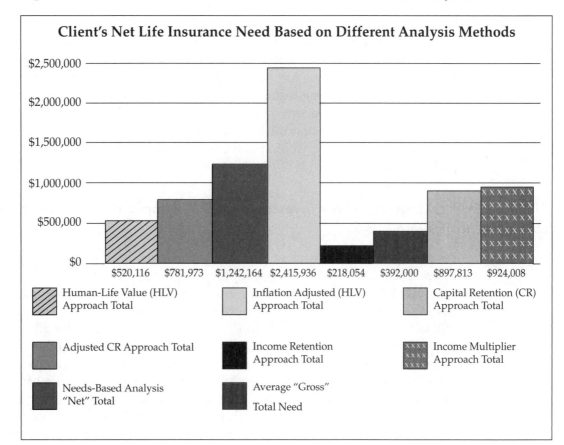

Once the amount of need is determined, that number must be converted into the most cost-effective purchase amount. **Face value break points** (e.g., more or less than $100,000 or more or less than $1 million), can significantly affect the cost of coverage. Companies refer to these price differentials as **insurance bands**, where more insurance could actually cost less than a lower amount in the previous band, or below the break point.

#Remember

Life insurance is sold in units. Each unit is equal to $1,000. Someone, for example, who purchases 100 units of insurance is purchasing $100,000 in face value coverage.

To illustrate, assume that a company's pricing bands are $500,000 to $999,999, followed by $1 million to $1,999,999, etc. Based on a projected need of $895,000, buying $1 million of coverage could actually be less expensive than the $865,000 because the cost of $1,000 of coverage decreases with progressively higher bands. This is only one among many underwriting considerations that can affect policy pricing. However, whether comparison shopping with an insurance professional or online, asking about the break points or bands, or experimenting with different amounts may provide significant cost savings and potentially more protection.

Life Insurance Planning Skills

When reviewing a client's current life insurance situation, as well as when framing recommendations, policy and contract features are major considerations. Implications for the income and estate tax situation of the client make the life insurance planning process more complex for some clients. Nevertheless, such considerations are important when drafting recommendations for new insurance products, if necessary, as well as when conducting periodic reviews of changes to a client's situation. An important role of the financial planner may be to work with the client and insurance, tax, and estate planning professionals, as applicable, to formulate or mitigate insurance planning issues.

Planning Skill 1: Understand the Investment and Tax Implications Associated with a Life Insurance Payout

Another potential adjustment that can be made to all of the life insurance estimation approaches presented in this chapter is to base the calculations on after-tax or "spendable" income. Because, in most cases, life insurance proceeds are income tax free, this methodology yields a more direct comparison to the income the survivor will actually be able to spend. To do this, simply substitute the after-tax income for the payment (PMT) previously shown. Although this adjustment has merit, care must be taken not to overestimate the tax advantages of life insurance proceeds. Generally, if the proceeds are received from a life insurance contract because of the death of the insured, the benefits are not considered taxable income and do not have to be reported. However, any earnings received on the death benefit would be considered taxable income. In other words, the periodic income derived from the invested settlement proceeds is taxable to the extent that it exceeds the original basis of the investment.

Another issue worthy of consideration is where the proceeds are invested. Generally, if the proceeds are taken as a lump sum and invested in taxable accounts, then the growth and/or income attributable to the account could be eligible for lower capital gains and qualified dividend tax rates. However, if the proceeds are left on deposit with the insurance company and paid as an installment or life annuity, then any interest received will be taxed at the beneficiary's marginal tax bracket.

Why does this matter when calculating life insurance need? The reason comes down to the following insight: the survivor can spend only after-tax income. Therefore, some discussion on how the proceeds would be received and taxed should be included in any comprehensive evaluation. IRS Publication 525, *Taxable and Nontaxable Income*, should be consulted for additional information on the extent to which life insurance proceeds are taxed.

Planning Skill 2: Understand and Differentiate Common Types of Insurance Products

An important step in the life insurance planning process, and certainly a step that must be completed before a financial planner can recommend additional or alternative life insurance, entails have a clear understanding of the different life insurance products available in the marketplace. Although there are numerous types and classifications of life insurance policies offered in the market, most fall within one of the following six categories:

1. **Term life insurance**: The most basic and least expensive life insurance policy, term life insurance provides coverage for a specific number of years, usually at a fixed annual premium rate. Although term policies can be renewable (this is an optional rider), new policies usually cost more, because the premium on term policies is tied to the age of the client, and older clients pay higher premiums. To overcome the problem of clients having to renew at higher premium costs and for longer terms than desired, some companies offer term policies that continue until age sixty-five or expected retirement age, but that can be purchased at any age.

> **Self-Test 4**
>
> All of the following require a policy holder to make a fixed premium payment, except:
>
> a. Whole Life
>
> b. Variable Life
>
> c. Universal Life
>
> d. None of the above

2. **Return-of-premium term insurance**: As the name implies, a return-of-premium term insurance policy refunds up to 100 percent of total premiums paid if the policy is held to the end of the term. In situations where a policy is terminated prematurely, only a portion of the premiums paid will be returned.

3. **Whole life insurance**: As the most basic form of **cash value insurance**, a whole life policy combines lifetime insurance protection with a continual buildup of cash value. Effectively, a portion of each premium payment is used to fund premiums associated with the purchase of life insurance, the costs associated with management of the policy, and cash value accumulation. A unique feature associated with whole life insurance is the level lifetime premium. *Loans* can be taken against the accrued cash value.

4. **Universal life insurance**: As an alternative cash value policy, universal life insurance allows a policy owner to increase, defer, or decrease the annual premium, and to withdraw accrued cash values (although this would reduce the policy's **death benefit**, which is defined as the policy's face value less outstanding loans and other expenses credited against the policy). Universal life insurance also allows a policy owner to change the face value periodically without **proof of insurability**. Like its cousin, whole life insurance, universal life policies build cash value on a guaranteed return basis (approximately 3 to 4 percent annually).

5. **Variable life insurance**: Variable life insurance offers policy owners a fixed annual premium; however, unlike whole- or universal life policies, a variable contract provides an opportunity to earn higher returns on the cash value of the policy. Accrued cash can be invested in stock, bond, and money market investments through subaccount funds. As such, the cash value and death benefit associated with a variable life insurance policy fluctuates over time. It is important to note that insurance companies rarely guarantee cash values within variable products.

6. **Variable universal life insurance (VUL):** As the name implies, variable universal life insurance is a blended product that borrows features from universal and variable policies. A VUL, as the product is sometimes known, offers policy owners flexible premiums and a wide variety of investment options within the cash account. As with all cash value policies, outstanding loans accrue interest and reduce the death benefit when paid.

Planning Skill 3: Know the Policy Characteristics When Choosing Between Cash Value and Term Policies

Before reviewing specific life insurance strategies, a planner should consider whether a client's current and projected needs are best met through a term or cash value policy. Figure 5.3 compares important attributes associated with term and cash value polices.

Figure 5.3 Comparison of Term and Cash Value Insurance Policy Characteristics

Characteristic	Term Renewable	Cash Value			
		Whole Life	Variable	Universal	VUL
Length of policy	1–30 years	Life of insured*	Life of insured*	Life of insured*	Life of insured*
Premium from year to year	Fixed or increasing	Fixed	Fixed	Flexible	Flexible
Cash value	No	Yes	Yes	Yes	Yes
Guaranteed cash value	NA	Yes	No	No	No
Interest earned on cash value	NA	Fixed	Based on investments chosen	Based on annually adjusted fixed rate	Based on investments chosen
Death benefits	Guaranteed	Guaranteed	Guaranteed minimum (may be less than face value)	Option A: guaranteed; Option B: guaranteed minimum (may be less than face value)	No guarantee (may be greater than or less than face value)
Ability to skip premiums	No	No	No	Yes	Yes

*Some policies terminate at a specified, but very advanced, age–typically no earlier than 95 years old.

NA = not applicable

The decision process involved when choosing between a term policy and a cash value policy must include several important factors. Figure 5.4 illustrates the general decision process use to select a life insurance product. The first factor is the goal of the policy. Will the policy be purchased to cover a temporary or permanent need? If the need is permanent or very long term, perhaps greater than twenty years, a client might want to consider a low-cost, cash value policy. Furthermore, if a financial planner determines that a client's current health status is poor or has the potential to deteriorate significantly, a cash value policy could be an appropriate recommendation. Cash value policies generally last for the life of a client (or at least to age one-hundred). Therefore, no additional medical tests would be required to maintain the policy, even if the client's subsequent risk class would make insurance prohibitively expensive. Some term policies are **guaranteed renewable** and do not require new medical tests. But the review cannot stop at the client's current health condition. Determining a client's family health history, lifestyle, and occupational risk factors can offer insights into the choice of a permanent or temporary type of coverage. For a client who reports numerous issues that could affect the underwriting decision, a permanent type of insurance could be more appropriate than a term policy.

Figure 5.4 Decision Tree for Choosing between a Cash Value Policy (CVP) and a Term Policy

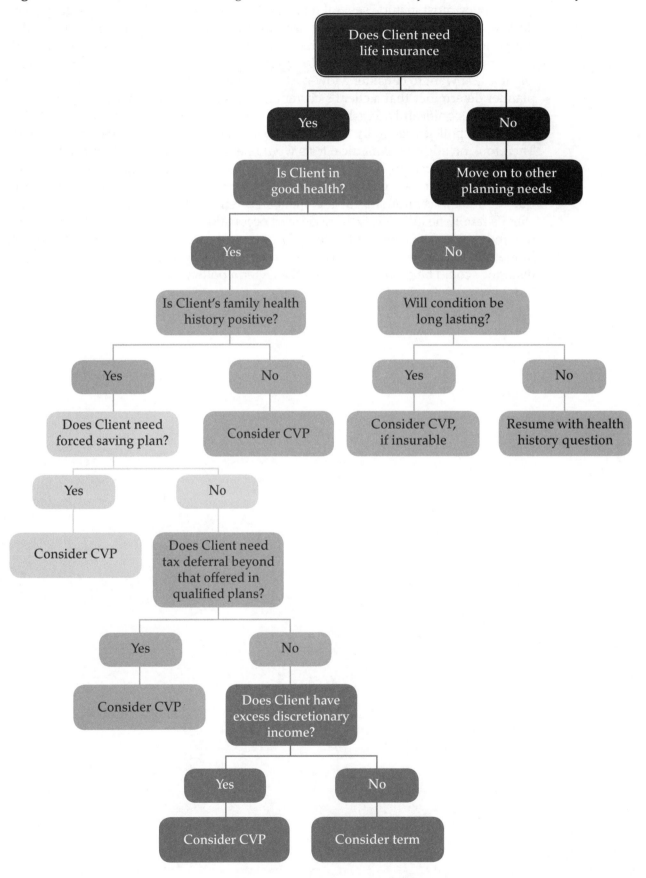

Medical history and coverage period are not the only important factors when determining which kind of policy to recommend. Cash value policies offer a savings component that is not generally available in a term policy. Under certain circumstances, a client might want the **forced savings** or investment availability of a cash value policy. Access to and the amount of tax-advantaged investments a client has available should be considered. Clients who earn significant yearly income will find that they are unable to take full advantage of 401(k), 403(b), 457(b), and other qualified defined contribution plans, leaving high levels of income subject to taxation. This is especially true for business

Twists on Term Insurance

Some new term policies, generally with a longer term, provide a return of some premiums, with payment of a death benefit after the policy term ends. Also, some term policies can be converted into permanent coverage.

owners. High income earning clients may need a way to invest a significant amount of money each year into other tax-deferred investments. Life insurance can serve this purpose. However, it is important to note that putting too much money into a life insurance contract can violate the seven-pay test and result in the contract being classified as a modified endowment contract (with less favorable tax treatment), as discussed later in this chapter.

Finally, term life policies provide coverage at a fraction of the cost of a cash value policy if the client's lifestyle, occupation, and health status suggest no underwriting concerns, and the client:

- qualifies for but does not maximize contributions to defined contributions plans, individual retirement accounts, and other forms of tax-advantaged investments;

- is not a business owner; and

- needs only temporary insurance coverage.

When a cash value policy is chosen, a few more considerations must be addressed. The following questions can be used to guide the decision-making process: Will the policy be funded in full at the time of purchase or over the life of the contract? Will the cash value policy offer an array of investment choices through subaccounts or simply be a "savings account" with the rate of return controlled by the insurance company? If a cash value insurance policy is selected, will it be whole life, universal life, variable life, or variable universal life (VUL)? The decision tree shown in Figure 5.5 can be used to gauge which cash value policy might be the most appropriate for a client.

Figure 5.5 Decision Tree to Guide the Choice of Cash Value Policy

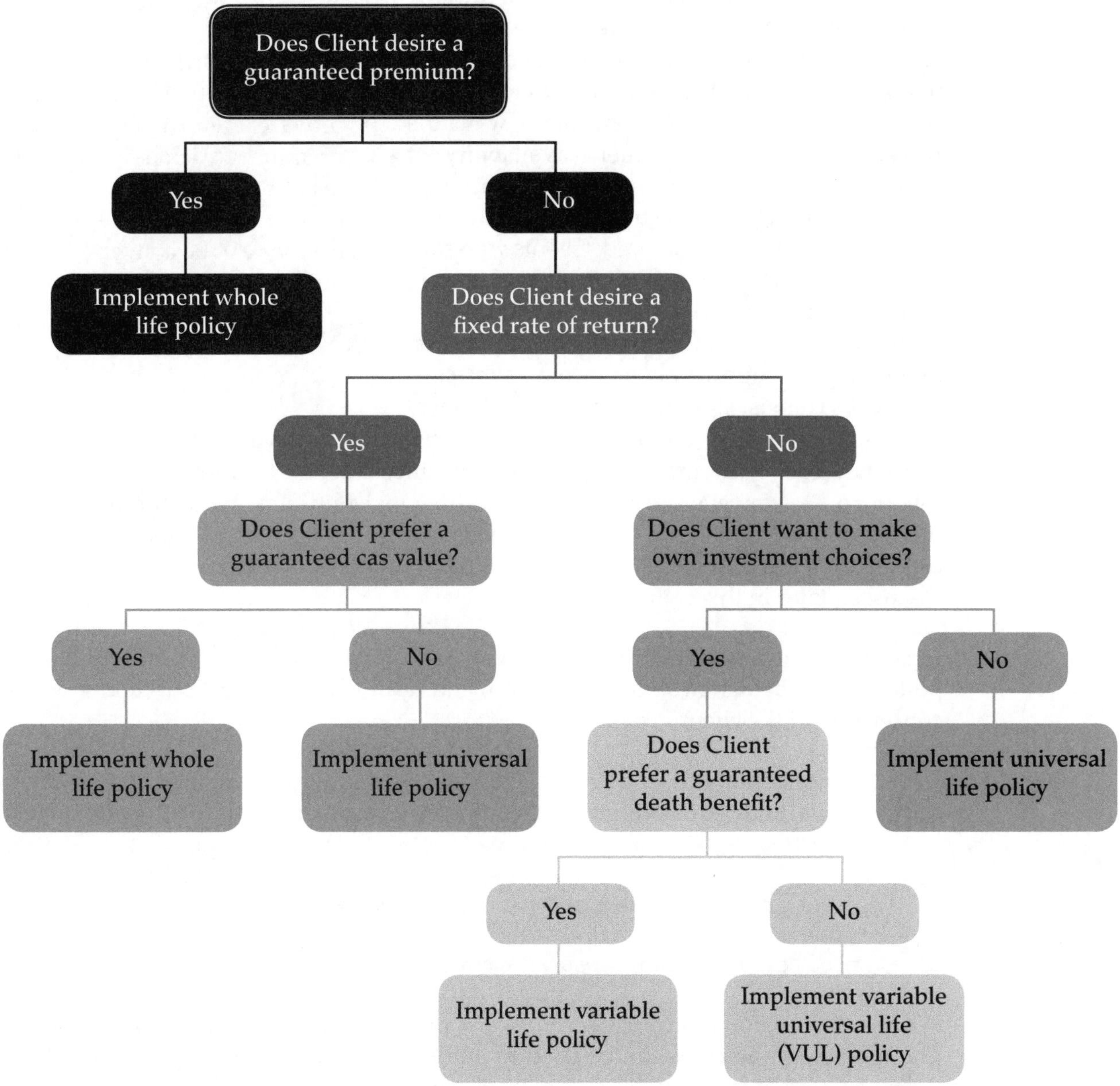

Planning Skill 4: Understand Common Life Insurance Terms and Definitions

Once all currently in-force policies have been identified, it is important to document the ownership, or titling, of each. Whenever a life insurance contract is underwritten, three parties must be identified within the contract. The **policy owner** is the person or entity who has the right to name one or more beneficiaries. The owner is also entitled to all participating dividends and has the responsibility for paying the insurance premium. Policy owners can, at their discretion, surrender, transfer, or cancel a policy. A policy owner is any person or entity with an insurable interest in the insured, so it can be the insured, a family member, an employer, or a trust. The policy owner must provide evidence of an **insurable interest**, which is defined as possibly incurring a financial loss resulting from the death of the insured. The **insured** named in a policy is the person whose death prompts payment of the insurance policy's face value.

The **beneficiary** can be a person or entity (e.g., trust, business, or nonprofit organization) who receives the proceeds from a policy at the death of the insured. Generally, an owner can change a beneficiary unless the beneficiary choice was considered irrevocable at the time the policy was issued. Two types of beneficiaries exist. A **primary beneficiary** receives the proceeds of a life insurance policy when the insured dies. A beneficiary can be designated revocable (can be changed) or irrevocable. When a beneficiary is named irrevocable, the owner cannot change the beneficiary on the policy without the prior consent of the irrevocable beneficiary. Naming an irrevocable beneficiary also changes the owner's ownership rights. The owner cannot receive dividends, take a loan against the policy, pledge the policy as collateral for a debt, or surrender the policy without the written permission of the irrevocable beneficiary. These examples of the right to change, use, modify, or benefit from a policy are typically referred to as **incidents of ownership**.

> **Self-Test 5**
>
> Which of the following is an incidents of ownership?
>
> a. The right to change the beneficiary.
>
> b. The ability to modify the contract.
>
> c. The right to use the policy as collateral.
>
> d. All of the above

A **contingent beneficiary** receives the proceeds in the event the primary beneficiary has predeceased the insured. Married clients with children often list their minor children as contingent beneficiaries to life insurance policies. Unfortunately, this can be a costly mistake, both financially and in relation to the speed at which policy proceeds can be distributed. Most states do not allow a child under the age of eighteen to own monetary assets. Therefore, most insurance companies will not pay benefits directly to a minor. Because children cannot legally receive a death benefit, if a guardian or a trust (with the minor as the beneficiary) has not been named in a will, then the court will appoint a guardian or require that a trust be set up to manage the proceeds from the life insurance payout. The insurance company can hold the assets for the minor until a court-approved or court-appointed guardian is named to oversee the distribution and investment of insurance proceeds for the minor child. Without proper planning for the distribution of the proceeds to a minor child, the court can require that funds be held in an FDIC-insured account. This safe alternative could, however, preclude sufficient earnings to meet the child's future needs.

An individual can be the owner, insured, and beneficiary of the same policy; however, this is not generally recommended. The most common form of ownership is for the insured to own the policy. However, estate tax consequences must be considered. The **face amount of the policy** (i.e., the dollar value of the policy when issued to be received by the beneficiary) will be included in the gross estate of an insured owner who possesses any incidents of ownership. The policy proceeds will also be included in the gross estate if the insured or "my estate" or "for the benefit of my estate" is named as the beneficiary. This might not be an estate tax problem right away because of the unlimited marital deduction, because any assets the insured/owner left to the spouse are exempt from federal estate taxes. However, the additional value could increase the estate value for the surviving spouse, thus making it subject to estate taxes—often referred to as a "second to die" issue. On the other hand, if the proceeds are payable to children of the insured with the insured as owner, then the proceeds would be subject to estate tax if the value of the estate exceeds the estate tax exclusion.

Even when each party of an insurance contract is a separate person or entity, another problem, known as an **unholy trinity**, can occur. Consider a situation where a wife owns a policy in which the husband is the insured and the non-minor children are the beneficiaries. When the husband dies, the children will receive the insurance proceeds on a tax-free basis; however, the surviving spouse, as the owner, could owe a *federal gift tax* on the policy proceeds if the amount exceeds the annual gift exclusion and the total amount of the wife's gifts exceeds the lifetime gift tax exemption amount. The situation can become more troublesome if the wife, while the husband is still alive, transfers ownership of the policy or changes the beneficiaries—both of which are legal actions available to owners.

Planning Skill 5: Recognize Approaches to Transferring Policy Ownership

Use Caution When Terminating a Policy

Underwriting issues are an important consideration in the decision to replace an insurance policy. The cost of insurance, based on the YPT formula, may be high suggesting that the policy should be replaced. However, a review of a client's insurability factors might suggest that it would be a mistake to cancel the policy because the client might either be unable to purchase or afford a new policy because of the higher risk classification. A basic financial planning rule is this: policies should only be canceled or terminated *until* after a new policy is in place.

Two methods are available to change the ownership of a policy: ownership can be transferred to another individual/ entity or to a trust. Transfer to another individual or entity with an insurable interest as a gift is irrevocable, and the value of the policy proceeds will be brought back into the estate if the transfer occurs within three years of the owner's death. If the current cash value plus any unearned premiums paid at the time of the gift exceed the annual gift tax exclusion ($14,000 in 2016), gift taxes are assessed and will be due upon the death of the original owner. Gift splitting with a spouse is allowed.

The second alternative is to establish an **irrevocable life insurance trust**, or **ILIT**, and transfer the policy ownership. To remove the policy from the estate, an owner must give up all incidents of ownership. There are costs related to establishing and managing an ILIT. With an ILIT, an owner can ensure that premiums are paid, and with careful planning for the trust, the insured can gift money to the trust up to the annual exclusion amount to pay the premiums. The new owner should immediately update the beneficiary form. Furthermore, owning life insurance in an ILIT is a very effective way to mitigate tax and privacy issues for domestic partners.

Planning Skill 6: Know How to Evaluate an Existing Policy

Once all currently in-force coverage is identified, it is likely that some policies should be retained while others should be replaced, canceled, or otherwise altered. Financial planners who make replacement recommendations without conducting a **policy replacement analysis** are overlooking an important portion of their professional responsibility to their clients. It is very important to review whether the forms and types of insurance held by a client are appropriate to meet the client's current and longer-term needs. If changes can be made to existing policies to better meet a client's needs, then every attempt should be made to do so.

There may be times when existing policies must be replaced. Whether because of a change in the client's situation or a change in the tax laws, trying to force fit older policies generally does not work well. Another issue that can arise is that the current policy could still be the right kind or face amount, but the insurance company's financial situation has changed. Given the importance of a well-managed company to invest insurance product assets potentially over several decades, it is important that financial planners assess each insurance company's financial strength and default risk. Five third-party rating agencies and their range of ratings are shown in Figure 5.6. It is wise for planners to encourage the use of products from companies rated "A" or higher by any of the rating agencies. A planner may need to recommend replacing insurance products issued by companies with lower ratings.

Figure 5.6 Third-Party Insurance Company Rating Agencies

Rating Agency	Safety Ratings	Criteria
A.M. Best	A++ to F	Insurance company's ability to meeting policyholder and contractual obligations based on four size categories.
Demotech's	A'' (Unsurpassed) to S (Substantial) to M (Moderate) to L (Licensed)	Measures of solvency
Fitch Ratings	AAA to D	Insurance company's claims-paying ability, financial fundamentals, capitalization, debt rating leverage, and asset quality.
Moody's	Aaa to C	Insurance company's ability to meet policyholder obligations by focusing on investment portfolio and asset/liability structure.
Standard & Poor's	AAA to C	Insurance company's claims-paying ability.
Weiss Ratings	A to F	Adherence to general accounting principles.

Next, attention can turn to policy cost considerations. Term policies can be compared on the basis of premium dollars per $1,000 of coverage, as long as comparisons are for similar periods and face amounts. The complexity of cash value policies demands more rigorous review. Financial planners use a number of methodologies to evaluate the cost-effectiveness of cash value life policies. Commonly used methods include the **traditional net cost method,**[1] the **interest-adjusted net cost method,**[2] the **internal rate of return yield method,**[3] and the **yearly price per thousand method** (also known as the **yearly rate of return method**).[4] One approach that provides a quick insight into the "maintain or replace" question for a cash value policy is the yearly-price-per-thousand formula.

The yearly-price-per-thousand formula is effective in determining the cost per thousand a client pays for a policy. Using established benchmark costs, it is possible to compare cash value policies based on the age of the insured. This method is particularly well suited for analyzing whole life and universal life insurance policies.

The information needed to calculate the yearly-price-per-thousand formula is generally available from the insurance company underwriting the policy. The **yearly-price-per-thousand method formula** is:

Equation 5.5: Yearly Price per Thousand of Coverage (YPT)

$$YPT = \left[\frac{(PMT + CV_0) \times (1 + i) - (CV_1 + Div)}{(DB - CV_1) \times (0.001)} \right]$$

YPT = yearly cost per thousand in coverage

PMT = annual premium payment

CV_0 = cash value at beginning of the year

CV_1 = cash value at end of the year

i = projected after-tax rate of return

Div = current policy dividend

DB = death benefit (most often face value)

The interest rate used in the formula should be the rate of interest that a financial planner and client estimate could be earned in another investment with similar safety and liquidity characteristics as those offered in a life insurance policy. The rate of return should be equivalent to a net after-tax yield. Once the cost per thousand of coverage is calculated, this amount is compared to benchmark price recommendations shown in Figure 5.7.

Figure 5.7 Benchmark Premium Prices Based on the Yearly-price-per-thousand Formula

Age of Client	Yearly Price per $1,000 (Benchmark)
Less than 30	$1.50
30–34	$2.00
35–39	$3.00
40–44	$4.00
45–49	$6.50
50–54	$10.00
55–59	$15.00
60–64	$25.00
65–69	$35.00
70–74	$50.00
75–79	$80.00
80–84	$125.00

Source: Adapted from Belth, J. M. *Life Insurance: A Consumer's Handbook*, 2nd Ed. (Bloomington, IN: Indiana University Press, 1985).

If the yearly-price-per-thousand formula cost is less than the benchmark price, the client should maintain the policy. If the cost is greater than the benchmark price but less than two times the benchmark price, the client should still retain the policy. Only when the cost per thousand is greater than two times the benchmark price should a client consider replacing or exchanging a policy. The new policy should be priced favorably according to the yearly-price-per-thousand formula guidelines.

In this example, the yearly-price-per-thousand formula was calculated for whole life policies owned by Adam and Katherine, two hypothetical clients. Note that the formula inputs are the same for both policies. However, the interpretation varies because of the couple's age difference. Adam is 36 years old and Katherine is thirty-four.

$$YPT = \left[\frac{(PMT + CV_0) \times (1 + i) - (CV_1 + Div)}{(DB - CV_1) \times (0.001)} \right]$$

$$YPT = \left[\frac{(600 + 475) \times (1{,}069) - (500 - 0)}{(500{,}000 - 500) \times (0.001)} \right] = \$13.11$$

$13.11 > \$6.00$ or two times the $3.00 benchmark

Determining the Tax Status of Insurance Policy Dividends

Dividends earned on life insurance and endowment policies are typically not taxable. The IRS considers dividends a return of premium to the client. However, dividends are taxable *if* total dividends received exceed total premiums paid. This is rarely the case. And, if dividends remain with the insurance company, and the dividends earn interest, the interest is fully taxable.

Adam is currently paying $13.11 per $1,000 of life insurance coverage, whereas the recommended benchmark for a male his age is $3.00 per $1,000 of life insurance coverage. Given that the premium cost per $1,000 of coverage is more than four times greater than the recommended yearly-price-per-thousand benchmark, a recommendation to replace the policy (assuming the coverage is needed) should be made. However, additional analysis might also be warranted to gain a better understanding about why Adam's premium is so high. It could be that Adam is a very poor underwriting risk, in which case his advisor may not be able to obtain a policy quote with a lower premium.

This type of analysis offers the client several benefits. First, Adam might be able to stop paying for an overpriced policy. If so, the premium savings can then be used to purchase additional life insurance, if needed, or redirected to other financial goals. Second, if the client is a poor underwriting risk, this could uncover additional planning needs. There may be a need for a larger emergency fund, to increase life coverage on other financial dependents, or to alter lifestyle or other habits to mitigate the detrimental underwriting factors. Alternative sources of insurance through Adam's employer or other groups could offer additional coverage.

Replacing or consolidating policies, for any reason, must be done with care. The financial planner must ensure that this recommendation is handled in the most advantageous manner possible, so that the client does not lose protection or incur undue additional expense. Furthermore, it is important that any existing policy not be terminated until a new policy is permanently in place.

Planning Skill 7: Use Policy Nonforfeiture Options to the Client's Advantage

Both state and federal laws offer consumers options for terminating life insurance policies. State laws specify standard nonforfeiture options that companies must offer policyholders. Further, the Internal Revenue Code offers certain tax advantages for policy ownership. These consumer protections, as well as their implications for use in life insurance planning, are briefly considered here.

A **nonforfeiture provision** is available to owners of cash value life insurance policies. This provision gives a policy owner the ability to use the cash value of a policy to maintain some life insurance coverage without paying additional premiums or subjecting the cash value to current income taxation. Owners of cash value policies have three broad alternatives if they discontinue premium payments (i.e., cancel the policy), as shown in the Figure 5.8.

Figure 5.8 Sample Whole life Insurance Nonforfeiture Table

End of Policy Year	Cash/Loan Value	Paid-up Insurance	Extended-term Insurance Years	Days
1	$14	$30	0	152
2	$174	$450	4	182
3	$338	$860	8	65
4	$506	$1,250	10	344
5	$676	$1,640	12	360
6	$879	$2,070	14	335
7	$1,084	$2,500	16	147
8	$1,293	$2,910	17	207
9	$1,504	$3,300	18	177
10	$1,719	$3,690	19	78
11	$1,908	$4,000	19	209
12	$2,099	$4,300	19	306
13	$2,294	$4,590	20	8
14	$2,490	$4,870	20	47
15	$2,690	$5,140	20	65
16	$2,891	$5,410	20	66
17	$3,095	$5,660	20	52
18	$3,301	$5,910	20	27
19	$3,508	$6,150	19	358
20	$3,718	$6,390	19	317
Age 60	$4,620	$7,200	18	111
Age 65	$5,504	$7,860	16	147

Source: Sample Life Insurance Policy (no date). Education and Community Services, American Council of Life Insurance, Washington, DC.

The hypothetical policy in the sample nonforfeiture table is for a 35-year-old male smoker; the first premium is $241.60 for a policy with a face value amount of $10,000. The premium includes a disability waiver of premium ($4.30) and an accidental death rider ($7.80). Together, these add $12.10 to the base premium of $229.50.

First, the client can request that the insurance company return the **cash surrender value** of the policy, as shown in the second column of Figure 5.8. The value of the cash received in excess of the net paid premiums is subject to federal and state income taxation. (Also, note that the amount in the second column is that available for a policy loan.) Second, the cash value of the policy can be used to purchase a fully **paid-up cash**

value policy. This will result in a significantly reduced face value policy, as shown in the third column. The benefit, however, is that no additional premiums will have to be paid. Third, the cash value can be used to purchase a **fully paid term policy**. The face value of the original cash value policy is retained in this case. The length of the term policy is then determined by the amount of the cash value available in the policy.

For example, as shown in the sample nonforfeiture table, at the end of thirteen years of premium payments, the surrender cash (or loan) value of $2,294 is available to the policy owner. Almost $5,000 of paid-up whole life coverage is available with no additional premium payments. Or the whole life policy could be converted to a paid-up twenty-year and eight-day term policy with a $10,000 face amount. Conversely, at the end of policy year 2, with a small cash value account of only $174, extended term coverage would be available for only four years and 182 days.

One of the nonforfeiture options could be appropriate for clients who purchased an overpriced policy or for clients who later find that a portion of the cash value distribution will be taxable. The nonforfeiture provision could also be useful to clients who made the mistake of buying a cash value policy when a more reasonably priced term policy would have provided the necessary protection. Retirees, or other insureds, that no longer need the insurance coverage or have dependents to support, may find that a smaller amount of coverage would be appropriate.

However, two caveats must be considered. First, the nonforfeiture option should not be implemented until a thorough analysis has been conducted and any new policy is in force. The analysis may need to include consultations with both insurance and tax professionals. Second, life insurance obtained by using a nonforfeiture option could be costly compared to policies available in the marketplace. Nevertheless, the continued insurance protection might be a better alternative than the cash value, depending on the need for cash or the amount of taxes due.

Although the insurance company will issue a 1099-R, showing the gross payout from surrendering the policy, proactive planners should calculate the tax consequences when advising clients on their options. To determine if taxes are due, calculate if the gross proceeds from the policy exceed the cost basis. If so, any taxable gain is subject to ordinary income tax and should be reported on the applicable income tax form as "other income." The following example illustrates the process for a $250,000 policy for a thirty-five-year-old non-smoker, who paid $4,430 in annual premiums for ten years.

Total premiums paid:	$44,300
Total dividends received:	-$12,404
Cost basis:	$31,896
Cash surrender value:	$55,487
Cost basis:	-$31,896
Taxable gain:	$23,591

Individual client situations, such as premiums paid for additional benefit riders or any outstanding loan amounts change the calculation. Dividends are not taxed upon surrender as they are normally considered to be a rebate or return of premium. This is true regardless of whether the dividends were taken as cash, used to pay premiums, or used to purchase additional paid-up coverage. If the cash surrender value does not exceed the cost basis, then the proceeds are received tax free and any "loss" does not offset gains from other investments. In the example above, the insured would owe $5,898 in taxes, assuming the 25 percent marginal tax bracket.

Planning Skill 8: Use a Section 1035 Exchange Option as a Way to Procure Different Coverage

A Section 1035 exchange is another alternative to the nonforfeiture options, especially if the policy has taxable appreciation. The Section 1035 exchange offers more options for **policy replacement**. Internal Revenue code Section 1035 allows for a policy owner to exchange a life insurance policy (**contract**) for another life insurance contract on a tax-free basis. In general, a **Section 1035 exchange** allows a policy owner to transfer the cash value from one policy to another without paying taxes on the distribution. This is substantially similar to a tax-free "rollover" of a policy's cash value.

Five specific types of Section 1035 exchanges are allowed.

1. A currently owned life policy for a newly issued policy;

2. An endowment contract policy for another endowment contract, with certain restrictions, or for an annuity contract;

3. A currently owned life policy for an annuity contract;

4. An annuity contract for another annuity contract; or

5. An annuity or life insurance contract for a long-term care contract.

In other words, it is possible to exchange a currently owned policy for another newly issued policy by the same or another insurance company. The process of transferring policies on a tax-free basis is analogous to conducting a custodian-to-custodian rollover of qualified retirement plan assets. Although Code section 1035 can be used to exchange life insurance policies, the majority of Section 1035 exchanges involve annuity contracts. Nevertheless, on the whole, a Section 1035 tax-free exchange strategy should be considered whenever a currently owned cash value policy is disadvantaged in terms of performance or premium cost. It is important to keep careful records of the exchange for tax purposes and to be certain the new policy is in force before cancelling the original policy.

Planning Skill 9: Use Accelerated Death Benefits or Viatical Settlements to Assist Clients with Health Issues

Chronically or terminally ill clients have several options available to access policy funds prior to the death of the insured. Policy provisions, known as living benefit riders or accelerated death benefits, may be available, depending on the policy. But they may not be available in the client's insurance products. The other option, known as a **viatical settlement**, involves the sale of a life insurance policy to a third party. In either case, the funds can be used to pay for medical or pharmaceutical expenses, caregivers or living expenses. These options benefit individuals who have exhausted other funds or who want the insurance proceeds to make the end of life more comfortable for themselves or others. For federal income tax purposes, the amount received by an insured client from an accelerated death benefit or a viatical settlement is treated as an amount paid under the life insurance contract by reason of the insured's death and thus is generally tax-free. For more information see Publication 525, Taxable and Nontaxable Income.

Although exact definitions may change from company to company, an insurance company may pay **accelerated death benefits** to the insured when the insured is critically, chronically or terminally ill. This is done with a policy feature or a rider(s) that is added to the policy either at the time of purchase or, in some cases, to a preexisting policy. If added, the cost of the rider must be considered relative to the client's perceived need or medical history, and cost comparisons among companies should be considered.

In the case of a policy feature or rider, a portion of the face value of the policy (e.g., typically a stated amount or percentage, such as 25 to 95 percent) is paid to the client once certain medical situations are documented, and the balance is paid at the death of the insured. Some states set specific limits on the percentage amount that can be paid out, while some restrictions are set by the insurance companies. Service or interest charges may apply, and there may be requirements that the policy be in effect for a stated period of time before accelerated benefits are available. Accelerated death benefits paid to the chronically ill on a **per diem** or other periodic basis are excludable up to a limit of $330 per day, per the IRS. Anything over that amount is considered taxable income.

Qualifications for benefits vary depending on the policy. A person with a **chronic illness** is one who has been medically certified, within the previous twelve months, to require:

1. substantial assistance because of the inability to perform at least two activities of daily living (i.e. eating, toileting, transferring, bathing, dressing, and continence); or

2. substantial supervision because of cognitive impairment.

Critical illness benefits are triggered by a diagnosis of specifically listed conditions, while the diagnosis of expected death within two years would trigger terminal illness benefits.

Viatical settlements occur when a terminally ill insured client sells a life insurance policy to a third party. Settlement values vary greatly, but would typically be for 40 to 85 percent of the death benefit and be most dependent of the insured's life expectancy. The viatical settlement provides the dying person with immediate funds; the face value of the policy is paid to the viatical holder at the death of the insured. Individual state law defines terminal illness. Generally someone has a **terminal illness** if life expectancy is twenty-four months or less from the date that a physician certifies that death is reasonably expected as a result of the insured's illness or physical condition. When considering a viatical settlement, it is important to consider immediate benefits to the insured, the household, and caregivers compared to the longer-term effect of no insurance proceeds for the beneficiary. If chosen, the cost of the viatical settlement should be compared across different companies to get the maximum benefit for the client.

Planning Skill 10: Use a Life Settlement to Assist Elderly Clients

For elderly clients who no longer need life insurance or estate tax protection, or can no longer afford the premium costs, **life settlements** or selling a policy to a life settlement company offers several benefits.   First, to be worthwhile, the settlement must be for more than the cash surrender value. Second, the client benefits from the immediate availability of the funds for reinvesting, supplementing income, or meeting medical needs that do not qualify for a viatical settlement. Third, the client avoids the premiums required to maintain the policy, which is a form of future savings or addition to the client's cash flow. At the death of the insured, the face value of the policy is paid to the settlement company.

When considering a life settlement, it is important to recognize that life settlement companies prefer that the insured be at least sixty-five to seventy years old with a policy providing a minimum face value of $250,000; some companies will consider $100,000 policies, depending on the age and health of the insured. Other guidelines apply that could affect the availability of a settlement offer. Policy owners with a life expectancy of less than twelve years are preferred, but those in declining health could receive a higher offer. The policy should have been in force for two years, and the client should be expected to live for at least two more years. Contingent on the cost basis of the policy, the cash surrender value, and the settlement offer, the life settlement payment could be taxable. If a life insurance policy is surrendered or sold for a lump sum amount prior to the death of the insured, any amount received in excess of the net premiums paid is taxable as income. Losses are not recognized for tax purposes. Fees or commissions also apply, so it is important to consider offers from multiple settlement firms to get the maximum benefit for the client.

Planning Skill 11: Identify the Role of Annuities in the Insurance Planning Process

Annuities, once considered the product choice of retirees and excessively risk-averse investors, have increasingly gained popularity as a way to lock in higher rates of return while reducing volatility risk. For many investors, annuity products have replaced fixed-income holdings in asset allocation models. Given the importance and use of annuities, it is important for financial planners to understand the definitions and general operating characteristics of these products.

Annuities are products marketed and sold by insurance companies, and they come in two general forms: deferred and immediate income, although it is also possible to purchase hybrid annuity products. A **deferred annuity** is a tax-deferred investment that can be funded with a lump sum, a series of payments, or a combination of these two approaches. When a deferred annuity is purchased, the owner must choose either a fixed or variable annuity option. Investors who are interested primarily in security and complete minimization of variability in the investment account typically purchase a **fixed annuity**. Fixed deferred annuities are similar to certificates of deposit in that the insurance company provides a guaranteed interest rate on the account balance for a fixed number of years. However, unlike certificates of deposit, FDIC insurance does not apply. At the end of the period, the interest rate credited to the account can be changed.

Variable deferred annuities tend to be popular with younger and more aggressive investors. The term **variable annuity** refers to the type of investments held within the annuity account. Whereas a fixed deferred annuity provides a guaranteed interest rate on assets in the annuity, the rate of return on a variable product is based on the investments held in the account. Usually, variable products offer mutual funds and guaranteed investment contracts as investment options. It is very important to note that, unlike typical mutual funds that can often be purchased without a commission, fund and investment choices within annuity products tend to be more expensive. Insurance companies typically charge fees and expenses above and beyond what the funds levy. Furthermore, almost all deferred annuity products contain **early distribution penalties** that can last up to fifteen years, meaning any distribution will be reduced by the **surrender charge**. Together, fees, expenses, and surrender charges make annuity products an expensive investment alternative.

Financial planners can recommend either a fixed or variable deferred annuity product to clients who have maximized their use of qualified retirement plans and other tax-deferred investment alternatives. Because a 10 percent penalty could be imposed on distributions before age 59½, these products are inappropriate for clients seeking short-term or emergency fund investment choices. It is also important to remember that annuities avoid probate by means of beneficiary designation. Account values can be paid as a lump sum over a period not to exceed five years, or as a lifetime stream of income at the death of the annuitant. A beneficiary spouse can elect to assume ownership of the annuity, thus maximizing the tax deferral of the product.

Immediate income annuities represent a fast growing segment of the annuity marketplace. Income annuities are usually purchased by retirees or others who need a guaranteed (although not federally insured) source of income for life or a fixed period of time. The primary difference between a deferred annuity and an income annuity is that immediate income annuity holders receive income from the annuity on a regular basis rather than deferring income to a later period. (A deferred annuity can be converted to an income annuity at a future point in time.) When a fixed-income annuity is purchased, the insurance company guarantees an income stream for a given period of time. Some annuity products can even include a **cost-of-living rider**, which is a form of inflation protection. It is important to note, however, that this guarantee is based on the insurer's claims-paying ability and financial strength. As is the case when purchasing any insurance product, financial planners should always assess the strength of an insurance company before basing a purchase recommendation on either the rate of return offered or the commission provided to the planner.

Although not as popular as fixed-income annuities, **immediate variable annuity** products are also available. To maintain certain tax advantages, insurance companies are required to guarantee income for life from a variable annuity; however, they are not required to guarantee the amount of each payment. In effect, the level of payout from a variable annuity depends on the investment choices made in the account. This product is most appropriate for younger clients who have a relatively high level of risk tolerance.

Distributions and rules associated with immediate annuities can get quite complex. Income payments from annuity products vary by company, but generally the client's gender, age, and purchase value are used to estimate either guaranteed or projected income from an annuity product. Those who choose a variable annuity can receive more or less than the projected annual income amount based on the underlying performance of the investments in the account. When a client is married, a **joint and survivors annuity distribution** choice can be selected. A 100 and 50 percent survivor benefit is traditional.

To illustrate the distribution of annuity income, consider a sixty-one-year old male client who purchases a $500,000 immediate fixed-income annuity.[5] A typical annuity product would guarantee him a monthly payment of $2,204. At death, his spouse, also age sixty-one, would receive no survivor benefit. A 100 percent guaranteed lifetime survivor benefit option would reduce the monthly income stream to $2,181, with all payments ending at the death of the wife. A 50 percent survivor option would generate $2,519 per month in current income and leave $1,259 per month to the surviving spouse, with all payments ending at her death.

> **Self-Test 7**
>
> Swarn would like to purchase an product that will provide him with lifetime income starting immediately. For planning purposes, he would like a guaranteed income stream for the remainder of his life. Swarn should purchase a(n):
>
> a. Deferred Annuity
>
> b. Variable Annuity
>
> c. Immediate Fixed Income Annuity
>
> d. Immediate Variable Income Annuity

Many financial planners and clients worry about the irrevocable nature of immediate income annuity products. Although it is true that if a traditional product is purchased (thus maximizing current monthly income) all asset values held in the annuity will revert to the insurance company at the death of the owner or last beneficiary, certain income distribution alternatives reduce the possibility of purchasing an annuity, receiving a few payments, passing away, and forfeiting the present value of the asset. Today, most insurance companies provide a ten- or twenty-year **guaranteed payout schedule**. Using the preceding example, if the client purchased a 100 percent survivor product with a twenty-year payout guarantee, the initial monthly payment would be $2,181 per month. If both the husband and wife were to pass away in less than twenty years, the insurance company would guarantee distributions to additional beneficiaries until the twenty-year period was fulfilled.

As this discussion highlights, the use of annuity products in a client's financial plan has grown beyond the retiree market. Today, many financial planners incorporate fixed-income annuity products into portfolios as a substitute for traditional fixed-income holdings. The risk-return tradeoff (the risk being the financial stability of the insurance company) must always be considered, but in cases where a guaranteed long-term fixed rate is needed, an annuity could be an important tool in the insurance and financial planning process. For clients who have maximized other forms of deferred savings, variable annuity products that allow financial planners to actively manage portfolio assets can also be powerful investment tools.

Life Insurance Planning Product & Procedural Strategies

Financial planners have a multitude of life insurance planning alternatives available to meet client objectives. It is the professional duty of each financial planner to continually improve product knowledge and keep abreast of new strategies and products that are appropriate for meeting client needs, even beyond the requirements for professional licensure and certification. The following is a brief review of common product and procedural strategies for financial planners to consider.

Product Strategy 1: Purchase a Whole Life Policy

For a client who demands greater product certainty, this strategy provides a fixed annual premium, guaranteed cash value, known rate of return, and guaranteed death benefit. Clients who are considered a substandard risk could find that whole life is the only type of cash value policy available. It is important to note, however, that whole life insurance does not allow clients to control the rate of return earned on cash value. Typically, the rate of return is quite modest— generally not more than 5 percent annually. Furthermore, both face value and premium are fixed, which reduces policy flexibility.

Product Strategy 2: Purchase a Universal Policy

Universal life provides clients with the opportunity to earn a conservative rate of return greater than that offered in a whole life policy. This strategy should be considered for clients who want a guaranteed fixed rate of return with the opportunity to earn more with improved performance of the insurance company's investments. Universal life also provides clients with some flexibility in terms of changing the annual premium.

Unlike a variable life policy, universal life does not allow a client to fully manage the assets—and consequently the rates of return—in the cash account. Also, it is unlikely that a client will earn more than a 1 to 2 percent real return over an extended period of time. The greatest shortcoming associated with universal life policies, however, is that unless the policy is properly funded and possibly prefunded, it is possible for the coverage to **lapse** (i.e., that coverage be terminated) because of nonpayment of premium and/or a reduction in cash value due to low rates of return earned on the cash account. Although lapsing is possible with any form of universal life policy, the flexibility associated with the frequency and amount of premium payments could make this a greater risk than for a variable universal life policy because of the availability of higher-risk, higher-return assets in which to invest with a VUL policy.

Product Strategy 3: Purchase a Variable Policy

This strategy offers clients the opportunity to manage their investments in the cash account, which makes it possible to earn a higher tax-advantaged rate of return. More diversification is possible than that provided by a whole- or universal life policy. This product is appropriate for clients who demand some guarantee in terms of annual premium, but who are also willing to assume greater investment risk over time. It is worth noting that variable life insurance is relatively inflexible. Premiums are fixed on a yearly basis, regardless of how well the cash value is invested, and the death benefit is typically fixed.

Product Strategy 4: Purchase a Variable Universal Life (VUL) Policy

Variable universal life insurance is the most flexible cash value policy. Premiums can be changed annually. The client can direct the investments in the cash account, and the death benefit can grow to exceed the face value. It is also possible to skip premium payments if the account earns a sufficiently high rate of return. This strategy also provides high-income clients with the opportunity to maximize diversified tax-advantaged savings more than in qualified defined contribution plans. Clients with an above-average financial risk tolerance could find this strategy appealing because it allows them to invest the cash value aggressively.

Keep in mind, however, that whenever a VUL policy is sold, the insurance company provides a cash value growth illustration to the client; some illustrations can be quite optimistic. The premium, based partially on the assumed rate of return, could be too low to fully fund the policy. A policy that assumes high returns in the subaccounts could be underfunded as a result of lower realized market returns achieved over the period. If a policy becomes underfunded, the insurance company will require the client to increase the premium. This strategy can also subject a client to relatively high administrative, insurance, and subaccount fees. Consequently, a client may need above-average returns on investments simply to cover administrative, premium, and interest costs.

Self-Test 8

Stephen, age 47, plans to retire at age 67. He is considering a $200,000 face value whole life policy. The annual premium is $4,000. Alternatively, he is thinking that he could buy a 20 year $200,000 face value term policy for $500 per year. If he implements a buy term and invest the difference strategy and can earn 8% annually, how much will be in his account when the term policy expires? Should he implement the strategy?

a. No, the $23,000 account value will be less than the face value of the whole life policy.

b. Yes, $160,000 account value will be more than the face value of the whole life policy.

c. Yes, the $183,000 account value will be more than the replacement value of the whole life policy.

d. No, the $200,000 account value will be less than the nonforfeiture value of the whole life policy.

Product Strategy 5: Purchase a Single-Premium Variable Universal Life Policy

This strategy allows a client to pay a one-time premium that will result in a higher guaranteed face value in the future. Some financial planners recommend this strategy as part of an estate reduction plan that allows clients to reposition assets to reduce estate taxes or to leverage assets for gifts to beneficiaries or charities. For example, an average fifty-year-old client can use a $10,000 one-time premium to purchase between

$25,000 and $30,000 of life insurance. As with any variable life insurance strategy, this approach can fail if the realized rate of return earned in the cash account falls below projections. Also, a single-premium policy is generally classified as a modified endowment contract (subject to less favorable tax treatment).

Product Strategy 6: Purchase a One-Year Term Policy

This strategy provides the maximum amount of pure coverage at the lowest annual cost and is most appropriate for a client who needs to avert possible income loss or asset replacement for one year or less. This strategy satisfies a temporary need caused by a change in employment or other life-cycle event that dramatically increases the need for insurance protection. Without a **guaranteed renewable provision** (i.e., the right to renew the policy on the policy's anniversary date at a higher premium without fear of denial), this strategy exposes the client to the possibility of becoming uninsurable when the policy terminates. This strategy also eliminates multiple-year cost savings and guarantees that the client will pay a higher premium when the new policy is issued.

Product Strategy 7: Purchase a Multiyear Term Policy

This strategy allows a client with a limited insurance budget to purchase the maximum amount of pure life insurance over an extended period of time. The annual premium is fixed for the term of the policy. Policies can be purchased with terms ranging from two to forty years. Usually, this strategy is presented as a **buy term and invest the difference** tactic based on the term policy premium and premium for a comparable cash value policy. Essentially, a client who buys term and invests the difference takes what would have been paid for a cash value policy and invests the difference between that premium and the cost of the term policy in a basket of stocks and bonds. Over time, the value of the investments should grow large enough to replace the face value of the term policy when the insurance coverage expires. This strategy can fail when a client fails to actually save the difference in premiums or when the investment rate of return achieved on the savings is below expectations. Regardless, however, because of the term nature of the insurance, coverage ceases at the end of the term, and the annual premium will increase upon policy renewal.

Product Strategy 8: Purchase a Return-of-Premium Term Policy

A return-of-premium term insurance policy is a hybrid between pure term and whole life insurance. These polices guarantee to repay all premiums to the policy owner if the insured outlives the term of the policy. If the insured dies during the term of the policy, the full face value is paid. This type of policy appeals to young, healthy clients who want some kind of return on their premium investment but do not want to spend the extra premium to purchase a cash value life insurance policy. Return-of-premium polices offer two significant advantages. First, the cost can be as much as 60 to 70 percent less than the premium for a cash value policy. Second, the returned premium can be received on a tax-free basis.

The primary disadvantage associated with this strategy deals with a client's self-discipline. If the client allows a policy to lapse, the return-of-premium option is of little value. Returned premiums seldom exceed 35 percent of actual premiums paid if a policy lapses. Another disadvantage is that the premiums repaid do not earn interest during the term of the policy. Therefore, the inflation-adjusted "time value of money" could be greatly reduced depending on the term of the policy. Obviously, the longer the term, the greater the loss of purchasing power. However, some money received could be better than no money returned.

Procedural Strategy 1: Purchase Insurance through a Group Term Policy

This strategy is designed for clients who are able to purchase life insurance on a pretax, group-rate basis, which makes the insurance very affordable. Coverage is typically available to any employee (or in some cases, members of fraternal, professional, or other groups), regardless of insurability factors. This provides at least a minimum level of insurance to pay for final debts and expenses. Aside from the benefits of guaranteed insurability and relatively low cost, lack of coverage diversification can be a major disadvantage of this strategy. If most or all of a client's life insurance is purchased through an employer, conversion to individual coverage is typically unavailable should the client cease working. Even a change in position with a reduction in salary could affect insurance coverage and cost. Payment of income taxes on employer-provided premiums (generally for coverage in excess of $50,000), also known as **Section 79 imputed income**, is another disadvantage.[6]

Procedural Strategy 2: Combine a Group Term Policy with a Low-Cost Private or Individual Policy

This combination insurance strategy is most appropriate for clients who have access to low priced group insurance, but also want the assurance of supplemental, continuous coverage of a private policy. This strategy is also appropriate for clients who anticipate leaving employment before retirement, or those who fear a **substandard risk classification** in the future due to health habits, medical history, or work history. As a precaution, insurance diversification and lifetime coverage can be assured by purchasing a cash value policy or guaranteed renewable term rather than depending solely on employer-provided coverage. The primary disadvantage associated with this strategy is that the additional insurance will probably be more expensive than group coverage and will not offer the ability to purchase coverage with pretax dollars. Furthermore, to be most cost effective, the purchase must be made at a relatively young age.

Procedural Strategy 3: Combine a "Base" Cash Value Policy with Group or Private Term Policies

This strategy offers the guarantee of permanent insurance protection coupled with the lower cost options of group or private term insurance. It offers clients increased flexibility to add lower cost term coverage during periods of high insurance coverage need (e.g., when children are young or in college), while maintaining a smaller "base" amount of permanent protection. Keep in mind that during the early years of strategy implementation, when client earnings are lower, the higher cost, cash value policy could limit the amount of coverage a client can afford relative to the amount of term insurance that could have been purchased.

Procedural Strategy 4: Include Conversion and Renewability Features in Term Policies

An attractive feature offered in most term polices is a **conversion provision**, which allows the policy owner to exchange a term policy for a cash value policy without proof of insurability. This rider is valuable for those who think that they could become uninsurable in the future or face a significantly higher risk classification. When purchasing a term policy, it is also possible to obtain a guaranteed renewable provision, which guarantees that the policy owner can renew the policy for an extended period of time without proof of insurability. A conversion provision usually has time limits. The guaranteed renewable provision does not guarantee a fixed premium rate, only the ability to lengthen the term of the policy regardless of underwriting considerations. Clients interested in locking in a steady annual premium should consider purchasing a cash value policy.

Procedural Strategy 5: Include a Disability Waiver Provision when Purchasing a Policy

Almost all policies provide a **disability waiver provision**. This optional provision enables an insurance policy to remain in effect during a period of a disability without the additional cost of continuing premium payments. In effect, this provision supplies a waiver of premiums if the policy owner becomes disabled. The probability of becoming disabled far exceeds the probability of premature death during most of a client's working years. Consequently, from a cost/benefit analysis perspective, this provision is generally worth the expense. A variation of the idea of continuing coverage for the client is a **waiver of premium for unemployment** if an individual is unemployed and eligible for unemployment benefits. Restrictions apply regarding how long premiums will be paid or how often the waiver can be used.

As with other policy provisions, the inclusion of the disability waiver or the unemployment waiver will increase the annual cost of a policy, sometimes substantially. The unemployment waiver provision may be offered as a no-cost rider or added for a fee. When recommending any rider, a client's situational factors and risk tolerance must be considered in the cost-benefit analysis in consultation with an insurance professional.

Self-Test 9

Graham was diagnosed with cancer. He underwent treatment and was found to be healthy and cancer free. However, Graham worries that in the future he might have a reoccurrence, which would affect his chances of obtaining life insurance. His budget is constrained and he can only afford a 10-year term policy. What feature or policy rider should Graham purchase to enable him to continue coverage in the future even if the cancer returns?

a. Guaranteed Renewable Provision

b. Conversion Provision

c. Unemployment Waiver Provision

d. Both a and b

Procedural Strategy 6: Beware of Modified Endowment Contracts

Modified endowment contract (MEC) status applies to any contract purchased after June 1988 that fails the **seven-pay test**. As defined by Internal Revenue Code section 7702A, the seven-pay test refers to any contract "if the accumulated amount paid under the contract at any time during the first seven contract years exceeds the sum of the net level premiums which would have been paid on or before such time if the contract provided for paid-up future benefits after the payment of seven level annual premiums." This basically means that if a contract could have been self-supporting after seven years based on the premiums of the first seven years and additional amounts were deposited, some of the tax benefits of the life insurance contract will be lost. The purpose of the test is to discourage policyholders from making very large premium payments during the first seven years of the contract to create a **paid-up policy** that leverages the tax advantaged status of the deposits. If a policy is an MEC, any death benefit provided under the contract will qualify for income tax-free treatment. However, any distribution—whether a loan, withdrawal, surrender, or settlement from an MEC—will be taxed on an income-first basis. Furthermore, if the insured is less than age 59½, a 10 percent penalty also applies to the taxable portion of most distributions.

Procedural Strategy 7: Know the Different Options to Access Policy Benefits and Avoid Income Taxes

In summary, both state and federal laws offer consumers options for terminating life insurance policies and accessing the benefits. These decisions could be prompted by a variety of reasons to meet both short- and long-term client needs ranging from a policy loan for an immediate need to a Section 1035 exchange for an entirely different insurance product. In each case the client's need for life insurance protection, available cash flow to pay premiums, and the tax implications of the alternative must be considered. The complexity of these decisions could involve collaboration with the client's insurance professional or tax consultant. A review of these options, discussed earlier in the chapter, is shown in Figure 5.9.

Figure 5.9 Options for Accessing Life Insurance Policy Proceeds

Action	Immediate Benefit	Effect on Face Value	Effect on Premiums	Tax Consequences
Nonforfeiture – surrender	Cash value accumulated in the policy	Policy contract ends	Ceases	Taxes due if the proceeds exceed the expenses of the policy
Nonforfeiture – paid up term		Face value remains constant, but only for the specified term	Ceases	None
Nonforfeiture – paid up whole life		Face value reduced based on policy cash	Ceases	None
Accelerated Death Benefits • Terminal • Critical • Chronic	Percentage of face value available to the insured	Reduced to percentage remaining, paid at death of the insured to the beneficiary	Continues	Generally, none, except in the case of critical care if the amount exceeds the tax free daily rate set by the IRS
Viatical Settlement (fees may apply)	Percentage of face value available to the terminally ill insured	At death of insured, full face value paid to the viatical settlement company	Ceases, paid by settlement company	Generally, none
Life Settlement (fees may apply)	Percentage of face value available to the elderly insured	At death of insured, full face value paid to the life settlement company	Ceases, paid by settlement company	Taxes due if the proceeds exceed the expenses of the policy

Procedural Strategy 8: Structure the Life Insurance Contract to Avoid Future Problems

Determining the face amount of coverage and the specific policy or policies to purchase—in other words, the strategy—is insufficient for making a sound client recommendation. More specifically, the recommendation should go beyond the strategy to clearly state how the life insurance policy contract should be structured. Considerations unique to life insurance recommendations include:

- who owns the policy;

- who receives the benefit from the policy, and

- how policy proceeds will be disbursed.

This attention to the structure of the policy contract promotes smooth and timely asset transfer by maximizing tax benefits and minimizing legal issues upon the death of the insured. When purchasing a policy, care must be taken to consider the income, gifting, and estate tax implications of potential scenarios. Periodically, during planner-client review meetings, it is important to reconsider the beneficiaries and ensure that they still match the client's wishes. Finally, after significant life or family events it is important to again review insurance policy contract features. The following reminders can be used to guide ongoing insurance reviews:

- Avoid having the insured as owner of the policy if the client's estate is likely to be greater than the federal estate tax exclusion amount.

- Avoid naming the policy owner or the owner's estate as beneficiary because of (1) possible estate tax or state inheritance tax implications, (2) lack of protection of the funds from creditors, and (3) delays with the probate court that will make the funds inaccessible.

- Avoid establishing a trust to manage life insurance proceeds and naming an individual as the beneficiary of the policy. The proceeds will go to the beneficiary instead of the trust.

- Avoid delays in updating the policy beneficiary after major life events. In a few states, divorce automatically revokes a beneficiary designation naming the ex-spouse. Otherwise, an ex-spouse could receive policy proceeds years after the divorce.

- Avoid naming only a single, primary beneficiary and opt instead for naming a primary beneficiary with one or two contingent beneficiaries. Should a sole beneficiary predecease the insured, the insurance proceeds would then be payable to the estate unless a second in-line contingent beneficiary (or two) is named.

- Avoid naming minor children as beneficiaries unless the will names a guardian or trust to manage the funds on behalf of the children. If the court has to appoint someone, there will be additional expense—paid from the insurance proceeds.

- Avoid stating a specific amount of policy proceeds to be paid to multiple beneficiaries, opting instead for a stated percentage of the policy proceeds. Because of dividends, outstanding loans, or other variations, the face value of the policy might not, at the time of death, be exactly the face amount initially stated in the distribution.

LIFE INSURANCE PLANNING FOR SPECIAL POPULATIONS

Life Insurance for the Small Business Owner

Life insurance plays an extremely important role for the owner of a small or closely held business because the business may be the primary source of income and perhaps the bulk of the client's net worth. When an owner dies, revenue can decline or cease and there may not be an easy way to extract value from the business to support the survivors. Many typical estate planning needs are amplified in the case of business ownership. Without an effective estate plan, including a **business succession plan**, the business may have to close or be liquidated to pay estate taxes. With the proper use of life insurance, a business owner can plan to provide the liquidity needed to pay any estate tax liability.

But beyond immediate liquidity needs, there are two additional reasons that life insurance is so critically important to small business owners: (1) key person insurance to protect the company and (2) buy-sell funding agreement to protect the partners.

Key person insurance is life insurance on the vital person or persons who are crucial to a business. The purpose of key person insurance is to help a company survive the financial loss associated with the death of the person who makes the business work. The business might not be viable without the services of the owner or another key person. Therefore, to ensure the continuation of the business, the company purchases a life insurance policy on the **key employee**(s), pays the premium(s), and is the beneficiary of the policy(ies). If the insured dies, the company receives the face value of the insurance. The company can then use insurance proceeds for expenses until it can find a replacement person, or if necessary, pay off debts, distribute money to investors, pay severance to employees, and close the business in an orderly fashion. In a tragic situation, key person insurance provides companies with options other than immediate bankruptcy.

A **buy/sell agreement** reduces the number of difficulties a business faces when an owner dies by allowing the business to continue. The agreement is typically between the owners, an owner and a family member, the owners and the business entity, or an owner and employees.

Buy-sell agreements are typically defined as either a cross-purchase plan or an entity purchase plan. In either case, in a partnership the agreement facilitates the surviving partner(s)' purchase of the deceased partner's business interest from the heirs or the estate at an agreed-upon price. Buy-sell agreements work similarly for limited liability companies and their members, and for corporations and their shareholders.

In a **cross-purchase plan,** each partner, not the partnership, buys a life insurance policy on each of the other partners. Each partner owns, pays the premiums, and is the beneficiary of the insurance policies on the other partners in an amount equal to each partner's investment or business equity as set forth in the buy/

sell agreement. At a partner's death, the other partners purchase the deceased partner's interest in the partnership.

In an **entity purchase plan** the individual partners enter into an agreement with the **partnership** (the legal entity representing the business), which owns, pays the premiums, and is the beneficiary of the policies. At a partner's death, the partnership purchases the deceased partner's interest in the partnership. This plan only works when more than two partners are involved.

However, any plan should include a funding method. There are several options for the future business owner to fund a buy-sell agreement, including borrowing funds, establishing a savings account within the company, or establishing an employee stock ownership plan. However, the death of an owner typically creates a significant financial burden on the business and its remaining partners. To mitigate this risk, many buy-sell agreements are established to be funded with the proceeds of life insurance, although life insurance used in this manner can be very expensive because of the size of the policy.

In either of these situations, a buy/sell agreement is executed as follows:

- An agreement is prepared that sets forth the entity or the prospective business owner's obligation to buy, the price of the business, and the method of payment. (The price should be periodically reviewed based on a current valuation of the business.)

- The entity or the prospective business owner purchases, funds, and is named the beneficiary of a life insurance policy on the current owner, as the insured.

- Upon the death of the owner, the death benefit of the insurance policy is used to buy the business, shares, or interest from the decedent's estate.

Because two-party partnerships are automatically dissolved with the death of one partner, a buy-sell agreement is especially important, but this business continuation method can be used with partnerships, limited liability companies, or closely held private corporations.

LIFE INSURANCE CONSIDERATIONS FOR DIVORCING COUPLES

Among the myriad issues that must be considered as part of a **divorce**, life insurance must not be overlooked. In fact, before a divorce is final such decisions should be resolved, and if new coverage is needed, the purchase should be completed. A purchase promised for later may not occur, or the ex-spouse may not be eligible to purchase new insurance. Knowing this before the final divorce decree means that an adjustment in the final settlement could be made.

Couples often have self-owned policies that name the spouse as beneficiary. When this is the case, the owner can simply change the beneficiary at the time of the divorce

Self-Test 10

What type of buy/sell agreement exists when each partner buys a life insurance policy on each of the other partners?

a. entity purchase plan

b. cross-purchase plan

c. key person plan

d. cross purpose plan

unless the ex-spouse is an irrevocable beneficiary, as described in this chapter, or other considerations apply.

Some couples cross-own their policies, where one spouse is the owner and beneficiary but the other spouse is the insured. This form of ownership may need to be altered or terminated upon divorce. But if gifting the policies to each other is a consideration, this should be done before the divorce to take advantage of marital gifting rules.

In some cases, one or both individuals might want to maintain the policy on the former spouse, assuming there is a continuing insurable interest. *Insurable interest* exists if there is financial reliance upon another person that would create hardship if the support ended. In instances where money or benefits are transferred directly from one party to another (e.g., spousal support or alimony, child support, continued insurance benefits as an agreement of decree) the insurable interest is clear. However, an insurable interest can remain after divorce for a number of reasons. By having life insurance in place, should the ex-spouse die, the proceeds of the policy could replace the stream of income support or be used to purchase health insurance or other benefits.

Minor children are possibly one of the most common reasons that an insurable interest would remain—and not just because of child support payments. In some cases, one parent might be granted primary custody of the child and the other parent provides health insurance for the child. Or a parent could be contributing to the future benefit of a child (e.g., a college fund). In these situations, the custodial parent could be granted the right to own a policy with the ex-spouse as the insured as long as the benefits are payable to the child or into a custodial account for the benefit of the child. This situation can also arise when the ex-spouse is unable or unwilling to self-own a policy because of the cost of ownership, an inability to purchase insurance for health or other reasons, or to avoid estate issues. In other cases, it may be done in lieu of alimony if the ex-spouse is in poor health or does not have much current income to distribute. Future policy proceeds can be given in lieu of current income.

Another consideration could be which spouse is responsible for the premium payment. As owner, the custodial parent described in this situation would be responsible, but by divorce decree the ex-spouse could be responsible even if not the owner. Thus, by decree the ex-spouse would have to pay the premiums. Divorce does not necessitate changes to a policy unless estate or divorce settlement plans mandate them. Still, life insurance should be reviewed as part of a divorce.

Mini-Case Problems

Theresa Cortez

1. Theresa Cortez is the primary breadwinner for a family of four. Her husband has been unable to work since the onset of severe vertigo 2½ years ago. Their two children are both in high school and, presumably, college bound. After attending your seminar about life insurance planning, she has come to you to determine whether she has enough life insurance. Besides the small disability check that her husband receives, she is the only source of income—albeit a good income of $84,000 per year. At your request, she has brought her most recent annual income and expense statement that shows the family's annual expenses of $55,000, annual taxes of $17,000, and savings of $12,000.

    Calculate Theresa's current insurance need using the Human Life Value approach for each of the following four scenarios, assuming her remaining working life is twenty-six years and the projected discount rate is 8.0 percent before taxes, compounded daily.

    a. Using her gross income.

    b. Using her gross income and a growth rate of 3.5 percent.

    c. Using her net income.

    d. Using her net income and a growth rate of 3.5 percent.

    Which of these four methods would result in the most reasonable estimation of insurance need?

John Wilson

2. John Wilson is a forty-two-year-old computer programmer, husband, and father of four. He wants to use the capital retention approach to determine how much life insurance he should purchase. Because of his $105,000 salary and their four children, his wife does not work outside the home. The family's current annual living expenses are approximately $75,000, including $8,000 in annual IRA contributions. He prefers to use the capital retention approach (CRA) so that he can be reasonably assured that his family will not exhaust the proceeds of his policy. However, he also wants to consider the possible reduction in expenses and apply a 70 percent replacement ratio to the calculation.

    a. Calculate John's insurance need using the capital retention approach, an after-tax discount rate of 5.5 percent, and assume end-of period payment of benefits.

    b. Calculate John's insurance need using the human life value approach (HLV), an after-tax discount rate of 5.5 percent, a remaining working life of twenty-five years, and assume end-of period payment of benefits.

    After your presentation, John was bewildered about why the HLV and CRA calculations resulted in significantly different insurance needs. Using the two formulas as a guide, explain to John why this result occurred.

Morgan Hanna

3.   Morgan Hanna is a thirty-two-year-old nurse. She is in good health and has applied for a new cash value life insurance policy. She is interested in knowing whether she should surrender her current policy and purchase the new policy offered through a AAA-rated firm. If all of the contract and company characteristics are similar, and the current face value of her policy is sufficient, should she maintain or replace her current policy? Assume the following factors:

*   Yearly premium: $1,900

*   Cash value at the beginning of the period: $13,456

*   Cash value at the end of the period: $13,927

*   Projected after-tax rate of return: 3.50 percent

*   Current policy dividend: $350

*   Death benefit: $200,000

Comprehensive Bedo Case—Life Insurance Analysis Questions

Before beginning the Bedo household life insurance analysis, it will be important to review assumptions related to salaries, assets, and client goals (e.g., funding education and retirement). When reviewing their current life insurance situation, note the proportion of insurance held by the Bedos from private policies and employer-provided group term policies. Evaluating the cost of these policies will also be beneficial. Use the following questions to guide the life insurance planning process.

1.   Develop a life insurance planning goal for the Bedos. When conceptualizing this goal, consider the following:

    a.   Is the goal developed in agreement with any or all goals and objectives that the clients have identified regarding life insurance planning?

    b.   What situational factors might influence their life insurance goals? Are these factors explicit, implied, or assumed? Is additional information required from the Bedos?

    c.   What is the desired outcome for the clients?

2.   Make a list of the lifestyle, occupational, and health underwriting factors that should be evaluated for the Bedos. How might this information be obtained? How might it be useful in the current life insurance situation analysis? Also, make a list of life events that could impact the life insurance planning analysis for Tyler and Mia and that should be reviewed at future client meetings.

3.   Develop a list of globally accepted, client-specific, or planner-generated planning assumptions that will structure the life insurance situation analysis.

4. Using the formulas or the Financial Facilitator, calculate both Tyler's and Mia's gross and additional life insurance need using each of the following approaches:

    a. Needs analysis approach

    b. Human life value approach

    c. Capital retention approach

    d. Income retention approach

    e. Income multiplier approach

5. How might these results change if a growth rate is applied to the desired benefit amount? What if the Bedos wanted to replace after-tax rather than gross income?

6. Using the life insurance calculation approach that best fits their situation or triangulation, state how much additional life insurance, if any, Tyler and Mia might need. Provide a brief, client-friendly explanation of how this number was determined. What graphic presentations might be used to convey this information to the clients?

7. Calculate the yearly price per thousand in coverage for Tyler's current whole life policy. Based on your findings, should Tyler consider replacing this policy? Provide a brief, client-friendly explanation of this analysis and the interpretation to include in the Bedos' plan. What graphic presentations might be used to convey this information to the clients?

8. Calculate the yearly price per thousand in coverage for Mia's current whole life policy. Based on your findings, should Mia consider canceling this policy or exchanging it for a term policy? Are there tax implications to consider? Provide a brief, client-friendly explanation of this analysis and the interpretation to include in the Bedos' plan.

9. As very responsible parents, the Bedos question if life insurance is needed for a child, and if so, what type of policy would be most appropriate? Provide a brief explanation of this analysis and the interpretation to include in the Bedos' plan.

10. Based on the information collected, financial advisors have a responsibility to fully document and inform clients of the analysis and results. This information can be communicated by letter or in a comprehensive or a modular plan. Using bullet points summarize your observations about Tyler's, Mia's, and Becky's current life insurance situation and the planning need(s) identified.

11. Based on the goals originally identified and the complete analysis, what product or procedural strategies might be most useful to satisfy the Bedos' life insurance protection needs? Be sure to consider strategies matched to the planning needs identified for each member of the household. When reviewing these strategies, be careful to consider the approximate cost of implementation, as well as the most likely outcome(s) associated with each strategy.

12. Write at least one primary and one alternative recommendation from select strategies in response to each planning need identified. More than one recommendation may be needed to address all of the planning needs. Include specific, defensible answers to the who, what, when, where, why, how, and how much implementation questions for each recommendation.

    a.   It is suggested that each recommendation be summarized in a Recommendation Form.

    b.   Assign a priority to each recommendation based on the likelihood of meeting client goals and desired outcomes. This prioritization will be important when recommendations from other core planning content areas are considered relative to the available discretionary funds for subsidizing all recommendations.

    c.   What considerations should be taken into account when naming beneficiaries to any new life insurance policies for the Bedos?

    d.   Comment briefly on the outcomes associated with each recommendation.

13. Prepare a tent to fifteen minute presentation for the Bedos of your observations and/or recommendation(s) for meeting their life insurance needs. Be sure to include visual aids, Excel handouts, and other materials that will make the recommendations more meaningful for the clients.

Chapter Resources

Baldwin, B., *The New Life Insurance Investment Advisor* (New York: McGraw Hill, 2002).

Belth, J. M., *Life Insurance: A Consumer's Handbook*, 2nd ed. (Bloomington, IN: Indiana University Press, 1985).

General life insurance and tax source: *Tax Facts on Life Insurance & Employee Benefits* (Cincinnati, OH: National Underwriter Company, published annually).

Leimberg, S. R.; Buck, K.; and Doyle, R.J. *The Tools & Techniques of Life Insurance Planning*, 6th ed. (Cincinnati, OH: National Underwriter Company, 2015).

Life and Health Insurance Foundation for Education, general life insurance information (www.naifa.org/consumer/life.cfm).

Self-Test Answers

1: c, 2: c, 3: b, 4: c, 5: d, 6: a, 7: c, 8: b, 9: d, 10: b

Endnotes

1.   The traditional net cost method subtracts total premiums paid from a policy's projected dividends plus cash surrender value. What remains is divided by the projected holding period. This equates to an annual cost of ownership. One criticism of this methodology is that the calculation does not account for the time value of money associated with premium payments. This evaluation procedure is not widely used because the calculation often results in a negative cost of ownership.

2.   This method of evaluation adjusts the traditional net cost estimate for the time value of money associated with premium payments.

3.   Sometimes called the net payment cost index, this approach assumes that premiums and policy dividends are accrued over a set period of time, typically 20 years, with a fixed rate of return (e.g., 4%) paid on the policy cash value. Total dividends are then subtracted from the total of all premium payments. This figure is then averaged, using a time value of money adjustment, to estimate an average annual net premium cost.

4.   Joseph Belth originally developed the yearly price per thousand method. A complete description of the method can be found in Belth, J. M., *Life Insurance: A Consumer's Handbook,* 2nd Ed. (Bloomington, IN: Indiana University Press, 1985).

5.   Calculations based on estimates from Fidelity Investments Guaranteed Income Estimator. Available at: gie.fidelity. com/estimator/gie/gielanding?refpr=annufixincom011.

6.   Issues related to Section 79 imputed income are addressed in Chapter 3 on Cash Flow Planning.

Chapter 6

Health Insurance Planning

Learning Objectives

1. Helping clients make choices that maximize benefits, reduce costs, increase tax-advantaged purchases, and facilitate peace of mind are good reasons to incorporate health insurance planning into every comprehensive review of a client's financial situation.

2. Arguably the most sweeping social legislation since the Great Depression, the Patient Protection and Affordable Care Act (PPACA) of 2010 has created dramatic shifts in the way consumers, financial planners, and policy makers view health care in the United States. Provisions of PPACA impact nearly every aspect of health care as it is currently provided. Over the next five to ten years, the health care environment will change significantly. It is imperative that financial planners stay abreast of legislative changes to help their clients maximize benefits, minimize costs, and reduce surprises resulting from PPACA both today and in the future.

3. Each client's financial, physical, and emotional situation is unique.

As discussed in this chapter, client situational factors need to be evaluated carefully when assessing and selecting appropriate health care plans, products, and services. Although the number of situational factors is almost limitless, this chapter highlights the need for financial planners to consider, at a minimum, the following client characteristics: (a) family health status and related health history; (b) family demographics, which can trigger insurance needs; (c) assets available for use in case of a catastrophic health claim; (d) lifestyle choices that can affect the availability of insurance benefits; (e) working in a hazardous profession or occupation; and (f) concerns over future unemployment, career changes, or retirement.

4. As discussed in the chapter, determining and quantifying a client's need for and selection of health care coverage is not an easy financial calculation. In some respects, this aspect of planning can best be described as a combination of art

Learning Objectives

and science. Rather than producing strictly a dollar need, as with a life insurance analysis, planning for health insurance focuses both on potential financial risks or needs to be met as well as the client's psychological needs (e.g., decreasing the financial fears associated with disease and discomfort). Helping clients deal with not only the financial realities associated with health care but also the worries associated with the unknown is one way to strengthen the client-planner relationship.

5. As noted in this chapter, it is important for financial planners to have a working knowledge of terms such as traditional indemnity; managed care plans such as HMO, PPO, POS, and EPO; and high-deductible health plans. Although each of these terms represents a type of health insurance coverage, each plan is distinct, offering advantages and disadvantages for clients. Other important terms include: (a) deductibles, (b) copayment levels, (c) coinsurance requirements, (d) policy stop-loss limits, (e) excluded coverages, (f) out-of-network restrictions, (g) premiums, and (h) access to COBRA and HIPAA benefits. Well-qualified financial planners should not only know the basic terms and provisions of health insurance products but also be able to summarize their associated strengths and weaknesses to clients.

6. As clients transition from working life toward retirement, they face many new challenges and opportunities. One common source of anxiety among those considering retirement deals with health care costs and health insurance alternatives. Even

clients who continue to work past age sixty-five must grapple with health insurance issues. Because of this, financial planners need a firm understanding of the key rules, guidelines, products, and services targeted toward seniors. Specifically, understanding how Medicare and Medigap policy coverage affects health insurance planning is essential. The monetary and psychic costs associated with hastily made Medicare and Medigap choices can easily come back to haunt clients and their financial advisors.

7. Assessing the role of Section 125 Plans and flexible spending arrangements (FSA)—also known as premium-conversion or premium-only plans—is an essential skill for financial planners interested in developing strong client-planner relationships that include a health insurance analysis. As noted in this chapter, FSAs are a useful tool not only from the perspective of paying out-of-pocket health care costs, but also from a cash flow and tax planning perspective. Clients who contribute to an FSA do so with pretax dollars. Contributions are exempt from state, federal, and Social Security taxes. Although there is a "use it or lose it" provision associated with FSAs, the ability to pay for health and dependent care costs with pretax dollars almost always outweighs the potential risks of losing unused savings.

8. Although the number of product and procedural strategies available to financial planners dealing with client health care issues is somewhat limited, there are ample opportunities to recommend strategies that increase

Learning Objectives

client cash flow and maximize client satisfaction. Exploring concepts related to the use of health savings accounts, flexible spending arrangements, high-deductible insurance plans, Medigap policies, and, of course, understanding provisions related to PPACA, provides an outstanding way to identify and recommend appropriate and reasonable health insurance strategies matched to a client's situation.

Key Terms

20 Percent Penalty

Archer Medical Savings Account

Cafeteria Plans

Cancer Insurance

Coinsurance

Consolidated Omnibus Budget
  Reconciliation Act (COBRA)

Coordination of Benefits

Copayment

Cost Sharing

Critical Illuness Policy

Deductible

Dependent Care FSA

Domestic Partner Benefits

End-Stage Renal Disease

Exclusive Provider Organization (EPO)

Expense Incurred Policy

First Diagnosis Critical Care Policy

First Occurrence Cancer Policy

Flexible Benefit Plans

Flexible Spending Arrangement (FSA)

Formulary

Health Care FSA

Health Insurance Exchange

Health Insurance Portability and
  Accountability Act (HIPAA)

Health Maintenance Organization (HMO)

Health Reimbursement Account (HRA)

Health Savings Account (HSA)

High Deductible Health Plan (HDHP)

Imputed Income

Initial Coverage Period

Insurance Rating Company

Limited Insurance Policy

Managed Care Plan

Medicare

Medicare + Choice Program

Medicare Advantage Program

Medicare Part A/B/C/D

Medicare Select Plan

Medigap

MSA

Out-of-Pocket Expenses

Pre-Existing Conditions

Preferred Provider Organization (PPO)

Premium

Premium-Conversion Plan

Premium-Only Plan

Preventative Services

Primary Care Provider

Qualifying Change-in-Status

Key Terms

Qualifying Event

Roth IRA

Salary Reduction Agreement

Section 125 Plans

Small Group COBRA Benefit

Specified Disease Policy

Standard Medicare Supplement

Stop-Loss Limit

Supplemental Health Policy

Tax Credits

The Patient Protection and Affordable Care Act (PPACA) of 2010

Traditional Indemnity Plan

Uniform Coverage

Use It or lose

CFP® Principal Knowledge Topics

D.23. Analysis and Evaluation of Risk Exposures

D.24. Health Insurance and Health Care Cost Management (Individual)

D.30. Insurance Needs Analysis

HEALTH INSURANCE PLANNING: DETERMINING THE NEED

Health insurance is a topic that goes beyond traditional financial planning. When working with clients, financial planners should anticipate the fear of financial loss associated with the costs of health care and related **out-of-pocket expenses**, which are defined as the maximum amount of unreimbursed expenses, and the **deductible** a client must pay before insurance benefits begin. Health coverage is one of the most complex types of insurance offered in the marketplace–whether through an employer, a private health insurance contract, or a governmental exchange. Although financial planners may or may not sell the actual insurance that they recommend, it is nevertheless important that planners understand the basic issues involved in medical insurance planning and policy selection.

Analyzing a client's current health insurance need is relatively straightforward, but nuances must be considered. Insurance information is typically collected during the data-gathering phase of the planning process. Issues to consider during this step include:

- family health status and related health history;

- family demographics that could trigger insurance needs;

- assets available for use in case of a catastrophic health claim;

- lifestyle choices that could influence the availability of insurance benefits;

- working in a hazardous profession or occupation; and

- concerns about future unemployment, career changes, or retirement.

The next step in analyzing the current situation focuses on reviewing the client's current coverage or tax-advantaged accounts. Gathering a variety of information about a client's health insurance situation is an important element associated with a thorough analysis.

Before considering specific health insurance planning strategies, a financial planner should determine whether a client's current and short-term needs are best met through a traditional indemnity health insurance plan, one of the managed care plan options, or a **high deductible health plan** (**HDHP**), which can be structured after either model. **Managed care plan** options attempt to manage access to and coordination of services while promoting efficient, high-quality care, all with the objective of controlling health care costs. The standard in- or out-of-network methods common to managed care plans are different than a **traditional indemnity plan** where the insured can obtain services from any provider, but typically at a higher premium and service fee. Figure 6.1 provides a comparison of the five primary health insurance plans available in the marketplace.

Health Insurance for Grown Children

Clients with children who are approaching age 26 and who do not have access to an employer-provided plan should consider purchasing a short-term individual health insurance policy or using a Health Insurance Exchange.

Preferred provider organization (PPO) plans, **point-of-service (POS)** plans, and **health maintenance organization (HMO)** plans are three of the most common managed care designs. The PPO offers the most flexibility in seeking health care, whereas the HMO is typically the most restrictive. The hybrid POS plan shares features of the PPO and HMO, whereas an **exclusive provider organization (EPO)** plan is similar to but more restrictive in its provider network than the HMO.

Figure 6.1 Comparison of Health Insurance Plans

Plan Type	Traditional Indemnity Plan	Preferred Provider Organization (PPO)	Point-of-service (POS) Plan	Health Maintenance (HMO)	High-Deductible Health Plan (HDHP)
Cost	Highest	Middle-high	Middle-low	Lowest of managed cost plans	Lowest of all plans available
Physician Choice	Least restrictive, but restrictions are increasing to control costs	Restricted to network; may go outside network with higher deductible and copayment	Restricted, but insured may see out-of-network provider for additional cost	Restricted	Depends on whether the HDHP is an indemnity, PPO, POS, or HMO plan, but certain requirements must be met to qualify as an HDHP. Offers copays for office visits only after the deductible has been met. For 2016, the minimum deductible for one insured is $1,300; $2,600 for families. Out-of-network providers can cost more than in-network providers.
Hospital Choice	Least restrictive, but restrictions are increasing to control costs	Restricted to network; may go outside network with higher deductible and copayment	Restricted to network	Restricted	Depends on whether the HDHP is an indemnity, PPO, POS, or HMO plan, but certain requirements must be met to qualify as an HDHP. Offers copays for office visits only after deductible has been met. For 2016, the minimum deductible for one insured is $1,300; $2,600 for families. Out-of-network providers can cost more than in-network providers.

Figure 6.1 Comparison of Health Insurance Plans (*cont'd*)

Appropriate for Whom?	Households that demand maximum choice	Households that would like some choice but with lower expenses than a traditional plan	Households that use medical services frequently, but occasionally visit out-of-network providers	Households that use medical services frequently	Households that are: • Generally healthy and medical expenses are limited to preventive care *OR* not healthy and typically hit the lower limits on catastrophic coverage in other plans and incur out-of-pocket expenses for exclusions (e.g., drug or other costs); • Financially disciplined savers who can fund the annual maximum of the HSA ($3,350 for individuals; $6,750 for families in 2016) to cover expenses; and • Comfortable with in-network providers to maximize savings.
Among Firms Offering Health Benefits, Availability of this Plan, 2015[1]	3%	50%	24%	16%	23%
Estimated Annual Group Plan Cost for a Family, 2015	No cost estimate provided due to limited availability	$18,469	$16,913	$17,248	$15,970

[1] **Source:** Kaiser/HRET Survey of Employer-Sponsored Health Benefits, 2015. Available at: kff.org/report-section/ehbs-2015-summary-of-findings/. Note: The reason the column does not sum to 100 percent is that some firms offer more than one type of plan.

Sources: C. Rapoport, Congressional Research Service. *Tax-Advantaged Accounts for Health Care Expenses: Side-by-Side Comparison.* Available at: assets.opencrs.com/rpts/RS21573_20100618.pdf.

J. Mulvey, Congressional Research Service. *Health Savings Accounts: Overview of Rules for 2011.* Available at: op.bna.com/mdw.nsf/id/plon-8csks5/$File/CRShsareport.pdf.

IRS Publication 969, *Health Savings Accounts and Other Tax-Favored Health Plans.*

Keep in mind that choices typically are limited to plans offered by a client's employer and that plan changes are severely restricted. While it may be possible to obtain coverage outside of an employer's plan, the cost to do so may be too high for most clients. Even so, it is important to explore client preferences that reflect both quantitative aspects of the analysis as well as qualitative or more intangible preferences. The latter may supersede cash flow issues, when something as personal as family health care is at stake.

Figure 6.2 identifies decision criteria to help address which type of health plan—traditional indemnity, PPO, POS, or HMO—may be the most appropriate. It is important to note that the same options can also be offered as an HDHP, so the decision criteria and research on the plan would be similar once the HDHP alternative has been chosen. Helping clients choose the type of health insurance that best matches lifestyle, health situation, medical usage, and anticipated wellness is an important consideration when making health insurance recommendations.

Self-Test 1

Which of the following health insurance plans offers the greatest flexibility in terms of health care provider choice and facility use?

a. PPO

b. Traditional Indemnity

c. HMO

d. HDHP

Figure 6.2 Health Insurance Plan Decision Tree

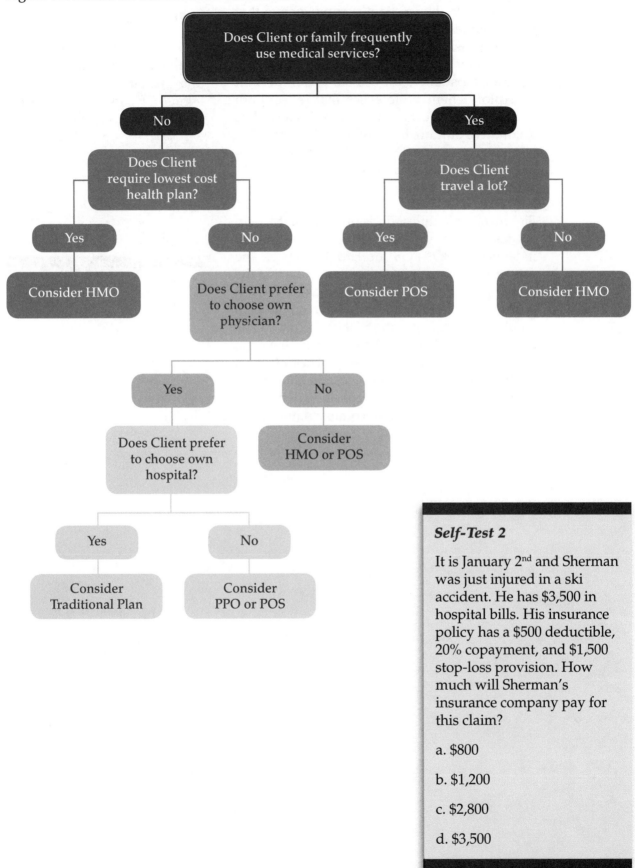

Property and Liability Insurance Planning Skills

Planning Skill 1: Understand the Terminology of Health Insurance

An important planning skill is the ability to identify and articulate the different terms and phrases associated with health insurance. The following include the most widely used health insurance terms and definitions:

- current deductible—amount the insured pays before the insurance company contributes;

- current copayment—fixed fee the insured pays for services in addition to what the insurance company will pay;

- current coinsurance—percentage of service expense paid by the insured above the deductible amount (e.g., if a plan has a 20 percent coinsurance clause, the insured is responsible for paying the deductible and 20 percent of each bill up to the maximum annual stop-loss limit);

- current **stop-loss limit**—the maximum amount of out-of-pocket expenses paid by an insured, which includes deductibles, copayments, and coinsurance (i.e., **cost sharing**);

> **Couples with Children**
>
> Special consideration must be given to couples with children. In cases where both parents are providing family coverage, the child's primary coverage will be determined by which parent's birthday comes first in the calendar year. In such cases, any coverage provided by the other parent, spouse, or guardian will be considered excess coverage for benefit purposes. In the case of unwed or divorced parents, the primary provider of coverage is generally the parent granted custody, unless determined otherwise by a court decree.

- excluded coverage—what a plan will not pay for (e.g., elective cosmetic surgery);

- out-of-network restrictions, freedom of choice, network of providers, and cost differentials if an HMO, PPO, POS, or EPO;

- current annual premium—the cost of insurance; and

- access to COBRA and HIPAA benefits (discussed later in the chapter).

Planning Skill 2: Recommending the Appropriate Plan

If a particular insurance plan is the only one available to a client, then the analysis stops here, aside from perhaps establishing a flexible spending account. The second and maybe more important way a financial planner can offer advice is in cases where more than one health plan is available, either by one employer, or for couples or partners, across both employers. If multiple plans are available, then a similar cost-benefit analysis should be conducted. For instance, some organizations provide employees with the choice of a traditional indemnity plan, a managed care plan (e.g., HMO, PPO, POS, or EPO), and/or a high-deductible health plan. To maximize benefits and control costs, a thorough analysis is needed, perhaps with the assistance of personnel from human resources or employee benefits or an independent health care insurance specialist.

On the basis of this information, a planner and client can begin to take action to adequately protect the health of the client's household while minimizing or eliminating duplicative coverage. It is also important to recognize that the choice of plan may change over the life cycle. Decisions about the **coordination of benefits** between two plans must also be considered, as well as the option for each spouse/partner to carry an individual plan, if no coverage is required for children. However, care must be taken when a high-deductible health plan is used because coverage by any other health plan is not permitted. Exceptions to this rule include accident, disability, dental, vision, long-term care, or specified disease insurance (e.g., cancer).

Planning Skill 3: Appreciate How the Patient Protection and Affordable Care Act (PPACA) of 2010 Changed the Health Insurance Marketplace

The **Patient Protection and Affordable Care Act of 2010** changed the health care planning environment dramatically. The law established Health Insurance Exchanges, expanded Medicaid coverage, and provided incentives for employers to offer health insurance. Additionally, the law strengthened consumer protections, limited premium increases, encouraged preventive care, and required all Americans to purchase health insurance. Even though the Act had a minimal impact on financial planning clientele—few clients lost their insurance coverage or encountered reduced coverage—the law did introduce several new issues that all financial planners need to incorporate into analyses of a client's health care insurance situation. The following discussion highlights these factors. More information about these and other features of the Act can be found at www.healthcare.gov.

- The Act effectively eliminated insurance restrictions based on pre-existing conditions; waiting periods are now banned.

- Programs are now in place to help those who are fifty-five or older obtain insurance prior to enrolling in Medicare at age sixty-five.

- Tax credits up to 50 percent of employer contributions to health insurance plan premiums help small businesses offer plans.

- Children up to age twenty-six can now stay on their parents' insurance regardless of financial dependence, student status, marital status, employment, or residency (some states, like New York, have even more generous laws).

- Lifetime limits on coverage are now prohibited.

- The Act banned rescissions in which insurance companies could drop someone from coverage due to a paperwork mistake after they got sick.

- Health insurance plans must provide preventative services without copayments, coinsurance, or deductibles.

- The Act formalized an appeals process for individuals and groups who feel that their insurance company has denied a claim in error.

- The choice of a primary care provider is guaranteed, assuming the provider is available to accept new patients.

- Direct access to OB/FYN services is guaranteed; further, insurance companies can no longer force an insured to use a network OB/GYN service provider.

- The Act prohibits employer sponsored plans from excluding employee participation based on salary or income.

- Lower income households receive subsidies to make health insurance premiums more affordable.

- The Act guarantees everyone access to health insurance without regard to age, sex, occupation, or health status.

Planning Skill 4: Understand the Characteristics of Health Savings and Flexible Spending Accounts and Other Plans

Another choice that aligns with the selection of health insurance is the use of a tax-advantaged account. Because these decisions must be coordinated, it is important that planners be aware of the features of each to help clients effectively manage their costs or save for the future. Four primary tax-advantaged accounts exist: (a) health care flexible spending arrangement (FSA), (b) health reimbursement account (HRA), (c) health savings account (HSA), and (d) Archer medical savings account (MSA).

A health *care FSA may be* funded through a voluntary salary reduction agreement. No employment tax or federal income tax withholding is deducted from an employee's contribution. The employer may also contribute. The FSA *can be used to reimburse the* participant for qualified medical expenses. An *HSA* is a tax-exempt trust or custodial account set up *in conjunction with a HDHP* that allows the participant to be reimbursed for qualified medical expenses. As a reminder, a HDHP has a higher annual deductible compared to other health plans, which means *participants* must pay more of their health care costs. HSAs can be used to meet these expenses. *Individuals* who are married or have a partner may not have a joint HSA. An HRA receive contributions from the employer only; *however, contributions are not included in a participant's income.* Employees may not contribute. Reimbursements from an HRA that are used to pay qualified medical expenses are not taxed. *Finally, MSA eligibility is restricted to employees of small employers and the self-employed,*

> ### Coordination Between Types of Tax-Advantage Accounts
>
> If a client is funding both an FSA and an HSA, funds from the FSA should be exhausted first so that funds can remain in the HSA for the future. Similarly, to the extent that qualified expenses could be reimbursed from either a FSA and a HRA, expenses from the FSA should be used first, typically to maintain the HRA balance.

which rules out participation for many taxpayers. MSAs have been phased out and replaced with HSAs, except for those who were eligible prior to December 31, 2007. MSA funding can continue, assuming the owner is still eligible, or the Archer MSA can be rolled over into an HSA. *Figure 6.3 compares aspects of these accounts (note: some of these options are also discussed later in this chapter).*

Figure 6.3 Comparison of Tax-Advantaged Accounts

	HSA	MISA	HRA	FSA
Pre-Tax Employee Contribution?	Yes	Yes, but only if employer does not contribute	No contribution from employee allowed	Yes
May Assets in Account be Invested?	Yes, using IRA instruments	Yes, using IRA instruments	No	No
Employer Contributions Allowed?	Yes	Yes	Yes	Yes
Rollover Allowed	Yes	Yes	No	No
Must Account be Linked to HDHP?	Yes	Yes	No	No
2016 Contribution Limit	$3,350 Individual $6,750 Family	IRA no longer allows funding	No limit	$2,550
May Account Assets be Rolled Over?	Yes	Yes	Yes	Only $500 may be rolled over to the new year

Source: U.S. Bureau of Labor Statistics: www.bls.gov/opub/mlr/cwc/consumer-driven-health-care-what-is-it-and-what-does-it-mean-for-employees-and-employers.pdf

Planning Skill 5: Medicare Planning and Eligibility

Generally, **Medicare** is available for people age sixty-five or older, younger people with disabilities, and people with *end-stage renal disease* (i.e., permanent kidney failure requiring dialysis or a transplant). Medicare has three primary parts. Part A is a hospital insurance plan. Part B is a voluntary medical insurance plan with a monthly premium. Part D is a prescription drug benefit. Those who did not pay Medicare taxes for at least ten years or were never married may not be eligible for Part A, but they may be able to purchase coverage if they are age sixty-five or older and a citizen or permanent resident of the United States. A brief description of Parts A, B, and D follows. To learn more about the changes in Medicare plans and benefits, see www.medicare.gov.

Medicare Part A, hospital insurance, helps cover costs for inpatient care in hospitals, critical access hospitals, and skilled nursing facilities. Benefits for the latter are available only following a related three day hospital stay. Part A also covers hospice care for the terminally ill and some home health services prescribed by a doctor, including durable medical equipment and supplies. In addition to services and supplies covered as part of hospital or skilled nursing home care, Part A includes coverage for pints of blood received at a hospital or skilled nursing facility. Although the costs of some benefits are fully covered, coinsurance and deductibles also may apply.

> *Self-Test 3*
>
> Which of the following Medicare coverages is typically a free benefit starting at age 65?
>
> a. Part A
>
> b. Part B
>
> c. Part D
>
> d. All of the above

Medicare Part B, medical insurance, provides benefits for doctors' services, outpatient hospital care, some home health services, and some other medical services excluded from Part A, such as the services of physical and occupational therapists or speech pathologists. Part B helps pay for these covered services and diagnostic testing and supplies when they are judged to be medically necessary. The listing of covered services is extensive, ranging from ambulance services when medically necessary to transplants, yet restrictions and limitations on services apply.

The base monthly Part B premium in 2016 was $121.80 for those with income less than $85,000 ($170,000 for those filing a joint tax return). The premium is higher for those with incomes that exceed this threshold. This monthly premium is generally deducted from the client's Social Security, Railroad Retirement, or Civil Service Retirement check. In addition to the monthly premium for Part B, annual deductible and coinsurance provisions also apply. Effective in 2007, premium charges for Part B are "means tested." In 2016, consumers with incomes in excess of $85,000, or $170,000 for couples, are required to pay a higher premium for Medicare Parts B and D, Medicare prescription drug coverage, with the premium prorated on the basis of income. Some programs are available to reduce Part B premiums for those with limited income.

Medicare Part D, Medicare prescription drug coverage, provides coverage for both brand-name and generic prescription drugs at participating pharmacies. Medicare prescription drug coverage provides protection for people who have very high prescription drug costs. Everyone with Medicare is eligible for this coverage, regardless of income and resources, health status, or current prescription expenses. The annual election period is from October 15 through December 7, during which time anyone with Medicare can enroll in Part D or change Part D plans. A client's decision to enroll in Part D depends on the kind of health care coverage available at retirement. Clients can join either a Medicare prescription drug plan or a Medicare Advantage Plan or other Medicare Health Plan that offers drug coverage. According to the Social Security Administration, when clients join Part D they will pay a monthly premium, which varies by plan, and a yearly deductible. Clients also pay a part of their prescription costs, including a copayment or coinsurance.

PPACA attempts to close the **Medicare doughnut hole**, or the coverage gap that many with Medicare Part D coverage and high prescription drug costs encounter annually. In 2016, the donut hole started when a drug plan pays a total of $3,310 in medication costs (typically referred to as the *initial coverage period*). Once a retiree reaches the coverage gap, they will pay 45 percent of the plan's cost for covered brand-name prescription drugs. Although the retiree pays 45 percent of the price for the brand-name drug, 95 percent of the price—what the retiree pays plus the 50 percent manufacturer discount payment—counts as an out-of-pockets expense which helps eliminate the coverage gap. What the drug plan pays toward the drug cost (5 percent of the price) and what the drug plan pays toward the dispensing fee (55 percent of the fee) are not counted towards the gap. By 2020, the coverage gap will be closed, in that individuals will pay only 25 percent of the cost of prescription drugs until the annual out-of-pocket spending limit is met. In 2016, individuals will pay 86 percent of the cost of covered generic drugs and 50 percent of the cost of covered brand-name drugs purchased in the doughnut hole. It is important to remember that individuals in the doughnut hole enter catastrophic coverage after their out-of-pocket expenses for drugs on the plan's **formulary**, or list of covered drugs, reaches the stated annual limit, and Part D payment for prescriptions resumes until the end of the year. The money spent on drugs that are not covered on the plan's formulary does not count toward the catastrophic coverage threshold. Medicare Part D coverage resets each year on January 1st.

The **Medicare + Choice program**, which is sometimes referred to as **Medicare Part C**, is an alternative to traditional Medicare programs. Part C coverage was ushered in as part of the Medicare Prescription Drug, Improvement, and Modernization Act of 2003. Medicare Part A and Part B coverage is required to be eligible. Medicare + Choice Plans allow consumers to seek benefits through a private health maintenance organization (HMO), a special needs plan for targeted audiences, a private fee-for-service plan (PFFS) through a private insurance company, or a preferred provider organization (PPO). (The latter two will probably cost more). Part C plans may include extra benefits such as prescription drugs, dental care, and routine physical and vision services.

Originally enacted in 1997, this program has been renamed the **Medicare Advantage Program** and was expanded in 2006 to offer more choices for both urban and rural consumers. For example, Congress created **special needs plans** to allow insurance companies to target enrollment to special needs individuals, including those who are (a) institutionalized, (b) dually eligible, and/or (c) suffering from severe or disabling chronic conditions. To identify Medicare Advantage Programs available in a geographic area and any extra benefits offered by these plans, visit the Medicare Personal Plan Finder at www.medicare.gov.

The **Medicare Advantage MSA** is an Archer MSA for those who are enrolled in Medicare Part A and Part B and have an HDHP that meets Medicare guidelines. The tax-exempt trust or custodial account is funded by the Medicare program—no personal contributions are allowed—to pay for qualified medical expenses of the account holder. Funds in the account can earn interest or dividends, grow tax-deferred, and are not taxed if used for qualified medical expenses. Medicare Advantage MSAs are administered through the Medicare program.[1]

A variety of expenses are not covered under either Medicare Part A or Part B. Some *exclusions* affect only select groups of Medicare beneficiaries (e.g., exclusions for acupuncture, cosmetic surgery, or health care received outside the United States). Other exclusions for routine physicals, eye care, foot care, dental care, hearing aids, or custodial care at home or in a nursing home affect far more consumers. In 2011, PPACA eliminated cost sharing (e.g., copayments, coinsurance, and deductibles) for select Medicare covered preventive services. It is important that financial planners and their clients be fully informed of both exclusions and covered services to more accurately project medical costs. Clients who assume that they are covered may find themselves exposed to unreimbursed costs if they use these services. Such knowledge can help planners develop strategies to cover these expenses with private sources of insurance, such as Medigap coverage, or through self-insurance techniques. Clients who overestimate the cost of care may unnecessarily limit their lifestyle, gifting, or spending for other goals to save more for future medical costs.

Self-Test 4

Mary Bell is going to join a HDHP at her work. Which of the following must she also contribute to at that time?

a. Health Savings Account

b. Roth 401(k)

c. Flexible Spending Account

d. Health Management Account

Health Insurance Planning Product & Procedural Strategies

After completing an analysis of a client's current and projected health plan needs, the second step in the analysis and evaluation of a client's financial status focuses on the array of strategies for choosing the most appropriate product(s), structuring the insurance contracts, coordinating benefits between contracts, coordinating benefits with social insurance, if applicable, and establishing or optimizing other tax-advantaged accounts to meet the client's needs. Increasing a client's confidence to handle the financial loss associated with serious or chronic illness, and to minimize the lingering financial and emotional effects of that loss, solidifies a strong client-planner working relationship.

The following array of strategies represent a cross-section of product and procedural approaches often used by financial planners to meet a client's health insurance needs over the life cycle. Understanding a client's needs, as well as preferences, on health care coverage can further inform the review of specific product and procedural strategies.

Product Strategy 1: Establish an HSA in Conjunction with a Qualified HDHP (For clients aged sixty-four or younger and not a dependent of another individual)

This strategy works well for self-employed clients, for those without access to cost efficient group plans, and those with access to qualifying HDHPs. The combination of a HSA and an HDHP offers a number of benefits to those who have minimal health care needs and want greater control over the cost of medical care and insurance. Because of the high-deductible plan, premiums are significantly lower than typical health care plans.

To qualify as a *HDHP* in 2016, an individual insurance plan must have at least a $1, 300 deductible and an annual stop-loss limit of no more than $6, 450. For a family plan to qualify, the deductible must be at least $2, 600, with a maximum stop-loss limit of $12,900.

The HSA is similar to an individual retirement account (IRA) for health care-related expenses. The client has access to a catastrophic health plan, and the benefit of an above-the-line tax deduction for post-tax contributions or a tax-exemption for pretax contributions to the account. If available to an employee, an HSA can be funded up to the 2016 contribution limit of $3,350 for an individual and $6,750 for a family, with pretax salary reductions or with employer contributions that may be available through a Section 125 Plan. Contributions are not subject to state or federal income tax or FICA withholding. A catch-up contribution of $1,000 is also available for persons aged fifty-five to sixty-four.

Assets in the account grow tax deferred as they accumulate. Distributions for qualifying medical expenses are excluded from income. Any funds remaining in the account not used for medical expenses can be used after age sixty-five for any purpose without penalty. Other allowable coverage includes dental and vision insurance as well as coverage for a specific disease or illness as long as it pays a specific dollar amount when the policy is triggered.

There are drawbacks associated with HSAs. Only clients covered by a qualifying HDHP are eligible for an HSA. Annual contribution limits as well as the allowable above-the-line tax deduction are limited, but they increase annually. Distributions made for any reason other than to pay for qualified medical expenses are subject to income taxes. In addition, such distributions are subject to a 20 percent penalty unless made after death, disability, or age sixty-five. Premiums paid for a high-deductible health plan are not eligible as an itemized tax deduction. Also, the participant must be younger than age sixty-five, the age of eligibility for Medicare. In addition, an account cannot be established if the participant is a dependent of another person.

HSA accounts provide financial planners an opportunity to add value to the client-planner relationship. HSAs are portable and require contributions to be managed, typically through mutual funds or bank accounts. As is the case whenever an investment is made, the custodian of the account should be evaluated in terms of investment alternatives, costs, and fee structure. Many smaller banks—and even some specialty banks—act as HSA trustees. They offer fixed-interest funds and other account types for qualified deposits.

Product Strategy 2: Maximize the Benefits of a Section 125 Plan (for Employed Clients)

Internal Revenue Code section 125 provides employees with several advantages for choosing, using, and paying for health insurance premiums, health care expenses, and other benefits. **Section 125 plans**, commonly known as **cafeteria plans** or **flexible benefit plans**, make it possible for employers to offer employees a choice between cash and a variety of nontaxable benefits. Such plans must allow employees to choose between two or more qualified benefits (i.e., life insurance, health insurance, accidental death and dismemberment, long-term disability insurance, child and dependent care costs or adoption assistance, group legal services, or medical expense reimbursement) and cash, or another taxable benefit that is treated as cash. Nontaxable benefits, such as disability insurance purchased with after-tax dollars, can also be included in a cafeteria plan.

The benefits chosen are typically paid for with pretax dollars through employee salary reduction agreements or "credits" provided by the employer. Employee contributions are made by contributing a portion of salary, on a pretax basis, to pay for qualified benefits. Salary reduction contributions are not considered to be actually or "constructively" received by the participant. Therefore, contributions are generally not considered wages for federal or state income tax purposes (some exclusions apply). Also, plan contributions generally are not subject to FICA withholdings. In addition, employer-provided credits, often stated in dollar amounts, are used to purchase qualified, or nontaxable, benefits. Although the credits may vary with employee age, service, or salary, the plan cannot offer an undue advantage to highly compensated employees.

> **Self-Test 5**
>
> All of the following are reasons someone may be allowed to make a change to their flexible benefit plan, EXCEPT:
>
> a. They were married last week.
>
> b. They just adopted a baby.
>
> c. They were in the hospital for surgery.
>
> d. Their spouse was fired.

Because of their complexity, cafeteria plans are generally available to those working in midsize to large firms. Self-employed clients are ineligible to establish these plans, although other tax advantages for health and retirement plan contributions are available to them.

Once an employee has elected benefits for a plan year, the choice can be changed only in limited circumstances. Under change-in-status rules, a plan may permit participants to revoke an election or make a new election with respect to accident and health coverage, dependent care expenses, group-term life insurance, or adoption assistance if a qualifying event occurs and the participant makes the change in a plan within thirty-one days of the qualifying event. **Qualifying change-in-status** events include:

- a change in legal marital status;

- a change in number of dependents or eligible family members;

- a change in employment status of the employee or changes affecting the employment of a covered family member;

- cases where the dependent satisfies or ceases to satisfy the requirements for eligibility;

- a change in residence for the employee, spouse, or dependent; and

- the commencement or termination of an adoption proceeding, for purposes of adoption assistance.

Medigap Caveats

It is illegal for an insurance company to sell clients a Medigap policy that substantially duplicates any existing coverage, including Medicare coverage.

A client can postpone purchasing a Medigap policy if working past age 65 and covered by employer-sponsored health insurance, or if not working but still covered by a spouse's employer-sponsored plan. Clients can still enroll in Medicare, but the employer-sponsored insurance will be the primary payer, and Medicare will be the secondary payer.

Medicare will pay any costs covered by Medicare that are not covered by the employer's plan. If clients find themselves in this situation, they may want to enroll in Medicare Part A, because it is free. Remember, however, that if clients enroll in Medicare Part B, the open enrollment period for Medigap begins at that time.

Many cafeteria plans offer a **salary reduction agreement**, or **premium-conversion plan,** or **premium-only plan** for the purchase of health or life insurance coverage. Pretax salary reduction agreements can also be used to fund an HSA and HDHP. A flexible spending arrangement, also referred to as a *flexible spending account* (FSA) is another tax-favored tool that allows employees to accumulate pretax dollars (exempt from state, federal, and Social Security taxes) through salary reductions for the reimbursement of select expenses. Both health care FSAs and dependent care FSAs are established and maintained in a similar manner. For both, allowable reimbursements are limited to those eligible for the medical deduction or the dependent care tax credit, respectively.

A health care FSA can be used to pay for cost sharing (e.g., copayments, coinsurance, and deductibles) as well as other medical, dental, or eye care costs not covered by health insurance. Over-the-counter drugs, vitamins, dietary supplements, and cosmetic procedures are excluded, but expenses for herbal remedies or a weight loss program, if prescribed by a physician as medically necessary, could be covered. As described in Figure 6.3, contributions to FSAs are limited.

A dependent care FSA can be used to pay for qualified dependent care expenses, such as child care and elder care costs incurred, when both spouses are employed, unless one is disabled or a full-time student. The maximum tax-free reimbursement for a dependent care FSA is $5,000 ($2,500 for a married employee filing separate tax returns), although income restrictions apply to determine the maximum allowable contribution.

It is important to recognize that the health care FSA and dependent care FSA differ on the uniform coverage, or risk-of-loss rule. **Uniform coverage** means that the maximum amount of reimbursement (i.e., the annual election) must be available to the health FSA participant at all times. For example, if an employee elects a monthly salary reduction of $100 for an FSA, then the annual election of $1,200 (less any prior year reimbursements) must be available for employee reimbursement at any time during the plan year without regard to the employee's actual accumulated balance. The plan may not accelerate the payment schedule based on the employee's prior claims. Conversely, the dependent care FSA account can reimburse only with funds deposited into the account, based on the monthly salary deductions available in the participant's account to date.

For both health and dependent care FSAs, reimbursements can be made only for claims incurred during the plan year and cannot be paid in advance. FSA expenses are treated as having been incurred when the participant is provided with the medical care or dependent care resulting in an expense, not when the participant is billed or pays for the care. Reimbursement requests can be submitted, with restrictions, after the plan year ends for expenses incurred during the plan year. The IRS now allows a 2½-month grace period for the use of health FSA assets before the **use it or lose** it provision applies; additionally, up to $500 may be carried forward to a new year.

Section 125 plan options usually must be chosen before the beginning of the plan year during the open enrollment period. Once established, adjustments to the amount of salary reduction during the year are not allowed, unless there is a qualifying change of family or work status. Careful estimates of out-of-pocket medical and dependent care expenses are necessary to avoid the loss of contributions if flexible spending accounts are used. Because of the "use it or lose it" rule, any balance remaining in the account at year-end will most likely be forfeited. Preplanning medical expenses to occur within one year is a way to coordinate the "bunching" of medical services as a way to avert the loss of account funds. In addition to non-qualifying health expenses, premiums for other health care coverage or for long-term care insurance are also excluded. Dependent care reimbursements from an FSA reduce the total dependent care expenses eligible for calculation of the dependent care credit.

> ### Over-the-Counter Drugs and HSAs, MSAs, FSAs, and HRAs
>
> Effective 2011, qualified distributions from an HSA, an Archer MSA, an FSA, or an HRA exclude over-the-counter (nonprescription) drugs. The IRS defines a medicine or drug as a qualified expense only if the medicine or drug (a) requires a prescription, (b) is available without prescription, and a prescription is written for it, or (c) is insulin. The PPACA also increased the tax on nonqualified distributions to 20%.

Product Strategy 3: Purchase a Medigap Policy to Supplement Medicare Coverage (for Clients Age Sixty-five or Older)

Traditional **Medigap** insurance is available to residents of most states. Medigap policies are sold by private insurance providers to pay for health care costs not provided by Medicare Parts A and B, such as out-of-pocket expenses for copays, co-insurance, or deductibles. Some Medigap plans also fill in for "gaps" in coverage not provided by Medicare Parts A and B. A few states—Massachusetts, Minnesota, and Wisconsin—have their own specific Medicare supplemental policies and are not considered here. Acceptance by an insurance company into a Medigap plan is guaranteed once a client reaches age sixty-five and enrolls in Medicare. Clients have six months to apply for a Medigap policy. Clients cannot be turned down, regardless of health status, if they apply within the six-month window. However, anyone covered by Medicaid or by a Medicare Advantage Plan is typically ineligible to purchase Medigap insurance.

Nearly all Medigap insurance is sold as a standardized plan that must meet federal and state laws. As shown in Figure 6.4, ten standard plans are available, ranging from the most basic coverage in Plan A to other plans, with different features, having different alphabetical titles up to Plan N. Every insurance company offering Medigap insurance is required to provide the same standard coverage for each plan, although premiums may differ significantly. Each company offering Medigap insurance must offer Plan A, but companies may have some, all, or none of the other plans available in a state or geographic region within a state. Basic benefits include:

- in-patient hospital care: covers the cost of Part A coinsurance and the cost of 365 extra days of hospital care during the client's lifetime after Medicare coverage ends;

- medical costs: covers the Part B coinsurance (generally 20 percent of Medicare-approved payment amount) or copayment amount, which may vary according to service; and

- blood: covers the first three pints of blood each year.

Figure 6.4 Standard Medicare Supplement, or Medigap, Plans and the Percentage of Costs Covered for Benefits

Benefits	A	B	C	D	F*	G	K*	L*	M	N
Part A coinsurance and hospital costs up to an additional 365 days after Medicare benefits are used	100%	100%	100%	100%	100%	100%	100%	100%	100%	100%
Part B coinsurance or copayment	100%	100%	100%	100%	100%	100%	50%	75%	100%	100%***
Blood (first 3 pints)	100%	100%	100%	100%	100%	100%	50%	75%	100%	100%
Part A hospice care coinsurance or copayment	100%	100%	100%	100%	100%	100%	50%	75%	100%	100%
Skilled nursing facility care coinsurance			100%	100%	100%	100%	50%	75%	100%	100%
Part A deductible		100%	100%	100%	100%	100%	50%	75%	50%	100%
Part B deductible			100%		100%					
Part B excess charges					100%	100%				
Foreign travel emergency care (up to plan limits)			100%	100%	100%	100%			100%	100%

Note: The Medicare supplement policy covers coinsurance only after the insured has paid the deductible (unless the supplement policy also covers the deductible).

*Plan F also offers a high-deductible plan. If this option is chosen, the insured must pay for Medicare covered costs up to the deductible amount before the Medicare supplement plan pays anything.

**Plans K and L do not include the entire benefit package. They offer catastrophic coverage at a lower premium. After meeting the annual out-of-pocket limit (i.e., $4,960 for Plan K and $2,480 for Plan L in 2016) and the annual Part B deductible, the Medicare supplement plan pays 100 percent of covered services for the rest of the calendar year.

***Plan N pays 100 percent of the Part B coinsurance, except for a copayment of up to $20 for some office visits and up to a $50 copayment for emergency room visits that do not result in an inpatient admission.

Source: Centers for Medicare and Medicaid Services. *Choosing a Medigap Policy: A Guide to Health Insurance for People with Medicare*, p 11. Available at: www.medicare.gov/Publications/Pubs/pdf/02110.pdf.

Another alternative is a **Medicare SELECT plan**. These plans are similar to traditional Medigap plans; however, SELECT coverage utilizes a managed care approach, similar to an HMO or PPO, where clients must use either an in-network or preferred provider, which can make the premiums less expensive than comparable plans.

Medigap insurance offers the advantages of a standardized insurance policy, with a range of supplemental coverage, for those on Medicare. With careful selection and attention to company ratings and consumer satisfaction rankings, a Medigap policy can be a cost-effective solution to the limitations of Medicare coverage. To make a cost-effective selection, financial planners and their clients should compare the projected Medigap premium with potential out-of-pocket costs for deductibles, coinsurance, and other health care needs not covered by Medicare. Medigap policies are particularly useful for clients who are not offered or cannot afford to continue any company-provided health benefits after retirement.

Self-Test 6

Midge would like to purchase a Medigap policy to cover very large, unexpected, and catastrophic expenses. She is also interested in a lower price plan. Midge should consider which of the following standard policies?

a. Plan D

b. Plan K

c. Plan N

d. Plan M

Product Strategy 4: Establish an HSA in Conjunction with a Qualified HDHP (for Young Adult Clients)

This strategy works well for young, healthy adults because it could provide another avenue to save for retirement. While a person is healthy, single, and without dependents it is a great time to maximize contributions to an HSA. Additionally, an HSA can be invested in a wide variety of risk- and age-appropriate investment assets.

Some health insurance pundits have even argued that under the right set of circumstances a person should invest in an HSA even before maximizing Roth or Traditional IRA contributions. While all original contributions to a Roth IRA can be withdrawn at any time, earnings withdrawn within five years of opening an account may be fully taxable and subject to a 10 percent early withdrawal penalty (if the owner is under age 59½). To withdraw earnings, in addition to the five-year rule, one of a number of qualifying events or exceptions must be met. One exception deals with unreimbursed health care expenses; however, to meet the exception rule, the unreimbursed health care expenses must exceed 10 percent of the account owner's AGI. No such limitation exists for HSA withdrawals, plus any money remaining in the account when the account owner reaches age sixty-five may be withdrawn for any reason without a tax penalty, although ordinary income tax will be owed.

Additionally, although the income-based phase-out limits on a Roth IRA are quite high, the phase-out on a deductible, Traditional IRA, if the account owner is eligible for a qualified retirement plan, is only relatively low (i.e., less than $75,000). Single clients with income exceeding the phase-out threshold could make a deductible contribution to an HSA even if they had maximized their Roth IRA contribution because HSA deposits are not included in the combined maximum funding levels.

As with all strategies, several caveats are worth noting. Overfunding an HSA in preference to a *Roth IRA* can create additional tax consequences at retirement given that qualified Roth IRA distributions are tax free, whereas distributions from an HSA at age sixty-five or after will be taxed at ordinary income tax rates. Also, the HSA acts more like a Traditional IRA than a Roth IRA in that contributions to an HSA are made on a pretax basis, but again are taxed upon withdrawal. An additional issue is that if the account owner must take a withdrawal from an HSA prior to age sixty-five and for a reason other than a qualified medical expense, the penalty on the withdrawal is 20 percent—twice the penalty rate on IRA accounts.

Product Strategy 5: Use Supplemental Health Policies Cautiously

Self-Test 7

When would it make sense to recommend the purchase of a specified disease policy?

a. When the policy is the primary source of health cost reimbursement.

b. When the client is having a difficult time funding other important financial goals.

c. When the client's health history indicates that there is a high likelihood of experiencing a major high cost illness.

d. All of the above.

Supplemental health policies are a form of **limited insurance coverage** that pay benefits for the actual diagnosis and/or treatment of a specific illness or complications arising from the treatment of a specific illness. **Cancer insurance** is the most common limited insurance policy. When clients ask about these forms of insurance it is best to be recommend caution. Supplemental insurance should never be used as a substitute for comprehensive health insurance or for supplemental Medicare coverage. A **critical illness policy** (also called a **specified disease policy**) provides hospital and medical benefits for other diseases in addition to cancer, such as heart disease, stroke and Alzheimer's disease.

Clients should always purchase insurance that provides the best coverage available for the cost that covers expenses regardless of the type of illness or injury involved. Supplemental policies and critical illness policies should only be recommended when a client can afford to coverage without threatening the accomplishment of other financial planning goals.

There are two traditional types of supplemental insurance policies. The first (sometimes known as an **expense incurred policy**) pays a percentage of all expenses up to the policy's maximum dollar limit. The second type (sometimes called an *indemnity policy*) also provides payments, but the payments are limited to a fixed dollar amount not the actual expenses incurred.

It is not uncommon for certain cancers (e.g., skin) to be excluded). Limited insurance and critical illness policies have provisions related to waiting periods, pre-existing conditions, and limits on duplicate coverage payments. The marketplace for these products is dynamic. For example, it is possible to purchase a **First Occurrence Cancer Policy** that pays a lump sum upon the first diagnosis of cancer. The benefit can range from $2,000 to over $100,000. A **first Diagnosis Critical Illness Policy** includes coverage for other specified illnesses, such as heart attack, stroke, or Alzheimer's disease, and pays a lump sum amount as defined in the policy.

In most states, consumers have a "free look" right that provides a minimum number of days to review and return a policy for any reason. One reason to cancel a purchase is a poor review for one of the following insurance rating companies:

- A.M. Best

- Demotech, Inc.

- Fitch

- Moody's

- Standard & Poor's

Self-Test 8

All of the following are qualifying events, EXCEPT:

a. Turning age 26

b. Turning age 65

c. Turning age 23

d. Dying at age 43

Procedural Strategy 1: Monitor Health Insurance Coverage and Encourage Clients to Do the Same

Financial planners should routinely conduct ongoing reviews of clients' health insurance plan coverage as part of the comprehensive financial planning process. This may seem redundant and unnecessary to clients; however, including this strategy as a specific recommendation, or in a structured client-planner to-do list, reminds clients that they too have a responsibility for staying abreast of plan changes and insurance triggers. Both financial planners and clients need to monitor the ongoing PPACA changes scheduled to occur over the next few years.

It is important to remember that in many cases, the flexibility to change a health plan within a given year will be severely constrained and likely limited to the plan's open enrollment period. Nevertheless, it is prudent to recommend that clients continue to monitor potential employer-provided and PPACA-mandated alternatives or modifications available to them or their spouse/partner, as well as any other household changes that could affect health care planning options.

Procedural Strategy 2: Use COBRA to Bridge Employment Termination or Continue Group Health Coverage for Dependents

The **Consolidated Omnibus Budget Reconciliation Act (COBRA)** of 1985 law requires employers with twenty or more employees offering group health plans to provide employees and certain family members the opportunity to continue group health coverage in a number of instances when coverage would otherwise have lapsed. The lapse must occur as the result of an employee **qualifying event**, defined as:

- voluntary or involuntary termination of employment, except in the case of gross misconduct;

- coverage termination due to a reduction in hours worked;

- eligibility for Medicare;

Coordination of Plan Changes

Most clients will be eligible to make changes only during the annual open-enrollment period or in response to a qualifying midyear event. Of course, these limitations do not apply if the client purchases an individual policy, but this is the exception and not the rule. As with any sound recommendation, health care recommendations must be developed in anticipation of events that could create coverage gaps or restrictions.

- divorce or legal separation; or

- death.

Two other nonemployee qualifying events also are included in COBRA: (a) dependents who cease to meet the dependency definition; and (b) the filing of Chapter 11 bankruptcy by the employer.

The employee must pay for the entire cost of continuing coverage through COBRA. The employee or qualified beneficiary may be charged 102 percent of the applicable premium for this benefit. Although expensive, coverage is available, whereas a privately provided individual policy might not be available, might offer more limited coverage, or be equally expensive.

Employers must send COBRA notifications to employees and their spouses when the employee is first covered under the group health plan. They must also send notices to both the employee and qualified beneficiaries whenever a qualifying event occurs. The latter notice must be sent within fourteen days of learning of the qualifying event.

Qualified beneficiaries have sixty days to elect continuation of coverage. The maximum period that this continued coverage must be provided is generally eighteen months, but in some cases it is thirty-six months. Depending on the state, there may be a *small group COBRA benefit* available. Given the time constraints, a timely response is required. Election of coverage continuation must occur within sixty days of employer-provided COBRA notification. The cost of insurance continuance can be 102 percent of total premiums, calculated as the employer and employee contributions and a 2 percent surcharge. Thus, it is possible that a policy that cost a client $2,500 annually as an employee may actually cost, for example, as much as $6,500 when COBRA benefits are used. The effect on cash flow must be weighed relative to the potential financial loss of an uninsured accident or illness for one or more household members.

Procedural Strategy 3: Maximize the Benefits of HIPAA to Extend COBRA Coverage

The original COBRA law was amended by the **Health Insurance Portability and Accountability Act (HIPAA)** of 1996. The first change dealt with the extension of COBRA coverage to disabled beneficiaries. COBRA required that the eighteen-month maximum coverage continuation period be extended to twenty-nine months if the qualified beneficiary was determined under the Social Security Act to have been disabled at the time of the qualifying event. HIPAA provided that if the disability existed at any time during the first sixty days of COBRA coverage, then the twenty-nine-month period applies. The twenty-nine-month period also applies to a nondisabled qualified beneficiary of the covered employee.

HIPAA also provide that a newborn infant or child placed for adoption with the covered employee during the period of COBRA coverage is entitled to receive COBRA continuation coverage as a qualified beneficiary. COBRA coverage can be terminated early for individuals who are covered under another group health plan. HIPAA provides that COBRA coverage can be cut short even if the new plan has a pre-existing condition exclusion unless the exclusion applies to a condition for which the insured is receiving treatment.

To take advantage of HIPAA, a person must prove that he or she was insured during the previous twelve months and has not been uninsured for more than sixty-three days. Workers who could be unemployed for more than sixty-three days should consider purchasing a (1) *COBRA bridge* or (2) an individual short-term policy to maintain continuous coverage, and thus avoid loss of coverage for pre-existing conditions.

Life events that should trigger either a COBRA or HIPPA discussion and necessitate a health care policy review include:

- childbirth;

- marriage/divorce/widowhood;

- employment change (especially retirement);

- a child reaching the age of twenty-six, if ineligible for an employer-provided plan; or

- a change in the overall health of the client or other household member.

In addition to coordinating the timing of plan changes, the client may also need to coordinate the timing of health care expenditures to maximize benefits. For example, the "bunching" of medical expenses in one year may allow a client to periodically satisfy the 10 percent floor for claiming an itemized tax deduction (7.5 percent for those age sixty-five and older). Conversely, the same strategy of bunching expenses can allow for more effective management of a health FSA or the coordination of periodic elective expenses (e.g., new eyeglass frames) with health FSA funding.

PROPERTY AND LIABILITY PLANNING FOR SPECIAL POPULATIONS

Health Insurance Planning for Same-Sex Couples

Rising costs and access to health care are recognized problems in the United States, but for **same sex couples**, taxes are an additional hurdle. Same sex couples who fail to marry may trigger extra taxes and complications when allocating resources for health care expenses. (The same is also true for non-married, opposite sex couples who choose to enroll in **domestic partner benefits**, although some employers bar access because the couple could marry and receive benefits.) The IRS considers the benefits received by a non-married, non-dependent spouse imputed income, and the cost of the benefit provided is added to the employee's ordinary income.

The **imputed income** can come in two ways. First, taxes are due on the imputed cost of the benefit—taxes not paid for benefits when received by married couples. Second, the additional imputed income could push the employee into a higher tax bracket, thus incurring additional taxes on other income. The company offering the benefits is also responsible for any additional income or payroll taxes due on the phantom income reported to the employee.

The same practice is applied if a partner's children are added to the health plan. In situations where one partner is the legal guardian of a child, it might be possible to co-adopt the child, thereby obtaining coverage. If the child is a dependent of the employee, coverage would be available.

To compensate, some employers choose to "gross up" an employee's income in the amount of the additional tax payment due. In January 2012, Ernst & Young LLP and its affiliates became the first Big Four accounting firm to offer this perk by reimbursing non-married lesbian, gay, bisexual, and transgender (LGBT) employees for the additional federal and state taxes paid on same-sex domestic partners' medical benefits in the United States. According to the Human Rights Campaign (HRC), more than thirty for-profit employers and municipalities offer the tax equalization benefit.[2] According to the HRC, calculating the gross-up amount is a two-step process. First, the taxes due on the fair market value of the benefit are calculated. Then, because that amount will be added to the employee's income and additional taxes will be due, that tax amount is also calculated. The sum of the two tax payments equals the gross-up amount for tax equalization.

The situation is worse if a client covers a domestic partner through an HDHP, despite the benefit of being eligible to contribute up to the annual maximum for a family account. If reimbursement is made from the HSA for a non-dependent domestic partner's health care expenses, the distribution is taxable and subject to an additional 20 percent penalty tax if the account owner is younger than age sixty-five. All HSA distributions for non-qualifying expenses are added to the annual gross income and subject to the 20 percent penalty tax.

However, a domestic partner covered by the HDHP may also be eligible to establish his or her own HSA, if eligible. To be eligible for an HSA, the partner cannot have other medical coverage or be claimed as the dependent of another taxpayer. Opening two HSAs allows each domestic partner to receive tax-free distributions from his or her individual account. This strategy also allows both partners to contribute up to the family coverage limit to each HSA; they are not constrained by the limit set for spouses.

Finally, if the domestic partner is the beneficiary of an HSA, all tax advantages end at the death of the account owner. The balance, or fair market value of the account, is taxable to the surviving domestic partner in the year of death. This is true for any HSA when the designated beneficiary is not a spouse.

Health Insurance Planning for Early Retirees

One of the biggest challenges for those who wish to retire early is finding and funding health care insurance. Clients may want to retire early for many reasons—to leave a job they dislike or find stressful, to pursue more leisure or volunteer activities, to take on more family responsibilities, or to pursue education or training for a second career. With fewer companies offering retiree health coverage, regardless of age, those who wish to retire prior to Medicare eligibility at age sixty-five may have to be creative.

The following list of alternatives could match the needs of some clients:

- Use a Health Insurance Exchange to obtain insurance coverage.

- If available, continue coverage through the employer, being sure to inquire about the coverage (same or more limited), the cost, the potential increase in premiums, and whether coverage is available until age sixty-five.

- For a couple or those with a partner, consider having one continue working to provide health insurance benefits while the other retires or cuts back to part-time work, assuming the domestic partner can be covered. However, this change must be planned to coordinate the addition of the spouse/partner to the coverage as a qualifying event (rules apply) or during open enrollment.

> ### Self-Test 9
>
> Link just quit his job and is considering extending his health insurance through COBRA. He paid $2,300 in premiums, while his employer paid $4,000. How much will his COBRA premium be if he uses this purchasing option?
>
> a. $2,300
>
> b. $2,346
>
> c. $6,300
>
> d. $6,426

- Seek part-time employment that includes access to health insurance.

- If the employer and the client are COBRA eligible, use the COBRA benefit to continue health insurance for the eighteen months before the client reaches age sixty-five. This could be an expensive alternative, because the client will be responsible for the full premium cost (employer and employee portions) and the 2 percent up-charge, but it would provide coverage for the employee, the spouse, and any dependents. Because of the continuous coverage, HIPAA protection would guarantee access to an independent policy, although the cost could be prohibitive.

- Purchase a private market policy, although this, too, could be a very expensive alternative, and health conditions could prohibit underwriting approval to secure an independent policy. When seeking coverage for a couple or family, it is important to inquire about pricing for individual and family coverage with an insurance broker with access to multiple companies, or to shop different companies individually. Age is a consideration for pricing, so purchasing individual policies could be cheaper than a family policy. If a family policy is purchased, it may be beneficial to do so in the name of the younger spouse so he/she will not lose coverage when the older spouse/partner transitions to Medicare.

- Consider any membership organizations, either professional, trade, or community/public service, that might offer group health insurance access. Coverage may be limited, but group rates could make this a more cost-effective option, especially for someone with few health issues. The cost and requirements to maintain group membership must also be considered.

Regardless of how badly a client may want to retire, an important caveat is not to act until health coverage and a budget with ample cash flow have been confirmed. Early retirement may be the goal, but not at the cost of jeopardizing the future.

Quantitative/Analytical Mini-Case Problems

Xuan Chen

1. Xuan Chen, a forty-year-old, unmarried client has been contributing to an HSA for the last three years using a salary reduction agreement through his employer. The stated effective annual rate on the account is 3 percent and the interest is compounded on a monthly basis. The client is in the 25 percent marginal federal tax bracket and the 5 percent marginal state tax bracket. Use this information to answer the following questions.

    a. How much money does the client currently have in the HSA if the client has deposited $200 per month and did not make any withdrawals?

    b. Because the client is in exceptionally good health, the client is also using this account as an additional retirement savings vehicle. How much money will the client have in the account at age 65 if the client maintains his current level of contribution?

    c. How much will the client have at age sixty-five if the client contributes $2,850 every year?

    d. How much will the client have at age sixty-five if the client contributes $2,850 every year if it is assumed that the contribution and catch-up provision limits increases to 2.5 percent each year? (Ignore any minimum or maximum dollar change limitations.)

So-hyun Joo

2. So-hyun Joo, a fifty-two-year-old client, has come to you for assistance with funding her HSA. Her doctor has told her that she will be facing knee replacement surgery within the next five years. She was also told that her out-of-pocket expenses (deductibles, copays, and various other uncovered expenses including rehabilitation) for the operation would total $4,000 if the operation happened today. Her open enrollment period is currently open. She plans to wait exactly five years for the surgery.

    How much money should she contribute on a monthly basis if the account pays a stated rate (APR) of 4 percent compounded quarterly. To determine her out-of-pocket expenses at the time of her surgery, inflate the current cost by an effective annual rate of 7 percent.

Ludwig Lindamood

3. Ludwig Lindamood has just accepted a position at a midsize firm that provides three health insurance plan choices for employees. Basic information about each plan is provided below (note: Plan C is a high-deductible health plan with a savings option). Ludwig must make a plan choice immediately. He can afford the annual premium for any of the plans and/or the HSA contribution. Although no one can predict a future health emergency, Ludwig estimates that he

will likely incur $500 in medical expenses during the next year. Given this forecast, what policy should he purchase to minimize his net health insurance cost for the year?

Plan Provisions	Plan A	Plan B	Plan C
Annual deductible	$300	$150	$1,500
Coinsurance	20%	35%	20%
Annual stop-loss limit	$1,400	$2,000	$3,000
HSA eligible	No	No	Yes
HSA yearly employer contribution	NA	NA	$400
HSA minimum employee contribution	NA	NA	$100
Yearly premium	$190	$175	$94

David Cohen

4.   David Cohen, a twenty-four-year-old, single, healthy male has just opened an HSA in conjunction with his qualified HDHP. He wants to determine how much the account might be worth if he funds it primarily for retirement purposes.

   a.   How much would the account be worth at age sixty-five if David makes a deposit of $3,100 per year for the next seven years before changing to his employer's standard health plan because of family health concerns and discontinuing contributions to the HSA? Assume that David earns only 3 percent per year for the next seven years while he might need the money, but after he changes plans he increases his risk and expects an annual return of 6 percent.

   b.   How much would the account be worth at age seventy if David makes the maximum deposit of $3,100 per year for the next eight years, but he also has to take a $5,500 qualified distribution at age twenty-eight? Assume that David earns only 2 percent per year for the next seven years while he might need the money, but after he changes plans he increases his risk and expects an annual return of 7 percent.

   c.   If David took a $10,000 nonqualified distribution from his HSA prior to age sixty-five, how much in federal income tax and penalties would he owe? Assume that he is in the 25 percent marginal tax bracket.

Comprehensive Bedo Case – Analysis Questions

Often, health insurance is overlooked in the planning process because it is generally employer provided. As such, the financial planner has little control over selection of the product or coverage. Health insurance assessment, however, should not be overlooked in the planning process. Adequate policy provisions, as should other aspects of coverage and the potential for future changes, should be evaluated.

Strategies using Section 125 Plan and FSA alternatives should also be developed based on the Bedos' annual health care spending patterns, deductibles, and copayments. Although it is unlikely that a planner would recommend that either Mia or Tyler purchase a private insurance policy, a cost analysis of other available policies offered during the open enrollment periods would be appropriate. The family's goal of living a financially satisfying life must be weighed against the relative costs of health care options.

1. Develop a health insurance planning goal for the Bedos. When conceptualizing this goal, consider the following.

    a. Is the goal developed in agreement with any or all goals and objectives that the clients have identified regarding health insurance planning?

    b. What situational factors might influence their health insurance goal? Are these factors explicit, implied, or assumed? Is additional information required from the Bedos? If so, what?

    c. What is the desired health insurance planning outcome for the clients?

2. Make a list of the lifestyle, occupational, and health factors that should be documented and evaluated for the Bedos. How might this information be obtained? How might it be useful in the current health insurance situation analysis? Also, make a list of life events that could affect the health insurance planning analysis for Tyler and Mia and that should be reviewed at subsequent client meetings.

3. Are there globally accepted, client-specific, or planner-generated planning assumptions that will influence the health insurance situation analysis? List the assumptions as they might appear in a plan.

4. Make a list of specific policy features that should be evaluated as part of the documentation and evaluation of the Bedos' health insurance planning efforts.

5. Conduct a current health insurance situation analysis for the Bedos. Be sure to assess the following:

    a. The after-tax costs of their current plans compared to purchasing an individual policy.

    b. The use of a tax-advantaged account as a health insurance planning tool.

    c.   How COBRA impacts health insurance planning for the Bedos.

    d. Should one of the Bedos' employers offer the option, would another managed care plan or high-deductible health plan and HSA be a viable option for this household? What criteria would be considered in this decision?

6. Summarize your observations about the Bedos' health insurance planning situation as they might appear in a client letter or plan.

7. Based on the goals originally identified and the completed analysis, what product or procedural strategies might be most useful to satisfy the Bedos' health insurance protection needs? When reviewing the strategies, be careful to consider an approximate cost of implementation, as well as the most likely outcome(s) associated with each strategy.

8. Write at least one primary and one alternative recommendation from selected strategies in response to each identified planning need. More than one recommendation may be needed to address all of the planning needs. Include specific, defensible answers to the who, what, when, where, why, how, and how much implementation questions for each recommendation.

    a. It is suggested that each strategy be summarized in a Recommendation Form.

    b. Assign a priority to each recommendation based on the likelihood of meeting client goals and desired outcomes. This priority will be important when recommendations from other core planning content areas are considered relative to the available discretionary funds for subsidizing all recommendations.

    c. Comment briefly on the outcomes associated with each recommendation.

9. Complete the following for the Health Insurance section of the Bedos' financial plan.

    a. Draft an introduction to this section of the plan (no more than one paragraph).

    b. Explain the purpose of an FSA and its potential benefit for the Bedos.

10. Prepare a ten- to fifteen-minute presentation for the Bedos of your observations and/or recommendation(s) for meeting their health insurance planning needs. Be sure to include visual aids or handouts.

Chapter Resources

Choosing a Medigap Policy: A Guide to Health Insurance for People with Medicare (www.medicare.gov/Publications/Pubs/pdf/02110.pdf).

General insurance information and quotes (www.insurance.com).

Health insurance cost information (www.nchc.org).

Health savings account information (www.hsabank.com, www.hsafinder.com, or www.treasury.gov/resource-center/faqs/Taxes/Pages/Health-Savings-Accounts.aspx.

Insurance Information Institute (www.iii.org/individuals/healthinsurance/).

IRS Publication 969, *Health Savings Accounts and Other Tax-Favored Health Plans*.

Medicare and You (www.medicare.gov/Publications/Pubs/pdf/10050.pdf).

Medicare information (www.medicare.gov).

Patient Protection and Affordable Care Act (PPACA) of 2010 (www.dol.gov/ebsa/healthreform/).

Section 125 Plan information (www.irs.gov/govt/fslg/article/0,,id=112720,00.html).

Your Guide to Medicare Medical Savings Account (MSA) Plans (www.medicare.gov/Publications/Pubs/pdf/11206.pdf).

Self-Test Answers

1: b, 2: c, 3: a, 4: a, 5: c, 6: b, 7: c, 8: c, 9: d

Endnotes

1. See www.medicare.gov or IRS Publication 969.

2. Human Rights Campaign. Domestic Partner Benefits: Grossing Up to Offset Imputed Income Tax. Available at: www.hrc.org/resources/entry/domestic-partner-benefits-grossing-up-to-offset-imputed-income-tax.

Chapter 7

Disability Insurance Planning

Learning Objectives

1. Any number of situational factors can affect a client's need for and selection of disability income coverage; however, some of the most critical factors include:

   a. the number of wage earners in the household;

   b. whether the client is providing support for minor children or disabled adults;

   c. the availability of assets or credit;

   d. whether the client has qualified for Social Security Disability Insurance;

   e. the hazard level of the client's job and whether he or she is self-employed;

   f. the client's lifestyle choices; and

   g. the client's risk tolerance.

2. Calculating the appropriate amount of disability insurance requires consideration of income and expenses, assets available to support lifestyle (i.e., bank accounts, undrawn lines of credit), and employee benefits (i.e., vacation and sick leave, Family Medical Leave Act (FMLA) availability, group disability policies). For example, a client might not have a short-term disability policy, but one may not be needed because of a generous leave policy from work (mitigation) or the availability of liquid assets (self-insurance). Again, several factors determine the amount of long-term disability coverage needed. A client could opt for a larger monthly replacement percentage and a longer elimination period or a lower replacement ratio and a shorter elimination period for roughly the same cost. In either case, it would be assumed that the client had assets that could be used to cover a gap or shortfall in benefits. Additionally, if there is another earner in the household and the household could meet monthly expenses on the income of the

Learning Objectives

remaining earner, there might be less need for coverage, or a smaller amount of coverage could be purchased.

3. Five basic questions must be answered when evaluating a disability policy:

   - How restrictive is the definition of disability?

   - How long does the insured have to wait before benefits are paid?

   - How much of a client's expenses (measured as a percentage of gross or net income) will be replaced during the benefit period?

   - Will the benefits remain fixed or will they increase with the rate of inflation?

   - How long will the benefits continue?

4. For purposes of disability insurance, disability can be classified broadly as either *own-occupation* or *any-occupation*, Any-occupation is the stricter classification, under which claimants are considered eligible to collect benefits only if their disability is severe enough to keep them from performing the duties required for any meaningful work. With an own-occupation policy, claimants are considered disabled and therefore eligible for benefits if they are unable to perform the duties required by their original or "own" job. In addition to these classifications of disability, a policy provision called a *residual benefits rider* is typically available for purchase. This rider offers added protection for partial disability or for claimants who can return to work on

a part-time basis. Finally, some policies offer a cost-of-living adjustment rider that continues to increase benefits as inflation increases.

5. In addition to traditional disability income replacement policies, a client might have access to or be eligible for Social Security Disability Income and/or Workers' Compensation insurance. To be eligible for SSDI a worker must be totally disabled and expect that disability to last for at least twelve continuous months. To be eligible for Workers' Compensation, the event that precipitated the disability must have occurred at work or when functioning in a working capacity. In addition, a disabled employee might have unused sick or personal leave that could be used for a short-term disability.

6. Many possible strategies can be recommended based on a client's situational factors and the quality of any in-place disability policies. Recommendations should generally center on a client's willingness and capacity to sustain the loss of income. Clients must be made aware that most disabilities not only reduce income but also increase expenses; therefore, recommendations should consider the likelihood and severity of any possible disability. Finally, strategies should also consider the policy provisions (e.g., inflation riders, classifications of disability, residual benefit clauses) that make the most sense for a client, because a client living in a dual-earner household or one with adequate access to assets might not need the same amount of coverage or a policy with many added provisions.

Key Terms

Any-Occupation

Automatic-Increase Disability Option

Average Premiums for Individual
Disability Insurance

Benefit Period

COLA

Contributory Disability Plan

Cost-of-living Adjustment (COLA) Rider

Decision Rules When Making a Disability
Insurance Recommendation

Definition of Occupation

Disability

Disability Insurance for High-Income
Earners

Disability Integration Clause

Disability Waiting Period

Disabled Children

Elimination Period

Future-increase Disability Option

Group Disability Plan Coverage

Group Disability Replacement Rider

Guaranteed-Renewable Disability
Provision

Incidence of Disability

Likelihood of Disability

Loss-of-Income Test

Modified Own-occupation

Mortgage Disability Insurance

Noncancelable Disability Provision

Own-Occupation

Own-Occupation Disability Coverage

Permanently Disabled

Probability of Becoming Disabled

Qualification Period

Quantitative/Analytical Mini-Case
Disability Problems

Rating Service

Recurrent Disability Provision

Replacement Ratio

Residual Benefit Rider

Residual Disability Provision

Short-term Disability Coverage

Social Security Disability Insurance

Social Security Disability Rider

Split-Definition Policy

Supplemental Security Income

Tax Credit for Disability Benefits

Taxability of Disability Benefits

Totally Disabled

Transgender

Wage Replacement Ratio

Waiver-of-Premium Clause

Workers Compensation

CFP® Principal Knowledge Topics

D.23. Analysis and evaluation of risk exposures

D.25. Disability income insurance (individual)

D.30. Insurance needs analysis

G.53. Social Security and Medicare

Systematic Financial Planning Process - Disability Insurance Planning

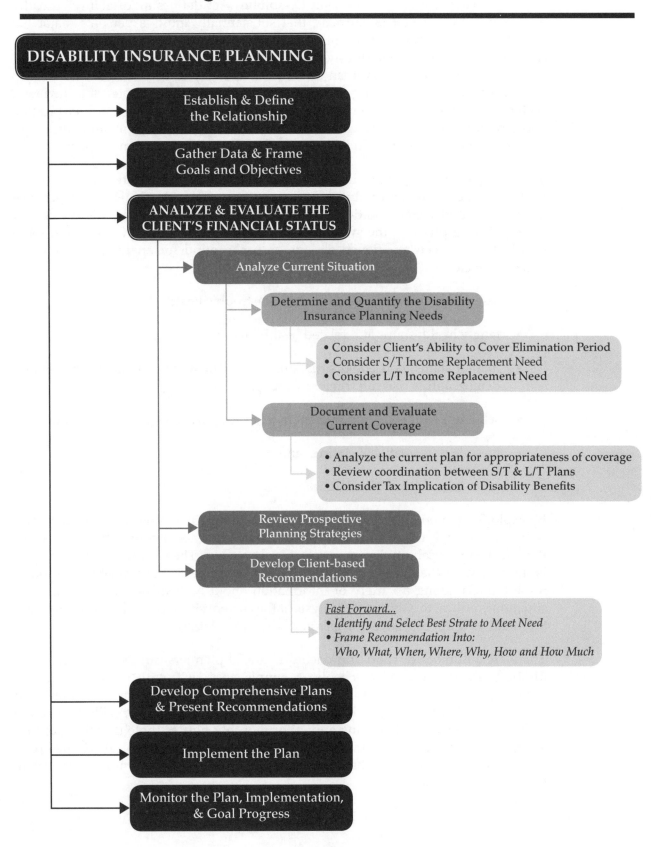

DISABILITY INSURANCE PLANNING

Establish & Define the Relationship

Gather Data & Frame Goals and Objectives

ANALYZE & EVALUATE THE CLIENT'S FINANCIAL STATUS

Analyze Current Situation

Determine and Quantify the Disability Insurance Planning Needs

- Consider Client's Ability to Cover Elimination Period
- Consider S/T Income Replacement Need
- Consider L/T Income Replacement Need

Document and Evaluate Current Coverage

- Analyze the current plan for appropriateness of coverage
- Review coordination between S/T & L/T Plans
- Consider Tax Implication of Disability Benefits

Review Prospective Planning Strategies

Develop Client-based Recommendations

Fast Forward...
- *Identify and Select Best Strate to Meet Need*
- *Frame Recommendation Into:*
  Who, What, When, Where, Why, How and How Much

Develop Comprehensive Plans & Present Recommendations

Implement the Plan

Monitor the Plan, Implementation, & Goal Progress

DISABILITY INSURANCE: DETERMINING THE NEED

Among those of working age, more are likely to become disabled than to die in any given year. The Americans with Disabilities Act defines a "disability" broadly as a physical or mental impairment that substantially limits a person's major life activities.[1] The incidence of disability varies based on many factors, including but not limited to gender, age, lifestyle, and occupation. Generally speaking, a forty-two-year-old worker is more than three times as likely to become disabled than to die during his or her working lifetime.[2] The purpose of this chapter is to review a method for determining a client's disability insurance need and to consider product and procedural strategies that can be used when making and implementing disability insurance recommendations in the context of a comprehensive financial plan.

Analyzing a client's current disability insurance coverage is relatively simple, but projecting the need for disability insurance protection clearly is not. Insurance information and client situational factors are collected during the discovery and data-gathering phase of the systematic planning process. Issues to evaluate, some of which have been mentioned already as background for analyzing the client's situation, include:

- assets available for use in case of a catastrophic health claim;

- family health status and related health history;

- marital status, household situation, number of wage earners or other family demographics that can trigger insurance needs;

- self-employment or employment in a hazardous profession or occupation;

- lifestyle or recreational choices; and

- attitudes, such as risk tolerance.

By exploring the possible future need for disability income protection and currently available coverage, the planner and client become informed of issues that could affect the selection of disability income protection strategies. The next step in the analysis is the review of the client's currently in-force coverage or the availability of other resources. Gathering a variety of information about a client's disability insurance situation is critical to a thorough analysis of the current situation and is the foundation for identifying appropriate strategies and recommendations.

There are a number of valid approaches financial planners can use to estimate the disability insurance need of clients. A simple approach, with an accompanying example, is shown below. In this example, the proposed policy is assumed to provide long-term coverage with a ninety-day elimination period. As illustrated, the estimate can be calculated using annual or monthly figures (note that the monthly estimates are rounded); however, since disability insurance is typically issued on a monthly dollar replacement basis, the monthly estimates may be more appropriate for most client situations.

Figure 7.1 Basic Approach to Estimate Disability Insurance Need

Inputs	Yearly Example	Monthly Example	Monthly Calculation
Determine Household Income Need in the Event of a Disability	$90,000	$7,500	
Determine an Appropriate Income Replacement Ratio	80%	80%	
Estimate Net Household Income Needed	$72,000	$6,000	$7,500 x 80%
Determine Spouse Income While Insured is Disabled	$50,000	$4,167	
Calculate Disability Need	$22,000	$1,833	$6,000 - $1,833
Long-Term Disability Benefits	$0	$0	
Social Security Disability Benefits	$0	$0	
Estimate Earnings from Assets while Insured is Disabled	$12,000	$1,000	
Sum of Disability Benefits + Earnings	$12,000	$1,000	$0 + $0 + $1,000
Calculate Long-Term Disability Insurance Need	$10,000	$833	$1,833 - $1,000
Estimate Short-Term (90 Day) Elimination Period Need	$5,500	$5,500	$1,833 x 3
Current Emergency Fund Value	$10,000		
Short-Term Disability Insurance Need	$0		$5,500 - $10,000

As illustrated, this hypothetical client needs a long-term disability policy that will pay $833 in monthly benefits. This estimate assumes that the policy will begin paying benefits ninety days after a covered disability. The emergency fund needed to cover the first ninety days of disability comes to $5,500; because the client has $10,000 currently saved, no short-term disability coverage is needed at this time. The next step in the planning process involves reviewing prospective product and procedural strategies related to disability insurance.

The key figure for determining an insurance need is generally based on an **income replacement ratio** of 60 percent to 70 percent of earned income. However, some planners prefer to estimate income needs more conservatively by using a 100 percent income replacement ratio. For example, assume that a client currently earns $90,000 per year before taxes. Using a 70 percent income replacement ratio, the client's total annual disability need is $63,000 of available, or after-tax, income. This amount is equivalent to the client's after-tax income before the disability, assuming a 30 percent combined federal and state marginal tax bracket. However, this seemingly straightforward estimation is complicated by three factors that must always be considered:

1. Disability insurance pays a fixed amount of monthly indemnity, but the amount that can be purchased is limited to prevent over-insurance, or the disincentive to return to work.

2. Disability policies often have a **disability integration clause**, also to protect against the moral hazard of over-insurance by instituting an offset for other benefits.

3. Disability benefits can be subject to income tax depending on whether the recipient paid the premiums and whether the premiums were paid with pretax or post-tax dollars.

Long-term policies are more important than short-term policies. A basic outcome of the financial planning process is an emergency savings fund or the identification of emergency sources of income. Self-insurance could be the best option for managing a short-term disability. By planning to use emergency funds, including cash assets, short-term liquid securities, or available lines of credit, clients can avoid the additional cost of short-term coverage. This could provide additional incentive to build and maintain an emergency fund and credit.

The greatest financial risk for most clients is a long period of disability. As such, the general rule is to purchase a long-term policy that provides benefits until age sixty-five or sixty-seven, when Social Security and other retirement benefits can be used to fund income needs. Short-term coverage, although important and perhaps the cheaper of the two options, should be a secondary consideration.

> **#Remember**
>
> Purchase a policy with an annual inflation adjustment to the benefit. Regardless of the percentage of income initially replaced, long-term benefits will soon become too low because of inflation.

Disability Insurance Planning Skills

Disability insurance planning may be the most important yet most frequently overlooked aspect of financial planning. This often happens because disability insurance may part of a client's employee benefits package, which has implications for the benefits provided as well as the taxation of those benefits. The incidence of personal bankruptcy has been closely linked to both medical expenses and job loss; so in the event of a disability the client could be facing both of these factors. Disability insurance could provide the necessary funding to help a client or family avoid, or at least mitigate, a potentially devastating financial loss.

Planning Skill 1: Know the Probability of Disability

As illustrated in Figure 7.2, the probability of becoming disabled for ninety days or longer is significantly greater than the probability of death until a client reaches age sixty or older, although on a continually decreasing basis. This information is important for a planner to understand because it illustrates the fact that the need for disability insurance actually decreases over time. This is more similar to life insurance than health insurance, where the need generally increases as a client ages.

Figure 7.2 Probability of Death or Disability by Age

Current Client Age	Probability of Death prior to Age 67[1]	Probability of Disability Lasting 90 Days or Longer prior to Age 65[2]
25	24%	54%
30	23%	52%
35	22%	50%
40	21%	48%
45	20%	45%
50	18%	39%
55	15%	32%
60	9%	9%

1. Calculation is a simple summation of the probability of death at every age from the current age to age 67. Social Security Administration, *Actuarial Publications, Period Life Table*. Available at www.ssa.gov/oact/STATS/table4c6.html.

2. National Association of Insurance Commissioners , *1985 Individual Disability Table A and B* as reported by Kenneth Black, Jr., and Harold D. Skipper, Jr., in *Life & Health Insurance*, 13th Ed. (Upper Saddle River, NJ: Prentice Hall, 2000), 149. Often referenced as 85CIDA or 85CIDB.

The reported *incidence of disability* can vary greatly from the raw data presented in the original 1985 Insurance Commissioners' study that still serves as the primary source for projecting the probability of disability.[3] For instance, some data are segmented not only by age, but also by cause of disability claim as shown in Figure 7.3, or by gender and occupation category of the claimant as shown in Figure 7.4.

Figure 7.3 Probability of Disability from Accident or Illness by Age

Current Client Age	Probability of Disability Lasting 90 Days or Longer prior to Age 65
25	40.3%
30	38.5%
35	36.5%
40	34.0%
45	30.5%
50	26.2%
55	20.5%

Source: New York Life, *Disability Income Worksheet*. Based on data from the 1985 National Association of Insurance Commissioners' Individual Disability Table A. Available at www.newyorklife.com/nyl/v/index.jsp?vgnextoid=9a7ba2b3019d2 210a2b3019d221024301cacRCRD. Often referenced as 85CIDA.

It is obvious that different occupations have differing incidences of disability; therefore, when determining whether to issue a policy and the applicable premium, underwriters take into account the *likelihood of disability* based on the applicant's profession. There are four basic classifications for disability insurance underwriting:

- Class 1—Professional;

- Class 2—Skilled;

- Class 3—Nonhazardous or light manual labor; and

- Class 4—Hazardous or heavy manual labor.

Figure 7.4 Probability of Disability by Occupational Class and Gender

Occupational Class	Probability of Disability (Lasting 90 Days or Longer prior to Age 65	
	Male	Female
1	18.0%	26.2%
2	33.3%	38.2%
3	46.1%	48.9%
4	49.2%	52.3%

Source: Adapted from Robert W. Beal, FSA, The *Real Risk of Disability in the U.S.* May 17, 2007, p. 7. Milliman, Inc. Available at www.lifehappens.org/media1/LIFEDIResearch.pdf. Based on 1985 National Association of Insurance Commissioners' Individual Disability Table A, often referenced as 85CIDA.

Planning Skill 2: Master the Key Terms of Disability Insurance Coverage

Before making a disability insurance recommendation it is important to recognize definitions and standard long-term disability policy options. Some of these key terms are outlined in Figure 7.5.

Figure 7.5 Long-term Disability Policy Definitions and Options Available

Option	Description	Options Available	Typical Selection
Elimination period	Period of time the insured must be totally disabled before benefits can begin	30, 60, 90, 180, or 365 days	Minimum: 180 days Preferred: Matched to short-term policy benefit period, paid leave available, or savings
Benefit period	Period of time the insurance company is obligated to pay the monthly disability benefits	3, 5, 10, or 20 years, until age 65, or lifetime	Minimum: 5 years Preferred: Age of eligibility for Social Security/Medicare
Qualification period	Period of time the insured must be totally disabled before residual benefits can begin	Same as elimination period	Minimum: 180 days Preferred: 30 days
Definition of occupation	Determines the conditions under which disability income benefits are paid	Own occupation or any occupation	Own occupation is preferred but should be coordinated with residual benefit rider
Residual benefit rider	Pays a partial benefit when the insured is not totally disabled	N/A	Recommended, but coordinated with definition of occupation
Cost-of-living adjustment (COLA) or inflation rider	Total disability and residual benefits each year are increased by a specified percentage	N/A	Recommended for maximum coverage, but expensive

Planning Skill 3: Understand the Tax Implications Associated with Disability Payments

For private or employer-provided policies, the **taxability of disability benefits** is based on who paid the annual premium during the plan year in which the disability occurs. For purposes of determining the extent of taxability, there are six basic premium payment scenarios, as shown in Figure 7.6.

Figure 7.6 Taxability of Disability Insurance Benefits Matrix

Scenario	Type of Policy	Premiums Paid by	Premiums Included in Income	Taxability of Benefits
1	Group	Employer	No	Yes
2	Group	Both	No	Yes
3	Group	Employer	Yes	No*
4	Group	Both	Yes	No*
5	Group	Employee	Yes	No*
6	Individual	Owner	N/A	No

* Taxes will be due on the portion of benefits attributable to any employer-paid premiums over the preceding three policy years.

If the client is insured through a group plan paid for completely by the employer and elects to exclude employer contributions from taxable income, any future benefit received is fully taxable to the employee. For employees who irrevocably elect to include the employer contributions as income (and therefore they are taxable in the current year), any benefits resulting from a disability occurring during the plan year would avoid taxation, prorated to the portion of employer-provided premium contributions made over the preceding three policy years.

If the premium cost is shared between the employer and the employee (i.e., a **contributory disability plan**), then taxes will be due on the portion of benefits attributable to the employer-paid premiums over the preceding three policy years. If the premium is paid completely by the insured with after-tax dollars, all benefits will be received tax free. When conducting a disability insurance analysis, it is very important that financial planners consider whether a client is better served to pay the taxes on the premiums received today or the benefits received in the future. Helping clients financially prepare for the unknown is a basic tenet of financial planning, and in this case client situational factors such as marital/partner situation, type of employment, self-employment, or recreational pursuits must be considered.

Planning Skill 4: Categorize Disability Insurance by Type

Of paramount importance is defining the type of disability coverage to purchase. Policies fall into two categories, **any-occupation** and **own-occupation,** based on the policy owner's ability to maintain gainful employment in a specific or nonspecific occupation. An any-occupation policy pays reduced or no benefits as long as the insured can maintain any employment, regardless of the level of skill or compensation relative to pre-disability employment. With an own-occupation policy, at least partial benefits are paid if the claimant cannot continue to hold gainful employment on a similar skill and compensation level as before the disabling event. Much more information on this topic, as well as modified own-occupation policies, are discussed in the Strategies section of this chapter.

Planning Skill 5: Identify Appropriate Insurance Company Selection Criteria

Given the long-term nature of most disabilities, it is important to match a product recommendation for a client with an insurer that is financially strong and stable. While it is possible to conduct an independent evaluation of an insurer, nearly all practicing financial planners rely on a **rating service** to help guide the selection of an insurance provider. The following firms make available insurance company ratings: A.M. Best Company, Fitch Rating, Moody's Investor Service, Standard & Poors, and Weiss Ratings. These firms consider each insurer's unique characteristics, including capitalization structure, asset and portfolio quality, risk exposures, profitability, liquidity, claim paying history, and financial stability. While each firm's rating system is different, most rank companies ranging from excellent to weak on a grading system, such as A+ to F.

Planning Skill 6: Estimate Average Premiums for an Individual Disability Policy

It is often difficult to obtain a disability insurance quote without undergoing the full underwriting process. However, it is possible to estimate premium costs for an average high-quality policy when writing a comprehensive financial plan in which disability insurance is not the primary client objective. The cost generally comes close to between 1 and 3 percent of a client's annual gross earned income.[4] The definition of disability or type of policy selected is the primary determinant of cost. It is up to the planner to adjust the premium to fit the needs of each client based on the elimination period, benefit period, and monthly benefit chosen. Extending the elimination period lowers the premium. As with most planning issues and estimates, it is best to over-estimate the premium than to be too conservative with disability cost estimates.

Planning Skill 7: Know When to Use a Liability Release Form

Protect yourself as a competent professional with a liability release form. If a client declines a recommendation to purchase disability insurance, a liability release should be signed. Thus, should the client, the client's spouse, or other family members question the lack of contingency planning to protect the household from a temporary or long-term loss of income, the planner is protected. The client's signature on the liability release acknowledges that the planner made a recommendation that was declined. But it is important that the advisor remain sensitive to and respectful of the client's choice when requesting a liability waiver.

Disability Insurance Product & Procedural Strategies

The following product and procedural strategies represent just a sampling of alternatives used by financial planners in practice. When planning for a client's disability protection, it is important to consider strategies for choosing the most appropriate product(s), structuring the insurance contracts, coordinating benefits between group and individual contracts, and coordinating benefits with social insurance, if applicable. Strategies to meet both short- and long-term needs must be considered, as well as coordination between the two.

Product Strategy 1: Purchase an Own-occupation Policy

The most generous disability insurance definition is known as *own-occupation disability coverage*. Under this definition, an insured receives benefits if, as the result of sickness or injury, the client is unable to perform the specific duties of his or her own occupation. The difference between the "own" and "any" occupation definitions is significant. It is quite possible that a client becomes disabled and unable to work in the chosen occupation but is able to perform the duties of another, unrelated occupation. In this case, if the client's coverage is any-occupation, no benefit is received. Most clients prefer an own-occupation policy.

The insurance industry is moving away from offering the more narrowly defined own-occupation policy; thus, own-occupation coverage could be more difficult to find. Policies that are available can be quite expensive. Insurance professionals report that a premium equivalent to 5 percent of a client's gross income is not unrealistic.

Product Strategy 2: Purchase a Modified Own-occupation Policy

Trends within the privately provided or non-group disability insurance market are ominous. Although own-occupation policies are appropriate for the majority of clients, finding such a policy is becoming increasingly difficult. Several insurance companies have either stopped offering own-occupation policies or significantly reduced the number of policies issued on a yearly basis. When and if an own-occupation policy can be obtained, the annual premium can be quite expensive.

The reason for this is the increasing number of claims being filed and the high costs associated with providing benefits to those who become disabled. Increasing costs are due, in part, to the types of disabilities that precipitate these claims. For instance, in the past nearly all disabilities were physical in nature. More recently, the number of mental and emotional disability claims has skyrocketed. This has had the most significant negative impact on coverage availability and premiums.

To meet the needs of the market while protecting the underwriting profitability of insurance companies, some firms have begun to offer modified own-occupation and split-definition disability policies (see below). A **modified own-occupation** policy is one that pays only if an insured is unable to engage in his or her chosen occupation and is also unable to work in a reasonable alternative occupation—or one for which the client is qualified by education, training, or experience. This strategy is appropriate in cases where a client does not qualify for an own-occupation policy or is unable to afford the premium for an own-occupation policy. The premium for a modified own-occupation policy can be significantly less than for an own-occupation policy.

Although the premium is less than for own-occupation coverage, some clients find that the premium still exceeds their insurance budget. A projection of 1 to 3 percent of gross client income provides a rough estimate of the premium cost for a disability policy, but elimination period, benefit period, age, optional riders, premium structure, occupational class, gender, state, health, amount and type of coverage, and benefit amount all influence cost.[5]

Product Strategy 3: Purchase a Split-definition Policy

A **split-definition policy** incorporates the preceding modified own-occupation definition with a short- and long-term disability definition. Specifically, to obtain benefits, the insured must be unable to engage in his or her own occupation for a certain period of time, usually two years. After the specified period, benefits are continued if the insured is unable to engage in a suitable and reasonable occupation.

It is apparent from these definitions that insurance companies want to encourage clients to re-enter the workforce as soon as possible. To this end, a **loss-of-income test** can also be used to determine benefit eligibility. This method considers earnings before the disability, earnings in the new position, and the maximum benefit coverage originally provided by the policy. If eligible, the insured receives a percentage of the maximum monthly benefits relative to the percentage of earned income lost between the two jobs.

This strategy is cost effective and a more readily available alternative than an own-occupation policy. The initial benefit period is contingent on the inability to perform all or the principal duties of the insured's occupation. This time offers the insured the opportunity for rehabilitation or other training, which could be necessary to pursue employment that is a reasonable match, or fit, according to prior training, education, or experience. The "split" in the definition and the coverage periods allows benefits to continue if the insured is unable to pursue related employment.

The initial period is typically two years, which may be insufficient for retraining, counseling, and therapy to adequately prepare the insured for re-entry into a related occupation. But benefits do not continue unless the insured is unable to function in any related occupation as defined by prior training, education, or experience.

Product Strategy 4: Purchase an Employer- or Group-provided Policy

This strategy allows a client to purchase **group disability plan coverage**, which typically costs less than a private policy. This strategy may use pretax dollars or, in some cases, taxable dollars. Medical examinations are usually not required. An initial waiting period might apply to new employees. Existing employees may be eligible to enroll only during an annual open-enrollment period.

Because of the pretax premiums, any benefits received are taxed at the recipient's current federal marginal tax bracket. This can be offset by the credit for the disabled, if the individual is eligible, including retirement for permanent and total disability. When disability benefits are included in gross income, a federal tax credit might be available to clients who are totally and permanently disabled. However, income guidelines and other restrictions apply in the calculation of the credit. For more information, see IRS Publication 524: *Credit for the Elderly or the Disabled* on the IRS website. If the option to pay premiums with after-tax dollars is available, any benefits received avoid taxation.

Coverage is typically standardized for an entire employment group. In a fluctuating job environment, primary coverage through an employer can be problematic. Disability coverage ends at termination of employment, leaving clients vulnerable to disability losses at the most inopportune time.

Product Strategy 5: Consider a Mortgage Disability Insurance Policy

This strategy offers a client another insurance alternative if the earned *income replacement ratio* is lower than needed to meet the majority of expenses, or if the individual is the sole source of income. Disability insurance offered through a mortgage company has additional drawbacks that are not generally mentioned at the time of sale. The insurance policy itself could be a fully restrictive policy, meaning that a client must be completely unable to engage in gainful employment to collect. Additionally, there may be a waiting period before it starts to pay, a time during which premiums must still be paid. This is not always the case, so research is necessary. Finally, the cost of such insurance is often based on the amount of the loan—so much per thousand dollars of coverage needed. Private disability insurance is based on the income needed and is usually a percentage of latest salary; thus, a client is probably able to draw more using this method than if the benefit payment was based on the mortgage alone.

Product Strategy 6: Purchase a Policy with a Social Security Rider

Monthly benefits for private or group coverage can be affected by policy provisions that coordinate the benefit amount with Social Security or workers' compensation benefits. Known as a **Social Security disability rider**, this provision decreases the amount of policy benefits paid if the insured meets both the policy definition of disability and qualifies for Social Security benefits. This rider should substantially reduce the policy premium. Group policies specifically offset Social Security in their contracts.

There are different types of Social Security offset riders in the individual market. In some instances, individual policy Social Security offset riders assure the client of a certain level of benefits if Social Security does not pay benefits. This is often the case because of the broadly defined any-occupation definition.

To encourage rehabilitation, the total combined benefit is less than the income received before the disability. For example, group benefits, which are typically limited to 60 to 70 percent of salary, are likely to be reduced if the insured is also eligible for Social Security or Workers' Compensation benefits.

Product Strategy 7: Ensure Continuation of Coverage by Including Appropriate Provisions

The availability of several provisions that help ensure continuity or continuation of coverage should be a key decision point when selecting a policy. A **group disability replacement rider** guarantees a client the ability to convert a certain percentage of the group disability benefit into an individual plan, thus making the group long-term disability policy portable. A **waiver-of-premium clause,** which pays all future premiums in the event of disability, is also an important provision to consider. Obviously it would not be beneficial for a disabled client to lose coverage because of nonpayment just when coverage is needed most.

A **guaranteed-renewable disability provision** protects the insured from policy cancellation by allowing the insured to renew a policy without proof of insurability. However, if available, a noncancelable policy is even better than a guaranteed-renewable policy. A **noncancelable disability provision** allows for the guaranteed renewal of the policy at a predetermined premium—an essential provision for controlling costs. The policy cannot be cancelled, and if desired, the insured can renew for a specific number of years or until age sixty-five or sixty-seven (depending on the policy).

Purchase a noncancelable and guaranteed-renewable policy, if available and affordable; otherwise, purchase a guaranteed-renewable policy. Including both riders is ideal, but these policies are typically offered only to low-risk occupational groups at a high premium. A guaranteed-renewable policy offers continual coverage subject to premium increases. But any premium increase applies to all policyholders in the same insurance classification and cannot be modified for individuals. Any premium increase must be approved by the state insurance department contingent on a company's adverse claims history.

Product Strategy 8: Purchase a Policy with a Recurrent Disability Provision

A common client question is, "What happens if I become disabled a second time as the result of a previous injury or illness?" It is not uncommon for an insured to become disabled, recover from the disability, return to the workforce, and then become disabled a second time.

It is important for those employed in high-risk professions to obtain a **recurrent disability provision** as part of the original disability contract. Recurrent disability provisions state that if a policyholder becomes disabled again within six months or up to one year, the disability will be considered a continuation of the previous claim. Without a recurrent disability provision, an insurance company can impose another elimination period before beginning benefits a second time.

The primary disadvantage associated with this strategy is that the addition of this provision adds to the cost of the policy. As with other provisions, this could negatively impact other short- and long-term financial objectives by diverting cash flow that could be used for other objectives.

Product Strategy 9: Purchase a Policy with Partial or Residual Benefit Provisions

The **residual disability provision** could be the most important rider available. A large percentage of all disability insurance claims either start or end in a residual disability claim. The basis of a residual claim is that those insured are either still or once again actively engaged in their occupation, but because of a sickness or injury they are suffering from either a loss of time and/or productivity or a loss of income.

The preferred residual provisions provide coverage based on lost income rather than on the loss of job responsibilities caused by a disability. The amount of the benefit is prorated according to the disability. For example, someone who is 50 percent disabled would receive a 50 percent benefit. Someone who was determined to be 30 percent disabled would receive a 30 percent benefit. It is assumed that the person will then work part time to increase monthly income. The primary disadvantage of this strategy is that it adds to the cost of the policy. However, this provision tends to add to the value of the policy because it pays benefits when policies without it would not. Most residual benefit provisions also institute a benefit floor of $250 to $500 to minimize the administrative cost of very small benefit payments.

Procedural Strategy 1: Do Not Purchase Group or Individual Disability Coverage and Rely on Social Security Benefits

The disability insurance definition used by the Social Security Administration is by far the most stringent. The qualification for coverage is based strictly on an any-occupation definition. To collect benefits, the insured must be currently eligible to receive Social Security benefits and be permanently and totally disabled. According to the Social Security Administration, *permanently disabled* means that the disability is expected to last at least twelve months, and *totally disabled* means that the insured is unable to work at any occupation. Furthermore, there is a five-month elimination period, and benefits do not include reimbursement for related medical expenses. Finally, the recipient is limited in the total amount of earned income per month they can receive (usually less than $1,800 is allowed).

> **#Remember**
>
> Depending on cost, availability and willingness to pay, recommend types of disability policies in this order for the best protection: own-occupation, modified own-occupation, and split-definition. Only after these policies have been explored should an any-occupation policy be considered.

The one advantage to Social Security coverage is that the cause of a disability does not have to be work related to qualify. So even if someone slipped in the shower, as long as the disability meets the other permanent and total criteria, benefits can be received after the elimination period. Given the restrictions on the definitions of permanent and total disability, the mandatory elimination period, and the lack of reimbursement for related medical expenses, the general recommendation for clients is not to rely solely on Social Security disability benefits. Consider these benefits only as a supplement to an existing long-term policy.

Each of these provisions adds to the cost of the policy. However, given their importance, each provision should be included unless the cost makes the underlying policy prohibitively expensive. The only other disadvantage to any of these provisions concerns the guaranteed-renewable provision. Although the policy cannot be cancelled for any reason other than nonpayment, this provision allows the insurance company to increase the annual premium for all individuals covered by the policy.

Procedural Strategy 2: Coordinate Noninsurance Strategies with Short-term Disability Coverage

For the average worker, the likelihood of short-term disability far exceeds that of long-term disability. Nonfinancial strategies such as maintaining a moderate reserve of employer-provided sick leave or vacation time could provide full salary and benefits for a short time. Emergency funds or other financial assets could be liquidated, if necessary, to extend the elimination period on a short-term policy and reduce premium cost. If group or individual short-term coverage is unavailable or judged to be too expensive, noninsurance strategies can be a cost-effective alternative; but client management is necessary.

Contingent on individual client and employer-provided benefits, noninsurance strategies might not be available, or there may be employer restrictions on sick leave or vacation reserves. Increasing the elimination period by increasing an emergency savings fund subjects a client to potentially significant opportunity costs. Higher rates of return could be sacrificed, or the untimely forced sale of assets could result in significant losses.

Procedural Strategy 3: Pursue Other Sources of Disability Benefits, when Applicable

Workers' Compensation is administered through state compensation boards and funded by participating employers. These programs grant benefits to employees who are injured at work or suffer a work-related illness. Although specific program provisions vary from state-to-state, benefits include medical treatment, partial wage replacement, and survivor benefits. In some states, clients might also be eligible for compulsory temporary benefits. These are basically state-sponsored disability insurance pools.

Generally the Workers' Compensation program can be thought of as a combination health and disability policy. But unlike Social Security benefits, Workers' Compensation covers only disabilities that occur during the normal course of employment. The other basic difference from Social Security is that employees are eligible for Workers' Compensation benefits for short-term, long-term, partial, and total disabilities.

Because of this broad coverage, some disabled workers can file claims with both Social Security and the state office of Workers' Compensation, but the combined benefit amount cannot exceed 80 percent of the workers' average current earnings. Clients who find themselves unemployed after a disability could be eligible for state-sponsored unemployment insurance, although some restrictions may apply and benefits generally end after thirty-nine weeks. Private unemployment insurance could also be available on a limited basis. However, the costs associated with this type of insurance are prohibitive and generally not worth the premiums. Benefits from private policies are related to previous earnings and typically equal no more than 50 percent of a person's earnings. This is further limited by a total dollar maximum monthly benefit. It is important to note that neither state-sponsored nor private unemployment benefits are designed for long-term disability situations.

Finally, settlements from a liability or negligence claim resulting from a disabling accident could provide assets or income. But this is a worst-case scenario and receipt of any financial benefits could potentially be delayed for years. Restrictions on applicability, availability, benefit amounts, and benefit periods limit the usefulness of these sources of disability benefits in the planning process. But for eligible clients, these benefits are a useful supplement that should not be overlooked.

Procedural Strategy 4: Increase the Waiting Period and Increase Emergency Savings Fund

Choose the longest **elimination period** that is financially feasible, but at least a ninety-day elimination period, because increasing the elimination period significantly lowers the annual premium. The financial planning process answers the question of how a client will fund living expenses during the elimination period. Expenses during this time can be covered from employer-compensated sick leave or other vacation time, emergency savings and other emergency income sources, or if necessary, supplemented with available lines of credit.

Extending the **disability waiting period** in a policy significantly reduces the cost of coverage for a short- or long-term disability policy. If a large enough emergency fund or other assets earmarked for liquidation are available, it may be possible to eliminate the need for short-term coverage. Compared to a 90-day wait period policy, a 180-day wait period can reduce the cost of long-term coverage by approximately 1 percent of a client's gross income. It is important to note that increasing the elimination period and increasing an emergency savings fund could subject a client to potentially significant opportunity costs. A client can sacrifice higher rates of return on assets held as emergency savings to implement this strategy. The untimely forced sale of assets earmarked for this purpose could result in significant losses.

Procedural Strategy 5: Reduce the Wage Replacement Ratio

This strategy reduces the premium cost relative to a policy with a higher wage replacement ratio. Reducing the amount of cash flow needed to fund a disability policy can provide a more cost-effective solution that ensures some income protection. It could allow for accumulating assets to meet this need as well as other household needs or goals.

Purchasing a policy with, for example, a 60 percent wage replacement ratio could leave a client underinsured. This could negatively impact other short- and long-term financial objectives, unless the client has the financial wherewithal to cover any possible difference between the benefit amount and actual living expenses. It is important to note that in most situations, this strategy should be reserved for two-income households. Reducing the replacement ratio can be a better alternative than no protection. But for many households, especially those already living at or beyond their means, further reducing available income could have an immediate disastrous effect on a client's disability cash flow situation.

DISABILITY PLANNING FOR SPECIAL POPULATIONS

Recommending Disability Insurance for High-Income Earners

Disability planning for the high income earner may seem like a Wall Street executive complaining that her bonus was cut by 80 percent to a mere $350,000. However, high-income earners, like moderate earners, are accustomed to a certain lifestyle. A disability could create serious financial repercussions. Multiple mortgages, private school tuition for children, and domestic help could all be considered fixed expenses not easily continued in the event of a disability.

Many disability insurance policies limit the maximum monthly benefit regardless of the stated percent of coverage. This is especially prevalent in-group policies. For example, a group disability policy could impose an absolute limit of $6,000 of monthly benefits or limit the amount of earned income includable in the benefits calculation to $120,000 of annual income. In either case, a high-income earner could face a situation where the group disability policy covers far less than the stated 60 percent of income.

Although many high-income earners might also have sizable net worth that could provide adequate unearned or investment income to fill the earnings gap, others might not have nearly enough to support their current lifestyle, which could create undue hardship on the earner's family. In these cases, the executive, doctor, or entertainer might want to purchase a supplemental disability income policy. These policies, although expensive, offer a much higher income limit—in some cases, $1 million or more—and are normally underwritten by specialty insurers, such as Lloyd's of London.

In addition to filling an income gap, a supplemental policy can provide an extra layer of financial protection that replaces a larger percentage of total compensation because it includes incentive pay, bonuses, or commissions as part of the earnings covered. Although moral hazard prohibits any policy from providing benefits greater than earned income, a supplemental policy can offer additional guarantees and enhanced portability.

The issue of disability insurance covering only earned income creates an additional issue for self-employed business owners—not all of whom are high-income earners, but they might be. Business owners often overlook the fact that their businesses generate income attributable to the owners' work that is not covered under the disability income insurance definition of *personal, earned income*. An example of this is a business that generates $250,000 of revenue per year based on the activities of the owner, but the owner draws a salary of only one-half that amount, choosing to reinvest the remainder in the company. That reinvestment would decrease or even cease as a result of a lost-time injury or illness and would not be replaced by a standard disability insurance policy. Strategies to prepare for this uncertainty are available, but the important point is not to overlook these issues when advising self-employed business owners.

Planning for Families with Disabled Children

Wage earners' disabilities have obvious emotional and financial repercussions. However, families with a disabled child, whether disabled from birth or as the result of an accident or illness, face very different financial planning hurdles. Although this situation does not fit the standard disability insurance planning need, because there is no loss of income, a disability to a child, whether psychological or physical, can be equally financially devastating and in extreme cases can mean a loss of income for life.

Social Security provides a financial safety net for such situations as long as the child's disability results in "marked and severe functional limitations" for at least twelve continuous months; this program is known as Supplemental Security Income (SSI).[6] In general, a child must meet the same eligibility requirements pertaining to disability status and income as an adult, but additionally the parents or caregiver's income must also be within eligibility limits if the child is under the age of eighteen. In addition to SSI, a minor child would also be eligible for state-provided medical services such as reduced-cost or free clinics.

Having a disabled child creates issues in addition to the obvious financial and emotional strain. Education planning can be much more complex. Instead of planning for college funding, a family or caregiver may be faced with determining the need, availability, and cost of a special education environment for grade school. Estate planning is another area that becomes more difficult when a child is receiving public aid. Bequeathing assets to a child with a physical disability may not be prudent, but bequeathing assets to a developmentally disabled child may be impossible or even illegal. In either case, a special-needs trust may be the most prudent way for parents to leave assets to a child without potentially disrupting or terminating the child's eligibility for Social Security or Medicaid benefits. The lesser-known support trust could be another vehicle for leaving assets to children; however, beneficiaries of such trusts are normally ineligible for financial assistance.

Once a child reaches the age of eighteen and is still eligible for Social Security benefits, then SSI can stop, and Social Security Disability Insurance (SSDI) should begin, provided the parent is insured under Social Security and is receiving retirement or disability benefits or is deceased.[7] The biggest difference between the two programs is that benefits paid under the SSDI benefit program are not need-based, meaning that the child could work for additional income, if able. Furthermore, if the child is ineligible for SSDI benefits because of the parent's status, the child can continue on SSI under certain circumstances.

Planning for a family with a disabled or special-needs child obviously takes a great deal of expertise given (1) the sensitivity of the planning and the advisor-client trust required and (2) the complexity of navigating the numerous legal, tax, and policy guidelines that must be followed.

Transgender Issues and Disability Insurance Planning

The term transgender refers to a person whose gender expression or identity differs from their birth sex. Disability insurance planning for transgender individuals, and others who have complex or sensitive medical histories, can be difficult. Each insurance carrier's rules differ, but in general, insurance companies are reluctant to issue a policy to anyone considering full or partial transgender surgery until after the surgery has been completed, the patient has been released from the hospital, and the patient has returned to work on a full-time basis.

Many insurance companies also require a full post-surgery medical evaluation to identify potential residual surgery issues, which can delay issuance of a policy for three or more years. When underwriting a policy for a transgender individual, it is common for insurers to evaluate the applicant's employment history, psychiatric and psychological state, and drug and alcohol history, in addition to factors related to the person's gender identity. Finally, some insurers will issue the new policy based on the person's gender indicated on the application, whereas other firms will base policy decisions and premiums based on the birth sex of the applicant. More information about transgender issues and insurance planning can be found at the Gay Lesbian Alliance Against Defamation website.

Mini-Case Problems

Tarek Framborgia

1. Tarek Framborgia is considering the purchase of a disability policy. He is currently thirty-five years old and earns $50,000 per year as a quality control engineer for a major industrial company. His greatest concern is that with his moderately strenuous job responsibilities and his potential for increasing earnings he be adequately covered should an off-the-job accident keep him from continuing his career. He has come to you with the following list of problems and questions.

   a. If I purchase a policy that pays a fixed benefit of 90 percent of my current salary, how long will it be before this amount covers only 70 percent of my future salary if I assume salary increases of 4 percent per year?

   b. Assuming the same policy as above, if I purchase a policy with a provision for future increases of $1,000 per year, how long will it cover at least 70 percent of my income?

   c. If I assume that both my salary and the inflation rate increase at 4% per year, and that there is no floor or ceiling to my potential benefit increases because I purchase both the COLA and future increase option provisions on the above policy, how much should my annual benefit be in twenty-five years?

Samantha O'Reilly

2. Samantha O'Reilly has come to your office for a second opinion about her individual long-term disability policy. She was told that her best option for reducing the cost of her policy was to choose a long elimination period. But she has become worried that she will not be able to pay her monthly expenses for the year-long elimination period. She has some savings, but she is afraid that is not enough.

    a. If her current annual salary is $43,000, her taxes are $8,000, and she just barely manages to fund her Roth IRA each year with $5,000, how much of an emergency fund would she need to meet only her living expenses?

    b. How long would it take her to achieve the emergency fund goal above if she currently has $18,500 saved, invests $300 per month, and earns an annual percentage yield or APY of 4.25 percent after taxes in her money market mutual fund.

    c. If she could reduce her elimination period to nine months for an additional premium of $10 per month, how much would she need to save on a monthly basis in the same money market account to reach her emergency fund goal within twelve months? Could she afford this savings payment if she suspended her IRA contribution for one year?

Deshawn Carter

3. Deshawn Carter has just received his open-enrollment notification and has asked you to assess his disability insurance coverage. He currently has a long-term, any-occupation disability policy available through his employer that pays a benefit of 80 percent of his $85,000 gross annual income. Deshawn previously elected to have his premiums deducted from his salary on a before-tax basis, and the premium dollars are not being added back into his taxable income. He has asked you to determine the net after-tax benefit he would receive should he become disabled under each of the following situations:

    a. No changes are made to his policy.

    b. He elects to have the pretax dollars used to pay his policy premiums added back into his taxable income. (Remember to remind Deshawn that this is an irrevocable election.)

    c. His employer has offered to pay 50 percent of the premium on his behalf, and Deshawn would elect to pay the other half of the premium with after-tax dollars. (Remember to address with Deshawn how the income tax impact of this election will change his net benefit over the next several years, assuming his salary remains static.)

Social Security Benefits Integration

4. One of your clients has just realized that her own-occupation disability policy has a Social Security benefits integration clause, meaning that her policy will have a dollar-for-dollar reduction in benefits paid if she qualifies for Social Security disability. According to her most recent Social Security benefits statement, she would be eligible for $1,325 per month for a permanent and total disability. How much would her disability policy pay as a monthly benefit under the following circumstances if her current annual salary is $62,000, her policy pays 70 percent of gross, and she pays for the policy with after-tax dollars?

a. Her disability meets the definition for her policy, but it doesn't meet the Social Security definition.

b. Her disability meets the definition for her policy and also meets the Social Security definition.

c. How much would her total combined monthly disability benefits equal if she meets both definitions of disability and her policy does not have a benefits integration clause? Why could this be problematic? In other words, why might this create a moral hazard?

Comprehensive Bedo Case—Disability Analysis Questions

Certain key data are needed before a disability needs analysis can be conducted for the Bedos. It is important to summarize the type of disability coverage currently in force for Tyler and Mia. Data such as the type of coverage available—short- or long-term—and the provider of the coverage—employer or private company—should be reviewed. Insurance company ratings and policy costs should also be considered. Other information needed to advise the Bedos includes the availability of Social Security benefits; the client's assumptions regarding the availability of these or other benefits; and the specific assets, expenses, or goals that the clients are willing to adjust in the event of a disability.

1. Develop a disability insurance planning goal for the Bedos. When conceptualizing this goal, consider the following:

    a. Is the goal developed in agreement with any or all goals and objectives that the clients have identified regarding disability insurance planning?

    b. What situational factors might influence their disability insurance goal? Are these factors explicit, implied, or assumed? Is additional information required from the Bedos, and if so, what?

    c. What is the disability insurance planning outcome desired for the clients?

2. Make a list of the lifestyle, occupational, and health factors that should be documented and evaluated for the Bedos. How might this information be obtained? How might it be useful in the current disability insurance situation analysis? Also, make a list of life events that could affect the disability insurance planning analysis for Tyler and Mia and should be reviewed at future client meetings.

3. Are there globally accepted, client-specific, or planner-generated planning assumptions that will influence the disability insurance situation analysis? List the assumptions as they might appear in a plan.

4. Make a list of specific policy features that should be evaluated as part of the documentation and evaluation of the Bedos' disability insurance planning efforts. For each feature, write a definition or explanation that could appear in this section of the plan or in the plan glossary.

5. Use the Financial Facilitator to calculate the income replacement need to be met by short- and long-term disability insurance for both Tyler and Mia, given their employer-provided policies.

    a. What is the resulting need if individually disabled?

    b.   What is the resulting need should they both be simultaneously disabled?

    c.   How does the assumption on qualification of Social Security benefits affect the calculation? Explain the advantages and disadvantages of planning for disability with or without Social Security benefits.

    d.   What are the tax implications of these benefits?

    e.   What are the implications for their emergency fund given the applicable waiting periods?

6.   Based on the information collected, financial advisors have a responsibility to fully document and inform clients of the analyses and results. This information can be communicated through a letter or via a comprehensive or modular plan. Summarize your observations about Tyler's and Mia's current disability insurance situation and the planning need(s) identified. Incorporate text, bullets, and graphics in your explanation.

7.   Based on the goals originally identified and the completed analysis, what product or procedural strategies might be most useful to satisfy the Bedos' disability insurance protection needs? Be sure to consider strategies matched to the planning needs identified for Tyler and Mia, individually. When reviewing the strategies, be careful to consider an approximate cost of implementation, as well as the most likely outcome(s) associated with each strategy.

8.   Write at least one primary and one alternative recommendation from the strategies selected in response to each identified planning need. More than one recommendation might be needed to address all of the planning needs. Include specific, defensible answers to the who, what, when, where, why, how, and how much implementation questions for each recommendation.

    a.   It is suggested that each recommendation be summarized in a Recommendation Form.

    b.   Assign a priority to each recommendation based on the likelihood of meeting client goals and desired outcomes. This priority will be important when recommendations from other core planning content areas are considered relative to the discretionary funds available to subsidize all recommendations.

    c.   Comment briefly on the outcomes associated with each recommendation.

9.   Complete the following for the Disability Insurance section of the Bedos' financial plan.

    a.   Outline the content to be included in this section of the plan. Given the segments written previously, which segments are missing?

    b.   Write the introduction to this section of the plan (no more than one to two paragraphs).

10. Prepare a ten- or fifteen-minute presentation for the Bedos of your observations and/or recommendation(s) for meeting their disability protection needs. Be sure to include visual aids, Excel handouts, and other materials that will make the recommendations more meaningful for the clients.

Chapter Resources

Council for Disability Awareness: www.disabilitycanhappen.org.

Disability Insurance Education—Glossary of Disability Insurance Terms: www.instantdisabilityinsurancequote.com/html/disability-insurance-education-glossary.html.

Elias, Stephen, and Kevin Urbatsch. *Special Needs Trusts: Protect Your Child's Financial Future.* Berkeley, CA: Nolo Press, 2011.

Gay Lesbian Alliance Against Defamation organization: www.glaad.org.

Insurance Information Institute–General disability insurance information: www.iii.org/fact–statistic/disability.

Information about Medicare: www.medicare.gov.

Nadworny, John W., and Cynthia R. Haddad. *The Special Needs Planning Guide: How to Prepare for Every Stage of Your Child's Life.* Baltimore: Brookes Publishing, 2007.

Rajput, Minoti. "Planning for Families of Children with Disabilities." *Journal of Financial Planning* August, 2001: 74–84.

Russell, L. Mark, and Arnold E. Grant. *Planning for the Future: Providing a Meaningful Life for a Child with a Disability after Your Death.* Planning for the Future, Inc., 2005.

Social Security Benefit Calculator (disability, retirement, survivor): www.socialsecurity.gov/planners/benefitcalculators.htm.

Stenken, Joseph F., *2016 Social Security & Medicare Facts.* Erlanger, KY: National Underwriter Company, 2015.

Endnotes

1. U.S. Equal Employment Opportunity Commission, *Facts About the Americans With Disabilities Act*. Available at www.eeoc.gov/eeoc/publications/fs-ada.cfm.

2. John R. Ingrisano, *The Disability Income Insurance Decision*. Available at www.aafpins.com/Old%20Web%20Site/aafpins/mono2.html.

3. "Report of the Committee to Recommend New Disability Tables for Valuation," *Transactions of the Society of Actuaries*, 37 (1985): 449–601. Available at www.soa.org/library/research/transactions-of-society-of-actuaries/1985/january/tsa85v3713.pdf.

4. AffordableInsuranceProtection.com, *How Much Does Disability Insurance Cost?* Available at www.affordableinsuranceprotection.com/disability_premiums.

5. Guardian Disability Insurance Brokerage, *Common Questions: How Much Does Disability Insurance Cost?* Available at www.disabilityquotes.com/disability-insurance/disability-insurance-cost.cfm.

6. Social Security Administration, *Benefits for Children with Disabilities*. Publication No. 05-10026, January 2012, ICN 455360. Available at www.ssa.gov/pubs/10026.html#a-0=0.

7. Social Security Administration, *Frequently Asked Questions: Benefits for Disabled Children*. Available at ssa-custhelp.ssa.gov/app/answers/detail/a_id/156/~/benefits-for-disabled-children.

Chapter 8

Long-Term Care Insurance Planning

Learning Objectives

1. The aging of the baby boomers coupled with a steady increase in life expectancy is fueling a rapid increase in the cost of and need for care for the elderly. This continuum of care includes home health care services, care at an adult day care center, in-home care, assisted living care, skilled nursing care, hospice care, and in some instances, a combination of these needs. As the annual cost of long-term care in the United States approaches $200 billion, providing care becomes either a direct client expense that financial planners must help their clients fund or an indirect expense paid for by the tax-funded Medicare and Medicaid programs. Thus, it is important for financial planners to help clients prepare to fund future long-term care expenses, for themselves or extended family members, as part of the comprehensive financial planning process. Central to long-term care planning is client education on the possible contribution of Medicare, Medicaid, insurance products, and self-insurance to meet future needs.

2. This chapter highlights the client situational factors necessary to analyze a client's need to purchase long-term care insurance or self-insure. Although planning for the uncertainty of long-term care needs is not an exact science, advisers typically focus on two issues: the client and the client's resources. Specifically a client's age, health, family health history, lifestyle choices, and occupational choices (i.e., risk triggers) can directly influence the likelihood of needing long-term care services. A client's financial and personal resources (network of family or friends) directly influence decisions regarding how to provide or pay for any necessary long-term care services. As part of this situational analysis, advisers often apply the rules linked to clients' net worth of less than $250,000, between $250,000 and $1.5 million, and over $1.5 million. These measures, clients' preferences, and projected care needs all play a role in influencing the decision to purchase long-term care insurance or to self-insure.

Learning Objectives

3. The need for long-term care insurance is based on (a) client preferences, (b) net worth, and (c)the projected need for care based on age, personal health, family health history, lifestyle choices, and occupational choice. The first two may be more easily identified, while the latter are more random. All three also significantly influence the projected cost of care and the amount of insurance to be purchased. Specifically, five factors are considered when quantifying the amount of insurance coverage to purchase the (1) range of services covered and benefit amount; (2) coverage period; (3) method by which benefits are paid (i.e., pool of money or indemnity); (4) elimination period; and (5) inflation rider to increase coverage limits.

4. Financial planners who are asked to evaluate an existing long-term care policy should first determine whether the client really needs coverage or if self-insurance is a better option. Then, factors that determine the amount of insurance needed as well as other riders that affect coverage should be reviewed. If the decision to discontinue a policy is made, a client has the option to (1) let the policy lapse; (2) exercise the nonforfeiture clause, if available; (3) exercise a contingent benefits nonforfeiture provision CBL, if available; or (4) exercise a Section 1035 exchange for another, more suitable long-term care insurance contract. With the latter option, care must be taken because the new policy premium will reflect the client's current age.

5. This chapter reviews linked-benefit (or hybrid) life and annuity products. These products offer clients the certainty of a base policy—death or annuity benefits, respectively—coupled with the availability of long-term care coverage, if needed. These products help clients manage the risk of paying for but not requiring long-term care protection, at the same time offering the certainty of estate protection or a policy benefit for heirs. Health underwriting may be less stringent or unnecessary—a benefit for some clients, but the single-sum payment may be a deterrent. Individual policy features can make hybrid policies less favorable than purchasing two separate policies if both are needed.

6. This chapter describes the benefit of a long-term care partnership plan. These plans are used to protect assets when qualifying for Medicaid. Medicaid requires clients to "spend down" assets to meet means tests (i.e., a maximum of $2,000 in countable assets owned in the individual's name, although this amount may vary by state), and a lien could be placed on any remaining assets for recovery by Medicaid for benefits paid. Conversely, assets transferred by an individual within sixty months of needing Medicaid benefits could trigger a penalty period and ineligibility for aid. Clients who wish to retain assets and avoid these rules could find a partnership plan, if available in their state, to be a good option that protects some level of assets for heirs or a legacy.

7. Long-term care insurance contracts typically are reimbursement plans that provide for a specific amount of coverage, or indemnity plans that pay for a specific period of time. Provisions that customize a policy include the elimination period, the inflation rider, the nonforfeiture clause, an accelerated

Learning Objectives

payment option, a restoration of benefits provision, a return of premium provision, the "bed hold" or reservation feature, and the spousal survivorship option. Additionally, policies can be guaranteed renewable or noncancelable and special provisions such as a joint policy or shared-care policy may be available only to couples. Policy discounts also may apply.

8. As illustrated in this chapter, numerous product and procedural strategies are available to advisers to customize long-term care planning recommendations to individual client needs. Strategies reflect differences in products available, product coverage and features, and the tax or other advantages of different products. Other strategies focus on client education to help clients choose between long-term care product options and self-insurance options. For many clients, a combination of strategies may be needed.

Key Terms

10 Percent AGI Threshold

Accelerated Payment Options

Activities of Saily Living (ADL)

Acute Care

Adult Day Care

Adverse Selection

American Association for Long-Term Care Insurance (AALTCI)

Annuity

Asset Based Products

Assisted Living Care

Bed Hold Provision

Benefit Bank

Chronic Care

Cognitive Disability

Contingent Benefits Nonforfeiture Benefits (CBL)

Continuing Care Retirement Communities

Cost-of-Living Adjustment (COLA)

Eimination Period

Expense-Reimbursement Contract

Extension of Benefits Option

Fee-for-Service Contract

First Dollar Coverage

Guaranteed Renewable

Health Insurance Portability and

Accountability (HIPAA)

Home Care

Hospice Care

Hybrid Product

Indemnity Plan

Indemnity Policy

Inflation Guard Rider

Inflation Rider

Integrated Policies

IRC Section 1035

Leverage Factor

Life Care Contract

Linked-Benefit Annuity

Linked-Benefit Products

Long-Term Care Insurance

Long-Term Care Rider

Long-Term Care Partnership Programs

Look-Back Period

Medicaid

Medicaid Planning

Medical Necessity

Modified Contract

Noncancelable

Nonexempt Transfer

Nonforfeiture Clause

Key Terms

Nursing Home

Nursing Home Care

Nursing Home Insurance

Partnership Plans

Patient Protection and Affordable Care
   Act (PPACA)

Penalty Period

Pool-of-Money Policy

Qualified

Reduced Paid-up Coverage Option

Reimbursement Plans

Reservation Feature

Residual Death Benefit

Restoration of Benefits Provision

Return of Premium Option

Return of Premium Provision

Risk Triggers

Shared-Care, Policy Rider

Shortened Benefit Period Option

Spousal Survivorship Option

Stated Period Policy

Waiver of Premium Provision

CFP® Principal Knowledge Topics

D.23. Analysis and Evaluation of risk exposures

D.26. Long-term care insurance (individual)

D.30. Insurance need analysis

Chapter Equations

Equation 8.1: Future Value (FV)

$$FV = PV (1 + i)^n$$

Equation 8.2: Present Value (PV)

$$PV = \frac{PMT}{i - g} \left(1 - \frac{(1 + g)^n}{(1 + i)^n} \right)$$

Equation 8.3: Future Annuity Payment

$$PMT = \frac{PV (i - g)}{\left(1 - \frac{(1 + g)^n}{(1 + i)^n} \right)}$$

Equation 8.4:

$$\text{Serial Rate} = \frac{(1 + i)}{(1 + g)} - 1$$

LONG-TERM CARE PLANNING: DETERMINING THE NEED

Once known as *nursing home insurance*, long-term care insurance continues to be redefined. Policies can cover a range of services from home health care, care at an adult day care center, in-home care, assisted living care, skilled nursing care, hospice care, or some combination of these needs. Various policies cover home modifications. Some policies also include benefits for respite care, which pays for substitute care given when a primary caregiver takes a vacation or break. A typical respite care clause will cover up to twenty-one days per calendar year of substitute care.

Because **long-term care insurance** coverage is designed for care that is not purely "medical care" and is not provided in a hospital, health insurance typically offers no coverage. Medicare offers only limited coverage under certain conditions. Hospitals provide **acute care**, or care that is immediate or short-term. Long-term care facilities provide for the progression of **chronic care** or care that may be continuous or long-term.

Long-term care facilities run the gamut from basic assisted living facilities that provide only domestic help to facilities with twenty-four-hour medical staff capable of dispensing medication and handling minor medical emergencies. With increased care comes increased cost. Facilities also offer a variety of living conditions, including group arrangements, semiprivate living quarters, and private rooms or even suites. With increased amenities and privacy come higher costs.

These costs are staggering and vary widely by geographic area. States such as Alaska, Massachusetts, and New York have, on average, higher costs of living, so facilities in those states are correspondingly more expensive. The median 2015 cost for semiprivate nursing home room was $80,300. Costs ranged from a low of $51,100 in Texas to $114,975 in Alaska.[1]

As these figures suggest, it is important for financial planners to estimate their clients' need for long-term care insurance. Analysis of a client's long-term care situation is built on information similar to that required for the analysis of health insurance needs. Issues to consider include:

- family health status and related health history;

- family demographics and preferences that can affect the need for care;

- assets available for care expenses, as well as the goals competing for those assets; and

- lifestyle and profession or occupational choices that could affect the future need for long-term care.

For example, the likelihood of developing Alzheimer's disease, the most common type of dementia, is greater for someone with a first-degree relative (i.e., a parent or sibling) who has the disease. For an individual with more than one first-degree relative diagnosed, the risks of the disease are even greater. Further complicating the analysis is consideration of the continuum of care that may begin at home, transition to an assisted living facility, and finally progress to a skilled nursing facility or what is typically called a *nursing home*.

The actual steps required to determine a long-term care insurance need are relatively straightforward. The process is show in Figure 8.1. The following inputs are needed: current age of client, assumed age at need, annual cost of care today, the long-term care inflation rate, the value of any funds set aside for long-term care expenses, the before tax-rate of return, the client's marginal tax bracket, and the expected increase in future savings for long-term expenses.

Figure 8.1 Long-Term Care Insurance Need Calculation

Client Data Input	Example	Calculation
Current Age	60	
Age LTC Benefits Begin	65	
Annual Cost of LTC	$50,000	Calculate FV of Cost N = 5 I/Y = 3 PV = $50,000 CPT FV = $57,964
Annual LTC Inflation Rate	3%	
Number of Years Benefits are Needed	3	
Before-Tax Rate of Return	8%	
Marginal Tax Bracket	25%	
Annual Increase in Savings	0%	
TOTAL LTC NEED		Calculate Need on First Day of Care 1. Determine After-Tax Return 8% x (1 - .25) = 6% 2. Calculate Serial Rate (1.08/1.03) – 1 = 2.91% 3. Calculate PV (Annuity Due) N = 3 I/Y = 2.91 PMT = $57,964 PV = $169,021
Current Value of Assets Set Aside for LTC Needs	$50,000	Calculate FV of Assets N = 5 I/Y = 8 PV = $50,000 FV = 73,466
NET LTC NEED		$169,021 - $73,466 = $95,555

As illustrated in this example, and using the equations listed at the beginning of this chapter, the client needs to purchase a policy that will pay total benefits equal to $95,555. Nearly every input used in a long-term care calculation is an assumption. As such, the derived estimates should be used only as a starting point in further discussions with clients.

Long-Term Care Insurance Planning Skills

Planners should base long-term care recommendations on a thorough review of a client's situation and projected needs. Determining need is not easy—although most companies will sell to clients between the ages of eighteen and eighty-four who are in reasonably good health and able to care for themselves. Unlike life insurance or health insurance that everyone eventually uses, long-term care insurance is truly a gamble. The analysis of a client's current situation begins by answering two important questions:

1. Does the client's current health, family medical history, or personal situation suggest that long-term care may be needed in the future?

2. Does the client have sufficient monetary resources or a family support network to "self-insure" in the event that long-term care may be needed in the future?

Self-Test 1

Pat has arthritis. She has trouble getting out of bed each morning, but she manages to make it through the day with the help of pain medications and a walker. Does Pat qualify for long-term care?

a. Yes because she cannot perform an ADL.

b. No because she still has functional abilities.

c. Yes because arthritis is an overarching trigger of benefits.

d. No because she does not yet exhibit dementia.

Notice that the first question does not address finances. This ordering is purposeful and based on the subjective factors that help characterize a client's situation and affect the pending decision. The emotion surrounding a client's decision to purchase long-term care insurance is second only to the decision to purchase life insurance. There is little reason to consider an objective assessment of the financial ramifications of long-term care without first addressing a client's fears, preferences, and even cultural biases about care.

Some of the concerns clients might face center not only on who will care for them, but also who will care for those for whom they have traditionally provided care and support. Guilt about the possibility of being unable to care for family can be a very powerful emotion. Other concerns surrounding a diagnosis or the need for custodial care might be more egocentric, such as feelings of shame, inadequacy, or failure. Women, who tend live longer than men, may be in greater need of paid care services. Single individuals, because of the lack of a family network, might require paid care services. The loss of privacy and the potential reversal of family roles are additional concerns, especially between parents and children. Besides these intrinsic barriers, home design, space limitations, or the geographic location of family members can pose even greater barriers for long-term care alternatives.

Although such fears may seem rational to clients or their children (if they are involved in the decision making), they can create barriers to open communication in the financial planning process. For example, a recent survey of adults ages eighteen to ninety revealed that more than 90 percent of respondents had not talked to their spouses, adult children, or parents about any of the following: their preferred long-term care option, the role of family members in managing care, and how to pay for long-term care.[2] Eighty-six percent of respondents in the same survey felt it was important for their financial professional to discuss long-term care with them, but only 9 percent of respondents had actually done so.[3]

A financial planning professional must be able to adequately empathize with these issues while encouraging clients to fully explore the biases that may shape decisions about long-term care needs. This could start by helping clients confront their understanding, or lack of knowledge, of the protection and limitations of Medicare, Medicaid, private insurance, and personal assets. Clients might also be ignorant of the range of care available or the associated costs. Allowing time for the discussion to evolve and approaching the conversation with sensitivity to the emotional and cognitive needs of the client are good strategies to encourage client action.

Planning Skill 1: Identify Activities of Daily Living

Eligibility for long-term care insurance benefits is based on functional ability, cognitive ability, or medical necessity. Functional ability is determined by the insured's ability to perform a certain number of **activities of daily living (ADLs)**, which measure the ability to perform routine personal care functions. Benefits begin when the insured is unable to perform two of the six activities (some policies may combine toileting and continence and require three of five ADLs) listed below:

1. Eating

2. Toileting (e.g., getting to, from, on, and off the toilet)

3. Transferring from a bed to a chair

4. Bathing

5. Dressing

6. Maintaining continence (e.g., ability to control bladder and bowel movements)

Cognitive disability, such as Alzheimer's disease or other dementias or organic cognitive disorders, is another eligibility trigger and one of the primary reasons for admission to a care facility today. The Alzheimer's Association reports, based on various studies, that at least half of elderly adult day care clients, almost half of nursing home residents, and 45 to 67 percent of the residents of assisted living facilities have Alzheimer's disease or another form of dementia.[4] Such mental incapacities are isolated triggers and should not be linked to any ADLs.

Medical necessity is the final qualification for long-term care insurance eligibility. A client is eligible for long-term care benefits if, as the result of an illness, injury, or chronic condition, the insured requires medically necessary care and assistance. Some policies require that a company representative perform the screening, but others allow the client's physician to do the assessment, which is typically considered the better option.

Planning Skill 2: Use Tax-Qualified Policies when Appropriate

Beyond the issue of eligibility for policy benefits is the related issue of policy eligibility for favorable tax treatment. The **Health Insurance Portability and Accountability Act (HIPAA)** of 1996, along with Internal Revenue Code (IRC) Section 7702B, set forth the requirements for long-term care policies to be considered "**qualified**" and therefore eligible for the premiums to be tax deductible and the benefits in excess of premiums paid to be excluded from income. To be considered a qualified policy, the benefit payment must be contingent on:

1. a chronic illness that lasts for at least ninety days;

2. the loss of at least two ADLs; and

3. severe cognitive impairment or impairment that requires supervision.

Tax qualification under HIPAA also precludes medical necessity as a stand-alone trigger for benefit payment. In addition to these benefit-related requirements, to claim the cost of premiums as a tax deduction the insured must also itemize tax deductions and claim medical expenses that exceed the adjusted gross income (AGI) limitation of 10 percent (or 7.5 percent if the client or client's spouse is sixty-five years of age or older).

The primary benefit of purchasing a tax-qualified policy is that the premiums may be tax-deductible, whereas no portion of the premium cost is a tax-deductible expense if the policy is not tax qualified. But the advantages of not purchasing a tax-qualified policy include unlimited benefits, less restrictive qualification for benefits, and a shorter qualification period. Given the AGI limitation and the age-based maximum deductibility of premium limits, as shown in Figure 8.2, this cost-reduction strategy will work only for clients who have substantial additional out-of-pocket medical expenses.

Figure 8.2 Maximum Deductibility for Eligible Long-Term Care Premiums, 2016

Attained Age in Year	Maximum Deduction per Person
40 or under	$390
41–50	$730
51–60	$1,460
61–70	$3,900
71 or over	$4,870
Source: Texas Department of Insurance	

For example, a fifty-year-old single client with an AGI of $50,000 per year would need to have more than $4,290 of other IRS Schedule A unreimbursed medical expenses to receive any tax benefit from the long-term care premium (($50,000 × 10%) ⊠ $710). But married clients, age sixty-two with the same AGI and each paying annual premiums of $3,000, would not require any additional out-of-pocket medical costs to qualify for the tax deduction. In this case, their deduction would be $1,000 (($3,000 × 2) – ($50,000 × 10%)). This would result in approximate tax savings of $1500 ($1,000 × 15%) assuming that they are in the 15 percent marginal tax bracket. It is important to note that these calculations reflect changes from the 2010 **Patient Protection and Affordable Care Act (PPACA)**, which increased the medical deduction threshold from 7.5 to 10 percent unless the taxpayer or spouse is age sixty-five or older. Regardless of the situation, the cost associated with the more restrictive benefit qualification must also be considered. It would be a disservice to the client, given the negligible tax savings, if the client was never eligible for benefits under the qualified plan but would have been eligible for benefits under a nonqualified plan.

Understanding eligibility for long-term care insurance benefits provides an important foundation for determining and quantifying a client's need for insurance coverage. This assessment is perhaps one of the most complex and subjective of any of the core financial planning content areas, and perhaps one of the most difficult to discuss.

Planning Skill 3: Understand the Triggers Associated with Long-Term Care Needs

By promoting the discussion of health, medical history, and caregiving preferences, a financial planner might be able to soothe a client's fears, enabling a more productive outcome. Certain personal, family, and lifestyle **risk triggers** should be closely reviewed when evaluating the potential need for long-term care expenses. In some cases, for example, family health history may be the most important evaluative factor for a planner to understand when helping a client analyze a potential need. Anticipating the probability of incurring assisted living or skilled nursing facility expenses, based in part on family history, will help determine whether and how much long-term care coverage is needed. Furthermore, awareness of a genetic health issue can also help determine when a policy should be purchased.

Specifically, the following risk triggers should be considered:

- personal health status (e.g., diabetes, alcoholism, high blood pressure);

- related family health history (e.g., coronary artery disease, cancer, Alzheimer's disease, or Parkinson's disease);

- lifestyle choices (e.g., high-risk activities, tobacco or other drug usage); or

- working in a hazardous profession or occupation (e.g., steel worker, emergency medical technician).

These triggers could compromise a client's future health status and increase the likelihood of needing chronic care or custodial care. Considered in conjunction with the client's care preferences and biases, both client and adviser will have a better idea of what challenges or financial demands the future may hold.

In addition to risk triggers, a client's age is another important factor when considering the need for and future cost of long-term care insurance. According to the *American Association for Long-Term Care Insurance (AALTCI)*, in 2007 only 3 percent of coverage claimants were under age sixty, compared to 55.2 percent of claimants who were eighty or older. Almost a third of claimants were between the ages of seventy and seventy-nine.[5] As a client ages, the likelihood of needing services may become more apparent. This phenomenon, known as **adverse selection**, is the tendency for persons with a greater chance of loss to seek coverage.

Adverse selection is controlled by the insurance company underwriting process, which results in higher premiums for those with greater need or more likelihood of making a policy claim. Therefore, the older the purchaser, the higher the periodic premiums, but the fewer premiums paid. The younger the purchaser, the lower the periodic premium, but the greater the number of premiums paid—unless a fixed-pay policy is chosen.

Clients under the age of forty typically are not advised to purchase a long-term care policy because the cost/benefit tradeoff makes long-term care coverage unfavorable for young clients. A young person who owns a policy is unlikely to make use of services for an extended period of time. As such, the opportunity cost associated with premium payments usually outweighs the benefits of being insured. Beyond the financial savings of delaying the purchase, clients under the age of forty are also more likely to have living parents or other family members who could help care for them in the event of a disability or illness that would otherwise have required a stay in a care facility.

Conversely, clients over the age of fifty-five typically should consider purchasing some sort of long-term care coverage. The reduced availability of an extended family network or of family members to care for an older adult, the increased immediacy of need, and the sheer cost of a long-term stay in a care facility make long-term care insurance at this stage of life very important for some clients. These same factors can be relevant regardless of a client's age. For example, a younger client with no extended family network, spouse, or partner to provide care may need and want a policy simply for peace of mind, so that if care is needed, coverage would be available.

By age sixty-five, clients should have a reasonable idea about their individual likelihood of need. After age seventy, policy cost and physical condition may eliminate the option. As reported in 2004 by *Consumer Reports*, a plan that costs a fifty-year-old $1,625 annually will cost a sixty-year-old $3,100 and a seventy-year-old $7,575. Furthermore, one out of four sixty-five-year-olds fails the physical and is rejected for long-term-care insurance. At age seventy-five, one in three is rejected.[6]

Planning Skill 4: Develop a Long-Term Care Insurance Purchase Strategy for Each Client

Owning long-term care insurance typically does not make financial sense for those under age forty, and many financial planners with clients in the forty to fifty-five age range take a wait-and-see approach. With college or wedding costs for children, as well as the need to accelerate retirement savings, discretionary cash flow may be insufficient to meet all financial goals. Although there may be many reasons to delay the purchase of long-term care insurance, an early purchase could be in a client's best interest. By purchasing a policy while younger and still working, a client has more income to meet financial obligations. For example, if a forty-five-year-old client purchased a twenty-pay policy, then the client's long-term care needs would be funded before or near the time of retirement. This would free up cash flow during retirement and protect the client from future premium increases.

Whereas a client's risk profile and age can offer insight into the need for long-term care insurance, a more definitive answer may come from the client's available monetary resources for funding care services. Assuming a client is at least age forty and that there is evidence to suggest that long-term care may be needed in the future, a client's situation analysis hinges on the retain-the-risk versus the insure-the-risk approach. This issue is addressed in the second question above, which asked, "Does the client have sufficient monetary resources or a family support network to 'self-insure'?"

The following rules can be used to help an adviser, in consultation with a client; answer the financial part of that question:

> **Rule 1:** If a client has a net worth between $250,000 and $1.5 million, exclusive of the value of the home, a long-term care policy may be worth considering. This type of client may not have sufficient resources to fully self-insure. If an extended stay in a care facility was needed, the cost would significantly reduce the client's net worth. Lifetime premiums, as a percentage of net worth, often indicate the need for long-term care coverage.

> **Rule 2:** Clients with a net worth in excess of $1.5 million, exclusive of home value, should consider self-insuring. Clients with this level of net worth can often afford to self-insure the risk of entering a care facility or fund needed services while remaining at home. Assuming an average stay in a care facility, usually quoted as thirty months, it is unlikely that this cost would deplete assets below $1 million for most clients, thus preserving wealth for other goals.

> **Rule 3:** Clients with a net worth less than $250,000, exclusive of home value, should consider self-insuring. Although this rule seems harsh, a client at this level of net worth would be expected to spend down assets and use Medicaid benefits to pay for an extended period of care, if necessary. The cost of premiums, in comparison to such a low level of net worth, makes purchasing a policy inefficient. But clients living in a Partnership Plan state, discussed earlier in the chapter, could purchase a lower-cost, state-certified policy and protect a certain level of assets while remaining Medicaid eligible. In addition to Medicaid qualification restrictions, clients could lose control over care decisions, and in-home care typically is not an option.

As with all "rules," exceptions apply. For example, consider a client with a net worth of $2 million who wants to preserve the money for a charitable or family legacy. To protect this wish, the client could purchase a long-term care policy, even though the cost of care is otherwise affordable. Another exception would be a married couple with $750,000 in assets who decides that the much younger spouse would care for the older spouse should chronic care be required. As long as the couple jointly reaches an informed decision, the choice to self-insure should be honored. Figure 8.3 summarizes how a client's age, family health history, or current financial situation can generally be incorporated into determining the need for long-term care insurance.

Figure 8.3 Long-Term Care Insurance Planning Decision Tree

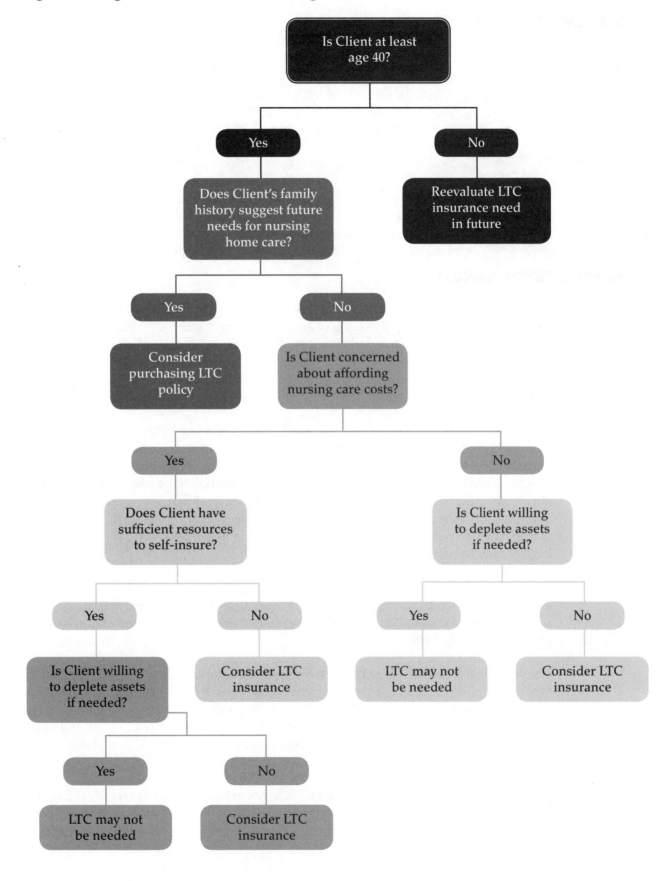

Planning Skill 5: Quantify a Long-Term Care Insurance Purchase Strategy for Each Client

Self-Test 3

Which of the following forms of care is not covered in a traditional long-term care policy?

a. nursing home care.

b. dementia care.

c. hospice care.

d. assisted living care.

Once the need for long-term care insurance has been established, attention must turn to the quantification of that need. Just as the determination of need is not always straightforward, neither is the decision regarding the amount of coverage to purchase. The continuum of services covered; differences in the respective costs of those services; and uncertainty regarding when, where, and how long services may be needed confound discussions on the amount of coverage. Additional factors, such as the ages of the client, spouse, or partner and the corresponding cost of coverage purchased now or later must be considered. A number of policy provisions are available to tailor a policy to a client's needs, but they may also add to premium cost. Conversely, experts caution that restricting coverage too much in an effort to reduce premiums may render the policy virtually useless.

When purchasing a long-term care policy, client and planner should consider several factors. The first factor is the range of services covered and the corresponding actual benefit amount. Most comprehensive long-term care insurance policies, or **integrated policies**, cover a range of services, although the amount of coverage may vary by service. The client may use **home care**, **adult day care**, **assisted living care**, **nursing home care**, or **hospice care** until the maximum benefit or the stated period expires.

The choice of maximum benefit is typically based on nursing home costs. But coverage amounts for other services vary and may be the same as the nursing home amount, a percentage of that amount contingent on the type of care used, or a smaller stated per-day coverage amount contingent on the service. Some policies cover only the insured, but others offer coverage for couples—a difference that can significantly affect the amount of coverage needed when matched to the needs of the client(s). Finally, it is important to note that policy benefits can be limited to specific coverage, such as facility-only or home-care only.

The majority of long-term care policies provide a specified "per-day" benefit. This amount can range from less than $100 to more than $300 per day. The appropriate amount should be based on a thorough review of facility costs in the area where the care is most likely to be received.

The second factor when quantifying coverage need is the length of the coverage period. Most policies offer coverage periods between two (or, in some states, a minimum of three) and five to seven years, although some may offer coverage for a lifetime. (The latter can be prohibitively expensive.) The length of coverage must be matched to the individual client's projected need for coverage, available resources, and ability to pay for the premiums.

The third factor considered when quantifying coverage need is how a policy pays the benefit. Some policies pay a full daily limit regardless of actual charges for long-term care services. In other words, the full cost of a day of service is "exhausted" regardless of actual cost, and with some older policies any excess benefit is lost. Most policies pay the actual amount of charges incurred up to the daily limit chosen. Still other policies provide a set dollar benefit that is not measured by calendar usage, but rather by a lifetime maximum dollar amount. For example, a four-year, $100-per-day policy would list a total benefit of $146,000 (4 × 100 × 365). But the insured's actual benefit received could vary depending on the type and length of care.

If the policy is a **pool-of-money policy**, also known as an **expense-reimbursement contract**, then regardless of the benefit per day received, the policy would pay $146,000 prior to expiration. If the policy is a *stated period policy*, or *indemnity policy*, however, then it will pay only for the specified period of years, whether or not the client receives the maximum $100-per-day benefit. In other words, the only way to receive the full $146,000 is to be eligible for the maximum per-day benefit for the full four years. A pool-of-money policy refers to the maximum lifetime benefit amount. A stated-period policy refers to benefits indemnified or paid over a period of time. Benefits from an individually owned long-term care policy are typically received tax free, except for benefits from an indemnity policy. Benefits are subject to federal tax only if the amount paid exceeds the higher of the cost of qualified long-term care or an IRS determined rate that varies by year.[7]

Clearly a pool-of-money, or expense-reimbursed, contract is superior to an indemnity contract. A pool of money might allow a client to extend a four-year benefit to longer-term coverage if the reimbursement did not require the maximum daily amount. In addition to direct reimbursement for services, other plans feature a per-diem cash payment based on the daily benefit amount and the number of eligible days in a payment cycle, regardless of the type of services used once eligibility is established. The cash payment option offers more flexibility because the recipient of the benefits determines how the money is spent.

The fourth factor to consider when quantifying the need for long-term care insurance is the **elimination period** of a policy. This factor affects the amount of proposed coverage, the cost of coverage (the longer the waiting period, the lower the premium), and the client resources available to pay for care during the waiting period. Almost all policies have waiting periods before benefits are payable, ranging from 0 days (known as **first-dollar coverage**) to, more commonly, fifteen to ninety days, although it can be as long as 365 days.

Policies define the days that count toward the elimination period or deductible differently, the primary consideration being "days of service," meaning how long the insured received paid care, or simply "calendar days." Some policies count actual qualifying service days or weeks (based on a defined number of qualifying days within a week), and they may count only consecutive days or random qualifying days over a period of time. Some policies also change the elimination period based on other factors, including previous stays in a care facility within the last twelve months, a hospital stay immediately preceding a move to a care facility, or a change in the insured's health.

#Remember

Long-term care costs continue to outpace inflation. It is reasonable to assume an annual cost of care increase between 4% and 5% annually.

The fifth factor to consider when quantifying coverage need is an inflationary increase in the cost of long-term care services. Although this can be important for any client, it is especially important for younger clients, because the difference between increasing service costs and policy benefits must be drawn from personal assets. An **inflation rider** provides an annual automatic increase in coverage limits in one of three ways. The annual inflation factor can be a simple fixed percentage, a compound fixed percentage, or it can be based on the Consumer Price Index or other measure of inflation. Policies typically offer a 2 percent to 5 percent inflationary increase, but other options may be available. Both the amount of increase and the kind of factor influence the cost of the rider, with choices that yield a greater increase in benefits, level of protection, or greater cost. Some sources refer to the inflation rider as a **cost-of-living adjustment**, or **COLA**.

A compound fixed percentage increase is recommended, unless clients are in their sixties or older, when a simple fixed percentage may offer sufficient protection. But clients should be cautioned that waiting until this age to purchase a policy will increase the cost and, depending on health status, could render them uninsurable. A second caution is also warranted. The inflationary increase should be automatic, not contingent on the insurability of the client, as some policies require.

Two more options for increasing coverage are available and can affect the amount of coverage purchased initially. A different inflation protection approach is a guaranteed purchase option that allows the insured to increase daily coverage automatically at periodic intervals (e.g., every three to five years) with no evidence of insurability. This provision offers additional flexibility, but it does increase the premium based on the insured's age at the time of exercise. If the option is not exercised, it is typically lost. Another option is to choose a significantly higher daily benefit than currently needed, with the idea that the cost of care will increase to or exceed the benefit amount. This can be more cost effective than adding an inflation rider. But higher-than-expected out-of-pocket costs may be necessary if the cost of care increases more than anticipated and no other inflation protection has been included.

Incidental to the consideration of inflationary increases in the cost of care is the issue of future premium costs relative to retirement income available. For those on a fixed income, premiums that were once affordable can, over time, become prohibitively expensive. Without a well-diversified retirement plan and ample savings, purchasing long-term care insurance that will subsequently lapse may not be the most productive use of premium dollars.

Although there may not be as many different policy types as other forms of insurance, the complexity and cost of long-term care policies can truly confound decision making for planners and clients. Emotional issues involved in the purchase decision add to this complexity. It is imperative that financial planners be familiar with the various aspects of the policy but, more importantly, with the process to help clients assess their situations. So for planners the question becomes who might need it and who might not? Answering that question requires both planner and client to recognize that a long-term care policy may be a cornerstone in protecting a client's financial well-being and provide confidence to face the future.

Long-Term Care Planning Product & Procedural Strategies

The long-term care planning landscape continues to change rapidly. Several important trends will have an impact on the way long-term care product recommendations are made in the future. Increasing premium costs, commonly described as double-digit and in some cases projected to be as high as 40 percent, have caught people with policies—and those seeking to purchase—by surprise, and they have significantly reduced sales.[8] High claims, a low-interest-rate environment, a low policy lapse rate, and a tendency toward adverse selection, among other factors, have forced several companies, such as MetLife, out of the long-term care market.

When purchasing long-term care insurance, it may be prudent to discuss with clients methods that optimize the cost/benefit ratio of the policy. One of the easiest ways to accomplish this, aside from adjusting the amount of the benefits, is to weigh the benefit period and the elimination period against the premium. A long benefit period and a short waiting period will result in a relatively expensive policy. Conversely, a policy with a short benefit period and a long waiting period may leave the client uninsured when insurance is most needed. A client's gender must also be considered. Because women tend to live longer than men, their benefit period may need to be longer. But if a client can afford the premium, a lifetime benefit, regardless of gender, may be best. When conducting such a cost/benefit analysis it is important to keep in mind that the average stay in a long-term care facility is thirty months; but the median length of stay, according to the AALTCI, is between twelve and thirty-six months. Clients have a 50 percent chance of incurring a stay of longer than three years.[9] To err on the side of caution, all of the following strategies assume that a client will spend at least three years in a long-term care facility and insure the projected total cost. The following product and procedural strategies provide an insight into some of the most widely used tools and techniques used by financial planners when helping clients navigate the long-term care insurance marketplace.

Product Strategy 1: Match the Appropriate Product to Each Client's Needs

More insurance companies are offering innovative products by packaging life insurance and long-term care products together, or by packaging annuity and long-term care products together. As a result of the Pension Protection Act of 2006 (the Act) insurance companies can offer life insurance and annuity products with a long-term care insurance rider, and the benefit payments would not be treated as taxable distributions of policy gains. This contributed to the availability of innovative linked-benefit products. Investments in the contract may fund the long-term care insurance rider, but neither that cost nor the benefits are taxed as a policy distribution. However, these expenses do reduce the investment in the contract, which may have implications if the contract is surrendered, or upon the death of the owner. This combining of products, often referred to as **linked-benefit products** or *asset-based products*, will provide additional choices—and complications—for consumers and financial planners.

The Act also modified the provisions of **IRC Section 1035** to allow for the tax-free exchange of a life insurance or annuity product to purchase a qualified long-term care policy, or the exchange of one long-term care policy for another. This change protects from taxation a client's gains from existing life insurance or annuity contracts by allowing their tax-free exchange for another product. These changes, which stemmed from the Pension Protection Act of 2006, made it possible for clients to protect their futures more easily by means of a deferred annuity with a long-term care benefit; to exchange an annuity or life insurance product to purchase a long-term care insurance policy; or to exchange an annuity or life insurance contract for a similar product with a qualified long-term care rider.

It is important to note that neither an annuity contract nor a traditional long-term care contract can be exchanged, tax-free, for a life insurance policy with or without a qualified long-term care rider. A nonqualified single-premium immediate annuity is also eligible for a tax-free exchange to purchase long-term care insurance. Care must be taken to handle the exchange appropriately through the insurance companies, with the advice of a tax professional, and to be certain that any death benefit surrendered (in the case of life insurance) is no longer needed.

Finally, **Partnership Plans** that started in the 1980s but became available to all states in the Deficit Reduction Act of 2005 are helping families meet long-term care insurance needs by providing tax and asset protection benefits. These plans encourage long-term care planning by linking insurance coverage and Medicaid eligibility, and they support the goal of reducing Medicaid spending for a rapidly increasing elderly population.

Financial planners must help clients develop a long-term care strategy regardless of a client's age, health status, or financial situation. As with other aspects of the planning process, the uncertainty of the future provides the context for the choices considered. For many, long-term care insurance offers the advantages of greater choice among care alternatives, including the option for the often-preferred in-home or in-community care, as opposed to residential or custodial care. For some, it eliminates or reduces the need for extended family to pay for care. For others, any private insurance delays dependence on Medicare or Medicaid, with their complicated federal and state regulations regarding eligibility for care, assets, and asset transfers. Those who cannot medically qualify for long-term insurance face these and other issues surrounding asset accumulation and preservation. Two product trends, linked-benefit products and partnership plans, offer planners and their clients' additional options. Discussions of both follow.

Product Strategy 2: Understand the Role of Long-Term Care and Life Insurance Combination Products

The question "what if I never need long-term care?" coupled with the expense of the insurance is a primary reason the average American fails to purchase long-term care coverage. Realizing that people feel constrained when faced with what they consider to be a lose-lose scenario, a number of firms within the insurance industry have created a product that combines the advantages of cash value life insurance with long-term care coverage. Financial planners and consumers have enthusiastically embraced these combination or hybrid products because clients perceive dual value—they obtain long-term care coverage while building cash value that can be used if the long-term care benefit is never needed.

Although products vary by company, most hybrid products add a long-term care rider to a cash-value (whole or universal) life insurance policy. Policies are available as a single premium or, in some cases, with a recurring premium. Regardless of the product, an accelerated benefits rider makes the policy death benefit available to pay for long-term care expenses. An **extension of benefits option** adds a multiple to the face value of a policy for additional long-term care expenses. For example, with this option, a $100,000 face value policy might provide an additional $200,000 in long-term care coverage. Both the death benefit of the policy and the extension of benefits would be available to pay long-term care costs. Unlike traditional long-term care policies that offer greater choice in the length of time qualifying care must be provided before policy benefits begin, a ninety- or one-hundred-day elimination period is common.

> **Self-Test 5**
>
> Afra currently needs long-term care assistance; however, her expenses fluctuate month-to-month. Which policy type will provide her with the highest average monthly benefit?
>
> a. Indemnity plan.
>
> b. Reimbursement plan.
>
> c. Extension plan.
>
> d. Partnership plan.

According to the AALTCI, insurance companies use different formulas when qualifying claims. **Reimbursement plans** repay actual expenses up to the policy maximum monthly benefit amount. Another approach is known as an **indemnity plan**, which pays a monthly maximum as long as the policyholder provides evidence of an ongoing need within covered expenditures. An indemnity plan tends to be more expensive. Policyholders determine the total long-term care amount and maximum monthly payment when purchasing a policy. Typical payment periods range from twenty-four to sixty months, although a few lifetime plans are also available. Policies may pay for a range of care options (in-home, assisted living, or adult day care) or be limited to nursing home care. Regardless of policy type, the benefit amount must fall within IRS-defined guidelines and conform to federal regulations for both life insurance and long-term care insurance coverage to maintain qualified tax status.

It is important to remember that clients must meet underwriting standards for a hybrid policy, but requirements vary by product. However, applying for a hybrid policy before it is needed is imperative. Some companies offer joint policies for couples, which may ease underwriting concerns if one spouse is reasonably healthy.

The following example, described by the AALTCI, illustrates how a linked-benefit life and long-term care plan works. A client with $400,000 in retirement assets is sixty years old and in good health. He plans to leave his nest egg to his adult children. The client could purchase a $200,000-face-value hybrid policy, naming his children as beneficiaries. By adding an extension of benefits rider, he could have up to $400,000 in long-term care coverage, or $6,000 per month for five years. Using a return of premium option, the client can cancel at any time and receive his premium payments back, but if necessary, the policy could protect the retirement assets intended for the heirs. Typically, the long-term care benefit rider is paid with a one-time premium of available assets. In 2011, the average premium was $65,000. A Section 1035 exchange of an existing life insurance policy could be used.

Product Strategy 3: Use Long-Term Care and Annuity Combination Products

Hybrid products combining *annuity* and long-term care features also appeal to clients who want protection for long-term care costs but fear that they will not ultimately need the coverage. Although features vary by company and individual product, several general product characteristics add to the appeal—and the complexity—of these hybrid annuity products. It is important to note that product availability also varies by state. Thus, working with a knowledgeable professional is important. Many financial planners, in the best interests of their clients and to remain within their competence limits, collaborate with someone who specializes in long-term care products once a client need has been established.

Both fixed and variable annuities may offer a *long-term care rider*, although fixed products are more common. Some linked-benefit annuity and long-term care products require health underwriting, and others do not. The latter feature is particularly attractive to those who may be uninsurable. However, the available term of long-term care benefits varies for these products. Annuities that do not require underwriting typically limit coverage to no more than thirty-six months, and longer benefit periods are available for products that require health underwriting. Of the products that do not require underwriting, some may be purchased before care is needed, and others can be purchased afterwards.

Funding options also vary by product. Lump-sum, or single, payments are required, but if funds are not available, a traditional annuity contract or a life insurance contract can be exchanged, through Section 1035, for an annuity with a long-term care rider. For annuities that require health underwriting, up to 60 percent of the value in a qualified account such as a 401(k) or IRA can be used through a Section 1035 exchange to purchase the product. This option can benefit couples, in that qualified funds of one spouse may be used to purchase a shared-benefit product that could offer protection for both. **Linked-benefit annuity** and long-term care products have certain disadvantages, including high surrender charges, low fixed returns on premiums, and the opportunity costs associated with funding long-term care insurance with a lump-sum payment rather than over time.

An example reported by Phipps may illustrate how this product can be used.[10] Consider a sixty-year-old female who purchases a twenty-year long-term-care fixed annuity with a 5 percent inflation-adjustment rider for long-term care coverage and a lump-sum premium of $50,000. This coverage provides the client with an initial $100,000 (two times the premium) in long-term care coverage for a maximum of the six-year benefit period. If no distributions are taken from the policy, the account will increase to $265,330 of long-term care coverage, or a maximum of $3,685 per month at the end of twenty years, assuming a 3.5 percent compound interest rate less administrative fees. If the long-term care coverage is not needed, the client may continue to defer the account value or begin taking distributions when the annuity matures. Upon her death, her heirs would receive the premium of $50,000 less any long-term care benefits paid *or* the accumulated annuity value, whichever is larger.

Despite the complexity of hybrid annuity products, the long-term care protection available, if needed, is typically based on four factors:

1. the amount of the single premium paid;

2. the term of benefits selected (generally four or six years);

3. the addition of an inflation factor and its amount (e.g., 3 percent or 5 percent); and

4. the multiplier (sometimes called the *leverage factor*) applied to the initial premium paid to determine the maximum long-term care benefit, typically 1.5 or two times if inflation protection is chosen *or* two or three times if inflation protection is not chosen.

> **Self-Test 6**
>
> The Medicaid look-back period is:
>
> a. 1 year
>
> b. 3 years
>
> c. 5 years
>
> d. Indefinite

Clients should be cautioned to fully understand and compare products prior to purchase. Also recall that, as a result of the Pension Protection Act of 2006 distributions for long-term care coverage are made on a tax-free basis. This tax savings could benefit a client who previously purchased a traditional annuity, but who could now purchase a hybrid product with a Section 1035 exchange and avoid the taxes that would have been paid on the gains in the original product.

Product Strategy 4: Integrate Partnership Plans with Medicaid

Medicaid is a federally funded program to provide health and long-term care services to those with few resources and very limited income. States administer the Medicaid program individually to provide nursing home care and, to a limited extent, in-home and community care services to those who meet financial and functional eligibility requirements. Medicaid will not pay for long-term custodial care for individuals until most of their assets have been spent and income is limited. **Medicaid planning** involves efforts to distribute or "spend down" assets to meet the means tests (i.e., a maximum of $2,000 in "countable" assets are owned in the individual's name, although this amount may vary by state) and other eligibility requirements for Medicaid long-term care benefits.

Financial planners are not allowed to recommend that clients forgo the purchase of a long-term care policy with the intent of spending down assets to become Medicaid eligible. When someone applies for Medicaid, the Medicaid agency reviews all transfers of assets that the applicant or his or her spouse have made in the prior sixty months; this is typically called the *look-back period*. Nonexempt transfers or transfers disallowed by Medicaid during this period cause the loss of Medicaid eligibility (what is called a *penalty period*) that begins when the individual is eligible for Medicaid benefits. The length of the penalty period is determined by dividing the value of the transferred asset by the average monthly private-pay rate for nursing facility care in the state. This penalty means that more of an individual's assets must be liquidated or, if unavailable, that the extended family may have to offer assistance.

According to the Omnibus Budget Reconciliation Act of 1993, each state has the right to reclaim the amount paid for the care of a Medicaid applicant. And because of the means testing to qualify for Medicaid, the home is usually the only property of substantial value that a Medicaid recipient is likely to own. But federal law also allows a married Medicaid recipient to transfer the home to his or her spouse without penalty. Then, should the spouse choose to protect the home, some states allow the spousal owner to gift the home to others. This creates a number of issues, beyond the obvious questions of whether the donor will be able to remain in the home. A second issue focuses on the donor's potential need for long-term care. If Medicaid was to be needed, all transfers within the prior sixty months would be reviewed, and any **nonexempt transfer** or a disallowed transfer of assets, during that prior five-year period would trigger a penalty period and ineligibility for aid. A third issue is the potential gift tax that could result.

When analyzing a client's capacity to fund a long-term stay in a care facility, financial planners must consider a client's desires regarding the location, the type of care anticipated, and family or charitable legacy relative to the assets available. Public/private partnership plans encourage long-term care planning by linking insurance coverage and Medicaid eligibility. Partnership programs, which are now available in more than thirty-five states, split the cost of custodial care between personal assets and state payments while allowing the recipient to maintain assets based on a predetermined formula established by the state.

Partnership plans encourage consumers to partner with a state-based program as they purchase qualified private long-term care insurance policies. Partnership-qualified policies are available from licensed insurance professionals and financial planners. To qualify, policies must meet state and federal partnership requirements. People who purchase a qualifying long-term care policy may still qualify for Medicaid after depleting their insurance benefits, provided they meet all other Medicaid eligibility criteria. In effect, a long-term care partnership program provides dollar-for-dollar asset protection. Each dollar paid by a partnership policy entitles a consumer to keep a dollar of assets sheltered from Medicaid recovery.

It is important to note that, although these plans help protect assets from liquidation, they do not waive the income limit or functional eligibility required for Medicaid—functional eligibility requirements that may exceed the eligibility requirements for the private policy that had been providing care services. Another downside of these partnerships is that benefits may or may not be portable from state to state, depending on individual state agreements that allow for reciprocity among states. Finally, Medicaid plans typically restrict coverage to services provided in a nursing home.

The increased availability of partnership plans further complicates long-term care planning for some clients. Advisers must be knowledgeable about the coordination of services and eligibility guidelines between private insurance and Medicaid coverage or be able to offer referrals to knowledgeable professionals who specialize in long-term care planning. Out-of-pocket expenses to supplement the cost of care provided by the private policy also must be considered.

Product Strategy 5: Purchase a Policy with a Lifetime Benefit Period and a 180-day Elimination Period

This strategy is appropriate in cases where the probability of needing skilled care for an extended period of time is high, based on defined risk triggers. Assuming a three-year or longer care period and having a 180-day elimination period results in the client self-funding for six months up front, but it ensures that the client will never exhaust coverage. This strategy is most suitable for clients who are predisposed to chronic diseases that could incapacitate them for years, such as Alzheimer's disease, severe osteoarthritis, Type 2 diabetes, or Parkinson's disease.

Two disadvantages are associated with this strategy. First, the cost of insurance for this level of coverage can be very high. Second, this strategy requires a client to maintain assets equivalent to the cost of care during the elimination period, which in light of current average monthly costs could equal $20,000 to $50,000, not including projected 5 percent increases in annual costs. An alternative to reduce the cost of coverage would be to extend the elimination period to a full year, if that option is available from the insurer and the client has enough assets to cover the cost. Another option would be to limit the lifetime benefit period, a feature that significantly increases the premium.

> *Self-Test 7*
>
> Zelda would like to purchase a LTC policy but her budget is very tight. She has a relatively large emergency savings fund already established. Which strategy will help reduce the annual premium she will need to pay for a LTC policy?
>
> a. Extend the elimination period.
>
> b. Increase the benefit amount.
>
> c. Increase the benefit period.
>
> d. Both b and c.

Product Strategy 6: Purchase a Long-Term Care Policy with a Four-Year Benefit Period and a Ninety-day Elimination Period

This strategy is appropriate in cases where the probability of needing skilled care for an extended period of time is moderate to average, based on defined risk triggers. Assuming a three-year care period and having a ninety-day elimination period result in the client self-funding for only ninety days up front. Even that could be offset by Medicare, if the client qualifies for coverage. This strategy is most suitable for a client who is predisposed to terminal coronary artery disease or stroke, where the length of stay is not as long and has a higher probability of meeting the requirements for Medicare coverage. Should the length of stay exceed the benefits, the family has some time to consider alternatives for meeting the cost of care. According to the AALTCI, only 12 percent of patients stay for an average of five years or more in a nursing home; the largest single group of patients, 30.3 percent, stays an average of one to three years.[11]

Three possible disadvantages are associated with this strategy. First, insurance for this level of coverage can be fairly expensive. Second, this strategy requires a client to maintain assets equivalent to the elimination period, in this case, $10,000 to $25,000, not including projected increases in annual costs. Third, the client could exhaust coverage should the long-term care extend beyond the four-year coverage period. A longer elimination period would reduce the cost of insurance, but it would increase the client's savings requirement.

Product Strategy 7: Purchase a Fixed-premium, Restricted-coverage Long-Term Care Policy with a Four-year Combined Benefit Period and a Ninety-day Elimination Period

This strategy is appropriate in cases where the probability of needing custodial care is average to low. The fixed premium results in a higher initial premium. Restricting the types of coverage reduces the overall cost of the insurance. One method of restricting the coverage would be to have two years of coverage for assisted living care and two years for nursing care. Assuming a three-year combined care period and having a ninety-day elimination period result in a client self-funding for three months up front. But as long as one type of care does not exceed two years, the client's coverage should not be exhausted.

The primary disadvantage associated with this strategy is that the total four-year benefit period would not be available for either assisted living or nursing care. Experts advise against limiting policy coverage to the point that the policy offers a false sense of security for the premiums paid but actually offers little protection. Eliminating benefits or key provisions from a comprehensive policy to make the premium affordable may be less effective than having no coverage at all.

Product Strategy 8: Purchase a Fixed-premium Long-Term Care Policy with a Two-year Benefit Period and a 180-day Elimination Period

This strategy is appropriate in cases where the probability of needing custodial care is average to low. Although fixing the premium results in a higher initial premium, it makes planning for expenses easier for the client. Assuming a three-year care period and having a 180-day elimination period result in the client self-funding for six months up front and six months at the end. If funding allows and the option is available, a one-year elimination period may be preferable because this option substantially reduces the cost of insurance and still requires the client to self-fund only one year of coverage.

The three primary disadvantages associated with this strategy are: (1) the cost of insurance may still be significant for some clients; (2) this strategy requires a client to maintain an emergency level of savings equivalent to the elimination period; and (3) the shorter coverage period could leave a client unprotected in the event of an abnormally long care period.

Product Strategy 9: Self-Insure the Long-Term Care Need

This strategy is appropriate in cases where the probability of needing custodial care is moderate to low. If a client's asset base is sufficient to support up to four years of expenses in today's dollars, long-term care insurance may not be needed. This strategy is particularly appropriate for clients with a net worth in excess of $1.5 million and whose insurance coverage and other assets are adequate to care for surviving family members.

If a client is strongly committed to leaving an inheritance to individuals or assets to charity, this strategy could significantly diminish the assets available. With nursing home care costs ranging from approximately $40,000 to $200,000 annually, contingent on location and care provided, the cost of even four years of nursing care can be a significant sum. Assisted living facility care is almost as expensive and often precedes a move to a nursing facility. Clients who want to leave a legacy should consider the benefits of a long-term care insurance policy.

Product Strategy 10: Self-Insure with a Life Insurance Backup

This strategy is best suited for a client whose asset base is sufficient to support at least partial funding of a long-term care stay. If a life insurance policy is available that allows for a living benefit to be paid for the costs associated with long-term care, even if the client is not terminally ill, then long-term care insurance may not be needed. This could be a good strategy for a client who has a life insurance need but wants added protection should nursing care, such as skilled care or hospice, be needed.

If a client is strongly committed to leaving an inheritance in the form of life insurance benefits, using the living benefit would reduce the amount of the legacy and/or leave the survivors underinsured at the time of death. This insurance should be purchased well in advance of possible need. Policies vary regarding the qualifications that must be met to receive the living benefit, so a complete understanding of the requirements as well as an evaluation of the cost of the rider should be considered.

Product Strategy 11: Self-Insure with a Medicaid Backup

This strategy is appropriate for clients with less than $250,000 in net worth, exclusive of the home. Clients with this asset profile may find that the premiums associated with long-term care insurance outweigh the benefits provided. It is possible that a client's asset base could be depleted if nursing home care is required, which would result in the client becoming dependent on Medicaid to pay for care.

Product Strategy 12: Take Advantage of Available Policy Discounts

In some states, a 10 to 30 percent discount is available for married couples who insure jointly with the same insurer. Another way of decreasing the cost of coverage for a married couple is by sharing a common benefit pool. Some individual plans allow couples to transfer benefits to each other from the same policy or sometimes between policies. A **spousal survivorship option**, available on some plans, requires both spouses to buy separate coverage. If one spouse dies after coverage has been in effect for a certain number of years, usually ten years, then the surviving spouse's policy becomes paid up. Finally, as with health insurance, long-term care insurance offers "good-health" discounts for people who do not take unnecessary health risks or have a history of debilitating diseases. Because policies vary so much by company, shopping for discounts in addition to other needed provisions can be time consuming. Working with a knowledgeable professional can reduce the time spent comparing policies.

Product Strategy 13: Use a Long-Term Care Partnership Program to Protect Client Assets

Long-term Care Partnership Programs allow policy owners to protect a portion or all of their assets if they ever need to apply for and use Medicaid services. Typically, clients should be encouraged to purchase a three- to five-year long-term care policy with a specific dollar amount of coverage. Should a client need long-term care coverage, the policy will pay benefits up to the maximum dollar amount of the policy, for example $250,000, over the policy term. After depleting the coverage, the client may qualify for Medicaid. These policies provide dollar-for-dollar protection of assets equal to the policy coverage limit (e.g., $250,000). That is, each dollar that a policy pays out entitles the client to shelter a dollar of assets from Medicaid.

Under provisions of the federal Deficit Reduction Act of 2005, each state is authorized to enact Partnership Programs, but not all states have done so. To qualify for asset protection, Partnership Program plans must be tax-qualified, include certain consumer protection provisions, and provide inflation protection.

Product Strategy 14: Purchase a Hybrid Life Insurance Policy with Long-Term Care Benefits

These cash value products, both whole life and universal, are ideal for clients who want to be protected against long-term care costs but desire to transfer any remaining assets to heirs. The policy protects assets and offers benefits even if the long-term care benefit is never needed. Underwriting may be more or less stringent than traditional long-term care policies, so purchasing early is prudent. Care should be taken that the policy provides benefits for a variety of care situations, not only nursing home care. Most policies do not provide for payment of benefits beyond five years, so clients anticipating the possibility of a longer stay because of medical or family history should consider a traditional long-term care policy. Despite potential future availability of assets for heirs, the initial purchase requires a sizeable lump sum for the single-premium payment, and returns on the life insurance policy are low.

Product Strategy 15: Purchase a Hybrid Deferred Annuity with Long-Term Care Benefits

Insurance companies are issuing both fixed- and variable-annuity products offering a guaranteed lifetime withdrawal option that includes the benefits of an annuity with a long-term care multiplier. Not all products require health underwriting, and for those that do, underwriting can be less strict than for a traditional long-term care policy. Once the qualifications for benefits are met (based on ADLs), there are few policy restrictions on how the funds are used to pay for care. Funds are received tax free, but the federal tax savings must be considered relative to the potentially lower return on the annuity when compared with other taxable investment options. The lump-sum payment is convenient for some purchasers who have chosen to self-insure but want the added security of the linked product and the tax benefits. The residual value also offers security, assuming no long-term care benefits are needed or the benefits do not exhaust the entire value.

Clients must be medically underwritten to quality for some products. A client in poor health will not have access to these hybrid annuity products but could have access to those that do not require underwriting. Clients must have significant assets available to (1) make the single premim payment, and (2) insure sufficient long-term care benefits, depending on projected need. Furthermore, because of surrender fees, clients must be certain that no part of the funds will be needed for the first five to ten years. And, once the policy matures, any withdrawals from the annuity will reduce the long-term care benefit. Returns on hybrid fixed annuities tend to be less than on traditional annuities, so projected need for long-term care coverage must be weighed against product returns on a hybrid product or the purchase of two traditional products (an annuity and long-term care insurance). Also, earnings on the current asset should be compared to earnings on the hybrid product before making the purchase. Finally, the hybrid must be purchased early enough to allow for the twenty-year maturity to fully access benefits.

Procedural Strategy 1: Purchase Policy No Earlier than Age Fifty to Fifty-Five

Clients younger than age fifty generally should not purchase long-term care insurance unless they know that they have a high likelihood of needing care at an early age and for an extended time. One possible scenario would be if a client knows of a genetic predisposition for early-onset Alzheimer's disease or Parkinson's disease and could be uninsurable in the future. Clients who wait until at least age fifty to purchase long-term care coverage implicitly self-insure the risk of needing long-term care coverage earlier than age fifty.

> ### Definition of a Couple
>
> Although definitions may vary by company, most apply a broad definition of couple when applied to long-term care products and riders. Typically a couple is defined as:
>
> • married;
>
> • partners (same- or opposite-sex) who live together for a specified period, often at least three years; or,
>
> • two people of the same generation (i.e., sibling, cousin, etc.) living together and sharing expenses for a specified period, often at least three years.

Procedural Strategy 2: Purchase a Joint Policy

It can be significantly less expensive for a married couple (or an unmarried couple that meets the policy definitional requirements) to purchase a joint policy than to purchase two individual policies with the same benefit amount and period. With this type of policy, the couple shares the pool of benefits, either individually or simultaneously. This can be a very useful strategy when both partners want long-term care coverage but only one has a high propensity for using the policy. Generally, this strategy should be recommended in situations where both spouses are close in age. Wide dispersions in age between spouses can trigger excessive policy premiums. However a joint policy allows the couple to maximize eligible tax deductibility for the premium when there is a difference in ages between the spouses.

Although the annual premium for this type of coverage is lower, the total benefit available for each spouse is also lower should both become benefit eligible. To compensate, a large inflation factor is recommended to increase the daily or monthly benefit should both members of the couple require benefits simultaneously. This strategy may be unsuitable for spouses who are of significantly different ages because of the higher premiums.

Procedural Strategy 3: Purchase Linked, or Shared-Care, Policy Riders

For a married couple (or an unmarried couple that meets the policy definitional requirements), benefits can be increased by linking individual policies with a shared-care rider, which essentially provides sequential access to the benefits available to each individual, thus doubling the benefit, if necessary. Benefits can be drawn on simultaneously by each spouse, but combining the benefits is only available after one spouse has exhausted individual coverage. Thus, assets will be needed to supplement the cost of care if benefit coverage is insufficient for all costs. Discounts can be available when spouses apply for coverage at the same time.

The shared-care rider adds to the cost of the policies, but it is cheaper than buying additional benefits. Linking policies with reduced individual benefits can be a workable strategy unless the cost of care for one partner exceeds the benefit available, thus requiring other assets to supplement that cost. The second spouse to need benefits will have access only to the remainder of his/her unused benefits, which could be insufficient.

Procedural Strategy 4: Increase the Coverage Period but Decrease the Daily Benefit

If a client has adequate funds to self-insure but does not want to risk the chance of depleting savings, then sharing the cost of care might be an excellent alternative strategy. By choosing a lower daily benefit, such as $75 or $100, and increasing the benefit period to five years or more, the client should have adequate protection in the event of an abnormally long care period. Without incorporating an **inflation guard rider** in the policy, choosing a low initial benefit amount could put undue strain on a client's finances, regardless of the coverage period. To offset this possibility, a planner could recommend a pool-of-money policy, rather than a stated period, or indemnity, policy so that a client can draw a higher amount, up to actual costs incurred, until the policy is exhausted.

Procedural Strategy 5: Educate Clients that Long-Term Care Costs Are Generally Not Covered by Medicare

Clients are often misinformed about Medicare coverage and may need guidance to prepare for unexpected long-term care costs. Medicare coverage for home care is limited to skilled-nursing care when homebound under a doctor's care. Skilled nursing home care, limited to one hundred days, is covered only within thirty days of a three-day or longer hospital stay. And hospice care in a Medicare-approved hospice is available only if a doctor certifies that the individual has six or fewer months to live. Furthermore, restrictions on the services covered, benefit periods, benefit payments, and client copayments apply in each situation. Without long-term care insurance and with only limited Medicare benefits, clients are effectively self-insuring against the costs associated with skilled nursing care. Unfortunately, these clients are often unaware of the actual costs involved, or how dramatically different the cost could be in one area or one type of facility versus another.

Implications for adult children who may provide care or share in the cost of insurance premiums or the cost of care services must also be considered. Although clients should not rely on Medicare as a long-term care provider, some clients may not be able to afford the cost of long-term care coverage.

Procedural Strategy 6: Tailor the Policy to the Client with Appropriate Provisions

Provisions customize the policy to better meet the needs of the client. Guaranteed renewability or better yet, noncancelability are recommended provisions that add to the cost of a policy. **Guaranteed renewable** means that as long as premiums are paid on time, the insurance company cannot cancel the policy, unless it does so for an entire risk category. But premiums can continue to increase. **Noncancelable** also means that the policy is in force as long as premiums are paid, but unlike the guaranteed renewable policy, premiums are fixed for the duration of the policy. Not all companies offer noncancelable policies; guaranteed renewable policies are more commonly available.

Some plans offer ways for clients to shorten the length of time that premiums are due. **Accelerated payment options** include ten-pay, twenty-pay, or pay-until-age-sixty-five options. Each of these payment options allows for a fixed payment period beyond which no further premiums are due. This can be a very beneficial feature for clients who can afford to "pre-pay" the higher premium, thus avoiding payment later when income may be reduced or medical expenses may have accelerated. The amount of the premiums no longer required could also become available for funding other goals.

Another feature available on some long-term care policies is the **restoration of benefits provision**. This feature is conditional and restores benefits that have been used under a policy, as long as the benefit pool has not been exhausted. For example, if a client has a six-year benefit policy and uses up five years of benefits, all of the policy benefits can be restored if they are not needed for a certain length of time, most likely twelve months. To trigger the restoration, a physician must certify that the insured no longer needs long-term care, and the insured must resume paying premiums if a waiver of premium had been granted.

The **return of premium provision** adds approximately 70 to 80 percent to the base premium, but it will repay the difference between premiums paid and benefits collected upon the insured's death. To collect on this feature, most insurers require the policy to have been in force for a certain period of time, such as ten years. Although this feature is moderately expensive, it may be a useful planning tool if a client is uncertain about the probability of using the policy but wants the assurance of coverage for care, if needed.

The **bed hold provision** or **reservation feature** preserves the bed or room in a long-term care facility should the client need to leave for a period of time, typically two weeks to two months, or for a certain cause, such as a stay in a hospital. In other words, the facility cannot "rent out" the room simply because it is temporarily unoccupied.

Self-Test 8

Roger, age 85, was released from the hospital 10 days ago after in-patient surgery (he did remain in the hospital overnight for observation). Since that time he has needed in-home care. Roger can expect Medicaid to pay for how many days of such care?

a. zero

b. 30 days

c. 100 days

d. unlimited

Self-Test 9

Rex believes that insurance of any type is a rip-off. He worries that if he does not need LTC care all the premiums paid will have been for nothing. However, he does not want to pay 100% of costs if he actually needs care. His financial planner has a solution. Which of the following provisions best serves Rex's need for insurance while providing some piece of mind?

a. Nonforfeiture clause.

b. Residual death benefit.

c. Return of premium provision.

d. accelerated payment option.

This can be a very valuable feature if care facility vacancies in the geographic area are at a premium.

A **residual death benefit** makes the full life insurance benefit available if the long-term care coverage feature is not used. Some policies provide a minimal residual death benefit to cover final expenses if all policy benefits are exhausted. Inflation protection can also be purchased. This additional feature provides some protection against increasing long-term care costs.

One of the most beneficial options that can be purchased with a long-term care policy is the **nonforfeiture clause**, especially if a client is younger or still in exceptional health. In some policies this is known as a **benefit bank**. This clause allows the insured to receive some residual benefit in the event of policy lapse or death before making a claim. Many states require nonforfeiture on policies, or the company may voluntarily offer it as an option. The nonforfeiture option adds to the cost of a basic policy premium—in some cases, as much as 40 percent, and by some estimates as much as 100 percent.[12] Different types of nonforfeiture options are available, and costs vary by company.

Nonforfeiture options are similar to those for cash value life insurance. These options include a reduced lifetime (or paid-up) benefit, a reduced benefit period, or a return of premium. The **reduced paid-up coverage option** provides that a specified amount of coverage is available until the death of the client, but the daily benefit is permanently reduced, and with some companies the coverage is limited to nursing home care. The **shortened benefit period option** provides the insured the benefit originally offered, but the duration of coverage is limited based on the dollar amount of the premiums paid. With the **return of premium option**, a percentage of the premiums paid is returned after policy lapse or death.

For insureds who did not purchase a nonforfeiture option, some policies offer **contingent benefits nonforfeiture benefits (CBL))** upon lapse. Based on a standardized table recommended by the National Association of Insurance Commissioners (NAIC) 2000 Model Act and Regulation, this benefit is available when a policy lapses because of increased premium cost. Availability of the option is based on a comparison of the insured's age and the percentage increase in premium cost, either for a single increase or for cumulative increases, compared to the initial premium amount. Like other nonforfeiture options, CBL is available only when required by state law or when voluntarily offered by the company. The options are reduced paid-up benefits (available indefinitely, but with a reduced daily benefit) or a shortened period of benefits (with the original coverage benefit available, but for a limited time).

For clients who are considering a long-term care policy lapse or replacement provision, financial planners must carefully study the nonforfeiture and CBL options available. In some cases, continuing a policy for even a short period of time can affect the nonforfeiture benefits available. As is true with other types of insurance, clients should be cautioned not to cancel a policy until another is in force. Furthermore, a pre-existing condition clause in the new policy could limit coverage initially. Also, premium costs will reflect the increased age of the client at the date of purchase. These are two distinct disadvantages that should not be overlooked.

Procedural Strategy 7: Use Tax-advantaged Methods to Purchase Long-Term Care Coverage

A portion of the long-term care premiums paid for a tax-qualifed policy may be eligible for a medical expense deduction for clients who own their own businesses (including S-corporation owners, LLC members, and partnership owners) and individual taxpayers who file Schedule A as part of IRS Form 1040. For individuals, tax-qualified long-term care insurance premiums paid for themselves, their spouses, or any tax dependents (e.g., parents) can be claimed as a personal medical expense.

Additionally, clients who purchase health insurance through a high-deductible plan and a health savings account (HSA) can use distributions from the HSA to pay long-term care insurance premiums up to a maximum eligible premium amount. This results in a pretax purchase method for long-term care insurance. Some states also offer tax incentives (i.e., deductions or credits) for long-term care premiums.

Keep in mind that the deductibility of long-term care premiums exclusive of the *10 percent AGI threshold* is available only to business owners. Individuals can deduct premiums only if all unreimbursed medical expenses, including long-term care premiums exceed 10 percent of AGI or 7.5 percent for those age sixty-five or older. If an HSA is used to purchase long-term care coverage, clients will lose the IRS Schedule A deduction. Bear in mind that distributions from Section 125 plans and flexible spending accounts may not be used to pay long-term care insurance premiums.

Procedural Strategy 8: Consider Group Long-Term Care Coverage

For those who need long-term care insurance, group coverage may be an acceptable option, especially for people who might not meet the underwriting standards to qualify for an individual policy. However, for those who can qualify individually, adverse selection may force healthy clients to pay increasing premiums to subsidize the costs of others in the group. Because of the group policy guaranteed or modified-guaranteed offering (i.e., little or no medical history or health underwriting required), adverse selection can result in large premium increases. Additionally, most group policies do not offer automatic inflation protection, but increases in coverage through a guaranteed purchase option, which is based on the age of the insured. Excercising this benefit can be expensive, so the benefits available may be quite limited as the client ages. Group long-term care premiums often appear to be inexpensive, but the policy limitations may actually make group insurance more expensive than an individual policy or self-insuring the costs via other assets.

LONG-TERM CARE PLANNING FOR SPECIAL POPULATIONS

Continuing Care Retirement Communities

According the to the AARP, **continuing care retirement communities** (CCRCs) combine independent living, assisted living, memory or special care, and skilled nursing home care in a tiered approach for those who want to prepare for health care need transitions. Rather than moving from one facility to another as health care needs change, a retiree enters a CCRC as an independent person living in a single-family home or apartment. When the need arises, the person can transfer to assisted living or nursing care facilities within the community. And for couples who need different types of care, the community can accommodate both needs while promoting independence and togetherness. Many CCRC residents prefer the notion of living in one location with an available continuum of care. Family members also like the idea of consistent friendships within the community as well as familiarity with the caregiving services. But CCRCs can be expensive. Clients who wish to consider this type of living arrangement in retirement should consider the costs and plan accordingly. According to AARP, Some CCRCs require nonrefundable entrance fees (e.g., $100,000 to $1 million) and monthly maintenance charges (e.g., $2,000 to $5,000).[13] It is also common for the monthly fee to increase over time and as the health care needs of the resident change.

Three CCRC contracts are common. The first is a **life care contract,** also called an *extensive contract*. This provides unlimited assisted living, medical treatment, and skilled nursing care over a resident's lifetime with no additional charges. A **modified contract** offers residents a choice of services for a predetermined period of time. At the end of that time period, additional services may be purchased. Finally, a **fee-for-service contract** provides access to a CCRC, but once assisted living and/or skilled nursing care is needed, the resident will be required to pay market rate for additional services and care.

When working with clients to select the appropriate CCRC facility, it is important to consider factors associated with the financial viability of the CCRC as well as other licensing and inspection reports. Qualitative issues to consider include facilities and grounds, staff, food, transportation, and interests shared with other residents. Third-party accreditation and review standards are available, such as from the Commission on Accreditation of Rehabilitation Facilities/Continuing Care Accreditation Commission (CARF/CCAC), or LeadingAge.

Long-Term Care Insurance Issues for Women

Women are particularly affected by the issue of long-term care. On one hand, they are more likely to be caregivers, by choice or because financial support for paid care is unavailable. On the other hand, women are more vulnerable to the need for paid care services because they live longer and spend more years of their lives alone, on average. Almost 70 percent of women age seventy-five or older, compared to about 30 percent of men, are widowed, divorced, or never married.[14] Older women also tend to have lower incomes and access to fewer resources. Consider the following statistics:

- Almost two-thirds of family caregivers, defined as those providing care and assistance for an older adult or someone with a chronic or disabling situation, are female (65 percent). The "average" U.S. caregiver is a forty-nine-year-old woman who works outside the home but spends about twenty hours each week providing unpaid care to her mother for nearly five years.[15]

- The Alzheimer's Association recently reported that 60 percent of family caregivers and other unpaid caregivers of people with Alzheimer's disease and other dementias are women. The caregivers are white (70 percent), married (66 percent), and aged fifty-five or older (56 percent). Nearly half of the caregivers (44 percent) work full or part time. Little relief for unpaid caregivers is available, because 50 percent of them live in the same household as the person with Alzheimer's or other dementias for whom they provide care.[16]

- AALTCI reported that longevity, an average of five years more than men, explains why women use more long-term care services than men. More than 70 percent of nursing home residents are women, and 75.7 percent of assisted living community residents are women. Of those who remain independent aged seventy-five or older, women are 60 percent more likely than men to need help with one or more ADLs.[17]

- Almost two-thirds of all Americans living with Alzheimer's disease are women. A larger proportion of women than men have Alzheimer's or other dementia primarily because women live longer than men, on average, not because women are more likely to develop dementia. According to the research, age-specific onset does not vary by gender.[18]

- When asked about what would be or has been a barrier to discussing long-term care, women were more worried than men (72 percent to 57 percent, respectively) about upsetting their families by talking about long-term care needs or options.[19]

- A 2011 study reported that, based on a representative sample of U.S. adults age twenty-five and older with an income of $50,000 and higher, men were twice as likely as women (69 and 31 percent, respectively) to have purchased long-term care insurance in the last six to ten years.[20]

- According to AALTCI, women represented just over 60 percent of the 2010 purchasers of life insurance policies with long-term care coverage. One-third (34 percent) of the women who purchased new life insurance policies with long-term care riders in 2010 were between the ages of fifty-five and sixty-four, and nearly 40 percent were between the ages of sixty-five and seventy-four. Male purchasers tended to be slightly older.[21]

Financial planners have an opportunity to empower women to change the course of their lives by discussing long-term care planning. For many individuals, the question focuses on whether there is a need. But for many women, whether thinking about themselves or others in their lives, the question may not be *if*, but *when*. Helping women understand their options and make informed choices by planning for that uncertainty is a value-added service that only a well-informed financial professional can provide.

Quantitative/Analytical Mini-Case Problems

Ambra Turco

1. Ambra Turco is age fifty and single. She is concerned about funding long-term care insurance costs in the future. Based on family history, she has determined the following:

   - She will likely need long-term care coverage beginning at age seventy-eight;

   - She will need coverage for six years;

   - Long-term care costs in her area are currently $72,000 per year;

   - Long-term care costs are increasing by 5 percent annually;

   - She can earn 7 percent on her savings and assets;

   - She currently earns $98,000 per year; and

   - She has saved $75,000 that she is willing to earmark for long-term care costs.

   Use this information to answer the following questions:

   a. What is the future value cost of long-term care coverage when Ambra enters a nursing facility?

   b. What is the total cost of coverage for six years when Ambra enters a nursing facility (present value of cost determined at age seventy-eight)?

   c. How long will Ambra's long-term care savings last when she enters a nursing facility?

   d. Assume that Ambra has other property valued at $250,000. If she is willing to use this asset to help pay for long-term care costs, does she need long-term care insurance at this time?

Dan and Terry Ogelsmith

2. Recently, a married couple—Dan and Terry Ogelsmith—requested that you assist them by writing a modular, or targeted, long-term care financial plan. The clients both turned fifty-four this month and are fairly wealthy but not rich. Specifically, they wanted to consider self-insuring for any long-term care costs. However, they do not know whether they have adequate assets to self-insure. Use the following client assumptions to answer their questions.

   - The current cost of an assisted living facility is $95 per day and the nursing care facility is $135 per day.

   - Cost of care will increase at an annual effective rate of 6 percent throughout the time period. Assume cost increases occur annually.

   - Both clients will simultaneously enter care facilities at age seventy-seven, spend three years in assisted living and one year in nursing care, and die at age eighty-one.

- For simplicity, assume that all expenses, whether premium payments or direct costs, are to be paid at the end of each year.

- The policy includes a *waiver of premium provision*. In other words, once the clients begin to receive benefits for a long-term care stay, premium payments cease.

- Premiums are not paid during the elimination period.

- The clients currently have $40,000 that could be set aside for long-term care expenses. But if long-term care insurance is purchased, this same account would be used to pay for the insurance premiums.

- The effective annual required rate of return on invested funds is 6.5 percent.

- For simplicity, assume that all months have thirty days.

Use this information to answer the following questions:

a. How much will assisted living care cost per year when the clients reach age seventy-seven?

b. How much will nursing care cost per year when the clients reach age eighty?

c. What is the total present value need for one person at age seventy-seven?

d. Given the future value of assets saved for long-term care needs compared to future costs, should the couple plan to self-insure the need?

Lakned Jones

3. Lakned Jones is fifty years old. He is working with you, his financial planner, to calculate his long-term care insurance need. Please use the following assumptions to calculate Lakned's net LTC need:

Current Annual Cost of LTC: $73,000

Age at which Lakned will need LTC Services: seventy

LTC Inflation Rate: 4.50 percent

Number of Years Benefits will be Needed: six

Before-Tax Rate of Return: 7 percent

Marginal Tax Bracket: 25 percent

Annual Increase in Savings: 0 percent

Current Value of Assets Set Aside for LTC Need: $100,000

Comprehensive Bedo Case – Analysis Questions

Long-term care insurance is sometimes overlooked because younger clients typically do not require this kind of coverage. Also, from a cost perspective, long-term care insurance is most appropriately purchased during a relatively short window of opportunity, between the ages of fifty and sixty-five. Although many clients may not need long-term care insurance, because of their age, health, or assets, it is still important to conduct a thorough long-term care analysis as part of a client's comprehensive insurance analysis.

The Bedo family's health status is an important consideration when considering long-term care coverage strategies. A review of Tyler's and Mia's health history and their access to long-term care coverage through their employers must be considered. The family's goal of living a financially satisfying life must be weighed against the potentially high costs of insuring both Tyler and Mia for long-term care expenses.

1. Develop a long-term care planning goal for the Bedos. When conceptualizing this goal, consider the following:

   a. Is the goal developed in agreement with any or all goals and objectives that the clients have identified regarding long-term care planning?

   b. What situational factors might influence their long-term care goal? Are these factors explicit, implied, or assumed? Is additional information required from the Bedos? If so, what?

   c. What is the desired long-term care planning outcome for the clients?

2. Make a list of the lifestyle, occupational, and health factors that should be documented and evaluated for the Bedos. How might this client information be obtained, or collected, from the Bedos? How might it be useful in the Bedos' long-term care situation analysis? Also, make a list of life events that could affect long-term care planning analysis for Tyler and Mia and that should be reviewed at future client meetings.

3. Are there globally accepted, client-specific, or planner-generated planning assumptions that will influence the long-term care situation analysis? List the assumptions as they might appear in a plan.

4. Make a list of specific policy features that should be evaluated as part of the documentation and evaluation of the Bedos' long-term care insurance planning efforts. For each feature, write a definition or explanation that could appear in this section of the plan or in the plan glossary.

5. Conduct a current long-term care situation analysis for the Bedos. Be sure to assess the following:

   a. Tyler's and Mia's need for long-term care insurance today.

   b. The Bedos' need for long-term care insurance in the future.

   c. How will Medicare or Medicaid benefits influence the Bedos' need for long-term care insurance?

   d. What, if any, are the tax implications of a policy purchase?

e.   What are the implications for their emergency fund, given different elimination periods?

6.   Summarize your observations about the Bedos' long-term care planning situation as they might appear in a client letter or plan. Incorporate text, bullets, or graphics in your explanation.

7.   Based on the goals originally identified and the completed analysis, what product or procedural strategies might be most useful to satisfy the Bedos' long-term care planning needs? When reviewing the strategies, be careful to consider the approximate cost of implementation as well as the most likely outcome(s) associated with each strategy.

8.   Write at least one primary and one alternative recommendation from selected strategies in response to each identified planning need. More than one recommendation may be needed to address all of the planning needs. For each recommendation, include specific, defensible answers to the who, what, when, where, why, how, and how much implementation questions.

a.   It is suggested that each recommendation be summarized in a Recommendation Form.

b.   Assign a priority to each recommendation based on the likelihood of meeting client goals and desired outcomes. This priority will be important when recommendations from other core planning content areas are considered relative to the available discretionary funds for subsidizing all recommendations.

c.   Comment briefly on the outcomes associated with each recommendation.

9.   Complete the following for the long-term care section of the Bedos' financial plan.

a.   Outline the content to be included in this section of the plan. Given the segments written above, which segments are missing?

b.   Write the introduction to this section of the plan (no more than one to two paragraphs).

10. Prepare a ten–fifteen-minute presentation for the Bedos of your observations and/or recommendation(s) for meeting their long-term care planning needs. Be sure to include visual aids or handouts.

Chapter Resources

AARP (www.aarp.org).

Administration on Aging (www.aoa.gov).

American Association for Long-Term Care Insurance (www.aaltci.org).

Commission on Accreditation of Rehabilitation Facilities/Continuing Care Accreditation Commission (CARF/CCAC) (www.carf.org/Providers.aspx?content=content/Accreditation/Opportunities/AS/CCAC.htm).

Comparison of Nursing Homes (www.medicare.gov/NHcompare).

Comprehensive long-term care insurance information (www.longtermcarelink.net).

LeadingAge (www.leadingage.org/).

Long-term Care Partnership Only (ltcpartnershiponly.com/index.html).

Medicare (www.medicare.gov).

National Clearinghouse for Long-term Care Information (www.longtermcare.gov).

Weiss Ratings (www.weissratings.com).

Self-Test Answers

1: b, 2: c, 3: d, 4: d, 5: a, 6: c, 7: a, 8: a, 9: c

Endnotes

1.   *Genworth 2011 Cost of Care Survey.* Available at: www.genworth.com/corporate/about-genworth/industry-expertise/cost-of-care.html.

2.   AgeWave/Harris Interactive, *America Talks: Protecting Our Families' Financial Futures.* Available at: pro.genworth.com/content/etc/medialib/genworth_v2/pdf/industry_expertise/retirement.Par.89331.File.pdf/America_Talks.pdf, pp. 34–35.

3.   AgeWave/Harris Interactive, *America Talks: Protecting Our Families' Financial Futures.*

4.   Alzheimer's Association, "2011 Alzheimer's Disease Facts and Figures," *Alzheimer's & Dementia* 7, no. 2 (2011): 40. Available at: www.alz.org/downloads/Facts_Figures_2011.pdf.

5.   American Association for Long-Term Care Insurance, *2008 LTCi Sourcebook.* Available at: www.aaltci.org/long-term-care-insurance/learning-center/fast-facts.php.

6.   "Do You Need Long-term-care Insurance? (CR Investigates)," *Consumer Reports* (2003). Available at: www.accessmylibrary.com/coms2/summary_0286-19498415_ITM.

7.   American Association for Long-Term Care Insurance, *Long-term Care Insurance Tax-deductibility Rules.* Available at: www.aaltci.org/long-term-care-insurance/learning-center/tax-for-business.php.

8.   Ingrid Case, "Long-Term Care: Crisis Brewing," *Financial Planning.* Available at: www.financial-planning.com/fp_issues/2011_4/crisis-brewing-2672143-1.html?zkPrintable=1&nopagination=1; also *Study Examines Long-term Care Insurance Rate Increases,* American Association for Long-Term Care Insurance. Available at: www.aaltci.org/news/long-term-care-insurance-association-news/study-examines-long-term-care-insurance-rate-increases.

9.   American Association for Long-Term Care Insurance. *2008 LTCi Sourcebook.* Available at: www.aaltci.org/long-term-care-insurance/learning-center/fast-facts.php.

10. J. L. Phipps *New: A Hybrid Annuity with LTC Coverage.* Available at: www.bankrate.com/finance/insurance/new-a-hybrid-annuity-with-ltc-coverage-1.aspx.

11. American Association for Long-term Care Insurance, *What Is the Probability You'll Need Long-term Care? Is Long-Term Care Insurance A Smart Financial Move?* Based on the 2008 LTCi Sourcebook. Available at: www.aaltci.org/long-term-care-insurance/learning-center/probability-long-term-care.php.

12. *What if You Cannot Afford to Continue Paying the Long Term Care Premium? Nonforfeiture Benefits in Long Term Care Insurance Policies.* Available at: law.freeadvice.com/insurance_law/long_term_care/can-not-afford-to-continue-paying-long-term-care.htm.

13. AARP, *Continuing Care Retirement Communities: What They Are and How They Work.* Available at: www.aarp.org/relationships/caregiving-resource-center/info-09-2010/ho_continuing_care_retirement_communities.html.

14. American Association for Long Term Care Insurance, *Long-term Care—Important Information for Women.* Available at: www.aaltci.org/long-term-care-insurance/learning-center/for-women.php.

15. Lynn Feinberg, Susan C. Reinhard, Ari Houser, and Rita Choula, *Valuing the Invaluable: 2011 Update The Growing Contributions and Costs of Family Caregiving* (Washington, DC: AARP Public Policy Institute), 1. Available at: assets.aarp.org/rgcenter/ppi/ltc/i51-caregiving.pdf.

16. Alzheimer's Association, *Facts and Figures*, 25.

17. American Association for Long Term Care Insurance, *Important Information for Women.*

18. Alzheimer's Association, *Facts and Figures*, 14.

19. AgeWave/Harris Interactive, *America Talks*, 30.

20. AgeWave/Harris Interactive, *America Talks*, 30.

21. American Association for Long Term Care Insurance, *Women Buy Majority Life—Long-term Care Insurance.* Available at: www.aaltci.org/news/long-term-care-insurance-association-news/women-buy-majority-life-long-term-care-insurance.

Chapter 9

Property and Liability Insurance Planning

Learning Objectives

1. The role of a property and liability insurance planning within the comprehensive financial planning process sometimes gets relegated to a quick review, especially when compared to life and long-term care planning issues. This is unfortunate. Although often overshadowed, issues related to property loss and liability exposure can influence almost every other aspect of a client's financial situation. It is imperative, as such, that financial planners adequately review and evaluate a client's personal, household, and family lifestyle issues as a way to identify threats that could lead to financial loss.

2. The risk management process can be defined as identifying, analyzing, and ranking a client's personal, household, and family lifestyle factors for potential threats that could lead to financial loss and identifying methods to reduce or eliminate the impact of that loss. Five risk reduction techniques can be used to manage client property and casualty risks: (1) *risk retention*, (2) *risk avoidance*,

(3) *risk reduction*, (4) *risk transference*, and (5) *risk sharing*. Insurance contracts represent an example of transferring and/or sharing risk with a third party.

3. **Risk control** refers to the ongoing process of identifying and analyzing the severity and likelihood of potential loss exposures. Issues related to maximum possible losses, maximum probable losses, and typical losses dominate the risk control process. Insurance companies regularly engage in risk control evaluations. This is one factor that determines the price of insurance. Additionally, insurance underwriters rely on insurance scores as a method for pricing policies. An insurance score is similar to a credit score. Both scores are calculated by considering a client's credit history, debt level, and previous financial behavior. Insurance firms use scores to predict premium payment history and the number of claims someone is likely to file. Low scores are generally associated with high insurance premiums.

Learning Objectives

4. Information and situational factors used to assess the need for property and liability insurance focus on the assets and lifestyle of a client's household. Initially, attention is focused on identifying all of the property to protect and the possible risk exposures associated with a client's activities and those of other family members. The risk management and control process is an ongoing activity. Financial planners can strengthen the client-planner relationship by periodically updating client information to maintain and improve a client's property and liability insurance protection. Minimally, financial planners should, at regular intervals, review client data related to (a) the names and addresses of all household members; (b) dwelling construction type; (c) dwelling or outbuilding improvements or additions; (d) changes in car ownership; (e) liability policy limits; (f) policy deductibles; and (g) homeowners and personal automobile policy schedules and endorsements. By including property and liability reviews in meetings with clients, issues related to property loss and/or liability exposure can be minimized both currently and in the future.

5. Although financial planners and clients collaborate with licensed insurance agents to manage the client's risk exposure, financial planners can play a significant role in the insurance planning process. It is important for financial planners to have a fundamental knowledge of typical liability exposures resulting from property ownership and the activities of a client's household. Planners also need to be competent in comparing different homeowners and personal automobile policy insurance types and provisions designed to manage client risk exposures. Through the data collection and discovery process, financial planners can develop a profile of a client's situation that enables them to advise clients on: (a) forms of coverage, (b) policy provisions, (c) excess liability planning, (d) flood/earthquake coverage, and (e) factors associated with premium rate determinations.

6. As this chapter highlights, *excess liability*, or umbrella, policy coverage is an essential tool that can be used to help clients manage exposure to insurance risk. Typically, financial planners recommend clients purchase at least $1 million in excess liability protection, although higher limits are sometimes more appropriate. To qualify for an umbrella policy, clients will be required to increase liability limits in both their homeowners and personal automobile policy coverage. Although implementation of this planning strategy will result in increased annual premium charges, the benefits associated with enhanced liability protection are generally well worth the cost.

7. A key calculation within the property and liability planning section of a financial plan involves determining whether clients are currently in conformity with the 80 percent rule. Although not universally used by all insurance companies, the 80 percent rule provides an indication of the level of reimbursement that will occur if a client incurs a loss and makes a claim against their homeowner's policy. If the amount of insurance on a structure,

Learning Objectives

divided by 80 percent of the applicable replacement cost, is equal to or greater than 1.0, then the homeowner will be reimbursed for the lesser of the replacement cost or the amount of the policy. If the result of the calculation is less than 1.0, the client will not qualify for full repair or replacement.

8. Ensuring that a client has adequate levels of property and liability insurance is an important aspect of financial planning, especially for those who are engaged in providing comprehensive financial planning services. The strategies presented in this chapter represent examples of insurance recommendations that can be incorporated into plans for clients who are either in the asset accumulation or asset preservation stage of the life cycle. Although recommendations will differ based on each client's unique situation, the fundamentals of property and liability insurance planning apply to all clients. Thus, identifying and recommending appropriate and reasonable insurance strategies is a measure of a financial planner's abilities and an important way to potentially help clients protect property, assets, and future income.

Key Terms

80 Percent Rule

Accidental Death and/or Personal Property Insurance Coverage

Actual Cash Value

All-Risk Policy

Appraisal

Attractive Nuisance

Auto Loan/Lease Coverage Endorsement

Aversion to Risk

Bodily Injury Coverage

Building Code Upgrade Endorsement

Burden of Proof

Catastrophic Losses

C-corporation

Cohabitant Form

Coinsurance Penalty

Collision Coverage

Collision Damage Waiver (CDW)

Combined Single-Limit Coverage

Comprehensive Coverage

Cost Per Square Foot

Deductible

Directors' and Officers' Liability Insurance

Earthquake Insurance

Endorsements

Endorsement

Excess Coverage

Excess Liability

Extended Replacement Cost Endorsement

Federal Emergency Management Agency (FEMA)

Floater Policy

Floaters

Flood Coverage

Flood Insurance

Gap

Good Student Discounts

Guaranteed Auto Protection

HO-3 Policy

Hold-Harmless Agreement

Home Business Insurance Endorsement

Home Safety Features

Homeowner's Coverage

Homestead Declaration

Homestead Exemption

Identity Theft

Indemnify

Inflation Endorsement

Inland Marine Policy

Insurance Contract

Insurance Score

Invasion of Privacy

Inventory

LDW

Key Terms

Libel

Loss Damage Waiver

Market Value

Maximum Possible Loss

Medical Payments Coverage

Multi-Policy Discount

Named Perils Policy

National Flood Insurance Program (NFIP)

Non-Collision Damage

Open Peril

Pair and Set Clause

PAP

Partnership

Peril

Personal Article Policies

Personal Article, Personal Effects Policy

Personal Automobile Policy

Personal Injury Coverage

Personal Liability

Personal Property Endorsement

Personal Property Policy

Property Damage Coverage

Property Exclusions

Replacement Cost

Replacement Cost Coverage Endorsement

Riders

Risk Avoidance

Risk Control

Risk Exposure

Risk Management

Risk Reduction

Risk Retention

Risk Sharing

Risk Tolerance Profile

Risk Transference

Scheduled Assets

S-corporation

Slander

Sole Proprietorship

Split-Limit Liability Coverage

Standard Policy Forms

State Minimum Liability Requirements

Strictly Liable

Typical Loss

Umbrella Liability Policy

Underinsured for Losses

Underinsured Motorists Insurance

Uninsured Motorists Insurance

Upside-Down

Write Your Own Company (WYO)

CFP® Principal Knowledge Topics

D.22. Principles of Risk and Insurance

D.23. Analysis and Evaluation of Risk Exposures

D.30. Insurance Needs Analysis

D.32. Property and Casualty Insurance

Chapter Equations

Equation 9.1: Coinsurance Penalty Reimbursement Amount

$$= \frac{\text{Amount of HO Insurance Coverage}}{80\% \times \text{Replacement Cost}} \times \text{Value of Loss} = \text{Value of Claim} - \text{Deductible}$$

PROPERTY AND LIABILITY INSURANCE: DETERMINING THE NEED

Like other insurance needs, analysis of a client's need for adequate property and liability coverage is essential within the financial planning process. For many clients, a large portion of net worth is associated with home equity. Uninsured damage or liability claims against the property can adversely affect this important investment. Without adequate liability coverage, for instance, a single accident or event could place a family's financial future in jeopardy and negatively impact the capacity to fund other financial goals. In today's increasingly litigious society, it is imperative that clients be protected from financial losses associated with personal property and casualty claims. Financial planners need to assess and discuss each client's unique property and liability insurance exposures or risk their clients having to invade financial assets to pay for losses that could have been transferred to a third party, such as an insurance company. Despite the fact the client may have consulted with insurance professionals, an oversight could be deemed a serious financial planning omission within a comprehensive financial plan.

> **#Remember**
>
> Dangerous attractive nuisances, like a swimming pool or a yard trampoline that attract children or others to your home, mean family fun but present a perilous opportunity for loss that requires additional insurance, especially liability, coverage.

Managing risks involves identifying, analyzing, and ranking a client's personal, household, and family lifestyle for potential threats that could lead to financial loss and identifying methods to reduce or eliminate the impact of that loss. In its simplest form, this is the premise underlying **risk management** methodologies. The success of any risk management method is contingent on timing. Recognizing a client's *risk exposure* after a loss has occurred is pointless. Thus, it is essential to take the time before a loss occurs to carefully evaluate risk exposures.

Five primary risk reduction techniques should be considered when analyzing a client's property and casualty insurance situation. Two of these techniques deal with reducing the likelihood of loss (i.e., **loss prevention**) and two deal with reducing the cost of loss. There is one additional possibility: **Risk retention** involves having the client accept the loss or gain resulting from a risk. Risk retention is an appropriate risk management strategy when the costs associated with insurance are significantly greater than the potential losses involved. By definition, any risk that is not prevented, avoided, or transferred is retained by the client. Sometimes retention is the only way to handle risk. There may be no economically viable option to prevent a risk or to indemnify a client for it (e.g., acts of war). Retention may also be the best way to deal with risks that are predictable and not costly.

Clients who do not want or cannot afford to retain the risk of loss may reduce or eliminate it. Clients can prevent a loss from occurring by reducing or, in the extreme, avoiding the behavior that could lead to a loss. Alternatively, a client can indemnify the loss by sharing or, in the extreme, transferring the cost of replacing missing, damaged, or stolen items.

The two primary methods of reducing, or controlling, the likelihood of a loss includes **risk avoidance** and **risk reduction**. However, both avoiding and reducing risk require a client to alter behavior, possessions, or their personal, household, or working environment. For instance, to avoid an auto theft loss, the client could choose not to own a car. This approach to risk management may not be feasible or even possible. Instead, the client may seek to reduce the likelihood of loss by safeguarding the car with a vehicle alarm or tracking system. This is an example of risk reduction.

If controlling the likelihood of loss is impractical, a client can **indemnify** the loss by sharing the cost associated with the risk with another person or organization, typically an insurance company. The two primary indemnification methods include **risk transferring** and **risk sharing**. Both of these methods establish an agreement or contract (e.g., an indemnity or **hold-harmless agreement** or *insurance contract*) prior to a loss. The agreement outlines the moral and financial responsibilities of both parties. When contractually transferring risk, clients (ideally with the help of their financial advisor) must identify potential risks, determine the likelihood of loss, and calculate the estimated financial exposure associated with that risk. Conversely, the insurance company determines the risks, probabilities, and costs associated with insuring the risks. Insurance is often the preferred risk management mechanism when risks pose the possibility of moderate or high financial loss but the anticipated frequency of loss is low or unpredictable.

A financial planner should strive to educate her clientele about the advantages associated with evaluating risk and engaging in **risk control** as an ongoing process that involves identifying and analyzing the severity and likelihood of potential loss exposures. To understand risk control is to recognize issues related to maximum possible loss, maximum probable loss, and typical losses, as well as the likelihood of each. The **maximum possible loss** is the largest loss that can occur. Theoretically, for liability purposes, there is no limit on the maximum possible loss because there generally is no way to be certain what a jury might award. The **maximum probable loss** is the greatest loss that has the highest probability of occurring. The **typical loss** is the one that occurs most frequently.

Safeguarding against the maximum possible loss requires insurance to cover *catastrophic losses*, regardless of how likely or unlikely it is that a catastrophic event might occur. When analyzing a client's **homeowner's (HO)** coverage, a financial planner should make certain that the limits of liability and property coverage shield the client from a potentially bankrupting financial responsibility. Additionally, clients may need coverage for property that they *assume* is protected, but the coverage is limited. An **endorsement** changes the policy, by modifying the scope of coverage, specifying some unique loss exposure, or adding insureds or locations for coverage. Typical endorsements, depending on the insurer, include guaranteed replacement cost coverage, inflation protection, identity theft, or modified coverage of assets that are included or *scheduled* for coverage, such as musical instruments or jewelry.

A thorough knowledge of a client's personal and financial situation is central to all aspects of financial planning, but nowhere is this more evident than when planning for property and casualty insurance. Seemingly mundane—and in some cases intrusive—questions about a client's home, personal property, pets, hobbies, autos, and driving habits must be considered. To complete a comprehensive assessment, the planner and client must explore issues concerning the client's lifestyle, the client's *aversion to risk*, property owned, and the ways in which property is used by members of the insured's household, including residence employees. This information provides the basis for determining property and liability insurance needs as well as appropriate product recommendations.

An important step in the assessment of a client's current situation focuses on gathering, summarizing, and analyzing all currently in-force property and liability policies. This entails conducting a comprehensive review of a client's HO, personal automobile, excess liability, and other miscellaneous policies. A basic checklist is shown in Figure 9.1.

Figure 9.1 Questions to Use When Assessing Property and Liability Insurance Coverage

Assesing Homeowners Insurance Coverage	Yes	No
Assessing Homeowners Insurance Coverage		
Is client's home insured for 100% replacement value rather than market value?		
Is coverage on the home at least 80% of the estimated replacement value?		
Has the home recently been appraised for its estimated replacement value?		
Does the policy have an inflation endorsement?		
Does the policy have a building code, sewer back-up, identity theft, or other endorsement?		
Has client made a household possessions inventory?		
Does client have a video or pictures to supplement the inventory?		
Is the household possessions inventory/documentation held in a safe place outside of the home?		
Does client's homeowners policy have adequate contents insurance protection?		
Does client need special coverage for collectibles and other hard-to-replace items?		
Does client have written appraisal for expensive items (silver, jewelry, furs, etc.)?		
Does client have endorsements or individual policies for these items?		
Does client carry comprehensive (open perils) coverage on household contents?		
Does client carry replacement cost coverage on household contents?		
Does client need/have coverage for any watercraft?		
Does client need extended theft coverage?		
Is coverage for medical payments to others sufficient?		
Is liability coverage sufficient? Is it coordinated with an umbrella policy?		
Does the deductible match client's ability to pay out of pocket for losses?		
Have all available discounts been taken?		
Does client own any seasonal residences that might need special insurance treatment?		
Does client own an historic home that might need special insurance treatment?		
Assessing Automobile Insurance Coverage	**Yes**	**No**
Are liability limits sufficient? Are they coordinated with an umbrella policy?		
Is coverage for medical payments to others sufficient?		
Is uninsured and under-insured motorist's coverage sufficient to protect the client, if needed?		
Does client still need comprehensive or collision coverage, given the age of the vehicle(s)?		
Does client have coverage for any off-road or recreational vehicles?		
Do deductibles match client's ability to pay for losses from cash flow or assets?		
Have all available discounts been taken?		

Figure 9.1 Questions to Use When Assessing Property and Liability Insurance Coverage (*cont'd*)

Assessing Liability Insurance Coverage	Yes	No
Does client have an umbrella liability policy?		
Does client have potential liability exposure from serving as an officer or director of a for-profit or not-for-profit organization?		
Does client have potential liability exposure resulting from volunteer activities?		
Does client have a nanny, housekeeper, or lawn/garden help?		
Are liability homeowners and auto policies coordinated with client's umbrella policy?		
Assessing Need for Flood and Earthquake Insurance	**Yes**	**No**
Does client need, or qualify for, flood insurance?		
If maximum losses were incurred, could client afford to pay damages from cash flow and/or assets?		
Does client need/have earthquake insurance?		
Can client afford the premium for flood or earthquake insurance?		

Two issues should guide the review. First, is the current level of coverage sufficient to insure property losses fully? Second, is the client adequately protected against liability claims? Each issue should be considered in greater depth; however, the questions presented in Figure 9.1 serve as the basis of this analysis.

Calculating the 80 Percent Rule

Two out of every three homes in the United States are underinsured. The average amount of under-insurance is 22 percent, with some homes underinsured by 60 percent or more.[1] As these statistics suggest, it is imperative that financial planners assess each client's home insurance coverage to ensure adequate reimbursement for potential losses. Some homeowner's policies include an **80 percent rule** (or "coinsurance" rule) to determine the level of reimbursement when a loss is incurred. The 80 percent rule provides one way to verify whether an HO policy limit is sufficient to provide full replacement for a major loss. Based on the value of the residence at the time of loss, if the amount of coverage is equal to 80 percent of the replacement cost, then full replacement of the damaged portion will be paid, up to the limits of the policy less the deductible, with no reduction for depreciation. If the insured does not carry insurance equal to at least 80 percent of the replacement cost, the insured is penalized through a coinsurance clause when the loss is paid.

> **#Remember**
>
> Although 80% coverage is the minimally acceptable level of coverage on the structure, 100% coverage with an inflation endorsement is a standard planning strategy.

Financial planners should remind clients that insurance is based on **replacement cost**, which is defined as the actual amount needed to rebuild or repair property, rather than the *market value* of that property. Market value may be higher or lower than replacement cost, depending on the geographic area in which the home is located. Although it is always a good idea to recommend a 90 to 100 percent replacement cost policy with inflation protection, it is essential that the 80 percent rule be met. Otherwise, a client may not be completely reimbursed for future losses or damage. The additional **inflation endorsement** ensures that property coverage automatically adjusts annually in response to rising prices. Some policies may include the inflation protection, without an additional endorsement.

If the amount of insurance on a structure, divided by 80 percent of the applicable replacement cost, is equal to or greater than 1.0, then the homeowner will be reimbursed for the lesser of the replacement cost or the amount of the policy. However, if the amount of insurance on the structure, divided by 80 percent of the applicable replacement cost, is less than 1.0, then the insured will not qualify for full repair or replacement. The reduction in reimbursement is sometimes referred to as a "coinsurance penalty." In this situation, the insured will be paid the actual cash value of the part of the structure damaged or destroyed less the deductible *or* the reimbursement amount calculated using the following formula:

Equation 9.1: Coinsurance penalty reimbursement amount

$$= \frac{\text{Amount of Insurance Coverage}}{80\% \times \text{Replacement Cost}} \times \text{Value of Loss} = \text{Value of Claim} - \text{Deductible}$$

The deductible amount will be subtracted from all settlements, regardless of whether the insured has met the 80 percent rule. **Actual cash value** settlements typically depreciate a property to account for its age. Replacement cost settlements typically do not include depreciation.

Assume, for example, that a client owns a home with a replacement value of $190,000. Unfortunately, over the years the policy has not kept pace with the rising values of real estate and the home is currently insured for only $130,000 with a $500 deductible. If the insured incurs a loss of $20,000, the insurance company will reimburse the client only $17,105, as shown below:

$$\left(\frac{\$130,000}{80\% \times \$190,000} \times \$20,000 \right) - \$500 = \$17,105 - \$500 = \$16,605$$

The $2,895 not reimbursed on the $20,000 claim is considered to be the client's **coinsurance penalty**. However, this is the reimbursement before applying the $500 deductible. Therefore, the actual amount received by the client will be $16,605. To maintain full reimbursement to the limit of the policy, the house should have been insured for a minimum of $152,000 ($190,000 multiplied by 80 percent).

In general, it is important to remember three rules when evaluating the current coverage limits on a client's home: (a) the 80 percent rule applies primarily to partial losses; (b) if the actual cash value exceeds the 80 percent rule limit, the insured receives the larger amount; and (c) the total reimbursement will never exceed the face amount of the policy less the deductible. Figure 9.2 provides guidance on how the 80 percent rule can impact client outcomes in the event of a loss. Most other coverage levels are determined as a percentage of the coverage on the structure; it is important to note that the ripple effect of under-insurance can have a significant effect on large losses.

#Remember

Deductible and premium amounts move in an inverse relationship. Increasing the deductible reduces the annual premium. The increased discretionary cash flow can be used to build an emergency fund to offset future insurance costs and losses. A homeowner's policy deductible of the lesser of $1,000 or 1% of the value of the dwelling is not uncommon.

Figure 9.2 Coverage and Coinsurance Illustration

Possible Coverage and Coinsurance Outcomes					
Amount of Insurance Coverage	Coverage Ratio to Property Value	Payment for Total Loss (Less $2,500)	Insured Coinsurance Percentage	Payment for Partial* Loss (Less $2,500)	Insured Coinsurance Penalty
$250,000	100%	$250,000	0%	$50,000	0%
$200,000	80%	$200,000	20%	$50,000	0%**
$150,000	60%	$150,000	(1- (60/80)) or 25%	$37,500	25%
$100,000	40%	$100,000	(1- (40/80)) or 50%	$25,000	50%
Based on a home value of $250,000 and an HO policy with a $2,500 deductible.					
* $50,000 loss					
** 80% rule					

Property and Liability Insurance Planning Skills

Beyond a lender's requirement for HO insurance or the state-mandated requirement of **personal automobile policy (PAP)** insurance to license a vehicle, most Americans think of property insurance in the context of replacing damaged, lost, or stolen property. Although the financial impact of property loss may be significant, by far the greater risk comes from liability claims resulting from the actions of the insured or members of the insured's household.

Factors that can affect the need for property and liability insurance parallel the issues that influence underwriting and the rating used to determine insurance costs. Although the factors that insurance companies use vary for HO and PAP insurance, two consistent and very important issues must be considered when determining the level of insurance coverage to recommend.

First is the territory or location of the property. Aside from moving, this factor is beyond the insured's control when purchasing HO or PAP insurance. Location influences the need for flood insurance or earthquake coverage. Retrofitting or modernizing a home to improve its disaster resistance may reduce policy costs and the potential for loss.

Second is the client's **insurance score**, which is calculated from data collected by the major national credit bureaus. The Federal Trade Commission defines an insurance score as a numerical summary of a person's past credit delinquencies, bankruptcies, debt ratio, credit-seeking behavior, credit history, and use of credit.[2] These factors are shown in Figure 9.3.

Figure 9.3 Factors That Contribute to an Insurance Score

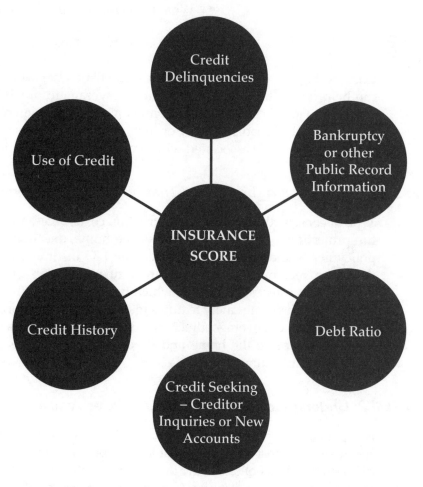

Insurance companies typically use insurance scores to estimate whether a person is likely to make premium payments and the number of claims someone is, in all likelihood, going to file over any period of time. A client's insurance score tends to be inversely correlated with claims costs. In other words, the lower the client's insurance score, the higher the likely cost of future claims and the higher the insurance premium. For clients with credit problems, efforts to reduce the reliance on credit and to make timely payments can, over time, improve their credit and insurance scores, both of which can impact other aspects of the client's financial life, primarily by reducing the cost of credit and insurance premiums.

Answering the question of how much a client needs in property and liability coverage is not a straightforward process. Most insurance experts agree on the need to transfer risk through insurance, but how much of that risk to transfer or the amount of protection to purchase is often a matter of interpretation. One approach that can be used to answer this important question involves considering the following issues:

- What is the maximum loss possible?

- What is the maximum loss probable?

- What is the typical loss?

Considering these questions in light of a client's net worth and *risk tolerance profile* can help frame the choice of how much coverage to purchase. Other factors unique to the individual client household must also be considered. The following planning skills provide a broad summary of some of these issues as well as the basic insurance concepts commonly associated with property and casualty insurance coverage.

Planning Skill 1: Understand the Factors That Influence HO Premiums

Type of construction and local construction costs, access to and quality of community fire protection, occupancy and use of the home, and home safety features all affect policy needs and costs for clients seeking HO insurance coverage. When providing insurance recommendations within a financial plan, it is important to include references to *home safety features*, which typically reduce the cost of insurance. Clients who enhance existing safety features may qualify for additional discounts. Policy type and the limits of coverage affect the cost of all policies. As such, issues surrounding the cost to replace the home and its contents should be carefully reviewed when conducting an insurance analysis.

Planning Skill 2: Understand the Types of HO Policies Available

HO policies are generally packaged as **standard policy forms**. Figure 9.4 compares seven of the most widely available HO policy forms. An important feature that differentiates HO policies is the protection from *perils*. A **named perils policy** protects against financial loss resulting from perils that are specifically named within a policy. **Open peril** is a term used to describe an **all-risk policy** that covers losses from all causes unless specifically excluded in an insurance contract. These exclusions typically include flood, earthquake, war, nuclear accident, and mold. Corresponding to these types of policies is the related issue of *burden of proof*. With a named perils policy, the homeowner (or renter) must provide evidence that the loss was caused by a named peril listed in the policy. In contrast, with the open peril policy, a loss is covered unless the insurance company can provide evidence that the loss was excluded from the policy.

Once the type of policy is chosen, both homeowners and renters have choices on the level of protection offered, or the policy's loss settlement clause. Some policies use **actual cash value (ACV)** as the basis for replacing property. Although typically applied to replacement of possessions, ACV may also apply to claims on a structure. Actual cash value provides reimbursement on the basis of the replacement value of the property less depreciation. Older property, whose age exceeds the specified useful life of "x" years, has no reimbursement value. Consequently, reimbursement could be pennies on the dollar relative to the value of the loss or the amount needed for even minimal replacement. "Market value" may be an analogy, as the reimbursement may be similar to the price of a used product (a three-year-old camera) whereas replacement cost coverage would pay for a similar camera to the one stolen.

> **Self-Test 2**
>
> Sienna owns a condominium in a college town. What type of HO policy does she need?
>
> a. HO 1
>
> b. HO 3
>
> c. HO 6
>
> d. HO 8

A **replacement cost coverage endorsement** provides for lost, stolen, or destroyed property to be replaced with equivalent property with no reductions for depreciation. Although slightly more expensive, replacement cost coverage is recommended in most situations.

Although not available in every state or from every insurance company, homeowners also may have the choice of **guaranteed replacement cost** or **extended replacement cost** for claims on the structure. With both, the amount paid on a claim to replace or repair the structure may exceed the amount of coverage on which the premium is based. Guaranteed replacement coverage pays the full amount, while extended replacement coverage pays a specified amount, typically 20 to 25 percent above the policy coverage limit. These endorsements protect the insured in the case of a total loss or when a natural disaster may cause widespread market increases in construction costs. But it is important to note that costs of upgrading the home to comply with current building codes are not typically included.

For clients who rent or own a condominium or cooperative, the 80 percent rule is not an effective measure of coverage. Other factors must be considered. Foremost is the named perils coverage on contents, which some clients may wish to extend to protect against all risks except specific exclusions. Clients protected by an HO-4 or HO-6 policy should include replacement cost and inflation guard (discussed later in the chapter) endorsements for maximum protection.

Condominium or cooperative owners must consider the level of coverage on unit property for which they are responsible, such as built-in cabinetry, appliances, or other surface treatments (e.g., carpet, tile, wall paper, etc.) relative to their actual cash value or replacement cost decision. Upgrading to replacement cost and inflation guard protection offers broader protection, but it will increase premium costs as well.

Figure 9.4 Typical HO Policy Forms and Coverage

Seven Forms of Homeowners Policies*						
Forms	Part A Dwelling	Part B Other Structures	Part C Personal Property	Part D Loss of Use	Part E Typical Personal Liability Limit	Part F Typical Medical Payments to Others Limit
Broad Form (HO-2) Named 16 perils policy¶¶	Replacement value	10% of dwelling coverage	50% of dwelling coverage actual cash value	30% of dwelling coverage	$100,000	$1,000 per person per incident
Special Form (HO-3) Named 16 perils policy for personal property	Does not apply	10% of dwelling coverage	50% of dwelling coverage actual cash value	30% of dwelling coverage	$100,000	$1,000 per person per incident
Contents Form (HO-4) Named 16 perils policy for personal property¶¶	Replacement value	Does not apply	Usually stated in dollar amount actual cash value	30% of personal property coverage	$100,000	$1,000 per person per incident
Comprehensive Form (HO-5) All perils, except specific exclusions	$1,000 - $5,000 minimum limited to semi-permanent features in the unit Market value of structure or cost to repair replace with functional equivalent	10% of dwelling coverage	50% of dwelling coverage Actual cash value	30% of dwelling coverage	$100,000	$1,000 per person per incident
Unit Owner's Form (HO-6) Named 16 perils policy¶¶		Does not apply, or included in Part A	Usually stated in dollar amount actual cash value	50% of personal property coverage	$100,000	$1,000 per person per incident
Modified Coverage Form (HO-8) Named 11 perils policy¶		10% of dwelling coverage	50% of dwelling coverage Actual cash value	10% of dwelling coverage	$100,000	$1,000 per person per incident

*Discussion here and throughout this chapter is based on the standard Insurance Service Office (ISO) policy forms used throughout the U.S. Policy variations may apply as some insurers use the American Association of Insurance Services (AAIS) forms, some insurers design their own forms, and in some instances, state mandated modifications may apply. For more information see www.iso.com.

#HO-1 policies are generally no longer available.

Figure 9.4 Typical HO Policy Forms and Coverage (*cont'd*)

¶ Named 11 perils typically include: (1) Fire or lightning; (2) windstorm or hail; (3) explosion; (4) riot or civil commotion; (5) damage caused by aircraft; (6) damage caused by vehicles; (7) smoke; (8) vandalism or malicious mischief; (9) theft; (10) volcanic eruption; and (11) falling objects.

¶¶ The additional 5 perils to total 16 include: (12) weight of ice, snow or sleet; (13) accidental discharge or overflow of water or steam from within plumbing, heating, air conditioning, automatic fire-protective sprinkler system, or from a household appliance; (14) sudden and accidental tearing apart, cracking, burning, or bulging of a steam or hot water heating system, an air conditioning or automatic fire-protective system; (15) freezing of a plumbing, heating, air conditioning, automatic, fire-protective sprinkler system, or of a household appliance; and (16) sudden and accidental damage from artificially generated electrical current (does not include loss to a tube, transistor or similar electronic component). For more information see the Insurance Information Institute at www.iii.org/policymakers/home/

Planning Skill 3: Recommend Coverage for Overlooked Personal Property

Beyond the basic limits of Part C coverage for personal property as shown in Figure 9.4, additional coverage is available for select items that are either inadequately covered or excluded from coverage under a HO policy. Jewelry, furs, firearms, collectibles/collections, musical instruments, art, precious and semiprecious metals, securities held in physical form, and business assets are some examples that may require additional coverage. Although a basic HO policy provides some coverage, the value of such items can quickly exceed the limits of coverage—typically $200 to $2,500—depending on the asset and the insurance company.

> **Self-Test 3**
>
> Which of the following assets would need a separate floater policy to fully insure for the value?
>
> a. Shotgun valued at $3,500.
>
> b. Diamond ring valued at $1,000.
>
> c. Guitar valued at $200.
>
> d. All of the above.

The provisions to extend personal property coverage, may be through a **personal property endorsement**, or rider on an existing polity or the addition of a **floater policy**. Originally called an *inland marine policy*, a floater is a separate mini-policy that "floats" coverage for an asset that frequently changes location—most often jewelry, firearms, art, or musical instruments. A **personal article, personal effects policy**, or **personal property policy** (different companies use different terms) works in much the same way as the personal property endorsement. Whereas an endorsement is an extension of an HO policy, a floater is a separate policy that may or may not be written by the same company and often has different features, including all risks coverage. This type of separate policy may benefit a client because the coverage allows for more flexibility in coverage limits and deductibles. The endorsement may be written to increase coverage on a specific asset basis, a class of asset basis, or a blanket basis for all classes of personal property otherwise limited in the policy.

A recent receipt for the purchase or a professional appraisal may be necessary to secure coverage. These costs, as well as the time and effort to complete a well-documented possessions inventory, may discourage some clients. But a quick tally of the potential financial losses, without the additional coverage, may persuade clients to add endorsements or floaters. Annual client reviews should include questions about any new property (i.e., not covered at the time of purchase) to ensure that adequate ongoing coverage is in place.

Planning Skill 4: Identify Other HO Insurance Exclusions

A client and her financial planner should consider other **property exclusions** that may be relevant. For example, theft of property typically is excluded from coverage for college-age students who vacate their dorm rooms or apartments for more than forty-five days during the summer or for alternative educational opportunities. Although an obscure circumstance, this question, as well as others, relating to coverage for property moved by a college student away from the insured residence should be considered because policies vary. Clients who operate a home business will find that insurance restrictions may require the addition of a **home business insurance endorsement**. HO policies typically include up to $2,500 of coverage for business property kept at home, but standard coverage characteristically excludes many business exposures from liability claims and losses of high-value business property.

Clients often worry about issues related to medical claims resulting from property ownership. The **medical payments coverage** (Part F) and liability coverage (Part E) of a HO policy extend beyond situations on the insured's property to liability losses caused by the activities of the insured, the activities of a residence employee in the course of employment, and the activities of an animal owned or cared for by the insured. It may be wise to increase the medical payments or liability coverage as a result of the athletic participation or hobbies of household members, as well as pet ownership. For example, some states have passed legislation making the owner of a dog that bites someone *strictly liable* for the injuries. Information about dog ownership often is considered when underwriters are rating and offering insurance coverage. Homeowners with swimming pools also may pay higher insurance premiums. Pools are generally considered to be an **attractive nuisance**. A knowledgeable insurance professional should be consulted to explore these issues and to ensure sufficient protection, either through the HO policy or in conjunction with an excess liability or umbrella policy, which is described in more detail later in the chapter.

> **#Remember**
>
> A standard HO policy may or may not provide coverage for "off-premises" property, such as in a storage facility. And, if covered, the perils may be more limited. Some storage facilities provide coverage, but clients should be warned: "Before you store, be sure you know." For example, banks do not insure safe deposit box content, so a jewelry floater would be needed.

Planning Skill 5: Make Sure Clients Protect Property from Mother Nature

Standard HO policies typically provide reimbursement for losses associated with fire (including wildfires), windstorms, hail, and freezing pipes. Standard policies, however, exclude damage caused by disasters, such as flooding and earthquakes, and for those who live in hurricane coastal areas, windstorms. Clients who live in areas prone to flooding must consider **flood coverage**. A lender may, in fact, require **flood insurance** before a mortgage can be acquired. Floods are the most common and widespread of all natural disasters, except for fire. The federal flood insurance requirement applies to any structures located in an eligible community or one that is designated a Special Flood Hazard Area in the emergency program.

The flood insurance program is administered by the Federal Insurance and Mitigation Administration (changed from the Federal Insurance Administration), which is part of **FEMA (Federal Emergency Management Agency)**. An insurance agent or broker may issue a policy directly from the **National Flood Insurance Program (NFIP),** or a client can secure coverage from a **write your own (WYO) company**. WYO companies are private insurance companies that provide flood insurance under a special arrangement with the NFIP. WYO companies provide and service policies, while the NFIP retains the risk, thus expanding the availability of flood protection to more homeowners and communities. Policies are also available for renters and condominium unit owners.

Flood insurance provides reimbursement for the overflow of inland or tidal waters and surface waters. Mudslides caused by a flood are also covered. Flood insurance will not cover damage from rain, snow, hail, sewer back-ups, or water damage that results from something a homeowner can control. As with all types of property insurance, premiums reflect the risk of loss, and a deductible does apply. According to the National Flood Insurance Program, the average annual cost of a flood insurance policy is $700.[3] The maximum deductible may be set by the mortgage lender, but as with other insurance, increases to the deductible will result in a reduced annual premium.

> **Self-Test 4**
>
> When Wookjae went to his basement the other day he noticed that he had several inches of water near the main drain. Which of the following potential causes would not be covered under his HO policy?
>
> a. An overflowing toilet on the first floor
>
> b. Sewer back-up, and he did not have the water back up and sump overflow endorsement.
>
> c. A leak in his roof as a result of damage sustained during a major rainstorm.
>
> d. All of the above

Despite the fact that all states have experienced earthquakes of varying magnitudes, and damage, neither the government or mortgage lenders mandate coverage. **Earthquake insurance** provides catastrophic coverage for those who live in areas prone to earthquakes and also provides coverage for landslide, mudslide, mudflow, mine subsidence, or other earth movement. Earthquake policies typically have deductibles equal to 10 to 25 percent of the policy limit. Some policies apply the deductible separately to the contents, the structure, and any unattached buildings, so care must be taken to carefully evaluate the policy.

As with all types of property insurance, premiums reflect the risk of loss, including location and the probability of an earthquake, as well as building materials and other structural considerations. Premiums for a $500,000 home in a high-risk earthquake community can run as high as $2,000 a year, with a deductible equal to 10 percent of the limit of coverage. In other parts of the country, an earthquake endorsement can be purchased much less expensively.

Some planners advise clients to self-insure against earthquake losses. Other planners argue that the cost of insurance plus the deductible is reasonable considering the unpredictability and potential magnitude of earthquake damage. The value of the home and potential replacement costs relative to the client's total net worth should be a major consideration. Earthquake damage to autos would be covered under comprehensive insurance, included in the automobile policy.

Planning Skill 6: Understand How Driver Characteristics Influence PAP Premiums

Driver characteristics, such as age, gender, marital status, and driving record, use of the auto, and number and types of cars covered are considerations in PAP insurance price and coverage analyses. How vehicles are used (e.g., for pleasure, commuting to work, or business or farm activities) significantly affects PAP prices and the liability limits needed. Driver education and *good student discounts* may be used to reduce premiums for households with young drivers, as may the discount for a college student away from home without a car.

Auto insurance is often viewed simply as a requirement to operate a motor vehicle. As shown in Figure 9.5, New Hampshire is the only state that does not have compulsory liability insurance minimums. Aside from the fact that *state minimum liability requirements* are generally inadequate, attention to the liability limits in a PAP is important for another reason. Typically the **split-limit liability coverage** chosen is the same amount of **uninsured** or **underinsured motorists insurance** offered by the policy. **Bodily injury coverage** and **property damage coverage** protect the insured from losses sustained as a result of an accident with an uninsured, or underinsured, driver. Studies by the Insurance Research Council, as reported by the Insurance Information Institute, suggest that approximately 12.6 percent of U.S. drivers may be uninsured. In Oklahoma, Florida, Mississippi, New Mexico, Michigan, and Tennessee, reportedly 20 percent or more of the drivers are uninsured.[4] Individuals who reside in areas where there is a concentration of uninsured drivers may want to consider higher limits for uninsured or underinsured motorists insurance. While a few more states require uninsured motorist coverage, only Connecticut, Illinois, Maryland, Minnesota, Nebraska, New Jersey, North Carolina, North Dakota, Oregon, South Dakota, and Virginia require drivers to carry underinsured motorist coverage.[5]

Figure 9.5 State Minimum PAP Split-Limit Liability Requirements

State/District	Split-limit Liability Minimums	State/District	Split-limit Liability Minimums
Alabama	25/50/25	Montana	25/50/20
Alaska	50/100/25	Nebraska	25/50/25
Arizona	15/30/10	Nevada	15/30/10
Arkansas	25/50/25	New Hampshire	25/50/25***
California	15/30/5	New Jersey	15/30/5
Colorado	25/50/15	New Mexico	25/50/10
Connecticut	20/40/10	New York	25/50/10
Delaware	15/30/10	North Carolina	30/60/25
Florida	10/20/10	North Dakota	25/50/25
Georgia	25/50/25	Ohio	25/50/25
Hawaii	20/40/10	Oklahoma	25/50/25
Idaho	25/50/15	Oregon	25/50/20
Illinois	25/50/20	Pennsylvania	15/30/5
Indiana	25/50/25*	Rhode Island	25/50/25
Iowa	20/40/15	South Carolina	25/50/25
Kansas	25/50/25**	South Dakota	25/50/25
Kentucky	25/50/10	Tennessee	25/50/15
Louisiana	15/30/25	Texas	30/60/25
Maine	50/100/25 + minimum of $1,000 for medical payments	Utah	25/65/15
Maryland	30/60/15	Vermont	25/50/10
Massachusetts	20/40/5	Virginia	25/50/20
Michigan	20/40/10	Washington	25/50/10
Minnesota	30/60/10	Wash D.C.	25/50/10
Mississippi	25/50/25	West Virginia	25/50/25
Missouri	25/50/10	Wisconsin	25/50/10
		Wyoming	25/50/20

Note: Some states allow the minimum requirement to be met with a combined single-limit policy. Coverage amounts vary by state. Some states require medical payments coverage; amounts vary by state.

*Effective July 1, 2017

** Effective January 1, 2017

***New Hampshire does not require the purchase of auto insurance, but drivers must be able to prove they can meet the New Hampshire Motor Vehicle Financial Responsibility Requirements in the event of an "at-fault" accident. The 25/50/25 minimum is recommended coverage.

Source: The Insurance Information Institute. Available at http://www.iii.org/issues_updates/compulsory-auto-uninsured-motorists.html

Planning Skill 7: Recognize the Need for Liability Coverage and How Split-Limit Requirements Are Too Low for Most Clients

Beyond the direct protection of an insured motorist, a secondary—and perhaps less obvious—protection is also available. Consider the example of a client who chooses split-limit coverage of $1 million/$1 million/$1 million liability coverage and uninsured or underinsured motorists insurance. The liability coverage protects the client's assets and future income from losses caused by an accident for which the client or the client's family members are determined to be at fault. Conversely, if the client is involved in an accident for which an uninsured or underinsured driver (for example, PAP with only $100,000 of liability insurance) is at fault, the client's PAP provides additional protection. Assuming the client was disabled as a result of the accident, the $100,000 would leave little, if any, coverage for lost income. The client's protection of $1 million might not replace a lifetime of income, but it would provide significantly more than that of an uninsured or underinsured driver and a PAP with lower coverage limits. Although this is no substitute for adequate disability insurance, for a client who spends significant time commuting or traveling for work, the additional PAP coverage could be relatively inexpensive protection for this isolated loss.

Planning Skill 8: Identify Other Auto Policy Considerations

In addition to understanding the basic components of a traditional PAP, financial planners are sometimes required to help clients deal with insurance issues related to leased cars and those where the insured is considered to be **upside-down**, meaning that they owe more on the car than the car is worth in the marketplace. An **auto loan/lease coverage endorsement** provides coverage for the potential gap between the actual cash value of an auto and the amount the insured owes on the auto loan or lease. If a vehicle is deemed a total loss after an accident, the owner may owe more on the vehicle than the insurance will pay as its actual cash value. **Guaranteed auto protection (GAP)** pays the difference between the actual cash value settlement and the remaining balance on the loan or lease.

> **#Remember**
>
> Although not common, some states allow owners to self-insure for auto losses. High net worth clients who drive exotic cars forego replacement due to damage and instead focus on paying liability claims only. The client posts a liability bond for an amount determined by the state.

Renting a car while on business or for personal reasons causes many clients anxiety. Whether to purchase the insurance offered by rental car companies can be a confusing issue. Normally, clients who carry **collision coverage**—a policy provision which covers damage to a policy holder's auto resulting from physical contact with another object—on their personal car will find that the coverage extends to rental cars as well. Usually **comprehensive coverage** also carries over to a rental car. This coverage provides reimbursement for *non-collision damage* or theft of the automobile; however, it is important to advise clients that they are responsible for paying the policy deductible and that the insurance company will consider the policy to be **excess coverage**, meaning the insurance company will look first to see whether the insured purchased coverage from the rental car company before paying a claim.

Drivers who have many claims on file with their insurance company, and those who are highly risk averse, should consider purchasing insurance as part of the rental agreement. Rental car insurance is known as a **loss damage waiver (LDW)** or a **collision damage waiver (CDW)**. Purchasing an LDW/CDW allows the insured to walk away from an accident, or if the car is stolen or vandalized, without having to pay a deductible, unless the rental company can show that the driver was reckless or driving while under the influence of drugs or alcohol. Costs for LDW/CDWs average between $7 and $20 per day. Sometimes clients will ask financial planners whether **accidental death and/or personal property insurance coverage** should be purchased when renting a car. Normally, the answer is no. The cost of accidental death insurance can be very high, and most often, reimbursement for lost personal property falls under a client's HO policy.

Planning Skill 9: Explore the Need for Excess Liability Coverage

Although clients often think of insurance as a tool to reimburse property losses, financial planners should be quick to point out that liability coverage may be a more important need for clients. Typical HO and PAP coverage provides basic levels of liability protection. Often, however, these limits are very low. In some states, for example, someone may drive legally with as little as $5,000 in liability coverage. Although it is possible and prudent for clients to purchase additional liability coverage of $300,000 to $500,000 on individual HO, auto, or watercraft policies, additional—and perhaps more cost-effective—coverage should be purchased through an **excess liability** or **umbrella liability policy**. These policies provide coverage for losses above HO and PAP liability limits. Higher HO and PAP liability coverage is typically required before an excess liability policy can be purchased. Umbrella contracts are not standardized, so coverage can vary. These insurance contracts also typically provide **personal injury coverage** (e.g., claims alleging *libel*, *slander*, or *invasion of privacy*) that may not be included in other policies.

Although $1 million is a typical minimum policy available in the marketplace, financial planners often recommend $2 million to $5 million in coverage. It is appropriate to roughly match the umbrella protection, at a minimum, to the client's net worth. But other factors, such as earnings potential, risk tolerance, personal risk and lifestyle profile, and the availability of assets to be attached to pay for a claim beyond the coverage of the policy, also must be considered.

Self-Test 5

Jim's wife recently hit a light pole in a parking lot. The accident was clearly his wife's fault. Jim can make a claim on his PAP using what coverage provision?

a. Collision for the car; property damage liability for the light pole.

b. Property damage liability for the car and light pole.

c. Comprehensive for the car; out of pocket payment for the light pole.

d. None of the above; the damage to both the car and the pole will be covered by the parking lot's commercial policy.

Planning Skill 10: Use a Homestead Exemption for Additional Liability Protection

Many states provide homeowners with the opportunity to protect a portion of home equity in a personal residence from creditors, which can include liability claims. This protection is provided through a **homestead exemption** or **declaration**. Protection may or may not be automatic, depending on the state. To qualify, a client must live in the residence, and it may be necessary to file a form with the local municipality. Equity protection amounts and guidelines vary by state.

Property and Liability Insurance Product & Procedural Strategies

Answering the key property and liability questions presented in Figure 9.1, and reviewing a client's current coverage and liability limits, can help financial planners and their clients discover gaps in current insurance coverage and opportunities to enhance in-force policies. Generally, these needs can require an increase in current coverage or the purchase of a new policy. The way an insurance contract is structured will affect the cost and amount of insurance obtained. The following discussion describes commonly used property and liability insurance strategies to meet a typical client's needs. When reviewing these strategies, it is important to consider that, in practice, financial planners often go beyond these basic tactics to help their clients navigate the complex property and casualty insurance environment.

Product Strategy 1: Purchase an HO-3 Policy with at Least $300,000 in Liability Coverage

An *HO-3 policy* provides the broadest open perils coverage available for a given structure. But, this type of policy covers personal property losses for named perils *only*. An endorsement to provide open perils coverage on the contents is available for those who prefer the most comprehensive coverage, assuming an HO-5 is unavailable. If the HO-3 provides only $100,000 in liability coverage, it should be increased to a minimum of $300,000, which is what many financial planners consider a minimum level of protection and in some cases required by the insurance company as a minimum for adding an umbrella policy. Increasingly, a minimum of $500,000 of liability protection is recommended. An umbrella policy can be added for additional liability protection. Choosing the open perils coverage on contents or the higher liability limit will add to the cost of the policy, but can be partially offset by a high deductible.

HO Rules

Four parameters can be used whenever an HO policy is recommended to a client. First, clients should purchase maximum liability protection, but never less than a $300,000 limit. This should be coordinated with an umbrella policy of at least $1 million. Second, the coverage should be as comprehensive as possible. Third, first-party losses should be paid on a replacement cost basis, with an annual inflation adjustment. Finally, any and all discounts should be explored, including higher deductibles. Premium discounts also may be earned by implementing property protection devices and by buying all policies from the same insurance company.

Product Strategy 2: Maximize HO Coverage with Endorsements

To personalize and maximize coverage, a wide variety of endorsements, such as a personal articles endorsement, personal injury endorsement, an identity theft endorsement, an inflation endorsement, or home office coverage, can be written as an addendum to a HO contract. These choices must be considered in light of a client's property, risk tolerance and emergency funds available for unreimbursed losses – as well as the projected probability for loss relative to the additional premium cost of the endorsement.

> **#Remember**
>
> Play it safe by recommending an in-home safe to store valuables and the verifications for property values. Buying a safe retains the risk and reduces the probability of loss. Purchasing insurance coverage (i.e., endorsement or floater) is a form of loss sharing.

But three endorsements may be broadly applicable. The first two are the *replacement cost endorsement* for the structure, the contents or both and the *inflation endorsement*. The need for these endorsements will vary with the individual insurer and the HO policy. The third is the **building code upgrade endorsement**. Whenever major repairs or reconstruction must occur, building codes mandate that the work must be updated to the standards of the current building code requirements. Bringing a home up to date in the affected area can significantly add to replacement costs. Some HO policies provide coverage that helps offset expenses associated with bringing a dwelling up to residential code standards after a loss; however, the amount of coverage is typically limited to 10 percent of the amount of insurance on the dwelling. Other policies provide no coverage for this necessary expense.

Product Strategy 3: Purchase Lowest-Cost PAP Coverage

It is possible to purchase PAP coverage with low split-limit liability coverage at a low cost; however, the least effective way to shop for automobile insurance involves comparing policies on premium alone. Although a policy with low liability limits may be purchased for a modest annual premium, buying automobile insurance on premium alone can be dangerous. First, a client is more likely to be underinsured for liability exposure. Second, low-cost insurance providers should be reviewed for financial stability, claims history, and customer satisfaction. Further, some low-cost policies require that claims be made via telephone or the internet. Although this often sounds reasonable before an accident, the inherent limitations of such claims adjustment procedures can be severe in a serious accident. Having a competent and well-trained agent is often worth the extra premium.

Product Strategy 4: Purchase at Least a $1 Million Umbrella Liability Policy

Rapidly increasing jury awards for liability claims have escalated the need for additional liability insurance to protect current assets and future income. High-net-worth clients are especially at risk for liability exposure. Unfortunately, the greater the perceived ability of an individual to pay, the greater the likelihood of a liability lawsuit. The annual cost of an umbrella policy is quite reasonable. A $1 million policy can be purchased for $300 or less annually in most cases. In addition to the additional financial protection it provides, an umbrella (excess liability) policy provides peace of mind. For a very modest annual cost, clients can sleep easier knowing that they are protected in case of a liability claim.

HO and PAP liability limits generally must be increased to obtain an umbrella policy. A minimum of $300,000 in liability coverage for a HO policy typically is required. Higher split-limit coverage, such as 250/500/100, or a $500,000 single limit, is normally required for PAP policies. An insured's HO policy or PAP provides the first level of coverage in case of litigation. Once these policy limits are reached, the umbrella policy provides additional protection up to the limits of the policy.

If the umbrella policy is used for a claim that is excluded from an HO or PAP, a deductible ranging from a low of perhaps $250 to as much as several thousand dollars may be imposed. For example, payment of a deductible would be required for a lawsuit that is excluded from HO coverage. This must be considered when establishing emergency fund needs.

Procedural Strategy 1: Drop Collision Coverage on Autos Six to Eight Years of Age or Older

The costs associated with repairing significant damage on most late model standard automobiles almost always exceeds the book value of the automobile. In such cases, an insurance company may elect not to repair the car. Rather, they may pay the insured the book value (minus the deductible) and declare the car a total loss. Paying premiums for collision coverage on a car in this situation may not be cost effective.

This strategy will reduce the premium and increase annual discretionary cash flow. However, the insured must recognize that, without physical damage protection, any loss other than an at-fault accident caused by another driver with insurance will mean that the insured must pay for all repair costs or replace the auto with another auto. This strategy is least effective when the insured drives a high value or collectible car. Also, the out-of-pocket expenses associated with a loss can still be quite high. This may require a client to hold more in liquid assets than might otherwise be desired.

PAP Rules

Four rules personal automobile policy rules should be followed. First, clients should obtain the maximum affordable level of liability coverage, which should be coordinated with coverage for uninsured and underinsured motorists and an umbrella policy. Second, medical expense coverage should be evaluated. Policy payments to others within the policy should be maximized if the insured frequently has passengers who are not family members. Third, clients need to take advantage of premium reductions for discounts and higher deductibles. Finally, collision insurance, which covers damage to a policy holder's auto resulting from physical contact with another object, should be monitored yearly and eliminated once the automobile's value drops substantially. It is also important to monitor comprehensive insurance coverage as well. In situations where a client owns an older car, comprehensive coverage can be reduced or eliminated as a way to decrease the annual premium.

Procedural Strategy 2: Choose the Highest Deductible a Client Can Afford

A higher deductible is preferred, unless the client has no emergency savings. Raising an HO policy deductible from $500 to $1,000 could save a client up to 25 percent in annual premium costs.[6] Similarly, raising a PAP deductible from $200 to $500 could reduce collision and comprehensive coverage costs by 15 to 30 percent, and increasing a deductible to $1,000 could save 40 percent percent or more in annual premium costs.[7] Because client out-of-pocket expenses will increase in case of a loss, this strategy requires clients to increase their emergency fund holdings, which may temporarily divert savings and assets from funding other goals. Financial planners should conduct a cost-benefit analysis to determine how long it will take to recoup costs if a claim occurs earlier or later in the savings process.

Procedural Strategy 3: Increase Liability Limits

In general, liability limits on an HO policy should be increased to a minimum of $300,000. Insurance experts often recommend that clients have a minimum of $100,000/$300,000/$100,000 in split-limit coverage on a PAP. A minimum of $500,000 **combined single-limit coverage** is recommended, with the insurance company paying covered liabilities up to this amount regardless of the distribution between bodily injury and property damage liability. Increasing liability coverage decreases the likelihood of being *underinsured for losses* caused to others. Furthermore, these amounts are generally the minimum required to purchase excess liability insurance. Increasing liability limits will result in an annual premium increase. But the premium cost must be considered relative to the protection of assets and future income, in the event of a large award from an at-fault accident. The increased premium cost can be partially offset by (1) comparing costs from different insurers; (2) taking advantage of all discounts; and (3) increasing the deductible on collision and comprehensive coverages, as generally no deductible applies to the liability coverage for auto on homeowner policies.

Procedural Strategy 4: Reduce Premiums with Discounts

Clients may be eligible for insurance premium discounts. For example, an older client who drives infrequently may be eligible for a low-mileage discount, and clients with teenagers or college-age children should inquire about good student discounts. In many states, it is also possible to receive a discount for taking a driver's education course. Clients who insure a home and automobile with a single insurer may receive a **multi-policy discount**. HO policy discounts may be available for smoke detectors or security systems, including dead-bolt locks. The only real disadvantage associated with this strategy is the amount of time involved in researching, requesting, or validating eligibility for certain discounts. There may be a significant opportunity cost between

---

Self-Test 6

Michael has split-limit coverage equal to 50/100/25. Yesterday Michael rear ended a new Mercedes as he was driving to work. The damage to the car totaled $33,000, while the medical bill for the other driver was $15,000. How much will Michael's insurance company pay (without regard to the deductible)?

a. $15,000

b. $33,000

c. $40,000

d. $48,000

the amount of time spent obtaining a discount and the amount of premium saved. Clients should instruct their insurance agent to recommend applicable discounts.

Procedural Strategy 5: Review Insurance Rates before Purchasing a New Car

Insurance rates are, in part, based on the type and value of the car being insured. Cars with lower repair rates will be less expensive to insure than those with higher repair rates. Likewise, a lower-priced car will be less expensive to insure than a more valuable one. Cars with outstanding safety records, passive restraint systems, and antitheft devices also generate lower premiums. Unfortunately, implementing this strategy can significantly limit a client's choice in automobiles. Additionally, adding features that will reduce premium costs may increase the overall cost of the vehicle. The best advice: when auto shopping is to check the cost of coverage on all models considered. Insurance premiums can vary significantly for autos that appear similar in style, features, and cost.

Procedural Strategy 6: Bundle HO and PAP Coverage to Reduce Annual Premiums

Self-Test 7

Joe, Lance, and Ann recently entered in a business arrangement. They are worried about getting sued if someone gets hurt using their product. Which of the following forms of business ownership will provide the least amount of liability protection?

a. C-Corporation

b. LLC

c. S-Corporation

d. Partnership

Clients, particularly those with a high insurance score, should shop aggressively for HO and PAP bundled coverage. The marketplace is competitive and discounts are widely available for those with a strong history of premium payment and a low incident level of filing claims. An easy way to reduce annual premiums involves bundling a PAP and HO policy together, using a replacement value endorsement. When determining the level of HO insurance to purchase, insurance agents and brokers often recommend using the *cost per square foot* associated with building in a local area as a guide. Average insurance rates, for bundled and unbundled policies, can be obtained at www.homeownersinsurance.com.

A clear disadvantage associated with bundling coverage relates to sometimes being held captive by one insurance company. Although a single provider may offer competitive rates on, for example, HO policies, there is no guarantee that the company will also be competitive with PAP coverage rates. It is important for financial planners to work with their clients to shop competitively for bundled policies that provide the lowest net premium cost.

Procedural Strategy 7: Use Appropriate Business Structure to Help Clients Limit Liability

Although not solely a property and casualty insurance issue, clients who own a business as a sole proprietorship who also use personal property as a function of their business need to understand that they are exposed to potential unlimited *personal liability* for claims against either the business or the individual. Normally, this liability cannot be controlled with an HO policy or an excess liability insurance contract. Although a *sole proprietorship* can be easy to manage, there are better alternatives to protect clients from liability. Five alternatives should be considered when working with small business owners. These alternatives, with a brief description, are listed below:

1. **C-corporation**: Limited liability for owners; relatively complex to manage. The corporate structure can provide an effective way to provide tax-advantaged fringe benefits for employees and owner-shareholders.

2. **S-corporation**: Limited liability for owners; income flows through from corporation to owners; may not have more than 100 shareholders.

3. **LLC**: Liability limited to member's contribution to firm; members rather than shareholders; less cumbersome than a corporation.

4. **LLP**: Liable for actions of all partners, but not liable for errors and omissions of partners.

5. **Partnership**: Liable for action of all partners; this form of business ownership provides little liability protection.

The costs, both financially and administratively, are higher for these arrangements than for sole proprietorships. Also, changing from a corporate structure back to a sole proprietorship can be expensive. Sometimes clients feel these costs outweigh the potential liability associated with owning a business; nonetheless, financial planners should always address liability exposure and recommend alternative forms of business ownership, when appropriate, within a comprehensive financial plan.

PROPERTY AND LIABILITY INSURANCE PLANNING FOR SPECIAL POPULATIONS

Planning for Special Situations

Whereas some core content planning areas present unique planning challenges for select segments of the population, property and liability risk management issues can be a challenge simply because of the property owned or lifestyle activities. Consider the following:

Jewelry Owners. Very few people typically walk around with thousands of dollars in their pocket? Yet, a diamond ring, wedding band, watch, or other jewelry could easily amount to $10,000 or more. Jewelry owners often make three common mistakes. First, they often assume that jewelry is covered by their HO policy, not realizing that relatively low limits apply (typically $2,500). Second, they do not understand that policies rarely cover loss, damage, or the loss of a diamond from the setting. Third, they forget that a deductible will also apply, further reducing the stated, limited protection. **Personal article policies**, which are relatively inexpensive, provide comprehensive jewelry coverage, typically without a required deductible. The annual premium for a personal article floater can be estimated using the following formula: Value of Property x 2 percent. For example, a ring valued at $5,000 could be insured for approximately $100 per year.

Another common mistake is the failure to periodically update jewelry appraisals based on fluctuations in the price of gold, silver, diamonds, or other precious stones and metals. Recommendations on how often new appraisals should be performed vary, but waiting more than, say, ten years is inadvisable. Without a current assessment, a gap in coverage could result in a loss—of not only the item of jewelry, but also in the amount of insurance proceeds to replace it.

A personal articles policy is an all-perils policy and protects from loss, theft, or damage to the item, as well as loss of gemstones and diamonds. A **pair and set clause** offers additional protection for items sold as a pair or a set, as in a matching diamond ring and wedding band or a pair of earrings. A broad form pays for full replacement of both items, but a standard form pays only to replace, or duplicate, the missing component. Personal articles policies typically include inflation protection, based on the purchase price or appraised value when insurance is initially purchased, and require no deductible.

Yet another common mistake is failure to maintain an up-to-date inventory. Appraisals required to purchase personal article policies (or to add a personal article endorsement) provide needed documentation, but it is still important to maintain a complete **inventory** of all jewelry. Care should be taken to continually update the inventory and buy coverage for new purchases. In fact, specialized insurance is available to protect items purchased during a specific time period, such as while traveling, so that insurance is immediately available until a personal articles policy or endorsement can be obtained.

Those Serving on Corporate or Nonprofit Organization Boards. Individuals are often honored, and quite motivated, to serve on the board of directors of a nonprofit organization. Most corporations and nonprofit organizations purchase **directors' and officers'** (D&O) liability insurance to protect those serving in this capacity. But if the coverage is inadequate or is not purchased, then a liability suit that names the officers and directors could expose their personal assets to any claims or jury awards. An excess, or umbrella, liability policy provides limited protection in this situation, specifically for bodily injury or property damage, but it may pay for the costs of defending the client. Another option is for the client to purchase a directors and officers liability policy to protect against non-bodily injury claims (e.g., discrimination or termination of employment) arising from misstatement, misleading statement, breach of duty, or errors and omissions. The policy may or may not provide for legal and court fees, and deductibles often apply.

Pet Lovers. The financial planning data collection and discovery process could reveal a family's love for animals. A family member might serve on a struggling, local animal shelter board; however, the client might never have considered how a dog bite at a shelter-sponsored event could threaten her personal wealth. A qualified insurance specialist is best equipped to address this possibility and to recommend the necessary insurance protection. A financial planner plays a valuable role in asking the questions to uncover the issue and to recommend that the necessary actions be taken. In this case, obtaining D&O insurance is a necessity. If the same person were to own a dangerous pet, such as a dog or exotic animal, they should check with their insurance agent to ensure that their HO and umbrella coverages are still valid. They may be required to obtain additional coverage or to remove the animal from their home.

Anyone Protecting Against Identity Theft. Clients may not have considered insurance coverage in the event of a stolen identity. In fact, according to the Federal

Trade Commission (FTC), one of their top consumer complaints continues to be identity theft.[8] Placing fraud alerts with credit reporting bureaus, shredding documents with personal or financial information, and using strong passwords are all recommended methods of prevention; there are times, however, when these measures fail. More than 13 million Americans reportedly were victims of identity theft in 2015, with a total fraud amount of $15 billion.[9] According to the *2016 Identity Fraud Study*, $112 billion was stolen over the past six years.[10] Identity theft can continue undetected until the victim checks his credit report, notices an incorrect charge on a credit card statement, or is contacted by a debt collector.

One method to mitigate such loss at the household level is to insure for it. Some HO policies provide at least a modest form of coverage. This may be limited to a particular type of transaction (e.g., forgery, electronic fund transfer, or credit card fraud) or a nominal amount of coverage (e.g., $500 to $1,000) depending on the company. The first layer of additional protection is available with an endorsement on the HO policy to enhance both the scope and coverage amount for a potential loss. Additional coverage may be available with an excess liability, or umbrella, policy.

Property and Liability Planning for Cohabitating Couples, Housemates, or Partners

Insurance companies can deny claims from an auto accident caused by a driver who routinely has access to a car but is not included on the policy as a driver or for a fire caused by a live-in partner or roommate who is not included on the HO policy. Often, property owners, of a car or home, may never suspect that they, and the actions of their partners, are not protected in these situations. So, what is required to provide protection for the property and potential liability claims against the owner's assets or future income? It depends! It is essential that financial planners review the titling—and insurance coverage—of jointly used assets as part of the insurance planning analysis.

Ongoing Monitoring

Completing periodic reviews of a client's insurance coverage is an important task. At a minimum, the actual insurance policy documents should be reviewed annually for accuracy -- with the client or the insurance professional:

- Names and addresses

- Social Security Numbers

- Dwelling construction type

- Dwelling or outbuilding additions

- Auto, motorcycle, or watercraft coverage

- Deductibles

- Schedules and endorsements

- Any new purchases that may require coverage

- Coordination of coverage if not purchased through the same company

If any item on a policy document is incorrect or inaccurate, immediate steps should be taken to correct it. Accurate documentation will lead to more efficient claims settlement should a loss occur.

Self-Test 8

Which of the following increase the property and liability premiums?

a. Decreasing the deductible.

b. Increasing the deductible.

c. Decreasing the amount of liability coverage.

d. Both b and c.

In the case of an auto, most companies will allow a multicar policy for unrelated individuals who share the same "garage address" for their vehicles. If this is unavailable or is not the method preferred by a nontraditional couple or housemates, then the other option is to add the partner or roommate to the auto policy of each of the insured's vehicles. With either method, the premium cost will be based on the driving records of both individuals. This is required for regular access to, and use of, the other partner's car. If access to the other's car is limited to a random, occasional occurrence, then it is not necessary to add the partner as a driver. If there is only one car, but both partners routinely drive it, then both must be named as insured drivers on the policy.

Similarly, if a home is owned by one partner, then coverage must be extended to the housemate or partner. Typically, HO policies are written to match the deed and protect only the insured and his or her immediate family. To extend coverage, several options are available. The non-owner's name may be added to the policy as an additional insured, although not all companies will allow this. Some companies add a rider, or **cohabitant form**, for an additional occupant. If this is not available or is not the method preferred by the clients, then the non-owner should purchase a renter's policy, even if no rent is actually being paid. The renters policy will provide protection for the personal property in the home, and more importantly, provide liability and other HO-4 coverage (for more information see Figure 9.4), if needed. If the home is rented, a joint renter's policy may be available; otherwise, each partner should purchase an individual policy.

Contingent on the insurance options chosen from these alternatives, a similar strategy may be available to purchase excess liability, or umbrella, insurance. State laws and company policies vary, so it is important to consult with an insurance professional. However, individuals who are not married or do not own property jointly typically cannot purchase an excess liability policy together; individual umbrella policies will be necessary. Either way, the protection should be matched, at a minimum, to the net worth of the individuals, and potentially to an even higher amount to protect assets adequately.

Mini-Case Problems

Ricardo Juarez

1. Ricardo Juarez is purchasing a HO insurance policy. He is very concerned about inflation and wants to make a determination about purchasing the optional inflation protection rider. He has identified several scenarios and wants to know how often he needs to revisit his coverage to maintain at least 80 percent of replacement cost. Base all calculations on an initial home value of $250,000 and initial coverage of 100 percent on the dwelling and contents.

    a. He believes that current housing prices will increase at 4 percent per year. How long will his coverage meet the 80 percent rule if he does not buy inflation protection? How long would he be covered if he purchases an inflation protection rider that offers annual compound increases of 3 percent?

b. Given the recent declines in housing values, he believes a recovery is coming and that housing prices will increase at 7 percent per year for the next five years before slowing to a permanent 4 percent annual appreciation rate. How long will his coverage meet the 80 percent rule? First assume that Ricardo does not purchase an inflation protection rider, and then assume that he purchases an inflation protection rider that offers annually compounded increases of 3 percent.

c. Ricardo believes that housing prices still have a ways to fall before any meaningful recovery. He believes that future housing prices will decrease at an annual rate of 4 percent for the next three years before the long-term trend of 5 percent annual increases resumes. Assuming that he does not purchase an inflation protection rider, how long will his coverage meet the 80 percent rule?

d. He believes that future price increases will be very unstable. With this uncertainty, he wants to have the inflation rider protection of 3 percent compounded annually. Assume actual housing price changes for the next five years are 3, -7, -2, 8, and 12 percent. Will his coverage meet the 80 percent rule at the end of this five-year period? What if he does not purchase the optional rider?

e. Based on the results from above, what can be said about how frequently insurance coverage needs to be reevaluated?

Narang Park

2. Your client, Narang Park, has coverage of $90,000 on a dwelling. The replacement value of the dwelling is $125,000. The policy coinsurance requirement is 80 percent. The client has chosen a $500 deductible. Calculate the amount of loss reimbursement a client should receive for each of the following losses.

a. The amount of the loss is $60,000.

b. The amount of the loss is $90,000.

c. The amount of the loss is $120,000.

Now assume that the client increases the amount of coverage to $105,000. To offset some of the premium increase, the client chose to increase the deductible to $1,050. The policy coinsurance requirement is 80 percent. The replacement value of the dwelling is $125,000. Calculate the amount of loss reimbursement for each of the following losses.

a. The amount of the loss is $90,000.

b. The amount of the loss is $105,000.

c. The amount of the loss is $120,000.

Comprehensive Bedo Case – Property and Liability Insurance Analysis Questions

Specific client data are needed to conduct a thorough property and liability analysis, which is why planners obtain a copy of the client's HO and personal automobile policies. The 80 percent rule should be reviewed in relation to the Bedos' HO coverage and the value of their property. Any personal property that might be excluded or have limited coverage should be identified for coverage with policy endorsements. Special attention should also be placed on examining liability limits in the HO, auto, or umbrella policies.

1. Develop one or more property and liability insurance planning goals for the Bedos. When conceptualizing this goal, consider the following:

    a. Is the goal(s) developed in agreement with any or all goals and objectives that the clients have identified regarding property and liability insurance planning?

    b. What situational factors might influence their property and liability insurance goal? Are these factors explicit, implied, or assumed? Is additional information required from the Bedos, and if so, what?

    c. What is the desired property and liability insurance planning outcome for the clients?

2. Make a list of the lifestyle factors or property ownership issues that should be documented and evaluated for the Bedos. How might this information be obtained? How might it be useful in the property and liability insurance situation analysis? Also, make a list of life events that could affect the property and liability insurance planning analysis for Tyler and Mia and that should be reviewed at future client meetings.

3. Are there globally accepted, client-specific, or planner-generated planning assumptions that will influence the property and casualty insurance situation analysis? List the assumptions as they might appear in a plan.

4. To determine and quantify the Bedos' current property and liability insurance planning needs thoroughly, assess the following:

    a. Possible liability exposures faced by the Bedos and implications for their insurance needs.

    b. Their current level of HO insurance coverage compared to industry benchmarks.

    c. The amount of liability coverage in the Bedos' HO policy compared to their possible liability exposure.

    d. The need for specific policy endorsements.

    e. The split-limit coverage limits on their personal automobile insurance policies.

    f. The need for Part D Coverage for Damage to Your Car automobile insurance coverage.

    g. The need for an umbrella, or excess liability, policy.

5. List and comment on other policy features that should be evaluated as part of the documentation and evaluation of the Bedos' property and liability insurance planning needs and efforts, including, but not limited to, the following.

    a. Do the Bedos have sufficient documentation to verify property or values in the event of a loss?

    b. Assume that the Bedos were shopping for a new car. What attributes of the car might result in a lower annual insurance premium?

6. Based on the information collected, financial advisors have a responsibility to fully document and inform clients of the analyses and results. This information may be communicated through a letter or a comprehensive or modular plan. Summarize your observations about Tyler and Mia's current property and liability insurance situation and the identified planning need(s). Be sure to discuss their homeowners, auto, and, if needed, excess liability insurance. Incorporate text, bullets, and graphics into your explanation.

7. Based on the goals originally identified and the completed analysis, what product or procedural strategies might be most useful to satisfy the Bedos' property and liability insurance protection needs? Be sure to consider strategies matched to the planning needs identified. When reviewing the strategies, be careful to consider the approximate cost of implementation, as well as the most likely outcome(s) associated with each strategy.

8. Write at least one primary and one alternative recommendation from the selected strategies in response to each identified planning need. More than one recommendation may be needed to address all of the planning needs. Include specific, defensible answers to the who, what, when, where, why, how, and how much implementation questions for each recommendation.

    a. It is suggested that each recommendation be summarized in a Recommendation Form.

    b. Assign a priority to each recommendation based on the likelihood of meeting client goals and desired outcomes. This priority will be important when recommendations from other core planning content areas are considered relative to the available discretionary funds for subsidizing all recommendations.

    c. Comment briefly on the outcomes associated with each recommendation.

9. Complete the following for the Property and Liability Insurance section of the Bedos' financial plan.

    a. Outline the content to be included in this section of the plan. Given the segments written above, which segments are missing?

    b. Write the introduction to this section of the plan (no more than one to two paragraphs).

    c. Define, explain, or interpret at least five policy features or concepts (e.g., the 80% rule) that would be included in this section of the plan. For each, write a definition or explanation that could appear in this section of the plan or in the plan glossary.

10. Prepare a ten–fifteen-minute presentation for the Bedos of your observations and/or recommendation(s) for meeting their property and casualty insurance needs. Be sure to include visual aids, Excel handouts, and other materials that will make the recommendations more meaningful for the clients.

Chapter Resources

Insurance Institute for Business and Home Safety (www.disastersafety.org).

Insurance Information Institute (www.iii.org).

National Flood Insurance Program (floodsmart.com or www.fema.gov/nfip/ or 1-800-638-6620).

Policy Forms Used by the Top 10 Homeowners' Insurance Groups in Nevada (doi.nv.gov/scs/Homeowners.aspx). Nevada is the only state offering this service to consumers, but other states are expected to follow this initiative.

Property Casualty Insurers Association of America (www.pciaa.net/web/sitehome.nsf/main).

United Policyholders™ Empowering the Insured (www.uphelp.org).

Self-Test Answers

1: b, 2: c, 3: a, 4: b, 5: a, 6: c, 7: d, 8: a

Endnotes

1. Nationwide. *Underinsurance: A Common Problem.* Available at www.nationwide.com/underinsurance.jsp.

2. Federal Trade Commission, *Credit-based Insurance Scores: Impacts on Consumers of Automobile Insurance.* Available at: www.ftc.gov/os/2007/07/P044804FACTA_Report_Credit-Based_Insurance_Scores.pdf, p. 1.

3. National Flood Insurance Program, Policy Rates. Available at www.floodsmart.gov/floodsmart/pages/residential_coverage/policy_rates.jsp.

4. Insurance Information Institute. *Uninsured Motorists.* Available at: www.iii.org/fact-statistic/uninsured-motorists

5. Insurance Information Institute, *Uninsured Motorists.*

6. Insurance Information Institute. *How to Save Money on Your Homeowners Insurance.* Available at: www.iii.org/article/how-to-save-money-on-your-homeowners-insurance

7. Insurance Information Institute. *How Can I Save Money on Auto Insurance?* Available at http://www.iii.org/articles/how-can-i-save-money.html.

8. Federal Trade Commission, *Top 10 Consumer Complaint Categories: Is Your Industry on the List?* Available at: www.ftc.gov/news-events/blogs/business-blog/2016/03/top-10-consumer-complaint-categories-your-industry-list.

9. Pascual, A., Marchini, K. and Miller, S. (February 2016). *2016 Identity Fraud: Fraud Hits an Inflection Point.* Available at: www.javelinstrategy.com/coverage-area/2016-identity-fraud-fraud-hits-inflection-point.

10. *Id.*

PART IV: Analyzing and Evaluating a Client's Financial Status to Plan for the Growth and Distribution of Assets

Chapter 10

Investment Planning

Learning Objectives

1. The development of an investment plan is based on an analysis of client situational and external economic factors, but foremost is the type of goals a client would like to achieve. The type of investment plan developed must match the goal(s) and time frame(s) identified with the client, taking into account the client's risk tolerance and risk capacity. The investment plan might be the most revisited portion of the financial plan because it is subject to so many client-driven events and economic changes. Ultimately, the soundness of investment choices is one of the primary determinants of success or failure in realizing future goals.

2. This chapter reviews the steps involved in conducting an investment planning analysis. First, a financial planner must understand the five situational factors that influence a client's investment planning. These include (1) risk tolerance, (2) expectations about future market conditions, (3) knowledge and experience, (4) time horizon, and (5) the capacity to handle risk. The first three factors are inferred, meaning that they are more reasoned than measured. The other two factors are more quantitative in nature because they can be more objectively measured. Next, the financial planner must determine the rate of return desired or required to meet the client's objectives. Unfortunately, sometimes a client's risk profile does not match the required portfolio. Once the desired rate is determined, appropriate asset classes can be selected and the financial planner can finally determine how to combine these asset classes into a single cohesive portfolio or, in some cases, multiple portfolios.

3. As discussed in this chapter, when allocating a client's assets, financial planners must consider not only the asset classes available, but also client situational and external asset allocation factors. Client situational asset allocation factors, which involve the goal of the client's portfolio and how aggressively the assets in the portfolio can be allocated within the risk comfort level of the client, are client-centric in

Learning Objectives

nature. Assets should not be allocated in the same way for a risk-averse client seeking some asset appreciation while attempting to preserve capital as for a client seeking maximum capital appreciation while minimizing potential tax liabilities. Investments are also allocated or reallocated based on external factors pertaining to the current and prospective economic landscape. Although external factors can be more easily quantified, interpreting the influence each may have on a portfolio can be more difficult; external factors encompass asset class returns, domestic interest rates, stock and bond yields, monetary and fiscal policies and inflation (see Chapter 3 for a review of these factors).

4. Financial planners often engage in different allocation approaches. Strategic asset allocation is the process of setting target allocations for each class of assets based on the long-term objective of a portfolio. The portfolio is then periodically rebalanced back to original asset allocation percentages. A strategic allocation of a portfolio is the most important determinant of total return. Tactical asset allocation, on the other hand, allows for more active management by setting a range of percentages in each asset class rather than a fixed target. This range gives a financial planner the ability to be more opportunistic about changing the allocations when longer-term economic conditions might favor one asset class over another. Two examples of tactical allocation strategies are sector rotation and core and satellite.

5. Once the five client factors of investment planning are established,

the financial planner can start combining them with a client's investment attitudes (e.g., social or religious preferences) and expectations about the future to build the client's investment profile. This chapter reviews the process of documenting a client's investment preferences and evaluating the alternatives, which is the basis of constructing an investment policy statement (IPS). An IPS guides the investment and management of a client's investments and is included in a client's investment plan as a (1) way to reduce financial planner liability through appropriate planning disclosure and (2) reminder to the client and planner of the importance of adhering to established guidelines.

6. This chapter explores the importance of using indexes appropriately. Indexes can be used track the performance of a select group of financial assets, but they are also useful as standards of measurement within a client's portfolio. For a meaningful comparison, it is important to select a benchmark that closely matches both the type of security and the corresponding level of risk. The simplest method for determining the best benchmark is to find one that generally fits the asset or asset class being evaluated, (e.g., large-cap fund versus large-cap benchmark). It is also recommended that a linear regression of returns be conducted to validate the similarity of the benchmark. With some additional work this analysis can also be performed for entire portfolios. Once an appropriate benchmark is identified, the next step in evaluating a portfolio is to calculate one or more performance statistics. There are two primary classes of performance measures: absolute

Learning Objectives

and ratio. Although different measures categorize risk differently, the precision of measurement is important to financial planners when attempting to make decisions about the effectiveness of a portfolio management or asset selection decision.

7. Clients tend to seek the help of a financial planner for investment planning guidance to increase the capital appreciation potential of their investments, to increase the amount of current income earned from their investments, and/or to reduce the amount of taxes paid on their investments. However, clients are often unaware of what might be necessary to increase their real, risk-adjusted, or after-tax returns. As noted in this chapter, nothing is more important than a financial planner's skill in matching one or more investment alternatives to a client's objective. However, selecting only a few from the vast array of choices takes a great deal of time and ability. Although the tendency when dealing with investments is to focus on specific products, this chapter illustrates the importance of following a procedure. Financial planners and clients often find that the simplest strategy makes for the best recommendation.

8. In many ways, the development and presentation of investment planning recommendations is the most important part of the systematic financial planning process. Although there may be a temptation to develop complex and intricate recommendations, this is not always appropriate or even necessary. Lack of implementation by the client is the leading cause of plan failure. Making plans easy to implement is important. Some of the best planning strategies accomplish more than one objective, such as hedging inflation while providing current income or maximizing long-term appreciation while minimizing tax consequence. As such, it is imperative that recommendations be easily understood, conceptually valid, and cost effective. As discussed in this chapter, it is of paramount importance when developing or choosing strategies to remember that a client's goals should dominate the decision-making process. Financial planners should always solicit a client's collaboration in decision making and implementation. For the majority of investment planning recommendations, a client should be able to quickly understand the reasoning behind each suggestion and the potential outcomes associated with implementation. This means that answers to the core implementation questions of who, what, when, where, why, how, and how much should be clear, concise, and understandable.

Key Terms

12b-1 Fees	Capital Preservation
A Shares	Cash
Accumulation Stage of the Life Cycle	Certificates of Deposit (CD)
Active Management	Client Situational Asset Allocation Factors
Aggressiveness	Client Situational Factors
Alpha	Close-End Fund
Annuity	Coefficient of Determination
Asset Allocation	Coefficient of Variation
Asset Allocation Framework	Collectibles
Asset Classification	Commodities
Average Return	Common Stock
B Shares	Consumer Price Index (CPI)
Back-End Load	Contingent Fee
Balanced Funds	Core Holdings
Benchmark	Core-and-Satellite Portfolios
Beta	Corporate Bond
Beta of the Market	Correlation
Bond Fund	Correlation Coefficient
Bond Rating Agencies	Covariance
Bond Yields	Covered Call Option
Break Points	Creation Unit
Business Risk	Credit Risk
Buy-and-Hold Investing Strategy	Currency Exchange Rates
C Shares	Current Income, Capital Appreciation
Call Option	Debt-to-Equity Ratio
Capital Asset Pricing Model (CAPM)	Default

Key Terms

Default Risk	Financial Life Cycle
Deferred Sales Charge	Financial Risk
Discounted Dividend Valuation Model	Firm Risk
Dispersion Around the Mean	Fitch Ratings
Distribution Stage of the Life Cycle	Five Investment Planning Factors
Diversification	Five-Asset-Class Model
Dividend Growth Model	Fixed-Income Market Indexes
Downside Deviation	Futures
Downside Risk	Geometric Mean
Dynamic Allocation Strategy	Geometric Median
Economic Cycle	Growth Funds
EE and I Savings Bonds	Growth Rates
Equity Market Indexes	Hard Assets
Europe, Australia, and Far East Index (EAFE)	Hedge Fund
	Holding Costs
Exchange Rate Risk	Income Funds
Exchange-Traded Fund (ETF)	Index Funds
Expectations	Index Options
Expected Return	Inflation Risk
Expected Risk-Adjusted Rate of Return	Information Ratio
Expense Ratio	Interest Rates
External Asset Allocation Factors	Internal Rate of Return
Family Dynamics	International Investing
FDIC Insured Bank Accounts	Investment Attitudes
Federal Agency Bonds	Investment Characteristics by Investment Type
Financial Assets	

Key Terms

Investment Expectations

Investment Knowledge and Experience

Investment Policy Statement (IPS)

Investment Profile

Investment Profile and Portfolio
  Summary Form

Investment Selection Matrix

Investment Style Stability

Investment-Grade Corporate Bonds

Investments Attitude Questionnaire

Jensen Performance Index

Jensen's Alpha

Junk Bonds

Laddered Fixed-Income Portfolio

Large Cap

Leading Economic Indicator

Liquidity

Liquidity Risk

Load

Log-Normal Probability

M2

Managed Fund

Management Fee

Market Index

Market Risk

Marketability

Markowitz

Mean

Mid-Cap

Modern Portfolio Theory

Modified Duration

Modigliani Measure

Monetary Policy

Money Market Funds

Moody's Rating

Mortgage-Backed Security

Municipal Bond

Mutual Fund

Naked Call Options

Naked Put Options

National Bureau of Economic
  Research (NBER)

Net Asset Value

No-Load Fund

Nominal Rate of Return

Options

Political Affiliations

Political Risk

Pooled-Asset Investment Company

Portfolio Construction

Portfolio Risk Guidelines

Portfolio Risk Measures

Key Terms

Portfolio Turnover	Risk Tolerance
Precious Metals	Risk-Averse Behavior
Preferred Stock	Risk-Free Rate
Price-to-Book Ratio	Risk-Free Rate of Return
Price-to-Earnings Ratio	S&P 500
Price-to-Sales Ratio	Satellite Investments
Profit Margin	Savings Accounts
Property Manager	Sector Funds
Prospectus	Sector Rotation
Protection Stage of the Life Cycle	Semi-Deviation
Put Option	Semi-Variance
Qualified Stock Dividends	Sensitivity Analysis
R^2	Sharpe Ratio
Range	Short-Term Loss
Real Estate	Small-Cap
Real Estate Investment Trust (REIT)	Socially Responsible Investing
Relative Portfolio Performance Measures	Sortino Ratio
Rental Real Estate	Speculative-Grade Corporate Bonds
Required Rate of Return	Standard & Poor's
Return on Equity	Standard Deviation
Reverse Engineering	Stock Fund
Risk and Return	Stock Yields
Risk Capacity	Strategic Asset Allocation
Risk Perception	Style Drift
Risk Premium	Supply and Demand
Risk Profile	Systematic Risk

Key Terms

Tactical Asset Allocation

Tax Efficiency

Tax Liabilities

Tax-Equivalent Formula

Tax-Free Rate

T-Bill

Three-Asset Class Model

Time Horizon

Time the Market

Tips

Total Risk

Trading Expenses

Treasury Bonds

Treasury Inflation-Protection Securities

Treasury/Government Agency Bond

Treynor Index

Undiversified Portfolios

Unit Investment Trust

Unsystematic Risk

Value Funds

Variable Annuity

Variance

Volatility

Warrants

Zero Coupon Bond

CFP® Principal Knowledge Topics

B.12. Economic Concepts

D.31. Insurance Policy and Company Selection

E.33. Characteristics, Uses and Taxation of Investment Vehicles

E.34. Types of Investment Risk

E.35. Quantitative Investment Concepts

E.36. Measures of Investment Returns

E.37. Asset Allocation and Portfolio Diversification

E.38. Bond and Stock Valuation Concepts

E.39. Portfolio Development and Analysis

E.40. Investment Strategies

E.41. Alternative Investments

Chapter Equations

Equation 10.1: Variance $\quad \sigma^2_i = \dfrac{1}{T-1} \sum\limits_{t=1}^{T} (r_{i,t} - \bar{r}_1)^2$

Equation 10.2: Semi-variance $\quad \sigma^2_i = \dfrac{0.5}{T-1} \sum\limits_{t=1}^{T} (r_{i,t} - \bar{r}_1)^2$

Equation 10.3: Coefficient of Variation $\quad CV = \dfrac{\sigma}{\bar{r}}$

Equation 10.4: Beta $\quad \beta = \dfrac{\sigma_{i,M}}{\sigma^2_M}$

Equation 10.5: Sharpe Ratio $\quad S_i = \dfrac{R_i + R_f}{\sigma_i}$

Equation 10.6: Modigliani Measure $\quad M^2_i = \left[R_f + \sigma_m \left(\dfrac{(R_i - R_f)}{\sigma_i} \right) \right] - R_m$

Equation 10.7: Treynor Index $\quad T_i = \dfrac{R_i - R_f}{\beta_i}$

Equation 10.8: Jensen's Alpha $\quad \alpha = R_p - [R_f + \beta\,[(R_m - R_f)]$

Equation 10.9: Information Ratio $\quad \text{IR} = \dfrac{(r_p - r_B)}{\sqrt{Var\,(r_p - r_B)}} = \dfrac{a}{E_T}$

Equation 10.10: Tax-free Rate = Taxable Rate x (1 - Marginal Tax Bracket)

Equation 10.11: Discounted Dividend Valuation Model $\quad Value = \dfrac{D_0\,(1 + g)}{(i - g)}$

Equation 10.12: Variance Average Return (AR) $= \dfrac{r_1 + r_2 + r_3 + \cdots + r_n}{n}$

Equation 10.13: Asset Variance $\quad \sigma^2 = X_t - \mu$

Equation 10.14: Asset Standard Deviation

$$\sigma_i^2 = \dfrac{(x_1 - \mu)^2 + (x_2 - \mu)^2 + (x_3 - \mu)^2 + \cdots + (x_4 - \mu)^2}{n-1}$$

Equation 10.15: Variance:

$$\sigma_i = \sqrt{\dfrac{(x_1 - \mu)^2 + (x_2 - \mu)^2 + (x_3 - \mu)^2 + \cdots + (x_4 - \mu)^2}{n-1}}$$

Equation 10.16: Required Return of Asset A to equalize the CV $= \dfrac{\sigma A}{\text{CV of Asset B}}$

Equation 10.17: Variance $\quad \sigma_{ij} = \sigma_i \sigma_j \rho_{ij}$

Equation 10.18: Variance $\quad \sigma_{ij} = \dfrac{1}{n-1} \sum_{t-1}^{n} (r_{i,t} - \mu_i)(r_{j,t} - \mu_j)$

Equation 10.19: Variance $\quad \rho_{i,j} = \dfrac{\sigma_{i,j}}{\sigma_i \sigma_j}$

Equation 10.20: Variance $\quad \sigma_p = \sqrt{w_i^2 \sigma_i^2 + w_j^2 \sigma_j^2 + 2w_i w_j \sigma_{ij}}$

Equation 10.21: Variance $E(r) = r_f + IP + DP + BP + \ldots$

Equation 10.22: Variance $E(r) = (p_1 \times r_1) + (p_2 \times r_2) + (p_{n-1} \times r_{n-1}) + \ldots + (p_n \times r_n)$

Equation 10.23: Capital Asset Pricing Model (CAPM) $R_{Exp} = R_f + \beta(R_m - R_f)$

Equation 10.24: Variance $\beta = (\sigma_p / \sigma_m) \times \rho_{p,m}$

INVESTMENT PLANNING: DETERMINING THE NEED

Analyzing a client's current investment management situation involves a combination of qualitative and quantitative assessments. To this end, investment planning is as much an art as it is a logical system based on fixed rules. A financial planner must understand a client's perspectives on wants and needs, idealism and reality, as well as a broad range of personal characteristics that can influence investment decisions.

The first step in the analysis of a client's current investment planning situation focuses on determining and quantifying the client's planning needs. Temperament, personality, attitudes, and beliefs are particularly salient factors in the development of efficient, effective, client specific recommendations. Too often, investment planning decisions are based initially on assets available, with insufficient consideration of other client situational factors that should be instrumental in the products and strategies chosen. Although the assessment of a client's investment planning need is multifaceted, most professionals agree that an investment plan should be based on five key interrelated factors. These **five investment planning factors** include:

> ### *Investments for Risk-Averse Clients*
>
> Occasionally, a client's risk tolerance is so low that a financial planner has almost no choice but to recommend very liquid insured assets (e.g., savings account, CDs, and money market deposit accounts). In the most severe cases, a client might require the sole use of FDIC insured bank accounts. It is then up to the financial planner to optimize the client's earning power while maintaining complete FDIC coverage of the client's accounts. For very risk-averse clients, an annuity may also be an appropriate asset suggestion. Annuities can be used as a tool to convince a client to invest in the market with a small safety net.

1. a client's risk tolerance

2. expectations about future market conditions

3. knowledge and experience

4. time horizon; and

5. the financial capacity to withstand risk.

The first three represent client situational factors that are inferred, meaning that they are more reasoned than measured. A more complete understanding of these and other situational factors should emerge from the evolving client-planner relationship that occurs during the discovery and data-gathering process involved in Step 2 of the systematic financial planning process. Insights into a client's temperament and personality, as well as attitudes, beliefs, and behaviors, should also guide a financial planner when formulating an investment plan. The last two factors, time horizon and financial capacity to withstand risk (or loss), are more quantitative in nature because they can be more easily measured.

Risk Perception

Financial planning studies conducted over the past decade have generally concluded that, holding other factors constant, clients with low levels of financial knowledge tend to view risk differently than clients with a high degree of financial knowledge,. This view of risk is commonly referred to as **risk perception**, and it is different from risk tolerance. It has been determined that risk tolerance does not dramatically change with knowledge, whereas risk perception does.[1]

It is essential to consider both qualitative and quantitative situational factors before and during the development of investment strategies. An increased focus on the codification of investment policy statements is an example of focusing on the "whole" client. For example, the investment plan, client communication, and client education might, of necessity, be quite different for a highly emotional and reactive client who is unduly influenced by short-term market trends than for a client who has a more tolerant, long-term outlook.

Arguably, the most important situational factor in the investment planning process is a client's **risk tolerance**—Factor 1—which is defined as the maximum level of uncertainty a client is willing to accept when making an investment decision that entails the possibility of a loss. Developing an understanding of, and an appreciation for, both the time and psychological dimensions of risk is essential.

It is possible for a client to have both a long time horizon and a low tolerance for risk. However, in almost all cases, a person's risk tolerance supersedes other influential factors in asset allocation choices. To help mitigate the effects of **risk-averse behavior**, a financial planner must be willing to explain to clients that goal achievement may be impossible in a given time horizon if the client is unwilling to accept higher risk. But even with additional coaching, if a client's tolerance for risk is low, it is likely that an aggressive strategy will be abandoned if the client is faced with prolonged losses.

The second factor influencing investment planning decisions involves managing a client's **expectations**—Factor 2. These expectations include what perceptions of a financial planner's abilities and skill set, the general economy, and most notably, achievable rates of return. The most successful financial planners rarely compete in the marketplace based on their ability to generate the highest possible rates of return. Instead, the best financial planners work daily to manage client expectations regarding performance in relation to reasonable benchmarks.

Consider a financial planner who suggests an allocation designed to achieve a 10 percent annualized return but only manages to generate an 8 percent return. The 8 percent return might be poor, average, or excellent in relation to the market environment. In fact, the return may be superior to almost all other strategies available; however, clients working with this financial planner might very well be disappointed. Some clients fire their financial planner because they expected a higher return and were not appropriately coached to understand the relative nature of investing.

Now consider a financial planner who consistently informs clients that a 6 percent return is reasonable, but over the course of three to five years the planner generates an 8 percent return for clients. Clients working with this financial planner are likely to feel that they have received a bonus. This demonstrates the importance of managing client expectations when it comes to investment returns. A financial planner should attempt to achieve the appropriate amount of risk-adjusted return, but in some cases it is wiser to "under-promise and over-deliver."

An investment plan should be tempered by a client's expectations and the client's satisfaction with their current financial situation. Managing expectations requires a financial planner not only to measure but also to understand the client's view of market trends, both past and future. It is, therefore, necessary to account for investment and economic expectations when developing investment plans. A person's outlook, be it negative or positive, should be used as a moderating factor when developing an investment plan.

Regardless of what financial planning model is used for investment planning, one of the first factors that should be reviewed before developing a specific investment plan are a client's goals and objectives. If goals have not been determined, it is essential to do so before proceeding with any investment planning. Without a clear understanding of the goal (e.g., new home, retirement, university endowment), when it must be funded, its time horizon (e.g., next year, ten years, at age sixty-five), and the amount of funding needed, it is unrealistic to assume that an investment plan can be drafted that will remain valid over time.

Figure 10.1 provides an example the type of questions that can be used to measure a client's expectations about the future economy and satisfaction with the client's current situation. Answers to the first question are particularly important when developing investment planning strategies. If a client truly believes that the economy will perform worse in the future, and if the financial planner concurs, the level of risk taken to meet a financial goal should be reduced accordingly. Similar adjustments, either positive or negative, can be made based on responses to other questions. For instance, if a client is dissatisfied with a chosen career, this could be an indicator that a career change is possible or that the potential for significant promotions or salary increases may be limited. It would be imprudent to invest a client's assets aggressively—thereby reducing **marketability** (i.e., the size and activity of a market that allows for an asset to be sold quickly) and **liquidity** (i.e., how quickly assets can be converted to cash)—if there is a possibility that those assets will be needed to fund job search expenses and other costs. Furthermore, the capacity to withstand **financial risk** (i.e., variability of returns) and the availability of assets to invest must be realistically assessed.

Self-Test 1

An investor's willingness to engage in a risky financial behavior in which she can lose money is called:

a. risk perception.

b. risk preference

c. risk tolerance.

d. risk capacity.

Figure 10.1 Examples of Expectation and Satisfaction Questions

1. Over the next five years, do you expect the U.S. economy, as a whole, to perform better, worse, or about the same as it has over the past five years?

    a. Perform better

    b. Perform worse

    c. Perform about the same

2. How satisfied are you with your current level of income?

    1 2 3 4 5 6 7 8 9 10
    Lowest level   Highest level

3. How satisfied are you with your present overall financial situation?

    1 2 3 4 5 6 7 8 9 10
    Lowest level   Highest level

4. Overall, how satisfied are you with your current job or position within your chosen career?

    1 2 3 4 5 6 7 8 9 10
    Lowest level   Highest level

5. Rate yourself on your level of knowledge about personal finance issues and investing.

    1 2 3 4 5 6 7 8 9 10
    Lowest level   Highest level

Use of Questionnaires

Expectation and attitude assessments can provide only a starting point in client-planner discussions. However, questionnaires and scale items are not necessarily prescriptive in and of themselves; it takes a financial planner's insights and experience to decipher the impact that temperament, personality, attitudes, and beliefs have on the investment planning process.

Additionally, a financial planner is expected to know the investment terrain and a client's level of **investment knowledge and experience**—Factor 3. Beyond the regulatory requirements of understanding a client's knowledge level, financial planners will have fewer objections to overcome if they present investment alternatives that the client already understands or has experience with. The fifth sample question from Figure 10.1 can be helpful to determine how much to reduce the variance of returns or overall volatility of a portfolio based on knowledge and experience.

Although the qualitative factors of investment planning are critical to the long-term viability of a plan, two quantitative factors—time horizon and risk—may be more important in the short term. Suggesting that a client invest heavily and aggressively in a retirement account is certainly sound advice if a client is fifty years old, risk tolerant, and retirement funding is the client's primary goal. But making the same suggestion to an equally risk tolerant twenty-five-year-old who does not have an emergency fund might ignore the time available to realize the goal or the financial capacity to take on the risk associated with this plan.

Time horizon—Factor 4—can is defined as the time period between goal formation and goal achievement. For instance, someone who starts planning for retirement at age twenty-five will find that time is a great ally. Someone else who waits until age fifty to plan for retirement will most likely discover that time is an enemy. The longer the time period between goal establishment and achievement allows a client to invest more conservatively and maintain the same likelihood of goal success. Another way of viewing a longer time horizon is that a client can invest less money on a periodic basis, at a higher expected rate of return, because there is less need to worry about short-term risk (i.e., volatility).

For example, assume that two clients have the same goal of saving $1 million by age sixty-five. Both have $250 per month available to save. One client is twenty-five years old. The other is thirty years old. In this situation, the older client would need an average rate of return of close to 13 percent to reach the goal. This is possible, but at what level of risk? Comparatively, the younger client needs only to average about 9 percent to achieve the same goal. This is also possible, even probable—and at a much lower level of risk. As the example illustrates, the greater amount of time a client can devote to saving and investing for a goal, the higher the likelihood that the client will accomplish the goal. Because **risk and return** in the securities market are highly positively correlated (i.e. risk and return generally move in the same direction), those with longer time horizons tend to be more likely to reach their financial objectives.

Finally, a client's capacity to accept risk is an important factor to consider when making investment plans. **Risk capacity**—Factor 5—measures the amount of financial cushion or the safety net available to a client both before and after an investment decision has been implemented. Some clients are not prepared to take risks with their investments because they simply do not have enough assets compared to their other financial obligations. Documenting and assessing a client's risk capacity is especially important when tempering initial portfolio risk profiles based on time horizon and risk attitude. Factors that increase risk capacity include having adequate insurance in place and funded, a well-funded emergency fund, a stable source of household income, low debt, and high savings. Without these factors in place, the maximum amount of risk that a client should be willing to

Evaluating Risk Capacity

A good way to assess a client's risk capacity involves a financial ratio analysis. Determining how many ratios meet prescribed benchmarks (see Chapter 3) and the availability of an emergency fund can provide an insight into the level of a client's capacity. A client who has several ratios that meet or exceed the benchmarks could have significant risk capacity. Excess capacity gives a client additional flexibility with long-term investments because the client has the capital to cover an unexpected expense without liquidating long-term assets. Another client who meets or exceeds only one or two ratios could be considered to have a lower capacity to handle risk. The need for additional liquidity and stability would indicate that a financial planner should not recommend long-term volatile investments, even if the client has the willingness to take on such risks.

take, given the client's time frame, risk tolerance, expectations, and attitudes, may be higher than what the client can fiscally afford to lose.

The second step when analyzing a client's current situation, and certainly a step that must be completed before a financial planner can recommend additional or alternative investments, entails documenting and evaluating all investment plans currently in place, whether assets are allocated or unallocated for a specific goal. An initial assessment might focus on the client's stage in the **financial life cycle** (e.g., whether a client is closer to the beginning or end of their working life) and whether current investment plans match life cycle objectives and other client characteristics. It must be noted that changing **family dynamics** (e.g., delayed marriage, remarried or re-partnered families) can limit the usefulness of the life cycle approach, but even broad generalizations can be very important when educating clients. The financial life cycle is typically conceptualized in three stages: protection, accumulation, and distribution. These categorizations provide direction and meaning by helping clients understand and anticipate how each financial decision can influence subsequent decisions. The following is a short discussion of how the investment focus, or overall objective, can change as a client progresses through life cycle stages.

During the **protection stage of the life cycle**, a client should develop a budget and emergency fund to meet unexpected expenses. Regrettably, some young clients can focus on the later stages too early and be unprepared for the unexpected. As a result, they can find themselves raiding investment assets in the event of an emergency. Having a financial planner focus on protection ensures that clients' future risk capacity matches or exceeds their risk tolerance. Also, having the tolerance to invest aggressively but lacking the capacity to do so can result in unnecessary frustration for both client and planner.

Next is the **accumulation stage of the life cycle**, during which a client begins to build wealth. This stage can last from twenty to forty years or longer. Generally, clients want to save for retirement, purchase a bigger home, fund a child's education, and/or buy a new car. This is just a sampling of items that may need to be funded at this stage of the life cycle. The financial planner's responsibility is to recommend actions that will enable the client to meet these savings objectives as efficiently as possible. By closely monitoring the client's investment profile for changes and reallocating the portfolio as necessary, a financial planner can safely and effectively guide the client through the most challenging stage of the client's financial life.

Although the last stage—**distribution stage of the life cycle**—may seem to be neatly separated from the accumulation stage by retirement, many clients continue to accumulate wealth well into retirement. At this point in the life cycle, the financial planner begins to suggest titling and gifting strategies that minimize potential asset transfer and estate planning difficulties. Portfolio allocation and reallocation also become much more intense because failure in this stage could be disastrous.

#Remember

A free financial risk-tolerance questionnaire is available at: njaes.rutgers.edu:8080/money/riskquiz/

This questionnaire has been validated with over 200,000 investors over the past 10 years.

Determining a Client's Investment Profile

Once the five initial factors of investment planning have been established (i.e., risk tolerance, expectations about future market conditions, knowledge and experience, time horizon, and capacity to withstand risk), a financial planner can begin to combine these characteristics into a client's **investment profile**. Initially, this can be estimated by looking at the client's time frame and risk tolerance for goal achievement. Figure 10.2 illustrates how the combination of time frame and risk tolerance can be used to estimate a baseline for investment risk (i.e., volatility) that would be appropriate for a given client goal.

Figure 10.2 Portfolio Risk Guidelines Based on Client Time Horizon and Risk Tolerance

Time Frame	High Risk Tolerance	Moderate Risk Tolerance	Low Risk Tolerance
10+ years	Aggressive	Moderately Aggressive	Moderate
7 to 10 years	Moderately Aggressive	Moderate	Moderate
3 to 7 years	Moderate	Moderate	Moderately Conservative
1 to 3 years	Moderately Conservative	Moderately Conservative	Conservative
Less than 1 year	Conservative	Conservative	Conservative

The fact that clients typically have more than one goal, each with a different time horizon, implies that multiple investment strategies need to be designed. To use this table, it is essential that a financial planner use a reliable and valid risk-assessment instrument. It is also important to remember that the guidelines shown in the table must be tempered by an assessment of a client's attitudes, expectations, and risk capacity. Given this caveat, however, the guidelines provide general guidance on the level of risk that could be appropriate for a client.

> *Example.* A client is saving for retirement in twenty years. After taking a risk-tolerance assessment quiz, it becomes apparent that the client is neither a real risk taker nor a risk avoider. Given the length of time as the primary factor, an aggressive portfolio could still be prescribed as a starting point in client discussions.

Knowing only a client's time frame and risk tolerance is not enough to formulate a profile or an effective investment plan. These factors alone tell less than half the story. To get a full picture of a client's investment profile, it is also important to assess a client's **investment attitudes** and **investment expectations**. For instance, some clients might be open to holding any type of investment within their portfolio, while others may prefer to employ screens to eliminate certain types of investments. Screens related to **socially responsible investing**, **religious beliefs**, or **political affiliations** are examples of how attitudes can affect the structure of an investment plan. Other types of attitudes need to be evaluated as well. It would be helpful, for example, to know whether a client is content with regard to the current level of investment income, taxes paid on investment earnings, and level of volatility.

Answers to these kinds of questions can help a financial planner to identify a client's risk profile. These inputs can also be used to shape investment recommendations. Figure 10.3 presents some attitudinal questions a financial planner can ask. A financial planner can use a client's strong preferences to better understand what might be driving a client to seek help with investments.

Figure 10.3 Client Investments Attitude Questionnaire

Name _____ Investment Attitudes Questionnaire					
Put an X in the box to the right that reflects your first reaction to the statement.	Strongly Disagree	Disagree	Neutral		Strongly Agree
1. Keeping pace with inflation is important to me.					
2. I am comfortable borrowing money to make a non-home purchase investment.					
3. Diversification is important to investment success.					
4. The current return I am making on my investments is acceptable.					
5. I need to earn more spendable income from my investments.					
6. I am comfortable with the volatility I experience with my current portfolio.					
7. Reducing the amount of taxes paid on my investments is a top priority.					
8. I am willing to risk being audited by the IRS in exchange for higher returns.					
9. I am willing to risk being audited by the IRS in exchange for paying less tax.					
10. My friends would tell you that I am a real risk taker.					

The process of documenting a client's investment preferences and evaluating alternatives is the basis of constructing an investment policy statement. An **investment policy statement (IPS)** is a document used to acknowledge agreement with and willingness to follow the parameters guiding the investment or management of a client's assets. The IPS, normally written by the financial planner and signed by both planner and client, integrates a client's risk tolerance, risk capacity, and investment philosophy with the financial planner's proposed investment methods to establish parameters for the investment strategies.

Some financial planners develop multiple IPSs individually matched to the investment management plan aligned with different client goals. For example, two investment policy statements might be necessary for managing retirement assets if risk tolerance factors and acceptable investment management strategies are very different for spouses or partners. Regardless of the number of statements, or where the IPS is situated in the written document, its inclusion is not only a necessity to lessen financial planner liability through appropriate planning disclosure, but also because of it is a vital link to the planning process and as a reminder to the client and planner of the importance of adhering to the established guidelines.

Matching a Client's Investment Profile to Portfolio

Taken together, a client's investment profile, consisting of time frame, risk tolerance, knowledge, expectations, and risk capacity, can be used as the basis for better understanding the client's current situation. Once this part of the current situation analysis is concluded, it is appropriate to look at portfolio characteristics in more detail. Specifically, it is important to document whether a client's current portfolio matches the client's investment profile and goals.

> *Example.* A client has a long-term time horizon, a moderate level of risk tolerance and financial knowledge, generally positive attitudes and expectations regarding investing, and an intermediate level of risk capacity, but a portfolio that is invested fairly conservatively. The financial planner may conclude that more portfolio risk could—and probably should—be taken by the client, thus increasing the expected return of the portfolio.

One of the key questions that should be asked before conducting current situation investment planning analysis is whether a client needs to make a portfolio change to better meet financial goals. There is no definite, quantitative way to answer this question. But distinct approaches can be employed to make the process easier.

The IPS and the Litiqious Environment

Today's litigious environment suggests that financial planners—even those whose investment advice is secondary to their planning activities—should use an IPS to disclose and document the professional expectations for the management and investment of client assets. Practicing full disclosure with a client signed IPS is a prudent procedure because it establishes a mutually agreed-upon standard of conduct while reducing the possibility of a future lawsuit brought by a client who claims misrepresentation or poor performance.

One approach to quantifying how a portfolio corresponds to a client's investment profile is to document relevant portfolio characteristics using a standardized form, and then compare these characteristics to market benchmarks. Figure 10.4 is one example of a form that can be used in this process.

Figure 10.4 Investment Profile and Portfolio Summary Form

Investment Profile and Portfolio Summary Form			
Client Investment Profile			
Qualitative	Circle the appropriate response.		
Risk tolerance	High	Moderate	Low
Knowledge/experience	High	Moderate	Low
Market expectations	Positive	Neutral	Negative
Quantitative			
Time horizon	Long	Intermediate	Short
Risk capacity	High	Moderate	Low
Client risk profile*		Client allocation profile**	
Portfolio Measures	**Current Statistics**	**Benchmark Statistics**	**Comparison to Benchmark**
Targeted portfolio allocation profile**			
Observed portfolio allocation profile**			
Portfolio statistics			
Beta			
Alpha			
R^2			
Sharpe ratio			
Treynor ratio			
Fixed income measures			
Bond duration			
Average bond quality			
Asset allocation (%)			
Cash			
U.S. stock			
Foreign stock			
Bond			
Other			
Sensitivity analysis			
3-year average return			
Worst 1-year loss			
Best 1-year gain			
Does portfolio match investment profile?	Yes No	Yes No	

* Scale: 5: High; 4: Above average; 3: Moderate; 2: Below average; 1: Low

** Scale: 6: Aggressive growth; 5: Growth; 4: Moderate growth; 3: Balanced growth; 2: Conservative growth; 1: Income

This form begins by documenting the situational factors that influence a client's investment profile. An investor's profile, based on these factors, is then determined. This form uses a five-step investment risk profile scale—5: High; 4: Above average; 3: Moderate; 2: Below average; 1: Low. A financial planner then matches these risk classes with recommended portfolio allocations.

The client portfolio allocation profile becomes the basis for choosing a benchmark portfolio. Benchmark statistics should then be entered into the table. For example, if a financial planner determines that a client's investment profile falls in the moderate range, then statistics for a balanced growth portfolio could be entered in the benchmark column. Next, relevant portfolio statistics should be summarized and actual portfolio statistics compared to the benchmark.

> **Self-Test 2**
>
> Ted is hoping to identify an index to benchmark his portfolio performance. He has determined the following R^2 values for four indexes. Which is the best index to use as his benchmark?
>
> a. S&P 500: $R^2 = .78$
>
> b. NASDAQ: $R^2 = .85$
>
> c. Wilshire 5000: $R^2 = .82$
>
> d. IFCI: $R^2 = .77$

Using Financial Market Benchmarks to Document the Need

A **market index** can be used by investors to track the performance of a select group of equities, bonds, or other investment groups. The news media typically report index performance as indicators of general market conditions or movements. Economists use the performance of market indexes as a **leading economic indicator**. Financial planners, on the other hand, find indexes to be useful as benchmarks or standards of measurement for client portfolio performance. For a meaningful comparison, it is important to select a **benchmark** that most closely matches both the type of security and the corresponding level of risk in inherent in a portfolio.

The simplest method for determining the best benchmark is to first find one or more benchmarks that seem to have a general fit; for example, the S&P 500 index as a benchmark for a large-cap stock fund or a portfolio made up of large U.S. equities. Next, it is best to perform a linear regression of historical returns of the asset versus the historical returns of the benchmark. A financial planner can then review the **coefficient of determination (R^2)**—this statistic indicates the amount of explained variance in portfolio performance that is accounted for by the index—for each regression and select the benchmark that results in the largest R^2. When evaluating R^2, it is important to remember that values can run a continuum from zero to one; the larger the R^2 the more that the variability in returns of the asset is explained by variability in returns of the benchmark.

It is common to benchmark portfolio performance. To gauge overall portfolio performance, the returns for several indexes, reported over the same time period, can be matched proportionately to the assets in the portfolio. In other words, weighted average returns can be used to compare based the actual portfolio and the matching benchmarks for corresponding market sectors. Information to track the performance of most securities over time should be readily available, either free from the online sources or from the financial planner's custodian, broker dealer, or other third-party source. Although numerous indexes track different market segments (nationally, regionally, and internationally), some of the most commonly used indexes are listed in Figures 10.5 and 10.6. It is worth noting that it a decision to purchase or sell a security should not be based solely on performance relative to a benchmark; security selection and portfolio development issues should consider other aspects of the client's situation as well.

Figure 10.5 Select Widely Used Equity Market Indexes

Corresponding Index by Provider				
Market Sector	**S&P/Barra**	**Russell**	**Morgan Stanley**	**Wilshire/DJ**
All U.S. stocks	S&P Total Mkt	3000	Market 2500	Wilshire 5000
U.S. Equity (Size segmented)				
Mega-cap	—	—	—	DJIA 30
Large-cap	S&P 500	1000	Large-cap 300	Wilshire 750
Mid-cap	S&P 400	Mid-cap	Mid-cap 450	Wilshire 500
Small-cap	S&P 600	2000	Small-cap 1750	Wilshire 1750
U.S. Equity (Style segmented)				
Large growth	Barra Growth	1000 Growth	—	Target large growth
Mid-growth	—	Mid-cap Growth	—	Target large value
Large value	Barra Value	1000 Value	—	Target mid-growth
Mid-value	—	Mid-cap Value	—	Target mid-value
U.S. Equity (Sector segmented)				
Consumer	S&P Consumer	—	—	—
Health care	S&P Health Care	—	—	DJ Health Care
Utilities	S&P Utilities	—	—	—
Financials	S&P Financials	—	—	DJ Insurance
Technology	S&P Technology	—	—	DJ Telecom
International Equity (Region segmented)				
Global	S&P Global 1200	—	AC World Index	—
International (non-emerging)	S&P 700	—	AC World Index (Ex. U.S.)	DJ Developed Mkts
Emerging market	IFCI	—	Emerging Markets	DJ Emerging Mkts & DJ Latin America

In some cases, a benchmark analysis can lead to quick and apparent conclusions. For example, a portfolio that carries a higher **risk profile**, as measured by *beta*, a lower annualized rate of return, and hence a negative *alpha* compared to the benchmark could lead to the conclusion that the client is taking too much risk for the return received. When faced with this situation, a financial planner could implement steps to reallocate the client's portfolio.

However, not all analyses are that simple. During the early 2000s, for instance, portfolios that were over-weighted in bonds and cash tended to outperform portfolios that were more balanced. These fixed-income heavy portfolios almost always showed betas that were lower, alphas that were higher, and returns that were superior to balanced portfolio indexes. On paper, these portfolios looked better than what might actually be the case going forward. Over the long run, it is worth remembering that risk and return are positively related. In the short term, this relationship might not hold true. To believe that risk and return will continue to be uncorrelated—as many investors did during the Great Recession—can lead to a serious underachievement of client goals if and when the relationship reverts back to normal.

Figure 10.6 Select Widely Used Fixed-Income Market Indexes

Corresponding Index by Provider			
Market Sector	S&P	Wilshire/DJ	Barclay's
All U.S. bonds	—	—	U.S. Universal
U.S. Treasury (Term segmented)			
Long-term	BG Cantor U.S. T-bond	—	
Intermediate	—		U.S. Treasury
Short-term	BG Cantor U.S. T-bill		—
TIPS	BG Cantor U.S. TIPS		U.S. Treasury TIPS
Corporate Debt (Quality segmented)			
U.S. Investment Grade	—	—	U.S. Long Credit
U.S. High-Yield	—	—	U.S. Corp High-Yield
International (Region segmented)			
Global	—	—	Multiverse
International	Int'l Corp Bond	—	Global Aggregate
Emerging market	—	—	Global Emerging Markets
Specialty			
Real Estate (REITS)	U.S. REIT	Wilshire RESI*	—
Global Real Estate	—	Global RESI*	—
U.S. municipal	Municipal Bond	—	U.S. Municipal
U.S. mortgage-backed	—	—	U.S. MBS
*Real Estate Securities Index			

Investment Planning Skills

Planning Skill 1: Use Reverse Engineering to Determine a Client's Required Rate of Return

> **Self-Test 3**
>
> Avery would like to retire in 20 years. If she needs $6.4 million on her first day of retirement, what is her required rate of return assuming she can save $5,000 per month?
>
> a. 3.14%
>
> b. 4.84%
>
> c. 7.90%
>
> d. 9.78%

There are times when investment decisions must be based on projected investment outcomes rather than current attitudes and financial circumstances. In such cases, rather than making allocations that happen to result in a certain rate of return, a financial planner and client can allocate a portfolio to achieve the necessary rate of return. This type of **reverse engineering** has advantages if all goes as planned; however, if the results are not achieved, then maintaining client satisfaction will be harder because the client might be less comfortable with the level of risk exposure or the amount of volatility.

An example of reverse engineering can be seen with a thirty-five-year-old client who wants to retire at age sixty-five with $1 million; if he has $250 to invest on a monthly basis, the portfolio must be allocated to achieve an annual rate of return of nearly 13 percent (ignoring the impact of income taxes). This rate of return is simply the **required rate of return** that achieves the objective. It does not consider the client's risk tolerance or risk capacity.

Calculating a required rate is a simple time value of money equation where the future value, in this example, is $1 million, the present value is $0, the periodic payment is $250, and the number of periods is 360 [(65 –35) x 12]. In practice, having a required rate of return dictate an asset allocation, rather than having the client's risk profile dictate the targeted return, is a dubious proposition and should be recommended only for a knowledgeable client with the capacity to accept the risk. The reason is simple. If the client's risk profile does not match the required portfolio, then the client will have a difficult choice to make. The client must adapt and learn to be comfortable with the additional risk required, increase the amount of money available for savings, reduce the desired goal amount, or delay goal achievement. Any of these compromises could derail an investment plan and undermine the client-planner relationship.

Planning Skill 2: Identify Appropriate Portfolio Components

Asset allocation represents the way a client's investment dollars are spread among different financial asset classes. **Financial assets** can be broken into many categories for asset allocation purposes, based on either the client's preferences or current and projected market conditions. Figure 10.7 briefly outlines the primary asset classes and a suggested use for each.

Figure 10.7 Summary of Investments by Asset Classification

Equity (stocks). The primary purpose of equity investing is capital appreciation. Stocks have historically had the highest asset returns after adjusting for inflation. A secondary purpose of current income is possible if investing in stocks that pay a high dividend.

Sub-classifications:

- Large-cap—stocks with a market capitalization over $10 billion. These stocks are typically mature, dividend-paying companies.

- Mid-cap—stocks with a market capitalization between $2 billion and $10 billion. These stocks may not pay dividends, but they have higher growth rate prospects than large-cap companies.

- Small-cap—stocks with a market capitalization under $2 billion. These stocks typically do not pay dividends because they are less mature but fast-growing companies that retain earnings to fuel growth.

- Debt (bonds). The primary purpose of debt investing is current income. Bonds typically pay interest on a regular and recurring basis without the possibility of interest reinvestment. A secondary purpose of capital appreciation is possible if investing in a declining interest rate environment.

Sub-classifications:

- Treasury/government agency—bonds issued by the Treasury Department or a federal government agency.

- Municipal—bonds issued by state and local governments. Can be further classified as general obligation bonds or revenue bonds.

- Corporate—bonds issued by public corporations. Can be further classified as investment-grade or high-yield issues.

- Zero coupon—bonds sold at a discount to par value that do not pay a periodic payment. Typically, these bonds are issued by the federal government in the form of Treasury Strips; however, other zero-coupon issues are available.

International. The primary purpose of international investing is capital appreciation, especially during times of superior international growth. Sub-classifications include the equity and debt of both developed markets and emerging markets.

Commodities. The primary purpose of investing in commodity assets, for the average investor, is capital appreciation, especially in times of rapid hard asset price growth. Commodities can serve as an inflation hedge. Sub-classifications include precious metals, natural resources, energy products, livestock, and agricultural products.

Real estate. The primary purpose of real estate investing is current income. Real estate investment trusts (REITs) typically pay dividends on a regular and recurring basis. Capital appreciation, as a secondary focus, is possible with some forms of direct real estate investment. Sub-classifications include raw land, agricultural, commercial, residential, and mortgage-backed obligations.

Planning Skill 3: Determine the Riskiness and Potential Returns of Different Financial Assets

When allocating a client's financial assets, financial planners must consider not only the asset classes available, but also client situational and external asset allocation factors. **Client situational asset allocation factors** are client-centric and involve answering two primary questions. First, what is the client's goal—**current income, capital appreciation** or **capital preservation**? Second, how aggressively allocated does the portfolio need to be to achieve the goal? **Aggressiveness** can be loosely defined as the amount of additional risk a portfolio is subject to in order to achieve a corresponding incremental increase in potential returns. In other words, the more aggressive the portfolio, the greater the expected return of the portfolio, but the higher the anticipated volatility—or risk.

Figure 10.8 summarizes the risk and return characteristics of commonly used investments. The level of aggressiveness required within an asset allocation structure depends heavily on the difference between the current value of invested assets and the desired level of invested assets. From a time value of money perspective, there are only two factors that control the difference between the amount of money initially (or periodically) invested and the desired future value of the portfolio: rate of return and time horizon. Unless a client wants to delay the realization of a goal, or is willing and able to invest more money, a financial planner's only choice is to increase the aggressiveness of the portfolio in an attempt to achieve a greater rate of return.

Figure 10.8 Summary of Investment Characteristics by Investment Type

Asset	Risk (Aggressiveness)			Potential Return	
	Liquidity	Marketability	Risk	Current Income	Capital Appreciation
Direct Investment					
Cash	High	High	Low	Low	None
Savings accounts	High	High	Low	Low	None
Certificates of deposit	Moderate	High	Low	None	Low to average
Treasury bills	High	High	Low	None	Low to average
Treasury bonds	High	High	Low	Low to average	Low to average
EE and I savings bonds	High	High	Low	None	Low to average
HH savings bonds	High	High	Low	Low to average	None
Federal agency bonds	High	High	Low	Average	Average
Municipal bonds	Moderate	Moderate	Moderate	Average	Average
Investment-grade corporate bonds	Moderate	High	Moderate	Average	Low
Speculative-grade corporate bonds	Moderate	Moderate	Moderate	High	Low to high
Zero-coupon bonds	Moderate	Moderate	Moderate	None	Average to high
Preferred stock	Moderate	Moderate to High	Moderate	Average to high	None to low
Common stock	Moderate to High	High	Moderate to High	Low to average	Low to high
Collectibles (coins, stamps, art, etc.)	Low	Low to moderate	High	None	Dependent on supply and demand

Figure 10.8 Summary of Investment Characteristics by Investment Type (*cont'd*)

Asset	Risk (Aggressiveness)			Potential Return	
	Liquidity	Marketability	Risk	Current Income	
Direct Investment					
Precious metals	Low to moderate	Moderate	Moderate to High	None	Dependent on supply and demand
Real estate	Low	Low	High	Low to high	Dependent on supply and demand
Indirect Investment					
Money market funds	High	High	Low	Low to average	None
Bond funds/ ETFs	High	High	Low	Average to high	Low to average
Stock funds/ ETFs	High	High	Moderate	Low to average	Average to high
Commodity funds	Moderate to High	Moderate to High	High	Low to average	Low to high
Real estate investment trusts (REITs)	Moderate to High	Moderate to High	High	Average to high	Low to average
Derivative Investment					
Options and Warrants	Low	Low to Moderate	High	None to average	Dependent on underlying security
Futures	Low	High	High	None	Dependent on underlying contracts

Investments are bought and sold not only because of changing investor goals, risk attitudes, and time horizons, but also because of changing external factors. **External asset allocation factors**, such as the current and prospective economic environment are not client-centric. The process of economically based asset allocation can be outlined by asking the following questions.

- What have been the recent and long-term returns of various asset classes?

- Are domestic **interest rates** (currently and projected) rising or falling?

- What is the difference in stock yields and bond yields?

- Is the projected **monetary policy** and fiscal policy of the United States conducive to strong long-term growth?

- Will the U.S. dollar rise or fall in value relative to foreign currencies?

- What are projected domestic and international **growth rates**?

- Will inflation or rising commodity prices stunt growth domestically or internationally?

- Will foreign investments offer superior risk-adjusted returns?

Planning Skill 4: Identify External Factors that Influence Asset Choices

It is important that the client understand why certain asset allocations are recommended. A financial planner must be careful not to overwhelm the client with too much financial or economic information. To begin the economic allocation process, it is common for financial planners to mentally segregate assets into a two-by-two investment selection matrix (Figure 10.9).

Figure 10.9 Investment Selection Matrix

		Goal	
		Appreciation	**Income**
Inflation	**High**	**Commodities**	**Real estate**
	Low	**Stocks**	**Bonds**

The matrix consists of stocks, bonds, commodities, and real estate (**hard assets** such as collectibles are typically not considered investment assets because their value is determined primarily by supply and demand). Each one of these categories offers advantages and disadvantages; however, the use of a strategic allocation approach that includes all types of assets often yields the greatest benefit. The basic premise behind this mental accounting is that real assets, such as commodities and real estate, often perform better than financial assets, like stocks and bonds, in times of high or increasing inflation; the opposite often holds true in times of low or decreasing inflation.

By considering the impact of economic conditions—particularly inflation—a financial planner can optimize portfolio allocation choices by changing the weight of a particular class of assets. An example of an allocation that might perform equally well in times of high or low inflation is a portfolio split 25 percent among each asset class. However, this might not work if a client wants to maximize current income. As noted here, a financial planner must change the portfolio based on both the economy and the client's goal.

The current income versus capital appreciation question helps a financial planner develop basic guidelines for the allocation that best suits the client. Typically, financial planners recommend real estate and bond holdings to maximize the income potential of a portfolio. Stock and commodity holdings are used to maximize the appreciation potential. However, a 25 percent equal allocation might not work if, for example, high inflation is anticipated.

The next question is whether the investment focus should be foreign or domestic. The primary outcomes associated with including foreign investments in a portfolio is risk reduction (i.e., a decrease in the *systematic risk* associated with investing in only one country or region). However, superior returns can also be achieved with international investing by capitalizing on changes in **currency exchange rates** or higher international growth rates associated with emerging or recovering markets. In either case, adding international diversification to an **asset allocation framework** can increase the overall risk-adjusted return of a client's portfolio.

The final question pertains to the current and projected interest rate environment. The rule for fixed-income securities (bonds) is that as rates rise values fall. Therefore, a financial planner should allocate a portfolio that is not overly sensitive to rising or falling interest rates. Returning to the original 25 percent balanced allocation example, it is easy to see that in a time of rising interest rates a financial planner might want to reduce the bond allocation to mitigate possible negative consequences.

Planning Skill 5: Master the Concept of Risk When Developing Asset Allocation Strategies

Once classes of appropriate assets have been selected, a financial planner must determine how to combine them into a cohesive portfolio. **Portfolio construction** begins with the client and is based on the client's risk tolerance, risk capacity, time horizon, and investment objectives. The construction of a portfolio should target a specific risk level. It is then up to the financial planner to optimize the return. Risk can be qualified either by *standard deviation* or *beta* (each is described in more detail later in the chapter), but it is important to remember that a client may not be satisfied with a significant potential or real loss even if the loss is less than that of the overall market.

Financial planners should use caution when attempting to risk-weight a portfolio. **Beta**, which is a risk measure relative to a benchmark, is representative only if the asset allocation model is very similar to the benchmark from which it was calculated. As such, risk-weighting only works if the R^2 of a portfolio, relative to the benchmark, is very high (i.e., .eighty or greater). A second issue arises from the fact that the *capital asset pricing model (CAPM)* derives beta using a linear regression model. Because all asset class betas are linear, the beta of a targeted portfolio becomes the weighted average beta of the underlying asset classes. More information about specific investment metrics is available in Appendix 10A, but the following is an example of the difference that can result from attempting to target a portfolio beta versus a portfolio standard deviation.

Consider the data in Figure 10.10. Assume a client has an asset allocation of 50 percent domestic equities, 25 percent international equities, 10 percent commodities, and 5 percent each to real estate, bonds, and cash. Given the data and allocation, it is possible to achieve a portfolio beta of 0.88 as indexed to the S&P 500. This portfolio has a standard deviation of 23.6. The S&P 500 has a standard deviation across the same period of only 21.1. Although the portfolio exhibits only 88 percent of the systematic risk of the market, it exhibits nearly 112 percent of the total variability of return. It is also possible to construct a portfolio with a beta of 0.92 with a standard deviation of only 20.8, which means the portfolio exhibits 92 percent of the systematic risk and 98 percent of the total risk.

Figure 10.10 Sample Risk and Return Statistics

Asset	10-year Arithmetic Average Return	5-year Standard Deviation	Asset Beta vs. Best Index
Equity 1	7.00	20.21	0.757
Equity 2	8.41	19.08	0.887
International equity	9.29	28.51	1.046
Real estate	17.10	35.19	1.131
Commodity	14.59	39.42	0.682
Real estate bond	5.93	3.18	1.058
Treasury bond	6.32	3.77	1.066
Corporate bond 1	10.33	13.09	1.372
Corporate bond 1	3.57	11.33	0.850
Money market	3.50	1.78	0.211

Based on this example, it should be obvious that portfolios with similar betas can have very different total risk profiles. Developing an asset allocation framework based on standard deviation that gives the client a strong understanding of how much the value of the portfolio can change over time in absolute terms rather than one based on beta, which explains the changes only in relative terms, can go a long way toward helping a financial planner manage a client's expectations.

Planning Skill 6: Determine the Appropriate Use of Strategic and Tactical Asset Allocation Models

Strategic asset allocation is the process of setting target (percentage) allocations for each class of asset based on the long-term objective of the portfolio. The portfolio is then periodically rebalanced back to the original asset allocation percentages. This is necessary because different asset classes appreciate and depreciate at varying rates and times in the market cycle. This is the basis of a **buy-and-hold investing strategy**, where strategic asset allocations change only as the client's goals and needs change.

Historically, the standard **three-asset-class model** has predominated, where a portfolio is divided among domestic equities, debt, and cash. However, based on continued research and in light of recent economic events, a more diversified approach has become more prevalent. Currently, a **five-asset-class model** is more common. In addition to the original three asset classes, real estate and commodities are often included when developing a strategic asset allocation. Greater emphasis is also placed on international equity and debt holdings.

For example, if a client wants a portfolio designed for maximum capital appreciation with tax minimization, with a secondary goal of maintaining purchasing power over an extended period of time, a financial planner might recommend a portfolio that is comprised of 50 percent domestic equities, 25 percent international equities, 10 percent commodities, and 5 percent each to real estate, zero-coupon bonds, and cash. This allocation can then be rebalanced annually to maintain these targets until a change in the client's situation dictates a reallocation. For instance, if a client were to lose her job, it might be prudent to alter the composition of the portfolio to reduce volatility.

In the long run, strategic allocations are the most important determinant of total return for a broadly diversified portfolio. **Tactical asset allocation**, on the other hand, allows for a more active management style by setting a range of percentages in each asset class (e.g., a domestic equity range of 45 percent to 60 percent) rather than a fixed target of 50 percent. The use of a range gives a financial planner the ability to be more opportunistic about changing allocations to match current market conditions. Based on economic forecasts, tactical allocations attempt to add value by overweighting asset classes that are expected to outperform on a relative basis and underweighting those expected to underperform. The value added can be measured with alpha. **Alpha** is calculated by subtracting expected returns (usually estimated using the *capital asset pricing model*) from actual portfolio returns. This should not be confused with attempting to **time the market** (i.e., predicting short-term swings in the market); rather, this approach opens the door for changes to an allocation when longer-term economic conditions might favor one asset class over another. For instance, having 5 percent of a portfolio invested in real estate might make very good sense over the long-term, but not having as much or any exposure to real estate in 2008 would have turned out to have been a very wise move.

To some extent, tactical asset allocation is a **dynamic allocation strategy** that actively adjusts the apportionment of a portfolio based on short- and long-term market forecasts, with the objective of increasing appreciation potential. **Sector rotation** is a basic form of tactical asset allocation in which an investor attempts to outperform a market index, such as the S&P 500, by tracking the *economic cycle*. Sector rotation, as in investment approach, was first introduced as a way to incorporate **National Bureau** of Economic Research (NBER) data on the business cycle into investment decisions. Proponents of the strategy use their analyses of the current phase of the business cycle, and relative currency valuations, to anticipate industrial and household demand for goods and services. For example, during an economic contraction, demand for commodities typically decreases, which then relaxes the general price pressure on downstream goods.

Another form of tactical allocation is the construction of **core-and-satellite portfolios**. The core-and-satellite investing style is designed to maximize returns while minimizing **trading expenses** and **tax liabilities**. The approach comprises two types of investments: **core holdings** and **satellite investments** (i.e., speculative or rotational). Financial planners who use this strategy first decide how much to allocate to core portfolio investments, which are those that an investor intends to hold through a number of business and market cycles. This is essentially the investor's strategic allocation. Often, core investments are held as index positions. Core investments are rarely managed tactically, resulting in high tax efficiency. The remainder of the assets can then be dedicated to the satellite portion of the portfolio. Satellite holdings are actively managed. These investments tend to be short-term holdings that allow a financial planner to position assets tactically for maximum capital gain potential.

This portfolio management approach is used to add alpha by enhancing the return of an asset class upswing by adding exposure to that class of assets. When an investor increases a position in or exposure to a market movement she is adding leverage. For example if a portfolio has a "normal" strategic allocation that results in a portfolio beta of 0.8, the market increases 12 percent, and the risk-free rate was 2 percent then, according to **capital asset pricing model** (**CAPM**) the portfolio should rise only 10 percent [2% + (0.8 x (12% − 2%))]. However, if the portfolio was changed to have a beta of 1.1, then CAPM would suggest that the portfolio should rise by 13 percent [2% + (1.1 x (12% − 2%))]. If the investor mistimes the market and increases the beta just before a market downturn of 12 percent, then the portfolio would have lost 13.4 percent [2% + (1.1 x (-12% − 2%))]. See the appendix for a complete discussion of the CAPM formula.

Planning Skill 7: Master the Application of Comparative Risk Statistics

Performance measures of excess performance can be separated into two categories: absolute measures and ratio measures. As summarized in Figure 10.11, various measures categorize risk differently and provide a more specific description of what risk is: **total risk** versus **downside risk** or **systematic risk** versus **unsystematic risk**. Total risk is a basic measure that quantifies the general likelihood of an unexpected outcome, whereas downside risk limits the quantification of risk to both unexpected and negative outcomes. Systematic risk measures quantify the risk inherent in the entire market, whereas unsystematic risk quantifies the risk associated with a single asset or asset class within a market.

Precision of measurement is important for a financial planner when attempting to make decisions about the effectiveness of portfolio management or asset selection choices. The more active the financial planner is in attempting to mitigate a specific type of risk, or maximize a return based on a particular investment philosophy, the more precise the financial planner must be in isolating those variables to make accurate comparisons.

Figure 10.11 Summary of Commonly Used Portfolio Risk Measures

Name (Symbol)	Definition/Formula
Variance (σ^2) (**Equation 10.1**) and Std deviation (σ)	These are absolute measures of the average variability or spread of periodic returns. This measures the *total risk* of unanticipated outcomes. $$\sigma^2_i = \frac{1}{T-1} \sum_{t=1}^{T} (r_{i,t} - \bar{r}_1)^2 \qquad \sigma = \sqrt{\sigma^2}$$
Semi-variance (σ^2) (**Equation 10.2**) and Semi-deviation (σ)	These are absolute measures of the average variability or spread of periodic returns that do not meet the targeted return: *downside risk*. $$\sigma^2_i = \frac{0.5}{T-1} \sum_{t=1}^{T} (r_{i,t} - \bar{r}_1)^2 \qquad \sigma = \sqrt{\sigma^2}$$ Formulas assume "normal" distribution. (For more information, see Appendix 10.A.)
Coefficient of variation (CV) (**Equation 10.3**)	This is a measure of dispersion of a probability distribution. It is defined as the ratio of the standard deviation (σ) to the mean (μ). Formula = $CV = \dfrac{\sigma}{\bar{r}}$
Coefficient of determination (R^2)	This is a measure of systematic, or market-related, variability. R2 ranges from 0 to 100 and reflects the percentage of an asset's movements that are explained by movements in the benchmark. The remainders (residuals) are a rough measure of the *unsystematic* component of risk. Formula = Linear regression-based
Beta (β) (**Equation 10.4**)	The beta coefficient is a measure of a security's volatility relative to the market. This is a "relative" measure of volatility. Because beta reflects only the market-related or *systematic* portion of a security's risk, it is a narrower measure than standard deviation. Formula = $\beta = \dfrac{\sigma_{i,M}}{\sigma^2_M}$

There are five performance statistics commonly used for risk-adjusted, return-based portfolio evaluations. The first two statistics are the Sharpe ratio and the Modigliani measure. These are based on a measure of total risk. The next two, the Treynor index and Jensen's alpha, are based on a measure of systematic risk. The final performance measure, the information ratio, is not actually a risk-based adjustment; rather, it tries to capture whether a financial planner or asset manager is enhancing portfolio performance through active management. Each statistical tool is described in greater detail below.

Sharpe Ratio

The **Sharpe ratio** standardizes portfolio performance in excess of the risk-free rate by the standard deviation of the portfolio. Higher Sharpe ratio scores are indicative of better risk-adjusted performance. However, the ratio is not useful unless an investor has a comparable portfolio to judge the score against. Additionally, because the Sharpe ratio uses a measure of **total risk** (i.e., standard deviation) for risk adjustment, a financial planner should use this method primarily for comparing **undiversified portfolios** or concentrated positions. The Sharpe ratio can be calculated using the following formula:

Equation 10.5: Sharpe Ratio

$$S_i = \frac{R_i + R_f}{\sigma_i}$$

Where:

S_i = Sharpe ratio

R_i = Actual return of the asset (or portfolio)

R_f = Risk-free rate

σ_i = Standard deviation of asset (or portfolio)

Example: First, assume that Laini's portfolio achieved an average annual return of 12 percent with an annualized standard deviation of 16 percent, and the market portfolio achieved an annual return of 13 percent with a standard deviation of 18 percent. Second, assume that a risk-free opportunity returned 5 percent per year. Applying the formula, Laini's Sharpe ratio would be (12 – 5)/16 = 0.437. But what does this mean? Without a point of comparison, it is hard to tell. By calculating the Sharpe ratio of the market for a comparison (13 – 5)/18 = 0.444, it can be determined that Laini's portfolio provided an inferior return compared to the market portfolio.

Modigliani Measure

The **Modigliani measure (M²)**, which calculates the absolute amount of risk-adjusted return within a portfolio, is based on the Sharpe ratio. The Modigliani measure helps put a portfolio's results into perspective by providing an intuitive estimate of what the return should have been given the amount of total risk taken. The calculation starts with the Sharpe ratio and then applies a risk adjustment to convert the Sharpe back into percentage return form, adding the risk-free rate, then subtracting the return of the market.

Equation 10.6: Modigliani Measure

$$M^2_i = \left[R_f + \sigma_m \left(\frac{(R_i - R_f)}{\sigma_i} \right) \right] - R_m$$

Where:

M^2 = Modigliani measure

R_f = Risk-free rate

R_i = Return of the asset or portfolio

σ_m = Standard deviation of the market or benchmark

σ_i = Standard deviation of the asset or portfolio

R_m = Return on the market

Example. Returning to the previous example and based on the formula above, Laini's M^2 measure is –0.125 percent. Although she returned 1 percent less than the market with a standard deviation less than the market, her risk-adjusted return remained negative. In other words, this is her risk-adjusted return. This coincides with the fact that the Sharpe ratio was lower than the market. This measure nicely quantifies the exact amount of risk-adjusted performance achieved by an investor.

Treynor Index

The **Treynor index** is also a measure of standardized risk-adjusted performance. Instead of using standard deviation as a measure of absolute volatility, the formula uses *beta* as a measure of **systematic risk**—risk that cannot be reduced through diversification. Just like the Sharpe ratio, the Treynor index outcome is useful only in terms of comparing one portfolio to another. Because the Treynor uses a systemic measure of risk, this index should be used only with well-diversified portfolios. A Treynor index score can be calculated using the following formula:

Equation 10.7: Treynor Index

$$T_i = \frac{R_i - R_f}{\beta_i}$$

Where:

T_i = Treynor index

R_p = Actual return of the portfolio

R_f = Risk-free rate

β = Beta

Example. Assume Jack's portfolio return was 12 percent, the risk-free rate was 3 percent, and the beta of Jack's portfolio was 0.85. The Treynor index for the portfolio would be 0.106 [(0.12 – 0.03)/0.85].

Jensen's Alpha

Another useful statistic is **Jensen's alpha** or the **Jensen Performance Index**. *Alpha* measures the relative under- or over-performance of a portfolio compared to a benchmark—typically a representative, diversified market portfolio. Alpha measures the difference between the actual returns of a portfolio and its expected risk-adjusted performance. The following formula is used to determine the Jensen alpha of a portfolio:

Equation 10.8: Jensen's Alpha

$$\alpha = R_p - [R_f + \beta (R_m - Rf)]$$

Where:

α = Alpha (derived from the assumption of investment risk)

R_p = Actual return of the portfolio

R_f = Risk-free rate

β = Beta

R_m = Return on the market

Notice that the calculation is based on the **CAPM** ($R_f + \beta(R_m - R_f)$). A positive alpha indicates that a portfolio exceeded expectations on a risk-adjusted basis. A negative alpha suggests that a portfolio underperformed the market on a risk-adjusted basis. A reallocation of assets might be warranted if a portfolio shows a long history of significant underperformance.

Example. Returning to Jack's portfolio from the previous example, if Jack actually earned a rate of return of 12 percent over the three-year period, he could conclude that on a risk-adjusted basis he did better than expected. His portfolio would have generated a positive alpha of 1.35 percent (12% - 10.65%). If the portfolio were managed by a financial planner, Jack could conclude that the financial planner added value above what would have been expected given the risk taken.

Information Ratio

The **information ratio** can be used to estimate the excess return of a portfolio (alpha) generated by active management compared to the standard deviation (tracking error of alpha) generated by the active management. This is most useful when a financial planner is attempting to "beat" a benchmark through superior asset selection or market timing. The information ratio differs from other ratios in that the benchmark is no longer the risk-free asset, as assumed in the Sharpe ratio and Treynor index. This ratio can be calculated using the following formula.

Equation 10.9: Information Ratio:

$$IR = \frac{(r_p - r_B)}{\sqrt{Var\ (r_p - r_B)}} = \frac{\alpha}{E_T}$$

Where:

IR   = Information ratio

α = Alpha (derived from active management, not solely investment risk) where alpha is the difference between the portfolio return and the benchmark return

ε_T = Tracking error of alpha where the error is the standard deviation of the alpha return

Example. If a financial planner achieved an annual alpha of 2.5 percent with an annualized tracking error of 6.25 percent, then the information ratio would be 0.4. What does 0.4 mean? Generally, a positive estimate is good sign.

Each of the measures discussed above are based on concepts imbedded in **modern portfolio theory**. This theory introduced the process of mean-variance optimization, its related statistics, and various other investment rules can be used to determine whether a client's portfolio is efficient. While data can and should be used to guide portfolio choices, professional judgment must also play a role in the decision-making process. Experience, knowledge, and skill help a financial planner determine whether a portfolio is appropriate for a client's needs considering the current economic situation, client attitudes and expectations, and an analysis of risk tolerance and capacity. The integrated nature of these, and other situational factors, makes investment planning challenging. Figure 10.12 provides a summary of the relative portfolio performance measures as illustrated in this chapter.

Figure 10.12 Summary of Relative Portfolio Performance Measures

Name (Symbol)	Definition/Formula
Sharpe ratio	A measure of risk-adjusted performance calculated by dividing the excess return of a portfolio by a measure of *total risk*. Higher values are desirable. This measure is most appropriate when analyzing portfolios where unsystematic risk is still prevalent. Formula = $S = \dfrac{E(r_i) - r_f}{\sigma_i}$
Modigliani measure (M^2)	A measure of risk-adjusted performance that results in a percentage measure for under- (negative values) or over- (positive values) performance, based on *total risk* within the asset or portfolio. Formula = $M^2_i = \left[R_f + \sigma_m \left(\dfrac{(R_i - R_f)}{\sigma_i} \right) \right] - R_m$
Treynor index	A measure of risk-adjusted performance calculated by dividing the excess return of a portfolio, return beyond the risk-free rate, by its beta. Higher values are desirable and indicate greater return per unit of *systematic* risk. This measure is most appropriate when analyzing portfolios where only systematic risk remains. Formula = $S = \dfrac{E(r_i) - r_f}{\beta_i}$
Jensen's alpha (α)	Return in excess of capital asset pricing model (CAPM) return. In other words, alpha is the difference between the security's actual performance and the performance anticipated in light of the security's *systematic risk* (beta) and the market's behavior. Formula = $\alpha = \bar{r}_i - E(r_i)$
Information ratio	A measure of risk-adjusted performance calculated by dividing the excess risk-adjusted return (alpha) of a portfolio by the tracking error (standard deviation of alpha). Higher values are desirable. This measure is most appropriate when analyzing actively managed portfolios where either market timing or asset selection is being used in an attempt to exceed a benchmark. Formula = $IR = \dfrac{\alpha}{E_T}$

Investment Planning Product & Procedural Strategies

Clients tend to seek the help of a financial planner for investment planning guidance for one of three reasons: (1) they want to increase the capital appreciation potential of their investments; (2) they want to increase the amount of current income earned from their investments; or (3) they want to reduce the amount of taxes paid on their

Self-Test 6

Rodney is considering two bonds to add to his portfolio. Bond A has a modified duration of 8.0. Bond B has a modified duration of 3.0. Rodney expects interest rates to fall over the next three years. Based solely on this information (assume the investments have equivalent bond ratings), which bond should he purchase?

a. Bond A

b. Bond B

c. Either Bond A or Bond B

d. Neither because both will lose money when rates fall.

investments. However, clients are often unaware of what may be necessary to increase their real return, their risk-adjusted return, or their after-tax return. It is up to the financial planner to help the client understand methods to measure returns and to determine a realistic return. In other words, it is a financial planner's job to manage client's expectations. The best financial planning strategies accomplish more than one objective, such as ones that hedge inflation and provide current income.

Because of the wide variety of investment products available, an equally diverse number of strategies can be used to meet client goals and objectives. Although the tendency when dealing with investments is to focus on specific products, the procedure involved in investment planning can be just as important. Take, for example, recommending the purchase of municipal bonds. This might be a great strategy for a client, unless it is poorly executed by purchasing the bonds within a tax-advantaged account. Because the rules for an IRA or other tax-deferred account determine whether a distribution is taxable or not, there is no benefit for earnings that originate from a tax-exempt interest. Although no rules forbid this investment strategy, a financial planner may be doing a client a great disservice by executing the strategy in this manner. Advising a client to double-check the beneficiary on a retirement account, or retitle a mutual fund so that both spouses are on the account are examples of procedural strategies.

The following product and procedure strategies represent just a few of the most commonly used techniques to help client's reach their financial goals. As noted above, each strategy should be matched and adapted to the unique needs of each client.

Product Strategy 1: Use Zero-Coupon Bonds if Anticipating Changes in Interest Rates

Zero-coupon bonds are purchased at a discount on their face value. These types of bonds pay no interest; instead, bond owners accrue interest over time. Zero-coupon bonds are unique in that maturity and duration of the bond are basically the same. This means that a bond with a maturity and **modified duration** (i.e., an estimate of the amount the value of a bond will increase or decrease as a result of a change in interest rates) of 5 years will typically move up or down by approximately 5 percent with a 1 percent change in interest rates over a one-year period. Someone who believes that interest rates are going to fall can speculate on rising bond prices by purchasing long-maturity zero-coupon bonds to obtain the maximum price appreciation. On the other hand, someone who believes that rates will increase could sell long-term zero-coupon bonds and replace them with short-maturity bonds.

It is important to keep in mind that investors who use zero-coupon bonds in their taxable portfolios should be aware that, although they receive no income from the bonds, all accrued interest is taxable in the year of accrual. Any capital gains captured from this strategy will also result in a tax liability. The price of zero-coupon bonds is sensitive to changes in interest rates.

Product Strategy 2: Adjust the Duration of the Bond Portfolio if Anticipating Changes in Interest Rates

The modified duration of a bond or bond portfolio tells an investor approximately how much a bond or portfolio will change in value in relation to a change in interest rates. A modified duration equal to five means that if interest rates increase by 1 percent over a one-year period the bond will decline in value by approximately 5 percent. If interest rates decline by 1 percent over a one-year period, the bond should increase by approximately 5 percent. Knowing this, an investor can adjust a bond portfolio's exposure to interest rate changes by adjusting duration. For instance, if a financial planner believes that interest rates will fall, the planner could increase the duration of the bond portfolio to capture the increase in principal that should accompany the interest rate change. If, on the other hand, interest rates are expected to increase, the duration of the bond portfolio could be reduced.

In general, this strategy is an effective way to reduce interest rate risk within a bond portfolio. However, duration can be misleading in certain situations. For instance, the duration of a **mortgage-backed security** is often misleading. If rates rise, mortgage-backed bond prices fall. If interest rates decline, these same bonds might not go up in value as much as their duration indicates because of the negative convexity induced by the fixed interest rates of the mortgages within the bond. The reason for this is that as interest rates decline, home owners tend to refinance their mortgages, leading to prepayment of mortgage loan obligations. This effectively reduces the duration and potential capital gain advantage of mortgage-backed securities.

Product Strategy 3: Increase Client Income by Investing in Real Estate Investment Trusts (REITs)

REITs are structured in a way that allows investors to pool their investments in a publicly traded company that then purchases a portfolio of real estate. REITs can invest in land, buildings, shopping centers, apartment buildings, offices, and mortgages. REIT investments are attractive for income-oriented investors because REITs are required to distribute 90 percent of the income received from rents, dividends, interest, and other gains, such as income from the sale of securities and property. Although REITs tend to be high-income-producing investments, several factors can make these securities problematic for some clients. First, real estate tends to be cyclical, and given that REITs can invest in local markets, rates of return earned on real estate assets are usually tied to local market conditions. There is no guarantee that currently high yields will persist into the future. Furthermore, lack of liquidity in the commercial real estate markets means that REITs carry more risk than other dividend-paying stocks.

Product Strategy 4: Increase Portfolio Income by Reducing Bond Quality Mix in a Portfolio

Because of the inverse relationship between bond quality and interest rates—the lower the grade, the higher the interest rate paid—clients who need additional income may want to include lower-grade speculative bonds (**junk bonds**) in their portfolios. One way to do this is through junk bond mutual funds, which provide diversification and professional management as a way to reduce the increased risk associated with this strategy. This strategy has many potential pitfalls. First, clients who purchase lower-grade bonds, especially junk bonds, run the risk that the bonds will not be redeemed because of **default**. Also, lower-grade bonds are more volatile whenever interest rates change. So, an increase in interest rates will result in a greater loss in value than would a similar higher-rated bond. Finally, junk bonds tend to trade more like stocks than bonds. This means that lower-grade bonds are impacted by both a company's financial situation and interest rates, which subjects the bond holder to greater overall risk.

Product Strategy 5: Reduce Tax Costs by Investing in Dividend-Paying Stocks

Taxes on **qualified stock dividends** are capped at 15 percent for taxpayers in the 25 percent marginal tax rate and above, and 0 percent for taxpayers who are in lower marginal tax brackets. This means that clients who need income from their investments should consider shifting assets toward dividend-paying stocks. The net after-tax yield, given the lower tax on dividends, means a higher return for clients. It is important to remember that some dividends from stock and bond mutual funds are not considered to be qualified for the lower tax rate. To take advantage of this strategy, a client might need to build a diversified portfolio of individual stocks. This means potentially higher transaction costs, which for smaller portfolios could negate the tax advantage of receiving dividends. Furthermore, the costs—particularly in time—to manage a stock portfolio may not be worth the marginal tax benefit.

> ### Self-Test 7
>
> Liana is currently in the 15% marginal tax bracket. She can purchase a AAA corporate bond with a 4% yield to maturity. Alternatively, she can purchase a AAA municipal bond that yields 3.25%. Which is the better option for Liana?
>
> a. Purchase the municipal bond because the tax-equivalent yield is higher.
>
> b. Purchase the corporate bond because the tax-equivalent bond is higher.
>
> c. Purchase either bond because the yields are equivalent.
>
> d. Purchase neither because she does not need a bond given her low marginal tax bracket.

Product Strategy 6: Decrease Tax Liability by Investing in Municipal Securities

One of the basic tenets of investing is that an analysis of tax-free yields compared to fully taxable yields should be conducted on a regular basis for those investing in fixed-income securities. Clients in the highest marginal tax brackets often find that municipal securities provide a higher after-tax return than similar fully taxable bonds, even if the initial yield is higher on the taxable bonds. The following **tax-equivalent formula** can be used to determine whether owning a tax-free bond investment is better than owning a taxable security.

Tax-free Rate = Taxable Rate x (1 - Marginal Tax Bracket)

For example, assume a client can earn 4 percent in a fully taxable bond fund and is in the 25 percent marginal federal tax bracket. The equivalent tax free rate is 3 percent (0.04 x [1 – 0.25]). The client would be just as well served by investing in a municipal bond fund with a yield of at least 3 percent.

This strategy is even more effective if a client purchases municipal securities from the state in which the client lives. In such cases, interest earned is usually both federal and state tax free. The primary disadvantage associated with this strategy is that sometimes a client will conduct a tax-equivalency calculation and determine that the relationship between taxable and tax-free rates is fixed. In fact, the relationship between rates can change frequently, meaning that this analysis should occur more frequently than it often does. Also, clients must be aware that municipal securities generally have a lower degree of liquidity and marketability than some corporate and nearly all federal government debt. The importance of assessing each credit agency's debt rating cannot be overemphasized.

Product Strategy 7: Invest in a Variable Annuity to Reduce Current Taxes

Variable annuities provide clients with multiple advantages. Notably, annuities can be tax efficient. Dividends, interest, and capital gains earned in any given year are deferred until a later date. This can be quite beneficial for clients who will be in a lower marginal tax bracket in retirement than today, and for clients who employ tactical asset allocation strategies resulting in many trades. Keep in mind that variable annuity products should be used only in situations where a client has a long-term investment horizon. This strategy is inappropriate for clients who need assets to fund short-term expenses, such as the purchase of a home, car, or business. Some variable annuity products can be quite expensive. Additionally, income distributions are taxed at the client's full marginal income tax bracket.

Product Strategy 8: Hedge Inflation in a Fixed-Income Portfolio with Treasury Inflation-Indexed Securities

Treasury inflation-protection securities (TIPS) are ten-year bonds issued by the federal government. Purchasing TIPS is a strategy designed to reduce inflation risk. The principal value of a TIP security is adjusted on a semiannual basis to account for inflation, as measured by the *consumer price index*. At maturity, the redemption price is equal to the greater of the inflation-adjusted principal amount or par value. The coupon rate for TIPS is fixed, but payments to bond holders can increase over time as the inflation-adjusted principal amount increases.

Several potential disadvantages are associated with TIPS. First, the initial coupon rate for new issues tends to be significantly less than yields on comparable non-inflation-adjusted debt. This means that if inflation stays quiescent or there is deflation, the bond holder will receive less annual income than other investors. Second, bond holders must pay taxes on the increase in the inflation-adjusted principal amount on a yearly basis, not at maturity. This is why TIPS make the most sense in tax-deferred portfolios.

Product Strategy 9: Hedge a Portfolio against Inflation with Hard Assets and Precious Metals

During times of high inflation, hard assets and precious metals tend to outperform other assets, especially fixed-income and equity assets. There are many reasons for this, but in general, the limited supply of these assets makes them an attractive alternative to other securities during inflationary times. The disadvantages associated with this strategy can offset the advantages of holding hard assets. First, hard assets and precious metals entail **holding costs** that can be substantial. A place needs to be devoted to holding the physical assets, and insurance may have to be purchased to guard their value in case of loss or theft. All of these costs work to erode the potential for gain that this strategy offers.

Also, the value of hard assets and precious metals is determined primarily by **supply and demand** factors. If a new supply enters the market, the value of the assets is almost certain to fall. When inflation becomes less of a factor, the value of hard assets tends to stagnate or fall.

Product Strategy 10: Protect a Client against Interest Rate Risks by Creating a Laddered Fixed-Income Portfolio

Clients often need to limit the maturity and duration of a fixed-income portfolio to reduce interest rate risk. Unfortunately, doing so usually reduces the level of income generated from the portfolio. One strategy to increase the average yield from a portfolio of fixed-income securities while limiting average portfolio maturity involves creating a ladder. For instance, a client could purchase equal dollar amounts of three-, six-, nine-, and twelve-month certificates of deposit (CDs). Whenever one CD matures, another twelve-month CD could be purchased. This plan provides a weighted average maturity of less than twelve months but a yield greater than that offered on a three-month CD. Furthermore, this strategy enhances a client's liquidity situation, because there is always a CD near maturity. Obviously, the strategy could be extended beyond twelve months by adding CDs with longer maturities. The same strategy can be used to develop bond portfolios.

It is important to note that although this strategy is relatively simple to implement, it requires constant monitoring to remain effective. New securities must be purchased on a regular basis. This makes analysis of the fixed-income market extremely important. Replacing securities that mature with assets of similar credit quality and yields requires more work than simply buying and holding one or a few securities.

Product Strategy 11: Purchase Rental Real Estate to Reduce Taxes and Generate Cash Flow

A client's comfort level, knowledge, and experience with certain types of investments often dictates which strategy will dominate an investment plan. Some clients prefer to invest directly in real estate rather than through stocks, bonds, and other investment assets. **Rental real estate** can provide clients with deferred capital gains, tax shelter, an inflation hedge, and cash flow. Lack of liquidity and potentially limited marketability are two significant disadvantages associated with this strategy. Clients who are

---

Self-Test 8

Nick is a gambler. He thinks that the value of a stock is going to drop dramatically over the next three months. Unfortunately, the price of the stock is several hundred dollars per share. Nick does not have enough money in his brokerage account to purchase 100 shares. What strategy can Nick use to bet that the price of the shares will fall without having to hold shares directly?

a. Buy a call option.

b. Sell a covered call option.

c. Buy a put option.

d. Sell a put option.

considering rental real estate must also remember that costs for ongoing operating expenses can sometimes escalate more quickly than rents in certain locations. This is especially true in cases where the client hires a management firm to handle all aspects of rental ownership. Another disadvantage associated with real estate investing is that it requires the temperament and skill of a trained **property manager** to consistently make money. For example, client owners of rental properties must sometimes be plumbers, electricians, painters, sales agents, and evictors. Not everyone is capable of performing these activities. It may be possible to hire a management firm to oversee properties, but the costs associated with management can erode the return on investment generated from a property.

Product Strategy 12: Understand the Purpose of Call and Put Options

Investors increasingly are looking for ways to hedge the inherent risks associated with investments in equities. **Options** provide one mechanism to reduce the risk related to owning a basket of securities. A **call option** allows an investor to purchase an asset at a predetermined price in the future. For example, an investor might believe that the price of a stock will increase in the future. Rather than purchase the shares directly, the investor can purchase a call option. If the stock should increase in value, the investor can "call" his or her broker, pay the predetermined price (which will be lower than the current stock price), and then sell the stock in the market for a higher price. The net result is a profit with very little initial investment.

A **put option** is a way for an investor to sell an asset at a predetermined price in the future. Put options are often used to hedge a portfolio of stocks. Say an investor owns a diversified portfolio. The investor is worried that the markets might fall. He or she could purchase a put option. If prices do indeed decline, the value of the portfolio will fall, but the value of the option will increase, thus hedging the portfolio. Put and call options can be purchased for individual securities or for larger baskets of investments; these are called **index options**.

The primary disadvantage associated with **option trading** is that each option purchased adds a cost to the investment process. It is important to note that options have a limited duration—usually from a few days to a few months. If an option is not exercised by the owner, the value eventually declines to zero. Additionally, if the option is exercised, the investor must also pay a commission on the shares acquired. Options are usually a good investment only in a volatile marketplace. This is the reason that some investors not only buy options, but they sell them as well.

For example, assume that a shareholder owns 100 shares of stock X. The investor believes that the stock price will remain about where it is for the next year. That shareholder could sell a call option into the marketplace. Basically, the investor is betting against the person who buys the option. The buyer believes the price will go higher, whereas the seller thinks the price will decline or stay the same. Some speculators sell **naked call options** and **naked put options**. This is a very risky approach to investing. A naked option writer sells calls and puts without actually owning the underlying security. If the price moves against the seller he or she will be forced to enter the market and pay market prices. This strategy exposes the seller to unlimited market risk. In summary, although options trading can be an effective way to hedge a portfolio against market risk, the costs associated with the strategy must be incorporated into the return expectations associated with investing.

Product Strategy 13: Write (Sell) Covered Calls to Increase Portfolio Income

Suppose a client owns a stock that has appreciated in value. The client would like to sell the stock to capture the profit, but at the same time would not mind holding the stock if income could be generated from the asset. Writing a **covered call option** could be a good strategy to achieve the client's objective. Writing a call option provides immediate premium income for the client, which effectively reduces the cost basis of the original stock. If the price of the stock goes up, the stock may be called away, but this results in generally the same outcome as selling the stock now. If the price of the stock should fall, the call option serves as a hedge, reducing or eliminating the loss on the stock price decline.

It is worth noting that opportunity costs are linked with this strategy. If the price of the stock goes up dramatically, the client will lose both the stock and the price appreciation. If the client purchases back the option, the client will pay much more than the premium earned originally, which will result in a reduced gain. Further, the commission associated with writing covered calls can be quite high, as a percentage of assets, for those selling one or a few options. The strategy is only cost effective if large blocks of options are traded.

Procedural Strategy 1: Balance Long- and Short-Term Tax Gain and Loss Selling to Maximum Tax Savings

This strategy is premised on the fact that only $3,000 in **short-term losses** can be used to offset regular income in any given year. If a client has more short-term losses than short- and long-term gains, those losses must be carried forward into future years. By matching investment losses with asset gains, it may be possible to minimize the negative impact of taxes on portfolio performance. Remember, it may not always be possible to match losses and gains. It might be better to take a short-term loss than to wait and potentially have the investment liquidated with no value at all.

Procedural Strategy 2: Reallocate the Current Portfolio to Match the Client's Changing Investment Profile

Reallocating portfolio assets can be counted as one of the most basic investment planning strategies available. Because risk and return are positively related, it is reasonable to assume that, over time, a portfolio invested more aggressively should outperform other less risky portfolios. However, as a client's time horizon, risk tolerance, or risk capacity changes, investment allocations should also change. Although this is an easy recommendation to make, actual implementation entails many pitfalls. For example, reallocating assets through the sale of existing assets and the purchase of new assets has tax implications as well as certain up-front costs. It is unreasonable to assume that asset returns will improve in the short term simply by taking more risk. This relationship holds true only over extended periods of time.

Procedural Strategy 3: Invest in Low-Cost Mutual Funds to Maximize Performance

Mutual funds represent the most widely used investment company product. Mutual funds are professionally managed, **pooled-asset investment companies** formed to meet a specific investment objective. In effect, mutual funds pool assets from a number of investors and then hire a portfolio manager who uses the assets to purchase stocks, bonds, or other assets. Mutual funds are an attractive investment choice for clients, because funds tend to provide diversification at a relatively low cost. Additionally, mutual funds provide investors of modest means access to professional management at very reasonable entry levels. Shares in some funds can be purchased for as little as $100. The most useful predictor of a fund's future performance is the **expense ratio**. Funds with lower expense ratios historically and empirically tend to outperform others. Figure 10.13 provides a summary reference of key mutual fund terminology.

Figure 10.13 Mutual Fund Terminology

Term	Definition
Mutual Fund	Pooled investment that can issue an unlimited number of shares.
Close-End Fund	Mutual fund with a fixed number of shares sold at one time as an initial public offering and later traded in the secondary market.
Unit Investment Trust	Pooled investment based on a single sale of shares; the trust has a predetermined dissolve date.
Hedge Fund	A private, unregistered investment pool is limited to accredited investors (i.e., wealthy sophisticated individuals).
Net Asset Value (NAV)	The price investors pay to purchase or sell shares in a fund.
Load	Commission (sales fee) paid by investor to purchase shares.
Deferred Sales Charge (Load)	Fee paid when shares are sold; sometimes called a contingent or back-end load.
Management Fee	Fee paid from a fund's net assets to pay for portfolio management services and trading fees.
12b-1 Fees	Fees paid from a fund's net assets to cover costs associated with marketing and selling a fund to new shareholders.
Expense Ratio	The total annual operating expenses of a fund.
No-Load Fund	A mutual fund that does not charge a sales commission to purchase shares.
Break Points	Dollar thresholds where the commission (load) is reduced for new purchases.
Classes of Funds • A Shares • B Shares • C Shares	• Funds that charge a front-tend load. • Funds that charge a back-end load. • Funds with a higher 12b-1 fee and a lower front- or back-end fee.

Figure 10.13 Mutual Fund Terminology (*cont'd*)

Term	Definition
Prospectus	A fund's selling document that outlines all applicable fees, expenses, and investment goals of the fund.

Types of Funds
 	
• Money Market Fund
 	
• Bond Fund
  » Corporate
  » Government
  » Municipal
 	
• Stock Fund
  » Growth Funds
  » Value Funds
  » Income Funds
  » Balanced Funds
  » Index Funds
  » Sector Funds
	
	• Fund to aims to maintain a constant $1 NAV.
	
	• Fund that invests primarily in fixed-income securities.
	
	• Fund that invests in stocks and other equities.

Source: Securities and Exchange Commission: www.sec.gov/investor/pubs/inwsmf.htm

Procedural Strategy 4: Consider Adding Exchange-Traded Funds to Client Portfolios

Exchange-traded funds (ETFs) are a popular investment company product. Unlike traditional mutual funds, ETFs can be traded throughout the day, similarly to a stock, bond, or option. This gives ETFs a unique advantage over funds while retaining most of the attributes offered by mutual funds. ETFs are distinguishable from mutual funds in two respects. First, very few ETFs are actively managed. Until recently, nearly all ETFs mimicked a market index, such as the S&P 500, Dow Jones Industrial Average, or other market indexes. Second, investment companies develop ETFs by using **creation units**, which are then pooled into baskets of securities. These baskets of securities mirror an underlying index, and these securities are bought and sold by investors. This allows an investor to purchase one or more units of an ETF, and when an ETF investor wishes to sell their investment they can either sell units to other investors on the secondary market or they can sell them back to the investment company, though this is rarely done.

An ETF investment strategy provides investors with multiple advantages, as summarized in Figure 10.14. In general, ETFs allow clients to develop well-diversified portfolios with low annual expenses. ETFs also offer liquidity and marketability to a greater extent than index mutual funds. Moreover, ETFs are completely transparent, which means that the exact components and weightings of securities held in the portfolios are always known. Mutual funds, on the other hand, are only partially transparent, because they have to make only their holdings known on a periodic basis, and even then they are allowed to delay the publication of the data for a certain period of time to protect their marketability.

Other ETF advantages include **tax efficiency** and **investment style stability**. ETFs are tax efficient because **portfolio turnover** is low or even zero, which results in few taxable distributions. ETFs also allow financial planners to develop portfolios with fixed allocations to certain market benchmarks. Unlike mutual funds that tend to exhibit **style drift**, investing via an ETF almost guarantees exposure to a chosen asset class and market.

Figure 10.14 Indirect Investment Ownership Comparison

Investment Attribute	ETF	Index Fund	Management Fund
Tradability	Can trade during market hours	Can trade once per day	Can trade once per day
Ability to sell short	Yes	No	No
Transparency	High	Moderate to high	Low to moderate
Diversification	Low to high	Moderate to high	Low to high
Tax efficiency	Very high	High	Low to high
Subject to style drift	Low	Low	Low to high

The primary disadvantage associated with ETFs is the lack of **active management**. Once an ETF is created, the underlying assets do not change. This means that the opportunity to outperform the market, on a risk-adjusted basis, is very low. Also, because ETFs are traded like stocks, clients incur trading commissions whenever shares are bought and sold.

Procedural Strategy 5: Use the Discounted Dividend Valuation Model to Value Shares of Stock

The **discounted dividend valuation model**, sometimes referred to as the **dividend growth model**, can be used to value a share of stock using the present value of all future dividends. This method of valuation provides a starting point in valuing a stock. The formula is:

$$Value = \frac{D_0 (1 + g)}{(i - g)}$$

Where,

D_0 = Current dividend

i = Required rate of return

g = Dividend growth rate

Self-Test 9

Kaylee is interested in buying a stock. The stock's price is currently $95 per share. Kaylee is a value investor—she likes bargains. If the stock currently pays a $4 dividend should she make the purchase if her required rate of return is 9% and the dividend is growing at 5% annually?

a. No, because the value of the stock is less than the stock price.

b. Yes, because the value of the stock is less than the stock price.

c. No, because the value of the stock is greater than the stock price.

d. Yes, because the stock price is less than the estimated value.

It is worth noting that the model relies on two unknown assumptions: the dollar amount of future dividends and the growth rate of those dividends. As such, estimated values vary dramatically based on the assumptions used to measure value. Also, if the dividend growth rate exceeds the required rate of return a null value is obtained.

Procedural Strategy 6: Calculate Key Financial Statement Ratios as a Stock Valuation Technique

The use of the following types of financial statement ratios can provide an important insight into the relative value of individual equities:

- **Profit margin**: net income/total sales

- **Return on equity**: net income/shareholder's equity

- **Debt-to-equity ratio**: long-term debt/shareholder's equity

- **Price-to-earnings ratio**: market capitalization/net income

- **Price-to-sales ratio**: market capitalization/total sales or total revenue

- **Price-to-book ratio**: market capitalization/shareholder's equity

Each of these ratios can also be determined on a per-share basis by dividing the answer by the number of shares outstanding. Keep in mind that financial ratios provide a picture only of past performance. Should a firm's sales, net income, debt, or other calculation inputs change, estimated values also change.

INVESTMENT PLANNING FOR SPECIAL POPULATIONS

Planning for the Suddenly Wealthy

From technology company founders to professional athletes to lottery winners, most people can think of someone who instantly became wealthy and famous. With the exception of entrepreneurs who built wealth from a business enterprise, many lottery winners and athletes end up in financial ruin as a result of their investment and lifestyle choices.

However, for each one of these individuals, there are hundreds, if not thousands, of others who instantly became much wealthier as the result of an insurance settlement, inheritance, trust, or retirement. It does not take a tremendous sum of money to completely change the financial situation for a family; a sum as small as $50,000 or $100,000 dollars can make an enormous difference. The impact of this money could be ten- or 1fifteen-fold in thirty-five or forty years if invested correctly. For example, a young family saving $5,000 per year for retirement would have about $550,000 saved in thirty years; however, with an additional $100,000 today, that sum would instead be more than $1 million more—a threefold increase. So, instead of a $44,000 per year retirement annuity, they would have a $121,000 annual retirement annuity (assuming a twenty-five-year time horizon and a 6 percent annual rate of return). But all too often the money is spent on comparatively frivolous items or on a general improvement in the immediate standard of living.

Sometimes people with sudden money engage in splurge spending. They purchase multiple houses, cars, and vacations beyond even what their new wealth can support. Perhaps even more meaningful is the emotional toll that a financial windfall can exact. Some recipients use the occasion to make excessive gifts to charity. Although seemingly a well-intended, such acts might spring from a feeling of unworthiness or from guilt about receiving the money.

Susan Bradley, a financial planner who has done groundbreaking work in the area of sudden wealth, described the inner experience of sudden money as resembling a chute of emotions.[2] This chute leads the recipient into a general state of emotion that includes fear, isolation, grief, and insecurity. These emotions can lead to resentment or even paranoia depending on the events that led to the windfall. The Money, Meaning, and Choices Institute (MMCI) even coined a phrase: "Sudden Wealth Syndrome." Susan Bradley determined that sudden wealth makes some people stop listening to trust advisers and start listening to those whom they should not. MMCI attributes this to "identity confusion."[3] Susan Bradley suggests not making any financial or emotionally charged decisions for an extended period of time after a windfall event. The National Endowment for Financial Education goes so far as to suggest that cash for six to twelve months of living expenses should be kept separate from the remainder of the windfall so recipients can mentally and emotionally adjust to their new status.[4]

Investment planning for the suddenly wealthy can take a lot of time and patience from both financial planner and client to ensure the long-term success of a plan. In the short-term, the plan might not focus on investing activities as much as it does on ensuring the general financial well-being of the client and the client's family.

Planning with Minority Investors

Based on the premise that investors should not put all their eggs in one basket, Lazetta Rainey Braxton, founder of Financial Fountains LLC in Chicago, posed the following question:

> What would happen if financial advisers applied the basic intent of [Modern Portfolio Theory] MPT to matters of racial diversity in the financial profession? Diversification theory would suggest that a firm's business relationships (portfolio) with intentionally diverse asset classes (racial and ethnic groups) can maximize a firm's return (profits and social equity) and minimize its risk (inability to attract and retain minorities as employees or clients and a loss of economic sustainability).[5]

Some background might be helpful for financial planners who wish to pursue Ms. Braxton's proposal:

- Before the real estate bubble burst in the Great Recession, real estate had historically been the favored investment among African-Americans. According to *The Ariel Investments 2010 Black Investors Survey*, for the first time in the twelve-year history of the survey, more African-Americans chose stocks and stock mutual funds as the "best investment overall" relative to real estate.[6] Less than a third of black and white respondents (30 and 27 percent, respectively) said real estate was the "best investment overall" as compared to 41 percent of black respondents and 55 percent of white respondents who picked equities.[7]

- Business ownership is a primary source of building wealth among Hispanics. African-Americans are nearly twice as likely as those in the general population (35 percent versus 19 percent) to have a dream of starting a small business.[8]

- After controlling for demographic and behavioral variables, African-Americans were 35 percent less likely than whites to be investors.[9] There is a positive relationship between income and investing for African-Americans—a relationship not found among whites—for whom income was not a determinant of investing. A subsequent study revealed that after controlling for demographic factors, whites were nearly twice as likely to be investors as African-Americans.[10]

- The failure to invest is also reflected in retirement savings. Based on data from 57 companies and almost 3 million participants, 66 percent of black employees and 65 percent of Hispanic employees participated in 401(k) plans, compared with 77 percent of white workers and 76 percent of Asian workers.[11] According to the results, regardless of age and income, black and Hispanic workers were less likely to participate and saved less in comparison to Asian workers, who had the highest savings rate. African-Americans also had the lowest rate of equity investments, and equity ownership differences for Asians and Hispanics as compared to Whites were minimal.

- Although less familiarity with investments has been identified as a possible contributing factor, research has shown that blacks and Hispanics have lower investment risk tolerance than whites, even after controlling for income and other household characteristics.[12]

Given these observations, what steps might be necessary to apply MPT principles to the financial planning profession? Several suggestions include:

- Increase education about investment principles to encourage a broader understanding of the market and increase familiarity with equities and other investments. Given that familiarity influences risk perceptions, this change, in addition to education on different investments, might increase tolerance for risk within the investment market.

- Increase the diversity of the financial services workforce to provide greater language and cultural variety to serve a broader clientele. Care must be taken that translations of documents are not only accurate, but also consistent with the culture.

- Focus on the importance of building strong client-planner relationships that are based on trust. Anecdotal reports from financial planners suggest that working with minority clients can take more time, but the dividend on that investment is referrals to an underserved market.

Quantitative/Analytical Mini-Case Problems

Tad and Tyler Mendoza

1. Use the information provided in the table below to calculate the weighted-average before-and-after tax rate of return of the portfolio held by Tad and Tyler Mendoza.

Asset	Allocation	Amount	Rate of Return Before Tax	Rate of Return After Tax
Fund A	Large growth	$75,000.00	9.00%	6.75%
Fund B	Mid-value	$100,000.00	8.00%	6.00%
Fund C	Money market	$94,000.00	2.00%	1.50%
Fund D	Small growth	$14,000.00	12.00%	9.00%
Fund E	Small value	$35,000.00	4.00%	3.00%
Fund F	High-quality bond	$45,000.00	3.00%	2.25%
Fund G	Low-quality bond	$112,000.00	5.00%	3.75%

TJ Bartlett

2. TJ Bartlett would like to know how her portfolio is doing. Use the information shown in the following table to calculate the statistics below. (Refer to Appendix 10A, if necessary, for a refresher on the formulas and purpose of each.)

Year	Portfolio Return	Market Return
1	12.00%	9.00%
2	9.00%	8.00%
3	22.00%	19.00%
4	-4.00%	-1.00%
5	2.00%	5.00%
6	25.00%	19.00%
7	15.00%	15.00%
8	-6.00%	-4.00%
9	11.00%	9.00%

a. Geometric average of portfolio and market

b. Arithmetic average of portfolio and market

c. Standard deviation of portfolio and market

Uma Johnson

3. Uma Johnson has been tracking the performance of her portfolio benchmarked against a passive index. Here are her returns over the past few years along with the return of the market index:

Year	Portfolio	Market Index
1	12%	9%
2	9%	8%
3	22%	19%
4	-4%	-1%
5	2%	5%
6	25%	19%
7	15%	15%
8	-6%	-4%
9	11%	9%

Based on Uma's data, answer the following questions:

a. What is the standard deviation of Uma's portfolio and the market index?

b. What is the geometric mean for her portfolio and the market index? How does this compare to the arithmetic mean?

c. What is the correlation between Uma's portfolio and the market index?

d. Based on the calculations from above, what is the beta of Uma's portfolio?

e. Assuming a risk-free rate of 2 percent, what is Uma's CAPM?

f. Has her portfolio done worse, the same, or better, on a risk-adjusted basis, compared to the market index? How do you know?

g. Given your calculations, what should Uma do with her portfolio?

Nick Baker

4. Nick Baker is considering hiring a money manager to manage a portion of his sizable portfolio. He has narrowed his choices to the following money management firms. Each firm's historical mean return, portfolio standard deviation, and the risk free rate is shown below:

	Benchmark	Manager 2	Manager 3	Manager 4	Manager 5
Mean	9.52%	16.00%	9.20%	18.00%	7.00%
Standard Deviation	10.65%	15.00%	5.60%	25.00%	6.00%
Risk-Free Rate	3.50%	3.50%	3.50%	3.50%	3.50%

Use this information to answer the following questions:

a. Which money manager took the most risk? Rank the money managers by the risk taken (highest to lowest).

b. Which money manager had the best risk-adjusted performance? Rank the money managers by the Sharpe ratio (highest to lowest).

c. Use the Modigliani measure to derive an estimate of what each money manager's return should have been given the amount of risk taken.

d. Which money manager should Nick hire? Why?

Chyna Snow

5. Chyna Snow considers herself to be a savvy value-oriented investor. She is always on the lookout for bargains in the market. Chyna is considering the purchase of one or more of the following stocks. Use the information provided below to estimate the value of each company's shares. Based on your analysis, which stock or stocks should Chyna purchase?

	Stock A	Stock B	Stock C	Stock D	Stock E
Current Price	$60.00	$25.75	$145.00	$9.35	$89.50
Current Dividend	$2.00	$1.85	$3.56	$0.80	$3.68
Dividend Yield	3.33%	7.18%	2.46%	8.56%	4.11%
Dividend Growth Rate	4.00%	3.50%	5.20%	2.50%	3.75%
Chyna's Required Rate of Return	9.40%	9.40%	9.40%	9.40%	9.40%

Comprehensive Bedo Case—Analysis Questions

Almost all of the Bedos' goals have an investment component. For example, saving for retirement, college, and a home addition all require the analysis of investment planning factors. Each investment-funded goal will require documentation of the Bedos' time horizon, risk tolerance, and investment attitudes for the goal—which could include investment restrictions imposed by the clients, expectations about the future, and risk capacity.

Furthermore, these facts could differ for each goal. For instance, the maximum amount of risk that the Bedos are comfortable taking for retirement might be different from the level of risk they are prepared to take with Becky's education funding. Thus, it is important to review the client information as well as relevant assumptions, tax rates, and the Bedos' global asset allocation structure.

Note: Sufficient information is not yet available to quantify the education planning need or the retirement planning needs for the Bedos; thus, all references to these goal as they relate to investment planning must be addressed in generalities, with the integration of the investment strategies for the education planning and retirement planning more fully resolved in Chapters 11 and 12, respectively.

1. Develop a list of investment-funded planning goals (e.g., emergency fund situation, retirement investment plan, education funding goal, and the art gallery and home improvement goals) for the Bedos. When conceptualizing these goals, consider the following:

   a. Is each goal developed in agreement with any or all goals and objectives that the clients have identified regarding investment planning?

   b. What situational factors might influence their investment-funded goals (e.g., emergency fund situation, retirement investment plan, education funding goal, and the art gallery and home improvement goals)? Are these factors explicit, implied, or assumed? Is additional information required from the Bedos?

   c. What is the desired outcome for the clients for each of these goals?

2. Make a list of life events that could impact these goals for Tyler and Mia and that should be reviewed at future client meetings. Some events could affect all of the goals, and others only certain goals.

3. Develop a list of globally accepted, client specific, or planner-generated planning assumptions that will structure the situational analysis and planning for each goal.

4. Summarize the Bedos' time horizon, risk tolerance, investment attitudes, economic expectations, and risk capacity for each of their investment-funded goals (e.g., emergency fund situation, retirement investment plan, education funding goal, and the art gallery and home improvement goals).

5. Summarize your observations about Tyler's and Mia's current planning efforts and the identified planning need(s) for each of the investment-funded goals (e.g., emergency fund situation, retirement investment plan, education funding goal, and the art gallery and home improvement goals). Complete an Investment Profile and Portfolio Summary Form for each goal to determine whether changes are needed. Incorporate text, bullets, and graphics in your explanation. For example, what information might be shown graphically, and specifically what kind of graphs might most effectively convey this analysis to the Bedos?

6. Based on the goals originally identified and the completed analysis, what product or procedural strategies might be most useful to satisfy the Bedos' planning need(s) for each of the investment-funded goals (e.g., emergency fund situation, retirement investment plan, education funding goal, and the art gallery and home improvement goals)? Be sure to consider strategies matched to the planning needs identified. When reviewing strategies, be careful to consider the approximate cost of implementation as well as the most likely outcome(s) associated with each strategy.

7. In response to each identified planning need for the investment-funded goals (e.g., emergency fund situation, retirement investment plan, education funding goal, and the art gallery and home improvement goals), write at least one primary and, if applicable, one alternative recommendation from the strategies selected. Include specific, defensible answers to the who, what, when, where, why, how, and how much implementation questions for each recommendation.

   a. It is suggested that each recommendation be summarized in a Recommendation Form.

   b. Assign a priority to each recommendation based on the likelihood of meeting client goals and desired outcomes. This priority will be important when recommendations from other core planning content areas are considered relative to the available discretionary funds for subsidizing all recommendations.

   c.   Comment briefly on the outcomes associated with each recommendation.

8.   Depending on the organization of the plan, a comprehensive plan might or might not include a discrete section on investment planning. It could be included in the plan to address all investment-funded goals, or investment planning information could be incorporated in the section corresponding to individual goals (e.g., education planning or retirement planning). Given these options, choose one approach and complete the following for the Bedos' financial plan:

   a.   Outline the content to be included in this section of the plan. Given the segments written above and/or elsewhere in other chapters related specifically to investment-funded goals, which segments are missing?

   b.   If applicable, write the introduction to this section of the plan (no more than one to two paragraphs).

   c.   Define, explain, or interpret at least five terms related to investment planning. For each, write a definition or explanation that could appear in a section of the plan or in the plan glossary.

9.   Prepare a ten–fifteen-minute presentation for the Bedos of your observations and/or recommendation(s) for meeting their investment planning goals. Be sure to include visual aids, Excel handouts, and other materials that will make the recommendations more meaningful for the clients.

Chapter Resources

Benninga, S. *Financial Modeling*, 3rd Ed. Boston: MIT Press, 2008.

Boone, N., and L. Lubitz. *Creating an Investment Policy Statement.* Denver, CO: FPA Press, 2004.

Investment Risk Tolerance Quiz (njaes.rutgers.edu/money/riskquiz/).

FinaMetrica Risk Profiling System (www.riskprofiling.com/home).

FINRA Mutual Fund Expense Analyzer (apps.finra.org/fundanalyzer/1/fa.aspx).

Leimberg, S., et al. *The Tools and Techniques of Investment Planning*, 3rd Ed. Cincinnati, OH: National Underwriter Company, 2014.

Murray, Nick. *Behavioral Investment Counseling*. Mattituck, NY: The Nick Murray Company, Inc., 2008.

Shefrin, H., & Mario Belotti. "Behavioral Finance: Biases, Mean-Variance Returns, and Risk Premiums." *CFA Institute Conference Proceedings Quarterly*. June (2007): 4–11. Available at: www.ifa.com/pdf/behavioralfinancecp.v24.n2.pdf.

Siegel, L.B. *Benchmarks and Investment Management*. Charlottesville, VA: CFA Institute, 2003.

Susan Bradley's Sudden Money Institute (www.suddenmoney.com).

Self-Test Answers

1: c, 2: b, 3: a, 4: d, 5: b, 6: a, 7: b, 8: c, 9: b, 10: c

Endnotes

1. Susan Bradley. *Sudden Money: Managing a Financial Windfall*. (New York: Wiley, 2000).

2. Money, Meaning and Choices Institute. *Sudden Wealth*. Available at: www.mmcinstitute.com/about-2/sudden-wealth-syndrome/.

3. National Endowment for Financial Education (NEFE). *Financial Psychology and Life-changing Events: Financial Windfall*. (Denver, CO: NEFE Press, 2004).

4. Lazetta Rainey Braxton, "Minorities Can Enrich Financial Services Industry," *Investment News*, August 15, 2010. Available at: www.investmentnews.com/apps/pbcs.dll/article?AID=/20100815/REG/308159998&cslet=UnhOY2lLVDlKL09aK2pjMXNkbTdUZmhxbytmcXVHMD0=.

5. Ariel Investments, *The Ariel Investments 2010 Black Investors Survey: Saving and Investing Among Higher Income African-American and White Americans*. Available at: www.arielinvestments.com/images/stories/landing_pages/Black_Investor/2010bisreportslides.pdf.

6. Ariel Investments, *2010 Black Investors Survey*, 7.

7. Prudential Financial Inc., "The African American Financial Experience," *2011 Prudential Research Study*. Available at: www.prudential.com/media/managed/aa/AAStudy.pdf.

8. Ariel Investments, *The Ariel Mutual Funds/Charles Schwab & Co., Inc. Black Investor Survey: Saving and Investing Among Higher Income African-American and White Americans*, June 2001. Available at: www.arielinvestments.com/landmark-surveys/.

9. Ariel Investments *Ariel-Schwab Black Investor Survey 2007*, 11. Available at: www.arielinvestments.com/landmark-surveys/.

10. Ariel Investments, *The Ariel/Hewitt Study: 401(k) Plans in Living Color: A Study of 401(k) Savings Racial Disparities Across Racial Groups*, 2009, 7. Available at: www.arielinvestments.com/images/stories/PDF/arielhewittstudy_finalweb_7.3.pdf.

11. Sherman D. Hanna, Cong Wang, and Yoonkyung Yuh, "Racial/Ethnic Differences in High Return Investment Ownership: A Decomposition Analysis," *Journal of Financial Counseling & Planning* 21, no. 2 (2010): 45–59. Available at6aa7f5c4a9901a3e1a1682793cd11f5a6b732d29.gripelements.com/pdf/vol_21_issue_2_hanna_wang_yuh.pdf.

Modern Portfolio (Mean-Variance) Review

WHAT CREATES "RETURN"

For an investment market to exist there must be investors or institutions with more money than they need, and others who need more money than they have. The interests of these two groups are at odds. Those who need money want access to it at the lowest possible cost. Those who have money want the greatest possible compensation— in fact; they demand two types of compensation for the use of their money. First, they want to be compensated for delaying the opportunity to spend the money. This minimum compensation that clients require for delaying consumption when they are unwilling to accept any other risk is called the **risk-free rate of return**.

The second form of compensation is for accepting risk, or the **risk premium**. Multiple risk premiums can be assigned to an investment. Equity investments typically are assigned risk premiums associated with business risk and market risk. Bonds, on the other hand, receive a risk premium for default risk and interest rate risk. International investments might have premiums for exchange rate risk, liquidity risk, or political risk. This is not to say that these risks and risk premiums are exclusive to any single investment class; these examples represent typical assignments. A general understanding of why investment returns are not static over time is crucial for financial planners because it affects portfolio construction and management.

WHAT CAUSES "VARIANCE" OF RETURNS

Default risk, or **credit risk**, is the risk that investors might not be paid what they are owed contractually. Because U.S. Treasury issues are backed by the full faith and credit of the U.S. government, these issues are said to be **default-risk free**. However other investments, such as money market mutual funds or bank accounts, are also virtually default-risk free and therefore offer similar rates of return.

The **Treasury bill** (T-bill) rate is often quoted as the **risk-free rate**, except even the risk-free rate of return is not totally free of risk. The T-bill rate is quoted as a **nominal rate of return**, and thus its return is influenced by inflation. However, because inflation affects all nominally priced investments, freedom from default risk earns the T-bill the "risk-free" designation as a shortcut term. A premium on the risk-free rate is needed for clients to be willing to accept any additional risk. The **risk premium** depends on the type, severity, and probability of the risk, as well as the time horizon of the investment.

When a client is considering investment in other corporate or municipal issues, either equity or debt, it is always prudent to consider the default or credit risk of the entity, but this is difficult to quantify. One approach is to review credit rating agencies' opinion of default risk using the information provided in Figure 10A.1.

Figure 10A.1 Bond Rating Agencies and Descriptions

| Investment Grade Bonds | | | |
Moody's	S&P	Fitch	Rating Description
Aaa	AAA	AAA	Highest investment bond rating
Aa	AA	AA	Very high investment grade rating
A	A	A	Medium investment grade rating
Baa	BBB	BBB	Lower investment grade rating
Speculative-Grade Bonds—High Yield			
Moody's	S&P	Fitch	Rating Description
Ba	BB	BB	Highest grade junk bond
B	B	B	Speculative grade junk bond
Caa	CCC	CCC	Low grade junk bond
Ca	CC	CC	Default grade junk bond
C	C	C	Issue that pays no interest
---	D	D	Issue in default

A lesser-known risk that became extremely important during the Great Recession is **liquidity risk**. This is the risk that an investor will not be able to convert an asset into cash in a timely manner or without a loss of value. For example, in the fall of 2008 many investors could not redeem assets from money market mutual funds in a timely manner because the investments underlying the portfolio had become illiquid, meaning that the mutual fund could not sell the asset for cash to process the shareholder's request. Although it is now known that the liquidity crisis was temporary, it created enough panic that investors are still nervous about money market mutual funds four years later.

Possibly the most costly risk faced by investors and non-investors alike is **inflation risk**. Consumers can spend either now or later. But to spend later in an inflationary environment means that a consumer will have to spend more money, in nominal terms, to purchase the same amount of goods and services. The purchasing power of the money declines over time. It is worth noting that the majority of individuals who keep their money in savings accounts generally do not receive adequate compensation for the inflation risk they take on. If, for instance, inflation averages 4 percent and an account earns only 1 percent in interest, the real purchasing power of the savings declines by approximately 3 percent annually— before taxes are incorporated into the calculation. Figure 10A.2 reports inflation as measured by the **Consumer Price Index (CPI)**.

Figure 10A.2 U.S. Annual Inflation Rates (1992–2015)

Year	Inflation Rate	Year	Inflation Rate
1992	2.9%	2004	3.3%
1993	2.7%	2005	3.4%
1994	2.7%	2006	2.5%
1995	2.5%	2007	4.1%
1996	3.3%	2008	0.1%
1997	1.7%	2009	2.7%
1998	1.6%	2010	1.6%
1999	2.7%	2011	3.2%
2000	3.4%	2012	2.1%
2001	1.6%	2013	1.5%
2002	2.4%	2014	1.6%
2003	1.9%	2015	0.5%

Source: U.S. Bureau of Labor Statistics, *Consumer Price Index History Table*. Available at: www.bls.gov/cpi/#tables.

Notice that inflation, averaging approximately a bit less than 2.5 percent, has remained relatively benign over the past decade. Yet, even at recent inflation rates, it would take about $180 in 2016 to purchase what could have been bought for $100 in 1992. For example, if inflation edged up to 5 percent on average, clients would lose half of their purchasing power about every fourteen years. To counteract this erosion of purchasing power, minimally clients expect compensation that offsets this reduction. Therefore, a financial planner should generally attempt to develop portfolios that can at least match the rate of inflation.

Risk is at the root of most clients' concerns when they make investments. Beyond individual sources of risk, investors face two primary forms of risk: systematic and unsystematic.

Systematic risk, also called **market risk**, is embedded in the system of financial markets. This type of risk generally cannot be eliminated through *diversification*. Assume, for example, that the markets experience a significant one-day drop in value, such as occurred in 1929 and 1987. Regardless of the amount of diversification within a portfolio, anyone invested in the stock market lost money on unhedged investments on those days.

Examples of systematic risks that investors face include **political risk** (regulatory or tax code) and **exchange rate risk**. Political changes can have a widespread impact on the markets. For U.S. investors, these can range from changes in the tax code to increased regulation of business. Political risks can be even more exaggerated if the portfolio contains overseas investments, particularly in emerging markets. Generally, the political systems in such countries are less developed and new leadership can signal dramatic change. U.S. investors who invest overseas must also account for changes in exchange rates. In general, a declining dollar makes U.S. exports and foreign investments more attractive. When the dollar strengthens against foreign currencies, U.S. investors can actually lose money on foreign investments, even if the investments make money nominally.

Another important type of systematic risk is the overall level of compensation investors require for taking risk. During the internet bubble of the late 1990s, investors were willing to accept little compensation for additional levels of risk. At any time, investors as a whole might demand more compensation for the risks they take, which causes the value of securities either to stop increasing (stagnate) or to start decreasing (deflate). This was the case immediately following September 11, 2001.

Unsystematic risk or **firm risk**, on the other hand, is a type of risk that can be managed and reduced through diversification. **Diversification** involves blending assets that are not highly correlated within a portfolio to reduce risk exposure. Business failure is perhaps the greatest unsystematic risk. Businesses can fail because of poor management (**business risk**) or for taking on too much debt (**financial risk**).

MODERN PORTFOLIO STATISTICS—MEAN-VARIANCE ANALYSIS

Asset Mean "Average"

As discussed in Chapter 2, the most basic investment statistic is the **average return**, known as the arithmetic average, or **mean**. It is sometimes designated by the Greek letter μ. Typically, this is an easily understood investment statistic, the one most sought after by investors, and the most quoted by investment providers. This statistic is also the basis of all other modern portfolio theory related statistics, such as variance, standard deviation, the coefficient of variation, and the Sharpe ratio. The formula is:

$$\text{Average Return} \quad (AR) = \frac{r_1 + r_2 + r_3 + \cdots + r_n}{n}$$

Where:

r = return for period

n = number of periods

However, unless a client is investing in a fixed-return asset, such as a bank CD, it is important to remember that most periodic returns vary over time. An average return tells only half of the story. Although returns should average out in the end, returns during any given period likely will be either above or below the expected long-term average. When returns vary around an average, most predictions of future returns assume that the average will prevail.

Asset Variance

One of the primary measures of risk deals with the fluctuation of individual returns around an average return. The greater the dispersion of returns, the higher the return volatility; hence, the higher the risk. The difference between the average return and the range of possible outcomes is known as **variance**, denoted by σ^2. Variance is calculated by subtracting each individual outcome from the average outcome and then squaring the difference, as shown below:

$$\sigma^2 = X_t - \mu$$

Where:

σ^2 = variance

X_t = outcome

μ = average (mean)

Although individual security variance statistic is informative, average variance is the more important statistic. This calculation simply involves adding variances together and then dividing the sum by one less than the number of outcomes in the sample, as illustrated below:

$$\sigma_i^2 = \frac{(x_1 - \mu)^2 + (x_2 - \mu)^2 + (x_3 - \mu)^2 + \cdots + (x_4 - \mu)^2}{n - 1}$$

Where:

n = number of observations or units

Example. Assets A and B have the following returns.

Nominal Rates of Return	Asset A	Asset B
2003	-12.0%	-2.9%
2004	4.2%	6.5%
2005	11.8%	9.0%
2006	6.1%	-3.7%
2007	9.3%	7.5%
Arithmetic mean	3.88%	3.28%

By applying the preceding formula, a financial planner can determine that Asset A has a variance of 0.00873 and Asset B has a variance of 0.00370.

Asset Standard Deviation

Standard deviation, denoted as a lower-case sigma (σ), is a risk measure related to and predicated on variance. Standard deviation is the square root of variance and is more often quoted and used in investment statistics than variance. Standard deviation can be very useful in determining the dispersion of possible—or past—outcomes in relation to an expected outcome. **Total risk**, which comprises systematic and unsystematic risk, is typically measured by standard deviation.

$$\sigma_i = \sqrt{\frac{(x_1 - \mu)^2 + (x_2 - \mu)^2 + (x_3 - \mu)^2 + \cdots + (x_4 - \mu)^2}{n - 1}}$$

Where:

σ = standard deviation

n = number of observations or units

r_i = actual return

μ = average return

Using the table of data from the variance example, it is apparent that, because the annual outcomes are different, the standard deviation will be greater than zero. (In fact, the only time that standard deviation and variance are zero is when all outcomes over the analysis period are identical.) Using the preceding formula, or applying the square root formula to the variance derived above, the standard deviations are as 9.34 percent and 6.08 percent, respectively for Assets A and B.

Asset Coefficient of Variation

The **coefficient of variation** (CV) is another measure of dispersion (**range**), but in this case it is a relative measure based on average returns. CV is a ratio of unit of risk per unit of return. Therefore, it is easy to see that, for this ratio, smaller numbers are superior to larger ones. CV is useful to compare the risks of various investments with different expected returns. Therefore, calculating the CV for a single asset provides little insight. The equation for CV is:

$$CV = \frac{\sigma}{\mu}$$

Where:

σ = standard deviation

μ = mean

Again, consider the same two possible investments, Asset A and Asset B. To determine which asset offers the greatest return for a given level of risk, the risk of each asset (standard deviation) must be divided by the average return of each asset (arithmetic mean).

Nominal Rates of Return	Asset A	Asset B
2003	-12.0%	-2.9%
2004	4.2%	6.5%
2005	11.8%	9.0%
2006	6.1%	-3.7%
2007	9.3%	7.5%
Arithmetic mean	3.88%	3.28%
Variance	0.87%	0.37%
Standard deviation	9.34%	6.08%

CV Asset A = 9.34/3.88 = 2.41

CV Asset B = 6.08/3.28 = 1.85

By comparing the two assets without an adjustment for risk, a financial planner might choose Asset A, the riskier asset, because of its higher average return. However, after calculating the CV for both assets, the financial planner would rightly conclude that Asset A does not offer enough additional return for the increased level of risk.

Another use of CV involves determining the appropriate level of return for an increased level of risk. Returning to the preceding example, a financial professional sees that Asset B experiences 1.85 points of risk for each point of return. Therefore, for the financial planner to choose Asset A, a similar or lower ratio is needed. It is possible to use the following formula to determine the level of return necessary for the level of risk associated with Asset A:

$$\text{Required return of Asset A to equalize the CV} = \frac{\sigma A}{\text{CV of Asset B}}$$

$$\text{Required return to select Asset A} = \frac{9.34\%}{1.85} = 5.05\%$$

Correlation and Covariance of Two Assets

Diversification is a method used to reduce the unsystematic risk in a portfolio. However, to maximize the benefit derived from diversification, it is important for a financial planner to select assets that do not react the same way to a given economic environment. **Covariance** and **correlation** are measures of the degree to which multiple assets move in tandem.

Covariance measures the linear relationship between two random variables. The formula for covariance is:

$$\sigma_{ij} = \sigma_i \sigma_j \rho_{ij}$$

Where:

σ_{ij} = covariance of assets i,j

σ = standard deviation

ρ_{ij} = correlation of assets i,j

Notice that the preceding formula for solving covariance and the formula for solving correlation are identical. The variables have simply been rearranged to isolate the unknown. Unfortunately, if both correlation and covariance are unknown, then the equation is rendered useless. Therefore, an alternative equation must be used, one that is not predicated on the other, but on the periodic returns of each asset. The formula to solve for covariance if the correlation is unknown is:

$$\sigma_{ij} = \frac{1}{n-1} \sum_{t-1}^{n} (r_{i,t} - \mu_i)(r_{j,t} - \mu_j)$$

Where:

σ_{ij} = covariance of assets i,j

n   = number of observations or units

r_i = actual return at each period "t"

μ = average return

The easier to interpret of these two statistics is the **correlation coefficient,** which scales covariance based on the product of the standard deviation of two measured assets. The correlation coefficient is often denoted by the Greek letter *rho* (ρ).

Correlation is measured on a scale of -1 to +1, with a value of zero indicating that there is no relationship between two variables. If assets are positively correlated, it means that as one asset rises (or falls) the other asset usually does the same. If the assets are negatively correlated, then as one asset rises the other asset falls, and as one asset falls the other asset rises. If assets are positively correlated to a degree of +1, meaning that they are perfectly correlated, then not only will both assets rise at the same time, they will rise at the same rate. The inverse of this is also true if the assets are perfectly inversely correlated (-1). The formula for correlation is:

$$\rho_{i,j} = \frac{\sigma_{i,j}}{\sigma_i \sigma_j}$$

Standard Deviation of a Two-Asset Portfolio

Now that all of the statistics about Assets A and B are known, the power of investment statistics can be applied to a combination of these two assets—a portfolio. Unfortunately, a financial planner cannot simply weight asset standard deviations to calculate the standard deviation of a portfolio as can be done with returns because this ignores the covariance of the assets when used in tandem. Instead, the following equation must be used to determine the standard deviation of a two-asset portfolio.

$$\sigma_p = \sqrt{w_i^2 \sigma_i^2 + w_j^2 \sigma_j^2 + 2w_i w_j \sigma_{ij}}$$

Where:

σ = standard deviation

w   = weight "allocation" of each asset

σ_{ij} = covariance

MODERN PORTFOLIO STATISTICS—USING PROBABILITIES

Expected Return

So far statistics have been calculated based on historical—or known—data. But as a common financial planning investment disclaimer states, "past performance does not guarantee future results." For a financial planner to plan, some assumptions about the future must be made. These assumptions become the basis of expectations.

Clients expect a certain level of return to compensate for a variety of risks. This **expected return**, denoted *E(r)*, can be mathematically calculated by adding the appropriate risk premiums to the risk-free rate of return, as follows.

$$E(r) = r_f + IP + DP + BP + \ldots$$

Where:

$E(r)$ = expected return

r_f = risk-free rate

IP   = inflation risk premium

DP   = default risk premium

BP   = business risk premium

For simplicity, these **risk premia** are typically grouped together as one aggregated risk premium that accounts for both systematic and unsystematic risks. Once an expected rate of return is calculated, it is important for a financial planner to determine whether rates of return available in the marketplace are adequate for the level of risk that the client is willing to accept. Also, a financial planner must perform a **sensitivity analysis** to determine how likely the projected returns are.

Expected Return (Using Probabilities)

One of a financial planner's most common tasks is to conduct a scenario analysis that considers possible outcomes under various market conditions. However, to facilitate client communication, these scenarios can be aggregated into the most likely outcome—or at least an average representation of the various scenarios.

Assigning and using probabilities is the easiest way to aggregate these outcomes. If a financial planner looks at three possible market conditions—boom, normal, and bust—and assigns each outcome a probability, then the planner can determine an "average" or most likely outcome.

> *Example*: A planner determines that in any given year there is a 20 percent likelihood of above-normal returns (boom), a 65 percent chance of average returns (normal), and a 15 percent possibility of below-normal returns (bust). The financial planner also determines that the corresponding returns would be 21 percent, 9 percent, and -12 percent, respectively. With this information, and using the following formula, the planner can calculate the most likely—or average—outcome to be 8.25 percent.

$$E(r) = (p_1 \times r_1) + (p_2 \times r_2) + (p_{n-1} \times r_{n-1}) + ... + (p_n \times r_n)$$

Where:

$E(r)$ = expected return

p = probability of outcome

r = return (outcome)

n = number of outcomes

$E(r) = (20\% \times 21\%) + (65\% \times 9\%) + (15\% \times -12\%) = 8.25$ percent

Standard Deviation and Confidence Levels

If returns are normally distributed, nearly 100 percent of all possible outcomes will fall within three standard deviations above or below the mean. As such, a financial planner can reasonably predict the minimum and maximum periodic return value for any period of time.

Risk can be quantified using measures of **volatility**. Standard deviation is a measure of historical returns as they are dispersed around an average. Although the standard deviation of a portfolio can change, financial planners usually assume that historical standard deviation is somewhat predictive of the future volatility of a portfolio. To use this measure of risk effectively, a financial planner needs to understand the following confidence levels.

1. Approximately 68 percent of all observations fall within one standard deviation of the mean.

2. Approximately 95 percent of all observations fall within two standard deviations of the mean.

3. Approximately 99 percent of all observations fall within three standard deviations of the mean.

> *Example.* A portfolio returned an average of 12 percent and the standard deviation was 15 percent. Applying the three confidence levels, a planner could be 68 percent

confident that a client's actual returns fell within a range of -3 percent and 27 percent (12% +/- 15%). A 95 percent confidence level would suggest that returns ranged from -18 percent to 42 percent (12% +/- 30% (2 × 15%)) in any given year. A 99 percent confidence level suggests that returns ranged from -33 percent to 57 percent (12% +/- 45% (3 × 15%)) in any given year.

Standard deviation plays a central role in helping financial planners understand the dynamics of portfolio management. The measure of standard deviation, along with covariance and variance, makes up the core basis of modern portfolio theory.

POSTMODERN PORTFOLIO STATISTICS

The two primary flaws of modern portfolio theory are that statistical analysis assumes that returns are normally (symmetrically) distributed around the mean, and that standard deviation is the appropriate measure of risk. Both of these assumptions tend to fail in practice. First, investment returns are not normally distributed; they are closer to log-normal with slightly negative (left) skewness. This is important because the normal distribution erroneously assumes that one-half of the outcomes are below the average outcome and one-half are above. Second, investors dislike a negative surprise more than they like positive surprises. Put another way, the risk of the undesirable outweighs the risk of the unknown, and standard deviation simply measures the likelihood of the unanticipated happening—whether the outcome is positive or negative. To overcome these shortcomings, Markowitz himself suggested that models based on semi-variance (focusing on downside risk) are preferable.

Log-Normal Distributions

The **log-normal probability** distribution arises from a continuous distribution of returns where the logarithm of those returns is normal, rather than the returns themselves being normal. This results is a distribution curve of returns that is skewed slightly to the left or right; it has been determined that, in developed markets, skewness is to the left. For a financial planner and client, this skewness means that the **geometric mean** (average) and the **geometric median** (50 percent level) are unequal. In other words, if a distribution is skewed to the left, then more than 50 percent of the outcomes are below the mean outcome.

Asset Semi-variance

Semi-variance generally can be defined as one-half of the original variance. If a financial planner is working with a normal distribution this assumption is correct. However, in the case of log-normal distributions, semi-variance is either greater than or less than one-half, depending on the direction of skewness and which side of the distribution is being measured.

Downside Risk (DR)

Because it was previously asserted that financial planners and clients dislike losses even more than they like gains, it makes sense to target the side of the distribution that fails to meet the standard rather than the side that exceeds it. In this case, the standard is the expected or mean outcome, and the side that fails is the left side where relative returns are negative (even if absolute returns can be either positive or negative). As an interesting note, the target could be defined as any minimum return deemed acceptable; for example, the **internal rate of return** that satisfies an investment objective could be used as the target. First, the semi-variance would be calculated by squaring only the negative deviations from the mean (all outcomes above the target would be entered as the target, thereby resulting in a squared difference of zero). Taking the square root of the sum of these squared deviations results in **semi-deviation**, also known as **downside deviation**, a measure of **downside risk**.

The Sortino Ratio

The most popular method for ranking investment opportunities is by ratio. Typically, the ratio is of excess return (return greater than a target) over a measure of risk (e.g., total [σ], systemic [β], negative outcome [DR]). Whereas the *Sharpe ratio* measures excess return over total risk and the *Treynor index/ratio* measures excess return over systemic risk, the **Sortino ratio** measures excess return over only the risk of negative outcomes, or *downside risk*. This ratio is very useful when attempting to determine the likelihood of a particular investment or strategy not meeting the minimum acceptable return when the distribution of outcomes is non-normal, which has been previously determined. This utility arises from the fact that the minimum acceptable return target can be any number; it is not limited to a simple arithmetic or geometric mean.

SENSITIVITY ANALYSIS: CAPITAL ASSET PRICING MODEL (CAPM)

CAPM as Expected Return

Once a financial planner knows the return on the market, the risk-free rate of return, and the beta of a portfolio, the planner can calculate an **expected risk-adjusted rate of return** for the portfolio. The formula used to calculate an expected rate of return is known as the **capital asset pricing model (CAPM)**. The CAPM formula is shown below:

$$R_{Exp} = R_f + \beta(R_m - R_f)$$

Where:

R_{Exp} = expected risk-adjusted rate of return

R_f = risk-free rate

β = beta

R_m = return on the market

The risk-free rate of return is most often indexed to Treasury bill rates, or other risk-free, short-term rates. Some financial planners use the ten-year rate to approximate the long-term horizon assumed of a stock holding or the one-year rate as a proxy for a one-year forecast horizon. The return on the market used most often for domestic portfolios is the S&P 500. However, other benchmarks can be used. For example, if a portfolio is composed of technology and internet stocks, the NASDAQ index could be an appropriate benchmark. A portfolio comprised primarily non-U.S. stocks might be benchmarked against the **Europe, Australia, and Far East (EAFE)** index.

> *Example.* Assume that Chris has a well-diversified retirement portfolio. Over the past three years, the beta of the portfolio was calculated to be 0.85. The risk-free rate at the time of the analysis was 3 percent, and the market returned 12 percent. What risk-adjusted return should Chris have received during the three-year period?
>
> CAPM Return = 0.03 + [0.85 x (0.12 – 0.03)] = 10.65 percent

This means that Chris should have received 10.65 percent on a risk-adjusted basis over the three-year period. Anything below this expected rate of return would suggest that Chris took unsystematic market risk that he was not compensated for.

Beta

The main weakness associated with measuring volatility using standard deviation is that it is security/portfolio specific. It is difficult to compare one portfolio against another using standard deviation. Many planners instead use **beta** as a measure of volatility to solve this problem. Beta is a relative measure of risk and is most often used as a measure of systematic risk in the stock market, but it can also measure the volatility of a portfolio compared to a market index. As noted above in the CAPM calculation, beta is used to determine an investor's expected rate of return.

Beta is generally estimated by using a linear regression for each asset, based on historical asset returns and the corresponding market returns. If standard deviation and correlation data are available, beta can also be measured as:

$$\beta = (\sigma_p / \sigma_m) \times \rho_{p,m}$$

Where:

σ_p = standard deviation of the portfolio

σ_m = standard deviation of the market

$\rho_{p,m}$ = correlation between portfolio and market

Example. Assume that the standard deviation of a portfolio of stocks is 14 percent and the standard deviation of a market index, such as the S&P 500, is 12 percent. If the correlation between the portfolio and market is 0.90, the beta of the stock portfolio will be 1.05 [(0.14 ÷ 0.12) × 0.90].

The **beta of the market** is, by definition, 1.00. Typically, the S&P 500 is used as the market index by U.S. investors. A portfolio with a beta of less than 1.00 is considered less volatile than the market. On the other hand, a beta of greater than 1.00 implies volatility in excess of the market. Beta is useful because the number can be used to tell a client approximately how much less or more volatile a portfolio is in comparison to the market. A beta of 1.10 indicates, for example, that a portfolio is approximately 10 percent more volatile than the index. Beta coefficients are theoretically continuous, meaning that scores can range from less than zero to a positive number. In practice, however, beta coefficients for diversified portfolios rarely exceed 4.0 on the high or -2.0 on the low side.

One note of caution in relation to beta is in order. Financial planners who use beta should do so only with well-diversified portfolios. Beta becomes very unstable and unreliable when used with single securities or non-diversified portfolios. In such cases, it is often best to use standard deviation as the measure of portfolio risk.

Education Planning

Learning Objectives

1. As the cost of a college education and college loan debt reach unprecedented heights, planning for education funding has become an important financial planning topic for parents, grandparents, and other family members. Planners have responded by assuming a more proactive role that goes beyond the projection of costs and needed investments to helping clients plan to maximize need- and merit-based aid, to choose tax-advantaged accounts, and to creatively combine strategies that help clients balance the cost of education against potentially negative consequences. These deleterious outcomes include a significantly reduced lifestyle during the college years, a significant reduction in retirement savings, or launching children with a heavy future commitment to repay college loans.

2. A wide range of personal client situational factors, both qualitative and quantitative, affect planning for education funding and the type of recommendations ultimately made.

Unknown situational information and the short time frame for planning with full information further complicate the planning process. Additionally, education funding is a highly emotional topic for parents and children, and a goal that many clients are willing to compromise other goals for, including retirement. Client attitudes, values, and expectations, which influence planning assumptions, may be more important and potentially problematic in education planning than in any other core content planning area. Thus, it is important that planners take the time to fully explore client situational factors as a foundation for the planning of education funding.

3. The complexity of planning for college education funding and the variety of alternative approaches advocated can make it difficult for clients to choose and implement the most effective strategies. Planners can help clients explore the emotional issues and understand the advantages and disadvantages of different accounts.

Learning Objectives

Access to and control of the funds, the timeline for accumulating and disbursing the funds, the effect on financial aid, and tax implications are primary considerations that must be evaluated. Tax consequences include (1) tax-deferred vs. taxable growth; (2) tax-free vs. taxable withdrawals; (3) annual income tax reductions from state incentives, the federal adjustment for interest paid, or the credit for costs incurred; and (4) shifting assets to potentially reduce or avoid estate taxes.

4. The availability of tax-deferred savings and tax-free withdrawals is limited to funding retirement, health care, and education. CESAs, Section 529 savings and prepaid plans, and Series EE bonds all offer these advantages, assuming all guidelines regarding income, purchase, and disbursement are met, as applicable. State tax incentives for the Section 529 accounts are another advantage, but they must be considered relative to account earnings, fees, and other features when choosing an in- or out-of-state account. Although these accounts are popular education savings alternatives, numerous other dedicated or dual-purpose accounts are available and offer unique benefits. Access to and control of funds, the timeline for accumulating and disbursing the funds, the effect on financial aid, and tax implications are important considerations to evaluate, relative to the individual client situation.

5. Merit-based and need-based funding (i.e., scholarships, loans, or grants) can significantly reduce or defer the cost of education for parents and students. A first step for everyone is to file the FAFSA annually. Despite the fact that financial planning clients may not be eligible for most need-based aid, family situational factors (i.e., size of family, multiple children in college, medical debt/issues, etc.) and the student's profile (i.e., talents, aptitude, extracurricular activities, discipline of study, etc.) could increase eligibility for financial assistance. Being proactive in selecting schools where the student is competitive, identifying college- and community-based sources of aid, and broadly applying for aid are important strategies. Finally, planners can add value by helping clients understand the federal and private educational loan programs as well as other possible sources for borrowing funds (i.e., home equity, retirement accounts, life insurance) to mitigate the funding need.

Key Terms

2503(c) Minor's Trust

401(k)

403(b)

Alternative Education Loans

American Opportunity Tax Credit (AOTC)

Client Situational Factors

College Scholarship Service/Financial Aid Form

Coverdell Education Savings Account (CESA)

Crummey Trust

Dependent Student

Discretionary Income

Education

EE Savings Bonds

Expected Family Contribution (EFC)

Federal Supplemental Educational Opportunity Grant

Financial Aid

Free Application for Federal Student Aid Form (FAFSA)

Funding Shortfall

Graduated Repayment

Grants

Higher Education

Home Equity Loan

Hope Scholarship Tax Credit

I Savings Bonds

Income Based Repayment

Income Contingent Repayment

Independent Student

Inflation Rate

Lifetime Learning Tax Credit (LLTC)

Loans

Need-Based Loan

Parent Loan for Undergraduate Students (PLUS)

Pell Grant

Perkins Loan

Post-Secondary Education

Postsecondary Institutions

Qualified Educational Expenses

Pay-As-You-Earn

Repayment Plans

Risk Tolerance

Roth Conversion

Roth IRA

Scholarships

Section 529 Savings Plan

Stafford Loan

Standard Repayment

Student Aid Report

Subsidized Loan

Tax Credit

Key Terms

Tuition

Uniform Gifts to Minors Act (UGMA)

Uniform Transfers to Minors Act (UTMA)

Unsubsidized Loan

Variable Universal Life Insurance

CFP® Principal Knowledge Topics

C.17. Education Needs Analysis

C.18. Education Savings vehicles

C.19. Financial aid

C.20. Gift/income tax strategies

C.21. Education financing

Chapter Equations

Equation 11.1: Future value of a lump sum $FV = PV (1 + i)^n$

Equation 11.2: Present value of a growing annuity $PV = \dfrac{PMT}{i - g} \left(1 - \dfrac{(1+g)^n}{(1+i)^n} \right)(1 + i)$

Equation 11.3: Present value of a lump sum $PV = \dfrac{FV}{(1 + i)^n}$

Equation 11.4: Present value of an annuity payment $PV = \dfrac{PMT}{i - g} \left(1 - \dfrac{(1+g)^n}{(1+i)^n} \right)$

Equation 11.5: Payment required to achieve a savings goal $PMT = \dfrac{PV(i - g)}{\left(1 - \dfrac{(1+g)^n}{(1+i)^n} \right)}$

EDUCATION PLANNING: DETERMINING THE NEED

Education funding is a primary concern for many clients and planners. Often it is this issue that prompts a client to seek professional planning services. Although parents tend to be the most interested in education planning, this is not the only group that can be involved. Frequently, grandparents and relatives have a stake in helping a family plan for a child's education. A grandparent's objective may be strictly to help fund the grandchildren's education. On the other hand, the objective might include reducing the taxable estate. So, depending on the client and situation, education planning can be important to clients with young children, clients with children who are about to enter college, and clients with grandchildren.

Families are increasingly turning to financial planners to help answer questions about funding future college costs. As such, it is important for advisers to have a working knowledge of the variety of tax-advantaged and non-tax-advantaged options available for individuals and families as they plan to fund education expenses. Taxes, timing, assets, income, competing financial goals, and a host of other considerations serve to further complicate a seemingly simple question, "How do we pay for college expenses?"

A number of interrelated steps are involved in the analysis of a client's education planning situation. Knowing one's client is the basis of all education funding and planning recommendations. To complete not only an education funding assessment but also a comprehensive financial plan, it is essential that a client's goals and objectives guide the process.

It is possible—and likely—that a wide range of personal client beliefs and expectations will affect the education funding analysis and the type of recommendations ultimately made. In fact, client attitudes and beliefs, especially as they are interpreted into planning assumptions, may be more important and potentially problematic in education planning than in any other core content planning area.

Getting to know client situational factors must precede actual quantitative analyses or the identification and review of strategies. Just as strategies in any planning area must be matched to the client, this customization must be considered in education planning. The timing of planning efforts, the assumptions needed (which can vary dramatically depending on the timing), and client situational factors can preclude the use of some otherwise beneficial strategies.

Education funding and planning strategies and recommendations must be consistent with a client's personal beliefs and values. Parents, guardians, or other family members may have different attitudes about how to pay for education either for themselves or their children; and planning for their children's education must often be balanced with planning for other goals—most often, retirement. A thorough assessment to determine and quantify education planning needs can help clients make decisions that are in closest alignment with their goals.

Two fundamental questions in education planning require answers: (1) how much will the education cost, and (2) how will these costs be paid? However, many underlying factors need to be considered. Foremost is not using the term *college* at first, but instead initiating these discussions as being about *education, higher education,* or *post-*

secondary education. These terms allow clients to acknowledge without bias that their children might or might not be interested in college, but that other options such as trade, technical, or arts programs may be the more likely choice. For some clients the topic of paying for education can focus on the cost of private elementary or secondary school rather than public education. The following general questions offer one way to explore some of the situational factors surrounding education planning:

- Do you plan to save enough to pay for higher education before the child enters the educational program?

- Do you plan to pay for the educational program after or while the child is enrolled in the educational program?

- Do you expect others to pay for the child's education?

- Do you plan to use some combination of the foregoing to pay for the child's education?

Once a client has defined the direction of the education planning effort, then focused planning with the client can begin. Although discussion in this chapter is limited to planning for college education expenses, the principles are applicable to planning for other types of education expenses as well.

Thoroughly and openly discussing these questions can help the adviser and client explore the range of client situational factors that impact education planning decisions. For example, some clients may firmly refuse to fully pay for college costs, although they are financially capable of doing so. Based on their values and attitudes, they may want the child to contribute through earnings or loans. Another client might insist on funding college costs to the exclusion of other planning needs. To such clients, it is important that their child not have to struggle for an education as they perhaps did. Although these scenarios are extreme, they illustrate how personality, values, attitudes, experience, and socioeconomic descriptors converge to influence education planning.

For example, clients who plan to accumulate funding before a child enters college will likely initiate disciplined savings early and focus on the desired amount. Those who plan to pay during or after the student attends college may be doing so by necessity or choice—because of a failure to start early, competing financial goals, life events that prevented or interrupted savings, or any number of other reasons. Such clients have no reservations about incurring debt through public or private sources, or postponing other goals to contribute to educational expenses. They, as well as the clients who plan on someone else paying, may expect the child to contribute through borrowing or working (summers, vacations, during the academic year, or through cooperative working/learning programs). Other parents may view student loan debt or employment during the academic year as an unnecessary burden on their child.

In addition to the child, others who will pay could include providers of scholarships and grants awarded on the basis of aptitude (e.g., scholastic, athletic, artistic), interest (e.g., leadership, community service), or need. Other family members might be expected to contribute insignificant or significant amounts before, during, or after college through direct or indirect gifts, trusts, or estate distributions. Finally, some parents are amenable to any combination of these funding approaches that will allow their children to attend the college of their choice.

The real significance of these personal beliefs in determining a client's planning need hinges on the application of these beliefs as assumptions in the planning process. As illustrated below, conducting an education funding assessment relies on several key assumptions, which frame the funding need and recommendations. However, these assumptions can be invalidated at any time and will likely change as a child ages.

The guidance given to a client who believes strongly that a child will receive financial assistance or not attend college will differ significantly from that given to a client committed to saving. Clients who trust that their child will receive financial aid for merit or need might consider funding retirement as an alternative goal or as a contingent source of education funding.

On the other hand, a client who is uncertain about financial aid could be directed toward tax-efficient strategies that will maximize account growth without jeopardizing available aid. However, should this client's child unexpectedly receive support, placing savings into qualified education savings plans could result in a significant opportunity cost and higher taxes. For example, if the assets held in a Coverdell Education Savings Account (CESA) are not used for educational purposes, any distributions become fully taxable and subject to a 10 percent penalty.

In summary, the choice of which or how much of each goal to fund is complicated by the uncertainty of the assumptions used when determining education funding needs. Prior to quantifying this need, planners should first understand what priority a client places on education planning and which assumptions to include in the planning. For some clients, education funding will be the highest priority. For others, education funding will rank below other financial planning goals. Many of these issues can be revealed during the discovery process of gathering data and framing goals and objectives, but if they are not, then a discussion focused on education planning should occur. Specific issues to address with a client include:

- Determining how much value a client or household places on receiving higher education;

- Prioritizing education planning within the comprehensive planning framework;

- Establishing the primary reason education funding is desired, including feelings of obligation or benevolence, as well as other tax considerations (e.g., preferences for tax-advantaged savings opportunities to defer or avoid income taxes, availability of income tax adjustments or credits reductions in estate taxes);

- Establishing guidelines regarding what the client or household believes is a reasonable amount to pay for a college education for one or more dependents;

- Identifying the level of control a client wants to retain in the management of assets devoted to education funding needs;

- Assessing a child's probability of receiving a scholarship or grant based on unique skills, abilities, or interests; and

- Determining a client's expectation of receiving financial aid.

Of these factors, some are wholly determined by the client, and the planner must respect them without judgment. Other fact-based considerations, such as preferences regarding taxes and control over the account, can be used by planners to directly influence the strategy recommendations. Once a planner has a solid understanding of a client's perceived roles, attitudes, and goals surrounding education planning, the next step is to determine the cost of this goal.

Education planning involves documenting a client's specific education funding objective(s), determining gross need, and then determining whether or not the client is on track to meet the objective(s) given all other assumptions about the funding situation. The conversation can be guided by the following questions.

1. When will the child(ren) begin college?

2. What type of college might the child(ren) want or be encouraged to attend?

3. How much are college costs increasing annually for this type of college?

4. What are projected costs for the targeted college when the child(ren) begins college?

5. How much of the projected college cost does the client intend to provide?

6. How much of the projected cost does the client expect to be funded by scholarships, grants, and loans?

7. Does the client currently have assets earmarked for this goal?

8. How much is the client, or other family members, currently saving for this goal?

9. Does education planning include funding for graduate education? (If so, the preceding questions must be reconsidered for this scenario.)

Assessing a client's educational funding needs is a relatively straightforward procedure. Figure 11.1 illustrates the information needed to complete a basic education funding needs analysis, the likely source of data, and the calculations required.

Figure 11.1 Summary of Data and Calculations for a College Savings Need Analysis

Data Needed for Analysis	Source of Data
Rate of return	Client/planner assumption
Years to complete college	Client/planner assumption
Initial additional periodic savings amount	Client/planner assumption
Initial periodic increase in savings amount	Client/planner assumption
Annual cost of college today	Planner research
College expense inflation rate	Planner research
Current age of child	Client data
College age of child	Client data
Present value of assets currently saved	Client data
Calculations Required for Analysis	**Completed by**
College real interest rate	Planner
Future value cost of college	Planner
Future value of assets currently saved	Planner
Future value of additional periodic savings	Planner

To complete the analysis, a financial planner must determine the rate of return most likely to be generated in the accounts in accordance with the risk tolerance of the account owner. The choice of a single rate-of-return figure may be overly simplistic because it is possible for clients to (1) have a combination of before- and after-tax investments earmarked for education, and/or (2) have an age-based portfolio where the rate of return will decrease over time as risk is removed from the portfolio and goal realization nears. It is also likely that some investments (e.g., U.S. Savings Bonds and Section 529 plans) will generate tax-free returns. Financial planners who would like to generate more precise figures should estimate returns for each possible before- and after-tax investment as well as for taxable and tax-free investments. Once individual account returns have been determined, the planner can then calculate the weighted-average return on which to base future value calculations.

Other information needed to complete an analysis includes the assumed rate of inflation for college expenses, the child's current age, expected age when entering college, and the number of years of college to be funded. The current cost of the college of choice is needed. Finally, the amount of assets already saved and a projected annual savings amount must be determined. The following is a step-by-step process[1] that can be used to conduct an education funding analysis.

#Remember

Visit collegecost.ed.gov/catc/default.aspx to get the latest information on college and university tuition inflation rates.

1. Determine the future value (FV) cost of education for a single year at the time the child begins college using the future value equation below, where the present value (PV) is the current annual cost of college, the interest rate (i) is the projected annual increase (inflation rate) in college cost, and n is the number of years until college begins.

Equation 11.1: Future value of a lump sum　$FV = PV(1 = i)^n$

2. Find the total cost of education (all years) at the time the child begins college using the present value of a growing annuity equation below, where the payment (PMT) is the first-year cost of college as calculated in Step 1. Because college is normally paid as an annuity, the annual increase in college cost is the growth rate, the estimated rate of return becomes the interest rate, and N is the number of years in college. This is also an annuity due because college tuition is typically paid at the beginning of each semester.

> **#Remember**
>
> Visit http://collegecost.ed.gov/catc/default.aspx to get the latest information on college and university tuition inflation rates.

Equation 11.2: Present value of a growing annuity　$PV = \dfrac{PMT}{i - g}\left(1 - \dfrac{(1+g)^n}{(1+i)^n}\right)(1 + i)$

3. To determine the cost of college today (as if the client were going to set aside the requisite amount immediately), calculate the present value of the total cost of education as discounted from the first year of college back to today using the present value of a lump sum equation below, where future value is the total cost in Step 2. The interest rate is the estimated rate of return, and n is the number of years until college begins.

Equation 11.3: Present value of a lump sum　$PV = \dfrac{FV}{(1 + i)^n}$

4. If money is already dedicated to this goal, subtract that amount from the total present cost of education in Step 3. The result is **funding shortfall**, which is the lump sum amount needed immediately to meet the education goal.

Funding Shortfall = Total Need - Amount Already Dedicated

5. If the client is going to fund the shortfall on a periodic basis, the planner needs to determine the monthly savings required until college begins by using the present value of an annuity payment formula, where the present value is the lump sum amount in Step 4. The inputs for the formula include the expected rate of return and the anticipated growth rate of the periodic payment, if applicable. Again, n is the number of years until college begins.

Equation 11.4: Present value of an annuity payment $PV = \dfrac{PMT}{i - g}\left(1 - \dfrac{(1+g)^n}{(1+i)^n}\right)$

Rearranging the formula to isolate PMT yields:

Equation 11.5: Payment required to achieve a savings goal $PMT = \dfrac{PV(i - g)}{\left(1 - \dfrac{(1+g)^n}{(1+i)^n}\right)}$

This payment is the required periodic payment, assuming that the client wants to save enough to achieve the goal without regard to other funding sources.

To illustrate this process, consider this example to determine a one-time lump sum payment (as well as monthly savings) to fully fund a child's education. The current annual cost of the preferred college is $12,000, and to ensure adequate funding the planner and client assume annual cost increases of 5 percent per year both before and during college. If the child is to begin college in exactly four years, will attend for four years, no money has been saved for this goal, and the planner projects an effective annual rate of return of 8.30 percent,[2] what is the required savings amount if the client is going to set aside the entire amount today? What is the required monthly savings amount?

1. Determine the future value cost of education for the first year of school.

   $FV @T_4 - \$12{,}000\,(1.05)^4 = \$14{,}586.08$

Input	Keystroke	Result
0	[PMT]	PMT = 0.00
12000 [+/-]	[PV]	PV = -12,000.00
5	[I/Y]	I/Y = 5.00
4	[N]	N = 4.00
[CPT]	[FV]	FV = 14,586.08

Note: The PV is input as a negative because an investment is an assumed outflow, and for this step the inflation rate is treated as an interest rate to determine the "inflated" cost of the goal.

2. Find the total cost of education (for all years) needed at the time the child begins college.

   $PV@T_4 = \dfrac{\$14{,}586.08}{0.083 - 0.05}\left(1 - \dfrac{(1.05)^4}{(1.083)^4}\right)(1.083) = \$55{,}731.37$

Input	Keystroke	Result
14586.08	[PMT]	PMT = 14,586.08
0	[FV]	FV = 0.00
3.1429*	[I/Y]	I/Y = 3.1429
4	[N]	N = 4.00
[CPT]	[PV]	PV = -55,731.37

*The calculator needs a serial rate to handle growing annuities. See Chapter 2 for details.

3. Determine the present value of the savings required as a lump sum.

$$PV@T_0 = \frac{\$55,731.37}{(1.083)^4} = \$40,512.20$$

Input	Keystroke	Result
0	[PMT]	PMT = 0.00
55731.37	[FV]	FV = 55,731.37
8.30	[I/Y]	I/Y = 8.30
4	[N]	N = 4.00
[CPT]	[PV]	PV = -40,512.20

4. There are no current savings, so the lump sum amount needed immediately to meet the education goal equals $40,512.20 ($40,512.20 - $0).

5. Determine the monthly savings needed to meet the education goals. (Note: To solve for a monthly payment, the planner must use the equivalent monthly rate for both the rate of return and the rate of payment growth, if applicable).

$$PMT = \frac{\$40,512.20(0.00667)}{\left(1 - \frac{1}{1.00667^{48}}\right)} = \$989.02$$

Self-Test 1

When calculating the total cost of education you should

a. assume a beginning payment for tuition.

b. assume an ending payment for tuition.

c. a constant $100,000 future value.

d. quarterly compounding of returns.

Input	Keystroke	Result
40512.20	[PV]	PV = 40,512.20
0.667*	[I/Y]	I/Y = 0.667
48	[N]	N = 4.00
0	[FV]	FV = 0
[CPT]	[PMT]	PMT = -989.02

*To calculate the monthly payment, either the interest rate must be in a monthly EPR format or the number of payments per year must be reset to 12.

6. Because the client did not indicate that any money was currently being contributed to the goal, monthly savings needed to meet the education goal equals $989.02.

Education Planning Skills

Clients who want to fund a child's education often face a tough dilemma. They sometimes must decide whether to save for potential college costs or fund retirement plans. The time horizons for saving for these goals are generally different, but they often overlap. Furthermore, a child may decide not to go to college or to go to a more or less expensive college, or the child could qualify for a scholarship or other financial aid.

One method to hedge the possibility that college expenses will be lower than expected, funded through other means, or simply unneeded is to fund both goals in one account. This means that future college costs, coupled with retirement funding needs, can be combined into one or more tax-deferred contribution plans. An employer-sponsored retirement plan, a Roth IRA, or a traditional IRA can be used to fund a portion of or all projected college costs.

#Remember

Help clients find the right college by finding a school with a College Scorecard: https://collegescorecard.ed.gov/

For example, if a Roth IRA is opened at least five years before education funding is needed, all contributions (but not earnings) can be taken out on a tax-free basis. If a client dips into account earnings to pay qualified higher education expenses before age 59½, the distributed earnings are generally taxable but free of the penalty tax on early distributions.

Any withdrawals from a traditional IRA would be taxable (except to the extent the distribution is attributable to nondeductible contributions, determined on a pro rata basis). To the extent the withdrawal is used to pay qualified higher education expenses, the penalty tax on early distributions would not apply.

In general, for purposes of the education exception to the penalty tax on early distributions, distributions are covered only to the extent that they do not exceed the qualified higher education expenses of the taxpayer, the taxpayer's wife, or the child or grandchild of either, and if the expenses are paid during the same year as the distribution. Eligible expenses include tuition, fees, books, supplies, and room and board for a student attending undergraduate or graduate school at least half-time.

Financial planners and their clients have numerous alternatives available as they plan for funding education expenses. In addition to commonly used education planning accounts, less common and less advantageous funding alternatives include insurance and home equity loans. Regular investment accounts (e.g., savings, mutual funds, or brokerage accounts) are another possibility, but generally they do not offer income tax benefits.

A variety of grants, loans, scholarships, and other financial aid sources are available. Others seek funding from private education loans or even family or personal loans. Students sometimes fund a part of the cost through summer jobs or on- or off-campus employment during the school term. Finally, some students pursue careers associated with loan forgiveness programs as a means to defray after-college repayment.

Few other core financial planning content areas offer such an extensive range of strategies with the opportunity to align availability, advantages, and disadvantages with a client's unique situation. Some of the most common education planning strategies are presented below, but they do not represent all of the creative approaches that can be considered.

Planning Skill 1: Be Creative When Developing College Funding Recommendations

Clients who want to fund a child's education often face a perplexing dilemma; namely, deciding whether to save for potential college costs or fund retirement plans. The time horizons for saving for these goals are generally different, but they often overlap. Furthermore, a child may decide not to go to college or to go to a more or less expensive college, or the child could qualify for a scholarship or other financial aid.

One method to hedge the possibility that college expenses will be lower than expected, funded through other means, or simply unneeded is to fund both goals in one account. This means that future college costs, coupled with retirement funding needs, can be combined into one or more tax-deferred contribution plans. An employer-sponsored retirement plan, a Roth IRA, or a traditional IRA can be used to fund a portion of or all projected college costs.

For example, if a Roth IRA is opened at least five years before education funding is needed, all contributions (but not earnings) can be taken out on a tax-free basis. If a client dips into account earnings to pay qualified higher education expenses before age 59½, the distributed earnings are generally taxable but free of the penalty tax on early distributions.

Any withdrawals from a traditional IRA would be taxable (except to the extent the distribution is attributable to nondeductible contributions, determined on a pro rata basis). To the extent the withdrawal is used to pay qualified higher education expenses, the penalty tax on early distributions would not apply.

In general, for purposes of the education exception to the penalty tax on early distributions, distributions are covered only to the extent that they do not exceed the qualified higher education expenses of the taxpayer, the taxpayer's wife, or the child or grandchild of either, and if the expenses are paid during the same year as the distribution. Eligible expenses include tuition, fees, books, supplies, and room and board for a student attending undergraduate or graduate school at least half-time.

Planning Skill 2: Evaluate and Recommend Appropriate College Funding Alternatives

Figure 11.2 illustrates some of the decisions that could influence the choice of college funding alternatives. These and other product and procedural strategies, as well as the associated advantages and disadvantages of each, are discussed below. It is likely that one or more strategies will be needed to achieve a client's education funding goals. Different strategies should be fully evaluated relative to a client's situation before combining them in a recommendation.

Figure 11.2 Decision Tree for Select Education Funding Strategies

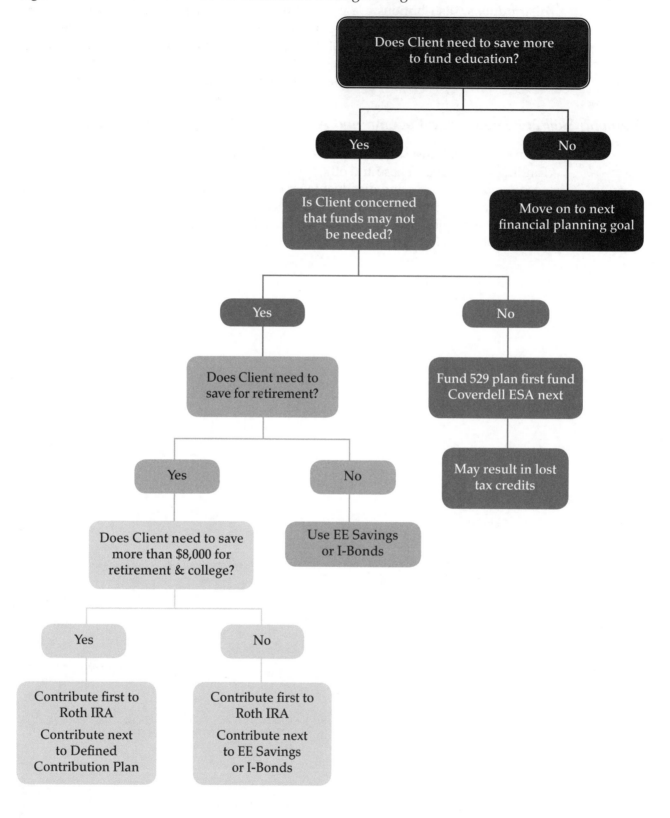

EDUCATION PLANNING PRODUCT & PROCEDURAL STRATEGIES

The following product and procedural strategies provide an insight into some of the most widely used educational planning tools and techniques used by financial planners on a day-to-day basis.

Product Strategy 1: Save for College Using a Section 529 plan

Section 529 savings plans, named after Section 529 of the Internal Revenue Code (IRC) that created them in 1996, offer a number of advantages for clients who want a tax-advantaged education funding tool.

First, a significant dollar amount can be contributed on an annual basis. This makes a Section 529 plan advantageous compared to a **Coverdell Education Savings Account (CESA)**, which is described in more detail later in the chapter. Second, investments in the account grow tax free, and withdrawals used for qualified college expenses are free from federal income tax. Third, some states offer state income tax advantages in addition to those offered by the federal government. States with an income tax often provide a state income tax exclusion for qualified withdrawals. Furthermore, most—but not all—states allow a deduction or credit for contributions to a Section 529 plan, and some offer direct grants or monetary incentives. Some states have "tax-parity" legislation that extends state tax deductions to residents investing in out-of-state Section 529 plans. The fourth benefit involves control over the account. The account owner maintains control over how funds are invested and distributed. A parent, grandparent, relative, or friend can establish an account for a designated beneficiary. The owner can even decide when withdrawals should be taken and for what purpose.

> **Self-Test 2**
>
> Which of the following statements is true?
>
> a. EE Savings bonds held in the name of a child can be used tax free for that child's college education expenses.
>
> b. § 529 assets may be used tax free to pay for tuition, fees, and books but not room or board.
>
> c. The maximum yearly § 529 contribution is the same as the limit for Roth IRA contributions.
>
> d. Both a and b

Another unique advantage of Section 529 plans involves their usefulness in estate planning. A client can contribute up to $70,000 to a Section 529 plan in 2016 without triggering the federal gift tax. In effect, by implementing this strategy a client can use up to five years of gift tax annual exclusions in one year. Joint tax filers can contribute twice as much, and there are no limits to the number of beneficiaries for gift tax purposes. In addition, amounts in a Section 529 plan account are generally not included in the account owner's gross estate for federal tax purposes.

A beneficiary can use Section 529 plan college savings program funds at any accredited college, university, technical, vocational, or graduate school anywhere in the United States. This means that withdrawals can be used to pay for expenses in Kansas, for instance, even though the Section 529 plan was sponsored by Nebraska.

Self-Test 3

Tamara's grandfather saved $49,000 in a 529 plan to help pay her college expenses. Because of other scholarships, Tamara needed used only $35,000 from the account. What options are available for her grandfather now?

a. Withdraw $14,000 and pay a 10% penalty.

b. Use the funds to help pay for Tamara's graduate school expenses.

c. Change the beneficiary of the account to another family member.

d. All of the above.

Furthermore, no income limitations or age restrictions are associated with Section 529 plans. Lifetime contribution limits for Section 529 plans are considerably higher than any other tax-advantaged college saving plan. The lifetime maximum contribution is based on each state's projected cost of college. In many states, the maximum lifetime contribution limit can exceed $250,000.

Advisers need to be aware of some potential drawbacks associated with Section 529 plans. A beneficiary could decide not to attend college or to attend a less expensive school. Earnings withdrawn for nonqualified expenses are generally subject to federal and state income tax as well as a 10 percent federal penalty tax. Instead of taking a nonqualified distribution, an account owner could transfer an account to another family member, including siblings, first cousins, spouses, and even back to the client.

Another potential problem involves investment choices within Section 529 plans. Nearly all states have pre-established asset allocation models that are used to direct investments within a plan. Accounts for young beneficiaries typically are invested aggressively, and in some cases annual management and maintenance fees can be high. Asset allocation typically becomes more conservative as the beneficiary ages. The choice of mutual funds within an account is almost always restricted, and historically the number of times an account owner can make changes within a plan has been limited to once a year.

Finally, investments held in the account are considered assets of the parent, and as such they increase the EFC for financial aid, but not as much as if the child held them.

A **Section 529 prepaid tuition plan** is a form of Section 529 plan that provides an opportunity to prefund college expenses. Three important issues must be acknowledged before using a Section 529 prepaid tuition plan. First, the amount of contribution is based on the age of the beneficiary and anticipated college costs in the state offering the plan. Second, the account owner has no control over how the account is invested. The sponsoring state manages the account and guarantees that tuition will be paid, regardless of account value. Third, and maybe most important, Section 529 prepaid tuition plans typically guarantee benefits only for public institutions within the state sponsoring the plan, although some plans offer more flexibility.

Product Strategy 2: Know the Options Available with Unspent Section 529 Plan Assets

While contributing to a Section 529 plan can be a good way to save for a child or grandchild's college education, there are times when money saved in a Section 529 plan is not used. When this occurs, clients have several options. One alternative is to withdraw the account balance as cash; however, doing so will cause the client to owe tax on the earnings, plus a penalty equal to 10 percent on account earnings. Another option is keep the money in the Section 529 plan. Doing so will allow a beneficiary to use the funds for graduate school expenses. An alternative is to change the recipient beneficiary. The only requirement is that the new beneficiary be a family member. In situations where Section 529 plan assets remain unspent because a beneficiary received a scholarship, it is possible for the client to withdraw money up to the value of the scholarship. Of course, the withdrawal will be taxable, but the distribution will not be penalized. The same holds true if the beneficiary becomes disabled or dies. Finally, there is no rush to make any changes to a Section 529 plan as long as the named beneficiary is still alive. The assets will continue to grow on a tax-free basis until used or withdrawn. In rare cases when no future beneficiary is anticipated, the client may decide to donate the account to a charity and receive a tax deduction (assuming the client itemized deductions).

Product Strategy 3: Save for College Using a CESA

A **Coverdell Education Savings Account** (CESA) can be used to help parents and grandparents save for a qualified beneficiary's education expenses. A CESA is a trust or custodial account set up for the purpose of paying qualified education expenses for a designated beneficiary. Principal and earnings from the account can be used to pay qualified higher education expenses, including tuition, fees, books, supplies, and equipment required for enrollment or attendance. Other expenses include amounts contributed to a qualified tuition program and room and board expenses. Distributions can be used to pay expenses at public, private, and religious elementary and secondary schools, as well as for postsecondary education expenses. This means that, unlike any other tax-advantaged program, a CESA can be used to pay for private day school expenses.

The designated beneficiary of a CESA must be under the age of eighteen when an account is established, unless the beneficiary has special needs. Any balance in a CESA must be distributed within thirty days after the date the beneficiary reaches age thirty, unless the beneficiary has special needs. There is no limit to the number of CESAs that can be established

Education Planning Tip: Traditional IRA Accounts

There is no hard-and-fast rule about the best time to convert a traditional IRA to a Roth IRA; however, there is a worst possible time—while your children are in college. Qualified retirement accounts are excluded from assets when calculating the EFC for financial aid; however, income derived from those sources is not. So, although a distribution from IRAs to pay qualified educational expenses is allowable and therefore will not trigger a tax penalty, it will count as income and could affect the income component of the EFC the following year.

A lesser-known consideration is the impact of conversion. Converting a traditional IRA to a Roth IRA is a taxable event. In other words, the amount of the conversion is typically taxable as ordinary income in the year of conversion, although there have been numerous temporary changes to this rule. So a planner must consider long-term tax implications of IRA distributions and conversions to the account owner, as well as the near-term financial aid implications to the dependent student of the account owner.

for one beneficiary. However, contributions can be made only in cash, and the total contributions made to all CESAs for any beneficiary in one tax year cannot be greater than $2,000. This means that a client cannot contribute $2,000 to an account while a grandparent contributes another $2,000. Also, contributions to CESAs are restricted by income phase-out rules.

The primary financial planning advantage associated with a CESA is that distributions are tax free to the extent the distribution does not exceed the beneficiary's qualified education expenses. If a distribution does exceed the beneficiary's qualified education expenses, a portion of the distribution is taxable. A CESA can be rolled over into a Section 529 plan. Also, the Hope Credit or the Lifetime Learning Credit can be claimed for certain qualified higher education expenses in the same year in which the student receives a tax-free withdrawal from a CESA. However, the distribution cannot be used for the same educational expenses for which the credit was taken.

Two limitations are associated with this college savings approach. First, many financial planning clients could find that their income exceeds threshold limits, making contributions out of the question. Second, and more importantly, the annual $2,000 contribution limit severely restricts the usefulness of this tool in accumulating assets for education.

To maximize this type of account, a client must start saving early in a child's life and save the maximum allowable each year. If, for instance, a client saved $2,000 each year for fifteen years earning 9 percent on average, the account would be worth only $58,722 at the end of the period. Also, if assets are not used by the child's thirtieth birthday and are not assigned to a close family member, the client will incur income tax and a 10 percent penalty on earnings that accumulated on a tax-free basis within the account.

Product Strategy 4: Save for College Using a Roth IRA

For those eligible to do so, contributing to a *Roth IRA* is an excellent strategy for clients who want to save for a contingent educational funding need, but who have a primary goal of saving for retirement. If funds are needed for college or other education needs, distributions of contributions can be received tax free as long as the Roth IRA has been open for at least five years. If earnings are withdrawn prior to age 59½ and used to pay qualified educational expenses, taxes may be due on such distributions, but the early distribution penalty will not apply.

The primary disadvantage associated with this strategy is that it is unlikely that enough funding can be generated to cover 100 percent of college costs at a moderate-to high-expense college. Reducing this retirement asset may benefit the child, who may have other education funding alternatives, but it could jeopardize the owner's retirement plan. Thus, this strategy may be more appropriate for a grandparent than a parent, depending on other situational factors. Additionally, distributions from Roth IRAs can adversely affect a subsequent financial aid application because of the increased income.

Product Strategy 5: Save for College Using Variable Universal Life (VUL) Insurance

This strategy, which is somewhat unorthodox outside the insurance industry, can be quite effective in meeting education funding goals. The principal advantages associated with this strategy include being able to maximize funding and investing in assets that can grow substantially over time. Ultimately, this strategy is beneficial if growth within the variable account is high enough to allow the client to take loans to pay for college expenses and have remaining assets generate returns to pay the interest and repayment charges. Also, if the insured dies, insurance proceeds could be used to pay for education.

The chief disadvantage associated with this strategy is that, to fully fund a VUL at the level necessary to accumulate a significant account value, a large face value policy is needed. The premium cost of such a policy can be prohibitive. Furthermore, ongoing administrative and subaccount fees can reduce overall rates of return on assets. Unless managed and invested well, a VUL can terminate with a zero cash balance. Also, rates credited by the insurer are reduced when a loan is made.

Product Strategy 6: Save for College Using Series EE and Series I Bonds

A parent's (or grandparent's) **EE savings bonds** can be cashed in tax free to pay for a child's (or grandchild's) college tuition. The amount that can be contributed on a yearly basis is higher ($30,000 for married clients) than what can be contributed to a CESA or traditional or Roth IRAs.

Individuals must meet certain requirements for distributions from EE and **I savings bonds** to be tax free. First, a client must be at least twenty-four years old on the first day of the month in which the bond was purchased. Second, when using bonds for a child's education, the bonds must be registered in the *client's and/or spouse's name*. A child can be listed as a beneficiary on the bond, but not as a co-owner. Third, if a client uses bonds for the client's own education, the bonds must be registered in the client's name. Finally, if a client is married and uses the bonds for educational purposes, the client must file a joint return to qualify for the exclusion.

Unlike distributions from CESAs, only payments made to *postsecondary institutions*, including colleges, universities, and vocational schools that meet the standards for federal assistance (such as guaranteed student loan programs) qualify for the program. **Qualified educational expenses** include tuition and fees such as lab fees and other required course expenses. Expenses paid for any course or other education involving sports, games, or hobbies qualify only if required as part of a degree- or certificate-granting program. The costs of books, room, and board are not considered qualified expenses. Savings bonds can be used to fund qualified state tuition plans, such as a Section 529 plan. When determining the amount of qualified expenses, a client must reduce the amount of total expenses by the amount of scholarships, fellowships, employer-provided educational assistance, and other forms of tuition reduction received. Finally, expenses must be incurred during the same tax year in which the bonds are redeemed.

Up to $30,000 in Series EE and Series I savings bonds can be purchased by married clients ($15,000 for single clients) in any given year. To exclude the interest from gross income, a client must use both the principal and interest from bonds sold to pay qualified expenses. If the amount of eligible bonds cashed during the year exceeds the amount of qualified educational expenses paid during the year, the amount of excludable interest is reduced using a pro rata formula. For example, assume that bond proceeds equal $20,000 ($16,000 principal and $4,000 interest) and the qualified educational expenses are $16,000. The amount of interest that can be excluded is $3,200 ([$16,000 expenses ÷ $20,000 proceeds] × $4,000 interest).

Like most tax benefits, certain household income limitations apply. The full interest exclusion is available only to clients with modified adjusted gross income (which includes the interest earned) under certain limits. Also, savings bonds are included as a parent asset, which can increase the EFC used in financial aid formulas. Furthermore, rates of return are relatively low, which limits a client's ability to fund expenses from interest earned. The early withdrawal penalty during the first five years and the relatively low rate of return require that this strategy be implemented well in advance of when the funds are needed.

Product Strategy 7: Use a Home Equity Loan to Pay for Additional College Expenses

This strategy is appropriate for clients who wish to borrow against their home equity to contribute to their child's education. In general, clients receive a tax deduction for the interest paid on a home equity loan (for up to $100,000 of debt) if they itemize deductions and are not subject to the Alternative Minimum Tax. Loan repayment typically ranges from five to fifteen years, and prepayment penalties may apply. Closing costs and other associated fees to establish and service the loan apply, and repayment begins immediately. Clients who use this strategy place a lien against their home equity that must be repaid over a number of years. If a child chose not to finish school or to use the proceeds of the loan for expenses other than college, the parents could have mortgaged their own financial future to fund something unintended.

Product Strategy 8: Use Retirement Accounts Rather than Education Savings Products to Save for College Expenses

Student financial aid formulas do not take into account assets held in defined contribution plans or self-employed retirement plans, such as Keoghs. By maximizing contributions to these plans, and then taking loans against account values if needed, it may be possible to reduce the expected family contribution when applying for financial aid. The primary disadvantage associated with this strategy is that if early withdrawals are needed, a 10 percent penalty may apply. Also, some private universities may require that retirement assets be listed for calculating the EFC for financial aid purposes.

Product Strategy 9: Use 401(k) and 403(b) Account Loans to Fund Education Expenses

Although not universal, many *401(k)* and some *403(b)* plans allow an account owner to borrow the greater of $50,000 or 50 percent of account value at any given time. Typically, loans can be taken for up to five years with a minimal rate of interest. This strategy allows a client to minimize the financial aid EFC by sheltering assets in a 401(k) or 403(b) plan, and then later use loan proceeds to pay for excess college expenses.

It is important to note that using retirement assets to fund a dependent child's college expenses could cause the parent's retirement plan to become underfunded. Once a loan is taken, loan proceeds stop earning market rates of return. An opportunity cost exists where the amount of interest repaid will almost always be less than the amount of interest and capital gains that could have been earned. Loan repayment starts immediately. If employment ends, the loan must be repaid in thirty days or less or taxes and penalties may apply.

> **Self-Test 4**
>
> Holub has a 401(k) account with a balance of $18,000. He would like to borrow from the account to help is son pay college expenses. What is the maximum loan Holub can take today?
>
> a. $50,000
>
> b. $25,000
>
> c. $18,000
>
> d. $9,000

Procedural Strategy 1: Consider the Advantages and Disadvantage of a Child Filing Taxes as an Independent Taxpayer

Often, clients assume that the best tax filing strategy is to claim a child as dependent for the maximum length of time possible. Other clients assume that the best way to maximize financial aid is to have the child file taxes as an independent taxpayer. Doing so could result in a client forfeiting a tax exemption or credit. However, not being claimed as a dependent on the parent's taxes does not confer independent student status on the child for financial aid purposes. The rules relating to independent student status for the purposes of filing for financial aid are different from those for tax purposes.

Several factors must be considered, including parental income, support for the child, the child's eligibility for financial aid, the parents' eligibility for the adjustment for education expenses or the education credit, and the marginal tax bracket of the parents. If the issue is isolated to taxes, generally the greater savings results from a parent continuing to claim the exemption. The benefit from savings on the client's income taxes may be negligible if the dependent could actually qualify as an independent student and receive maximum financial aid. However, it is important that both issues, the potential impact on income taxes and the impact on financial aid eligibility, be considered separately or in combination depending on the individual client situation.

Procedural Strategy 2: Recommend Appropriate Student Financial Aid Alternatives to Meet Client Funding Needs

Financial aid comes in three basic forms: (1) **scholarships**, (2) **loans**, and (3) **grants**. Nearly all scholarships offered in the United States are university or program specific. However, a number of national scholarships are available. Scholarships can be either need or merit based. Students interested in scholarships should generally apply through their university, college, and academic unit.

Federal student loans are available through as Stafford loans (Perkins loans were discontinued in 2015). **Stafford loans** are federally sponsored loans for educational expenses. Prior to July 2010, Stafford loans were offered under the Federal Family Education Loan Program, and funds were provided by private banks and credit unions. But after passage of the Health Care and Education Reconciliation Act of 2010, the Federal Direct Loan Program handles all Stafford loan processing, while the federal government provides funding directly by through participating schools.

There are two types of Stafford loans, **subsidized** and **unsubsidized**. The subsidized Stafford loan is a *need-based loan* where the federal government pays the interest for the student on the loan as long as the student is enrolled at least half-time. Unsubsidized Stafford loans are available to all students (who are eligible for federal aid) regardless of need. The unsubsidized Stafford loan accrues interest from the date of disbursement. Both loans offer payment deferral, meaning the student is not required to make interest payments while attending college at least half-time, and both offer a six-month grace period after the deferment period ends before repayment is required.

Annual loan limits for undergraduate students are determined by their grade level and dependency status. Interest rates on Stafford Loans are quite reasonable—the rates are set periodically by Congressional Act. Loans disbursed prior to July 2006 carried a variable interest rate capped at 8.25 percent.[3] Some currently enrolled students may hold a Perkins loan, which is a need-based loan that charges a flat 5 percent interest rate, allows repayment to be deferred until nine months following graduation, and features a ten-year repayment period.[4] These loans were discontinued after 2015.

Parents rather than students apply for the **Parent Loan for Undergraduate Students (PLUS)**. A PLUS loan can be taken out for an amount equal to the difference between the college-defined cost of attendance and all other financial aid received. For loans disbursed prior to July 2006, the interest was variable based on market conditions and capped at 9 percent; however, loans disbursed since that time have rates ranging from 7.9 percent to 6.41 percent annually.[5] A primary difference between Stafford and PLUS loans is that PLUS loans require repayment beginning approximately sixty days after the loan is fully disbursed rather than being deferred until graduation.

> **#Remember**
>
> A Pay As You Earn repayment plans generally limit debt repayments to 10% of the borrower's discretionary income, but never more than the standard 10-year repayment plan amount

All Direct Loan Program loans offer a variety of **repayment plans**, as listed below:

- *Standard repayment*—up to ten years, with a minimum monthly payment of $50.[6]

- *Extended repayment*—up to twenty-five years, with the option of fixed or graduated payments (increasing every two years); must have more than $30,000 in qualifying debt to be eligible).[7]

- *Graduated repayment*—up to ten years (or twenty years if also qualified under the extended plan) with payment increasing every two years. Later payments are prohibited from being more than three times any other payment on the loan.[8]

- *Income contingent repayment*—an applicant income-based formula capped at 20 percent of discretionary income with a repayment period of twenty-five years, after which any outstanding balance is forgiven but taxed as current income.[9] The annual payment calculation is based on adjusted gross income (AGI), plus spouse's income (if applicable), family size, and the total amount of Federal Direct Loans.

- *Income based repayment*—maximum repayment period can exceed ten years, but it is only available to those experiencing partial financial hardship; under certain circumstances, loan cancellation may be available.[10] Payment may adjust annually matched to income. Partial financial hardship is determined by a calculation where, under a standard ten-year repayment plan for all eligible loans, the total annual payment due exceeds 15 percent of discretionary income.[11] The Health Care and Education Reconciliation Act, passed in 2010, reduced the maximum payment percentage from 15 to 10 percent and also reduces the forgiveness of any remaining loan balance from twenty-five years to twenty. These changes are effective for new borrowers of new loans made on or after July 1, 2014.[12]

Beginning in 2015, any US citizen who had ever borrowed money using a federal government loan, either for college or graduate school, can enroll in the **pay-as-you-earn** debt repayment program. This program sets the maximum monthly debt repayment equal to 10 percent of a borrower's **discretionary income**, which is defined as adjusted gross income (AGI) less 150 percent of the poverty level. Under the rules, payments can be made for twenty years. For those with graduate student debt the repayment period can be extended to twenty-five years. At the end of the period (i.e., either twenty or twenty-five years), any remaining balance is forgiven; however, all amounts forgiven are subject to regular income taxes. Two things are worth remembering. First, parents who took

> **#Remember**
>
> Visit the Federal Student Aid website to learn more about repayment options
>
> studentaid.ed.gov/sa/ repay-loans/understand/ plans/income-driven

out loans to pay for a child's college costs are not eligible for pay-as-you-earn. Second, while this repayment plan will appeal to many people, it is important that clients be reminded that more interest will be paid over the life of the loan.

Procedural Strategy 3: Evaluate the Use of Alternative Educational Loans and Grants

Supplemental loans can be obtained to fund unpaid educational costs. These private education loans, also known as *alternative education loans*, are available through private lenders. Private education loans tend to cost more than education loans offered by the federal government, but they are less expensive than credit card debt. Loans are not subsidized and origination, guarantee, or repayment fees may apply. Repayment is typically deferred while a student is in school (interest payments may be paid or deferred), and the repayment periods can be as long as those of direct loans, although such features vary by lender.

Pell grants are the most widely recognized form of federal education funding support. A federal **Pell grant** is a tax-free gift to a student to offset college expenses; it is awarded based on family need as determined by the EFC. Universities and colleges can award **Federal Supplemental Educational Opportunity Grants** directly to needy students. Priority for these need-based federal grants is given to federal Pell grant recipients. Some states and universities also provide grants, but almost always such grants are based on need rather than merit.

Procedural Strategy 4: Plan for FASFA Requirements

For most forms of financial aid, some component of need or expected contribution is used to determine eligibility or availability. Therefore, a common planning need for clients who are not averse to "working the system" is working with the four factors that influence perceived need on the **Free Application for Federal Student Aid (FASFA)** form. Planners and clients must determine not only the amount of money that will be available for college expenses, but who will own that money. Ownership is important because the percentage of assets required to fund college costs depends on whether the assets are held in the child's, parent's, or guardian's name. Dependent students are expected to contribute 20 percent of assets and 50 percent of income to education expenses, and parents are expected to contribute only 22 percent – 47 percent of assets and 2.6 percent – 5.6 percent of income.[13] These amounts differ for independent students.

Armed with some knowledge of the financial aid system, a planner can advise parents regarding how to work more proactively with high school staff and targeted college financial aid programs to determine more accurately the likelihood of merit- or need-based financial assistance. The same strategy can be applied to identifying institutions, both public and private, that could offer the most assistance given the student's profile. Finally, this information, plus projected payment scenarios, can help parents feel more comfortable about taking on education loan debt for themselves or their children.

Procedural Strategy 5: Fund a 2503(c) Minor's Trust before the Child Reaches Age Twenty-one

Funding a **2503(c) minor's trust** completes a gift to a minor under Internal Revenue Code section 2503(c), thereby removing the assets from the estate of the grantor while maintaining some level of control over the distribution and use of the assets. There are caveats to consider before implementing this strategy. Gifts made to the trust are irrevocable and must be made before the child turns twenty-one. Additionally, all of the proceeds from the trust must be used for the benefit of the beneficiary prior to the age of twenty-one, unless a "window" is provided to the beneficiary immediately following the twenty-first birthday, which grants the beneficiary access before it converts into a *Crummey trust*. As with all trusts, set-up and administration fees can be quite high in comparison to the corpus of the trust. Finally, trust assets are considered assets of the child, and income derived from the trust is income to the child; therefore, it will have a significant impact on financial aid contribution calculations.

Procedural Strategy 6: Fund a Crummey Trust

Funding a **Crummey trust** completes a gift to a minor by allowing temporary access to the gift, thereby removing the assets from the estate of the grantor while maintaining some level of control over the distribution and use of the assets. Another benefit is that Crummey trusts, unlike Section 2503(c) trusts, can name multiple beneficiaries. Gifts made to the trust are irrevocable. As with all trusts, set-up and administration fees can be quite high in comparison to the corpus of the trust. Finally, trust assets are considered assets of the child, and income derived from the trust is income to the child; therefore, it will have a significant impact on financial aid contribution calculations.

Procedural Strategy 7: Shift UGMA/UTMA Assets Two Years Before the Child Turns Age Eighteen

Current financial aid formulas penalize families when a child holds sizable assets in **UGMA/UTMA** accounts. Although a parent cannot take back money held in a UGMA/UTMA account, it may be possible to use account assets to purchase goods and services for a child above and beyond items generally thought of as basic living expenses. For example, assets can be used to pay tuition to a precollege camp. Doing so increases the likelihood of receiving a larger financial aid award. This strategy should be recommended with caution. Gifts made to an UGMA/UTMA account are irrevocable. They should not be used for the benefit of a parent or guardian or for costs that are deemed to be basic expenses the parent or guardian may be obligated to pay. Also, the effectiveness of this strategy disappears if account transfers are not made at least two years before filing for financial aid.

Procedural Strategy 8: Use EE Savings Bonds to Fund a Section 529 Plan

Although discussed previously, this strategy is worth reviewing again. Proceeds from the sale of *Series EE* and *Series I* savings bonds can be received tax free when used either to pay for a family member's educational expenses or when funding a Section 529 plan or a CESA. Several requirements must be met. The account beneficiary must be the client, the client's spouse, or a dependent of the client. To qualify for the interest exclusion, the bonds must be issued in the parent's name and purchased after 1989, must be used to pay for qualified higher education expenses or funding a Section 529 plan or CESA, and the parent must meet the modified AGI guidelines for the interest exclusion (income phase-outs apply). Those filing "married filing separately" are ineligible for the exclusion. This allows savings bonds to be used on a tax-free basis to earn a potentially higher rate of return in a Section 529 plan. Furthermore, because many states provide an incentive to contribute to an in-state (and in some instances an out-of-state) Section 529 plan, doing so can yield a higher overall tax benefit. By transferring savings bond assets to a Section 529 plan, a client limits the availability and use of these assets for other goals, especially if the client's child does not need to use account assets for education.

Procedural Strategy 9: Increase Annual Savings Dedicated to Goal

One final and obvious strategy involves increasing the amount of savings dedicated to the education funding goal. The more that can be saved on a monthly or yearly basis, the more likely that the goal will be met. It may be possible to involve grandparents or other family or friends in this effort. This strategy is based on the premise that the client or others have additional discretionary cash flow and unallocated savings to contribute to the educational goal. If this assumption is incorrect, this strategy will not work.

Procedural Strategy 10: Decrease the Level of Support Assumption

Clients who attempt to achieve an education funding objective but still find themselves coming short of their goal may want to consider decreasing the cost-of-college assumption used in the analysis. Although it is nice to want to fund a child's full educational costs at an expensive university, it may be fiscally impossible. Therefore, reducing the cost to be covered and focusing on obtaining scholarships, grants, and loans may be a way to meet at least a portion of future educational costs. It is important to remember, however, that reducing the support assumption and instead relying on a child to receive grants and scholarships can be a problematic approach to planning. The uncertainty associated with grants and scholarships makes these sources of funding difficult to predict. An unrealistic reliance on these forms of funding can leave a client significantly short of actual future assets to fund these expenses. This alone would be detrimental, but it can also limit alternative funding planning.

Procedural Strategy 11: Increase the Risk/Return Trade-off Assumptions

Clients may underestimate their *risk tolerance* when accumulating assets for education funding needs. This especially applies when funding efforts are postponed (not initiated when the children are young) and therefore the time horizon for goal attainment is shortened. If this is the case, this strategy calls for the client to reallocate assets to increase the rate of return on savings. Increasing the rate of return on investment assets will amplify the compounding of returns, which helps make an education goal more achievable.

Not all educational funding products allow a client to systematically change the asset allocation of savings to increase returns. For instance, many Section 529 savings plans use a fixed asset allocation based on the beneficiary's age. In other words, the risk exposure in the portfolio decreases as the beneficiary gets closer to college age. Also, if a *Roth IRA* or retirement plan is used to partially offset college costs, increasing the return may not match well with the return assumptions used in the retirement plan.

Procedural Strategy 12: Decrease Assumed College Inflation Rate

One factor that drives the future high cost of funding educational goals is the constant increase in the price of **tuition** and **fees**. One way to manipulate an educational funding analysis is to decrease the assumed rate of tuition inflation. Doing so will make the future cost of education appear more affordable; that is, the amount of savings necessary will be less. The **inflation rate** for college costs varies over time and by type of institution, but valid data on which to base

> ### Self-Test 5
>
> Which of the following educational tax credits is Liana eligible to receive if her adjusted gross income is $185,000 and she is single?
>
> a. American Opportunity Tax Credit
>
> b. Hope Scholarship Tax Credit
>
> c. Lifetime Learning Tax Credit
>
> d. None of the above.

assumptions are available. However, once a reasonable inflation rate has been chosen, it is unwise to "cook" the numbers simply to assuage a client's concerns. A better alternative is to explain the discrepancy in funding the education goal and to consider other alternatives.

This is a complicated strategy that should be used only in extreme cases where the cost of college is significantly more than the projected future value of client educational assets. In effect, decreasing the tuition inflation rate assumption goes against twenty years of historical data, which suggest that tuition costs will continue to rise, with some projections indicating double-digit increases. But it may give the client some solace that their efforts will pay off as long as the actual rate of inflation is less than originally projected.

Procedural Strategy 13: Assign the Correct Priority to Paying off Student Loan Debt

Because the interest rate on student loans is in many cases substantially lower than other forms of borrowing, the cost of servicing this debt is relatively inexpensive. The debtor may be better served by maximizing cash flows to other goals, such as building an emergency fund, rather than paying off the student loan debt more quickly. This will enhances liquidity and reduces the likelihood that other, more expensive types of borrowing are incurred because of unforeseen circumstances. By diverting money from student loan debt service, the borrower will incur greater interest expense over the life of the loan. However, the interest might be tax deductible.

Procedural Strategy 14: Use Educational Tax Credits Appropriately

The **American Opportunity Tax Credit** (AOTC) was originally introduced as an enhancement to the **Hope Scholarship Tax Credit**. The AOTC is scheduled to expire at the beginning of 2018. Currently, the AOTC allows a tax credit up to 100 percent of qualified tuition and related expenses for each eligible student up to a maximum of $2,500. Additionally, up to 40 percent of the credit may be refundable. The *tax credit* can be used for four years of an eligible student's postsecondary education. Generally, the credit can be claimed if a client pays qualified tuition and related higher education expenses for an eligible student (including the client). The availability of the credit phases out when modified adjusted gross income (MAGI) reaches $90,000 for a single filer and $180,000 for joint filers. It is important to remember that those who file "married filing separately" may not claim the tax credit.[14]

The **Lifetime Learning Tax Credit (LLTC)** allows clients to claim a credit on 20 percent of the first $10,000 in college expenses. The maximum credit of $2,000 is per taxpayer. Expenses such as room and board, insurance, and transportation are not eligible. The LLTC is useful for clients who are funding a child's or their own education to acquire or enhance job skills. This can include part-time enrollment in college courses, trade school courses, and graduate courses. Income phase outs apply. In 2016, single taxpayers with income exceeding $65,000 and married taxpayers with incomes in excess of $130,000 were not eligible for the credit.

Procedural Strategy 15: Mitigate the Funding Need with Financial Aid

In some situations, a client's situational factors or beliefs could require a planner to determine alternatives to cover the projected cost of education, but in other cases the estimated cost of education may be so exorbitant that additional, cost mitigation methods are necessary. An important service a planner can provide is to help a client better understand the financial aid system and how planning choices can affect the likelihood of receiving aid. It is likely that nearly all clients (or their children) will apply for financial aid at some point in the educational planning process. In fact, this should be encouraged, regardless of family income.

It is important that parents and children start to discuss acceptable college costs early, and financial aid planning should begin in earnest no later than the child's junior year in high school. The longer planning is postponed, the more likely the chance to exercise certain strategies to increase financial aid offers will be lost. The following discussion highlights some of the most popular forms of financial aid available today and how a client, working with a financial planner, can assess the current situation to determine financial aid availability.

The first step involves understanding the basic financial aid application process. Information related to parent and student income and assets is input into a form called the **Free Application for Federal Student Aid (FAFSA)**, which can be opened, completed, and saved at the Department of Education Web site.[15] (Some private colleges and universities also require families to complete a **College Scholarship Service (CSS)/Financial Aid Form**). Once the application has been completed online or via paper submission, a *Student Aid Report* is sent to the client. This report provides the client with an **expected family contribution (EFC),** an indicator of a family's ability to pay for college. Schools use it to determine a student's eligibility for various financial assistance programs.

Eligibility may vary among schools. If the cost of college is higher than the EFC, the student could be eligible for need-based student financial aid. Four financial factors influence the expected family contribution for a dependent student: (1) the parents' income; (2) the parents' assets; (3) the child's income; and (4) the child's assets. Parental income includes all sources of income, taxable and nontaxable, received by the parents in the previous year. Certain adjustments are made.

Because student status is significant in determining financial aid, it is important to understand the difference between a dependent and an independent student. Except for some exceptional circumstances, a student is considered a **dependent student** for financial aid purposes unless one of the criteria for independent student status is met. For financial aid purposes, students are not automatically independent if parents stop claiming them as a tax exemption or refuse to provide support for college education. A common misconception is that not being claimed on a parent's income tax for two years establishes the child as an independent student. *Tax status and federal financial aid status are not the same.* To qualify as an **independent student** for financial aid purposes, children must:

> *Self-Test 6*
>
> Jelen joined the US Marines right out of high school. He is now 21 years of age and applying for financial aid at a local college. Which of the following applies to Jelen?
>
> a. He qualifies as an independent student?
>
> b. Given his age, he is considered a dependent student.
>
> c. If he uses resources from his family he will be considered a dependent students.
>
> d. He only qualifies as an independent student if he is also married.

- be twenty-four years of age or older during the year they apply for financial aid;

- be married;

- have legal dependents of their own (i.e., provide more than half of their support);

- be enrolled in graduate school;

- since turning age thirteen, be a ward of the court, be in foster care, or have both parents deceased;

- be a veteran of the U.S armed forces or serving on active duty;

- be (or have been) an emancipated minor or in legal guardianship;

- be homeless or at risk of being homeless as defined (criteria apply); or

- be judged "independent" by a university administrator, even though the preceding criteria do not apply but documentation for the extenuating circumstance is provided.

A questionnaire to determine dependency is available at www.finaid.org/calculators/dependency.phtml.

Procedural Strategy 16: Identify How Traditional IRA Accounts can be Used for Education Planning

There is no hard-and-fast rule about the best time to convert a traditional IRA to a Roth IRA (a *Roth conversion*); however, there is a worst possible time—while your clients' children are in college. Qualified retirement accounts are excluded from assets when calculating the EFC for financial aid; however, income derived from those sources is not. So, although a distribution from IRAs to pay qualified educational expenses is allowable and therefore will not trigger a tax penalty, it will count as income and could affect the income component of the EFC the following year.

A lesser-known consideration is the impact of conversion. Converting a traditional IRA to a Roth IRA is a taxable event. In other words, the amount of the conversion is typically taxable as ordinary income in the year of conversion, although there have been numerous temporary changes to this rule. So a planner must consider long-term tax implications of IRA distributions and conversions to the account owner, as well as the near-term financial aid implications to the dependent student of the account owner.

Self-Test 7

Which of the following will have the greatest impact on a family's expected contribution for funding college expenses?

a. A grandparent's 529 plan held for one of the family's children.

b. A $10,000 529 plan account balance held by a parent for a child.

c. $20,000 held in an UGMA account.

d. $250,000 held in a 401(k) plan by a parent.

Procedural Strategy 17: Evaluate the Impact Asset Ownership Can Have on an Educational Plan and Financial Aid

Tax planning and education planning may be the most difficult financial objectives to jointly optimize, because many of the most attractive options from an ongoing income tax liability perspective (e.g., Section 529 plans, CESAs) could interfere with the ability to also claim an education tax credit. Figure 11.3 summarizes this information for some of the more widely used funding alternatives.

Figure 11.3 Potential Impact of Asset Ownership on Financial Aid and Tax Credits

Educational Savings Plan	Change in Expected Family Contribution	Hope and Lifetime Learning Tax Credit Impact
Assets Owned by the Dependent Student		
UGMA/UTMA	Increased (20% of balance)*	No impact
§ 529 savings plan (UGMA/UTMA)	Increased (2.6% – 5.6% of balance)*	Expenses paid with distribution cannot be claimed for tax credit**
Coverdell Education Savings Account (CESA)	Increased (2.6 %– 5.6% of balance)*	Expenses paid with distribution cannot be claimed for tax credit**
Crummey trust[1]	Increased (20% of balance)*	No impact
Assets Owned by the Parent		
§ 529 savings plan	Increased (2.6% – 5.6% of balance)*	Expenses paid with distribution cannot be claimed for tax credit**
Series EE savings bonds (tax-free education withdrawals)	Increased (2.6% – 5.6% of balance)*	Expenses paid with distribution cannot be claimed for tax credit**
Retirement plans	None	No impact
Variable universal life insurance	None	No impact
Assets Owned by Others (e.g., Grandparent) but with Student as Beneficiary		
§ 529 savings plan	None***	Expenses paid with distributions cannot be claimed for tax credit**

*Hurley, Joseph F. (2011). *Family guide to college savings 2011–2012*, JFH Innovative, LLC, Pittsford, NY.

**Clients can take distributions from these plans. However, distributions must be spent on expenses not already claimed with the Hope or Lifetime Learning Credits.

***Distributions from plans owned by a third party will be added back as income on the FAFSA.

1. A Crummey trust allows the beneficiary a window of opportunity to access the gift made, thereby completing the gift and removing the donated amount from the estate of the donor, although the intent is for the money to remain in the trust for a specified purpose or time period.

Procedural Strategy 18: Prioritize Strategies to Help Clients Meet their Education Funding Goals

Developing education planning recommendations follows the same general process used in other areas of financial planning. Specifically, education planning recommendations flow directly from a client's primary education funding objective. Recommendations should evolve from both a quantitative analysis of a client's current situation and a review of situational factors, such as the expectations of the child receiving financial aid, the client's willingness to fund certain expenses while not funding others, and the level of control a client wishes to maintain over assets and savings. These personal expectations and attitudes strongly influence the type of recommendations that are most suitable for a client.

The process of combining education funding strategies into one or more client-specific recommendations depends on a number of factors. At least initially, the choice of appropriate strategies may be driven by the education planning need. Figure 11.4 illustrates a hierarchical approach that can be used to select appropriate strategies for a client recommendation.

Figure 11.4: Ranking and Using Education Funding Strategies

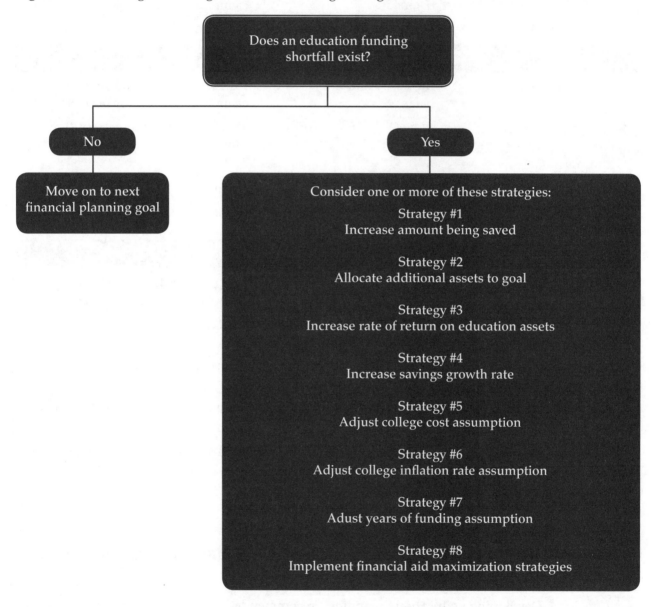

Before a recommendation is presented to a client, steps should be taken to confirm that the recommendation meets both the education funding need and the client's stated expectations. For instance, recommending that a client reduce the college cost assumption to make funding feasible could run contrary to a client's strong desire to have the child attend an expensive university. It may be better, in a situation similar to this, to determine whether the client would be willing to maintain the high cost assumption but realize that only a portion of the child's education costs can be funded. Such a candid approach helps the planner more effectively manage client expectations. It also enables the client to consider other options to maximize goal funding relative to any trade-offs in lifestyle that may be called for or the attainment of other goals. An overriding objective of comprehensive financial planning is to empower clients to make these decisions more effectively.

Education Planning for Special Populations

Thoughts on Planning for College Education Challenges

Rapidly increasing college costs coupled with a weak stock market and poor employment conditions have parents and students anxious about college costs and college debt. It is important that students and planners be familiar with a variety of education planning strategies. Consider the following ideas for targeted client groups:

Divorced Parents. According to an article in the *Journal of Family Issues*, parental contributions to education funding decline after divorce.[16] Married parents meet 77 percent of tuition costs and contribute about 8 percent of their income to a child's college expenses, whereas divorced parents meet only 42 percent of their children's financial needs and contribute only about 6 percent of their income.[17] This is attributable to all of the usual factors, but the resultant impact on education planning can be mitigated by careful divorce planning.

State laws differ in their treatment of parental support for education; some may require payments for college expenses, although most do not. Without an agreement in the divorce decree, there may be no legal requirement for educational expense assistance. Financial aid officers may require documentation of the noncustodial parent's legal obligation to assist with college expenses, because financial aid depends on only the custodial parent's (and, if applicable, the new spouse's) income and assets unless there is legal documentation of required support.

Parents with Credit Issues: Whereas unsubsidized Stafford loans do not require a credit check, collateral, or cosigner for the student, this is not true for PLUS loans, which are offered to parents. (It should be noted, however, that students who are currently in default on any federal student loans may not be eligible to receive any form of federal financial aid.) Parents who have a weak credit history because of late payments, foreclosure, or other issues related to the market downturn or loss of employment will likely be ineligible. In this case, once the parent is denied, the child will be eligible to borrow a maximum of $57,500 total debt via Stafford loans, the same amount as an independent undergraduate, instead of the maximum $31,000 available to a dependent undergraduate. Regardless of a student's status, the subsidized Stafford loan amount, if eligible, is limited to $23,000. Annual limits apply and the maximum loan amount is not guaranteed. Private student loans are another alternative, but they lack the consumer protections of federal loans, so shopping to compare terms and conditions is important.

Parents with credit issues may be well served to write or visit the financial aid office to explain how recent events such as unemployment, reduction of income, or other circumstances have negatively impacted their capacity to pay for college expenses and to request reconsideration for financial aid. It is also important to remind clients that EFC and award packages are unique to each institution, and in some cases, flexibility regarding awards rests with the financial aid administrator.

Parents with High-school-age Students: The recommendation to "start early" typically refers to saving for college, but it also applies to setting parameters for which colleges or universities are or are not affordable. In fact, this conversation should occur two to three years *before* high school graduation for several reasons. First, it avoids the emotional dilemma when a parent and child must agree that an institution, perhaps the child's top choice, is simply too expensive to consider. Second, it can motivate the child to more proactively develop a competitive application for the schools identified or to be more responsible in seeking employment or saving for college expenses. Finally, narrowing the list saves on the cost of visits to schools and application fees, although these are marginal expenses.

Deborah Fox of Fox College Funding LLC suggests that a "college match" can yield significant savings, perhaps as much as the cost of a year or more. This idea means perhaps not applying to the parents' alma mater or the big-name state university, but to select colleges where academic record, talents, extracurricular activities, or field of study place the student in the top 20 to 25 percent of applicants.[18] This strategy yields merit aid—another form of financial aid that is not need-based—and could be available at private or public institutions.

Parents with Children in College. Results of a Fidelity Investments® fifth national College Savings Indicator study revealed that more parents and children are making sacrifices to pay for college compared to anytime in the recent past. Consider the startling statistics:[19]

- 59 percent report having a child work part-time, compared to 49 percent in 2007;

- 48 percent report having a child live at home and commute, compared to 38 percent in 2007;

- 46 percent report asking the child to help pay for college, compared to 36 percent in 2007;

- 44 percent report asking the child to graduate in fewer semesters, compared to 13 percent in 2007;

- 44 percent report encouraging the child to attend a public college or university, compared to 34 percent in 2007;

- 18 percent report having the nonworking spouse go back to work, as opposed to 11 percent in 2007; and

- 17 percent report a parent getting a second job, compared to 11 percent in 2007.

Planning for education typically focuses on principles related to timing (start early), taxes (take advantage of tax-deferred accounts), and priorities (there are more options to fund education than retirement). But the true value of the planner-client relationship may be more evident in the creativity to suggest additional funding alternatives, such as those listed above, and to help clients recognize that they or their children are not alone in making lifestyle changes to fund education.

Quantitative/Analytical Mini-Case Problems

Johanna and Ryan Younan

1. Johanna and Ryan just put their two boys (grades 6 and 2) on their respective school buses for the first day of school and realized that they are growing up fast. So they called you and stated that they wanted to save, starting today, at the beginning of every month for the next six years (until the older child goes to college) to pay for one-half of school expenses for both children. You know that tuition, room, and board this year cost $18,000 at their selected school, and you expect 5 percent effective annual inflation for education expenses. They also said that they know the children's grandparents are going to make a gift of $48,000 toward this cause in exactly three years.

    Assume that both children attend the same college for four years each. Also assume that the annual tuition bill is due at the beginning of each academic year, and the first payment is exactly seventy-two months away. How much money will they need to invest on a monthly basis to meet their education goal assuming a required effective annual rate of 10.471 percent (10 percent APR with monthly compounding)?

Balik Antone

2. Balik Atone, a new financial planning client, wants to begin a savings program for her eight-year-old son. She has been reading about the various accounts available for college savings programs, but she is confused about which type of account would be best. Her primary concerns are taxes, account ownership, and flexibility. She has developed a list of questions that she would like answered at the next meeting.

    a. Which account would allow for the greatest flexibility given that she is a single mother, is not expecting to have any additional children, and is not absolutely certain that her son will attend college?

    b. Given the following account assumptions, which account would require the lowest monthly contribution to attain her goal of saving $50,000 in ten years? (The savings goal ends at the beginning of her son's first year of college.) Assume that she makes a fixed payment at the end of each month for the next 120 months. Also assume that any account set-up fees or annual fees are paid on a monthly basis in addition to the required savings deposit.

	Account Type		
	Nonqualified	Roth IRA	§ 529 plan
Projected market gross annual return	9.5%	9.5%	9.5%
Annual expense ratio (target date fund)	0.0%	1.1%	1.1%
Program fees*	0.0%	0.0%	0.6%
Annual account fee	$0	$12.00	$24.00
Annual applicable tax rate**	20.0%	0.0%	0.0%
*Program fees include management and state administration fees.			
**Assume that all withdrawals from qualified accounts are used for a qualified purpose and therefore are not subject to income tax or early withdrawal penalties.			

c.   Depending on the account type chosen in part b, who should "own" the account, assuming her son has earned income? Consider both financial aid eligibility and flexibility of use.

Broderick Baatz

3.   Broderick Baatz, an independent student, graduated from college in May 2016 with $37,000 (not including accrued interest charges) in unsubsidized Stafford Loan debt and realized that he is in over his head. He has come to you for answers. Answer the questions based on the following disbursement schedule:

Disbursement Date	Total Disbursement Amount	Interest Rate
Aug 2012	$8,000	6.8%
Aug 2013	$9,000	6.8%
Aug 2014	$10,000	6.8%
Aug 2015	$10,000	6.8%

a.   What was the actual aggregated balance on his loans the August after he graduated?

b.   What is the monthly payment if he chooses the standard ten-year repayment plan?

c.   How much will he pay in total to pay off the aggregate loan? How much interest will he pay, assuming all payments are made as agreed?

d.   What is the monthly payment if he chooses the extended twenty-year repayment plan?

e.   How much will he pay in total to pay off the aggregate loan? How much interest will he pay, assuming all payments are made as agreed?

f.   How much additional interest would Broderick pay if he chose the extended payment option?

Rahel Osei

4.   Rahel Osei, a dependent student, graduated from college in May 2015 with the maximum ($31,000) allowable amount in Stafford Loan debt; however, this was far less than the total cost of her schooling. Additionally, her parents had planned far enough in advance that Rahel demonstrated each year sufficient financial need to qualify for the maximum amount under the subsidized loan program. Her parents are wondering how much their planning paid off, so they have posed the following questions to you. Base your analysis on the disbursement schedule.

Disbursement Date	Total Disbursement Amount	Subsidized Amount	Unsubsidized Interest Rate	Subsidized Interest Rate
Aug 2012	$5,500	$3,500	6.8% (APR)	6.8% (APR)
Aug 2013	$6,500	$4,500	6.8%	6.0%
Aug 2014	$7,500	$5,500	6.8%	5.6%
Aug 2015	$7,500	$5,500	6.8%	4.5%

a.   What was the actual total balance on her loans the August after she graduated?

b.   How much total interest did Rahel avoid on her subsidized loans during college and since her graduation (the subsidy continues during the six-month grace period) as a result of the subsidy?

c.   What is the combined monthly payment, based on the standard ten0-year repayment plan, for her subsidized loans?

d.   What would her combined monthly payment have been if her loans had not been subsidized? (Although not completely accurate, assume that the balance in August was still the same.)

e.   How much additional interest would Rahel have paid if she had not qualified for any subsidized loans?

f.   How much was the subsidy worth? (Hint: Add the answer in part b to the answer in part e.)

Comprehensive Bedo Case—Analysis Questions

Determining the Bedos' education funding need is fundamentally a comparison of total assets needed and the total value of assets saved to date. The Bedos want to fund 100 percent of four years of college for Becky, who is age five and is assumed to start college at age eightee. The current cost of college is $10,000 per semester. It will be important to review the following: assets currently used for education funding, the rate of return on assets used for education funding, the growth rate of savings, and the assumed rate of inflation for college costs.

Once the cost of their education goal has been established, planning strategies must be incorporated into a recommendation to empower the Bedos to achieve it. It is essential to review the case for assumptions regarding which assets they are willing to allocate to their education funding goal and to ascertain the maximum amount of risk they are willing to take with their education fund assets.

Use the following questions to guide the education planning process.

1. Develop one or more education planning goals for the Bedo household. When conceptualizing this goal(s), consider the following:

   a. Is the goal(s) developed in agreement with any or all goals and objectives that the clients have identified regarding education planning?

   b. What situational factors might influence their education planning goal? Are these factors explicit, implied, or assumed? Is additional information required from the Bedos, and if so, what?

   c. What is the desired education planning outcome for the clients?

2. Are there globally accepted, client-specific, or planner-generated planning assumptions that will influence the education planning situation analysis? List the assumptions as they might appear in a plan.

3. To determine and quantify the Bedos' current education planning need, thoroughly consider the following:

   a. The future value of one year of college when Becky turns age eighteen

   b. The total amount of assets needed when Becky turns eighteen to fully fund four years of college

   c. The amount the Bedos need to save annually to meet their education goal(s)

4. List and discuss some of the advantages and disadvantages associated with an in-state Section 529 plan. Should the Bedos consider plans offered by other states, and if so, which state?

5. Summarize your observations about Tyler's and Mia's current education planning efforts and the planning need(s) identified. Incorporate text, bullets, and graphics in your explanation. For example, what information might be shown graphically, and specifically what kind of graphs might convey the analysis to the Bedos most effectively?

6. Based on the goals originally identified and the completed analysis, which product or procedural strategies might be most useful to satisfy the Bedos' education planning needs? Be sure to consider strategies matched to the planning needs identified. When reviewing strategies, be careful to consider the approximate cost of implementation as well as the most likely outcome(s) associated with each strategy.

7. Write at least one primary and one alternative recommendation from the selected strategies in response to each identified planning need. Include specific, defensible answers to the who, what, when, where, why, how, and how much implementation questions for each recommendation.

a.   It is suggested that each recommendation be summarized in a recommendation form.

b.   Assign a priority to each recommendation based on the likelihood of meeting client goals and desired outcomes. This priority will be important when recommendations from other core planning content areas are considered in relation to the discretionary funds available for subsidizing all recommendations.

c.   Comment briefly on the outcomes associated with each recommendation.

8.   Complete the following for the Education Planning section of the Bedos' financial plan.

a.   Outline the content to be included in this section of the plan. Given the segments written above, which segments are missing?

b.   Write the introduction to this section of the plan (no more than one or two paragraphs).

c.   Define, explain, or interpret at least five terms or concepts related to education planning. For each, write a definition or explanation that could appear in this section of the plan or in the plan glossary.

9.   Prepare a ten- to fifteen-minute presentation for the Bedos of your observations and/or recommendation(s) regarding their education planning. Be sure to include visual aids or handouts.

Chapter Resources

Bassonette, Zac. *Debt-Free U: How I Paid for an Outstanding College Education Without Loans, Scholarships, or Mooching off My Parents.* New York, Penguin Group, 2010.

Darvis, Rick. *College Solution: A Roadmap to Selecting Your Best Strategy to Fund College And Retirement...without Going Broke.* Mason City, IA, Stone People Publishing Co., 2005.

Department of Education, *2012–2013 Expected Family Contribution Formula Guide* (January 2012 Update) can be found at: www.ifap.ed.gov/efcformulaguide/attachments/010512EFCFormula Guide1213.pdf.

Federal student financial aid information can be found at www.studentaid.ed.gov.

For information regarding tax benefits for education, see IRS Publication 970, available online at: www.irs.gov/publications/p970/index.html.

Information about student loans and the Free Application for Federal Student Aid (FAFSA) can be found at www.fafsa.ed.gov.

Information about loans available for higher education can be found at www.finaid.org.

National Institute of Certified College Planners (NICCP) can be found at: university.niccp.com/default.aspx.

The Princeton Review and Kalman Chany. *Paying for College Without Going Broke, 2012 Edition (College Admissions Guides)*. Framingham, MA: The Princeton Review, 2011.

Self-Test Answers

1: a, 2: a, 3: d, 4: d, 5: a, 6: c.

Endnotes

1. This process assumes that periodic savings payments occur at the end of each period; that periodic saving payments for college will cease when the child begins college; and that the annual college expense payment occurs at the beginning of each school year. All of these assumptions can be changed to fit the individual situation, but corresponding changes in the calculations will be necessary.

2. An effective annual rate (EAR) of 8.30% is equivalent to an 8% rate compounded monthly.

3. Department of Education, Student Loans Overview, *Fiscal Year 2012 Budget Request*. Available at: www2.ed.gov/about/overview/budget/budget12/justifications/s-loansoverview.pdf, p. S-12.

4. FinAid, The Smart Student™ Guide to Financial Aid. *Student Loans*. Available at: www.finaid.org/loans/studentloan.phtml.

5. FinAid, The Smart Student™ Guide to Financial Aid. *Parent Loans*. Available at: www.finaid.org/loans/parentloan.phtml and edvisors.com. See also "Interest Rates and Fees on PLUS Loans:, available at: www.edvisors.com/college-loans/federal/parent-plus/interest-rates/.

6. Department of Education. Federal Student Aid. Direct Loans. *Repayment Plans*. Available at: www.direct.ed.gov/RepayCalc/dlindex2.html.

7. Department of Education, *Repayment Plans*.

8. *Id.*

9. *Id.*

10. *Id.*

11. Equal Justice Works. *Partial Financial Hardship*. Available at: www.equaljusticeworks.org/resources/student-debt-relief/income-based-repayment/partial-financial-hardship.

12. FinAid, The Smart Student™ Guide to Financial Aid. *Health Care and Education Reconciliation Act of 2010*. Available at: www.finaid.org/educators/20100330hcera.phtml.

13. Joseph F. Hurley, *Family Guide to College Savings 2011–2012* (Pittsford, NY: JFH Innovative, 2011), 66.

14. Additional information is available online at IRS, *American Opportunity Credit*, at: www.irs.gov/publications/p970/ch02.html#d0e1386.

15. See www.fafsa.ed.gov.

16. R. Turley and M. Desmond, "Contributions to College Costs by Married, Divorced, and Remarried Parents," *Journal of Family Issues* 32, no. 6 (2011): 767–790.

17. R. Turley and M. Desmond, "Contributions to College Costs."

18. Donald Jay Korn, Financial Planning, *College Panic*. Available at: www.financial-planning.com/fp_issues/2009_8/college-panic-2663445-1.html. For additional information, see Deborah Fox, Financial Planning, *Coming up Short*. Available at: www.financial-planning.com/fp_issues/2009_1/coming-up-short2638481-1.html.

19. Fidelity.com, *Fidelity® Study Finds Significant Shifts Over Five-Year Period in How Families Tackle Rising College Costs*. Available at: www.fidelity.com/inside-fidelity/individual-investing/csi-2011.

Chapter 12

Retirement Planning

Learning Objectives

1. This chapter highlights the importance of retirement planning in the comprehensive financial planning process. For nearly all clients, planning and saving for retirement requires a significant commitment to resource allocation. In addition to issues related to the use of cash flow to build a retirement nest egg, clients, working with their financial planner, must also grapple with questions related to housing preferences, recreational choices, and overall lifestyle factors as they plan for retirement. Clients who postpone tasks associated with retirement planning will find that the strategies, tools, and techniques available to reach retirement goals are limited. Financial planners can serve their clientele well by promoting early and ongoing retirement planning activities.

2. Although retirement planning entails a high degree of quantitative analysis, it is essential that financial planners account for client situational factors that could uniquely affect a client's retirement planning goals. As illustrated in this chapter, the following lifestyle issues can impact the process associated with retirement planning: retirement attitudes, early retirement aspirations, postretirement work attitudes, leisure activity hopes and dreams, health status, and relocation preferences.

3. Conducting a retirement capital needs analysis is a key aspect of the retirement planning process. The steps involved in calculating capital depletion, capital preservation, and inflation-adjusted approaches require the application of time value of money concepts. It is each financial planner's responsibility to develop assumptions related to rates of return, inflation, life expectancy, and timing of payments, and to balance these assumptions against each client's retirement aspirations and financial goals.

4. Competent financial planners must have a sufficient working knowledge of the Social Security system to help their clients plan for retirement. Even for

Learning Objectives

clients with other sources of retirement income, Social Security benefits tend to be a significant source of fixed income during retirement. Because of this, issues related to retiring either before or after their normal retirement age create complexities that require planners to incorporate both qualitative and quantitative client data into distribution analyses. It is not enough to rely on general planning rules when helping clients make decisions related to the timing of retirement or the receipt of Social Security benefits. Rather, when making Social Security recommendations, financial planners must account for a client's life expectancy, the need for Social Security benefits as a source of income, the probability a client will work while retired, and other factors.

5. Although qualified retirement plans such as 401(k) arrangements often dominate how clients think about saving for retirement, it is important for financial planners to understand that retirement savings can occur using both qualified and non-qualified products. Qualified plans provide an immediate tax reduction and tax deferral for plan participants; further, employers receive a current tax deduction for qualified plan contributions. These features make qualified plans attractive options for most clients as they begin to save for retirement. Unfortunately, qualified plans come with many restrictions; caps on employee and employer contributions are significant constraints. As such, financial planners may find that non-qualified products can be used to help clients more effectively reach their retirement goals. Annuity products and non-qualified plans (e.g., rabbi

and secular trusts) can be added to the product mix to help ensure that clients are best able to reach their retirement goals, and once in retirement, maintain an adequate standard of living.

7. Although the tendency of many financial planners—and their clients—is to focus on capital accumulation issues in the retirement planning process, it is equally important to develop retirement plan withdrawal strategies that match a client's income needs and life expectancy. Deterministic modeling techniques can be used to generate simplified income distribution projections. These projections can be presented to clients mathematically and graphically. Planners should also be familiar with stochastic modeling theory as an alternative to deterministic approaches to distribution planning.

8. Rules related to qualified plan and IRA distributions are complex. Factors related to early retirement, job transfers, and the use of plan assets for nonretirement purposes each have an impact on a client's retirement plan, as well as tax and cash flow implications. Understanding what might trigger a taxable distribution and federal tax penalty is considered a minimal standard of competency for financial planners. In addition, the ability to identify and calculate required minimum distributions (RMDs), exceptions to distribution rules, and QDRO exemptions is an essential skill for financial planners. Finally, understanding issues related to IRA rollovers and annuity distribution alternatives represent a characteristic of competency among financial planners.

Key Terms

10 Percent Penalty

401(k) Plan

403(b) Tax-Sheltered Annuity

457 Plan

Age 70½

Annual Additions

Annuities

Annuitization

Annuity Payouts

Average Indexed Monthly Earnings (AIME)

Capital Depletion Approach

Capital Depletion Withdrawal Method

Capital Needs Analysis

Capital Preservation Approach

Capital Preservation Method

Mapital Withdrawal Process

Claim-and-Suspend

Client Situational Factors

Combined Social Security Income

Compensation for IRA Purposes

Conversion

Deferred Income Annuity (DIA)

Defined Benefit Plan

Defined Contribution

Delay Social Security

Deterministic Models

Disclaim

Early Distribution Penalty

Elective Deferral

Employee Retirement Income Security Act (ERISA)

Employee Stock Ownership Plan (ESOP)

Employer-Sponsored Plan

Exclusion Ratio

Fiduciary

Fixed Annuity

Fixed Payment Annuity

Forfeitures

Fully Insured

Glide Path Portfolio

Guaranteed Annuities

Guaranteed Lifetime Annuity

Health Status

Highly Compensated Employee (HCE)

Home Equity

Inclusion Ratio

Individual Retirement Arrangement (IRA)

Inflation-Adjusted Capital Preservation Approach

Inherited IRA

IRA Asset Protection

IRS Publication 590

Key Terms

Joint and Last Survivor Life Expectancy
  Table

Joint and Survivor Annuity

Keogh Plan

Key Employee

Legacy

Legacy Pool

Life Annuity

Life with Period Certain Annuity

Longevity Annuity

Lump Sum Distribution

Maximum Annual Addition

Minimum Required Distribution (MRD)

Money Purchase Plan

Monte Carlo Modeling

Non-Qualified Deferred Compensation
  Plan (NQDC)

Non-Qualified Plan

Non-Random Deterministic Withdrawal
  Model

Non-Spouse Beneficiary

Normal Retirement Age (NRA)

Pension Benefit Guaranty Corporation
  (PBGC)

Pension Maximization

Pension Plan

Pensions

Period-Certain Annuity

PIA

Postpone Retirement

Primary Insurance Amount

Profit-Sharing Plan

Qualified Domestic Relations Order
  (QDRO)

Qualified Longevity Annuity Contract

Qualified Plan Coverage Rules

Qualified Retirement Plans

Rabbi Trust

Recharacterization

Replacement Ratio

Required Minimum Distribution

Retirement Annuity

Retirement Assets

Retirement Capital Needs Analysis

Retirement Income Funding Goal

Retirement Planning

Reverse Mortgage

Rollover

Roth 401(k)

Roth IRA Conversion

Safe Harbor 401(k) Plan

Secular Trust

Sequence Risk

Shortfall Risk

Key Terms

SIMPLE 401(k) Plan

Simplified Employee Pension

Social Security

Social Security Administration

Social Security Benefit Estimator

Social Security Benefits

Spousal Benefit

Step Transaction Doctrine

Stochastic Modeling

Stochastic Retirement Withdrawal Models

Stock Bonus Plan

Survivor Social Security Benefits

Target-Date Maturity Funds

Tax-Free Funding Level

Three-Legged Stool

Transfer

Transfer Incident to Divorce

Trustee-to-Trustee Transfer

Uniform Lifetime Table

Unit-Benefit Formula

Variable Annuity

Variable Universal Life (VUL) Insurance

Younger Spouse Exception

CFP® Principal Knowledge Topics

D.27. Annuities

G.52. Retirement Needs Analysis

G.53. Social Security and Medicare

G.55. Types of Retirement Plans

G.56. Qualified Plan Rules and Options

G.57. Other Tax-Advantaged Retirement Plans

G.58. Regulatory Considerations

G.59. Key Factors Affecting Plan Selection for Businesses

G.60. Distribution Rules and Taxation

G.61. Retirement Income and Distribution Strategies

Chapter Equations

Equation 12.1: Present value of a growing annuity $PVGA_n = \dfrac{PMT_1}{(i-g)} \left[1 - \dfrac{(1+g)^n}{(1+i)^n} \right] (1+i)$

Equation 12.2: Present Value $PV_n = \dfrac{FV}{(1+i)^n}$

Equation 12.3: Serial Rate $= \dfrac{(1+i)}{(1+g)} - 1$

RETIREMENT PLANNING: DETERMINING THE NEED

When viewed historically, **retirement planning**—the process of helping a client to define and prepare for retirement by developing strategies for asset accumulation, asset distribution, and monitoring of plan progress—can be seen as a relatively new phenomenon. Prior to the industrial revolution, people rarely planned to retire in the way retirement is defined today, nor did they live as long to spend as many years in retirement. Nearly everyone worked until they could work no longer. Those who did outlive their working careers relied on the charity of family, friends, religious groups, or community resources for assistance with elder needs. Today, beyond leaving one's primary source of employment, which most agree on, retirement can mean pursuing part-time or full-time employment in the same or a different occupation. Or it can mean pursuing leisure or volunteer activities. Although retirement activities can vary widely, for most people retirement represents a longer life segment—offering both opportunities and challenges.

Depending on an individual financial planner's business model and scope of services provided, retirement planning services can focus on one or two perspectives: the employer's or the employee's. In some situations, a client can be both. Financial planners can also advise employees who might be constrained by plan offerings through their employers. In some cases, planners must seek better alternatives because of plan limitations. This chapter provides an overview of the analysis and evaluation process undertaken by financial planners when reviewing a client's current retirement planning situation. This chapter also reviews common retirement planning strategies that can be used to meet retirement objectives. Because the average working client is the main focus, little attention is given to planning for clients who are self-employed, owners/partners in a closely held business, or highly compensated executives who might have privileged "golden handcuffs" or other non-qualified plan arrangements that can affect the timing of and resources available for retirement.

Prior to beginning a quantitative retirement analysis, either pre- or post-retirement, it is important to review lifestyle and client situational factors that may impact retirement planning assumptions. Client situational factors to consider from the perspective of the client and spouse, partner, or significant other include the following:

- attitude about retiring, or specifically about retiring early;

- motivation for retiring or retiring early;

- willingness to continue working in another firm or industry;

- willingness to establish a consulting practice or other business venture;

- types of personal, leisure, or volunteer activities that the individual(s) would engage in while retired;

- health status;

- willingness to relocate, either to a specific designation or to a lower-cost area; and

- willingness or need to provide support for other family members (e.g., children, grandchildren, parents, in-laws).

Although all pre-retirees should analyze the following quantitative financial factors to assess fiscal readiness, those considering early retirement must carefully consider the:

- ability of their accumulated asset base, plus other forms of income, to provide adequate retirement income;

- impact of early retirement on Social Security benefits;

- impact of early retirement on defined benefit plan distributions;

- effect of retirement on health benefits;

- impact of early retirement on the working status of a spouse or partner;

- tax implications of lump-sum benefits (e.g., unused sick and vacation days) received from an employer; and

- relocation and retirement transition expenses.

Retirement Needs Calculations

Once a client and planner have envisioned the ideal—or perhaps most likely—lifestyle and income picture for retirement, considering both the active and inactive years associated with aging, attention must turn to quantifying the cost of the projected retirement need. Fundamentally, *retirement planning* involves (a) documenting a client's specific retirement income funding goal, (b) determining gross need over a client's life expectancy, and (c) determining whether the client is on track to meet the asset accumulation objective given all other assumptions about the funding situation. Although the analytical approach may appear straightforward, these three essential components of the projection must be accurately matched to a client's situation. Each is now briefly considered.

> **#Remember**
>
> Visit the following website to obtain an estimate of a client's life expectancy:
>
> socialsecurity.gov/planners/lifeexpectancy.html

The retirement needs analysis process begins by calculating an income or living expense **replacement ratio**. This is a widely used tool used by financial planners to estimate a client's *retirement income funding goal*. An accepted generalization is that a client will need 70 to 80 percent of currently available income in retirement. That is, the target should be to replace at least 70 percent of current income on the client's first day of retirement. In general, low- and high-income-earning households need the highest replacement ratios.

Assume, for example, that a client currently earns $169,000 annually. If it is determined that the client needs to replace 80 percent of this amount in retirement, their income funding goal becomes $135,200. This amount should be reduced by guaranteed sources of retirement income, such as expected defined benefit payments, Social Security, and annuity payments. The result is the dollar amount need in a capital needs analysis. Because the figure is in today's dollars, a future value estimate needs to be made using an inflation rate assumption and the number of periods between the retirement date and the current period as the period input.

Determining the gross pool of assets needed over a client's life expectancy involves conducting a traditional **retirement capital needs analysis**. This projection determines the capital needed from all sources to support a client's estimated retirement income requirement, while allowing for the effects of inflation over a client's life expectancy. Three types of *capital needs analysis* are typically used by financial planners: (1) capital depletion, (2) capital preservation, and (3) inflation-adjusted. Each is based on relatively simple time value of money equations.

The financial planner must make several assumptions, in consultation with the client, before calculating retirement estimates. The first assumption involves determining whether contributions toward the retirement goal will grow or remain fixed. That is to say, will each subsequent payment increase by a predetermined amount, such as the inflation rate? In effect, this assumption comes down to using a fixed annuity or a geometric varying annuity assumption. A second assumption involves the length of the retirement period or the number of years that the client will engage in saving for the goal. The third assumption involves determining the rate of return expected during retirement. Once these calculation inputs have been determined, the financial planner—again working closely with the client—must calculate the amount of the first retirement payment. The amount of this payment should be based on the client's current (or projected) income. The projection could simply be an estimated target value, such as a dollar figure (e.g., $100,000) or a percentage of current living expenses. Once all variables are known, the planner can calculate the amount required to fully fund the level of savings needed on an annual basis to meet the accumulated asset objective as of the retirement date.

To facilitate the presentation of these calculations, two loosely defined terms are used. First is the **retirement annuity**, which is the amount of money required to fund a client's retirement over a given period. Second is the **legacy pool**. This is the amount of money that a client wants remaining at the end of the retirement period. This could be the amount the client wants to bequeath to others.

The **capital depletion approach**, when used to estimate the capital required to fund income needs on the first day of retirement, assumes that at the end of the retirement planning period no additional client assets will remain available to the client or heirs. In other words, all client assets available for retirement will be depleted by the time of the client's death. Therefore, the legacy pool value will be zero and can be ignored for this approach. Here is an example.

> *Example:* Assume a client desires to fund a retirement account with enough money to last for thirty years. The financial planner knows that the client wants the first payment to be $100,000 and occur at the beginning of the first year of retirement. [The $100,000 figure can either be an assumption or it can be based on taking a client's current household income multiplied by the income replacement ratio, less any guaranteed forms of retirement income, such as Social Security, and inflated to the date of retirement (i.e., a future value calculation).] Further, the planner knows that subsequent payments are to increase 4 percent annually to keep pace with anticipated inflation. Assuming an effective annual rate of 10 percent, how much money will the client need at retirement? Using the present value of a growing annuity, it can be determined that the client requires $1,492,564.

Equation 12.1: Present value of a growing annuity $PVGA_n$

$$PVGA_n = \frac{PMT_1}{(i-g)} \left[1 - \frac{(1+g)^n}{(1+i)^n} \right] (1+i)$$

Where,

i = 10%

g = 4%

PMT_1 = $100,000

n = 30

$$PVGA_n = \frac{\$100,000}{(0.10 - 0.04)} \left[1 - \frac{(1.04)^{30}}{(1.10)^{30}} \right] (1.10) = \$1,492,564$$

The capital depletion method results in the lowest retirement annuity need because it is assumed that the client will deplete the account over the course of retirement. Many clients are uncomfortable with the fundamental assumption of depleting all assets over their life expectancy. First, there is the possibility of outliving the available assets. Second, the capital depletion approach leaves nothing as a legacy to heirs or charities. In cases where the minimum capital depletion scenario can be satisfied with asset projections, the financial planner should also calculate the retirement need using the **capital preservation approach**.

To determine the legacy pool needed to preserve a client's capital so that the client's asset base does not decline during retirement, the financial planner must conduct one additional time value of money calculation. As with the previous approach, the retirement annuity figure must be estimated. The legacy pool should then be added to the present value of the retirement annuity to determine a new amount needed on the first day of retirement. In effect, the present value of the legacy pool grows while the present value of the retirement annuity is depleted. At the end of the planning period, the client should have exactly the same nominal amount available that they had on the first day of retirement. The following example illustrates the steps necessary to estimate a capital preservation retirement annuity.

> *Example:* Return to the previous example where a client requires a growing annuity with a beginning payment of $100,000. However, in addition, the client desires to leave a legacy equal to the beginning value of the retirement annuity. Given these assumptions, the client needs to accumulate only an additional $85,537 by the first day of retirement. This is the amount that will result in a future value equal to $1,492,564 at the client's death. Using this approach, the client needs a total of $1,578,101 saved at retirement ($1,492,564 + $85,537). The present value of a lump sum is used to solve for the additional amount needed.

Equation 12.2: Present Value $PV_n = \dfrac{FV}{(1 + i)^n}$

Where,

$i = 10\%$

$FV = \$1,492,564$ (the amount needed to fund the retirement annuity)

$n = 30$

$$PV_n = \frac{\$1,492,564}{(1.1)^{30}} = \$85,537$$

In cases where capital preservation can be achieved, a third retirement needs estimation can be used: **inflation-adjusted capital preservation approach**. It may be possible not only to preserve a client's assets, but also to account for inflation such that at life expectancy the real value of the retirement assets is equal to the nominal value at retirement. The following illustration example extends the case from above.

> *Example:* Return to the previous example where a client requires a growing annuity with a beginning payment of $100,000. However, in addition, the client wishes to leave a legacy with an ending purchasing power equal to the beginning purchasing power of the retirement annuity. To maintain equivalent purchasing power, the client needs to a have an additional $277,429 saved at the time of retirement. Using this approach, the client needs a total of $1,769,993 saved on the first day of retirement ($1,492,564 + $277,429).

Equation 12.3: Serial Rate

$$\text{Serial Rate} = \frac{(1+i)}{(1+g)} - 1$$

$$\text{Serial Rate} = \frac{(1.10)}{(1.04)} - 1 = 5.77\%$$

Using the serial rate, the following present value equation is used to calculate the required additional amount needed to preserve the purchasing power of the client's legacy.

$$PV_n = \frac{FV}{(1+i)^n}$$

Where,

i = 5.77%

FV = $1,492,564 (The inflation-adjusted amount desired at the end of retirement.)

n = 30

$$PV_n = \frac{\$1,492,564}{(1.0577)^{30}} = \$277,429$$

Once the retirement annuity figure has been determined, the financial planner must estimate the future value of retirement assets and savings. These assets will be used, in most client situations, to generate income as an element of the retirement annuity. Making appropriate rate of return, inflation, and tax rate assumptions is important at this stage of the analysis. Assume that a client currently has twenty-four year remaining until retirement, can earn an annualized rate of return equal to 7 percent, has 401(k) assets of $86,000, and is saving $9,000 per year (including employer matching contributions). Using these figures, a financial planner would estimate the future value as follows: (a) 401(k) = $436,224 and (b) savings = $523,590. These amounts would then be subtracted from the capital needs analysis estimate to determine a surplus or shortfall need. If a shortfall exists, a time value of money calculation can be used to pinpoint the amount of additional annual savings needed.

Retirement Distribution Calculations

There are multiple ways to calculate the optimal withdrawal strategy for a client. Some financial planners use a simple heuristic, such as the 4 percent rule, which states that a retiree can safely withdraw 4 percent of the value of savings each year during each year of retirement. The academic literature offers a multitude of similar strategies, ranging from withdrawals based on increasing equity holdings over retirement to reducing the safe distribution to 4 percent or less. Two other approaches are widely used. The first **capital withdrawal process** is based on a **deterministic model**. Deterministic models use a static, or constant, mean return throughout the modeling period provide and provide a very elementary projection on which to base a safe withdrawal strategy. Stochastic models add variability to distribution calculations. The following discussion highlights steps necessary to estimate withdrawals using a deterministic model.

> **Self-Test 1**
>
> What is the inflation-adjusted rate of return (serial rate) if the investment return is 12 percent and the annual inflation rate is 3 percent?
>
> a. 7.84%
>
> b. 8.74%
>
> c. 9.00%
>
> d. 15.36%

1. Determine the value of the pool of available assets at the beginning of retirement. Although not all client assets will be used to fund retirement (e.g., home equity), assets that can be used should be valued at the market value as of the projected date of retirement.

2. Choose a reasonable after-tax rate of return for retirement. A financial planner should always take into account a client's risk tolerance, expectations, time horizon, and preferences (e.g., asset class limitations) when establishing a rate of return projection. The return should not subject a client's assets to risks beyond those necessary to achieve the desired standard of living.

3. Choose a realistic average rate of inflation during retirement, or determine the client's desired rate of increase for the retirement annuity. Although not always the case, it does not hurt to be conservative in this choice (i.e., to slightly overstate projected inflation). Just as investment losses are more detrimental early in the withdrawal period, high inflation early in the withdrawal period can create lasting problems for meeting a client's desired standard of living.

4. Calculate the inflation-adjusted rate of return applicable to the client using the serial interest rate formula:

$$\text{Serial Rate} = \frac{(1 + i)}{(1 + g)} - 1$$

5. Determine the client's life expectancy. A client's individual life expectancy can be estimated using the Single Life Expectancy Table shown in Figure 12.1. If a client is married, the client and spouse's joint and survivor life expectancy (i.e., how long at least one of them will live, or until both will be deceased) can

be determined using a joint and survivor life expectancy table. These tables should be used as a starting point in the analysis. Other important information, including a person's ancestral life expectancy patterns, current health, occupation, and hobbies, can be used to increase or decrease assumptions regarding a client's life expectancy. For planners who want a conservative estimate, using a table factor life expectancy and adding at least five years is worth considering.

Figure 12.1 Single Life Expectancy Table

Age	Divisor	Age	Divisor

Single-life Expectancy Table[1]			
Age	Divisor	Age	Divisor
56	28.7	84	8.1
57	27.9	85	7.6
58	27.0	86	7.1
59	26.1	87	6.7
60	25.2	88	6.3
61	24.4	89	5.9
62	23.5	90	5.5
63	22.7	91	5.2
64	21.8	92	4.9
65	21.0	93	4.6
66	20.2	94	4.3
67	19.4	95	4.1
68	18.6	96	3.8
69	17.8	97	3.6
70	17.0	98	3.4
71	16.3	99	3.1
72	15.5	100	2.9
73	14.8	101	2.7
74	14.1	102	2.5
75	13.4	103	2.3
76	12.7	104	2.1
77	12.1	105	1.9
78	11.4	106	1.7
79	10.8	107	1.5
80	10.2	108	1.4
81	9.7	109	1.2
82	9.1	110	1.1
83	8.6	111+	1.0

1. For ages 0 to 55, see IRS Publication 590, Individual Retirement Arrangements (IRAs).

Source: https://www.irs.gov/publications/p590a/

6. Calculate the withdrawal amount. There are two basic methods that can be used for this step. Both methods can be adjusted to account for inflation to preserve purchasing power. If so, withdrawals will increase each year to reflect inflation.

The first method assumes a depletion of all assets at the end of the client's life expectancy (i.e., at the end of retirement), which is referred to as the **capital depletion withdrawal method** or approach. This method is based on a growth-adjusted present value of an annuity due calculation.

Example: Assume retirement assets equal $500,000 at the time of retirement, that yearly distributions will increase by 4 percent, assets earn 8 percent annually, and retirement is planned to last for twenty years, at which time assets will be depleted. The amount that can be withdrawn at the beginning of the first year equals $34,947; this amount would then be increased by 4 percent in each succeeding year.

$$\text{Serial Rate} = \frac{(1+i)}{(1+g)} - 1 = \frac{1.08}{1.04} - 1 = 3.846\%$$

$$\$500,000 = \frac{PMT}{0.03846}\left(1 - \frac{1}{1.03846^{20}}\right)(1.03846)$$

$$PMT = \frac{\$500,000 \times 0.03846}{(1 - 1.03846^{-20}) \times 1.03846} = \$34,947$$

Where,

i = 3.846%

FV = 0

PV = $500,000

n = 20

Solving for PMT also returns approximately $34,947; this is an annuity due estimate.

The second distribution approach is called the **capital preservation method** or approach. This method assumes that the client's assets at retirement will be preserved throughout the client's lifetime. The capital preservation method can also increase the capital each year to reflect inflation. Payments can be determined using a present value of a growing perpetuity due calculation.

Example: Assume retirement assets equal $500,000 at the time of retirement, that yearly distributions will increase by 4 percent, assets earn 8 percent annually, and retirement is planned to last for twenty years, at which time assets would still be equal to the inflation-adjusted future value of $500,000. The amount that can be withdrawn at the beginning of the first year equals $18,519; this amount will then increase by 4 percent in each succeeding year. Using the same serial rate as before:

$$\$500{,}000 = \frac{PMT}{0.03846}\left(1 - \frac{1}{1.03846^{20}}\right)(1.03846) + \frac{\$500{,}000(1.04^{20})}{1.08^{20}}$$

$$\$500{,}000 = \frac{PMT}{0.03846}\left(1 - \frac{1}{1.03846^{20}}\right)(1.03846) + \$235{,}050.77$$

$$\$500{,}000 - \$235{,}050.77 = \frac{PMT}{0.03846}\left(1 - \frac{1}{1.03846^{20}}\right)(1.03846)$$

What is actually available to support retirement is the difference in the $500,000 saved and the $235,050.77 needed to ensure the inflation-adjusted future value of the account.

$$PMT = \frac{\$264{,}949.23 \times 0.03846}{(1 - 1.03846^{-20}) \times 1.03846} = \$18{,}519$$

Note: In this case a calculator cannot handle this problem directly with the TVM keys because there is a future value involved and serial rates typically cannot be used to directly solve for future values. Therefore, the present value of the remaining balance must be subtracted before beginning. Again, the calculator should be set to beginning-of-period payments.

Where,

$I = 3.846\%$

$FV = 0$

$PV = \$264{,}949.23$

$n = 20$

Solving for PMT also returns approximately $18,519.

Thought about another way, the present value of the account is increasing in perpetuity by the rate of inflation. So, if the account is always increasing in value at a rate equal to increases in the annual withdrawal, then it turns out to be a simple present value of a growing perpetuity.

$$\$500,000 = \frac{PMT}{0.08 - 0.04} (1.08)$$

$$PMT = \frac{\$500,000 \times (0.08 - 0.04)}{1.08} = \$18,519$$

A *non-random deterministic withdrawal model* can be developed to help clients gain an idea of how long their retirement account balances will remain funded. Figure 12.2 illustrates how Excel can be used to project estimated withdrawal amounts for a client who enters retirement at age sixty-five with $100,000 in assets. The data in Figure 12.2 are based on the following assumptions:

- A 5 percent annualized before-tax rate of return,

- A 3 percent annualized inflation rate,

- A 4 percent annual distribution rate,

- A distribution rate that increases by the rate of inflation, and

- A *required minimum distribution* (RMD) based on the Uniform Life Table.

Figure 12.2 Deterministic Withdrawal Illustration

Age of Client	Beginning Balance	Yearly Distribution	Distribution Rate (percent)
65	$500,000	$20,000	4.00
66	$504,000	$20,600	4.09
67	$507,570	$21,218	4.18
68	$510,670	$21,855	4.28
69	$513,256	$22,510	4.39
70	$515,283	$23,185	4.50
71	$516,702	$23,881	4.62
72	$517,462	$24,597	4.75
73	$517,508	$25,335	4.90
74	$516,781	$26,095	5.05
75	$515,220	$26,878	5.22
76	$512,759	$27,685	5.40
77	$509,328	$28,515	5.60
78	$504,853	$29,371	5.82
79	$499,257	$30,252	6.06
80	$492,455	$31,159	6.33
81	$484,361	$32,094	6.63
82	$474,880	$33,057	6.96
83	$463,914	$34,049	7.34
84	$451,359	$35,070	7.77
85	$437,103	$36,122	8.26
86	$421,030	$37,206	8.84
87	$403,015	$38,322	9.51
88	$382,928	$39,472	10.31
89	$360,629	$40,656	11.27
90	$335,972	$41,876	12.46
91	$308,801	$43,132	13.97
92	$278,952	$44,426	15.93
93	$246,253	$45,759	18.58
94	$210,519	$47,131	22.39
95	$171,557	$48,545	28.30
96	$129,163	$50,002	38.71
97	$83,119	$51,502	61.96
98	$33,198	$33,198	100.00
99	0	0	0.00

The first column in Figure 12.2 reports the client's age from sixty-five to an assumed death at age ninety-nine. The second column documents the client's account balance adjusted for annual withdrawal and account earnings. The third column shows the annual 4 percent distribution, adjusted for inflation. The effective distribution rate shown in the last column was estimated by dividing the yearly distribution amount by the beginning balance. Over time, the effective distribution rate will rise in response to inflation.

Stochastic retirement withdrawal models are another way financial planners estimate retirement withdrawals. **Stochastic modeling**, or what is known as **Monte Carlo modeling**, has gained favor as a projection tool for withdrawal analyses. A stochastic approach randomizes rate-of-return, inflation, and life expectancy assumptions using thousands of data point observations to estimate features of plan success or failure. The primary drawback to stochastic models is the need to use software or advanced data worksheet applications. While certainly not impossible, it would be very time intensive to use a calculator as a stochastic modeling tool.

RETIREMENT PLANNING SKILLS

Developing retirement planning strategies and recommendations involves integrating qualitative and quantitative client situational factors. It is important to determine at the outset a client's goals, dreams, and aspirations for retirement. Where clients want to live, what they want to do, and how they will spend or donate money are all critically important factors to know before making recommendations. Examples of quantitative factors include asset values and savings amounts, and assumptions related to rates of return, inflation, and life expectancies. Once these factors have been reviewed, it is time to consider outputs from the estimates to quantify the client's retirement planning situation.

At the end of the retirement situation analysis, an advisor will know whether a client is on track to meet retirement goals, based on all planning assumptions. If so, few changes in the plan may be needed. If, on the other hand, the client's current retirement assets and savings approaches are insufficient to meet stated goals, it will be necessary to help the client implement changes to meet the retirement objectives.

Planning for retirement can encompass decades of planning to identify and implement the most effective accumulation and distribution strategies responsive to changing financial, economic, and tax environments. Some of the most commonly used retirement planning strategies, both product and procedural, are illustrated below. The tools and techniques listed are only a sampling of the techniques used in practice.

Planning Skill 1: Balance Contributions to Tax-Deferred Plans and IRAs

This strategy is premised on the notion that saving money on a tax-deferred basis is one of the best ways to accumulate wealth for retirement. The choice of which type of plan to use—an *employer-sponsored plan* or an IRA—is complicated. Figure 12.3 provides a rudimentary decision tree to help determine funding priorities based on plan type.

Figure 12.3 Choosing between a Defined Contribution Plan and IRA Contributions

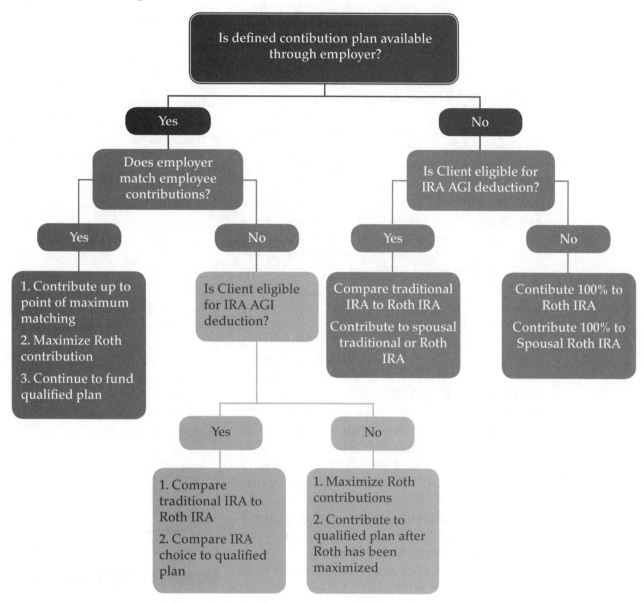

As shown in the decision tree, clients should be encouraged to contribute to a defined contribution plan when employer matching is available. Maximizing the match is important. If, for example, an employer matches dollar-for-dollar on the first 4 percent of contributions, a client would be foolish to pass up this offer. In effect, the employer is guaranteeing the client an immediate 100 percent return on contributions up to 4 percent, and that is before any earnings are generated from the contribution.

Next, benefits associated with employer-sponsored plans must be compared to advantages offered by IRAs. In many cases, contributing either to a tax-deductible or Roth IRA may be more beneficial than contributing to a defined contribution plan. If eligible, the tax-deductible plan offers an immediate income tax savings and tax-deferred growth, whereas the Roth offers the advantages of tax-deferred growth and tax-exempt earnings if the distribution rules are followed. Furthermore, IRAs offer more freedom of account choice than employer-provided plan offerings.

Once deductible or Roth IRA contributions have been maximized, clients who can afford additional contributions up to the maximum allowable limits should contribute to qualified and other employer retirement plans (e.g., 403(b) and 457 plans). These plans provide immediate income tax reduction and tax deferral on account growth.

The greatest limitation associated with this strategy is that not all clients will be able to fully implement each stage of the recommendation. This is especially true for a **highly compensated employee (HCE)**, which is defined as anyone who was a "5 percent owner" at any time during the year or anyone who receives IRS defined high compensation (the figure changes yearly but is more than $120,000) and, if elected by the employer, is in the top 20 percent of employees based upon compensation. A **key employee** is someone who is (a) an officer with relatively high income (e.g., more than $170,000), (b) a 5 percent owner, or (c) a 1 percent owner with high compensation. Highly compensated employee contributions to a 401(k) plan can be limited by the contributions made by non-highly-compensated employees. Also, higher-income clients typically cannot deduct traditional IRA contributions, and they may be unable to contribute to a Roth IRA. Other disadvantages include potential penalties associated with early withdrawals and the possibility of paying higher taxes if the client's marginal rate is higher once distributions begin. Other clients may not have available discretionary cash flow to benefit from multiple accounts.

In 2016, the Department of Labor (DOL) introduced new rules that impact the way financial planners provide advice regarding retirement plans. According to the DOL, a financial planner who provides recommendations to clients regarding ERISA regulated retirement plans or IRAs must provide advice using fiduciary investment standards. Recommendations made either directly or indirectly fall under the fiduciary rule.

Financial planners who receive some compensation in the form of commission need to pay particular attention to this rule. Suitability standards still apply for advice and recommendations made in traditional asset management and brokerage situations.

Learn more about the rule at: https://www.dol.gov/ebsa/newsroom/fs-conflict-of-interest.html

Planning Skill 2: Understand the Role of Insurance Company Products in Retirement Planning

Nearly everyone's fear after retirement is outliving their money. In the academic community this is known as **shortfall risk**, or the percentage of time a portfolio will run short of the money needed to pay distributions. Spitzer summarized the trade-offs involved when making distribution choices in retirement in relation to shortfall risk. His primary conclusions were as follows.[1] First, the use of *annuities* reduces shortfall risk significantly. The difference in risk falls from 0 percent with 100 percent annuitization to 6 percent without the use of annuities. Second, the use of annuities reduces a client's gross estate dramatically. Whereas, without annuitization someone can expect their final estate to be 150 percent of their starting portfolio value, the use of annuities reduces this amount to about 20 percent. In other words, retirees must choose between legacy and security. Retirees who are more interested in retirement income security, versus leaving heirs a legacy, should consider the use of annuitization as a retirement planning distribution tool.

Annuitized distributions provide a way to manage retirement income. Annuitization is basically an underwriting process where the issuer of an annuity—in the United States this must be an insurance company—determines the likely remaining life span of the annuitant, thereby calculating the cost of guaranteeing the stream of periodic payments to the annuitant. The annuity product is actually an insurance wrapper of sorts that guarantees the payment stream, but the client's assets are used to make the payments.

Self-Test 2

An annuity that provides a beneficiary with a stream of income that has little market risk is known as a(n):

a. Variable annuity

b. Period-certain annuity

c. Life annuity

d. Fixed annuity

Annuitization provides greater certainty of income for longer periods of time while also reducing the asset base subject to RMD, because the IRS assumes that the periodic payments from an annuity will suffice for the RMD. This last point effectively increases the after-tax rate of return for assets held in annuity accounts.

Annuitization is basically an irrevocable choice of planned distribution, and it comes in one of three basic forms: fixed period, single lifetime, or joint lifetime. Annuitization shifts the shortfall risk to the underwriter, because the annuitant could still outlive the principal but cannot outlive the payment stream, assuming a life annuity. Because of the underwriting and the guarantees provided, canceling or surrendering an annuity contract can be quite expensive, so the choice of an annuitized distribution should be made carefully.

Annuity payments are based on two factors: (1) the assets underlying the contract, and (2) the desired length of time the contractually obligated payments last. Two basic categories of annuities are available: fixed and variable. In return for a lump sum payment or series of payments, a **fixed annuity** provides an income stream based on a fixed, guaranteed interest rate, similar to a fixed income security or bank account. This option carries very little to no market risk. **Variable annuity** products, on the other hand, can offer clients a higher degree of inflation protection in exchange for an element of risk. Instead of providing a client with a fixed rate of return, variable annuities make payments based on the returns generated from the value of the securities in the portfolio. This option can offer a higher payout as long as market conditions are favorable, but in exchange the annuitant has chosen to accept a certain degree of market risk and payout variability.

A case can be made against retirees' use of annuities; the case is strongest against life annuities. A **life annuity** pays out either a fixed or inflation-adjusted stream of income for as long as the annuitant lives. If all goes as planned, in other words if a client dies when expected based on the mortality tables, then "nobody wins." However, if the client outlives the forecast, then the insurance company must continue to pay;

whereas without the insurance guarantee the client would theoretically have run out of money. If the client dies prematurely, any remaining principal balance in the annuity is forfeited at death. As a result, life annuities generally appeal only to individuals who have an above-average life expectancy and very high risk aversion.

A strong case can be made for the use of a **guaranteed annuity.** Although less commonly available in the marketplace, a **fixed payment** (or **period-certain**) **annuity** provides either a fixed or inflation-adjusted payout for a specific number of years, usually five, ten, twenty, or thirty years, regardless of how long the annuitant lives. In this case, the annuitant could outlive the payment stream, but if the annuitant were to die prematurely a secondary beneficiary would continue to receive payment until the end of the guaranteed period. The use of guaranteed annuities is warranted as a retiree's income increases, risk aversion increases, and overall equity and bond market volatility intensify.[2]

Some annuities combine certain aspects of both life and guaranteed annuities. **Guaranteed lifetime annuities**, as the name implies, provide lifetime income to a client. Most lifetime annuities cease payments upon the client's death (also as the name implies). However, it is possible to obtain annuities with a guaranteed minimum number of distribution years; these are sometimes referred to as a **life with period certain annuities**. If an annuitant were to die during the "period certain," then payments would continue to a secondary beneficiary until the end of that period.

Planning Skill 3: Use a Systematic Approach When Analyzing a Client's Current Retirement Planning Situation

Analyzing a client's current retirement planning situation involves documenting and evaluating all current retirement planning strategies. This type of analysis should consider four questions:

1. Is the amount of money the client is saving enough to meet the goal (discussed in the previous section)?

2. Is the client optimizing the asset class mix to ensure the best risk-adjusted return (discussed in Chapter 10 on investment planning)?

3. Is the client utilizing the optimal types of accounts (i.e., qualified or pretax versus non-qualified or post-tax) to ensure the best tax-adjusted return?

4. Is the client maintaining adequate financial flexibility to meet changing goals or emergencies?

Although question 1 may be the most important aspect to review early in the accumulation phase of retirement planning, question 4 becomes more important to evaluate as a client nears or enters retirement. Questions 2 and 3 represent important planning issues across the life cycle, as well as issues that might need to be reconsidered because of changes in the economy or market or tax policy changes.

Retirement Planning Product & Procedural Strategies

The following product and procedural strategies provide an insight into some of the most widely used retirement planning tools and techniques used by financial planners on a day-to-day basis.

Product Strategy 1: Increase Contributions to Retirement Plans and IRAs

Assuming that a client's retirement goals and assumptions are realistic, one of the simplest strategies for meeting the retirement accumulation goal is to allocate additional assets and savings to the retirement plan. Certain defined contribution plans and some IRA-based plans allow employees fifty years of age or older to make catch-up contributions beyond the maximum annual allowable contribution. The contribution catch-up information shown in Figure 12.4 summarizes catch-up provisions as they apply to 401(k), 403(b), 457, and IRA plans. This strategy has the advantage of taking already accumulated assets or unaccounted-for sources of cash flow to build retirement wealth.

> ### Self-Test 3
>
> Kala will turn age 57 this year. She currently contributes to a 401(k) plan and wants to make an IRA contribution. Is she eligible to use the catch-up provision?
>
> a. Yes, because she is older than age 50.
>
> b. No, because she is an active participant in a 401(k) plan.
>
> c. Yes, because she is not eligible for a 401(k) catch up.
>
> d. No, because she is less than age 59½.

Figure 12.4 Retirement Plan Catch-up Provisions

Plan	2016 and beyond	
401(k)	$6,500 Indexed to inflation in $500 increments	
Roth 401(k)	$6,500	
403(b)	$6,500 Indexed to inflation in $500 increments	
457	$6,500 Indexed to inflation in $500 increments	
SIMPLE IRAs and SIMPLE 401(k) plans	$3,000 Indexed to inflation in $500 increments	
IRA	$1,000	$1,000

It is important to note that reallocating assets and savings toward retirement plan goals could jeopardize other important financial planning goals, including building an emergency fund, funding insurance needs, and paying for education expenses. However, depending on the type of account used, some retirement savings can still offer options for certain expenses. Using a Roth IRA, for example, can be a way to save for retirement while providing a secondary source of education funding if needed.

Product Strategy 2: Fully Fund an Individual Retirement Agreement/ Arrangement

Assuming that a client has contributed to a defined contribution plan to the point of receiving the maximum employer match, investing in an IRA should be the next consideration. The choice of traditional or Roth IRA generally depends on two factors: (1) the ability to deduct contributions to a traditional IRA and (2) the marginal tax rates at the time of contribution and withdrawal. Clients who are eligible to make tax-deductible contributions generally find a traditional IRA attractive whenever the marginal tax rate will be lower when the client retires and distributions are made. Clients who are eligible to make contributions to Roth IRAs will generally find a Roth IRA attractive if marginal tax rates will be higher after retirement (assuming Roth IRA distributions are qualified). The Roth IRA is generally a better choice when a contribution to a traditional IRA is not deductible, unless contributions cannot be made to a Roth IRA. Figure 12.5 illustrates how tax rates impact IRA funding decisions. Furthermore, in some cases it may be worth fully funding a client and spouse Roth IRA before also contributing to a qualified plan, especially in cases where employer matching is unavailable.

Figure 12.5 Impact of Tax Rates on Traditional and Roth IRA Distributions

Type	Contribution	Contribution Tax Rate	Distribution Tax Rate	After-tax Distribution
Traditional IRA	$5,000	25%	25%	$13,659
Roth IRA	$3,750	25%	25%	$13,659
Traditional IRA	$5,000	25%	15%	$15,481
Roth IRA	$3,750	25%	15%	$13,659
Traditional IRA	$5,000	15%	25%	$13,659
Roth IRA	$4,250	15%	25%	$15,481

This table is based on the following assumptions:
- Number of years until distribution = 15
- Rate of return = 9%
- Roth IRA contribution = traditional IRA contribution × (1 – pre-retirement tax rate)
- Roth distribution is qualified

Choosing to contribute to either a traditional or Roth IRA before funding a qualified plan means that a client will lose an important tax reduction tool (i.e., the ability to fund qualified retirement savings with pretax dollars). Another disadvantage is that contributions to and accumulations in IRAs are not always protected from creditors. *IRA asset protection* differs from state to state. Furthermore, deductible contributions to a traditional IRA or contributions to a Roth IRA may be unavailable because of phase-outs based on modified AGI. It is worth noting, as well, that many high income earners may be phased-out of participation and unable to contribute.

Product Strategy 3: Elect Pension Maximization

Pension maximization generally starts by taking a 100 percent single life payout from a defined benefit plan or annuity. As a result of the single life payout, the monthly benefit will be significantly larger than a comparable joint and survivor annuity payout. Under a pension maximization arrangement, the extra amount is then used to purchase life insurance, which is used to fund a survivor's income need if the participant predeceases the spouse. If a permanent form of insurance is used, a portion of the cash value can be used in later years to supplement retirement income. Pension maximization will not work when a client is uninsurable. The strategy also might not work when a client's life expectancy is significantly longer than an affordable term of insurance, or when the amount of insurance that can be purchased is insufficient to fund the difference between the single life payout and the joint and survivor payout.

Product Strategy 4: Use a Reverse Mortgage to Increase Retirement Income

A **reverse mortgage** is a type of loan that is generally provided to a client on either a monthly payout or a line of credit basis. No interest or principal is due until the end of the mortgage term. Payments received by a client are not taxable. Payments received do not impact Social Security or Medicare benefits. Although a reverse mortgage allows a client to convert a portion of home equity to current income while living in the home, it is possible that all equity will be used by the end of the loan term, leaving nothing for the client or heirs. Furthermore, if a client saves a portion of the payments received, this could negatively affect Medicaid and Supplemental Security Income eligibility. Additionally, interest paid is not deductible until the end of the loan term. Finally, reverse mortgages have come under intense federal and state scrutiny because of generally high lender fees and expenses. The costs associated with these products could, in some cases, exceed the benefits.

Product Strategy 5: Use Variable Universal Life as a Retirement Planning Tool

In some cases, a highly compensated client needs to shelter income and assets to such an extent that qualified plans are of modest help. For example, a highly paid executive might quickly exhaust his or her ability to shelter assets in an employer plan due to maximum annual contribution limits. It is also likely, given the executive's income level, that the client cannot make a contribution to a Roth IRA because of phase-outs based on income. What is an executive to do? One solution might be for the firm to implement a non-qualified retirement plan. This can be an expensive option. It could also be a risky alternative for the executive, because assets held in a non-qualified plan could be subject to firm creditors. One realistic solution for solving this issue involves the use of a variable universal life insurance policy.

A **variable universal life policy** (**VUL**) can provide a method for a client (or the client's employer) to change the face value of a policy and yearly premiums paid. In effect, a VUL allows a client to purchase a term insurance policy while also investing in tax-deferred mutual funds. If invested appropriately, the cash account can grow in value over time. Unlike qualified plans that restrict annual contributions, a VUL can accept very large annual premiums. In fact, a VUL can easily be funded with multiples of the yearly limit applied to qualified defined contribution plans. Furthermore, the cash value in such accounts is sheltered from taxes and creditors. In most cases, the client owns the account outright.

Once the cash value of an account generates enough annual income to cover policy expenses (called the *tax-free funding level*), all additional earnings and premiums work to increase cash values, for example, assume that an executive is ready to retire. Also assume that over the course of 20 or 30 years, the executive funded the VUL to the fullest extent. If the account has gone up in value, the executive can start to take policy loans out against the value of the account. The insurance company will charge interest on these loans, but the executive generally owes no tax on the borrowed amounts unless he or she failed to make a loan payment. With a large enough account cash balance, the interest plus insurance expenses can continue to be covered by account earnings. Year after year, the executive can borrow money from the account.

Obviously, multiple factors come into play using this type of planning technique. First, the level of funding necessary to make the scenario realistic over time is quite large. Second, and most importantly, the client must invest aggressively over the VUL holding period. It is important to note that the account value must be of such size at the time of retirement to meet ongoing retirement income needs and also pay interest and insurance expenses. Another disadvantage is that this strategy is appropriate in only a limited number of cases, which limits the usefulness of the product in meeting the needs of many clients. If the policy is a modified endowment contract, loan payments are treated as taxable distributions to the extent that cash value exceeds investment in the contract.

Product Strategy 6: Use Glide Path Portfolios That Match a Client's Investment Time Horizon

A retirement **glide path portfolio** refers to the allocation of investments within a retirement account, most often mutual funds, which automatically adjust from risky to conservative as the client/investor ages. The glide path refers to the notion that the portfolio slowly adjusts to an increasingly conservative asset allocation the closer to retirement or the target-date maturity of the fund. At that time, the portfolio will be almost entirely in Treasury securities or other low risk/return assets and the client will have the choice of continuing to own the fund, purchasing an annuity, or reallocating the assets into the retirement income portfolio. These products provide two main advantages. First, the need to reallocate holdings is eliminated. Second, portfolio risk falls as the client's risk capacity declines.

It is worth noting that the term glide path portfolio is a marketing term used to describe what are generally known as *target-date maturity funds*. Although each company that provides a target-date product defines the glide path differently, all funds using this strategy reduce equity exposure over time. Depending on the reallocation from equity to low risk/return assets, this can run counter to academic studies showing that nearly everyone, regardless of age, should have some exposure to equities as an inflation and longevity hedge. By following a traditional glide path strategy, clients could find that their overall portfolio is too conservative based on the ratio of these retirement assets within the client's broader portfolio. For example, fixed-income assets (e.g., Social Security benefits, pensions, annuities, bond holdings, etc.) tend to make up a high percentage of income sources for the majority of U.S. retirees. Care must be taken that when glide path portfolios are included in the broader portfolio the allocation to fixed-income securities is not too great.

Product Strategy 7: Understand the Role Played by Joint and Survivor Annuities

The foregoing discussion assumes that a client is unmarried or has elected a single life payout. However, an additional annuitization choice must be made available for married individuals investing money from an IRA or qualified account. In such plans, it is illegal for a married person to exclude a spouse from receiving a survivor annuity unless the spouse signs a notarized affidavit waiving rights to the annuity payment. **Joint and survivor annuities** provide annuity payments for the lives of the client and a surviving beneficiary, typically a spouse. Choosing a joint and survivor annuity will initially result in a reduced benefit. Typical examples of joint and survivor annuities include 50 percent, 66 2/3 percent, and 100 percent annuity payouts. For example, a 100 percent annuity would continue the annuity payout at 100 percent of what was received before the first annuitant's death. A 50 percent joint and survivor annuity will pay one-half of the payout to the survivor for the survivor's life.

> *Self-Test 4*
>
> If Basia elects a 100% joint and survivor annuity what will occur?
>
> a. She must obtain her husband's permission.
>
> b. She can expect a greater payout than if she elected another annuity.
>
> c. She can expect a reduced payout compared to another annuity.
>
> d. She must pass a physical examination first.

Product Strategy 8: Incorporate Deferred Income Annuity Strategies into a Client's Retirement Plan

As the name implies, a **deferred income annuity** (DIA) provides an income stream to a retired client at some later point in retirement. A special subset of DIA is a *longevity annuity*, which starts payments after age seventy-five. The difference between a DIA and an immediate annuity payment can be quite large. Based on a $100,000 purchase, an immediate annuity might pay out $5,400 per year (assuming a return-of-premium feature). A similar DIA that starts payments at age seventy-five will generate about $10,500 per year. A DIA will appeal to conservative clients who want a guaranteed source of lifetime income. The IRS changed minimum distribution regulations in July 2014. The new regulations allow *qualifying longevity annuity contracts* (QLAC) to be excluded from minimum distribution rules that usually begin when a client turns age 70½. This means that current required distributions can be reduced, which might allow for a greater legacy transfer at death (assuming a return-of-premium policy is purchased).

In order for a DIA contract to be qualifying the amount used to fund the annuity is limited to 25 percent of the client's total retirement holdings. Also, distributions cannot be postponed beyond age 85. While a DIA carries a lower overall commission rate, few DIA products provide inflation protection. Additionally, some insurance pundits believe that the internal rates of turn are too low to make these products viable for most clients.

Procedural Strategy 1: Begin a Retirement Needs Analysis Using the Capital Depletion Method

Figure 12.6 outlines the hierarchical steps to follow when evaluating a client's current situation. The decision tree begins by asking whether a client needs additional savings to meet a capital depletion objective. If the answer is yes, a series of assumption changes and strategies is presented, beginning with allocating additional resources to the goal. If these adjustments do not allow a client to meet the retirement savings goal, the planner is prompted to determine the client's willingness to reduce the income needed in retirement. The process continues until the capital depletion projection is achieved for the client's life expectancy. However, caution must be exercised when changing planning assumptions to ensure that the assumptions are valid and defensible. Overly conservative estimates could compromise a client's current standard of living, and assumptions that are too generous could seriously threaten retirement funding by generating savings recommendations that would be insufficient if rate of return or inflation estimates deviate significantly from reality.

Once the capital depletion model is fully funded, the focus of potential funding strategies proceeds to Step Two at any point on the decision tree shown in Figure 12.6. Here, attention turns to projecting the funding needed for the capital preservation and inflation-adjusted models, depending on the client's preferences.

Figure 12.6 Decision Tree for Determining Retirement Planning Strategy

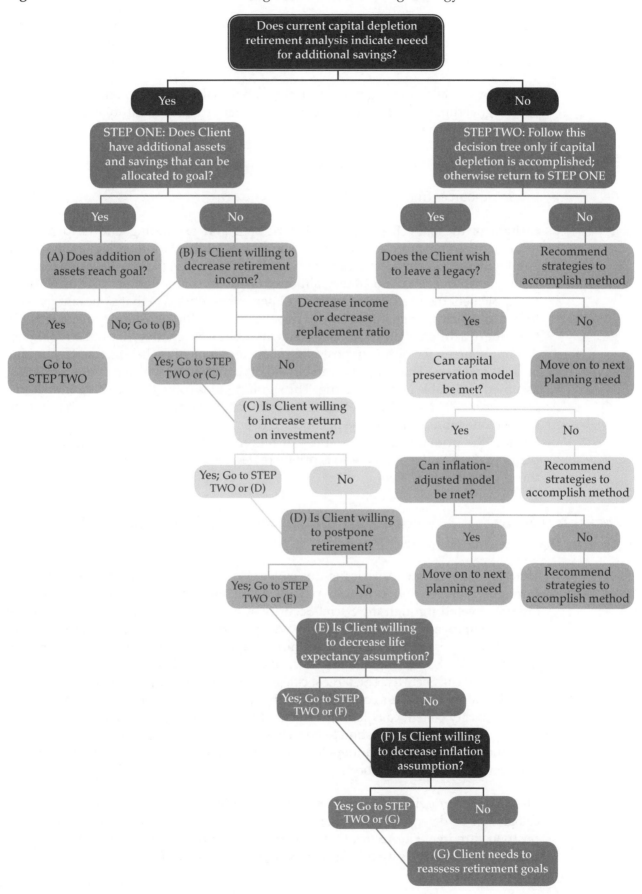

Procedural Strategy 2: Identify Sources of Retirement Income

Financial planners often use the analogy of the *three-legged stool* as a framework for considering a client's retirement planning situation. The three commonly identified legs of the stool supporting retirement are

1. resources from the government through Social Security benefits—a government-backed retirement system that provides monthly inflation-adjusted benefits;

2. resources from employer-provided retirement plans; and

3. resources from personal savings.

In light of the Baby Boom generation's recent and expanding efforts to redefine retirement, some professionals have suggested adding another leg to the stool: employment during retirement and the use of home equity. A Fidelity Research Institute Retirement Index report noted that, although 60 percent of pre-retirees plan on working to supplement their retirement income, 22 percent of retirees in that same survey were forced into early retirement because of poor health.[3] So although employment, either in the same or a different professional pursuit, may be an alternative, like other retirement funding sources, the option of postretirement employment is characterized by unique benefits and risks. The same also can be said of home equity, which prior to 2007, most assumed was stable or appreciating. The significant loss of value resulting from home losses post-2008 eroded the retirement portfolios of many pre-retirees, forcing them to postpone retirement because of concerns over the value and liquidity of real estate. Each of the primary funding sources of retirement (i.e., Social Security, retirement plans, savings, and employment) is briefly reviewed to establish the framework of the three- or four-legged stool.

Procedural Strategy 3: Incorporate Social Security Claiming Strategies into the Retirement Planning Process

Virtually all working Americans are covered by Social Security, which is funded through employee and employer payroll deductions. A few categories of workers are not covered through the Social Security system. For instance, certain municipal or state employees whose employers have opted out of the system are exempt from Social Security taxes. Federal workers hired before 1984 are generally not covered by Social Security. Some religious ministers and Christian Science practitioners can also opt out of Social Security. The largest category of privately employed exempt workers includes railroad workers covered under the Railroad Retirement Act. Although most Social Security benefit calculations can be estimated online, customized to the client's earnings record online, or estimated by a Social Security representative, it is important that students and novice planners have a working knowledge of Social Security terms and benefit calculation methods.

The *Social Security Administration* uses an **average indexed monthly earnings (AIME)** calculation to determine a worker's Social Security benefit upon early, regular, or postponed retirement. According to the Social Security Administration, two primary calculations need to be made, consecutively, to arrive at AIME.[4]

The first calculation is the adjustment for inflation of the retiree's top thirty-five years of earnings, not to exceed the Social Security maximum taxable income in that specific year. (Fewer years may sometimes be used.) The calculation begins by dividing the current national average wage index by the national average wage index in the year the individual incurred wages. This calculation is made for each year. This indexing adjustment is completed for all years with the exception of the most recent two years. The total indexed earnings amount is then divided by the total number of months in those years.

The second calculation involves multiplying each year's earnings by the index calculated for that specific year. This effectively adjusts each year's earnings to the current year's wages, as indexed for inflation. Calculation outcomes are added together and then divided by the number of months to arrive at AIME. AIME is then used to calculate the Social Security **primary insurance amount (PIA)**, which is a term used to describe the monthly benefit.[5]

> **Self-Test 5**
>
> Thalia's normal retirement age is 67. She plans to retire at age 63. Based on this, how much will her Social Security benefit be reduced?
>
> a. 5%
>
> b. 20%
>
> c. 25%
>
> d. 30%

Social Security benefits are generally based on an average of the thirty-five years of highest earnings, although the PIA is specifically used to determine retirement, disability, and survivor benefits that are paid *monthly* to a single individual. According to the Social Security Administration, PIA is calculated by first determining the worker's AIME, a factor the Social Security Administration provides. The PIA calculation is as follows:

PIA = 90% of the first $X of AIME

+ 32% of the AIME in excess of $X and less than $Y

+ 15% of the AIME in excess of $Y

In the preceding equation, $X and $Y are called *bend points*, which are adjusted annually according to the national average wage index. Although the figures change annually, the following examples are based on the value for $X as $767 and the value for $Y as $4,624. PIA is the amount the worker will receive for retirement at full retirement age.

> *Example*: Irina Dalakis, a forty-year-old account executive for a major pharmaceutical company, has begun to wonder how much she can expect to receive as a monthly benefit from Social Security to supplement her other retirement savings. Based on her AIME of $6,875, she would receive $2,262.00 per month in retirement benefit.[6]

$PIA = (0.90 \times 767) + (0.32 \times (4{,}624 - 767)) + (0.15 \times (6{,}875 - 4{,}624))$

$PIA = \$691.30 + \$1{,}234.24 + \$337.65$

$PIA = \$2{,}262.19$

It is important to note that PIA is reduced or increased for early or delayed retirement. When designing a retirement plan, it is important to remember that those who are eligible for Social Security may receive retirement, disability, survivorship, and Medicare benefits concurrently. A small lump sum death benefit of $255 is also available to survivors of a fully insured person.

To be **fully insured** in the Social Security system, a client must generally have forty quarters of employment coverage. It is possible to be *currently* rather than *fully* insured. Individuals with at least six quarters of coverage credits in the last thirteen quarters are considered currently insured.

Procedural Strategy 4: Differentiate Between Normal, Early, and Delayed Social Security Claiming Strategies

A client who is fully insured is entitled to Social Security benefits at retirement. **Normal retirement age** (**NRA**) is sixty-five for clients born before 1938. The NRA increases in two month increments for every year an individual is born between 1938 and 1943. Anyone born from 1943 to 1954 has a normal retirement age of sixty-six years. For anyone born from 1955 to 1960, the NRA increases in two month intervals until age sixty-seven. Age sixty-seven is currently the maximum Social Security normal retirement age.

It is possible to retire prior to the NRA. Age sixty-two is the earliest age at which Social Security retirement benefits can be received. A retiree's monthly benefit is reduced by 5/9 of 1 percent for every month of early retirement for the first 36 months, and by 5/12 of 1 percent for every month in excess of thirty-six. Someone whose NRA is sixty-six and who claims benefits at age sixty-four, for example, will receive a 13.33 percent reduction in benefits (5/9 × 0.01 × 24). Someone who's NRA is sixty-seven, who claims benefits at age sixty-two, will receive a *30 percent reduction in benefits*, as shown below:

[(5/9 x 0.01 x 36) + (5/12 x 0.01 x 24)]

Clients also can *delay* the receipt of Social Security benefits. Doing so results in a permanent increase in benefits. The actual increase depends on the age of the client, but generally a worker can expect between a 6.5 percent and 8 percent increase in benefits for every year of deferment between the normal retirement age and age seventy.

Procedural Strategy 5: Evaluate Social Security Survivorship Rules

For retirement planning purposes, **survivor Social Security benefits** are available to the spouse of an insured individual. A spouse who has no work history or a limited work history can draw Social Security benefits based on their spouse's work history. The payment is typically 50 percent of the insured's benefit, but this can be reduced if the surviving spouse is younger than the insured. Although several states currently recognize same-sex marriage, federal laws do not.[7] This means that rules associated with Social Security benefits and qualified retirement plans do not provide the same ownership or beneficiary clauses as those provided to same-sex couples. This effectively means that there are no survivorship benefits available through Social Security for same-sex couples, nor are joint-and-survivor benefits provided automatically under ERISA-covered defined benefit or cash-balance plans, discussed later in this chapter.

The Social Security Administration regularly sends statements to persons covered by Social Security that provide an estimate of future Social Security benefits in today's dollars, based on actual Social Security wages. Another easy way to estimate a client's approximate annual benefit in today's dollars is to use the Social Security Benefit Estimator on the Internet at www.socialsecurity.gov/OACT/quickcalc/index.html. This tool can be used to estimate how much a client and spouse can expect to receive at retirement.

Procedural Strategy 6: Recommend Early Retirement When Appropriate

A question commonly asked of financial planners is whether a client should take early Social Security retirement benefits. Before answering this question, the planner should perform a present value break-even calculation to determine the best time to begin drawing the benefit. Issues to consider when addressing this question include the client's life expectancy, current earnings projections, prospects for salary increases, and other employment opportunities. Other recommend that a single person should take early Social Security benefits only if the rate of return earned on the benefits exceeds the inflation rate by 5 percent.[8]

In effect, the client who postpones retirement benefits is wagering that he or she will live long enough to recoup the opportunity cost associated with delaying the benefit, and as such, the client must earn a sufficient real return to break even on the reduced benefit received. As long as the recipient's age and health profile matches statistical averages, the 5 percent rule is usually appropriate. Someone who takes an early benefit may think that having additional cash flow now rather than later is worthwhile both financially and psychologically. As suggested by the 5 percent rule, this may be true if the early paid benefits can be saved and reinvested at a rate higher than inflation.

It is important to take into account possible tax issues when helping clients make decisions regarding the timing of benefits. Social Security payments can increase a client's income tax liability. The amount of benefits subject to tax depends on each client's combined income (not solely adjusted gross income [AGI]) and filing status. **Combined Social Security income** is the sum of AGI, tax-exempt interest, and one-half the Social Security benefit. For example, if the combined income of a single filer in 2016 is between $25,000 and $34,000, up to 50 percent of Social Security benefits could be taxed. If the combined income of a single filer is more than $34,000, up to 85 percent of the benefits can be taxed. For those filing joint returns, break points are $32,000 and $44,000, respectively. For married individuals filing separate returns, the break point is $0.

A person who retires before their NRA and receives Social Security retirement benefits can lose some or all of the benefits by working. Retirees who have not yet reached their NRA for all of 2016 can earn up to $15,720 without losing benefits. If earnings exceed this amount, part of the Social Security benefit is lost; the penalty in lost benefits is severe. For every $2 a client earns above this amount, $1 in benefits is lost. For those who will reach their NRA in 2016, the Social Security Administration will deduct $1 from benefits for each $3 earned above $41,880 until the month a client reaches full retirement age. After NRA has been reached, a retiree can earn an unlimited dollar amount without penalty.

Procedural Strategy 7: Use Qualified Employee Plans Appropriately

Self-Test 6

Sarita participates in a defined benefit pension plan. Her firm uses the following unit-benefit formula: 2% of final pay for each year of service. If Sarita works for 20 years and has a final year income of $160,000 how much will she receive from the pension?

a. $58,000

b. $64,000

c. $4,800,000

d. $6,400,000

Employer-provided retirement plans can be broadly categorized as either qualified or non-qualified. **Qualified retirement plans** are recognized and described in the IRC. Qualified plans provide employees and employers certain tax advantages because they meet qualifications established by tax law. Contributions to an employee's qualified retirement plan are generally excluded from current taxable income. Employers enjoy an immediate tax deduction for contributions made to a qualified retirement plan for their employees. Although certain rules place limits on contributions, it is possible for some employers to offer more than one kind of plan.

Qualified retirement plans can be further differentiated into two categories: defined benefit plans and defined contribution plans. A **defined benefit plan**, or **pension plan,** provides a specific guaranteed benefit at retirement that is usually calculated using a **unit-benefit formula** typically based on a percentage of salary and years of service. For example, a benefit of 1.5 percent of final pay for each year of service up to twenty-five years is common. Using this formula, someone who has worked at a firm for twenty years would be eligible to receive 30 percent of final pay as a yearly benefit in retirement for the remainder of the retiree's life. Again, no joint and survivor benefits are provided automatically under ERISA-covered defined benefit or cash-balance plans.

A **defined contribution** plan provides an individual account for each participant and offers benefits to employees based on the value of that account upon retirement. The most common form of employer-provided retirement plan in the United States is the defined contribution plan.

The most common type of qualified plan is a 401(k) plan. A **401(k) plan** offers employees the opportunity to contribute pretax dollars to their accounts. Many plans provide some form of matching contribution by the employer. A 401(k) plan can also include a **Roth 401(k)** feature, which allows the contribution of after-tax dollars. Two specialized types of 401(k) plan designs are available: the **SIMPLE 401(k) plan** and the **safe harbor 401(k) plan**.

Defined contribution plans include all **profit-sharing plans**, as well as **stock bonus plans** and **employee stock ownership plans (ESOP). Money purchase plans** and **target benefit plans** are also included. Certain types of retirement plans are not technically qualified plans, yet they operate in a similar manner and provide tax-deferred earnings growth. Examples include **simplified employee pension** accounts (SEP accounts) and **Keogh plan** accounts for small businesses, **403(b) tax-sheltered annuities** for nonprofit employers, and **457 plans** for state, local, and municipal government employers. Figure 12.7 provides summary data for each of these defined contribution plans.

Figure 12.7 A Comparison of the Funding Characteristics of Defined Contribution Plans for 2016

Plan Type	Maximum Contribution on per Participant (Elective Deferral)	Maximum Annual Addition[1] per Participant (based on Max. Compensation of ($265,000)[2]	Mandatory Yearly Employer Contributions?	CODA/ 401(k) Permitted?	Forfeitures Generally Required to be Redistributed	In-Service Withdrawls Allowed?	Immediate Mandatory Vesting for Employer Contributions?
Large-employer-sponsored Plans							
Money purchase	After-tax allowed	The lesser of 100% of income or $53,000	Yes	No	Yes	No, but loans are allowed	No
Target benefit	Not allowed	The lesser of 100% of income or $53,000	Yes	No	Yes	No	No
Profit-sharing	Not allowed	The lesser of 100% of income or $53,000	No[3]	Yes	Yes	Yes	No
Stock bonus	$53,000	The lesser of 100% of income or $53,000	No[3]	Yes	Yes	Yes	No
ESOP	$53,000	The lesser of 100% of income or $53,000	No[3]	Yes	Yes	Yes	No
401(k)[4]	$18,000 + $6,000 age 50+ catch-up	The lesser of 100% of income or $53,000	No	NA	No	Yes	No
Roth 401(k)	$18,000 + $6,000 age 50+ catch-up (after-tax)	The lesser of 100% of income or $53,000	No	NA	No	Yes; after 5 years of participation, or age 59½	No
Thrift and savings	Varies	The lesser of 100% of income or $53,000	Generally, yes	No	Yes	Yes	No
403(b)[4]	$18,000 + $6,000 age 50+ catch-up	The lesser of 100% of income or $53,000	No	No	No	Yes	Yes

Figure 12.7 A Comparison of the Funding Characteristics of Defined Contribution Plans for 2016

Plan Type	Maximum Contribution on per Participant (Elective Deferral)	Maximum Annual Addition[1] per Participant (based on Max. Compensation of ($265,000)[2]	Mandatory Yearly Employer Contributions?	CODA/ 401(k) Permitted?	Forfeitures Generally Required to be Redistributed	In-Service Withdrawls Allowed?	Immediate Mandatory Vesting for Employer Contributions? *(cont'd)*
Large-employer-sponsored Plans							
457[4]	$18,000 + $6,000 age 50+ catch-up or 100% of compensation	$18,000 or 100% of compensation	Not allowed	No	NA	Yes; unforeseen emergency only	NA
Small-business-sponsored Plans							
SEP[5]	Not allowed	The lesser of 25% of net earnings or $53,000	No	No	NA	Yes; same as IRA	Yes
SARSEP/ 408(k)[6]	The lesser of 25% of compensation or $18,000	The lesser of 25% of net earnings or $53,000	No	No	NA	Yes; same as IRA	Yes
Keogh[5] money purchase	Employees may not contribute	Up to 25% of earned income	Yes	No	Yes	No	No
Keogh[5] profit-sharing	Employees may not contribute	Up to 25% of earned income	No[3]	No	Yes	Yes; after 5 years of participation, or age 59½	No
SIMPLE IRA	$12,500 + $3,000 age 50+ catch-up	See[7] below	Yes	No	NA	Yes; same as IRA	Yes
SIMPLE 401(k)[4, 8]	$12,500 + $3,000 age 50+ catch-up	$20,450 or $23,450 age 50+	Yes	Yes	NA	Yes; same as IRA	Yes

1. Annual additions are equal to the sum of employer contributions, employee contributions, both deductible and nondeductible, and unvested forfeitures.
2. There is an additional limitation on the maximum amount of employer contribution that is tax-deductible to the employer.
3. No mandatory annual employer contributions required, but employers must make substantial and regular contributions.
4. A targeted, non-refundable tax credit for low- to moderate-income savers is available for 401(k), 403(b), 457(b), and IRA contributions.
5. SEP and KEOGH: the effective maximum contribution percentage takes into account net earnings instead of total compensation.
6. Salary Reduction (SAR) SEPs have not been eligible for new establishment since 1997.
7. For a SIMPLE IRA, employers must make either a dollar-for-dollar matching contribution up to 3 percent of an employee's compensation (can elect to lower the percentage to no less than 1 percent for no more than 2 out of 5 years ending in the current year), or 2 percent of compensation for all eligible employees earning at least $5,000 regardless of elected salary reductions.
8. The maximum total contribution to a SIMPLE 401(k) plan for 2016 is $18,850 (salary deferral of $12,500 + 3 percent contribution of maximum salary of $265,000 + catch-up contributions). The maximum permitted contribution for a SIMPLE 401(k) plan is the maximum elective deferral plus the 3 percent matching contribution.

Procedural Strategy 8: Use Non-Qualified Employer Provided Plans Within the Funding Mix

Employers may find that nondiscrimination rules and dollar limits placed on qualified plans restrict the usefulness of these retirement planning tools, especially as a means for providing benefits to executives and highly compensated employees. **Non-qualified plans** give employers more flexibility in offering benefits to these select groups, but they generally offer fewer tax advantages. An example of a non-qualified plan is a **non-qualified deferred compensation plan** (**NQDC**), which is defined as an agreement between an employer and employee where the employee agrees to accept payments at some specified time in the future. Employees are sometimes allowed to contribute to an NQDC, in which case contributions are considered fully vested. However, employer contributions are not as secure compared to contributions to a similar qualified plan. In exchange for less security, an employee can be compensated with contributions far exceeding current limits on qualified plans.

> *Self-Test 7*
>
> Reyna, age 55, earns $46,000 per year. What is the maximum in annual additions that can be contributed to her qualified 401(k) account?
>
> a. $18,000
>
> b. $24,000
>
> c. $46,000
>
> d. $53,000

Two non-qualified deferred compensation arrangements are commonly used by employers when benefit plans are negotiated with highly compensated employees: rabbi and secular trusts. A **rabbi trust** is an irrevocable arrangement between an employer and employee. (The name stems from the first trust assessed by the IRS in which a congregation established this type of arrangement for its rabbi.) Under this agreement, the trust is considered to be unfunded, meaning that the employee cannot access assets until all contractual obligations have been met (typically at retirement). Because the plan is unfunded, the employer cannot deduct contributions to the trust until distributions are made. The employee is not taxed until he or she receives a trust distribution (e.g., upon retirement, death, disability, or employment termination). Because of the non-qualified status of the plan, assets held in the trust are subject to claims of the employer's creditors in case of bankruptcy. A **secular trust** provides employees additional security. Assets held in the trust are not subject to creditor claims against the employer. However, because the assets are more secure, all employer contributions to the plan are immediately taxable to the employee.

Procedural Strategy 9: Use Personal Savings Within the Funding Mix

Nearly all Americans who hope to retire comfortably must rely on their own willingness and ability to save money. Thus, it is important to generate a pool of assets, combined with those from qualified and non-qualified sources, which will be large enough to generate income during a client's retirement years.

The traditional or Roth **individual retirement arrangement** or **agreement (IRA)** is typically one of the first personal retirement savings vehicle recommended, assuming an individual has earned income. IRAs provide an option to grow assets on a tax-deferred (traditional) or tax-free (Roth) distribution basis, which offers financial planning clients unique tax benefits not available with other personal savings alternatives. Characteristics of traditional and Roth IRAs are summarized in Figure 12.8.

As illustrated in Figure 12.8, some features are common to both types of IRAs. First, almost any type of investment can be purchased, excluding life insurance and collectibles. Second, IRAs cannot be used as collateral for a loan. Third, under federal bankruptcy law, IRAs enjoy limited (up to $1 million) protection from creditors.

Beyond the taxation differences of traditional and Roth IRAs, there are four distinct types of IRAs, determined by funding source: contributory, rollover, inherited, and spousal. The contributory IRA is what most people are familiar with as the IRA with the funding limitation and earned income requirement. However, the other three types do not have an earned income requirement and only the spousal IRA has an annual funding limit. The option to fund a spousal IRA for a non-working married partner is another benefit for couples seeking additional alternatives for retirement savings.

Rollover IRA and **inherited IRA** accounts are distinctive for two reasons. The owner cannot contribute to these accounts after establishment and these IRAs may not be commingled. This means that the owner cannot combine assets from one IRA with those of another, with one exception: the rollover IRA is funded with assets that were originally contributed to another qualified retirement account (e.g. 401(k), 403(b), etc.) and distributed, typically as the result of a separation of service. The inherited IRA is an account originally funded by another person, with the original owner bequeathing the account to an heir. Multiple inherited IRAs from the same owner and of the same type (e.g., traditional or Roth), can be combined, or commingled, if all rules are followed.

Figure 12.8 A Comparison of Traditional and Roth IRAs

Feature	Traditional IRA	Roth IRA
Eligibility	Must receive earned income in the year of contribution Up to the calendar year when age 70½ is reached Spousal IRA—Up to the calendar year when the spouse is age 70½	Must receive earned income in the year of contribution 2016 modified adjusted gross income(MAGI) phase-out Single filers: $117,000–$132,000 Joint filers: $184,000–$194,000 Spousal IRA—Any age
Maximum annual contribution	Lesser of $6,000 or 100 percent of earned income in 2016 plus $1,000 catch-up for those age 50 or older Spousal: See specific rules regarding nonworking or low-earning spouses Rollover: No limit or income guidelines for rollover contributions	
Federal income tax treatment of contributions	Fully deductible for those ineligible for an employer plan (an exception applies for a non-employer eligible spouse who files a joint return if MAGI exceeds $194,000 for 2016) or if eligible below a certain AGI (in 2016: $98,000 joint or $61,000 single) Partially deductible for employees eligible for an employer plan with MAGI within a certain range (in 2016: $98,000–$118,000 joint or $61,000–$71,000 single) Nondeductible for employees eligible for an employer plan with MAGI above a certain amount (in 2016: $118,000 joint or $71,000 single)	Not deductible Taxable portion of traditional IRA conversion taxed at ordinary income rates
Earnings	Earnings grow tax deferred. Distributions of earnings and *tax-deductible* contributions are taxable.	Earnings grow tax deferred. Qualified distributions of earnings and contributions are exempt from federal taxation.
Tax on qualified distribution	Money from a qualified distribution of earnings and/or tax-deductible contributions is included in gross income for federal income tax purposes.	Money from a qualified distribution is *not* included in gross income for federal income tax purposes.
Tax on Withdrawals of Contributions?	Yes, unless the contributions were not tax-deductible	No, because no tax deduction was received for the contributions.

Figure 12.8 A Comparison of Traditional and Roth IRAs (*cont'd*)

Feature	Traditional IRA	Roth IRA
Tax on Distribution of Earnings?	Yes	Yes, unless the distribution is "qualified" meaning that: • The account is open for 5 years AND, • Distribution made on or after age 59½; or • Distribution made to the estate or a beneficiary of the owner upon death of the owner; or • Distribution made to the owner after meeting the definition of disabled according to the IRS code; or • Distribution used to pay for qualified first-time homebuyer expenses.
Is There a 10 percent Penalty on Withdrawals?	Yes <u>on both tax-deductible contributions and earnings</u>, unless: • Penalty-free withdrawals available for any reason after age 59½, or for the following prior to age 59½. However, income tax may apply. • Withdrawal occurs because of the IRA owner's disability or death • Withdrawal meets 72t standards. • Withdrawal used to pay for unreimbursed medical expenses that exceed 7½ percent of adjusted gross income (AGI). • Withdrawal used to pay medical insurance premiums after the IRA owner has received unemployment compensation for more than 12 weeks. • Withdrawal used to pay the costs of a first-time home purchase ($10,000 lifetime maximum). • Withdrawal used to pay for the qualified expenses of higher education for the IRA owner and/ or eligible family members.	Yes <u>on earnings only</u>, unless: • Penalty-free withdrawals available for any reason after age 59½, or for the following prior to age 59½. However, income tax may apply. • Withdrawal occurs because of the IRA owner's disability or death. • Withdrawal meets 72t standards. • Withdrawal used to pay for unreimbursed medical expenses that exceed 7½ percent of adjusted gross income (AGI). • Withdrawal used to pay medical insurance premiums after the IRA owner has received unemployment compensation for more than 12 weeks. • Withdrawal used to pay the costs of a first-time home purchase ($10,000 lifetime maximum). • Withdrawal used to pay for the qualified expenses of higher education for the IRA owner and/ or eligible family members.

Figure 12.8 A Comparison of Traditional and Roth IRAs (*cont'd*)

Feature	Traditional IRA	Roth IRA
Required Minimum Distributions	Must begin by April 1 of the next year after attaining age 70½.	No required minimum distributions.
Penalty Tax for Insufficient Distributions	Penalty of 50 percent of the amount that should have been distributed	No penalties apply.
Penalty for Excess Contributions	6 percent	6 percent
Compensation for IRA Purposes	1. Wages and Salaries 2. Commissions 3. Self-Employment Income 4. Alimony and Separate Maintenance 5. Military Differential Pay 6. Non-taxable Combat Pay	

Procedural Strategy 10: Apply Inherited IRA Rules Correctly

It is important for financial planners to understand rules related to the inheritance of IRAs as a way to help clients avoid paying unnecessary taxes and penalties. The following points highlight important inherited IRA rules for non-spousal beneficiaries:[9]

1. When a *non-spouse beneficiary* inherits an IRA, he or she must either begin lifetime distributions by December 31 of the year after the year of the decedent's death or choose a five-year distribution alternative. The five-year distribution is available only if the owner died before the required distribution beginning date for a traditional IRA. If the five-year distribution plan is chosen, the beneficiary can elect to revert to a lifetime distribution plan as long as the first distribution was made by December 31 of the year following the decedent's death.

2. The *10 percent penalty* for distributions prior to age 59½ does not apply to inherited IRAs; only taxes would be due upon distribution. The sixty-day rollover rule does not apply to inherited IRAs; any distribution is subject to tax.

3. Non-spouse beneficiaries cannot roll over inherited IRAs into an existing or new IRA, but they can transfer the funds to a new custodian or combine multiple inherited IRA accounts of the same type and from the same owner into one account. Care must be taken in titling the account according to IRS requirements, as follows: "IRA FBO Jane Smith as beneficiary of Dan Brown" or "IRA FBO Dan Brown (dec'd); Jane Smith (beneficiary)."

4. Non-spouse beneficiaries may not convert an inherited IRA into a Roth IRA or an inherited Roth IRA.

5. When calculating required minimum distributions (RMDs), inherited IRAs must remain separate from other IRAs owned by the beneficiary. RMDs are discussed later in this chapter; for more information, see IRS Publication 590, *Individual Retirement Arrangements (IRAs)*.

Most rules are similar for a spouse who inherits an IRA, although a spouse can roll over an inherited IRA into an existing or new IRA of the same type, which allows for more discretion on the RMDs from a traditional account. Figure 12.9 illustrates these general rules. However, extreme caution is warranted when working with a client inheriting spousal retirement assets or IRAs because the options are contingent on several different factors (e.g., age of spouse at death, age of surviving spouse, financial situation and the need for and timing of need for assets, potential estate tax situation of the surviving spouse), including the following:

- Transfer the inherited assets into an inherited IRA with rules similar to that for a non-spousal inherited IRA; or

- Roll over the assets into an existing or new IRA with the RMD based on the age of the surviving spouse; or

- Roll over or convert the assets into a new or existing Roth IRA; or

- *Disclaim*, within nine months of the spouse's death, all or part of the inherited assets.

Finally, an important caveat is the reminder that clients complete the necessary documentation to establish a beneficiary(ies) for an inherited IRA or a new spousal IRA funded with inherited assets. This is important to ensure that the client's wishes for bequeathing the assets are satisfied and to protect the client's estate from potential additional estate taxation.

Figure 12.9 Decision Tree for Planning for an Inherited IRA

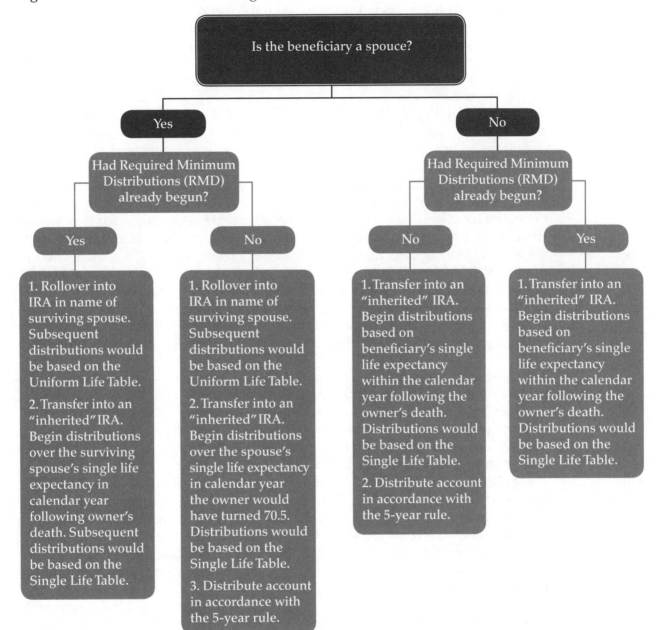

Procedural Strategy 11: Understand IRA Transfer, Rollover, and Conversion Rules

There are the two primary ways to move assets between qualified accounts without incurring an income tax liability: transfer and rollover. Typically, a **transfer** refers to moving assets directly from one custodian to another without the owner of the account ever taking possession of the funds. This is the most typical method for moving funds from one IRA account to another. The other method for moving funds from an employer-sponsored plan into an IRA is called a **rollover,** and there are two forms: indirect and direct. In the case of an *indirect rollover* the owner takes temporary (sixty days or fewer) ownership—called *constructive receipt*—of the funds. The original custodian sends the assets to the owner, who then sends them to the new custodian, thereby completing the rollover. The *direct rollover* method works the same as the transfer, where the owner never has constructive receipt of the funds.

Another method for moving funds—**conversion**—creates an income tax liability. Converting a traditional IRA to a Roth IRA is a strategy frequently used to gain the benefits of the Roth IRA. In its most basic form, a **Roth IRA conversion** occurs when a client converts assets held in a traditional IRA into a Roth IRA. Conversion triggers income tax in the year of the conversion on the value of the account (excluding any non-tax-deductible contributions that were previously taxed) on the day of the conversion. This allows the assets to continue to grow tax deferred with the option of making withdrawals on a tax-free basis. Because of the tax implications, and the potential to push some clients into a higher tax bracket, care must be taken when using this strategy. Some or all of a conversion can be undone (called a **recharacterization)** should the tax situation, the cash flow to pay the taxes, or the value of the accounts decline significantly. Undoing a Roth conversion involves moving the money from the Roth IRA back to a traditional IRA using the custodian's forms for a Roth recharacterization. It is also possible to execute a partial recharacterization and move part of a Roth IRA back to a traditional IRA. However, care must be taken to follow the rules carefully for a conversion and recharacterization, regarding both the process and the time line.

Beginning in 2010, income limits associated with Roth conversions were removed. This was the result of the Tax Increase Prevention and Reconciliation Act of 2005. The Act, however, did not eliminate the income restrictions associated with Roth contributions, thereby creating a significant tax loophole. High-income clients, clients who believe that their marginal tax rate will be higher in retirement than it is currently, and those who wish to postpone RMDs are the most anxious to hold wealth in Roth IRAs. These clients are also the most likely to convert traditional IRA assets into Roth IRAs. This is where the loophole comes into play. High-earning households typically are excluded from contributing to a Roth IRA, but not to non-deductible traditional IRAs. Some planners have recommended, therefore, that high-income clients contribute the maximum allowed to a traditional IRA. They are then encouraged to convert the IRA to a Roth. Because both transactions include only after-tax contributions, the strategy has no immediate tax consequences.

Although this strategy is being used, financial planners should be forewarned that the IRS requires IRA aggregating for calculating taxes due on conversions. If a client holds any pre-tax IRA assets, it is likely that this conversion strategy will trigger income taxation.[10] Further, some have argued that the IRS could assert the **step transaction doctrine**, which states that a series of actions taken to complete a single comprehensive transaction will be taxed on the overall economic outcome of the transaction. That is, the IRS may conclude that clients who use this type of conversion strategy constructively made an improper Roth IRA contribution. As such, this loophole should be used with great caution.

Procedural Strategy 12: Understand Social Security Eligibility for Divorced Clients

Increasingly, financial planners are called on to help clients prepare for retirement prior to, after, or during a divorce. It is important to understand how divorce can impact a client's eligibility for Social Security benefits. According to the Social Security Administration, if a client is divorced (even if the other person has since remarried), the client can qualify for benefits on the record of the ex-spouse. This is an important consideration for many women who were primary homemakers without an earnings record. To receive benefits, a client must:

- have been married to the ex-spouse for at least ten years;

- have been divorced at least two years;

- be at least sixty-two years old;

- be unmarried; and

- be ineligible for an equal or higher benefit on his or her own work or someone else's work.

These eligibility rules can place some clients in a financially awkward position. For example, if a client was married for less than ten years, he or she might not be eligible for benefits under the ex-spouse's record. The rules also prohibit a client from remarrying; however, clients sometimes marry first only to discover that their benefits have been lost. The primary disadvantage for younger divorced clients under current rules is that to receive benefits and/or to be considered insured for Medicare, the client may have to reenter the workplace to establish an income record.

Procedural Strategy 13: Consider IRA Transfer Rules when Advising Clients about Rollover Alternatives

The IRS currently allows assets to be transferred tax free from a qualified retirement plan or another IRA to an IRA. Three transfers are allowed. A **trustee-to-trustee transfer** occurs when one trustee directly moves a client's assets to another trustee. Because there is no distribution to the client, the transfer is tax free. According to the IRS, because this type of transfer is not a rollover, it is not affected by the one-year waiting period required between rollovers. The second transfer is called a *rollover*. An **IRA rollover** is a tax-free distribution of cash or other assets from a retirement plan made directly to a client. It is the client's responsibility to contribute assets to the IRA. Clients must generally roll over the entire contribution by the sixtieth day after receiving the distribution. The third transfer method is known as *transfers incident to divorce*. If assets in a traditional IRA are transferred from an ex-spouse to your client via a divorce or separate maintenance decree, the assets held in the IRA, starting from the date of the transfer, are treated as belonging to the client. The transfer is tax free.

Knowing the transfer rules is important as a tool for reducing tax liabilities and penalties. If a client fails to roll over a distribution within sixty days, in the absence of a waiver, the client must treat the amount as a taxable distribution. These amounts are taxable in the year distributed, even if the sixty-day period expires the next year. For clients under age 59½, it is likely that they will have to pay a 10 percent additional tax on early distributions. It is also important to note another disadvantage associated with a rollover. Generally, if a client makes a tax-free rollover of any part of a distribution from a traditional IRA, he or she cannot, within a one-year period, make a tax-free rollover of any later distribution from that same IRA. Clients are also prohibited from making a tax-free rollover of any amount distributed within the same one-year period from the IRA into which they made the tax-free rollover. The one-year period begins on the date that clients receive an IRA distribution, not the date they roll it into an IRA. There is third disadvantage. If an eligible rollover distribution is paid directly to a client, the payer must withhold 20 percent for federal tax purposes. This rule applies even if the client plans to roll over the distribution to a traditional IRA.

Procedural Strategy 14: Tap Home Equity for Retirement Needs

A Fidelity Research Institute report noted that some financial planning experts now refer to home equity as the fourth leg of the retirement funding stool—although this source of funding has come under pressure since the real estate collapse of the late 2000s.[11] The emotional tie to the asset, a desire to retire in the home, or the desire to convey the asset to heirs are influential factors that should be considered when adding home equity as a retirement asset. Nevertheless, the home can represent, either by necessity or choice, one of the largest retirement assets for many clients. A significant advantage associated with home equity is the tax-advantaged nature of the asset. A couple can exempt from taxes gains of up to $500,000 (or $250,000 for a single filer) generated from the sale of a principal residence. A common planning recommendation involves having clients who are entering retirement consider using the proceeds from the sale of their home to buy a smaller house and using the balance of the proceeds to supplement retirement income.

Procedural Strategy 15: Meeting the Need—Decrease Projected Income or Living Expense Requirements

A shortfall in retirement savings could exist even after committing unallocated assets and savings toward the retirement goal. It is possible that the amount of income or living expenses being replaced is too high. This strategy calls for the client to reevaluate the retirement income need. By reducing the need, it might be possible to use existing resources to fully fund retirement. Emotionally, asking a client to reassess his or her income need can be quite difficult. Some clients could interpret this suggestion as indicating that they are extravagant. Also, it is possible that the client's income need is realistic and that income cannot be cut without seriously decreasing a client's quality of life in retirement.

Procedural Strategy 16: Meeting the Need—Adjust the Life Expectancy Assumption

Changing the years in retirement assumption (i.e., life expectancy) is one way to decrease a client's total asset need without decreasing the projected amount of annual income received. The obvious disadvantage associated with this strategy is that a client could outlive the accumulated asset base. The fiscal and emotional strain on the client and other family members could be devastating. Elderly individuals who have planned well for retirement often worry about outliving their resources. Adjusting the life expectancy assumption, unless there is valid information on which to base this decision, could mislead a client and further limit alternative retirement saving options or available spending reductions.

Procedural Strategy 17: Meeting the Need—Increase Rate-of-Return Assumptions

Increasing the rate-of-return assumption within retirement planning models is the easiest way to obtain the theoretical feasibility of retirement goals. Hypothetically, it is possible to meet retirement objectives, holding all other inputs static, by increasing portfolio returns. Rate-of-return assumptions must be based on a combination of a client's time horizon, risk tolerance, capacity for risk taking, asset class preference, and expectations about the future. Assuming a rate of return that is higher than is commensurate with a client's risk profile almost inevitably leads to plan failure. So, even though it is theoretically possible to make a retirement plan work by increasing portfolio return assumptions, in practical terms it may not be possible to actually manage assets in a way that generates such returns without exposing the client to greater levels of risk. Further, overestimating expected returns in a portfolio might subject a financial planner to suitability challenges if returns are not realized.

Procedural Strategy 18: Meeting the Need—Postpone Retirement

It may be reasonable to recommend that a client postpone retirement one or more years. The advantage of this strategy is that it generally results in a higher Social Security benefit. The strategy also allows existing assets to grow for additional years. This strategy may not be feasible for clients who face forced retirement because of medical problems or loss of employment. Also, this strategy forces clients to work longer than hoped and expected, which can result in a reduced level of morale and willingness to maintain proactive financial planning strategies. As an alternative, in situations where one spouse will earn more by claiming a *spousal benefit* rather than their own Social Security benefit, a good strategy involves having the high-earning spouse file for benefits at NRA. This allows the low-earning partner to file for spousal benefits. The higher-earning partner can then, if desired, halt his or her request, thus allowing the benefit value to increase. Even though the high-earning spouse will not receive a benefit, the spousal benefit will be paid immediately. This popular claiming strategy is called *claim-and-suspend*.

Procedural Strategy 19: Meeting the Need—Decrease the Inflation Rate Retirement Assumption

In cases where adjusting other assumptions leaves a client short of their capital accumulation goal, another strategy is to reduce the assumed inflation rate for the retirement time period. This will result in a lower assumed gross asset need at retirement, which will make the value of assets and savings appear more likely to meet client needs. Implementing this strategy is fraught with risk. Inflation is often the greatest financial risk facing retirees on a fixed income. If actual inflation exceeds the assumed level, then it is likely that a client's assets will quickly be depleted over the course of the client's life.

Procedural Strategy 20: Meeting the Need—Decrease the Income Replacement Ratio

This strategy calls for decreasing a client's income need while in retirement. The advantage of this strategy is that decreasing the percentage of income projected to be replaced will result in a lower total funding need at the date of retirement. Implementing this strategy could reduce a client's standard of living to a level that is less than preferable, and in an extreme situation, unrealistic. The ultimate consequence is less money to fund leisure activities, gifting strategies, travel, entertainment, or other expenses.

Procedural Strategy 21: Meeting the Need—Continue to Work (Part-Time) while in Retirement

This strategy has the dual advantage of providing additional cash flow in retirement while providing meaningful activity for the client while retired. For some executives and former business owners, this could mean periodic consulting. For others, it might mean working a permanent part-time job. The additional cash flow reduces the amount of retirement income to be replaced from assets, savings, and retirement plans. Working while retired is also an excellent way to keep both mind and body active. Some retirees find that their dreams of retirement are larger than the reality, and employment provides some with the opportunity to contribute to society in a meaningful way.

It is worth remembering that working while retired can have a significantly negative impact on Social Security benefits. Clients who receive Social Security benefits before reaching NRA are limited in the amount that can be earned without losing benefits. Another disadvantage associated with this strategy is that for many clients the thought of working defeats the goal of retiring. This, like many of the procedural strategies presented, can have a negative impact on attitudes and willingness to continue planning.

Procedural Strategy 22: Understand Qualified Plan Coverage Rules

When designing or evaluating a qualified retirement plan for an organization (e.g., a small business owner) it is important to understand the following coverage eligibility rules:

- Defined benefit plans must benefit the lesser of 40 percent of eligible employees or fifty eligible employees.

- Defined contribution plans must provide a benefit to 70 percent or more of

    o non-highly compensated employees, or

    o the ratio of non-highly compensated employees to highly compensated employees, or o the average benefit ratio for non-highly compensated employees to highly compensated employees must be at least 70 percent, and

o the plan must not be nondiscriminatory.

Any plan that fails these coverage rules is considered non-qualified for tax purposes, resulting in lost tax deductions for the organization and potential loss of tax deferral for employees.

Procedural Strategy 23: Understand Who Could Be Excluded from a Qualified Retirement Plan

Providing a qualified retirement plan can often be an expensive benefit for businesses. By understanding who could be excluded from plan participation, it is possible to save plan expenses for a business owner client. In general, anyone under the age of twenty-one or those who work less than 1,000 hours per year can be excluded. Any employee who has worked for 1,000 hours in a twelve-month period and is at least twenty-one years of age is eligible for plan participation.

Excluding certain employees from a qualified plan can result in reduced productivity, resulting in higher employee turnover. Furthermore, business owners must weigh the potentially negative effects of excluding employees (e.g., low morale) against the actual dollar amount saved in benefit costs.

Procedural Strategy 24: Include Post-Retirement Income Tax Considerations when Conducting a Retirement Needs Analysis

An important factor determining the feasibility of a retirement needs analysis involves the client's place of residence. Each state taxes pension benefits—and in some cases even Social Security benefits—differently. Various sources, such as Kiplinger, AARP, and the National Conference of State Legislatures, provide a state-by-state comparison of taxes—income, sales, and real estate, for example—levied on retirees. By understanding the income tax status of Social Security and private, state, and federal pensions at the state level, a financial planner can provide a more accurate income projection. For example, some states like Nebraska, Rhode Island, North Dakota, Utah, and Vermont offer no income tax exemptions for Social Security or pension benefits.[12] Other states, such as Georgia, exempt Social Security benefits and up to $35,000 of retirement income from state taxation; Kentucky also exempts Social Security benefits from state income taxes plus more than $41,000 per person of retirement income, including public and private pensions and annuities.[13] It is important to remember that for some clients, it may be impossible to relocate to a state that provides a more competitive tax environment. There might also be situations when a client would rather pay higher taxes than move. Under such circumstances, this tax information should be used to help clients plan for avoiding or paying taxes rather than as a comparison of tax havens.

Procedural Strategy 25: Understand the Role Played by the Pension Benefit Guaranty Corporation in Retirement Planning

The **Pension Benefit Guaranty Corporation** (**PBGC**) was created when President Ford signed the Employee Retirement Income Security Act (*ERISA*) into law in 1974. The primary role of the PBGC is to protect participants in qualified defined benefit plans from losing benefits when a plan is terminated because of underfunding. PBGC is a government corporation that serves the role of insuring pension plan account balances; however, PBGC insurance covers only a fraction of the benefit level of a terminated pension plan. PBGC benefits are based on an employee's age, the previous promised defined benefit plan payout, and the amount of plan benefits that remain after plan termination. PBGC insurance is funded by premiums collected from pension plan sponsors (based on a premium per participant), earnings from assets held by PBGC, and recoveries from the sponsors of terminated defined benefit plans.

Procedural Strategy 26: Incorporate Sequence of Returns Risk into Planning Assumptions

Deterministic models sometimes fail as a result of **sequence risk**. This is the risk associated with receiving a below-average return during the first few years of distributions compared to earning higher returns later. Clients who begin distributions just before a market decline must earn higher rates in the future to reach their average return need. This means that the likelihood of having an asset shortfall is greater for such clients. Furthermore, these potential errors in retirement projections demonstrate the need for an ongoing client-planner relationship, where planners can continually update projections and advise a client on needed changes.

Procedural Strategy 27: Choose an Appropriate Withdrawal or Distribution Plan

Traditionally, financial planners have been trained to think of retirement planning in terms of asset accumulation and investment growth, with the ultimate objective being the development of a retirement nest egg. Little thought went into an equally important planning issue—how clients should structure withdrawals from accumulated savings when they retire.

Upon retirement, retirees face an important question regarding the distribution of income from accumulated savings. Financial advisors typically recommend that clients withdraw funds from taxable accounts before taking distributions from qualified retirement plans (e.g., a 401(k), 403(b), 457 plan) to maximize the tax deferral of the other accounts.[14] Assets held in tax-free accounts (e.g., a Roth IRA) should be distributed last. Two exceptions to this general rule exist. First, clients who will not take meaningful distributions prior to death may want to withdraw from tax-deferred accounts first to obtain the maximum step-up in basis on other assets at the time of death. Second, whenever the after-tax return on taxable accounts exceeds the return on qualified tax-deferred account assets, distributions from the tax-deferred accounts should occur first.[15] The one caveat to the second point is obviously the risk aspect, because higher returns normally mean higher risk.

Procedural Strategy 28: Understand the Tax Implications of Withdrawal Choices

Taking distributions from taxable accounts can offer some tax advantages. Lower rates have recently been available for long-term capital gains, and a client may be able to time the taxation of any capital gains, further reducing the average tax rate by looking for offsetting capital losses. In certain circumstances, taking distributions from these investments first could actually reduce income taxes. Postponing the redemption of tax-deferred accounts, taxed as ordinary income when withdrawn, allows these accounts to continue growing on a tax-deferred basis. Assuming the rules for tax-free distributions from Roth accounts are met, leaving those accounts until last allows for a longer period of tax-deferred growth and tax-free distributions.

Financial planners and their clients have the most flexibility in choosing the distribution method that best meets the client's needs when working with non-qualified accounts or with IRAs because employer-sponsored qualified retirement accounts may have additional limitations on withdrawal options. Employers often require employees who separate from service to take a distribution. Distributions from qualified plans (401(k), 403(b), 457 plan, etc.) can generally be made in a couple of ways. Accumulated assets can, depending on plan policy, be left in the plan itself, which may allow the client to take distributions as needed—on a regular periodic or irregular basis. Or the employer may require the former employee to take a lump sum distribution of all plan assets.

A client who takes a *lump sum distribution* from a qualified defined contribution plan must be given the opportunity to roll over the proceeds of the distribution into an IRA or other eligible qualified plan. Once the plan assets have been rolled over to an IRA, the client has the same distribution options as for any other IRA account. The following discussion examines two forms of distribution and associated income tax considerations. For taxation purposes, there are two categories of distribution payments:

1. Non-annuitized payments (e.g., lump sum "one-time" distributions, discretionary installment payments, irregular distributions)

2. Annuitized payments

Most qualified retirement plans offer lump sum distributions. Clients who take a lump sum distribution will trigger a 20 percent federal income tax withholding requirement. The IRS requires plan sponsors who issue lump sum payments to withhold taxes as a way to ensure that the recipient can pay any tax liability. The benefit of a lump sum payment is that the total account value (minus taxes) is available to make an investment or purchase. The drawback is that a client will lose tax-deferred compounding of the earnings. This disadvantage is another reason why financial planners often suggest that a client roll over the account balance into an IRA or other eligible plan. Rollovers allow retirement assets to be managed in a way that preserves the tax-deferral of the retirement account proceeds.

Additionally, a plan participant could opt, if available, for discretionary periodic withdrawals, which could be done on a planned or an ad hoc basis. This is in fact the most common method for handling distributions because it maintains the greatest flexibility and can be matched most closely to the deterministic withdrawal streams discussed earlier in the chapter.

If an annuity or other periodic taxable distribution option is taken, all or a portion of the payments received will most likely be taxable. If the annuity is inside an IRA, then the entire payment is taxable as ordinary income, but if the annuity is not within an IRA then any return of principal is not taxed. In other words, the extent to which the distributions are taxed is based on the adjusted taxable basis of plan assets. In a case where all contributions to a plan are made with "pretax" dollars, meaning that the IRS has not collected tax revenue on the money invested, as is the case with most employer-sponsored retirement plans, then all distributions from the plan will be fully taxable. At the other extreme are Roth accounts, either IRA or 401(k)/403(b). Assets held in these accounts are based on money contributed to the plan that was taxed prior to deposit. Thus, distributions from the plan will be exempt from federal taxation in most cases.

Procedural Strategy 29: Estimate Taxation of Annuity Payouts

Distribution planning becomes more difficult when some of the assets have been contributed on a pretax basis and some on an after-tax basis, or when there is some other reason why the adjusted tax basis is not zero. In these situations, annuity distributions from a traditional IRA (or any tax-qualified annuity) are taxed using an **inclusion ratio** (or the inverse **exclusion ratio**). The taxable portion of a periodic distribution can generally be estimated using the following formula.

Inclusion Ratio =

$$\frac{\text{(Annual Distribution x Expected Distribution Time) - Aftertax Contributions}}{\text{Annual Distribution x Expected Distribution Time}}$$

Example: Assume a client retires and receives a $2,000 monthly annuity payout, and that the client's life expectancy is twenty years. If the client contributed $150,000 to the annuity, 68.75 percent of each distribution would be subject to income taxes, based on the formula.

$$\text{Inclusion Ratio} = \frac{(\$2,000 \times 240) - \$150,000}{\$2,000 \times 240} = 68.75\%$$

Procedural Strategy 30: Estimate Required Minimum Distributions Correctly

A **required minimum distribution (RMD)**, also referred to by some sources as *minimum required distributions*, or MRDs, is a mandatory distribution from a qualified plan, traditional IRA, or other plan. An RMD generally must begin by April 1of the year following the year in which the retiree turns age 70½. (Different rules may apply to pre-1987 contributions to 403(b) plans.) Certain plans might permit employees (other than 5 percent owners) to wait until April 1 of the year following retirement, if not later. This delayed option is not available for IRAs. A penalty of 50 percent applies to the extent that RMDs are not made. Generally, RMDs are computed by dividing the account balance at the end of the preceding year by the client's life expectancy factor, based on one of three tables: (a) the Uniform Lifetime Table, (b) the Single Life Expectancy Table (for use by beneficiaries), or (c) the Joint and Last Survivor Life Expectancy Table (for the use of owners whose spouses are more than 10 years younger and are the sole beneficiaries of their IRAs). The appropriate table to use depends on the type of account, beneficiaries, and ages of the account owner and beneficiary. Lifetime distributions are generally based on the Uniform Lifetime Table factors shown in Figure12.7.

> **#Remember**
>
> Learn more about required minimum distributions by visiting the IRS website: www.irs.gov/Retirement-Plans/Required-Minimum-Distributions-for-IRA-Beneficiaries

Figure12.7 Uniform Lifetime Table

Uniform Lifetime Table			
Age	Divisor	Age	Divisor
70	27.4	94	9.1
71	26.5	95	8.6
72	25.6	96	8.1
73	24.7	97	7.6
74	23.8	98	7.1
75	22.9	99	6.7
76	22.0	100	6.3
77	21.2	101	5.9
78	20.3	102	5.5
79	19.5	103	5.2
80	18.7	104	4.9
81	17.9	105	4.5
82	17.1	106	4.2
83	16.3	107	3.9
84	15.5	108	3.7
85	14.8	109	3.4
86	14.1	110	3.1
87	13.4	111	2.9
88	12.7	112	2.6
89	12.0	113	2.4
90	11.4	114	2.1
91	10.8	115 +	1.9
92	10.2		
93	9.6		

Source: IRS. *Individual Retirement Arrangements (IRAs)*, Publication 590, p. 102. Available at: www.irs.gov/pub/irs-pdf/p590.pdf.

The Uniform Lifetime Table can be used by all IRA owners (i.e., unmarried owners; owners whose spouses are fewer than ten years younger; owners for whom the spouse is not the sole beneficiary) except under the following circumstances:

- IRA owners for whom the sole beneficiary of the account is a spouse who is more than ten years younger than the owner. In that situation, the Joint Life Expectancy Table is used, thereby reducing the RMD to preserve tax-deferred earnings.

- Inherited IRA owners (non-spousal or spousal if titled as an inherited IRA). In this situation, the Single Life Expectancy Table is used.

Example: Assume that an individual turned age eighty-two this year and has a traditional IRA valued at $100,000 at the end of the previous year. The planner would simply divide $100,000 by 17.1 to determine the current year MRD of $5,848.

The **younger spouse exception** provides a longer payout for IRA owners whose sole beneficiary is a spouse who is younger by more than 10 years and the only beneficiary of the account. These owners can calculate their lifetime RMD based on the ages of both owner and spouse, using a Joint and Last Survivor Life Expectancy Table. This effectively reduces the amount of the required distribution, thereby preserving the tax-deferred status of the account balance.[16]

Procedural Strategy 31: Calculate Early Distribution Penalties Correctly

Most distributions from qualified plans before age 59½ are subject to federal and state income taxation and could be subject to a 10 percent early distribution penalty. The following exceptions from the *early distribution penalty* are available for certain distributions:

- Distributions made at the death of the owner/participant.

- Distributions attributable to the disability of the owner/participant.

- Certain distributions made in the form of substantially equal periodic payments over the life of the person (or lives of the person and a beneficiary).

- Distributions to the extent of medical expenses that exceed 7.5 percent of a person's adjusted gross income.

- Distributions made to someone age fifty-five or older who has separated from service (this exception does not apply to IRAs).

- Certain distributions ordered by a court, such as a qualified domestic relations order (QDRO) (not applicable to IRAs).

- Distributions to the extent of health insurance premiums paid during unemployment (IRAs only, not applicable to qualified plans).

- Distributions to the extent of certain college costs (not applicable to qualified plans).

- Certain distributions for the first-time purchase of a home, up to $10,000 (not applicable to qualified plans).

RETIREMENT PLANNING FOR SPECIAL POPULATIONS

Retirement Planning for Young Adults

For the first time in nearly a century, an entire generation of Americans has grown up watching their parents lose their savings, their homes, their cars, and their jobs. In addition, Ponzi schemes have instilled distrust and heightened the fear of many potential investors. These factors have resulted in a younger generation that is investing as conservatively as their parents and grandparents.[17] Not since the Great Depression has there been such a financially devastating course of events as the decade of the 2000s. Just as the Depression shaped the saving and spending habits of what is commonly known as the Traditional generation, the Internet bubble and housing crisis have shaped and will continue to shape the financial habits and paradigms of the Millennial generation.

The names Millennials, Gen Y, or Echo Boomers typically identify those born between 1980 and 1995; this generation comprises nearly eighty million Americans. Other date ranges often cited for the Millennial or Gen Y generation include 1977 to 1998 or 1980 to 2000. People born in this period were between ages one and sixteen when the dot-com bubble burst and between ages eight and twenty-three when the housing collapse nearly brought down the entire financial system. This group is clearly cautious when evaluating investment and retirement risks. In fact, according to an MFS Investing Sentiment Survey, 40 percent of Millennials agreed with the statement "I will never feel comfortable investing in the stock market."[18] But in the same survey, 62 percent agreed that they enjoy investing.[19] This is a difficult dichotomy to overcome in the planning process.

Two additional issues to consider are that (1) Millennials will be the most indebted group of college graduates in the history of the United States, and (2) they will be the best-connected, most well-informed group in the history of the United States. But they are also new to the world of personal finance—a personal financial world that has become more complex—and a world where it is becoming apparent that learning how to manage money has evolved into a life skill. These are major issues for young people and for those who strive to provide financial advice to young people. On the bright side, this group seems to be more serious about savings, but in what?

Data points to younger generation investors who prefer to invest in tangible assets rather than purely financial ones; assets such as land, gold, energy, mineral rights, and bank deposits seem to be more in vogue than at any time since the 1930s. Coincidentally, energy and tangible assets such as gold have enjoyed sustained rallies for much of the Millennials' lives. But those who have watched their parents lose their retirement account values to accounting fraud (e.g., Enron), Ponzi schemes (e.g., Bernie Madoff), greed (e.g., Global Crossing, Inc), arrogance (e.g., AIG), or ignorance (e.g., Lehman Brothers) are looking for more stable returns, guarantees, and income generation in their own retirement accounts.

One final issue is that this generation will have to plan for a retirement that is practically devoid of private, corporate-sponsored pension plans. Although this avenue of retirement savings has been in decline since the 1970s, at least some members of all of the previous generations had access to a defined-benefit plan; now, that is almost solely reserved for government employees. In 1977 nearly two-thirds of active participants in employer-sponsored retirement plans were covered by a defined benefit; however, by 2007 that ratio had fallen to 22.5 percent.[20]

In summary, the Millennials enjoy investing, but they do not trust the stock market. They are willing to save, but not willing to risk; and they have an appetite for investing in asset classes that, in the long-term, perform no better than inflation.[21]

Retirement Planning for Divorcing Couples

Divorce is hard enough without the IRS getting involved, but that is exactly what will happen without careful planning and advice to protect a couple's retirement accounts. In the past, a couple's largest asset was their home; however, in the wake of the housing collapse, it is often their retirement accounts. Liquidating a 401(k) or IRA to be able to give half to the former spouse can leave both with about 25 percent of its pretax value. In this division, the only partner to get half is Uncle Sam. In the event of a divorce, liquidating a qualified retirement account will result in a taxable event, where 25 percent to 40 percent will be owed in income taxes and another 10 percent tax penalty will apply for early distribution: divorce does not qualify as a hardship withdrawal.

Fortunately, a divorce court can approve a tax-exempt transfer of assets from the qualified account of one spouse into the qualified account of the other. This is known as a **transfer incident to divorce**. A **qualified domestic relations order (QDRO)** can be used to divide pension rights, or other accounts covered under ERISA, between spouses. This way any potential tax liability can be shared or avoided. A QDRO may be issued as part of the divorce decree, as part of the property settlement, or as a separate order. A QDRO establishes rights and protections pertaining to the division of assets that the divorce decree may not. In some marriages, only one spouse contributes to a retirement plan because the other spouse may not work or earn enough to contribute. Upon separation or divorce, a QDRO provides the mechanism to divide the retirement account without incurring current taxes or penalties.

It may appear to be easier to split an IRA account than to divide employer-provided retirement plans. A common mistake is to plan to use the unlimited spousal gifting rules, but these rules do not apply to qualified accounts. Although a divorcing couple will not necessarily need a QDRO to divide IRA accounts, they will need the court to mandate the tax-free division of property under Section 408(d)(6) of the Internal Revenue Code.

Near-retirees Retirement Planning Efforts

Much of this chapter was written assuming that a client has several years remaining before retirement. Near-retirees are often defined as those who are age fifty to fifty-five or older; other authors use the term to refer to someone within five or so years of retirement. Regardless of the exact age or number of years until retirement, these clients have a different set of planning needs than someone twenty-five or more years away from retirement who is concerned only with wealth accumulation. For one thing, the near-retiree should already have a fairly sizable retirement nest egg, so the primary planning issue might be wealth preservation instead of wealth accumulation, although this is not always the case. The concern could be how to significantly increase savings and take advantage of account catch-up provisions to more quickly save for retirement, if the retirement nest egg has not been sufficiently funded.

The client's questions could also be focused on distribution, such as, "How much income can be safely distributed annually from accumulated assets?" In other words, what will be the client's standard of living in retirement? How might a few more working years, full- or part-time, impact retirement income? Or conversely, if the client retires sooner, are retirement assets sufficient to provide for income and legacy goals? Documenting and evaluating a client's current situation in relation to post-retirement planning issues is just as— if not more—important than dealing with pre-retirement accumulation planning concerns. Although the future is still uncertain, time horizon and other assumptions might be based more on fact than conjecture, as can be the case in the early years of retirement planning.

Quantitative/Analytical Mini-Case Problems

Marybeth and Anneal Yao

1. Marybeth and Anneal Yao are beginning to contemplate retirement. They have saved a total of $500,000 for retirement and they are each just forty-five years old. They realize that they have not saved sufficiently to be able to retire early, fully retire without some part-time employment, or replace 100 percent of their preretirement income. But they are willing to explore different avenues.

    Marybeth and Anneal have a combined annual income of $125,000 and believe that their salaries will keep pace with inflation at 4 percent per year. They are also comfortable assuming that the effective annual rate of return for their retirement assets will be 9 percent before retirement and 6.5 percent after retirement. For now, Marybeth wants to keep the planning simple, projecting that they will both die in exactly forty years and that their retirement assets will be depleted with the exception of $100,000 to cover funeral and burial costs. Lastly, they do not want to continue saving after they retire (either partly or fully).

    As their financial planner, provide some assistance with these calculations. The two primary options are listed below. Considering all previous information, which outcome requires the lowest monthly (end-of-month) contribution if they also require that their retirement annuity grow by 4 percent per year to keep pace with inflation? (Ignore the effects of income taxes and social security on the answer.)

a. To retire at age fifty-five with an income replacement ratio of 60 percent.

b. To retire at age sixty-five with an income replacement ratio of 100 percent.

Tara Woodyard

2. Tara Woodyard, age forty-four, plans to retire at age sixty-seven. Her life expectancy, accounting for family medical history, is age ninety-seven. Tara is single and currently earns $56,000 per year as a university librarian. At her normal retirement age she expects to receive $28,700 in Social Security benefits (today's dollars). She will also receive a small defined benefit pension in the amount of $13,500 from a local municipality. She has come to you to determine whether she is on track to meet her retirement goals. Use the following assumptions and information to answer the questions that follow:

- She would like to use a 90 percent income replacement ratio, based on current earnings.

- She is currently contributing $2,400 per year into a 403(b) plan [no employer match].

- Inflation is assumed to be 3.50 percent.

- She can earn a 6.50 percent after-tax rate of return on assets before retirement.

- She can earn a 4.50 percent after-tax rate of return on assets after retirement.

a. How much does Tara need, on her first day of retirement, to fund a capital depletion model of retirement?

b. Given her current level of savings, is Tara on target to reach her retirement goal?

c. If she has a shortfall, how much more must she save per year to reach her goal?

d. If she would like to obtain a capital preservation goal for retirement, how much will she need to have saved on her first day of retirement?

e. Given a capital preservation goal, is she saving enough on a yearly basis currently?

f. How much, in total, must she save yearly to reach a capital preservation model of retirement?

Annette Robinson

3. Annette Robinson is a sixty-three-year-old recent widow and is attempting to do some tax and investment planning pertaining to her late husband's traditional IRA account. She has sought your advice as to the best course of action. She has informed you that her husband was sixty-nine at the time of his death and had not begun taking his RMD.

a. What are the three distribution methods available to Annette?

b. Which method should she choose to maximize tax deferral? Based on the appropriate life table, how much would her first required distribution be? When would this distribution happen?

c. Which method should she choose to maximize the distribution? Based on the appropriate life table, how much would her first required distribution be? When would this distribution happen?

d. Which alternative would not have been available had her husband begun his required distributions?

e. If Annette had been younger than fifty-nine, which alternative would allow her to take distributions without incurring the tax penalty?

Lyle and Melissa Murray

4. Lyle and Melissa Murray plan to retire when Lyle turns age sixty-five, even though his normal retirement age is sixty-seven. Lyle has worked at the same firm for over thirty years. Melissa has worked only occasional temporary jobs over her lifetime. The Murrays have a few questions about Lyle's defined benefit pension benefit and their expected Social Security benefits. Use the following information to answer their questions:

Lyle must choose from the following four defined benefit plan distribution options:

1. $3,000 for life with no survivor benefit

2. $2,700 for life with a 50 percent survivor benefit

3. $2,350 for life with a 67 percent survivor benefit

4. $2,000 for life with a 100 percent survivor benefit

a. Assuming that (a) Lyle lives ten years after retiring, (b) Melissa lives an additional ten years beyond Lyle's passing, and (c) the pension has no cost of living adjustment, which of the four alternatives should they choose in order to maximize their combined lifetime benefit?

b. What benefit alternative should they choose if Lyle lives another twenty years beyond retirement and Melissa lives an additional ten years beyond that?

c. If Lyle's Social Security retirement benefit at age sixty-seven is $2,300 per month, how much will they receive in yearly benefits if they both claim benefits when Lyle turns age sixty-five?

Comprehensive Bedo Case – Analysis Questions

Tyler and Mia have clearly stated that they would like to retire at age sixty-two, and they would like their plan to include reduced Social Security benefits. The first step in the analysis involves working with relevant assumptions, such as before- and after-retirement inflation rate and marginal tax rate assumptions, savings rates, and portfolio values to determine whether they are on track to meet their retirement goal. If the answer is negative, it will be necessary to determine which assets and savings sources are available for the retirement goal. As a reminder, it is important to work through the retirement planning needs assessment in a logical, step-by-step order.

Every attempt should be made to achieve the Bedos' retirement goal using the capital depletion method. Only after attempting to meet this goal should changes in assumptions be made. Once the funding need is met using the capital depletion method, the next step is to attempt to fund retirement using the capital preservation method. If this goal can be met, the third step is to attempt to implement an inflation-adjusted approach. In other words, it is important to show the Bedos that different alternatives exist and that each alternative has both advantages and disadvantages.

Use the following questions to guide the retirement planning process.

1. Develop a retirement planning goal for the Bedos. When conceptualizing this goal, consider the following.

    a. Is the goal developed in agreement with any or all goals and objectives that the clients have identified regarding retirement planning?

    b. What situational factors might influence their retirement planning goal? Are these factors explicit, implied, or assumed? Is additional information required from the Bedos, and if, so what?

    c. What is the desired retirement planning outcome for the clients?

2. Make a list of life events that could affect the retirement plans for Tyler and Mia and that should be reviewed at future client meetings.

3. Are there globally accepted, client-specific, or planner-generated planning assumptions that will influence the retirement planning situation analysis? List the assumptions as they might appear in a plan.

4. Calculate the following for the Bedos:

    a. The total value, in current dollars, of assets that have been accumulated by the Bedos for retirement.

    b. The value at retirement of the retirement assets (including planned future contributions) using the current weighted average rate of return for the retirement assets.

    c. The net amount of income needed in today's dollars that must be replaced to meet the Bedos' retirement goal.

    d. The amount of assets needed to completely fund the Bedos' retirement, starting at age sixty-two, using a capital depletion assumption.

e. The additional savings the Bedos need at age sixty-two to meet a capital preservation retirement goal using the assumed after-tax rate of return.

f. The amount needed to be saved annually to fund an inflation-adjusted retirement scenario using the assumed after-tax rate of return.

g. The amount the Bedos need to save monthly to fully fund their future home expansion using the assumed after-tax rate of return.

h. The amount the Bedos need to save monthly to fully fund Mia's art gallery in retirement using the assumed after-tax rate of return.

5. Clients often request a modular plan for retirement goals. Using text, bullets, and graphics, summarize your observations about Tyler and Mia's retirement planning situation and the identified planning need(s). Based on the information collected, fully document and inform the Bedos of the analyses and results.

6. Based on the goals originally identified and the completed analysis, what product or procedural strategies might be most useful to satisfy the Bedos' retirement planning needs? Be sure to consider strategies matched to Tyler and Mia's identified planning needs, individually and as a couple. When reviewing the strategies, be careful to consider the approximate cost of implementation as well as the most likely outcome(s) associated with each strategy.

7. Write at least one primary and one alternative recommendation from the selected strategies in response to each identified retirement planning need. More than one recommendation may be needed to address all planning needs. Include specific, defensible answers to the who, what, when, where, why, how, and how much implementation questions for each recommendation.

a. It is suggested that each recommendation be summarized in a Recommendation Form.

b. Assign a priority to each recommendation based on the likelihood of meeting client goals and desired outcomes. This priority will be important when recommendations from other core planning content areas are considered relative to the available discretionary funds for subsidizing all recommendations.

c. Comment briefly on the outcomes associated with each recommendation.

8. Complete the following for the Retirement Planning section of the Bedos' financial plan.

a. Outline the content to be included in this section of the plan. Given the segments written above, what segments are missing?

b. Write the introduction to this section of the plan (no more than one or two paragraphs).

c. Write an explanation of the capital depletion approach, the capital preservation approach, and the inflation-adjusted approach to retirement planning.

9. Prepare a ten–fifteen-minute presentation for the Bedos of your observations and/or recommendation(s) for meeting their retirement planning goals. Be sure to include visual aids, Excel handouts, and other materials that will make the recommendations more meaningful for the clients.

Chapter Resources

Academic papers on sustainable withdrawal rates (research category) (www.planipedia.org/index.php/Sustainable_Withdrawal_Rates_).

Department of Labor site for Qualified Retirement Plan information (www.dol.gov/ebsa/publications/wyskapr.html).

Leimberg, Stephan R., et al. *Tools & Techniques of Retirement Income Planning*. Cincinnati, OH: National Underwriter Company, 2007.

Mortality tables (www.cdc.gov/nchs/nvss/mortality_tables.htm).

Social Security Benefit Estimator (www.socialsecurity.gov/OACT/quickcalc/index.html).

Stenken, Joseph F. *Social Security & Medicare Facts*. Erlanger, KY: National Underwriter Company, 2014.

Wagner, William J. *Ultimate IRA Resource* (including IRA Calculator), 3rd Ed. Cincinnati, OH: National Underwriter Company, 2006.

Self-Test Answers

1: b, 2: d, 3: a, 4: c, 5: c, 6: b, 7: c

Endnotes

1. J. J. Spitzer, "Managing a Retirement Portfolio: Do Annuities Provide More Safety?" *Journal of Financial Counseling and Planning, 20 no.* 1 (2009): 58–69.

2. M. A. Milevsky and V. R. Young, "Annuitization and Asset Allocation," *Journal of Economic Dynamics & Control, 31* (2007): 3138 –3177.

3. Fidelity Research Institute. (2007, March). "The Fidelity Research Institute Index." Research Insights Brief. Summary report available at: nsresearch.com/media/Mar.12.07_Retirement.pdf.

4. Social Security Administration. *Social Security Benefit Amounts*. Available at: www.ssa.gov/OACT/COLA/Benefits.html.

5. A complete calculation example can be found at: www.ssa.gov/oact/ProgData/retirebenefit1.html.

6. Social Security benefits are always rounded down to the next lower dollar. For more information, see www.ssa.gov/oact/ProgData/retirebenefit2.html.

7. See Marriage/Relationship Recognition Law by state to identify states that recognize same-sex marriage. Available from the Human Rights Campaign at: www.hrc.org/laws_and_elections/state.asp.

8. Lemons, D., "When to start collecting Social Security Benefits: A Break-even Analysis," *Journal of Financial Planning 25,* no. 1 (2012): 52–60.

9.   Caudill, A., "Inherited IRA myths." *Journal of Financial Services Professionals*, 65 no. 5 (2011): 38–41.

10. For more information on the tax loophole, see: www.kitces.com/blog/archives/242-Dodging-The-Income-Limits-on-Roth-Contributions-Strategy-Or-Abuse.html.

11. Fidelity Research Institute, "The Equity You Live In: The Home as a Retirement Savings and Income Option," *Research Insights Report* (2007). Summary report available at: www.capitalfundinggroup.com/EquityYouLiveIn1__1_.pdf.

12. National Conference of State Legislatures, *State Personal Income Taxes on Pensions & Retirement Income: Tax Year 2010.* Available at: www.ncsl.org/documents/fiscal/TaxonPensions2011.pdf , pp. 9, 10, and 11.

13. Kiplinger, *Retiree Tax Heavens (and Hells).* Available at: www.kiplinger.com/tools/retiree_map/.

14. W. Reichenstein, "Tax-efficient sequencing of account to tap in retirement." *Trends and Issues*, TIAA-CREF Institute, (2006, October). Available at: www.tiaa-crefinstitute.org/ucm/groups/content/@ap_ucm_p_tcp_docs/documents/document/tiaa02029501.pdf.

15. J. J. Spitzer and S. Singh, "Extending Retirement Payouts by Optimizing the Sequence of Withdrawals," *Journal of Financial Planning*, 19 *no.* 4 (2006): 52–61.

16. See IRS Publication 590 at: www.irs.gov/publications/p590/ar02.html for this table.

17. Marksjarvis, G. "Gen Y: Time Is on Your Side with the Stock Market." *The Bulletin.* September 22, 2011. Available at: www.bendbulletin.com/apps/pbcs.dll/article?AID=/20110922/NEWS0107/109220343/1163/1163&nav_category=1163&template=print.

18. MFS Investment Management. *MFS Investing Sentiment Survey Offers Insight into Generation Y Investing Behaviors.* Available at: www.mfs.com/wps/portal/mfs/us-investor/market-outlooks/news-room/press-releases/!ut/p/c5/04_SB8K8xLLM9MSSzPy8xBz9CP0os3j_QKNAf3MPIwN342BnAyMXE39j01BjQ5cAI6B8JLK8j4UjUN7fLczbLMDA3dKQgG4_j_zcVP2C3IhyAEF8gjE!/dl3/d3/L2dBISEvZ0FBIS9nQSEh/?contentId=templatedata%2finternet%2farticle%2fdata%2fnews%2fpr_sentiment2011_geny_part5.

19. MFS Investment Management, *Investing Sentiment Survey.*

20. Department of Treasury. *Statistical Trends in Retirement Plans.* August 9, 2010. Figure 3, p. 7. Text available at: www.treasury.gov/tigta/auditreports/2010reports/201010097fr.pdf.

21. Information about the inflation-adjusted performance of popular asset classes: www.investorsfriend.com/asset_performance.htm.

Chapter 13

Estate Planning

Learning Objectives

1. In some respects, estate planning is the most integrative of the core financial planning topics. As this chapter highlights, almost every aspect of a client's financial life affects, to some extent, estate planning issues. Additionally, each client's unique situation helps shape the type of recommendations that a financial planner makes. Some clients have a strong desire to minimize taxes. Others desire privacy. Still other clients wish to share their wealth with family and community organizations. These examples suggest that no single strategy or tool is always appropriate when framing estate recommendations. It is imperative that each financial planner, working with his or her clientele and collaborative professionals, develop recommendations that can be implemented in a way that maximizes each client's unique financial and lifestyle goals.

2. The estate plan should accomplish three objectives including: (a) planning for the cost-effective transfer of assets in a way that is consistent with the client's wishes through the preservation the estate: (b) providing for survivors or other financial or charitable needs; and (c) planning for the client's final wishes regarding incapacitation and other end-of-life decisions.

3. Before embarking upon a quantitative review of a client's estate planning situation, it is important for financial planners to identify influential situational factors and questions that can be asked to help determine a client's estate planning needs. Obtaining a clear idea of a client's values, social position, and culture can help shape an estate plan. In addition, asking questions related to privacy desires, feelings about taxation and charitable giving, and special needs are equally important factors shaping the way in which estate planning recommendations are formulated.

4. When determining and evaluating the factors associated with a client's estate tax liability, financial planners must

Learning Objectives

have a keen understanding of both the definitions and applications of several key terms. For example, differentiating between a client's gross and taxable estate and the process used to arrive at the taxable estate is important. Additionally, understanding how the unified credit applies to both taxable gifts and asset transfers is important when estimating a client's estate tax liability. The ability to describe and determine the annual gift exclusion and how gift splitting affects the value of a client's estate plays an equally important role in shaping tax calculations.

5. Four critical steps are associated with describing and calculating a client's estate tax liability. First, the value of the client's gross estate must be estimated. Second, the taxable estate must be calculated by subtracting from the gross estate funeral and administrative expenses, debts, taxes, charitable donations, and any marital transfers. Third, the value of taxable lifetime gifts must be added back into the taxable estate figure—unless the gift taxes were paid at the time the gift was made. This results in what is known as the adjusted taxable estate. The fourth and final step involves determining the tax payable. To arrive at this figure, the remaining exclusion amount is subtracted from the adjusted taxable estate. What remains is subject to taxation. Alternatively, the tax can be calculated first and the applicable credit amount can be subtracted to determine remaining liability.

6. The Tax Relief Act of 2010 had a significant impact on the type of estate planning calculations and recommendations being made in the financial services marketplace. The Act created the portable estate exemption, which effectively shields approximately $11 million from federal estate taxation for married couples. The Act changed the way many financial planners counsel clients. For example, A-B trust arrangements were once commonly recommended as a strategy to maximize the unified credit available to married couples. A-B trusts, although still recommended, are no longer as widely used because the portable estate exemption accomplishes the same objective with less cost. Other changes resulting from the Act include linking the estate and gift tax and eliminating previous restrictions on stepped-up basis.

7. Few aspects of financial planning provide as many opportunities to recommend strategies to meet multiple client goals as the estate planning process. When viewed holistically, the estate planning process can be seen as a unifying procedure that helps clients better understand the lifetime accumulation, preservation, and ultimate distribution of assets.

Key Terms

2503(b) Trust

2503(c) Trust

30 Percent Deduction Rule

50 Percent Deduction Rule

529 Plan

A Trust

A-B Trust Arrangement

Adjusted Taxable Gifts

Advance Medical Directive (AMD)

Age of Majority

Agent Alternated Valuation Date

Annual Exclusion

Applicable Credit Amount

Applicable Exclusion Amount

ATROs

Attorney-in-Fact

Automatic Temporary Restraining Orders

Avoid Probate

B Trust

Bargain Sale

Beneficiary

Buy-Sell Agreement Bypass Trust
   Catalog Value

Charitable Deduction

Charitable Giving

Charitable Lead Trust (CLT)

Charitable Remainder Annuity
   Trust (CRAT)

Charitable Remainder Unitrust
   Trust (CRUT)

Client Situational Factors

Codicil

Community Property

Complex Trust

Conflicts of Interest

Credit

Credit Shelter Bypass Trust

Cross-Purchase Agreement

Custodian

Custody Agreement

Decedent

Declaration

Defective Grantor Trust

Direct Skip

Directive to Physicians

Disclaimer

Divorce

Donation

Donee

Donor

Donor-Advised Charitable Fund

Durable

Durable Power of Attorney

Durable Power of Attorney for Health Care

ERISA

Key Terms

Entity Purchase Agreement

Estate Liquidity

Estate Planning

Estate Tax

Estate Tax Exclusion

Exclusion Amount

Fair Market Value of Assets

Family Conflicts

Family Law Restraining Orders

Family Limited Partnership (FLP)

Foreign Death Tax Credit

Form 706

Form 709

General Partnership Interest

General Power of Attorney

Generation

Generation-Skipping Transfer

Generation-Skipping Transfer Tax (GSTT)

Gift

Gift Leaseback

Gift Splitting

Gift Tax

Gift Tax Annual Exclusion

Gift Tax Return

Grantor

Grantor Retained Annuity Trust (GRAT)

Grantor Trust

Gross Estate

Incapacitation

Incapacity

Income Beneficiary

Income in Respect of a Decedent (IRD)

Inheritance

Installment Sale

Interpolated Terminal Reserve

Intera-Family Loan

Irrevocable Life Insurance Trust (ILIT)

Irrevocable Trust

IRS Form 1041

Joint Tenancy with Right of Survivorship (JTWROS)

Legal Separation

Letter of Last Instruction

Life Insurance

Lifetime Taxable Gifts

Limited Liability Company (LLC)

Limited Partnership

Living Trust

Living Will

Marital Deduction

Marital Deduction Trust

Market Value

Medical Directive

Medical POA

Key Terms

Medical Power of Attorney

Nonprofit Organizations

Ordinary Income Property

Over-Qualifying the Spouse's Estate

Payable on Death

Personal Representative

POA Trust

POD

Pooled Income Fund

Portability

Portable Estate Exemption

Powerholder

Privacy

Private Annuity

Private Foundation

Probate

Probate Fees

Proxy

Public Foundation

QTIP Trust

Qualified Disclaimer

Qualified Marital Transfer

Qualified Personal Residence Trust (QPRT)

Qualified Terminable Interest Property (QTIP)

Remainder Beneficiary

Remaindermen

Retitling

Revocable Trust

Self-Cancelling Installment Note (SCIN)

Simple Trust

Skip Person

Springing Power of Attorney

Standard Family Trust

Step-Up in Basis

Tax Basis

Taxable Estate

Taxable Gift

Tenancy by the Entirety

Tenancy in Common

Testamentary Trust

Transfer on Death (TOD)

Trust

Unified Credit

Uniform Gifts to Minors Act (UGMA)

Uniform Transfers to Minors Act (UMTA)

Unlimited Marital Deduction

UTMA

Viatical Settlement

Wait-and-See Buy-Sell Agreement

Will

CFP® Principal Knowledge Topics

H.63. Characteristics and Consequences of Property Titling

H.64. Strategies to Transfer Property

H.65. Estate Planning Documents

H.66. Gift and Estate Tax Compliance and Tax Calculation

H.67. Sources of Estate Liquidity

H.68. Types, Features, and Taxation of Trusts

H.69. Marital Deduction

H.70. Intra-Family and Other Business Transfer Techniques

H.71. Postmortem Estate Planning Techniques

H. 72. Estate Planning for Non-Traditional Relationships

Chapter Equations

While there are many equations used in the estate planning process, the calculations tend to be rather straightforward. Figure 13.1 summarizes the steps involved when calculating a potential estate tax liability.

Figure 13.1 Estate Planning Calculation Process

Step	Calculation	Notes			
1.	Calculate Gross Estate	Calculation is based on the fair market value at date of death or alternate date value of the decedent's ownership interest			
2.	Calculate the Taxable Estate	Subtract Funeral/Burial Expenses, Estate Administration and Legal Expenses, Outstanding Liabilities, Income Taxes, Executor Fees, Charitable Contributions, and other reductions, including the **Qualified Marital Transfer**, directly attributable to the decedent			
3.	Add back Adjusted Taxable Gifts				
4.	Estimate Tax liability based on Estate and Gift Tax Rates	**For Taxable Estates Between...**	**And ...**	**You'll Pay This Amount of Tax...**	**Plus, You'll Pay This Percentage on the Amount in Excess of the Lower Limit**
		$0	$10,000	$0	18%
		$10,000	$20,000	$1,800	20%
		$20,000	$40,000	$3,800	22%
		$40,000	$60,000	$8,200	24%
		$60,000	$80,000	$13,000	26%
		$80,000	$100,000	$18,200	28%
		$100,000	$150,000	$23,800	30%
		$150,000	$250,000	$38,800	32%
		$250,000	$500,000	$70,800	34%
		$500,000	$750,000	$155,800	37%
		$750,000	$1,000,000	$248,300	39%
		$1,000,000	-----------	$345,800	40%
5.	Subtract Tax on Adjusted Taxable Gifts				
6.	Equals Tentative Estate Tax				
7.	Subtract Credits	In 2016, the **applicable exclusion amount** was $5,450,000, which was equivalent to a **applicable credit amount** of $2,125,800			
8.	Equals Estate Tax Liability				

ESTATE PLANNING: DETERMINING THE NEED

Estate planning deals with the ownership and distribution of client assets. From a financial planning perspective, **estate planning** involves helping clients make decisions about the accumulation, preservation, and ultimate distribution of assets. Estate planning also involves providing advice on other end-of-life decisions, including custodial and guardianship situations for incapacitation or minor children. Estate planning is an essential part of any well-conceived financial plan. An estate planning analysis can identify potential weaknesses in a client's financial situation that can reduce assets available for beneficiaries, charities, or other legacy goals. Steps taken to analyze a client's situation and to develop estate planning recommendations can serve multiple outcomes. First, estate planning recommendations can maximize a client's financial assets via potential savings on taxes and estate settlement costs. Second, a well-crafted estate plan can protect a client's privacy. Third, estate planning can help ensure that legacy goals are achieved. Fourth, estate planning can give clients peace of mind by confirming that their final financial and life wishes will be enacted. The purpose of this chapter is review core estate planning calculation and to present a broad range of estate and gift taxes strategies.

Reviewing life goals with a client can be an important foundation for establishing estate planning preferences. A number of key questions can be used to determine a client's estate planning preferences and better assess client estate planning and estate liquidity needs. Answers to these questions directly impact the size or distribution of an estate. In situations where the estate is not large enough to trigger estate tax issues, other financial issues threaten to reduce the estate, or if not planned for properly they can create other problems for heirs.

Before considering these questions, it is important to clarify whether the client, and if applicable the spouse or partner, is a US citizen. Specifically, planning needs differ for noncitizens or resident aliens and can affect asset titling, gifts, estate transfers, and estate taxes. Property owned in the United States must be probated in a US court, so similar considerations apply. It is generally important for noncitizens to have US estate planning documents, even if documents were prepared in another country. Because citizenship adds another layer of difficulty to the estate planning process, it is a critical consideration. Another critical consideration is a client's marital status, because estate planning for domestic partners is more complicated, as described later in this chapter. Additional questions to determine a client's estate planning needs are listed below:

- Does the client wish to avoid probate (i.e., the legal and public procedure that validates a will and the distribution of assets as described in a will) or reduce probate assets?

- Is reduction of state death taxes a primary client need?

- Is protection of assets from creditors a concern?

- Is reduction of income taxes a primary client need?

- Does the client want to leave some or most of the estate to a spouse or partner?

- Are there special needs (e.g., mental or emotional health issues, retardation, physical handicaps) or other financial management issues that must be considered?

- Does the client have a desire to leave some or most of the estate to children? If yes, are they minor children or children with special needs, regardless of age?

- If an estate is to be left to children, will each child share equally, and if a child should predecease the parent, how will that child's share be distributed?

- Does the client want to leave some or most of the estate to other dependents besides spouse, partner, or children? If yes, are there special needs (e.g., mental or emotional health issues, mental or physical handicaps) or other financial management issues that must be considered?

- Does the client wish to leave a charitable bequest? If charitable giving is a priority, which organizations are most important?

- Does the client have financial or managerial ties to a small business or a closely or privately held business that must be planned for within or outside of the estate plan?

- Which assets will be used to pay for final expenses and debt reduction?

- Is preplanning for a medical situation or emergency or long-term care an important client objective?

- Does the client have any special wishes that should be accounted for in the estate plan?

> **Self-Test 1**
>
> Which of the following are allowable deductions from the adjusted gross estate when estimating a client's taxable estate?
>
> a. Qualified charitable deduction.
>
> b. Marital deduction.
>
> c. Deduction for taxes paid.
>
> d. All of the above.

Each of these questions can lead to an in-depth discussion between a financial planner and client—and in some cases spouses, partners, or other family members—about life goals, legacies, estate planning objectives, and end-of-life issues. Answers to these and similar questions can then be used as background for initiating an assessment of a client's estate plan.

The Estate Tax Calculation

A number of steps are involved in the analysis of a client's current estate planning situation. Although a client's values, social position, or culture are influential situational factors in determining and quantifying planning needs for all core planning content areas, these factors are particularly ubiquitous in estate planning. Sensitivity to a client's family, cultural, and religious beliefs and attitudes is an important financial planner consideration. Estate planning needs can run the gamut from bequests to immediate or extended family members or friends to providing care or a trust for a cherished pet. The prevalence of remarriages and other nontraditional family relationships, as well as the need for multigenerational planning, further complicate and, in some situations, challenge traditional property law.

The primary estate planning calculation centers on estimating the federal estate tax liability. The calculation hinges on the value of the client's **taxable estate** (i.e., the taxable value of assets owned by a decedent at his or her death) relative to the federal estate tax threshold—a figure currently close to $6 million.

The **estate tax** is a levy on a client's right to transfer property at death and is based on the value of the client's taxable estate at the time of death. A client's taxable estate is the gross estate less allowable deductions. The gross estate includes the fair market value of all property that the client owned or had an interest in at the time of death, or in some cases within three years of death. IRS Form 706 is used to account for these assets. The *fair market value of assets* at a client's death or as of an alternative valuation date is used, whichever will result in the most advantageous cost basis for the distributed assets. The assets included in the gross estate consist of cash and securities, real estate, revocable trusts, business interests, and other assets, as listed below:

- Life insurance proceeds payable to the estate or, if the client held incidents of ownership in the policy, to the client's heirs;

- The value of certain annuities payable to the estate or heirs;

- The value of certain property transferred within three years before death; and

- Trusts or other interests established by the client or others in which the client had certain interests or powers.

A client's *taxable estate* is determined by subtracting certain deductions from the gross estate. Allowable deductions include outstanding mortgages and other debts as well as the following deductions used to determine the taxable estate:

- Expenses of estate administration: funeral expenses paid out of the estate, debts owed at the time of death, taxes, and certain estate losses;

- Marital deductions, including all property passing to a surviving spouse;

- Charitable deductions; and

- The state death tax deduction.

It is important to deduct only the portion of a liability attributable to the client. Only the part of a client's debt attributable to a listed asset is deductible. For example, married couples holding a principal residence as joint tenants with right of survivorship (JTWROS) can list only half of the fair market value of the property as an asset. As such, the deceased client can deduct only one-half of the outstanding mortgage balance.

> **#Remember**
>
> Keep up to date on estate tax rates, the marital deduction, the unified credit, and other important data by visiting the IRS website yearly: www.irs.gov/Businesses/Small-Businesses-&-Self-Employed/Estate-Tax

A **marital deduction** is available for the value of all property that passes from one spouse to another. Under current law, the marital deduction is unlimited, meaning that one spouse can leave all of his or her assets to a spouse free of estate and gift taxes. A **charitable deduction** is available for the value of the property that passes to a charity or qualified non-profit organization.

After the net amount is computed, the **adjusted taxable gifts** or the value of lifetime taxable gifts made after 1976 are added to this figure, resulting in the taxable estate. The tax is then computed on the new balance or taxable estate. Tax is also calculated on the adjusted taxable gifts and subtracted from the tax on the taxable estate. The tax is also reduced by the available **unified credit** and other available credits, such as the credit for prior taxes paid or a foreign death tax credit. A **credit** is the dollar amount that reduces or eliminates a tax.

An additional tax, beyond the standard estate tax calculation, may be necessary for **income in respect of a decedent** (IRD). This tax is based on any income that the deceased person was entitled to receive prior to death but that was not actually received until after death. Examples of IRD include salary earned but not paid until after the taxpayer's death, retirement account distributions, royalties, rents, dividends, interest, and other similar forms of income. IRD items must be included in the decedent's gross estate and the beneficiary of the income is then taxed at the beneficiary's marginal tax rate. However, the beneficiary might be able to deduct his or her portion of any estate taxes generated by the inclusion of the IRD.

ESTATE PLANNING SKILLS

Two important considerations should be reviewed before identifying estate planning strategies. First, it is important to consider what might be considered basic estate planning strategies before introducing more complex tactics. Never assume that a client, regardless of wealth or income, has necessary, basic documents in place, such as a *will*, *power of attorney* (*POA*), *living will*, or *advance medical directive* (*AMD*). This means that although there are opportunities for a financial planner to develop multifaceted estate planning strategies, these should generally wait until the fundamental aspects of estate planning have been addressed.

It is important to remember that financial planners who are not attorneys should proceed carefully when developing and presenting estate planning recommendations. It is illegal for non-attorneys to draft legal documents for clients. The best approach is to work collaboratively with the client and the attorney on estate planning issues. This method of planning preserves the planner's fiduciary responsibility to act in the best interest of the client but limits the possibility of being sued by a client who later feels that a strategy was inappropriate; it also limits exposure to penalties for the unauthorized practice of law. Most importantly, a collaborative approach between planner and attorney will likely provide a better outcome for the client because of the insights available from the planner's more comprehensive knowledge of the client situation. Finally, planner recommendations should include a **disclaimer**, such as "Prior to implementing these recommendations, please confirm these suggestions with an attorney."

The strategies related to an estate planning analysis can range from basic to extremely complex. The intent of this section is to provide examples of common (i.e., fundamental) estate planning strategies. Readers interested in developing more complex strategies and recommendations should consider *Principles of Estate Planning 2nd Edition*, published by the National Underwriter Company.

Planning Skill 1: Understand Trust Terminology

Given the number of potential tax liabilities, it may be advisable to explore the use of trusts in addition to gifting strategies. A **trust** is an arrangement that grants a trustee legal title to assets. A trustee is required to act as a fiduciary when managing assets for the benefit of trust beneficiaries. In most cases, a **beneficiary** is the person who holds the beneficial title to trust assets. In general, trust income is passed directly from the trust to the **income beneficiary**, as opposed to the **remainder beneficiary**—the person or entity entitled to receive the assets upon termination of the trust. Often the income and remainder beneficiary are the same person or entity. It is also possible for a trust to have only income beneficiaries.

There are two main types of trusts: **testamentary trusts**, funded upon death; and **living trusts**, funded prior to death. The most common type of testamentary trust is a **standard family trust** (also known as an **A-B trust arrangement**), a legal tool established to hold assets and transfer income to a surviving spouse without the surviving spouse actually taking ownership of the assets. Upon the death of the surviving spouse, a trustee then distributes the remaining assets to beneficiaries, often referred to as *remaindermen*.

In addition to the distinction between living and testamentary trusts, living trusts can also be sub-classified as either irrevocable or revocable. **Revocable trusts** are also known as **grantor trusts,** because the trust or trust assets can be revoked or modified by the grantor. **Irrevocable trusts**, as the name implies, cannot be modified, amended, or revoked by the grantor; only the trustee has this authority according to trust document guidelines.

Planning Skill 2: Make Sure Stakeholders are Informed when Appointing Others in an Estate Plan

Clients are well served by financial planners who help them carefully consider potential family conflicts, conflicts of interest, or the qualifications required for those appointed to serve a function within an estate plan (e.g., a guardian for children or the executor of a will). Individuals chosen must fully understand and accept the responsibilities inherent in their appointed role. This also extends to medical providers and other family or household members who should be fully informed of a client's end-of-life preferences and decisions. For example, copies of the living will, AMD, or medical power of attorney should be distributed among appropriate medical, financial, and legal professionals, as well as the spouse, partner, or family.

Emotional distress and perhaps a loss of *privacy* are the primary disadvantages of this strategy. Although family discussions may be uncomfortable, it is critical that guardians and executors be informed of the choice and are willing to serve. Furthermore, it is important for these appointees to understand their financial obligations. Certainly, any preliminary distress will be less traumatic than disclosing this information after the death of the client, or failing to appoint anyone so that court involvement is necessary.

Planning Skill 3: Use Aspects of the Tax Relief Act of 2010 When Developing Estate Planning Strategies

On December 16, 2010, Congress passed the Tax Relief, Unemployment Insurance Reauthorization, and Job Creation Act of 2010 (the Act). This legislation extended estate, gift, and generation-skipping transfer taxes (GSTT) but increased the exemption threshold and lowered the marginal tax rates. The Act also indexed the exemption amount to inflation. Finally, the legislation reunified the estate and **gift tax** rate, so that a single lifetime exemption can be used for both lifetime gifts and/ or upon-death bequests.

The *unified credit* applies to both the gift tax and the estate tax and is subtracted from any gift or estate tax that a client may owe. The credit amount is 2016 was $2,125,800, which effectively exempts $5,430,000 from estate and gift taxes, although this credit is reduced based on the decedent's lifetime taxable gifts. An estate tax return for a US citizen or resident needs to be filed only if the gross estate exceeds the applicable exclusion amount. Once an estate exceeds the exemption amount, the maximum tax rate applied is 40 percent.

The Act also allowed for the *portability* of any unused exemption; in other words, The Act allowed an executor of a deceased spouse's estate to transfer any unused exemption to the surviving spouse. The **portable estate exemption**, allows the unused portion of a spouse's **estate tax exclusion** (i.e., the amount of assets that can be transferred tax free at the death of a client) to be shifted to the surviving spouse. This means that even if the first-to-die spouse fails to use his or her entire exemption, the unused estate exemption can be utilized by the second-to-die spouse. In effect, the portable estate exemption allows approximately $11 million for a married couple in 2016 to be sheltered from taxes. The Act makes it a good idea for all clients to file IRS Form 706 to maintain the portable estate exemption, even if the first-to-die's estate is not taxable.

EDUCATION PLANNING PRODUCT & PROCEDURAL STRATEGIES

The following product and procedural strategies provide an insight into some of the most widely used estate planning tools and techniques used by financial planners on a daily.

Product Strategy 1: Prepare a Will

This estate planning strategy should be the first advice given to a client who does not currently have a will and those whose wills are out of date. A **will** ensures that a client's wishes are followed appropriately rather than relying on the intestate laws of the client's state of residence.

> **Self-Test 3**
>
> Dying without a valid will and having state law dictate the distribution of assets is called:
>
> a. Intestate succession
>
> b. Testate succession
>
> c. Inter-vivo succession
>
> d. Ancillary succession

When reviewing a client's current will, planners should look for signs that a change or **codicil** might be needed. The following list includes a number of indicators that a client's will or estate plan should be reviewed by an attorney.

- The will was drafted more than five years ago.

- The client has additional beneficiaries who are not listed in the will.

- The client now has fewer beneficiaries than are listed in the will.

- There has been a major change in the beneficiaries' family or financial circumstances.

- The client has indicated verbally that the client wishes to distribute assets differently from what is listed.

- The client's health has diminished since drafting the will.

- The client's marital status has changed since drafting the will (marriage, remarriage, divorce, or death of a spouse).

- The birth or adoption of one or more grandchildren has occurred.

- A significant estate planning law was passed since the date of the will or the date of the last review, if any.

- There has been a significant increase or decrease in the client's wealth or income since the will was drafted.

- The client has purchased additional life insurance.

- The client has started a business.

- A change in the named guardian is needed.

- A change in the executor or contingent executor is needed.

- Property has been purchased in a different state.

- The client has moved, thereby changing the state of residence.

It is important for clients to recognize that having a valid will does not avoid *probate* and the associated disadvantages. It is important to remind them that, upon the death of a decedent, a will becomes a public document through the probate system. The value of the assets conveyed in the will is subject to probate fees, and in some states the probate process can be lengthy and expensive. The cost of a will might also be a deterrent; clients can expect to pay between $200 and $750 for a basic attorney-drafted will, and the cost increases with the complexity of the situation. Finally, this is often the most resisted recommendation of any in a financial plan. Planners must patiently encourage clients to act rather than postpone preparation of this important estate planning document.

> **Self-Test 4**
>
> A springing power of attorney (POA):
>
> a. becomes active immediately upon signature.
>
> b. only at incapacitation.
>
> c. only at a doctor's discretion.
>
> d. after a specific event, as described in the POA document, occurs.

Product Strategy 2: Write a Letter of Last Instruction

All clients should write a letter of last instructions. This letter can include special wishes that might not otherwise be included in a will or trust document. For example, a client can specify where the client would like to be buried, the name of the caterer that the client would like to use at the funeral, and other requests. Clients who write a letter of last instructions should take care to update the letter whenever they redraft their will or other legal documents. Great confusion can result if more than one letter is found at the date of death.

Product Strategy 3: Prepare a Living Will, Power of Attorney, or Advance Medical Directive

A **living will** is a legal document that establishes the medical situations in which a client no longer desires life-sustaining or life-prolonging treatment. A living will is essentially a document that involves the client and the client's physician, and it often includes wishes regarding the use of cardiopulmonary resuscitation, intravenous therapy for nutrition or medication, feeding tubes, and ventilators for artificial breathing. However, it is very important that the family be informed of an individual's wishes. A living will might also be known as a *declaration* or **directive to physicians** or in some states as an *advance medical directive*. Typically, a living will is relevant only in situations of terminal illness or injury when an individual is incapable of making care decisions.

An alternative to a living will is a **durable power of attorney for health care**, also called a **medical power of attorney**. This legal document appoints another person, called an **agent, attorney-in-fact**, or **proxy**, to make health care decisions for the client when the client is unable to do so as a result of physical or mental incapacitation. The addition of the term *durable* makes this or another power of attorney remain in effect or take effect in the event of mental incompetence. The agent can make decisions for nonterminal situations or, if a living will is available, help ensure compliance with the individual's wishes.

Generally, a **medical directive** or **advance medical directive** combines the protection of a living will in terminal situations with the broader powers of a durable power of attorney for health care into one document. A proxy or attorney-in-fact is appointed, as well as a contingent individual, or successor agent, should the primary person be unavailable to serve. Neither the medical power of attorney nor the medical directive obligates the agent or proxy with financial responsibility for the costs of medical care.

A power of attorney appoints a person or organization to handle a client's affairs. A *durable power of attorney* remains in effect or takes effect in the event of subsequent disability or incapacity. A power of attorney can be general, giving broad powers for most—if not all—financial affairs, or be limited to a specific list of responsibilities. With an extremely broad general power of attorney, a client might, in effect, give a third party "all legal powers that I have myself." A *powerholder* with an unlimited power of attorney may or may not be able to make gifts to him- or herself or family members; this will depend on state law and the prior history of the client. Powers of attorney are relatively inexpensive to establish, simple, private, and flexible. Courts also universally recognize powers of attorney.

When planning for *incapacitation* and overall health care issues, clients should be encouraged to have a living will and a medical power of attorney, as well as a power of attorney for financial affairs. In this way, the client's care and death decisions can be made confidentially using state-specific documents, and the client's financial affairs can be managed with a power of attorney.

The greatest disadvantage associated with this strategy is psychological, not fiscal. Planners may face resistance among clients when this strategy is presented. Some clients find the thought of planning for their own incapacity and the sharing of decision-making authority difficult and uncomfortable. As a result, some clients might resist implementing this strategy, but planners must patiently encourage client consideration. The use of a **springing power of attorney** (i.e., powers available only after a specific event, such as an illness or disability, and perhaps after validation by a physician) is one alternative. Clients should also be assured that the power of attorney can be revoked at any time. Depending on individual state law, an attorney or witnesses may or may not be required, so minimal costs might be involved. Clients who own property or live for periods of time in different states each year should exercise particular caution with these documents, because state reciprocity may not apply.

Product Strategy 4: Use Trusts for Incapacity Planning

Because a trust transfers the rights of ownership to a third-party trustee, a trust is a useful strategy to financially provide for a person or persons unable to care for themselves because of legal or medical incapacity. **Incapacity** can be defined in several ways, including lack of ability, lack of legal standing, lack of legal power, or the inability to plan, delegate, provide for, or manage one's legal and financial affairs. Medical incapacity is usually the result of illness or accident, whereas legal incapacity is most common in situations where minor children or developmentally disabled adults are involved. Less acknowledged are situations where an adult has maladaptive behaviors such as a drug or gambling addiction, legal issues, behavioral problems, or a history of poor financial decision making. Trusts are often established in response to the need to provide care for incapacity. However, in some situations, clients should be proactive in planning for their own incapacity. Individuals who fail to plan for the possibility of incapacity face potential risks and costs, including:

- placing the management of their assets and health decisions under the control of a third party;

- the loss of standing to direct the distribution of assets to heirs and charities before and after death;

- the inability to legally execute or delegate their own financial affairs; or

- the possibility of depleting family assets because of legal battles associated with conservatorship issues.

Product Strategy 5: Understand How Trusts are Taxed

All income and deductions associated with a revocable trust are treated as part of the grantor's individual tax return, although grantors are required to complete the entity part of **IRS Form 1041**. At the death of the grantor, the executor of a grantor's estate is also required to file IRS Form 1041 for the revocable trust.

An irrevocable trust, on the other hand, is considered a separate entity from the grantor, and as such, IRS Form 1041 must be completed each year that the trust has remaining income. With an irrevocable trust, income that is distributed is taxed first to beneficiaries. If income remains in the trust, the trust itself is subject to trust tax rates and must file IRS Form 1041 and pay applicable income taxes. If the trust has more than $600 in gross income, or if one of the beneficiaries is a nonresident alien, the filing can become more complicated.

One of the disadvantages of using trusts can be the higher trust tax rate assessed to income that remains within the trust. However, this may not be a disadvantage depending on the sources of income within the trust and the marginal tax rate of trust beneficiaries. The IRS classifies all trusts as simple or complex for the purposes of annual income taxes; complex trusts, whether living or testamentary, are subject to their own tax rates as reported on IRS Form 1041. The Internal Revenue Code (IRC) defines a simple trust as one that:

- distributes its income, instead of allowing discretionary distributions;

- makes no mandatory or discretionary distributions of principal; and

- makes no distributions to or has any principal set aside for charity.

Should the trust not meet the preceding criteria, it is classified as a complex trust and is subject to trust income tax rates for that tax year.

Product Strategy 6: Use Appropriate Property Titling Techniques

Titling assets properly is one tool to help manage a client's estate plan. Generally, whenever someone is added to the title of a property the IRS considers it a **taxable gift** to the new owner equal to the fair market value of the new ownership position. Understanding when a taxable gift might be incurred can save a client significant gift and estate taxes. If the original owner can make a withdrawal from the asset account without the permission of the new owner, no gift tax will be due until the new owner takes a distribution. For example, no gift tax is due when a joint owner is added to a bank account until the new owner makes a withdrawal. As an interesting note, if a security is held in street name, no gift tax is incurred upon joint titling; however, if a security is held JTWROS, a gift tax may be incurred.

Separate property is:

- Property a client owned before marriage;

- Property client and spouse agreed to convert to community property under state law;

- Property purchased with separate funds;

- Money a client earns while living in a non-community property state.

- Property received as a gift or inheritance.

- Community property is:

- Any property acquired during marriage while living is a community property state if the property was commingled with spouse or purchased with community assets.

The following titling methods can be used for property owned by more than one person:

- *Tenancy in common*: Used by two or more individuals; ownership interests need not be equal; each owner can sell, exchange, or otherwise dispose of his or her interest without the consent of the other owners; there are no survivorship rights.

- *Joint tenancy with right of survivorship* (JTWROS): Used by two or more individuals; ownership is equal among owners; ownership passes automatically to survivors upon the death of an owner; ownership can be terminated by death, mutual agreement, and divorce.

- *Tenancy by the entirety*: Used only by married couples; survivorship interest passes automatically to the surviving spouse.

- *Community property*: Used only by married couples living and acquiring property in community property states; survivorship interest does not automatically pass to the surviving spouse.

In the case of JTWROS and **tenancy in common**, creditors can access the value of the co-owner's interest. Only tenancy by the entirety protects a couple's home from creditor or liability claims against one member of the couple. Some states, such as Virginia, also allow married couples to title investment assets as tenants by the entirety. Potential gift taxes can arise with a change in titling.

Ten states provide married couples with an alternative to **tenancy by the entirety**, which is a common form of titling for property owned by a married couple. Alaska, Arizona, California, Idaho, Louisiana, Nevada, New Mexico, Texas, Washington, and Wisconsin each have a form of community property law. **Community property** refers to all assets obtained while a couple is married. Each spouse legally owns one-half of each asset purchased as community property.

Community property is unique, however, in that any property owned by a spouse prior to marriage remains the sole property of that spouse unless it is commingled with community property assets. Furthermore, if a spouse receives a gift or inheritance while married, those assets remain the separate property of the spouse.

One advantage associated with community property titling is that, upon the death of one spouse, all assets receive a 100 percent step-up in basis. This compares favorably to the 50 percent **step-up in basis** for assets held by spouses as **JTWROS** (i.e., titling procedure in which ownership of an asset transfers automatically at death to the surviving owners) or as tenancy by the entirety. Few banks, title companies, or other financial service firms automatically title marital assets as community property. A financial planner who fails to guide his or her community property clientele in the appropriate use of this titling option could cause clients to pay higher taxes in the future because of the lost step-up in basis associated with JTWROS titling.

> ### Self-Test 5
>
> Malek and Nelda were married and had lived in Nevada their entire life. Nelda recently passed away. Their home was valued at $500,000 at Nelda's death. Their basis in the home was $100,000. What in Malek's new basis in the property?
>
> a. $50,000
>
> b. $100,000
>
> c. $250,000
>
> d. $500,000

Product Strategy 7: Use a Qualified Disclaimer to Transfer Property

One way to transfer ownership is through the use of a **qualified disclaimer**. According to IRC § 2518, a "qualified disclaimer" refers to "an irrevocable and unqualified refusal by a person to accept an interest in property."[1] For the disclaimer to be qualified, it must meet the following guidelines:

- It must be in writing.

- It must be received no later than nine months after the bequest is made, or if the beneficiary is a minor at the time of the bequest, no later than nine months after the child reaches the age of twenty-one.

- The beneficiary must not accept any interest or benefit from the bequest.

- The beneficiary must not maintain any control or interest concerning who is to receive (inherit) the asset after filing the disclaimer.

Disclaimed assets are treated as though they were never transferred, which allows them to be transferred to another person or entity. This strategy can be useful in situations where the beneficiary already has a sizable estate and additional assets are not needed or desired. For a disclaimer to be qualified for federal and state tax purposes, the written disclaimer must be in compliance with IRC § 2518, as well as any state disclaimer statues that might apply. This can be an effective tool in the estate planning process.

Product Strategy 8: Avoid Probate by Using a Living Trust

Two reasons to consider establishing a *living trust* (i.e., a trust created during a client's life) are minimization of probate involvement and the publicity surrounding public documentation of a family's financial situation at a client's death. Other advantages include continuation of income and distributions to heirs from assets held in the trust after the death of the client, the ability of a trustee to manage assets, and the likely appropriate distribution of assets to heirs at the client's death. Other advantages include reducing the possibility of someone claiming that asset transfers were against the decedent's wishes and a reduction in legal costs for those with property in more than one state.

A significant disadvantage associated with this strategy is that clients sometimes confuse avoiding probate with avoiding estate taxation. Assets held in a revocable living trust are included in the client's gross estate for estate tax purposes. Also, income that is taxable to the trust, rather than to the grantor or the beneficiaries, is generally taxed at a higher rate (e.g., tax rates on trusts are based on compressed income tax brackets). Furthermore, although living trusts are effective in helping a client *avoid probate*, unless all titled assets are retitled or originally titled in the name of the trust, this goal may not be achieved.

Product Strategy 9: Establish an A-B Trust Arrangement for Clients with a High Net Worth

An *A-B trust arrangement* is another name for a strategy using a **credit shelter bypass trust** with a *marital deduction trust* (also known as a *standard family trust*). This technique can save a high-net-worth family substantial amounts in estate tax if properly implemented. In effect, this strategy guarantees that both spouses will maximize the use of their estate tax **unified credit** applicable exclusion amount. This strategy can also be an effective way to guarantee that a surviving spouse receives annual income but avoids some of the pitfalls of asset ownership, with the remaining assets going to ultimate beneficiaries upon the death of the surviving spouse.

In this arrangement, the *marital trust*—the A Trust—is established at the same time as the **bypass trust**—the B Trust—is created. The marital trust is typically funded with

---

Self-Test 6

Which of the following assets is not subject to probate?

a. Personal residence owned with a child.

b. Life insurance proceeds paid to a non-insured beneficiary.

c. Property titled as tenants in common.

d. Brokerage account.

all of the assets in excess of the estate tax unified credit applicable exclusion amount using the *unlimited marital deduction*. The marital trust is usually either a **POA trust** or a **QTIP trust**. In either of these types of trust arrangements, the surviving spouse must be given an income interest in the trust. In the POA trust, the spouse must also be given a general power of appointment over trust assets. As a result, marital trust assets are generally included in the surviving spouse's gross estate. For this reason, a bypass trust is also established, which is funded with assets protected by the unified credit of the first spouse to die. The bypass trust ensures that the first spouse does not lose use of his or her estate tax unified credit; but the trust bypasses the surviving spouse's estate.

When the Tax Relief Act of 2010 created the portable estate exemption, it effectively eliminated the need for most A-B trust arrangements. This law allows a surviving spouse to utilize any unused exclusion amount from the first-to-die spouse. As long as the couple was married at the date of the first death and the surviving spouse elects the exemption on IRS Form 706, the full value of a joint estate, approximately $11 million, can be sheltered from federal estate taxes in 2016. A-B trust arrangements will continue to be used regardless of the federal exclusion amount. These trusts allow for asset protection, particularly for those with estates exceeding $10.75 million. Assets in a B trust are generally inaccessible to creditors. A-B trusts also provide asset protection in cases where the surviving spouse remarries. If the portable estate exemption is elected and the surviving spouse remarries, the exemption amount could be reduced.

This strategy has some disadvantages. First, establishing the trust agreements requires that all other estate planning documents be revised, including the "evening out" of assets through retitling. (Remember: jointly held assets pass via property laws.) Retitling could result in a sizable upfront cost in both time and money for clients. This makes the strategy less attractive for clients whose combined assets are not, or will not be, greater than the estate tax unified credit applicable exclusion amount in the future. Second, the irrevocable nature of the bypass trust means that the surviving spouse generally can access only income generated from assets, which could limit the spouse's standard of living if the assets fail to generate adequate income in the future.

Product Strategy 10: Decrease Estate Tax Liability and Generate Income by Using a CRAT, CRUT, or Pooled Income Fund

This estate planning process is designed to benefit a charity while enhancing a client's financial situation. If proper gift planning is conducted and ultimately implemented, it may be possible to accomplish several distinct goals simultaneously. First, income tax liability can be reduced. The amount of the income tax charitable deduction is affected by the type and use of the asset given. Second, gift and estate taxes can be lessened. Third, benefits can be provided to charitable organizations. Fourth, giving can provide the donor a feeling of goodwill.

#Remember

Charitable lead trusts pay beneficiaries a percent of the value of assets in the trust; the charity is allowed to use the asset(s) for the term of the trust; at the end of the term, the assets are transferred to the donor's heirs without fit or estate tax.

Charitable giving involves providing gifts of money, income, and assets to charitable organizations. To qualify for a charitable donation, a client must give assets to a recognized charity in the United States, a US territory, or a political subdivision. *Nonprofit organizations* include most religious, scientific, and charitable organizations, some fraternal societies and associations, and certain veterans associations and organizations. To receive a tax deduction and exclude assets from an estate, a client should consider outright gifts, as well as using one or more of the following trust arrangements: a charitable remainder annuity trust, a charitable remainder unitrust, a pooled income fund, or a charitable lead trust.

When a client contributes to a **charitable remainder annuity trust (CRAT)**, the non-charitable beneficiary generally receives, on an annual basis, a fixed annuity payment equal to or greater than 5 percent, but not more than 50 percent of the initial net fair market value of the trust. The benefit may be structured as an annuity for life or a term certain. Once established, no additional contributions can be made to the CRAT. At the end of the term, the remainder goes to charity.

A **charitable remainder unitrust trust (CRUT)** is similar to a CRAT, but fundamentally different in the way in which payments are made to the beneficiary. The noncharitable beneficiary generally receives, annually, a payment equal to a fixed percentage between 5 percent and 50 percent of the assets held in the trust as revalued on an annual basis. The benefit can be structured as a unitrust for life or a term certain. In some instances, payments are set at the lower of the unitrust amount or trust income, with or without a make-up provision. This means that distributions can be limited to earnings, and there is no requirement to use principal to pay beneficiaries. Further, additional donations to a CRUT are allowed. At the end of the term, the remainder goes to charity.

A **pooled income fund** is a charitable device created and maintained by a charity. The donor makes an irrevocable gift that is pooled with similar gifts from other donors. The charity manages the commingled assets, and payments based on the income earned by the account are made to beneficiaries on a pro-rata basis for life. At the end of the term, the remainder goes to charity.

It is important to remember that gifts made to charitable organizations are irrevocable. It is also possible that payments from these trusts will not keep pace with inflation over time. Because a unitrust is a variable annuity, a CRUT can provide a hedge against this. In general, clients must be committed to the charity and acknowledge that the use of their donated assets might not represent their values or choices in the future. The irrevocable nature of charitable gifts is something each client must weigh against the qualitative and quantitative benefits received.

Product Strategy 11: Establish a Donor-advised Charitable Fund

A **donor-advised charitable fund** is an irrevocable account established by a custodian to accept, manage, and distribute donations to a client's chosen charities. The donor, while losing access to the assets for personal use, controls which charity receives a donation, when the donation will be made, how often the donation will be granted, and how much will be distributed. Although distributions cannot be used for pledges, private benefit, or political contributions, any legitimate charitable activity can receive benefits from a donor-advised fund.

The primary advantage associated with establishing a donor-advised charitable fund is that, although contributions are irrevocable, the client retains control over the timing and amount of annual distributions to a charity. Furthermore, the client can generally determine which charity will receive distributions. This choice can change yearly, so if a charitable organization veers from the client's objectives for giving, a different charity can be chosen in subsequent years.

There are tax advantages as well. Just like a regular charitable contribution, assets transferred to a donor-advised fund reduce a client's gross estate. Gifts of appreciated stock offer the added benefit to the donor of avoiding the capital gains on the appreciation. A portion of contributions can also be used to reduce federal income tax liability through an itemized deduction.

Several disadvantages are associated with this strategy. First, the number of donor-advised charitable fund providers is relatively limited, although financial services providers like Charles Schwab, Fidelity, and Vanguard offer these services. Second, the costs associated with such funds can be quite high. Annual fees of 2 to 5 percent are common, but they are still more reasonable than establishing a private foundation. Third, unlike CRATs and CRUTs, the donor cannot retain the right to receive payments.

Product Strategy 12: Establish a Foundation for Certain Clients

Private and public foundations are tax-advantaged entities that allow individuals to donate goods, services, and assets while receiving an income tax deduction (assuming the donor itemizes deductions). **Private foundations** generally receive their asset contributions from one or a few sources. Assets are then used to fund the ongoing operations of a charity or nonprofit organization. **Public foundations** typically receive funding from a wider public audience. Assets are then used to support a variety of community charities. Caps on the deductibility of contributions exist. The maximum deductibility for cash donations to private foundations is capped at 30 percent of adjusted gross income. Cash donations to public foundations are capped at 50 percent of adjusted gross income. Private foundations have very strict reporting requirements that require disclosure of asset values and donation sources. Private foundations must, by law, also distribute the equivalent of 5 percent of the fair market value of all investable assets per year.

Product Strategy 13: Decrease the Gross Estate by Contributing to a Section 529 Plan

This strategy works well when a client's objective is to help save for a child or grandchild's education while reducing his or her own estate tax liability. A single client can contribute up to five years of annual exclusion gifts to a § **529 plan** for a beneficiary in any given year (once every five years) gift tax free. By making five years of contributions in one year, a married couple can contribute $140,000 on a tax-free basis (2 × 5 × $14,000 **gift tax annual exclusion**) per child in 2016. Clients who use this strategy need to remember that if they elect to contribute the maximum amount allowable in a given year, they generally cannot make another tax-free contribution for five years. Furthermore, the client will be required to file a gift tax return at the time of the contribution to account for the gift.

Product Strategy 14: Establish a Qualified Personal Residence Trust (QPRT) or Grantor Retained Annuity Trust (GRAT) to Reduce Estate Liability

A **qualified personal residence trust (QPRT)** is designed to hold a client's home for later transfer to an heir(s). QPRTs are used by clients who would like to reduce the value of their gross estate in the future but still retain the right to live in their house, which may be their single greatest asset. If a client outlives the term of the trust, the property is transferred to the beneficiary. At that point, the client can generally continue to live in the property by agreeing to pay rent (based on an independent appraiser's fair market value rental) to the new property owner. If the client should die before the trust terminates, the full value of the home is included in the client's gross estate.

A **grantor retained annuity trust (GRAT)** is similar to a QPRT, but instead of holding a personal residence the trust holds other assets, such as stocks, bonds, mutual funds, and income-producing real estate. The trust makes annuity payments to the grantor for a certain number of years. At the trust's termination, the assets are transferred to the trust's beneficiaries.

> *Self-Test 7*
>
> Tyler would like to reduce the value of his gross estate by transferring ownership of his home to his daughter; however, he is worried that he will not have a place to live. Tyler should consider establishing a
>
> a. QPRT
>
> b. GRAT
>
> c. CRAT
>
> d. Limited Partnership

QPRTs and GRATs can be effective tools for reducing a client's gross estate while providing the client with immediate access to housing or an annuity stream. Implementing this strategy allows a client to remove a potentially rapidly appreciating personal residence or other assets from the client's estate if the client can outlive the term of the trust.

Several disadvantages are associated with this strategy. The trust is generally includable in the grantor's gross estate if the grantor dies during the trust term. Although the value of the property can be excluded from the gross estate if the grantor survives the trust term, the client could owe a gift tax on the present value of the remainder in the QPRT or GRAT. The shorter the term of the trust, the higher the potential gift tax will be. However, the longer the term, the more likely that the client will not outlive the trust term, which would defeat the purpose of the strategy.

Even though the QPRT owns the client's personal residence, it is the client's responsibility to pay all expenses related to upkeep, insurance, and taxes on the property. Also, if a client should outlive the duration of a QPRT, the client would need to negotiate with the owners of the property to continue living in the house.

Product Strategy 15: Establish a Family Limited Partnership

A **family limited partnership (FLP)** is a tool that can be used by high-net-worth business-owner clients to reduce estate tax liability, decrease income tax liability, and transfer ownership of a business to relatives over time. In the simplest form of an FLP, a client establishes a *limited partnership*, keeping a general partnership interest in it as well as some limited partnership interests. This enables the client to retain control over the day-to-day activities of the business. Initially, some limited partnership interests can be given or sold to family members. Over time, the client gives interests in the limited partnership to children, grandchildren, and other family members.

As income is generated in the business, the limited partners report their share of earnings. This can help a client reduce current tax liabilities. However, unearned income of a child under age nineteen (twenty-four if a full-time student) is generally taxable to the child at the parent's marginal tax rate.

> *Family Limited Partnerships:*
>
> • Allow parents to transfer wealth to their children a discount to FMV
>
> • Allow parents to transfer income tax liabilities to others in a lower bracket
>
> • Allow parents to retain some control over the transferred property
>
> • Offer limited liability to the partners, although the parents continue to have unlimited liability as the general partners

Over time, however, the real advantage of this technique is that it is possible to transfer ownership of a privately held firm from one generation to another on a tax-free basis, using a combination of the gift tax annual exclusion and the unified credit. Furthermore, valuation discounts are often available for transfers of minority interests and lack of marketability.

Some key disadvantages are associated with this strategy. First, even though a partnership can be established with relatively few upfront costs, the actual partnership document must be thorough and the parties need to continually observe partnership formalities to obtain tax benefits. Second, ongoing costs can become high because of accounting issues. Third, by establishing a partnership, the client may be taking on general liability for family members that the client might not otherwise want. Fourth, a gift tax might apply if future partnership gifts exceed the annual exclusion. Finally, implementing this strategy can result in a higher probability of being audited. An alternative involves the establishment of a *limited liability company* (LLC).

Product Strategy 16: Use an Irrevocable Life Insurance Trust to Reduce Gross Estate

An **irrevocable life insurance trust** (ILIT) strategy can be one of the best ways to remove a high-value asset from a client's gross estate. Using this strategy, a client transfers an existing life insurance policy to a trust. Premiums are then funded using the gift tax annual exclusion (i.e., the client gifts the premium amount to the trust, which then pays the insurance premium). Assuming the grantor-insured lives for more than three years after the gift, this has the advantage of removing the life insurance policy from the gross estate and allows for further estate reduction by using annual gifts to fund premium payments. Of course, if the trustee purchases the policy on the client's life using trust assets, the insured never has an incident of ownership and there is much greater assurance that policy proceeds will be estate tax excludable.

A significant disadvantage associated with this strategy is that the transfer of ownership in a life insurance policy is considered a gift. If the value of the gift exceeds or for some reason does not qualify for the gift tax annual exclusion, a client may have to use up some or all of his or her unified credit and perhaps owe gift tax. Another disadvantage is that the cost of establishing and maintaining an ILIT to some extent offsets the tax benefits gained.

Product Strategy 17: Establish a QTIP Trust When Applicable

A **QTIP trust** is often used to obtain a marital deduction for **qualified terminable interest property (QTIP)**. These trusts are useful for divorced individuals entering a remarriage with children, or when a wealthy spouse wishes to ensure adequate income for the surviving spouse but has a strong desire to be sure that at the spouse's death assets remaining in the trust will pass to the wealthy spouse's children. Two important rules apply to the use of QTIP trusts:

1. The surviving spouse must be given the right to all income from the trust (paid at least annually).

2. No one can be given the right to direct that the property will go to anyone else as long as the surviving spouse is alive.

If these rules are met, assets passing to the trust become eligible for the marital deduction. Property that remains in the trust after the surviving spouse's death then goes to the beneficiary originally named by the donor or decedent. Like any marital deduction trust, a QTIP trust is subject to estate tax at the surviving spouse's death. That is, QTIP trusts are ineffective tools for those wishing to reduce or eliminate estate tax liabilities.

Product Strategy 18: Reduce Taxes by Using a Charitable Lead Trust

A **charitable lead trust** (CLT) allows a client to gift assets to a charity, receive a tax deduction for the gift, and potentially reduce estate taxes. Unlike other charitable gifting strategies, a CLT provides a charity with an annuity income rather than assets. At the end of the annuity period, e.g., twenty years, any assets remaining in the trust are distributed to the client's remainder beneficiaries (e.g., children, grandchildren, trusts). The longer the term of the annuity payment, the larger the tax deduction and reduction in estate value will be.

For estate tax purposes, the return of the asset to the remainder beneficiary is considered a gift; however, the gift value is based on current market interest rates and the present value of the assets when donated, not the appreciated value. IRS rules make the use of a CLT strategy complicated. Gifts to CLTs do not qualify for the annual gift exclusion.

Also, the IRS will impose a tax on the sale or exchange of property in a CLT within the first two years. Finally, a CLT could be disallowed if the IRS suspects self-dealing.

Product Strategy 19: Use Intra-Family and Other Business Transfer Techniques When Appropriate

Clients who own one or more businesses and those who have substantial real estate holdings need to preplan ways to transfer these assets to co-owners, heirs, and other beneficiaries. Buy-sell agreements are used to facilitate the transfer of business ownership to other owners. The simplest type of agreement outlines the manner in which the ownership interest of one owner will be transferred to other owners, usually through the use of company assets. An entity purchase agreement can be used for this purpose. In this case, the company owns life insurance with each business owner as the insured and the company as the beneficiary. An alternative is a cross-purchase agreement where each business owner purchases a life insurance policy naming themselves as the beneficiary and the other owners as the insureds. A third option is a wait-and-see buy-sell agreement. Within this strategy the business is given the first right to purchase a deceased owner's interest in the firm, after which the remaining owners are given an opportunity to purchase the decedent's shares. Financial planners should ensure that a client has incorporated the following into any buy-sell agreement: wording that clarifies who is and is not covered by the agreement, what events beyond death might trigger the agreement, the buyout price, and how often the agreement should be reviewed and revised.

When considering family transfers, clients are often faced with the dual goals of reducing gift tax liabilities and ensuring family unity. Providing gifts while retaining an interest in an asset is one way to remove the value of an asset from a client's estate over time. A *grantor retained annuity trust* can be used to facilitate this process. With this type of trust, a donor gifts property to a trust and receives an annual payout from the trust for a pre-determined number of years. At the end of the period the remaining value is passed to one or more beneficiaries, thereby reducing both gift and estate taxes. A *qualified personal residence trust* is a special form of grantor retained annuity trust that helps transfer a home to beneficiaries. Some financial planners also use *defective grantor trusts*. These types of trusts are established so that the grantor is liable for income taxes, which reduces distributions from the trust and ensures a larger transfer later in time. GRATs, GRUTs, QPRTs, and some charitable lead trusts are all examples of intentionally defective grantor trusts.

Self-Test 8

Which of the following requires each business owner to purchase life insurance on the life of each other business owner?

a. entity purchase agreement

b. wait-and-see buy-sell agreement

c. cross-purchase agreement

d. bargain sale

Advantages of an installment sale include deferral of capital gains, removing an asset from the gross estate, and helping family members acquire property.

If the transferred property is a business, vacation home, or primary residence then the borrower may deduct the interest paid

Several additional strategies can be used to facilitate intra-family transfers. The first involves an *intra-family loan* where one family member loans money to another for the purchase of the lender's property. No gift tax consequences are involved in the loan is an arms-length transaction; however, if the loan's rate of interest is zero or below the market the foregone interest may be considered imputed income. The second approach involves the establishment of a *private annuity*. With this strategy the older family member purchases a lifetime income from the obligor— the younger family member—using assets from the elder's estate. The annuity becomes an uninsured promise to pay, but sometimes a life insurance policy is purchased on the obligor's life to ensure income payments to the annuitant. When the annuitant dies (the elder family member) the property's basis is adjusted for the annuity payments already made, which may generate a tax liability for the obligor. As long at the present value of the payments is equal to or more than the fair market value of the property used to purchase the annuity the property will be excluded from the gross estate.

Sometimes a *self-cancelling installment note (SCIN)* is used to facilitate intra-family transfers. An *installment sale* occurs when an older family member sells property to someone younger in the family using a loan. This is a SCIN if the loan automatically cancels after the death of the seller. The principal amount of the note is based on the seller's life expectancy. If the buyer and seller are not related, any cancelled payments are excluded from the gross estate but are taxed as income if respect of a decedent; however, if the parties are related this strategy can get complex, which explain why this strategy is rarely used.

Occasionally a business owning family will use a *gift leaseback* strategy. Using this technique, a parent would gift a depreciated asset to a child but continue to use the asset in the business. The parent and child then enter into a lease agreement where the parent makes tax-deductible payments to the child for use of the asset. The income is taxable to the child. As long as the value of the gift is below the annual gift exclusion amount the gift tax can be avoided. Finally, some families use a *bargain sale* to facilitate intra-family transfers. This occurs when the sales price of an item is less than the fair market value. The difference is considered a tax gift from the seller to the buyer if it exceeds the annual gift exclusion amount. The purchaser adopts either the seller's carried over basis or the amount paid, whichever is larger.

Procedural Strategy 1: Ensure That Each Client Has Appropriate Estate Planning Documents in Place

According to a 2011 ABC News poll, only 50 percent of all US adults have a will—a document written to direct the distribution of one's property at death, and even fewer—only 42 percent—have a *living will, health care proxy,* or *advance medical directive* (AMD) for directing end-of-life or health care decisions (i.e., someone a client appoints, such as a family member or friend, to make health care decisions for the client if the client is unable to make his or her own decision).[2]

A planner must evaluate the strategies, products, or legal techniques a client is currently using to accumulate, preserve, and distribute assets over time. Although no one but an attorney should ever draft a legal document, every planner who performs comprehensive financial planning should help clients think through the complex issues associated with planning an estate. As part of this review, it is imperative that financial planners determine whether a client (and spouse or partner) possesses any of the following documents, when they were drafted, and whether they are still applicable.

- **Client will(s):** A legal document outlining how property will be transferred at death

- **Letter(s) of last instruction**: A document written to a significant other (usually a spouse) to provides directions regarding the execution of a client's will

- **Codicil**: An attachment or amendment to an existing will

- **Power of attorney** (medical or financial): A legal document appointing another person to act for the client if the client becomes incapacitated

- **Living will** or **advance medical directive** (AMD): A directive written for the use of a physician or hospital that outlines a client's wishes regarding medical and end-of-life treatment in the event of the client's incapacitation

In addition to these legal documents, any prepaid, contracted, or even informal final arrangements should also be discussed and the location of any contracts determined, if applicable. Finally, it is important to verify and review the following documents to develop a comprehensive profile of the client situation and confirm locations for future use.

- Birth certificate(s) for all household members

- Marriage certificate(s) and/or divorce decree(s)

- All in-force insurance policies with beneficiary designations

- Life, health, long-term care, and annuity policies and beneficiary designation form(s) for individual and group policies

- Title(s) to personal property and deed(s) to real property in the state of residence or other states

- Inventory of any special property such as jewelry, fine art, or a collection (e.g., stamps, coins, wine, firearms) including a schedule of beneficiaries

- Brokerage account statements or other evidence of security ownership (e.g., stock certificates)

- Business agreements and documentation for any outstanding unpaid debts or unsettled legal claims

- Income tax returns for the previous three years

- The location of a safety deposit box, an inventory of contents, the location of key(s), and a determination of whether state law requires that the box be sealed until inventoried by a representative of the court

Procedural Strategy 2: Use a Legal Document Checklist

After reviewing a client's current estate plan, a variety of issues may need to be addressed. These will help the planner focus on strategies to form recommendations for the client. A client's last will and testament often needs immediate remedial attention. The checklist shown in Figure 13.2 will help novice planners and students assess a client's current will and end-of-life documentation to determine whether legal documents should be retained or rewritten.

Figure 13.2 Estate Planning Documentation Checklist

Estate Planning Documentation Checklist		
Question	**Yes**	**No**
1. Is the client's name correct on all documents?		
2. Is the spouse's or partner's name correct on all documents?		
3. Are the children's names and ages (if applicable) correct on all documents?		
4. Is the executor properly named?		
5. Is a guardian for dependent children named?		
6. If named, is the guardian still the appropriate choice?		
7. Are special bequests adequately identified?		
8. Are charitable bequests up to date and adequately identified?		
9. Is the simultaneous death clause appropriate for the state of residence?		
10. Are trust documents referred to in the will?		
11. Does the will refer to a particular trust if a trust exists?		
12. Have trusts, other than testamentary trusts, been		
13. Have special considerations been made for parents?		
14. Have special considerations been made for siblings?		
15. Have special considerations been made for grandchildren?		
16. Are codicils up to date and accurate?		
17. Does the client have a power of attorney in place? If so, what kind and what powers are included?		
18. Has the client written a letter of last instructions?		
19. Depending on the state of residence and need, has the client drafted:		
• a living will?		
• an advance medical directive?		
• a medical power of attorney?		
• a HIPAA authorization?		
20. Does the client share time in different states? If so, are all documents appropriate and in place?		
21. Is there a current list of all financial professionals, including the estate attorney, available for the survivors or the executor?		

Procedural Strategy 3: Use Annual Gifts to Reduce a Client's Gross Estate

One of the most effective ways to decrease a client's gross estate involves taking full advantage of the $14,000 (in 2016) **gift tax annual exclusion** per donee. Using this strategy, a client can give up to $14,000 per year gift tax free to as many individuals (related or not) as the client desires. Married couples can double gifts through gift-splitting techniques and provide up to $28,000 per year to each donee gift tax free. It is possible to reduce an estate substantially over time simply by systematically making gifts to one or more persons. The primary disadvantage associated with this strategy is that, once a gift has been made, the transfer is irrevocable. Further, gifts to others cannot be used to generate income for the donor. Gifts of more than $14,000 (in 2016) effectively decrease a client's unified credit and subject the donor to gift taxation.

#Remember

- Present gifts greater than the annual exclusion are currently taxable.

- Future interest gifts are currently taxable.

- No gift tax is due as long as the current gift plus all lifetime gifts do not exceed the applicable exclusion amount.

Procedural Strategy 4: Increase Charitable Giving to Reduce Estate Tax

Lifetime charitable giving provides clients with three primary advantages. First, gifts typically can be deducted, at least in part, as an itemized deduction for federal income tax purposes. Second, the full value of gifts made to qualified charities reduces a client's gross estate, which can reduce tax liability. Third, if established through a CRAT, CRUT, or pooled income fund, charitable gifts can also provide lifetime payments to, for example, the donor and the donor's spouse. Like all giving strategies, donating assets to charity results in loss of use of the property. Gifts are irrevocable, regardless of whether a client has a change of heart at a later date or needs the assets back to fund other goals. Issues related to family disagreements over charitable donations should also be considered.

Self-Test 9

At what age can the beneficiary of a 2503(b) trust elect to access the asset(s)?

a. Any time before age 30.

b. At age 18.

c. At age 21.

d. At a time described in the trust document.

Procedural Strategy 5: Make Gifts to Custodial Accounts (UGMA/UTMA)

State laws for custodian accounts are titled either **Uniform Gifts to Minors Act (UGMA)** or **Uniform Transfers to Minors Act (UTMA)**. If a UGMA/UTMA is used, an adult must be named *custodian* of the account. When a child reaches the *age of majority*, which is typically age eighteen or twenty-one depending on the state of the child's residence, the assets become the full property of the young person.

Certain tax advantages are associated with using UGMA/UTMA. First, the donor's gross estate can generally be reduced through the use of annual gifts. Second, income-producing assets can be shifted to children and grandchildren in a way that possibly reduces the total amount of income tax paid. Gifts to custodial accounts qualify for the annual exclusion for both gift tax and generation-skipping transfer tax purposes.

It is important to keep in mind several disadvantages associated with this strategy. To begin with, all gifts to custodial accounts are irrevocable, and upon the child's age of majority—typically eighteen or twenty-one—the assets become the sole property of the child. Unearned income of a child under age nineteen (twenty-four if a full-time student) is generally taxable to the child at the parent's marginal tax rate. The loss of property use and the inability to guarantee that assets will be used for a specific purpose make this strategy problematic for some clients.

Procedural Strategy 6: Make Gifts to § 2503(b) or 2503(c) Trusts for Minor Child

Certain trusts can be used to transfer assets to minor children and grandchildren using the gift tax annual exclusion. A **§ 2503(b) trust** generally requires the income from assets held in the trust to be distributed for the child's benefit at least annually. However, the principal need not be distributed at the age of majority.

A **§ 2503(c) trust** allows all income to grow within the trust, but distribution of trust assets must generally occur at the child's age of majority. A § 2503(c) trust is similar to UGMA/UTMA in this respect, but different in that a clause can be inserted into the trust document that gives the child a right to demand distribution from the trust for a limited period of time upon reaching the age of majority. If the distribution is not requested within this time period, the trust can continue into later years. Unlike a gift under UGMA/UTMA, the property can remain within the trust beyond the child's age of majority.

With either trust, the asset and the income from the asset are no longer available to the donor. Furthermore, if a § 2503(b) trust is used, income generated within the trust must be distributed at least annually to the child.

Procedural Strategy 7: Adding Co-owners to Accounts

Many times clients feel an emotional obligation to add family members to accounts. If they want the account to pass automatically at death, clients should consider using a **payable on death (POD)** or **transfer on death (TOD)** account. A POD is used for bank accounts, and a TOD is used for security titling. Clients are sometimes tempted to use forms of co-ownership as a way to avoid probate.

Although adding a spouse, child, or other person as a co-owner to property may sound like an attractive strategy initially, the long-term ramifications of this strategy can be quite negative. For example, co-owning all assets with a spouse almost guarantees that assets will transfer directly to the spouse through the unlimited marital deduction. This could result in *over-qualifying the spouse's estate* for the marital deduction, resulting in more federal estate tax due at the surviving spouse's death than might otherwise have been the case. Adding a co-owner other than a spouse to property can result in gift tax. Additionally, co-owners can lose the ability to receive a full step-up in basis on co-owned property. Finally, care is needed to avoid a conflict with POD or TOD arrangements that take precedence over intentions stated in the will.

Procedural Strategy 8: Make Complete and Appropriate Use of Property Transfer Law by Using Beneficiary Designations

One of the simplest ways to reduce *probate fees* and retain client privacy is to ensure that all financial assets have designated beneficiaries and contingent beneficiaries, and that these designations are kept up to date. Changes precipitated by a death, divorce, or other personal situation should not be overlooked. Like many other estate planning issues, beneficiary designations require clients to face their mortality and make choices. Too often, no designation is made or "payable to the estate" is chosen by default.

Procedural Strategy 9: Take Care to Accurately Account for Life Insurance in the Gross Estate

It is important to know when and how much life insurance is included in a client's gross estate. The face value of a policy is always included if a decedent owns the insurance and is the insured. The face value amount is reduced by any outstanding policy loans and accrued dividends. If the decedent owns the policy but is not the insured, the *interpolated terminal reserve* value of the policy plus any unearned premium will likely be included in the gross estate. Often, this value is close to the cash value of a non-term policy. Failing to account for the appropriate value of life insurance in the gross estate can produce significant estate miscalculations.

Procedural Strategy 10: Valuing Art and Collectibles

The valuation of art, collectibles, and other keepsakes owned by a deceased relative often causes heirs confusion. Two values exist: the *catalog value*, available for most items; and the *market value*. Catalog values are used primarily for insurance purposes; however, heirs sometimes assume that an inventory based on catalog values is equivalent to market value. This is rarely true. In the case of collectibles, such as stamps and books, market value may be as little as 20 percent of the unadjusted (for condition of the item[s]) catalog value.[3] That is, a collection will almost always generate less in cash value than the cost it would take to replace the collection. In some situations, catalog and market values tend to be close. The valuation of precious metals, for example, usually falls much closer to catalog valuation. When reporting the worth of a valuable collection for estate planning purposes, it is important to work with an experienced appraiser who can translate catalog values into market values.

Procedural Strategy 11: Incorporate Gift Tax Planning into a Client's Overall Estate Plan

The federal **gift tax** is linked to the estate tax. Planning for gifting does require additional strategizing. Under current law, gifts are taxable to the giver (**donor**) rather than the receiver (**donee**). The gift tax applies to transfers of property by

gift and occurs whenever property (including money) or the use of or income from property is given without expectation of receiving something of at least equal value in return. Additionally, if a client sells something at less than its full value, or if an interest-free or reduced-interest loan is made, the IRS will most likely consider a portion of the sale a gift.

The general rule is that any gift is a taxable gift. However, there are certain exceptions to this rule. Generally, the following gifts are not taxable:

- Annual gifts that do not exceed the exclusion for the calendar year;

- Gifts to a client's US citizen spouse (limits apply for a non-US citizen spouse);

- Tuition expenses a client pays directly to the educational institution for the benefit of someone else;

- Medical expenses a client pays directly to the institution or person providing care for the benefit of someone else;

- Gifts to a political organization for its use; and

- Gifts to qualified charities (a deduction is available for these contributions).

A separate *annual exclusion* applies to each person to whom a client makes a gift. In 2016, the annual exclusion was $14,000, indexed to inflation. In general, a client can give up to $14,000 to any number of people in 2016. As long as the gift value is equal to or less than $14,000, none of the gift amount is taxable. If a client is married, the client and spouse can effectively give up to $28,000 to the same person without making a taxable gift; this is known as **gift splitting**.

Generally, clients need not file a **gift tax return**, IRS Form 709, unless they give someone other than a spouse money or property worth more than the annual exclusion. Although a return may be required, no actual gift tax will become payable until cumulative lifetime taxable giving exceeds the applicable exclusion amount. Clients who give money or assets to others are primarily responsible for the payment of the gift tax. When discussing gift tax issues with clients, it is important to remind them that the person who receives the gift generally will not have to pay any federal gift tax.

> *Example.* Assume that a client gifts $25,000 to her son, $25,000 to her daughter, $8,000 to her niece, and $2,500 each to the seven other members of her bridge group; all gifts are made within the same calendar year—in this example, 2016. Although the client made gifts totaling $75,500, each gift is treated separately. After applying the $14,000 annual exclusion, none of the individual gifts under $14,000 are taxable; only the individual gift amounts in excess of $14,000 to each child are taxable. The gift tax will be calculated on the $22,000 [($25,000 ⊠ $14,000) × 2] in non-excludable gifts. Because the gift to each child is taxable, the client must file IRS Form 709 to claim the gifts, although the client could opt to subtract the tax from her unified credit rather than pay the tax.

Tax basis must also be considered when gifting property in that the donee's basis will be different depending on whether the property was received as a "gift" or an *inheritance*. When property is inherited, the donee's tax basis becomes the value of the property as of the donor's date of death (or alternate valuation date if chosen by the custodian of the estate); however, if the property is transferred as a gift, then the donee does not receive a step-up in basis, meaning the donee's original tax basis still applies.

> *Example.* Your parent left you the family farm, which has an original tax basis of $145,000, but the market value is $500,000. If the farm was received as a gift and then sold for the market value, you would owe capital gains tax on the $355,000 difference between the basis and sales price. Additionally, your parent might be responsible for gift tax on the $487,000 difference between the annual exclusion and the market value. However, if you inherited the property upon death, then you would not owe any capital gains tax on the sale, and so long as the total value of lifetime taxable gifts did not exceed the exclusion, your parent's estate would not owe any estate tax on the transfer.

Some financial transactions are difficult to classify as a gift. Adding a joint tenant to a bank account is not considered a gift until the new owner withdraws the funds. But adding a joint tenant to real estate is a gift if the new owner has the right to sell the interest in the property, even if the owner does not exercise this right. (It is important to note that adding joint owners to assets will override the distributions directed by the will because property law supersedes the instructions of the will or probate rulings.)

Finally, it is important to realize that although many other taxes can be filed jointly, gift tax returns are filed on an individual basis. So, if a married couple gives a single person a gift in excess of twice the annual exclusion, then the gift would be evenly split and each spouse would need to file individual IRS Forms 709 for one-half of the amount in excess of twice the exclusion amount.

Procedural Strategy 12: Account for a Possible Generation-Skipping Transfer Tax

A **generation-skipping transfer tax** (**GSTT**) is a levy on the portion of an estate that skips over one generation. Any gift or property assignment to someone two or more generations below the person making the transfer (or 37½ years younger that the donee, known as a **skip person**) is generally considered a **generation-skipping transfer**. Typically, a generation skip occurs when a distribution is made from a grandparent to a grandchild, thereby skipping a *generation*. This is known as a **direct skip**. Direct skips can occur whether the donor/decedent is living or deceased, but in cases where the death of the middle generation occurs before the gift is made, the GSTT tax is avoided. The tax can also be avoided whenever a donor/decedent and beneficiary are not related and the beneficiary is at least 37½ years younger than the donor.[4] Transfers to a trust—as well as certain transfers within or from a trust—are subject to the GSTT tax; such transfers are taxed at the highest estate tax rate in effect at the time of transfer.

Procedural Strategy 13: Elect Correct Estate Valuation Date

The *personal representative* of a decedent's estate may choose to value assets for tax purpose as the fair market value on the date of death or the value six months after death. The use of the **alternate valuation date** is appropriate whenever estate assets have decreased in value during the six months after death. A few caveats are worth noting. First, if a decedent's property is sold or distributed within the six month period the alternate valuation date may not be used. Second, if the alternated date is used all assets must be valued using the technique. Additionally, any estate that owes generation-skipping transfer taxes may not use an alternate valuation date. The personal representative must elect the alternate valuation date within one year of the estate tax return filing date. Extensions are not allowed.

> **#Remember**
>
> When valuing an estate, the following must be added back to arrive at an appropriate gross estate figure:
>
> - Gifts made within 3 years of death;
>
> - Transfer of a life insurance policy within 3 years of death;
>
> - Transfers where the decedent retained an interest in the transferred property;

Procedural Strategy 14: Identify Sources of Estate Liquidity

At death, the surviving family or estate is typically faced with immediate expenses; however, in some cases a decedent's assets may be frozen, making access to cash and other liquid assets difficult. Immediate expenses include funeral costs, medical bills, debts, probate costs, and possibly state and federal taxes. Identifying sources of **estate liquidity** prior to death is an important financial planning function.

In addition to cash and cash equivalents held by the decedent, the three primary sources of estate liquidity include life insurance, loans, and asset sales. Life insurance is widely used to meet a liquidity need. It is important to note, however, that if the beneficiary of a decedent's life insurance policy is the estate the proceeds will be included in the decedent's gross estate. Additionally, if the IRS deems life insurance proceeds as essential to the payment of taxes, claims, and other estate expenses the death benefit will be included in the gross estate. This is true even if the beneficiary is an ILIT or another person who is legally obliged to pay the decedent's final expenses. It may be possible to use a policy's accelerated death benefit or to sell the policy to a **viatical settlement** company if death is imminent.

The second liquidity strategy involves pledging unencumbered property held by the estate as security for a short-term loan. It may also be possible to borrow from a decedent's ILIT. The third option involves selling assets. Assets that are included in the gross estate typically receive a step-up in basis. Note that this strategy does not work for *ordinary income property*, such as 401(k), 403(b), annuity, and savings bond assets. Shortly after the decedent's death assets can be sold with little, if any, income tax liability. It may also be possible to sell assets to a decedent's ILIT. Another liquidity source for some clients are assets from a closely held business.

ESTATE PLANNING FOR SPECIAL POPULATIONS

Estate Planning for Domestic Partners without Civil Unions

Nearly 14 million US households were classified as unmarried by the Census in 2010. Of these, 10 percent represent same-sex couples.[5] Without proper planning, many of the health care and end-of-life rights that exist for married couples may be nonexistent for non-married couples regardless of the sexual orientation of the partners. As with many issues dealing with end-of-life and estate planning, the regulations and governing laws vary from state to state and, in some cases, are in nearly constant flux. So the best advice a planner can give to domestic partners is that if there is any question regarding rights or privileges, do not rely on general state procedures; rather, create a legal document that is allowable under the law. It is important for unmarried couples to execute detailed and legally enforceable instructions; the primary documents used for this are the *general power of attorney* (POA), the *medical POA* or advance medical directive (AMD), the appropriate trust documentation, and custodial documentation, if applicable.

Designating a **proxy** (also known in some states as an **attorney-in-fact** or **agent**) to make decisions regarding financial affairs (via a general, durable, or springing POA) or medical affairs (via a medical POA) is important protection. By executing a POA, a client can decide who will be the agent should the client become unable to act or make decisions. Without a POA, someone else—most likely an immediate family member—will have to petition a court to be appointed guardian and/or conservator to handle financial matters. This process can be expensive and the family member may not be the client's choice to have this decision-making authority. In addition to financial affairs, assisting a client with a plan for health care decision making during a period of disability or incapacitation is crucial. Virginia law, for example, provides an order of priority for making medical decisions; it includes guardian, spouse, child over age 18, parents, adult siblings, and other blood relatives, but makes no mention of a partner. Issues as seemingly simple as visitation rights and the ability to make financial and health care decisions for a partner may not exist unless a couple has updated health care proxies, living wills, AMDs or medical POAs (depending on the state of residence) and durable POAs in place. Without these documents, decisions regarding finances and health matters can revert to family or government-appointed guardians. Only through the execution of state-specific documents can a client guarantee that a domestic partner has rights and the ability to assist with financial and medical issues.

Another concern—potentially greater for same-sex couples—is avoiding courts, because all aspects of a last will and testament become public record during probate. The probate process means notifying potential heirs, thus giving them a chance to contest the will. Therefore, trust documentation should be in place for the disposition of any estate. Although a will may be important for other reasons, a revocable living trust can serve as a substitute for a will, thereby avoiding the probate process and keeping the transfer of assets confidential—and in most cases, uncontestable.

Finally, should the clients have children, it is advisable to draft a shared *custody agreement* if allowable under state law. Some states allow the legal parent to draft a contract for shared custody with a domestic partner. This could be very helpful in keeping the family together if the biological or legal parent dies; however the reverse is also true in that if the family breaks up, custody would still be shared.

Although having comprehensive estate and financial planning documents in place is important for everyone, it is especially important for unmarried couples. If the proper estate planning documents are not in place, then a domestic partner will likely have no rights in making financial or medical decisions on the client's behalf and might not inherit from the estate if the client passes away intestate or without a living trust. Whereas most clients do not like discussing such matters, the issues raised by this process can save time and money, avoid unnecessary litigation and disputes, and ensure that their wishes are followed and their partners respected.[6]

Estate Planning for Newly Separated or Divorced

Although state laws differ greatly regarding spousal rights, they all agree on one thing: your spouse is your spouse until a **divorce** is final. This can cause a great deal of difficulty, especially when the divorce is contested by one party or children are involved. In some states, uncontested divorce between spouses with no common children can be completed after six months of legal separation; however, this is the best-case scenario. On the other end of the spectrum, divorces can take years to resolve. This lag creates the need to carefully consider all aspects of an estate plan, including but not limited to wills, trust beneficiaries, qualified account beneficiaries, the custody of minor children, medical and durable powers of attorney, and life insurance contacts.

Divorce is really a two-phase process. Phase one is the *legal separation*—when two people are still married but realize that the marriage no longer works and will not continue, and it is not simply physical separation. Phase two is divorce—when the request for the dissolution of the marriage is granted by the court system. The period of legal separation is messier in that the soon-to-be ex-spouse still retains marital rights.

If a client has estate planning documents in place with the current spouse, the client should consider revoking and restating all of the estate planning documents before filing for divorce. In California, for example, the spouse who is contemplating divorce is not mandated to notify his or her spouse of any changes in estate planning documents, life insurance beneficiary designations, or retirement account beneficiary designations. However, the client may not be able to change these documents after filing a petition for divorce because California, ironically enough, and some other states issue *Family Law Restraining Orders*, sometimes called ATROs (*automatic temporary restraining orders*), which prevent certain activities from occurring during the divorce proceedings.[7]

These restraining orders do not allow the revocation of a trust, the changing of life insurance beneficiaries, or the changing of retirement plan or IRA account beneficiaries, among other constraints and limitations. The intent is to maintain the status quo of assets and ownership interests until the division of assets is final. So what was changeable before filing is no longer. However, if a client has already filed for divorce, the client should be able to update the will, financial POA, and AMDs.

Although other states, notably Arizona, automatically change spousal rights upon the granting of divorce, Arizona law dictates that (1) a divorced person's will remain valid, but the ex-spouse is disqualified as a potential beneficiary of the estate; (2) if one or both spouses should die before any joint marital property trust is dissolved as part of the divorce settlement, each spouse's share of the trust is distributed as if there were no surviving spouse; (3) an ex-spouse is automatically removed as an agent named in a financial or health care power of attorney, as a beneficiary on life insurance contracts, as a beneficiary for accounts with pay-on-death, transfer-on-death and in-trust-for designations; and (4) any property held as JTWROS automatically converts to tenancy in common so that the property will no longer automatically pass to the survivor.[8]

Qualified retirement accounts are notoriously difficult because of *ERISA*, the federal law governing such accounts. The US Supreme Court has ruled that plan administrators can rely solely on beneficiary designations. Thus, an ex-spouse remains a beneficiary of one of these plans until the plan participant submits a new beneficiary designation.[9] In fact this ruling upholds an ex-spouse's claim on residual assets even after the death of the account owner. Although this ruling does not extend to IRA accounts, the IRA custodian will likely treat the ex-spouse as beneficiary if the custodian has no knowledge of the divorce, so funds could be legally but inadvertently distributed to a former spouse. The best advice that planners can offer a recently divorced client is to systematically update all documentation that mentions the former spouse to ensure that the client's wishes for property ownership and division are met.

Quantitative/Analytical Mini-Case Problems

Sandomir and Rasia Kolbe

1. Sandomir and Rasia Kolbe, ages fifty-eight and fifty-seven respectively, and their three grown children recently attended Sandomier's father's funeral in Poland. They realized that they did not know the effect of federal estate tax on their own estate, nor did they have any legal documentation supporting end-of-life medical or financial decisions. So upon returning home, Rasia called her mother for a recommendation regarding financial professionals to interview. Her mother suggested an attorney for the legal documents and her own financial planner for other estate planning needs. Assume all family members are US citizens. Financial information for the Kolbe family follows:

Current Division of Assets				
Assets	Total	Sandomir	Rasia	Joint
Cash and Savings	$83,500	$4,500	$7,000	$72,000
Securities and annuities (nonqualified)	$625,000	$0	$0	$625,000
Securities and annuities (qualified)	$55,000	$0	$55,000	$0
Retirement plans	$605,000	$425,000	$180,000	$0
Automobiles	$105,000	$0	$0	$105,000
Personal property	$150,000	$0	$0	$150,000
Residence	$500,000	$0	$0	$500,000
Other real estate	$350,000	$0	$0	$350,000
Business interests	$225,000	$0	$225,000	$0
Life insurance (see table below)	$164,000	$84,000	$80,000	$0
Total assets	$2,862,500	$513,500	$547,000	$1,802,000

Current Life Insurance Information					
	Face Value	Cash Value	Owner	Insured	Beneficiary
Life Policy # 1 (Term)	$220,000	$0	Employer	Sandomir	Sandomir
Life Policy # 2 (Whole)	$250,000	$45,000	Sandomir	Sandomir	Rasia
Life Policy # 3 (Whole)	$150,000	$30,000	Rasia	Sandomir	Children
Life Policy # 4 (Term)	$20,000	$0	Rasia	Rasia	Sandomir
Life Policy # 5 (VUL)	$300,000	$50,000	Rasia	Rasia	Sandomir
Life Policy # 6 (Whole)	$50,000	$9,000	Sandomir	Rasia	Sandomir
Life Policy # 7 (Whole)	$150,000	$30,000	Sandomir	Rasia	Children
Total life insurance	$1,140,000	$164,000			

Based on the Kolbes' financial information, the lawyer and the financial planner jointly made these recommendations.

Recommendation 1: Establish testamentary trusts for both Sandomir and Rasia.

Recommendation 2: Retitle assets in preparation of funding trusts.

Recommendation 3: Transfer life insurance ownership to the three children.

To assist the Kolbes in their estate planning, answer the following questions.

a. What type of trust(s) might be recommended in keeping with the clients' desires of minimizing estate taxes, maximizing privacy, and easing ownership transfer?

b. How might the assets be retitled to ensure that all trusts can be adequately funded?

c. What are some of the challenges associated with transferring ownership of the insurance policies to the children? Describe some of the problems with the current life insurance designations. What other strategies could also be considered for alleviating any potential estate, gift, or income tax issues?

d. Besides completing wills and trust documents, what other legal documents should the Kolbes consider?

Jane and John Williams

2. Assume the following estate planning information for Jane and her spouse John.

	Client (Jane)	Spouse (John)	Joint*
Assets	$6,300,000	$1,200,000	$500,000
Debts			$100,000
Funeral	$20,000	$20,000	
Estate administration	$20,000	$20,000	
Charitable contribution	$20,000	$20,000	
Marital plan	A/B	A/B	

*Jointly owned with right of survivorship between client and spouse Assume exclusion amount of $5,450,000

a. If Jane were to pass away first, in 2016, what is her tax liability before the marital deduction?

b. If John were to pass away first, in 2016, what is his tax liability before the marital deduction?

c. Using the portable estate exemption, how much of their combined estate is taxable in 2016?

d. If Jane and John fail to take advantage of the portable estate exemption by forgetting to file IRS Form 706 at the death of the first spouse, will there be a tax liability in 2016, assuming the second spouse also passes shortly thereafter? Describe an estate planning strategy that can be used to minimize any estate tax liability in this situation.

Brenda Chatterjee

3. Brenda Chatterjee is wealthy, single, and generous. During the previous year she made the following gifts:

    • Gift of stock to the local art museum (a 501(c)(3) nonprofit organization): $245,000

    • College tuition payment for niece: $29,000 made directly to the institution

    • Medical bills for elderly neighbor: $18,000 paid directly to the hospital

    • Home down payment gift to daughter: $30,000 paid directly to the mortgage lender

    • Cash gift to son: $17,000

    • Use the gift tax rates shown below as a guide to answer the following questions:

For Taxable Gifts Between ...	And ...	You'll Pay This Amount of Tax ...	Plus, You'll Pay This Percentage on the Amount in Excess of the Lower Limit
$0	$10,000	$0	18%
$10,000	$20,000	$1,800	20%
$20,000	$40,000	$3,800	22%
$40,000	$60,000	$8,200	24%
$60,000	$80,000	$13,000	26%
$80,000	$100,000	$18,200	28%
$100,000	$150,000	$23,800	30%
$150,000	$250,000	$38,800	32%
$250,000	$500,000	$70,800	34%
$500,000	$750,000	$155,800	37%
$750,000	$1,000,000	$248,300	39%
$1,000,000	-----------	$345,800	40%

    a. What is the total amount of taxable gifts in 2016?

    b. What is Brenda's gift tax liability in 2016?

    c. Assuming a unified credit of $2,125,800, what alternatives does Brenda have in terms of paying the gift tax liability?

Comprehensive Bedo Case—Analysis Questions

Before beginning the estate planning analysis for the Bedos, it is important to review case details related to asset ownership, liabilities, and other assumptions, including estate tax growth rates. A review of the household net worth statement will help with the gross estate calculation for both Tyler and Mia. *The effect of state taxes paid should be ignored for purposes of the case narrative.*

An assumption must be made as to who will predecease whom. It is typical to assume that the primary breadwinner of the household dies first. In this case, this means that Tyler predeceases Mia.

Tyler's gross estate would, therefore, include one-half of all jointly held property plus the fair market value of any other personally owned assets, including life insurance. Funeral and administrative expenses and debts should be deducted to arrive at Tyler's adjusted gross estate. For this purpose, debt is limited to a lien, mortgage, or other form of debt that is attached to assets included in the estate. Tyler's taxable estate should then be calculated. The use of the unlimited marital deduction ought to be considered in the initial analysis.

A similar analysis should be conducted for Mia. It is possible that upon Mia's death federal estate tax may be due.

Use the following questions to guide you through the estate planning process:

1. Develop an estate planning goal for the Bedos. When conceptualizing this goal, consider the following.

    a. Is the goal developed in agreement with any or all goals and objectives that the clients have identified regarding estate planning?

    b. What situational factors might influence their estate planning goals? Are these factors explicit, implied, or assumed? Is additional information required from the Bedos?

    c. Identify life events that could affect the estate planning analysis for Tyler and Mia and that should be reviewed at future client meetings.

    d. What is the desired outcome for the clients?

2. Develop a list of globally accepted, client-specific, or planner-generated planning assumptions that will structure the estate planning situation analysis.

3. Calculate the following scenarios for the Bedo household as part of the analysis of their current estate planning situation. For each scenario, ignore any applicable state estate taxes.

    a. Scenario 1. The amount of federal estate tax due if Tyler were to predecease Mia and they both died in 2016.

    b. Scenario 2. The amount of federal estate tax due if Mia were to predecease Tyler and they both died in 2016.

4. Evaluate and comment upon the following:

    a. The appropriateness of Tyler's current will.

    b. The appropriateness of Mia's current will.

    c. Given their current situation, what other estate planning documents should the Bedos have in place?

5. A planner's observations and results from analyses can be communicated through a letter or a comprehensive or modular plan. Using some combination of text, bullets, or graphics, summarize your observations about the estate planning situation and the identified planning need(s) of the Bedo household.

6. Based on the goals originally identified and the completed analysis, what product or procedural strategies might be most useful to improve the Bedos' estate planning situation? Be sure to consider strategies matched to the planning needs identified for each member of the household. When reviewing strategies, be careful to consider the approximate cost of implementation as well as the most likely outcome(s) associated with each strategy.

7. Write at least one primary and one alternative recommendation from selected strategies in response to each identified planning need. More than one recommendation may be needed to address all of the planning needs. Include specific, defensible answers to the *who, what, when, where, why, how,* and *how much* implementation questions for each recommendation.

    a. It is suggested that each recommendation be summarized in a Recommendation Form.

    b. Assign a priority to each recommendation based on the likelihood of meeting client goals and desired outcomes. This priority will be important when recommendations from other core planning content areas are considered relative to the available discretionary funds for subsidizing all recommendations.

    c. What considerations should be taken into account when naming beneficiaries to any new life insurance policies for the Bedos?

    d. Comment briefly on the outcomes associated with each recommendation.

8. Complete the following for the estate planning section of the Bedos' financial plan.

    a. Outline the content to be included in this section of the plan. Given the preceding segments written, which segments are missing? What disclaimers, if any, could be important to include in this section of the plan?

    b. Draft an introduction to this section of the plan (no more than one paragraph).

    b. Identify at least five terms, concepts, or planning strategies that could be included in this section of the plan. For each, write a definition or explanation that would be helpful to the typical client with limited knowledge of estate planning.

9. Prepare a ten–fifteen-minute presentation for the Bedos of your observations and/or recommendation(s) for meeting their estate planning needs. Be sure to include visual aids, Excel handouts, and other materials that will make the recommendations more meaningful for the clients.

Chapter Resources

Garrett, S., and D. A. Neiman. *Money without Matrimony: The Unmarried Couple's Guide to Financial Security*. Chicago: Dearborn, 2005.

Hertz, F. C., and E. Doskow. *Making It Legal: A Guide to Same-sex Marriage, Domestic Partnerships, and Civil Unions*. Berkeley, CA: Nolo Press, 2009.

IRS Publication 950: Information on the unified credit (www.irs.gov/publications/p950/ar02.html).

IRS Form 706 filing instructions for 2015 (www.irs.gov/pub/irs-pdf/i706.pdf).

Leimberg, S. R., J. H. Ellis, S. N. Kandell, R. G. Miller, T. C. Polacek, and M. S. Rosenbloom. *Tools & Techniques of Estate Planning, 17th Edition*. Erlanger, KY: National Underwriter Company, 2015.

Pride Planners (professional association dedicated to same-sex and non-married financial and estate planning) (www.prideplanners.org).

Self-Test Answers

1: d, 2: a, 3: a, 4: d, 5: d, 6: b, 7: a, 8: c, 9: d.

Endnotes

1. Legal Information Institute, Cornell University Law School, 26 USC § 2518 – Disclaimers. Available at: www.law.cornell.edu/uscode/text/26/2518.

2. Gary Langer, *Poll: Americans Not Planning for the Future*. Available at abcnews.go.com/Business/story?id=86992&page=1#.TvpMeZg5tFI.

3. Napoleon, Philatelic Estate Disposition for the Novice, *American Philatelist*. Available at: stamps.org/userfiles/file/Estate/PhilatelicEstateDispositionfortheNovice.pdf, p. 159.

4. *IRS Form 706 Instructions: Generation Assignment*. Available at www.irs.gov/instructions/i706gst/ch01.html.

5. R. F. Stolz, "Estate Planning for Unmarried Couples: What Financial Planners Need to Know," *Journal of Financial Planning* 25, no. 2 (2012): 20–24.

6. Additional information and planning techniques for same-sex couples can be found at www.fpanet.org/journal/BetweentheIssues/LastMonth/Articles/PlanningIdeasandConsiderationsforUnmarriedCouples/.

7. California Family Law Form 110 (FL110) Summons Pertaining to Divorce. Available at: www.courts.ca.gov/documents/fl110.pdf.

8. Arizona State Legislature, Title 25-318, *Disposition of Property; Retroactivity; Notice to Creditors; Assignment of Debts; Contempt of Court._*Available at: www.azleg.state.az.us/FormatDocument.asp?inDoc=/ars/25/00318.htm&Title=25&DocType=ARS.

9. Legal Information Institute, Cornell University Law School, *Kennedy* v. *Plan Administrator for DuPont*, Case No. 07-636. Opinion available online at www.law.cornell.edu/supct/html/07-636.ZS.html.

PART V: Review of the Process

Chapter 14—Moving From Strategies to Plan Development

Moving From Strategies to Plan Development

Learning Objectives

1. The **systematic financial planning process** promoted by CFP Board and other organizations provides a proven and consistent method for practicing financial planning. Through uniform practice of the planning process it is possible to develop the reflexive professional proficiency to conduct analyses, interpret the results in the many dimensions of a client's financial situation, develop recommendations, and synthesize them into a viable, affordable plan matched to client' needs. This chapter provides several forms to facilitate this practice, including a Recommendation Form, a Comprehensive Planning Checklist, a Recommendation Impact Form, an Available Cash Flow and Other Assets Tracker Form, and an Implementation Checklist.

2. Client-based recommendations evolve from the data collection and discovery processes that occur as part of the planner-client relationship. Recommendations should be matched to the client's planning needs;

   however, recommendations must also reflect the situational factors that characterize the client and to a lesser extent, the financial planner and the planner's business model. **Alternative recommendations** should be offered to give the client choices; keep in mind, however, that available resources (i.e., discretionary cash flow, savings, and investments) are major determinants of recommendations that are included in a financial plan. This chapter provides several methods to deal with resource constraints, such as staggering the funding of recommendations and downsizing goals.

3. Several issues guide the development of a plan. Fundamentally, the issues relate to the tenuous balance between planning for what is important to the client and planning for what the client can afford. These two factors are not mutually exclusive, nor are they always compatible. Three issues guide the development of a financial plan: (1) whether all necessary recommendations have been identified, (2) whether the

Learning Objectives

consequences of the recommendations have been identified, and (3) whether the recommendations are affordable. The first two questions align with a client's goal orientation, whereas the third question, as well as identification of alternative funding options, corresponds to the cash flow position of a client.

4. The presentation of a plan is the primary outcome associated with the financial planning process. This outcome impacts a financial planner's business development and each client's access to financial planning advice, products, and services. The presentation should educate the client, motivate client action, and objectively project potential outcomes for the client. Clients may be asked to make decisions about alternatives in the plan and their willingness to implement it.

5. This chapter discusses the **seven implementation questions** of *who, what, when, where, why, how*, and *how much* that can be used to guide the development of action-oriented recommendations. The same questions are reflected directly or indirectly in several of the forms included in this chapter. In particular, the Implementation Checklist integrates these questions by tracking the financial impact of the recommendations on the client's cash flow and net worth. Although seemingly simplistic, these questions challenge planners to plan in detail for the implementation of multiple recommendations as well as the associated cash flows.

6. As discussed in this chapter, and contingent on the financial planner-client engagement agreement, plan implementation and monitoring can include all or some of the following activities: (1) following the plan and its match to the client's life situation as well as the changing regulatory, economic, tax, and market environments; (2) following the implementation of the plan and the need for continued implementation of delayed recommendations or other necessary actions; (3) following the viability and success of the products and services implemented; and (4) following the outcomes to date and progress toward the client's goals. Few aspects of a financial plan can be evaluated in isolation because the monitoring of previous actions should continue into the future. These should then be integrated into future recommendations.

7. Monitoring the use of products and services in a financial plan is essential as a way to keep the plan current, effective, and responsive to a client's life. Without continued monitoring, a plan can become obsolete. Responsibility for monitoring can rest with the client, the financial planner, other professionals, product or service providers, or no one. Ideally, the financial planner serves as the primary person of contact in terms of ongoing monitoring and all aspects of continued implementation. It is important to remember that not all clients want to delegate, and not all business models or planner-client engagements support anything more than periodic or isolated monitoring. The tension between what needs to be done and who does it, if anyone, is important to resolve because monitoring adds value for the both client and financial planner.

Key Terms

Act in the Client's Best Interest

Actionable Recommendation

Alternative Recommendations

Attitudes

Beliefs

Cash flow

Cash Flow Orientation

Cash Flow and Other Assets Tracker Form

Client Expectations

Client-Centered Recommendations

Complementary Recommendations

Comprehensive Financial Plan

Comprehensive Planning Checklist

Concerns

Cost-Benefit Analysis

Cross-Impact Analysis

Delayed Implementation

Disclaimers

Discretionary Cash Flow

Downsize

Educate

Effective Presentation

Experience

Family History

Fears

Financial Capacity

Financial Goals

Financial Interactions

Financial Knowledge

Funding Sources

Goal Orientation

How

How Much

Immediate Implementation

Impact Analysis

Implementation

Implementation Checklist

Investment Policy Statement

Lack of Confidence

Liability Release

Life Transitions

Marketing Skills

Medical Model

Meetings

Modular Plan

Money Dcripts

Motivate

Multiple Goals

Net Worth

Newsletters

Ongoing Plan Monitoring

Ongoing Review

Periodic Evaluation

Personality

Key Terms

Plan Development

Planner-Client Relationship

Planning

Prioritize

Process of Plan Development

Professional Referral

Professionalism

Promising Results

Ranking Goals

Recommendation Alternatives

Recommendation Form

Recommendation Impact Form

Recommendation Questions

Risk Tolerance

Selling

Seven Implementation Questions

Situational Factors

Systematic Financial Planning Process

Targeted Financial Plan

Temperament

Timeliness

To-Do List

What

When

Where

Who

Why

CFP® Student-Centered Learning Objectives

B8. Financial planning process

B10. Cash flow management

B11. Financing Strategies

B14. Client and planner attitudes, values, biases and behavioral finance

B15. Principles of communication and counseling

STRATEGIES TO PLAN DEVELOPMENT: DETERMINING THE NEED

The purpose of this chapter is twofold. First, the chapter revisits the systematic six-step financial planning process. The chapter presents a method by which client-specific recommendations developed in each of the core content planning areas in Chapters 3 through 13 can be prioritized, integrated, and funded for formulation into a comprehensive financial plan to present to a client. Second, a summary of plan implementation and monitoring is presented.

Although developing financial planning strategies to meet specific client goals and objectives is an important part of the financial planning process, this activity is not an end in itself. Three more equally important steps crucial for client success must be addressed in the systematic financial planning process:

1. Financial planning strategies, once chosen, must be integrated into a comprehensive (or modular) plan, and then presented as client recommendations.

2. The plan and recommendations must be implemented. In some respects, this step in the process is the most important. Without implementation, the plan and recommendations are nothing more than a "hoped for" outcome.

3. Implemented recommendations must be monitored to ensure that a client is progressing toward the goals and that the plan and recommendations continue to be appropriately matched to the client's life and the economic, tax, and legal environments.

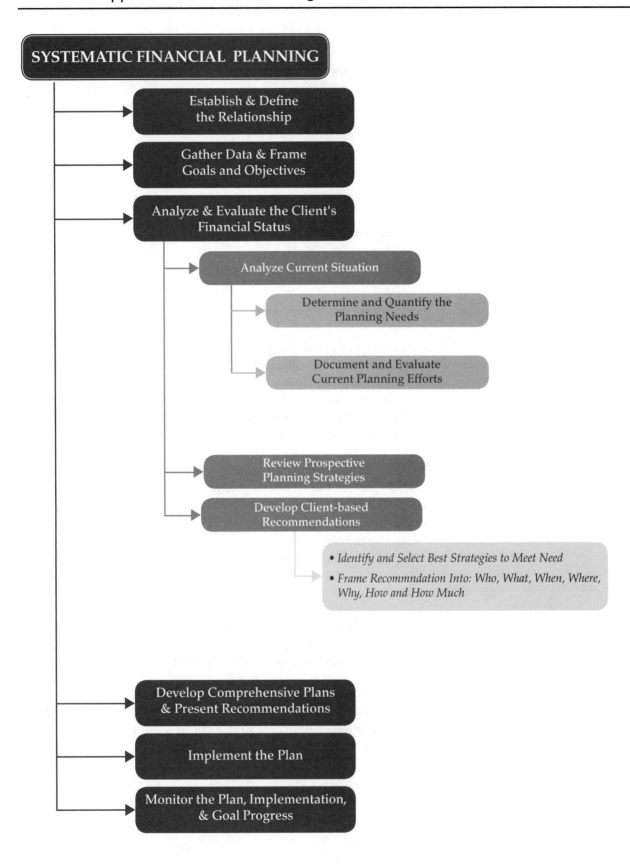

Which financial planning strategies should a financial planner recommend to a client? In a perfect world, the answer is simple: Choose strategies that best meet the client's goals and objectives and implement each one. In practice, however, this approach is difficult to follow and seldom used. This is an impractical approach when a client's financial resources do not allow full and complete implementation. The procedure also fails when a client's goals conflict, or when the client does not accept some of the financial planner's recommendations.

It is essential that a client and financial planner be able to prioritize recommendations relative to the goals and objectives. **Ranking goals** and the associated recommendations may require a client to make difficult choices among planning needs that reflect personal wants, desires, and needs and financial planner-recommended needs that the client may not have identified. This is particularly true for clients with insufficient assets, savings, and discretionary cash flow to fund all recommendations. Clients may need to grapple with questions such as, "Is retirement more important than funding my child's education?" and "Is funding a future goal more important than maintaining current lifestyle choices?" It is such dilemmas that suggest three important practices in the planning process:

1. A financial planner must have broad insight into the client's perspective to guide the formulation of the recommendations into a plan; this comes from knowing the client.

2. That same knowledge of the client and the need to resolve planning dilemmas supports the practice of offering the client alternatives or options for goal achievement.

3. When resources are limited and a client has multiple goals that are ranked similarly (e.g., retirement and education funding), it may be necessary for a financial planner to look for strategies that can be used to meet **multiple goals**.

For example, funding a Roth IRA is a strategy that can be used to meet a portion of an education funding need as well as a retirement objective. This strategy can be a powerful recommendation for a client with limited financial resources, assuming that the client has maximized any applicable employer match in a qualified retirement plan.

Central to the theme of recommendation development is the concept that a client's **temperament, personality, preferences, attitudes, family history, financial knowledge**, and **experience** must also be used to shape the recommendations. This information, which is typically gathered during the client data collection and discovery step of the financial planning process, plays a key role in helping determine which strategies might make the most effective recommendations. For example, assume that a client has a strong aversion to investing in gambling, alcohol, and tobacco stocks, and a decision must be made to recommend investing in either an index fund or a diversified socially screened mutual fund. In this situation, it is likely that the client's preference for a socially screened portfolio will outweigh other factors in the recommendation decision. (Formalizing these preferences in an *investment policy statement* would be an important approach to guide the financial planning process.)

It is also important for financial planners to take into account their own temperament, **risk tolerance**, personality, knowledge, experience, and biases when selecting strategies and making recommendations. It is very difficult for any planner to be totally objective and consider the client's goals and preferences exclusively. This is not to imply that planners are biased; each financial planner—like most other professionals—has preferred strategies. For example, some planners use variable universal life insurance as the primary tool in recommendations designed to help clients save for multiple financial goals. Other planners find the use of variable universal life insurance products inappropriate for the majority of their clientele. Rather than debate who is right or wrong, the best practice is for planners to know their clients and themselves. By acknowledging preferences and other factors, planners can be forthright in their communication with clients as well as their own assessment of the objectivity of their planning approach.

The idea that a client might not actually implement all recommendations sometimes comes as a surprise to those who have been trained using case study methodologies. In nearly all case studies, a client's situation lends itself to multiple "solutions" to satisfy a client's goals. The planner's recommendations might even include issues not identified by the client. The case study methodology gives students practice in the art (creativity) and science (analysis) of generating **client-centered recommendations**. It is common to find that case study clients have sufficient assets, savings, and discretionary cash flow to fund all goals and objectives—a characterization often not true of the "typical" client (depending on the business model of the planner). What students find difficult in such situations is prioritizing client needs and conceptualizing comprehensive and integrated plans—that the client can afford—to meet the needs. This can even be true of a modular plan, where implementation must be integrated into the client's current financial situation. In practice, however, few clients have sufficient financial resources to implement all recommendations.

In these situations, there are no definitive standards of practice to help a financial planner determine which strategies should be recommended to a client or in what priority recommendations should be ranked. An overriding question might be, "Which recommendation will potentially cause the most harm to the client if it is *not* implemented?" In many respects, these decisions result from professional judgment gained through study, experience, and personal knowledge applied to a client's unique character and situational factors.

A Recommendation Form—presented later in the chapter—as part of the systematic planning process, can assist financial planners focus on essential issues to include in an actionable recommendation. This useful planning tool summarizes the answers to the seven critical recommendation questions of *who, what, when, where, why, how,* and *how much* into one simple format. When initially identifying possible recommendations, the form is useful for summarizing and projecting the costs and benefits of the recommendations in meeting client goals. As the plan develops, it may be necessary to combine, sort, and rank recommendations from other core content planning areas, and the forms can quickly be revised for the costs and benefits of each recommendation. Once final, the forms can be used to document information for planning staff or to communicate with the client. Possibly one of the most beneficial uses of the form is documenting the titling of assets and beneficiary designations.

Strategy and Plan Development Skills[1]

Planning Skill 1: Resolving Recommendation Conflicts

Developing appropriate client-based recommendations is of primary importance within the context of the systematic financial planning process. Resolving the multiple issues inherent in even a simple comprehensive case involves the development and integration of recommendations from multiple strategies that originate from the core content planning areas. As illustrated in Figure 14.1, strategies lead to recommendations, which lead to plans. Keep in mind, however, that just as midnight balances yesterday and today, plans must balance on the axis between the **goal orientation** and **cash flow orientation** to planning, both of which ground the financial planning process in a client situation. In other words, the plan must balance equally the commitment to achieving the client's goals and the reality of the assets, or cash flow, available to fund those goals.

Figure 14.1 The Process of Plan Development

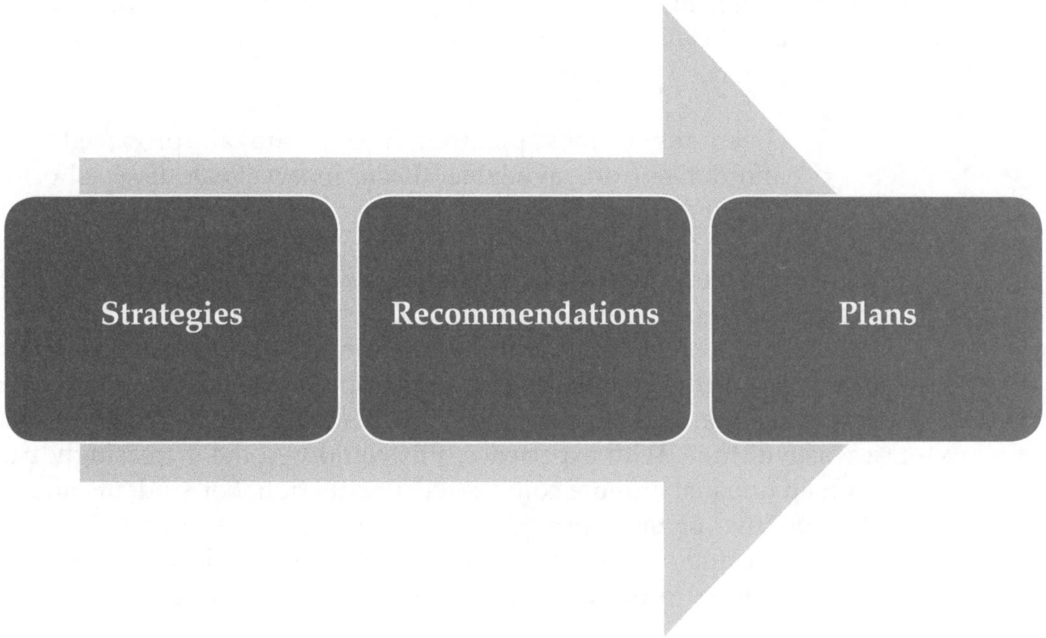

| Strategies | Recommendations | Plans |

Self-Test 1

Farrell would like to retire in 9 years. His retirement income goal will require accumulating $7.5 million on the first day of retirement. He currently has $2.0 million saved. If Farrell is risk averse, which of the following would be an appropriate financial planning recommendation?

a. Increase the risk of his portfolio in order to generate a 16 percent annualized return.

b. Counsel Farrell to reevaluate his income need in retirement.

c. Suggest that Farrell postpone retirement as a way to increase his savings.

d. Both b and c are appropriate.

Attention to **cash flow** (which can include discretionary income as well as other available assets) ensures that the plan is realistic and affordable, both in the current planning period and projecting into the future. The **goal orientation** ensures that the plan represents the client's values, needs, and desires interpreted into their most important goals both now and in the future. As one goal is accomplished, a new goal can be identified and new recommendations initiated. Careful tracking of cash flow ensures that funding one goal does not expose the client to unwarranted risk or leave the client unprepared for unexpected negative financial consequences. Although it is important that the financial plan maximize and stabilize cash flow across the client's planning period, the significance of the goals motivates sustained client commitment. In summary, both a goal orientation and a cash flow orientation are necessary for a successful plan, yet neither can fully protect the client from the unknowns of life, which can derail even the best plan.

Planning Skill 2: Developing a Financial Plan

The constantly evolving relationship between a financial planner and client grounds the financial planning process and **plan development**. Mutually agreed-on goals and client situational factors serve as the foundation of the analysis of each core content area and the identification of possible strategies. Using knowledge of the applicable strategies, the available **funding sources** (i.e., all sources of income, assets, employee benefits, inheritance), and the client situation, the planner proposes actionable client-based recommendations. These recommendations are manipulated and molded into a comprehensive plan or, when applicable and if multiple recommendations are made, into a targeted plan.

The development of a comprehensive plan occurs in response to the following three questions:

1. Given the client's planning needs, have all recommendations been identified and a preliminary priority assigned?

2. Given the client's planning needs, what are the impacts or consequences, beneficial and detrimental, that could result from implementing all of the proposed recommendations?

3. Given the client's planning needs, are all proposed recommendations affordable from available discretionary cash flow, short-term or liquid savings, or other assets?

Answering these questions with confidence is a complex and intellectually challenging exercise that truly represents the professional judgment gained from experience. Repeated use of the forms and checklists in the systematic financial planning process provides a method to build the expertise to manage this dynamic part of the planning process. Some might assert that the forms are excessive, tedious, and perhaps even a waste of time. With experience, this could become increasingly true —until faced with an unusual or more complex client situation. For students and novice planners, the objective of the repeated use of the forms is to build the capacity —in both knowledge and skill—to offer financial planning advice confidently. This framework of professional proficiency, practiced consistently, will foster the almost reflexive ability to formulate well-crafted comprehensive financial plans for clients. The following is a discussion of the significance of each question and the related forms that guide the process.

Planning Skill 3: Identifying and Prioritizing Recommendations

A **Recommendation Form** (Figure 14.1) completed for each of the recommendations developed in the systematic financial planning process, can be used to answer the seven questions of implementation (i.e., who, what, when, where, why, how, and how much) required for an **actionable recommendation**. The forms help financial planners quickly identify the cost and priority of each recommendation. It is helpful to have this valuable information easily accessible when comparing competing recommendations across the core content planning areas. Up to this point, these recommendations may have been considered only relative to other recommendations developed for a particular core content planning area. To develop a plan, recommendations from one core content area (e.g., life insurance) must compete against recommendations from another core content area (e.g., education planning), assuming there is insufficient funding for all recommendations, as is often the case. Also, cost and priority can easily be revised as all of the recommendations are considered in relationship to each other.

> **Recommendation and Implementation Questions**
>
> When developing and presenting recommendations it is important to address seven implementation question:
>
> 1. Who should implement?
>
> 2. What should be done?
>
> 3. When should the recommendation be implemented?
>
> 4. Where should implementation take place?
>
> 5. Why should the client implement?
>
> 6. How should implementation occur?
>
> 7. How much is needed and/or how much will implementation cost?

Planning Skill 4: Practice Using a Recommendation Form

Figure 14.2 show a completed *Recommendation Form* for a client who is being directed towards the purchase of a variable universal life (VUL) insurance policy. As discussed in Chapter 5, a VUL policy bundles pure life insurance with a cash account that can be invested in a mix of asset classes via subaccounts within the policy. As the name implies, a VUL policy is a hybrid product that is similar to a variable policy in the types of investments allowed in the cash account and comparable to a universal policy because the policy owner has the option of flexible premiums. Depending on the return from cash account investment choices, the policy death benefit could be substantially higher than the policy face value. Conversely, if invested imprudently or during periods when rates of return on equity investments are low or negative, the policy could lapse with no cash value.

The use of a VUL strategy is most appropriate for investment savvy clients who want to maximize tax-advantaged savings while providing beneficiaries with a base amount of life insurance proceeds. A target client might want an investment vehicle that allows tax-deferral of savings beyond what is typically available in a defined contribution retirement plan or other tax-advantaged investments. A high-net-worth/high-income client could, theoretically, overfund a VUL policy by annually contributing five- and six-figure amounts to the policy. However, the face value of the policy would have to be quite large to accept this type of funding.

The success of the VUL strategy is contingent on two factors. First, the client must be willing to overfund the policy for many years. Second, the client must invest the cash account in fairly aggressive investments to achieve a high annualized rate of return. In a bull market, the VUL policy strategy can work extremely well to build nontaxable wealth. Following this strategy, clients can take loans against their policy, spend the loan proceeds, and simply repay the loan interest. In effect, the client creates a tax-free retirement portfolio, and upon death the beneficiaries reap a substantial tax-free windfall.

A VUL recommendation could be presented using an Insurance Recommendation Form, such as that shown in Figure 14.2.

Figure 14.2 The Life Insurance Recommendation Form

Planning Recommendation Form				
Financial Planning Content Area		Life insurance and investments		
Client Goal		Maximize tax-qualified investment opportunities		
Recommendation No.:	1	**Priority (1–6) lowest to highest:**		5
Projected/Target Value ($)		$500,000 (face value)		
Product Profile				
Type		Variable universal life policy		
Duration		Lifetime		
Provider		Northern Nevada Insurance Company		
Funding Cost per Period ($)		$6,000 annually		
Maintenance Cost per Period ($)		$0		
Current Income Tax Status		Tax-qualified	X	Taxable	
Projected Rate of Return		7% (with a guaranteed minimum of 1.5% on fixed-asset account.)		
Major Policy Provisions		1. Loan provision 2. Automatic premium loans 3. Waiver of premium for periods of disability (restrictions apply)		
Procedural Factors				
Implement by Whom		Planner		Client	X
Implementation Date or Time Frame		Immediate		
Implementation Procedure		Contact Northern Nevada Life Company		
Ownership Factors				
Owner(s)		Mary E. Jones		
Form of Ownership		Sole		
Insured(s)		John D. Jones		
Custodial Account		Yes		No	X
Custodian		NA		
In Trust For (ITF)		Yes		No	X
Transfer on Death (TOD)		Yes	X	No	
Beneficiary(ies)		Mary E. Jones, spouse (100%)		
Contingent Beneficiary(ies)		William I. and Sarah B. Jones, children (50% each)		
Proposed Benefit		Immediate life insurance protection with the added benefit of accumulating tax-advantaged assets for use during retirement.		

In this example, the Joneses are high net worth clients who are experienced, risk-tolerant investors seeking additional tax-advantaged investments. John does not have sufficient life insurance, and they are comfortable with the advantages and potential disadvantages of a VUL policy. To avoid future estate tax issues for John, it is recommended that Mary own the policy. She is identified as the primary beneficiary, with their college-age children identified as the contingent beneficiaries. Note that the contract would be structured with loan and automatic premium loan provisions, both of which are central to the effective use of this product recommendation. Because of concerns over John's family medical history and his extensive career-related travel, he, Mary, and their planner agree that a disability waiver is important to include, although it would add to the cost of the policy. Finally, the form summarizes other specific information needed to implement the recommendation, as well as the projected immediate and long-term benefit to the Jones household.

Planning Skill 5: Formalize Plan Development Using a Comprehensive Planning Checklist

Another form used in the systematic planning process—the **Comprehensive Planning Checklist**—challenges financial planners to carefully consider important questions related to each of the core content planning areas. In essence, this form, shown in Appendix 14A, helps answer the broader question, "Has anything been overlooked?"

Although these forms and questions do not address comprehensive or sophisticated analysis of every client situation, they do challenge a financial planner to carefully consider important factors related to each of the core content planning areas. These forms provide a mechanism of self-assessment to ensure that oversights have not occurred. The Comprehensive Planning Checklist provides a framework for reviewing and summarizing a client's individual circumstances in each of the core planning areas, as well as fundamental interactions across planning areas, as represented by the "⟺" symbol. Keep in mind that it is impossible to encapsulate a process as broad and dynamic as financial planning in a simple form. This limitation cannot be overlooked. However, the checklist offers the advantage of focusing attention on the most common planning needs and patterns of interaction, whether developing a targeted or a comprehensive plan

Planning Skill 6: Identify the Consequences of Implementing Proposed Recommendations

Just as financial planning recommendations are not made in a vacuum; neither do the projected consequences of implementing recommendations occur independently. Implementing one recommendation tends to have a ripple effect throughout a client's financial plan, as shown in Figure 14.3, which summarizes some of the most common results, or **financial interactions**, that might be generated by frequently used recommendations. Because of the far ranging effects of seemingly simple recommendations, it is important for financial planners to incorporate an **impact analysis** as part of the systematic planning process.

A review of these impacts may suggest that additional strategies should be considered to meet a client's financial goals and objectives. Consider, for example, the relatively simple recommendation to purchase additional life insurance. If the insurance is owned by the insured who is also the client, or if the beneficiary is the estate of the insured, the insurance will be included in the client's gross estate. If the amount of the insurance is substantial, this inclusion could trigger an estate tax liability. In practice, a **cross-impact analysis** would indicate that the client ought to reconsider the ownership and titling of the insurance and/or take steps to reposition assets to reduce potential estate tax liabilities. Although there are strategies for changing ownership in the future, conducting an impact analysis encourages financial planners to be proactive and thorough in planning rather than reactive in the future.

Self-Test 2

Nelda recommended that her client pay off high interest credit card debt using money from the client's money market account. Which of the following will likely occur when this recommendation is implemented?

a. The client's level of discretionary cash flow will decrease.

b. The client's net worth will increase.

c. The client's net worth will decrease.

d. The client's level of discretionary cash flow will increase.

Figure 14.3 Financial Interaction Examples that Have Multiple Impacts on a Client's Financial Situation

Recommendation	Potential Result
Refinance mortgage (results will vary depending on whether closing costs are/are not included or if cash is/is not taken)	1. Change cash flow 2. Change net worth[a] 3. Change tax liability
Restructure debt	1. Change cash flow 2. Change net worth 3. Change tax liability
Change federal tax withholding	1. Change cash flow
Change state tax withholding	1. Change cash flow
Reallocate non-qualified portfolio assets	1. Change cash flow (only if earnings are not reinvested) 2. Change net worth[b] 3. Change tax liability

Figure 14.3 Financial Interaction Examples that Have Multiple Impacts on a Client's Financial Situation (*cont'd*)

Recommendation	Potential Result
Liquidate non-qualified portfolio assets	1. Change cash flow (only if earnings are not reinvested)
	2. Possible change in net worth depending on how the assets are used[b]
	3. Change tax liability
Increase retirement savings	1. Change cash flow
	2. Change net worth
	3. Change tax liability
	4. Change estate tax situation
Purchase additional life insurance	1. Change cash flow
	2. Possible change in net worth depending on type of insurance
	3. Change estate tax situation
Retitle assets	1. Change cash flow
	2. Change net worth
	3. Change tax liability
	4. Change estate tax situation
Begin gift strategies	1. Change cash flow
	2. Change net worth
	3. Change tax liability
	4. Change estate tax situation
a Assuming closing costs are paid from assets rather than current income	
b Transaction costs or sales charges may apply	

Planning Skill 7: Identify the Impact of Recommendations Using a Recommendation Impact Form

The use of a **Recommendation Impact Form** offers a systematic method to verify that any potential interactions among the recommendations have not been overlooked. This form should be completed for each recommendation and then revised, if necessary, as final recommendations are determined. Should cash flow or other assets be insufficient for funding all recommendations, completing the **Recommendation Impact Form** shown in Figure 14.4 can help financial planners identify mutually exclusive recommendations that could be integrated and achieved by another multipurpose planning product or procedure.

Figure 14.4 Recommendation Impact Form

Recommendation Impact Form					
Recommendation:					
Recommendation No.					
Planner Decision	Accept		Reject		Modify	
Client Decision	Accept		Reject		Modify	
Financial Impact					
Annual impact on cash-flow ($)					
Immediate impact on net worth ($)					

Planning Issue	Degree of Significance				Notes
	Major	Modest	Minor	None	
Financial situation—cash management					
Tax planning					
Life insurance planning					
Health insurance planning					
Disability insurance planning					
LTC insurance planning					
Property and liability insurance planning					
Investment planning					
Education or other special needs planning					
Retirement planning					
Estate planning					
Other planning need					
Other planning need					

By seriously considering the impact of each recommendation on the other core content planning areas financial planners can gain new insights into the client situation that otherwise might never have been considered. Likewise, if an financial planner cannot reasonably and knowledgeably assess the impact of the recommendations, more research or consultation with other professionals may be warranted. As such, the systematic approach, which may justifiably be criticized for stifling creativity, could actually encourage a greater depth and range of thinking. Ultimately, it is important that a consistent approach be used to rank and order recommendations in a way that is comfortable for the financial planner. To be effective, whatever approach is chosen must encourage the financial planning professional the freedom and responsibility to shift paradigms when analyzing and reviewing a client's situation.

Although integrating core financial planning content areas is beyond the scope of engagement of an financial planner focused on single-issue analysis, whether offering advice or promoting product sales, the importance of the impact analysis should not be overlooked. Projecting the integration of all recommendations using impact analysis ensures financial planners that a client has enough discretionary cash flow and assets to fully fund—and continue funding—all recommendations. Furthermore, the impact analysis gives financial planners another perspective on the logic and assumptions upon which a plan is based. The Planning Recommendation Form, the Comprehensive Planning Checklist, and the Recommendation Impact Form can help financial planners fully integrate plan recommendations. The systematic approach depends on the repeated use of planning forms and protocols to guide and document the planning process. With repeated use, this process should become so routine that basic norms of practice will be established and applied with every client.

Planning Skill 8: Determine if Proposed Recommendations are Affordable and Develop Strategies in Cases Where Choices must be Made

In addition to the impact of recommendations, funding recommendations is another critical issue that must be resolved before a plan can be finalized. Developing a financial plan is the culmination and integration of available cash flow, assets, and the goals most critical to a client. Although creative options may be available, generally financial planners and clients are limited to considering one or more of the following **recommendation alternatives**, which are summarized in Figure 14.5.

- Fully fund the most important recommendation in support of the goal determined by the planner and the client; prioritize other recommendations and corresponding goals or planning needs and apply the remaining funds.

- Agree to fund all recommendations, but stagger their implementation over a reasonable period of time that will not adversely affect the client's financial situation. This approach assumes that additional assets will become available to facilitate future funding as the result of an influx of income, assets, or the completion of goal funding, thus freeing up money to be redirected to another goal(s).

- Reconsider the recommendations and "downsize" or reduce one or more of the suggested funding alternatives so that all recommendations receive some funding.

- Review mutually exclusive recommendations that might be integrated and achieved through a different multipurpose planning product or procedure (e.g., a Roth IRA or life insurance).

- Prioritize the recommendations and goals, fund those that are most important, and eliminate or postpone other recommendations.

- Increase available funding for all or some of the recommendations. This might be done by reducing spending (for goods, services, or debt) or by increasing personal income, liquidating assets, or reallocating other assets for higher earnings.

Figure 14.5 Alternative Options for Funding Recommendations

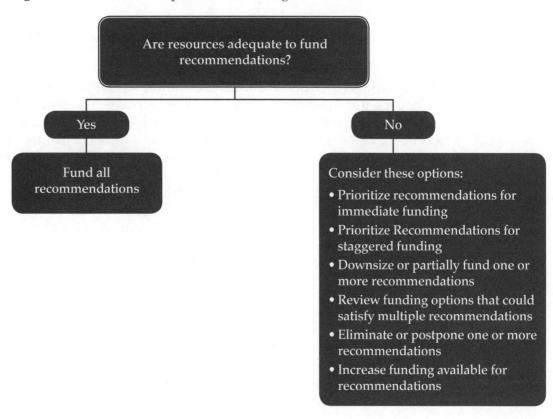

The priority for funding usually centers on the recommendations that most closely match a client's goals or that provide protection from the greatest perceived risk of loss. **Complementary recommendations** that can be used to meet more than one goal might also emerge as a priority. For instance, recommending that a client fund a Roth IRA can serve the dual goals of saving for retirement and a child's college expenses.

Although comprehensive plans are more complex, the synthesis of goals and funding strategies applies to both comprehensive and targeted (or modular) plans. The same is true of analysis in support of product sales, because a client must be convinced that the product fulfills a recognized need or goal and is worthy of funding. If funding is insufficient, the planner, working from knowledge of the client situation or directly with the client, must conduct a **cost-benefit analysis** to determine the best use of available funds relative to the proposed recommendations.

Planning Skill 9: Track Cash Flow and Net Worth Before and After Making a Recommendation

While it is always good practice to consider the impact of recommendations and funding alternatives, it is a planner's responsibility to also diligently track the financial effects of proposed recommendations. This can be done by systematically tracking changes in cash flow and net worth before and after making a recommendation. A financial plan is contingent on the availability of **discretionary cash flow**, savings, or other available assets to actually fund the recommendations. As such, there is one absolute rule that successful financial planners must incorporate into their professional practices: In addition to thoroughly and objectively justifying the choice of recommendations in a client's plan, planners must also clearly explain to the client how costs associated with the plan can be funded. One way to ensure that all recommendations can be implemented is to track cash flow and asset changes at the same time recommendations are determined.

An effective way to monitor funding is to use a **Cash Flow and Other Assets Tracking Form**, which can be easily developed using Excel™. A completed form, shown in Figure 14.6, illustrates how this planning tool can be used to document the effects of each recommendation on cash flow and net worth. The tracker's principal purpose is to help financial planners document that sufficient cash flow, savings, and assets are available to implement recommendations.

Figure 14.6 Available Cash Flow and Other Assets Tracker Form

	(Cost)/Benefit	Frequency (single/annual)	Discretionary Cash Flow	Monetary Assets	Other Assets	Liabilities	Net Worth
Annual Cash Flow Tracker							
				Running Balances			
Recommendation			($1,300)	$9,500	$42,000	$12,000	$39,500
Payment savings from mortgage refinance	$2,800	A	$2,800	$0	$0	$0	$0
			$1,500	$9,500	$42,000	$12,000	$39,500
Pay mortgage closing costs	($1,300)	S	$0	$0	($1,300)	$0	($1,300)
			$1,500	$9,500	$40,700	$12,000	$38,200
Pay-off credit card debt	($12,000)	S	$0	$0	($12,000)	($12,000)	$0
			$1,500	$9,500	$28,700	$0	$38,200
Payment savings from paying off credit card debt	$5,900	A	$5,900	$0	$0	$0	$0
			$7,400	$9,500	$28,700	$0	$38,200
Purchase life insurance	($1,000)	A	($1,000)	$0	$0	$0	$0
			$6,400	$9,500	$28,700	$0	$38,200
Increase education funding	($4,400)	A	($4,400)	$0	$4,400	$0	$4,400
			$2,000	$9,500	$33,100	$0	$42,600
Take $2,000 out of savings and contribute to an IRA	($2,000)	S	$0	($2,000)	$2,000	$0	$0
			$2,000	$7,500	$35,100	$0	$42,600
Final Balance			$2,000	$7,500	$35,100	$0	$42,600
Aggregate Change			$3,300	($2,000)	($6,900)	($12,000)	$3,100

In this example, the client begins the financial planning process with a discretionary cash flow equal to -$1,300. In other words, the client was "short" more than $100 per month, which probably contributed to the credit card debt of $12,000. The client has "unallocated" savings equal to $3,000 and another $42,000 in unallocated assets in a money market account and miscellaneous investments. Unallocated funds are those not specifically designated for goal accomplishment, other than for an emergency fund or other savings.

Initially, the financial planner recommends that the client refinance the mortgage. This results in a $2,800 per year decrease in expenses (ignoring any income tax changes, and assuming that the refinancing will not subject the client to the Alternative Minimum Tax). The decrease in annual expense flows directly to the client's discretionary cash flow, which is now a positive $1,500 (-$1,300 + $2,800). However, refinancing the mortgage also results in $1,300 in closing costs, which is paid from unallocated assets. This reduces the assets available for other purposes to $40,700. Implementing an immediate payoff of the credit cards further reduces unallocated assets by $12,000 to $28,700. Implementation of the recommendation also results in a $5,900 increase in discretionary cash flow because the client will no longer be making monthly credit card payments. This brings the available discretionary cash flow balance to a total of $7,400.

Purchasing life insurance at an annual cost of $1,000 and saving $4,000 annually for a college fund further reduces available cash flow to $2,000. In this scenario, the financial planner and client agreed that maintaining such flexibility is important for the household. Implementing a recommendation to reallocate the $2,000 of unallocated savings toward retirement reduces that account from $3,000 to $1,000. The client now has enough cash flow, savings, and assets to implement all recommendations but will utilize $2,000 of the unallocated savings and more than $13,000 in unallocated assets. Projected final balances equal $2,000 for available annual cash flow, $1,000 of unallocated savings, and a remaining balance of $28,700 ignoring any applicable taxes or transaction costs.

As noted, the Cash Flow and Other Assets Tracking Form is a useful tool to confirm that sufficient cash flow, savings, and assets are available to implement recommendations. Additionally, if several recommendations are competing for funding, both the Recommendation Form and the Available Cash Flow and Other Assets Tracker Form can be modified easily to reflect final recommendation features. Once finalized, the forms can be used to document this information for planning staff or to communicate information to the client. The Recommendation Forms are useful to summarize and project the costs and benefits of individual recommendations to meet client goals. The tracker form is an effective tool for communicating the costs of individual recommendations—and the entire plan—to the client.

Planning Skill 10: Document an Implementation Procedure for Plan Recommendations

In addition to the other issues, a financial plan must also provide a realistic and workable road map for the actions required, immediately and in the future, to give the client the greatest likelihood of protecting and growing assets. One of the most effective ways to motivate client action involves systematically summarizing recommendations so that implementation does not seem overwhelming. An **Implementation Checklist** bridges the gap between tracking the financial implications of the plan and summarizing the information needed to describe and implement each recommendation. As such, the Implementation Checklist provides an abridged plan that can be a useful reference for planning staff and client.

An Implementation Checklist that summarizes all recommendations is a useful tool in both modular and comprehensive plans. However, checklists can also be completed for each core content planning area or for specific segments of time. For example, a client with staggered goals or goals with staggered or changing funding schedules might best be served by having one checklist for each of several six-month periods. Moreover, in some instances one comprehensive checklist may suffice, contingent on the complexity of the plan or the client's role in implementing it. An Implementation Checklist for Doug and Emily is shown in Figure 14.7. The form summarizes five recommendations for Doug and Emily using the framework of the seven questions of implementation to guide recommendations and their subsequent implementation. Changes to Doug and Emily's cash flow and net worth situation are also explained. A realistic and defensible summary of projected results can motivate and sustain client action—and provide a valuable foundation for writing a plan.

Figure 14.7 Implementation Checklist for Doug & Emily Miscatt

Implementation Checklist for Doug & Emily Miscatt							
Recommendation	Who	When	Where	Why	How	Cash Flow Impact	Net Worth Impact
(What)						(How Much)	
Refinance your home mortgage at 5.875 percent for 25 years.	Doug and Emily	Start the process this week; interest rates are volatile.	First National Bank offers this loan with no points and $1,300 in closing costs.	Refinancing your mortgage will increase your monthly/ yearly cash flow.	Meet with Tommy Links to complete the mortgage application or use the online application portal. Sell $1,300 of XYX Mutual Fund. No taxes will be paid because of carry-over losses.	+ $2,800	-$1,300
Pay off all credit card balances.	Doug and Emily	Within the month	Discover and Best Buy	This will eliminate high-interest debt by using liquid, low-earning assets to increase your cash flow.	Sell $12,000 of XYX Mutual Fund to pay the balances on your Discover and Best Buy cards. No taxes will be paid because of carry-over losses. Pay any outstanding balances each month.	+ $5,900	None

Figure 14.7 Implementation Checklist for Doug & Emily Miscatt (*cont'd*)

Recommendation (What)	Who	When	Where	Why	How	Cash Flow Impact	Net Worth Impact
						(How Much)	
Purchase a $75,000 whole-life policy for Doug.	Doug and Emily	Within the next 6 weeks	With the Cia and Associates Insurance	This will provide permanent life insurance in response to Doug's concerns over family health history and financial risk.	Meet with an insurance professional at Cia & Associates Insurance Brokerage to complete the application.	($1,000)	None
Increase your quarterly contribution by an additional $1,100.	Doug and Emily	Time of the next quarterly payment	With the existing Anystate 529 Savings Plan	This will allow you to meet your goal of having $50,000 saved for Freddy's education.	Increase the amount of your quarterly check or electronic payment to $2,500.	($4,400)	+$4,400
Total Impact of Recommendations on Cash Flow and Net Worth						+$3,300	+$3,100
Discretionary Cash Flow after Implementing Recommendations						$2,000	
Net Worth after Implementing Recommendations						$42,600	

Planning Skill 11: Choose the Appropriate Plan Type for a Client—Targeted, Module, or Comprehensive

Conceptualization of a plan may require a financial planner to analyze competing recommendations, strategies, goals, or other client specific information to formulate the most cost effective, risk-adjusted plan for meeting a client's needs. What appeared initially, or in isolation, to be the best recommendation may subsequently have to be modified or abandoned when considered in relation to all other planning recommendations, needs, restrictions, or choices. Ultimately, every financial plan evolves from this linear yet more realistic recursive process.

One of the challenges facing planners who write **comprehensive financial plans** is how to account for the integrative nature of recommendations, implementation, and monitoring in the plan. The analysis, recommendations, and projected outcomes must be completely integrated into each individual section of the plan as well as across all core content planning areas.

Targeted financial plans, focused on only one or two goals, are less challenging, but they still must clearly communicate analysis, recommendations, and projected outcomes. Similarly, **modular plans** that deal with a few core planning topics should include all the elements associated with appropriate strategic development. Regardless of the type of plan prepared, it must clearly reflect a client's **situational factors** and goals. In other words, the plan must resonate with the individuality of the client and be adaptable to the client's financial lifestyle. That is not to say that changes in the client's financial situation will not be warranted or recommended, but that the changes must be in alignment with the client's ability to cope with and implement the changes.

Planning Skill 12: Use a Consistent Plan Writing Approach

When writing a financial plan, the following suggestions may be helpful:

1. Describe the current situation for each of the core content areas as if no other recommendations have been made or implemented.

2. Present all recommendations within a core content section (e.g., the retirement planning section) on the basis of the current situation analysis.

3. Describe alternatives or alternative outcomes in client circumstances where a recommendation in one core content area is based on the implementation of a recommendation in another core content area. For example, show *alternative recommendations* and alternative outcomes when education funding is done with or without gifting from grandparents.

4. Conclude a plan by illustrating a client's projected situation assuming all recommendations are implemented.

The fourth rule implies that a reanalysis and recalculation of certain client data should occur. Minimally, the following information should be recalculated to project the client's financial situation in one year (or some other time frame), assuming that recommendations are implemented:

- Available discretionary cash flow;

- *Net worth* balance;

Self-Test 3

George is a sole practitioner with a successful financial planning practice. When he meets with a prospective client he makes it clear that he will only work the person if he can conduct a review and provide recommendations on the following content topics: (a) cash flow/net worth, (b) taxes, (c) insurance, (d) retirement, (e) investments, (f) retirement, and (g) estate. Given George's requirements, you can classify him as engaging in:

a. Targeted Financial Planning.

b. Modular Financial Planning.

c. Comprehensive Financial Planning.

d. Both a and b.

- Income tax situation; and

- Estate tax situation (when applicable).

Recalculating estimates associated with these plan elements to reflect projected outcomes is another way to motivate clients. For instance, if a client can be shown that refinancing debt, reallocating portfolio assets, purchasing additional forms of insurance, and implementing other recommendations will result in positive outcomes, it is more likely that the client will take action. Revised cash flow, net worth, income tax, and estate tax projections can be included as a separate section in the plan or in an appendix. Some financial planners incorporate future projections (tabular or graphic) for each core content planning area of the plan. Different time frames coordinated to the individual goal or planning need can be used to project the short-, intermediate-, or long-term impact of the successfully implemented recommendation(s) on the client's future.

Either approach helps clients grasp how recommendations are integrative within a plan, and to see the potential impact of financial planning. However, it is extremely important that any projections include appropriate **disclaimers** (e.g., "past performance is no guarantee of future returns," "all projections are based on historical data, which may not be reflected in future returns," "projections are hypothetical") so as not to mislead clients or give the impression of guaranteed returns or outcomes. Other disclaimers include reminders to the client that "This plan is based on data provided by the client as of [specified date]" or "Please consult your tax or legal professional for assistance in reviewing and implementing these recommendations."

Planning Skill 13: Develop a Method for Presenting Financial Plan to Clients

Although advocates for the profession of financial planning have worked hard to dissociate **financial planning** from **selling**, in practice sales and **marketing skills** are integral to a financial planner's success. A financial planner actually is selling something, explicitly or implicitly, from the obvious (i.e., financial advice, products, or services) to something more subtle (i.e., client education or a suggested change in a client's attitudes, money scripts, or behaviors). Regardless of a planner's business model, the presentation to a client is the opportunity to "close the deal" for both financial planner and client. Without revenue, a planner cannot remain in business, but without planning advice, products, or services, the client's life could also be very different.

A well designed plan is the foundation of an **effective presentation** to clients. Such plans and presentations are easier for clients to understand and more likely to motivate client action. Good presentations are the result of effective communication (involving both verbal and nonverbal communication skills as well as the written and graphic messages in the plan, handouts, or PowerPoint), thorough preparation, and genuine concern for the client. The financial planner, in the roles of trusted adviser, educator, or mediator, must offer explanations to engage the client and empower the client to make decisions about plan alternatives. As these decisions are resolved, a final plan will emerge for the client's acceptance. Training and experience are critical to successful client presentations that motivate action by projecting but not *promising results*.

Ultimately, the decision to implement some or all recommendations rests with the client. If a client decides on a course of action contrary to the plan, or if rejected recommendations could potentially jeopardize the client's financial situation in the future or raise questions about the professional judgment of the planner, a **liability release** signed by the client should be considered. This stage of the planning process should end with a realistic plan for achieving the client's financial and life goals and lay the foundation for what could potentially be a long-term planner-client relationship.

To build such a relationship, clients and financial planners are best served by unbiased presentations that acknowledge that tax, legislative, economic, or personal life-changing events positively or negatively affect planning projections. Periodic reviews and adjustments (i.e., monitoring) offers clients the greatest likelihood of reaching financial goals.

> **Self-Test 4**
>
> Successful financial planners must possess which of the following skills?
>
> a. Sales Aptitude.
>
> b. Marketing Knowledge.
>
> c. Presentation Know-How.
>
> d. All of the above.

Planning Skill 14: Help Clients Take Action Through Plan Implementation

Implementation refers to putting a recommendation into action. Sometimes a financial planner performs the action or coordinates implementation, and at other times the client or other professionals direct implementation. Without a thorough, defensible, and easily understood description of how each recommendation can be implemented, it is likely that some clients will fail to do so, or fail to be convinced by the recommendations. Some financial planners argue that providing clients with a reasonable implementation plan could, in fact, be the most important part of a financial plan.

Implementation hinges on three key interrelated factors. First, recommendations need to be put in place—that is, action must be taken. A financial plan that is not implemented is of little value to anyone. Second, it is essential that a client have the **financial capacity** to implement recommendations. Where monies to fund a recommendation should come from, or where cash assets should be deposited, has to be clearly

> **Self-Test 5**
>
> Which of the following professionals might a comprehensive financial planner refer her client to implement a plan recommendation?
>
> a. A stock broker to obtain a portfolio review.
>
> b. Property and casualty insurance agent to purchase homeowner's coverage.
>
> c. Accountant to conduct an estate evaluation.
>
> d. All of the above.

identified. Finally, the effects of implementation on a client's discretionary cash flow and net worth situation ought to be shown. Financial planners can avoid oversights by using the seven questions in the systematic financial planning process to guide recommendations and implementation.

Planning Skill 15: Provide Guidance to Clients on the Implementation Process

Once a financial planner and client agree on a plan, implementation begins. A recommendation is only as good as the planner's, client's, or other professionals' ability—working together or independently—to effectively implement it. In the simplest terms, *who* will do *what*, and *where* should it be done? Depending on a financial planner's business model and the products or services offered, plan implementation approaches differ among planners, and perhaps even across clients served by the same planner. Some financial planners will take most, if not all, of the responsibility for carrying out various aspects of the plan and ask little of the client (assuming such authority is granted). Other financial planners will inform or assist the client, who has primary responsibility for executing some or all of the recommendations.

Some recommendations might require clients to work with professionals with whom they have an existing relationship (e.g., an insurance agent, broker, or banker), and other recommendations will require the forging of new relationships. Providing clients with a **professional referral** is one method to help a client move from recognition that action needs to be taken to actually implementing recommendations. If referrals are made, clients should be notified if fees are shared between the planner and consulting professionals. Planners often consider themselves the hub of a wheel as they facilitate plan implementation in collaboration with the client and multiple other parties (e.g., the client's accountant, attorney, trust administrator, or personal assistant).

In conjunction with the question of *who* are the issues of *what* and *where*. The latter may refer, literally, to the place a client must go to access the provider of a recommended product or service (e.g., a URL or mailing address). *What* represents the variety of traditional insurance, investment, retirement, and other ancillary financial planning products and services that emanate from the strategies identified in the systematic financial planning process to a wide range of concierge services. For example, some financial planners provide high net worth clients a variety of time- and money-saving services (e.g., shopping and negotiating transportation or mortgages, or handling routine bill payment for themselves or extended family members).

Another important detail is providing answers to what should be done. *What*, in this instance, can also refer to the client information that may be shared with other professionals, contingent on client disclosure agreements or the scope of the agreement giving a financial planner the authority to act on the client's behalf. In some instances, the client will be the go-between among all of the financial service providers. In other cases, the client will sign a disclosure document that allows the financial planner to contact other providers (e.g., tax preparer, lawyer, trust administrator) directly. Such situations require the utmost care and trust in the planner-client relationship, and the boundaries of authority must be clearly documented.

Planning Skill 16: Document Why and When Implementation Should Occur

Regardless of the range of a financial planner's products or services, or whether the client is solely or partly responsible for implementing recommendations, ultimately the actual implementation rests with the client. Although it is often assumed that clients acting in their own best interest will put plans into action, this is not always the case. The implementation issues of *why* and *when* can become inextricably intertwined. Regardless of the reason for inaction, lack of implementation is the single greatest deterrent to meeting financial goals. Therefore, it is imperative that planners take steps to examine—and in some cases supervise or facilitate—the **timeliness** and effectiveness of client implementation if such responsibilities are part of their business plan and the engagement agreed to with the client.

One function of a financial planner is to use a plan and its presentation effectively to **educate** and **motivate** a client regarding (1) *why* the recommendations are viable solutions to the client's concerns and (2) *when* implementation should occur to best meet the client's objective in a timely manner. Because a client pays for a plan does not mean that the client will necessarily be motivated to act. It may be necessary to remind the client that, without proper implementation, the ability to reach long-term financial goals is jeopardized. Other clients may know logically *why* they should implement, but emotional or other barriers (e.g., fear, lack of time or knowledge, or avoidance of difficult decisions) could be significant deterrents to *when* they implement. Recall that **temperament, personality, beliefs, attitudes**, and **money scripts** are significant influences in a client's financial life.

Keeping clients motivated to take action in the short term and over the longer term is a trait that separates the best planners from the rest. Furthermore, it takes careful attention to detail to keep the implementation and outcome of a plan on track. For example, it is important that clients realize and commit—both intellectually and personally—to the complexities of implementation. It is equally important to acknowledge that the implementation of the recommendation and the fulfillment of the goal may occur in different time frames, as outlined in the following examples:

- Immediate implementation and immediate completion (e.g., filing a change-of-beneficiary form for a retirement account).

- Immediate implementation and delayed completion (e.g., opening a Section 529 plan and contributing $500 per month for the next five years to fund the client's education goal).

- Delayed implementation and immediate completion (e.g., opening a flexible spending account and changing the health insurance plan during the next open enrollment six months in the future).

- Delayed implementation and delayed completion (e.g., increasing retirement savings by $500 per month in five years once the Section 529 plan is fully funded).

The meaning of "**immediate implementation** or **delayed implementation**" is fairly obvious, but the meaning of "immediate or delayed completion" is not as transparent. A goal that is completed immediately, such as paying off credit card debt, suggests that there is very little or no continuous action needed to achieve the desired result. However, if the results require periodic or continuous action and/or **ongoing plan monitoring**, then the goal should be categorized as a delayed-completion goal. Typically this type of goal requires more commitment and effort by both client and planner to see through to fruition.

Planning Skill 17: Document How Implementation Steps Should Take Place

Two additional implementation must be addressed by a financial planner; specifically, financial planners need to provide guidance to clients regarding *how* a recommendation should be implemented and *how much* it will cost to implement. These points may appear simplistic given the range of business models, recommendations, and products and services available, but issues related to cost and convenience are important regardless of how implementation is handled. One of the most effective ways to motivate client action involves systematically summarizing recommendations so that implementation can be easily understood and accomplished. The use of an Implementation Checklist, as described earlier in the chapter, can guide implementation within each core content area, across different periods of time, or as a comprehensive summary of the entire plan. Another way to motivate action is to create specific to-do lists for clients. Altfest[2] suggested that financial planners provided a **to-do list** after a plan is delivered to a client with a follow-up phone call from someone on the financial planner's staff to ask whether the client had any difficulty in taking action. In this way, a client can be motivated to take action to report back that a recommendation was successfully implemented.

Financial planners are often adept at answering the *how much* question, but frequently they are much less comfortable with helping clients address the fears and concerns associated with *how*. The results of the client goal analysis, built on defensible assumptions and sound analytical approaches, will yield an answer to the question of *how much should be purchased, saved, or invested*. The financial planner's technical knowledge and the use of an Implementation Checklist can provide the client with concise implementation instructions for *how* to put the recommendations into action. Note, however, that **fears** and **concerns** about *how* may have a more significant impact on the client than even an experienced financial planner recognizes at first.

Planning Skill 18: Manage Client Expectations During the Implementation Process

A client may be apprehensive about having insufficient financial knowledge, experience, or perseverance to implement the plans. Implicitly, the client's fears or attitudes about money could be a source of anxiety. What a financial planner might interpret as reluctance to implement could actually be the client's lack of **confidence** to implement—regardless of the amount of income available or the logical benefit to the client. At this juncture of the financial planning process, a financial planner's sensitivity to the impact of these client situational factors is an important first step toward gaining the skill and confidence needed to explore these issues with clients. Such efforts to fully understand and respect the client's issues contribute to a more trusting **planner-client relationship**.

Managing **client expectations** is yet another area of concern. Too often a client assumes that if a plan is executed perfectly, the financial planner's recommendations will result in the projected outcome—with no deviations. But the client may not fully understand that the financial planner (1) built the recommendation on the best (but imperfect) information available at the time; (2) used professional judgment to determine the best (but not foolproof) course of action; and (3) framed both the action and the expected outcome on the basis of mutually agreed-upon assumptions (some of which could ultimately prove invalid). Managing client expectations when implementing and monitoring a plan hinges on three important concepts:

1. The client needs to acknowledge that the plan is based on the information provided to the planner; consequently, withholding relevant information, giving "socially acceptable" answers, or otherwise knowingly or unknowingly misleading the financial planner will result in an unsound plan.

2. The client should be fully informed of the function and formulation of hypothetical projections in the financial planning process.

3. The client must be educated about financial trends and economic issues to provide a valid and reliable context for gauging plan results.

The last point can be accomplished through pre-planned financial planner-client interactions, such as periodic monitoring **meetings**, **newsletters**, or Website postings. These also provide opportunities for an financial planner to continue to assist and motivate the client to **act in the client's best interest**.

Planning Skill 19: Develop and Use an Ongoing Plan Monitoring Process

Sometimes it is easy to lose track of *why* a financial plan has been written. The real reason that clients need a comprehensive financial plan is to ensure that their short-, intermediate-, and long-term **financial goals** are met. Only by looking at how all components of a client's financial life fit together can a full picture of financial threats, opportunities, and successes be drawn. Likewise, whether or not a client is on target to meet goals can be determined only by tracking and monitoring client outcomes. Monitoring a client's situation enables a planner to determine the client's progress toward goals as well as the client's response to other economic or personal/life event changes. Continued monitoring also affords an opportunity for financial planners to add value to the planner-client relationship by helping clients respond to situations, reduce anxiety, and feel in control of and confident about their financial situation. Monitoring a financial plan entails periodic evaluation of:

- the *plan* as a malleable element in a client's life responsive to the client's changing situation and goals;

- the *effectiveness of the plan* as a comprehensive approach to meeting a client's needs in the current regulatory, economic, tax, and market environments;

- the *implementation* of the recommendations made to date;

- the viability of the *products and services* incorporated into the implementation and their continued usefulness to meet the client's needs; and

- the *outcomes* associated with the recommendations and the progress toward goal achievement.

It is important to recognize that monitoring can incorporate **periodic evaluation** or **ongoing review** of products and services. The extent of these monitoring activities—whether periodic or ongoing—varies with the financial planner's business model and agreed-on engagement with the client. However monitoring is conducted, this last step in the financial planning process is important for the following reasons:

> **Self-Test 6**
>
> All of the following are acceptable reasons to conduct an ongoing review of a client's situation, EXCEPT:
>
> a. To encourage client implementation of plan recommendations.
>
> b. To strengthen the planner-client relationship.
>
> c. To sell additional products, such as life insurance or annuities.
>
> d. To anticipate the changing needs of a client.

1. Monitoring compels a financial planner to stay in touch with a client to assess how well the plan is meeting the client's life and financial goals and objectives. Innovative financial planners will try to anticipate their clients' changing needs and facilitate dialogue to identify potential responses. It is equally important to encourage clients to proactively initiate questions in response to changing wants, needs, life cycle events, or life transitions (e.g., planning in anticipation of a divorce; a marriage, with or without a prenuptial agreement; or the birth of a child). Periodic contact from a financial planner can motivate a client to continue to take action or initiate changes, which can benefit the client's financial situation as well as the financial planner from a continuous revenue stream.

2. Periodic monitoring of a client's situation ensures that previously made recommendations, products, and services are still appropriate and useful for the client's situation. A client's needs, attitudes, or capacity to fund goals can change dramatically. It is essential, therefore, that a planner who is engaged by a client on a long-term basis periodically monitor both quantitative data and qualitative, or situational, life issues. Examples of quantitative product criteria for review include product and provider performance, product and provider ratings, fees and expenses, and other features unique to the product in question, such as the need for portfolio rebalancing.

3. Monitoring keeps a financial planner and client on track to (1) make time-sensitive changes in response to the client's need or changes in the economy, the stock market, or taxes; (2) determine how implemented recommendations, and the underlying products, have affected (or are affecting) other areas of the client's financial plan; or (3) implement recommendations that were delayed until a future date (e.g., redirecting funds from a Section 529 plan to retirement savings because a college savings goal has been met). In this respect, monitoring involves assessing the cross-impact of one recommendation on other areas of a client's financial situation after implementation, just as they were projected before implementation.

4. Monitoring provides an opportunity for a financial planner and client to celebrate what has been accomplished. Despite the **professionalism** required of planner-client relationships, often there is a genuine personal relationship and mutual concern for the well-being of the financial planner and client. Monitoring activities foster that relationship and provide an opportunity to express appreciation.

Planning Skill 20: Develop Strategies to Deal with Client and Plan Changes

Monitoring is multifaceted and integrative. Few aspects of a financial plan can be evaluated in isolation, even when considering a core content planning area. Significant changes to a plan may entail reevaluation of a client's planning needs or priorities, including analysis of the client's situation, identification of prospective strategies, and development and presentation of recommendations. Depending on the extent of the changes, new recommendations may be needed for an isolated goal or core content planning area, or for several goals integrated across multiple areas of the plan. Without consistent monitoring, a client's plan can inadvertently become obsolete, and an obsolete plan defeats the purpose of proactive planning.

> **Self-Test 7**
>
> Who is the least likely to engage in ongoing plan monitoring?
>
> a. Financial planners who work on an hourly fee basis.
>
> b. Financial planners who write comprehensive financial plans.
>
> c. Financial planners who meet with their clients quarterly.
>
> d. Both b and c.

With an understanding of *what* this step of the systematic financial planning process entails and *when* monitoring should occur, it is important to consider *who* does monitoring. Monitoring can be the responsibility of

- the client;

- the planner, or the planner in coordination with other product or service providers (recall the idea of the planner as the hub of the wheel that coordinates implementation and monitoring);

- a variety of product or service providers with no coordination; or

- no one.

A financial planner's business model and scope of the established planner-client relationship generally set the parameters for monitoring, which can vary widely. Some aspects of monitoring pertain only to planners who are soliciting an ongoing relationship (i.e., for services, products, or servicing products) with their clients. Some financial planners are consistently involved with their clients, offering counsel on how to achieve financial and life goals. For financial planners who conduct their practices akin to a **medical model** (i.e., with a treat-as-needed approach), or for these creating *modular plans* (e.g., on a single problem, issue, or core content planning area), monitoring may be beyond the scope of the planner-client engagement. The financial planner may not have the opportunity to follow up with a client because implementation and monitoring are the client's responsibility and the client may or may not re-engage the financial planner for to review and evaluate progress. In a more sales-based or product-delivery type model, service may not include monitoring of the situation once a product is sold to meet a specific need. Monitoring may be limited to periodic review of the client's progress on a multiple-year schedule.

For the greatest likelihood of client success, a financial plan must be responsive to change. The plan must mature in concert with the client and the life cycle progression just as it must be responsive to unforeseen events or the need for different products or services. Failure to monitor the implementation and results of the recommendations is inconsistent with the intent of the financial planning process. Unfortunately, though, that is sometimes the case and likely detrimental to client and financial planner, both of whom are missing opportunities. During the monitoring stage a competent financial planner can demonstrate the value added benefit of the planner-client relationship. This requires that both the personal relationship and business relationships between planner and client support such a trust-based exchange.

Quantitative/Analytical Mini-Case Problems

Adam and Kate Ford

1. You are preparing to meet with Adam and Kate Ford, and their three-week-old baby girl Cooper. They have lived life to the fullest but have recently realized that all of this excess is going to seriously jeopardize their long-term finances. They have done a fair job of saving but have also habitually overspent their annual income by financing the difference on credit cards, which has resulted in $17,000 in credit card balances. In the last year Kate and Adam have attempted to make significant changes in their spending and have excellent financial records. They have enlisted your help.

   You have numerous recommendations for them pertaining to almost every aspect of their financial lives, particularly for insurance and retirement planning, and you have compiled a list of these recommendations along with the associated cost and frequency of payment. One of your first recommendations is to build a $10,000 emergency fund, because you never know what might happen with a newborn. Currently the only monetary asset is a five-year, $15,000 bank CD that Adam inherited from his great-aunt. Luckily, it is coming due in a few months, so they will be able to access the money. They also have $85,000 in other financial assets and $26,170 in nonmortgage liabilities.

   When you started your analysis, you realized that Adam and Kate had only $2,250 in annual discretionary cash flow, so you knew that you had to recommend that they reallocate some assets and organize some of their debt. Given the low interest rate environment, they had inquired with a local lender and wanted your advice on a mortgage refinance. You determined that they could take out $32,500 of their home equity and still be approved for a 5.75 percent twenty-year mortgage, which would give them enough to pay the $6,330 in closing costs and pay off their credit card debt, with the remainder going toward their home equity line of credit (HELOC). The payment on the new mortgage is only $40 less than their old mortgage, but they did not want to extend the term beyond twenty years. Besides, the reduction in the HELOC balance also reduces that monthly payment by $125.

Now that they have a child, you think that they should each have life insurance (Adam was actually over insured, given his company benefits); they should reevaluate their property and casualty insurance coverage and see an attorney to get their affairs in order. Finally, Kate has informed you that their parents are going to provide generously for Cooper's education, so you are comfortable recommending that they reduce funding there to accomplish some additional goals, namely saving for retirement. You have sketched out your recommendations in the following table.

Recommendation Summary	Annual Value (Cost) / Benefit	Frequency of (Cost) / Benefit
Refinance the mortgage (5.75 percent, $158,300, 15 yrs.) with cash out	$480	Annual
Use the cash out proceeds to pay closing costs, HELOC ,and high-interest credit cards	$32,500	Single
Closing costs and points for the refinance	($6,330)	Single
Pay off high-rate (16.5 percent) credit card balances	($17,000)	Single
Pay down variable-rate (6.5 percent) HELOC	($9,170)	Single
Reduce HELOC payment ($125/mo)	$1,500	Annual
Eliminate credit card payments ($510/mo)	$6,120	Annual
Liquidate mutual fund (fund emergency fund account)	$10,000	Single
Liquidate CD upon maturity (fund emergency fund account)	$4,000	Single
Allocate money from CD and mutual fund to emergency savings account	($14,000)	Single
Federal tax refund	$1,956	Single
Reduce education funding , Cooper	$1,800	Annual
Drop $1 million term life insurance, Adam	$600	Annual
Purchase $1 million term life insurance, Kate	($770)	Annual
Enhance property and casualty insurance (homeowners, auto, umbrella)	($850)	Annual
Increase 401(k) contribution, Adam	($1,500)	Annual
Increase 403(b) contribution, Kate	($1,500)	Annual
Contribute to Roth IRA, Adam	($3,000)	Annual
Contribute to Roth IRA, Kate	($3,000)	Annual
Plan estate (wills, general power of attorney, letter of last instruction, and advance medical directive)	($1,000)	Single
Financial planning fee	($2,500)	Single

To prepare for the meeting, you need to:

a.   Complete a Recommendation Form and an Impact Form for at least one of the recommendations to explain your planning process to Adam and Kate.

b.   Complete a Comprehensive Planning Form to ensure that no planning needs have been overlooked.

c.   Complete a Cash Flow and Other Assets Tracker to determine the aggregate impact of your recommendations on their discretionary cash flow and net worth.

Marco Summerville

2.   Marco is planning to implement several financial planning recommendations within the next few weeks. He wants to make sure that he has the cash flow and asset position to implement each recommendation. Help Marco calculate the net effect of each recommendation on his discretionary cash flow (DCF) and net worth position as show below:

Recommendation / Action	Amount	Benefit / Cost	DCF	Assets
Opening Balance			$5,300	$41,000
Refinance Mortgage	$9,000	Benefit		
Refinancing Costs	$5,000	Cost		
Pay-Off Credit Cards	$23,000	Cost		
Reduction in Credit Card Payments	$4,600	Benefit		
Transfer Credit Card Payments to IRA	$4,600	Cost		
Purchase Term Life Insurance	$2,300	Cost		
Reallocate Portfolio (Trading Commissions)	$3,600	Cost		

Comprehensive Bedo Case—Analysis Questions

Before finalizing the recommendations and integrating them into a comprehensive plan to help the Bedos meet their financial goals, it is important to review all of the assumptions related to Tyler's and Mia's temperament, personality, attitudes, family history, financial knowledge, experience, and other factors. Finally, the Planning Recommendation Forms resulting from the independent situation analysis conducted for each of the core planning areas must be reviewed. Do recommendations serve to meet the Bedos' primary goals and objectives and at the same time reflect their situational factors? Use the following questions to guide the plan development, implementation, and monitoring steps of the financial planning process.

1. For each of the core content planning areas, one or more planning goals were identified for the Bedo household. When conceptualizing the comprehensive plan, consider the following:

   a. Are the goal(s) in agreement with any or all goals and objectives that the clients have identified?

   b. What is the desired outcome for the clients? Are there planner-identified needs or outcomes that must be presented to the Bedos?

   c. What situational factors might influence their ranking of these goals? Are these factors explicit, implied, or assumed? Is additional information required from the Bedos, and if so, what?

   d. Have all globally accepted, client-specific, or planner-generated planning assumptions been identified and considered? List the assumptions as they might appear in a plan.

2. Review all of the Planning Recommendation Forms prepared for the primary and alternative recommendations for each core content planning area. Then, considering the forms and the Bedos' goals, complete the Comprehensive Planning Checklist.

3. For each recommendation (primary and alternative, where applicable), complete a Recommendation Impact Form to review the cross-impacts of each recommendation.

4. Based on the priority originally assigned to each recommendation, review the priorities relative to the knowledge of the entire client situation. Be sure to consider the likelihood of meeting the clients' goals and desired outcomes, as well as the approach that will most effectively protect and grow assets. Sequence all of the recommendations to reflect these priorities.

5. Given these priorities and their corresponding goals and recommendations, and the Bedos' discretionary cash flow and other available assets, choose the most important recommendation(s) to fund first. Which recommendations, if any might be (1) downsized or (2) postponed to increase funding opportunities for more immediate recommendations? Be sure to review the preceding for ideas regarding how to meet the Bedos' goals most effectively and efficiently. Do current recommendations utilize the Bedos' resources to the highest and best use?

6. Financial planners are encouraged to provide clients with alternative approaches to reach the same goal, when applicable. Does this situation apply to the Bedos? What alternatives might realistically be offered to them? Are there any recommendations that, in consultation with the Bedos, might be eliminated given their goals, temperaments, personalities, attitudes, and financial knowledge and experience? Are there recommendations that the Bedos might choose to ignore?

7. Once the recommendations with the greatest likelihood of effectively and efficiently meeting the Bedos' goals and objectives are finally identified, summarize the financial impacts of each recommendation made using a Cash Flow and Other Assets Tracking Form. Make adjustments as needed to match the recommendations to the cash flow and assets available.

8. Develop an Implementation Checklist to clarify all of the details to be stated in response to the seven key questions.

9. Conduct a cross-impact analysis for the Bedos one year in the future by recalculating and projecting the following, assuming all recommendations will be implemented as planned:

    a. the cash flow situation;

    b. the household net worth;

    c. the income tax situation; and

    d. the estate and estate tax situation.

10. Develop a summary of the goals and recommendations that comprise the Bedos' plan. Based on the initial drafts written in Chapters 3 through 13 and the revisions made during plan development, clearly state each recommendation. Be sure to state specific, defensible answers to the *who, what, when, where, why, how,* and *how much* implementation questions for each recommendation. (Refer to the Implementation Checklist.) As assigned, prepare this as a Summary of Goals and Assumptions, as an Executive Summary, or as a Summary of Goals, Observations, and Recommendations for inclusion in the plan.

11. What barriers might a planner face when working with the Bedos that could lessen their motivation or timely action to implement recommendations? What approaches might be incorporated in the plan, included in the presentation, or both to help motivate the Bedos to take action?

12. Using the short presentations prepared in Chapters 3 through 13 of your observations and/or recommendation(s) and the final integrated plan develop a presentation for the Bedos. As assigned, the presentation could be a summary, highlighting only the goals, recommendations, and implementation *or* a longer presentation could provide a more detailed explanation of the entire planning process. Be sure to include visual aids, Excel handouts, and other materials that will make the plan more meaningful to Tyler and Mia.

13. Monitoring, in its most multifaceted and integrative form, involves a review of the client's life situation and its relationship to the plan, the implementation of the plan, the viability of the products and services chosen, and outcomes to date. Develop a list of three to five questions or issues representing each of these components to review with the Bedos at their first annual review meeting. How might those questions change by the time of the fifth annual review? Be specific.

14. For one of the following situations, list the most important situational factors and conceptual planning issues for the affected core content planning areas if the Bedos reported that:

    a. Tyler or Mia wanted to stop work and go to law school, with a substantial projected salary increase in five years.

    b. Mia was pregnant and for health or personal reasons needed to stop working for a few years.

    c. Tyler or Mia received a promotion resulting in a $10,000 annual salary increase.

Chapter Resources

Certified Financial Planner Board of Standards, Inc. (www.cfp.net).

Insurance company ratings can be monitored at:

A.M. Best Company (www.ambest.com)

Fitch Ratings (www.fitchratings.com)

Moody's Investor Service (www.moodys.com/cust/default.asp).

Lytton, R., J. Grable, and D. Klock. *The Process of Financial Planning: Developing a Financial Plan,* 2nd Ed. Erlanger, KY: National Underwriter, 2012.

Self-Test Answers

1: d, 2: d, 3: c, 4: d, 5: b, 6: c, 7: a.

Endnotes

1. This section of the chapter was excerpted from the companion text, R. Lytton, J. Grable, and D. Klock, *The Process of Financial Planning: Developing a Financial Plan* (Cincinnati, OH: National Underwriter, 2006).

2. K. C. Altfest, *Keeping Clients for Life: How to Build a Successful Financial Practice* (New York: John Wiley and Sons, 2001).

Comprehensive Planning Checklist

Comprehensive Planning Checklist for _____				
Cash Flow Analysis to Maximize Client's Discretionary Cash Flow			**Recommendation Needed?**	
1. Has planner reviewed financial ratios and compared them to benchmarks?	Yes	No	Yes	No
2. Have steps been taken to designate savings or other assets for use as an emergency fund or source of emergency income?	Yes	No	Yes	No
3. Has planner reviewed client budget or income and expense statement for possible expense reductions?	Yes	No	Yes	No
4. Has planner verified that the client is able and willing to proactively save money on a regular basis?	Yes	No	Yes	No
5. Have debt reduction or debt restructuring alternatives been reviewed?	Yes	No	Yes	No
6. Have mortgage refinancing alternatives been reviewed?	Yes	No	Yes	No
7. Are there other client-specific cash management issues to consider?	Yes	No	Yes	No
Tax Analysis to Minimize Taxes and Maximize Client's Discretionary Cash Flow			**Recommendation Needed?**	
8. Have tax projections for 1, 3, or 5 years been done to guide the planning process?	Yes	No	Yes	No
9. Has client income tax withholding been matched to tax liability?	Yes	No	Yes	No
10. Has client FICA withholding been matched to FICA liabilities?	Yes	No	Yes	No
11. Has planner reviewed client's tax situation to ensure that other tax-reduction opportunities have not been overlooked?	Yes	No	Yes	No

Tax Analysis to Minimize Taxes and Maximize Client's Discretionary Cash Flow (cont'd)			Recommendation Needed?	
12. Is the client currently subject to the AMT? Have projections been made for the next 1, 3, or 5 years?	Yes	No	Yes	No
13. Has planner checked to determine whether client is maximizing tax-reducing insurance alternatives? a. Health flexible spending account? b. Dependent care flexible spending account? c. Employer provided life, health, disability, or LTC benefits? d. Any other § 125 cafeteria plan benefits?	Yes	No	Yes	No
14. Are there other client-specific tax management issues to consider?	Yes	No	Yes	No

Insurance Analysis to Limit Client's Household Risk Exposures			Recommendation Needed?	
15. Has a life insurance analysis been conducted?	Yes	No	Yes	No
16. Has a disability insurance analysis been conducted?	Yes	No	Yes	No
17. Has a long-term care (LTC) insurance analysis been conducted?	Yes	No	Yes	No
18. Has a health insurance analysis been conducted?	Yes	No	Yes	No
19. Has a property, casualty, and liability insurance analysis been conducted?	Yes	No	Yes	No
20. Are there other client-specific risk management issues to consider?	Yes	No	Yes	No

Investment Planning Analysis to Maximize Client's Return			Recommendation Needed?	
21. Has an investment funding goal been identified?	Yes	No	Yes	No
22. Is the client on track to meet the targeted amount and date?	Yes	No	Yes	No
23. Are asset allocation and investments suitable given the client's time horizon, risk tolerance, and other assumptions?	Yes	No	Yes	No
24. Is the client fully benefiting from tax-advantaged investments?	Yes	No	Yes	No
25. Are there other client-specific investment planning issues to consider?	Yes	No	Yes	No

Education or Special Needs Planning Analysis to Maximize Client's Return			Recommendation Needed?	
26. Has an education funding goal been identified?	Yes	No	Yes	No
27. Is the client on track to meet the targeted amount and date?	Yes	No	Yes	No
28. Are asset allocation and investments suitable given the client's time horizon, risk tolerance, and other assumptions?	Yes	No	Yes	No
29. Is the client fully benefiting from tax-advantaged accounts?	Yes	No	Yes	No
30. Are there other client-specific education planning issues to consider?	Yes	No	Yes	No
31. Has a special needs funding goal(s) been identified? Is the client on track to meet the targeted amount(s) and date(s)?	Yes	No	Yes	No
32. Are asset allocation and investments suitable given the client's time horizon, risk tolerance, and other assumptions?	Yes	No	Yes	No
33. Are there other client-specific special needs planning issues to consider?	Yes	No	Yes	No

Retirement Planning Analysis to Maximize Client's Return			Recommendation Needed?	
34. Has a retirement funding goal been identified?	Yes	No	Yes	No
35. Is the client on track to meet the targeted amount and date?	Yes	No	Yes	No
36. Are asset allocation and investments suitable given the client's time horizon, risk tolerance, and other assumptions?	Yes	No	Yes	No
37. Is the client fully benefiting from any available match?	Yes	No	Yes	No
38. Is the client fully benefiting from tax-advantaged accounts?	Yes	No	Yes	No
39. Are other retirement funds available?	Yes	No	Yes	No
40. Are there other client-specific retirement planning issues to consider?	Yes	No	Yes	No

Estate Planning Analysis to Minimize Estate Taxes and Ensure Client's Final Wishes			Recommendation Needed?	
41. Has the client begun giving assets to dependents, other family members, or charity?	Yes	No	Yes	No

Estate Planning Analysis to Minimize Estate Taxes and Ensure Client's Final Wishes (*cont'd*)			Recommendation Needed?	
42. Are documents in place to distribute property and provide for dependents, heirs, or charities?	Yes	No	Yes	No
43. Have steps been taken to minimize probate, estate, or inheritance taxes?	Yes	No	Yes	No
44. Have steps been taken to minimize settlement costs, including legal and accounting fees?	Yes	No	Yes	No
45. Are funds available, or plans in place, for the payment of estate taxes and settlement expenses?	Yes	No	Yes	No
46. Are documents in place to guide incapacitation or other end-of-life decisions?	Yes	No	Yes	No
47. Are documents in place to care for, or name guardians for, children or other financial dependents?	Yes	No	Yes	No
48. Are documents in place to care for a pet, if applicable?	Yes	No	Yes	No
49. Has a letter of last instructions been prepared to provide for the distribution of personal and digital assets (i.e. accounts, music, pictures, etc.) as well as other final wishes?	Yes	No	Yes	No
50. Are there other client-specific estate planning issues to consider?	Yes	No	Yes	No

Cross-planning Analysis: Have the Following Interactions Been Considered?			Recommendation Needed?	
51. Net worth <=> insurance?	Yes	No	Yes	No
52. Income taxes <=> insurance?	Yes	No	Yes	No
a. Health flexible spending accounts?	Yes	No	Yes	No
b. Dependent care flexible spending accounts?	Yes	No	Yes	No
c. Employer-provided life, health, disability, and LTC benefits?	Yes	Yes	Yes	No
53. Income taxes <=> mortgage refinance?	Yes	No	Yes	No
54. Life insurance <=> estate planning?	Yes	No	Yes	No
55. Life/LTC hybrid <=> life insurance?	Yes	No	Yes	No
56. LTC <=> estate planning?	Yes	No	Yes	No
57. Education funding <=> estate planning?	Yes	No	Yes	No
58. Education funding <=> income tax planning?	Yes	No	Yes	No
59. Investment planning <=> income tax planning?	Yes	No	Yes	No
60. Retirement planning <=> income tax planning?	Yes	No	Yes	No

Writing Sample

The ultimate outcome associated with the development of financial planning strategies is the development of a written financial plan. The following is an example of how an analysis of a client's situation can be written for inclusion in a comprehensive financial plan. The sample represents a review of a client's current estate planning situation. Typically, each section within a written plan would follow the same format, which includes a broad description of the purpose, a presentation of important definitions, a review of the client's current situation, observations, recommendations, and an implementation strategy. When appropriate alternative recommendations and implications associated with recommendations should be included.

ESTATE PLANNING

Objective of an Estate Planning Analysis:

Estate planning involves a review and analysis of a client's accumulation, protection, and distribution of assets. An outcome associated with estate planning is a more effective and efficient management of assets, a reduction in gift and estate taxes, protection in the case of incapacitation, and a proactive approach to the distribution of assets after death.

Key Definitions

- **Will:** A legal declaration stating how each client wishes his or her assets to be distributed at death. Assets transferred via a will are to probate.

- **Living Will**: A legal document enabling an individual to direct his or her wishes regarding life sustaining medical treatment in the event of medical incapacitation; in some states this is called a medical directive or a document directing health care.

- **Power of Attorney:** A document naming an agent to transact business for a client (principal); some power of attorney are limited, whereas other have few limitation or time restraints.

- **Durable Power of Attorney**: A broad power of attorney that is not terminated by the incapacity or disability of the client (principal).

- **Medical/Healthcare Power of Attorney**: A document allowing a proxy (trusted individual) to direct health care decisions not specifically addressed in a living will; this document is also referred to as a health care proxy.

- **Revocable Trust**: A trust created by the client (grantor) that can be amended, revoked, or changed by the client's during the client's lifetime.

- **Irrevocable Trust**: A trust that cannot be amended or revoked during the grantors lifetime.

- **Probate:** The legal process of distributing assets according to state law.

Current Situation

- As a same sex couple you are entitled to the rights and privileges outlined in the Defense of Marriage Act (DOMA).

- The federal estate tax exemption currently is $5.45 million.

- Your current state of residence has an estate tax exemption of $1.0 million, with a 16 percent flat tax on all amounts exceeding $1.0 million.

- Your current state does allow spouses to leave an unlimited amount to each other via gift or estate transfer. As such, LBGT spouses can now leave unlimited amounts free of state tax.

- As a couple, you currently own your principle residence as joint tenants with rights of survivorship (JWTROS).

    o This means that your respective gross estate values are approximately $3.75 million each.

    o Your taxable estate values, based on final expenses of $100,000 each, state transfer taxes, and charitable donations are $3.5 million each.

- You each currently have a living will and medical power or attorney; each document specifies spousal authority for health care directives.

- You each currently have a will, drafted by an attorney, outlining your wishes for the transfer of property interests at death.

- Your retirement accounts have named beneficiaries: your spouse is the primary beneficiary.

Observations

We are pleased to see that you, as a couple, have been proactive in planning for the management and disposition of your assets. Decisions on healthcare and later life distribution of assets represent potential conflicts between surviving family members and spouses. Taking the time now to ensure that your family understands your wishes in the case of incapacitation or death is something we applaud. The fact that you both have established appropriate estate planning documents, such as wills, living wills, and healthcare powers of attorney, provides you with a strong foundation for future financial planning. Additionally, we commend you for already having established a working relationship with a reputable estate attorney. This relationship will continue to serve you as your family situation evolves.

We did notice that you have already designated each other as beneficiaries on your respective retirement accounts. Be sure to confirm with your employer that the beneficiary designations are current. You may wish to add a secondary beneficiary to each account as well.

Our analysis shows that should one or both of you pass away, now or within the next few years, you will owe no federal gift or estate tax. The value of your current gross estates falls below the federal minimum guidelines. You may, however, incur a state estate tax.

Finally, we believe that you have established a solid foundation for your estate plan. However, a few items do need your immediate attention. Implementing the recommendations discussed below will significantly strengthen the protection and distribution of your asset situation.

Recommendations

We recommend the following actions be implemented within the next three to six months. While we are ready to provide our expertise to ensure your estate plan synchronizes with your comprehensive financial plan, it is important to note that several of the recommendations require implementation through your estate attorney. An implementation guideline has been included at the end of this discussion to help facilitate implementation. This implementation timeline represents a best case recommendation because time periods involving establishing a trust can vary greatly by attorney expediency and costs:

Establish Durable Power of Attorney Documents: While you already have health care powers of attorney, giving your spouse the right to make health care decisions for you in the case you become incapacitated seriously ill, you each also need a durable power of attorney. This type of power of attorney provides your spouse broad decision making power over financial manners, rather than medical issues. These documents can be written to 'spring' into effect by an event such as incapacitation or disability. The cost of implementation will be approximately $1,000.

Establish Irrevocable Life Insurance Trust (ILIT): Creating an ILIT to hold your cash value life insurance policies is one way to reduce possible state estate taxes in the future. After a period of three years, following the transfer of policies into the trust, the death benefit or proceeds of any policy within the trust will be excluded from the policy owner's estate. When the transfer takes place, the ILIT will be the new owner of the policy. The ILIT will also be named the beneficiary of each policy. Proceeds paid to the trust can still be used to pay for any costs stemming from death of the insured, such as burial costs, administration costs, and taxes. The cost of implementation will be approximately $1,200.

Establish Revocable Trust: Currently, all of your property is owned JTWROS. Since you are currently considering purchase a vacation home out of state, we recommend that you establish a family revocable trust. Technically, this is called an inter-vivos (during lifetime) revocable trust or a living trust. The trust should be created with using guidance from your estate attorney. In this case, you may name each other as co-trustees, which will allow you to maintain control of all trust assets. You will, of course, still be responsible for all debts and tax liabilities resulting from trust activities. Your current wills should be amended to 'pour over' any outside assets into the trust at death. You should fund the trust with your individual cash accounts, non-retirement brokerage accounts, tangible personal property (furniture, art, clothing, cars, etc.), and business interests. Assets within the trusts avoid probate and will be distributed by the trustee per the terms of the trust documents.

Due to their revocable status, you (as grantors) will retain the rights to revoke or alter the trust at any time. This characteristic does mean that the value of assets within the trust will be included in your gross estates at death, but you will avoid probate. We estimate that the cost of implementation will be approximately $4,500, which includes drafting of new wills.

Use 'Payable on Death' Designations on Applicable Accounts: Any non-jointly held money market, certificate of deposit (CD), or cash accounts should be designated as payable on death (POD). A POD automatically transfers interests to another party. In your case, the POD should name the other spouse as the account beneficiary. When used appropriately, any account transferred POD will bypass the probate process. The use of a POD is not needed if the account is owned by your revocable trust. There is no cost associated with implementation.

Draft Letters of Last Instruction; This document, while not legally binding, does serve as a written notice regarding your last wishes regarding the disposition of your body and other assets not specifically named in your trust or will. There is no cost to implementation; your attorney can assist with this when your wills are revised.

Implementation Procedure

Recommendation	Who	Where	When	How	Cash Flow Impact	Net Worth Impact
Draft Durable Powers of Attorney	Naomi and Pat	Estate Attorney's Office	Immediately	Pay Fees from Money Market Account	$0	-$1,000
Establish ILITs	Naomi	Estate Attorney's Office	Within the Next Six Months	Pay Fees from Money Market Account	$0	-$1,200
Establish Revocable Living Trust	Naomi and Pat	Estate Attorney's Office	Within the Next Three Months	Pay Fees from Savings Account	$0	-$4,500
Transfer Assets to Trust	Naomi and Pat	Estate Attorney's Office	Within the Next Three Months and Ongoing	Begin Retitling Assets with Each Institution or Governmental Agency	$0	$0
Add POD Designations (Optional)	Naomi and Pat	Banks and Credit Unions	Immediately	Visit Each Bank and Credit Union Where You Have an Account	$0	$0
Draft Letter of Last Instructions	Naomi and Pat	Estate Attorney Office	Immediately; update when wills are adjusted	Work with Attorney in Drafting the Letters	$0	$0

Implications

The implementation of each recommendation, coupled with implementation of other recommendations provided in this comprehensive financial plan, provide a solid foundation for your financial future. These recommendations, in particular, will help you develop and maintain an effective estate plan ensuring private, efficient, and cost effective management of your estates following incapacitation and/or death.

As noted above, you currently are not subject to a gift or estate tax at the federal level. You may be subject to a state estate transfer tax however. Any transfers of wealth exceeding the federal and state exemptions, at the death of the second spouse, will be subject to estate taxes under a federal marginal rate scale and a 16 percent levy at the state level. However, portability will allow you to pass on an unlimited amount to your surviving spouse outside of taxation.

We believe that like a financial plan, an estate plan is a living document. You should plan to revisit estate issues at least annually with us and your estate attorney. We will continue to work with both you and your estate attorney to ensure your plan is current and effective, given the information provided to us by you. Should you have any questions please contact us.

PART VI: Financial Planning— Case Studies

Case 1: The Zimmer Case

Case 2: The Ande Case

Case 3: The Roth Case

Case 4: The Shim Case

Case 5: The Butterfield Case

Case 6: The Little Case

Case 7: The Contrell Case

Case 8: The Alpha Case

Case 9: The Edwards Case

Case 10: The Mayfield Case

Case 11: The Dion Case

Case 12: The Graham Case

Case 13: The Tun Case

Case 14: The Menjivar Case

Case 15: The Case of the Good Gone Bad

Introduction to Case Studies

This appendix includes fifteen mini-cases: (a) nine ten-question mini-cases; (b) five twenty-question cases; and (c) an ethics case. In general, the mini-cases are designed to test both definitional and basic applied financial planning concepts. The longer twenty-question cases provide more detail in terms of background, assumptions, and complications. Additionally, each of the longer cases, although comprehensive in context, focuses on one central theme, as follows:

1. **Graham case:** general financial planning

2. **Cantrell case:** investment planning

3. **Mayfield case:** retirement planning

4. **Butterfield Case:** insurance planning

5. **Tun Case:** education planning

Instructors and students interested in additional writing applications will find these cases appropriate for use as either modular/targeted or comprehensive financial planning narratives. That is, each case contains more information than needed to answer the core multiple-choice questions. (Instructions are provided with answers in the Instructor's Manual.) These longer cases also include open-ended discussion questions.

The ethics case is intended to be used as an interactive in-class exercise. It is designed to be lighthearted and obvious in the planner's violation of multiple professional standards. The case is designed to assess key Certified Financial Planner ™ Board of Standards, Inc., (CFP Board) *Code of Ethics and Professional Responsibility* terms, rules, and standards.

Before beginning work on these cases, it is important to remember the following case assumptions:

1. Case information and assumptions can be linked to the Financial Facilitator spreadsheet package provided with the book. Using the assumptions provided, financial planning students should generally be able to use the spreadsheets to arrive at mathematical solutions to all core financial planning problems (e.g., cash flow, net worth, retirement). This does not mean, however, that the cases can be solved only by using the spreadsheet package. To the contrary; it is possible to solve each case using traditional calculators, formulas, and commercially available software.

2. Assumptions within a particular case are divided into sections. For example, each case has unique assumptions related to insurance planning, retirement planning, estate planning, etc. Students should use only the assumptions provided in each section to solve math and strategic planning questions related to that section. In other words, it is possible—and likely—that rate-of-return assumptions, for instance, will be different for insurance and retirement planning purposes. When solving any question, students should use the assumptions related to the specific section. Furthermore, it is important to remember that case assumptions, particularly those related to rate-of-return data, will be different from data in the current market environment. It is essential, however, to use only the information provided in each case when answering the questions. Bringing in additional assumptions, return data, or other information from the "real world" will result in wrong answers and frustration.

3. Readers (e.g., instructors and students) who would like to add realism to each case may want to consider changing the Anystate and Anycity location assumption to a specific state. Income tax information was originally developed for each case based on a model state, as shown below:

   • Graham case: Arizona

   • Cantrell case: South Dakota

   • Mayfield case: Ohio

   • Butterfield case: Virginia

   • Tun case: Georgia

Case 1

The Zimmer Case

A FINANCIAL SITUATION MINI-CASE

Today's date is December 31, 20XX, and Bonita Zimmer has stopped by your office for her year-end annual financial planning review. The following narrative provides important details about Bonita.

Bonita just turned thirty years of age. She lives in a house that she purchased three years ago for $110,000, right before housing prices began to skyrocket. She was fortunate to purchase the home with $18,000 in down payment money received from her father (who is married) and a loan for the remainder. She was able to obtain a 6.5 percent thirty-year mortgage.

Bonita is a hard worker and good saver. Over the past eight years—since graduating from college—she has accumulated a nice-sized nest egg. Figure VI.1 summarizes her asset and liability situation.

Figure VI.1 Bonita Zimmer's Assets and Liabilities

Assets	Value	Liabilities	Value
Savings account	$9,000	Mortgage balance	$88,704
Checking account	$2,000	Credit card balances	$3,200
6-month CD	$2,500	Car loan	$9,500
Principal residence	$367,000		
Car	$12,000	**Total assets**	$403,500
Personal property	$11,000	**Total liabilities**	$101,404
		Net worth	$302,096

Bonita has been saving for an emergency fund. Her goal is to maintain a liquid account balance equal to six months of total expenses. Figure VI.2 summarizes Bonita's income and expense situation. Note that Bonita lives in an income tax-free state.

Figure VI.2 Bonita Zimmer's Income and Expenses

Income or Expense	Amount (Yearly)
Income	
Annual income	$55,000
Reinvested interest income	$400
Expenses	
Mortgage payment	$6,978
Real estate taxes and insurance	$2,200
Utilities	$2,400
Groceries	$3,000
Dining out	$2,400
Credit card payments	$960
Car payments	$4,400
Gas	$900
Auto insurance	$1,200
Auto and household maintenance	$1,800
Entertainment	$3,200
Federal taxes	$6,540
FICA	$4,320
Personal care	$1,500
Clothing	$3,000
Charitable donations	$2,200
Gifts to others	$3,000
Miscellaneous expenses	$2,400
Reinvested interest	$400

Please use this information to answer the following case questions.[1]

Case Questions

1. If Bonita sells her current residence for full fair market value (excluding commissions and closing costs), and she purchases a new residence for $180,000 in the same calendar year, the amount of proceeds subject to capital gains tax is:

---

1.   Questions 6, 7, and 8 are from "Released CFP® Certification Examination Questions," "2004 Case Scenario and Questions," and "1994 & 1996 Certification Exam Questions." Copyright © 2008, Certified Financial Planner Board of Standards, Inc. All rights reserved. Used with permission.

    a. $7,000

    b. $28,296

    c. $187,000

    d. $257,000

2.   Which of the following statements is true assuming that the money Bonita received for the down payment on her house from her father was a gift rather than a loan?

    I.   Bonita must pay a gift tax on the amount that exceeds the gift tax annual exclusion.

    II.   Her father should have filed a gift-splitting election with the IRS to avoid incurring a gift tax liability.

    III.   Bonita should have filed a gift-splitting declaration with the IRS to avoid incurring a gift tax liability.

    IV.   The basis in the house is increased by the amount of any taxes paid on the down payment gift.

    a.   II only

    b.   I and III only

    c.   II and IV only

    d.   III and IV only

    e.   I, III, and IV only

3.   Bonita is concerned that she could be overextended on her monthly mortgage payment. Do you agree with her?

    a.   Yes, because her total debt-to-income ratio exceeds the accepted benchmark of 36 percent of gross income.

    b.   No, because her monthly housing cost-to-income ratio is less than the accepted benchmark of 28 percent of gross income.

    c.   Yes, because her monthly housing cost-to-income ratio is greater than the accepted benchmark of 28 percent of gross income.

    d.   No, because her monetary assets are greater than six months of total expenses, which allows her to overextend her monthly mortgage obligation.

4.   Which of the following statements is correct regarding Bonita's cash flow situation?

    a.   Her level of discretionary cash flow, if used for savings, is below the recommended benchmark average of 10 percent of gross income.

    b.   Her level of expenditures for principal, interest, tax, insurance (PITI), and other debt payments exceeds the recommended maximum of 36 percent of gross income.

    c.   She needs to save additional money in liquid assets to achieve her six-month emergency fund goal.

    d.   Both (a) and (c) are correct.

    e.   Answers (a), (b), and (c) are correct.

5.   Bonita has been dating Jason for nine months. He has proposed marriage. If Bonita accepts the proposal and they purchase a home together after they get married, which method can they use to title the property that will provide automatic survivorship rights, assuming they live in a non-community property state?

        I.   Joint tenants with right of survivorship (JTWROS).

        II.   Tenants by the entirety.

        III. Tenants in common.

    a.   I only

    b.   II only

    c.   I and II only

    d.   I and III only

    e.   II and III only

6.   Bonita is considering changing jobs and plans to roll over the vested portion of her qualified retirement plan into either an IRA or the qualified retirement plan of her new employer. Reasons why a direct rollover into the new plan, rather than an IRA, would be more appropriate include which of the following?

        I.   The new employer's plan is the only way Bonita can get a distribution at retirement in the form of a life annuity.

        II.   The new employer's plan contains a provision for loans.

        III. There will be no tax penalty if a lump sum benefit is withdrawn from the new plan at early retirement after attaining age fifty.

        IV. Lump sum withdrawals from the new employer's plan after age 59½ will be eligible for five- or ten-year forward-averaging.

    a.   II only

    b.   I and III only

    c.   II and III only

d. II and IV only

7. Bonita received a bequest of one-hundred shares of XYZ stock from a relative who died on March 1 of this year. The relative bought the stock at a total cost of $5,500. The value of the one-hundred shares of XYZ stock was $5,750 on March 1. On July 1, Bonita sells the stock for $6,250, incurring expenses for the sale of $250. The taxable gain on the sale will be a:

a. $250 long-term capital gain.

b. $250 short-term capital gain.

c. $500 long-term capital gain.

d. $500 short-term capital gain.

8. Bonita is considering establishing a trust for her mother that will pay out $1,000 each month. The trust department will act as trustee. Bonita will retain the right to revoke the trust and be the remainder beneficiary of the trust. If the trust earns $15,000 for the year, who must pay the income tax on earnings?

a. Bonita pays on $15,000.

b. Bonita's mother pays on $12,000, the trust on $3,000.

c. Bonita's mother pays on $12,000, Bonita on $3,000.

d. The trust pays on $15,000.

9. If Bonita and Jason do get married and buy a house, they have identified two mortgage alternatives when taking out a loan. The first alternative is a thirty-year 7 percent mortgage with five discount points to be paid at closing. The second alternative is an 8 percent mortgage with two discount points to be paid at closing. Assuming they can qualify for either loan, which of the following aspects should Bonita and Jason consider when choosing between these two alternatives?

I.   Monthly PMI expenses.

II.   Estimated length of ownership.

III. Monthly utility expenses.

IV. Cash currently available.

a. I and II only

b. II only

c. II and IV only

d. IV only

e. I, III, and IV

10. Bonita is considering purchasing an expensive piece of jewelry next month. The local jeweler is offering a three-year financing plan to help her pay for the jewels. For the purposes of preparing Bonita's financial statements for next year, you should:

    I.   List the jewels as an investment asset.

    II.   List the loan amount as a current or short-term liability.

    III. List the jewels as a use asset.

    IV. List the loan payment as a fixed expense on the income and expense statement.

  a. I and II only

  b. II and III only

  c. III and IV only

  d. I and IV only

  e. II and IV only

Case 2

The Ande Case

A TAX PLANNING MINI-CASE

Today's date is July 1. Larry and Lolita Ande, both age forty-four, are reviewing their tax situation for the current year. They have been married for a number of years and have one adult child. They file their own tax returns, and this is the first time they have had questions about their tax situation. Figure VI.3 summarizes their financial position for tax purposes. Use this information to answer their tax questions.

Figure VI.3 The Andes' Annual Tax Position

Tax Item	Amount
Larry's earnings	$50,000
Lolita's earnings	$43,000
Federal tax withholdings	$12,300
State income tax withholdings	$4,100
State and local sales taxes paid	$2,300
FICA withholdings	$6,273
Bank account interest*	$1,600
State tax refund from previous year	$900
Home mortgage interest paid	$5,300
Real estate taxes paid	$1,800
Charitable contributions	$4,000
Unreimbursed medical expenses	$800

Figure VI.3 The Andes' Annual Tax Position (*cont'd*)

Tax Item	Amount
Stock ownership: United Motor Company**	Current value: $4,000
	Basis: $8,000
	Face value: $100,000
	Cash value: $7,800
	Owner: Larry
	Beneficiary: Lolita
	Insured: Larry
Whole-life insurance policy	Policy dividend: $300

*They earn 4% on their account balance. Short-duration municipal bond funds are currently yielding 3.4%.

**They purchased the stock three months ago and still own the stock today.

The Andes itemized deductions for their federal return last year. Currently, neither Larry nor Lolita has access to a qualified retirement plan through their work, and they have not funded IRAs up to this point. They have access to a § 125 flexible spending account through Lolita's employer. To date, they have not funded the account. Open enrollment for the § 125 account lasts for the next thirty days. For the purposes of solving this case, use the tax information shown in Figure VI.4.

Figure VI.4 Marginal Tax Rate, Deduction, and Exemption Amounts

Taxable Income	Tax Rate
$16,050 or less	10%
$16,050 to $65,100	15%
$65,100 to $131,450	25%
$131,450 to $200,300	28%
$200,300 to $357,700	33%
Over $357,700	35%
Standard deduction	$10,900
Personal exemption	$3,500

Please use this information to answer the following case questions.

Case Questions

1. Which of the following statements is true?

    I.   If Larry were to pass away this year, Lolita would be required to claim the face value of the life insurance received for federal income tax purposes.

    II. If Larry uses a transit pass valued at $100 per month given to him by his employer to commute to and from work, he will be required to add the value of the pass to his income for tax purposes.

    III. If the Andes want to reduce gross income for tax purposes, they could contribute to a flexible spending plan to cover the cost of unreimbursed medical expenses.

    IV. Although the face value of the life insurance policy would be tax free to Lolita if Larry were to pass away, the cash value would be fully taxable as income at the federal level.

    a.   II only

    b.   III only

    c.   I and III only

    d.   II and IV only

    e.   II, III, and IV only

2. Larry and Lolita are considering moving their bank account balance to a safe municipal bond mutual fund. Before making the switch, they should be aware of which of the following?

    I.   Given their federal marginal tax bracket, the bank account provides a higher after-tax yield.

    II. Interest and capital appreciation from the municipal bond fund is federally income tax exempt.

    III. Interest from the bonds will be state income tax free if the bonds held in the fund are from the state where the Andes live.

    IV. Municipal bond interest that is used to reinvest in the fund will grow on a tax-free basis.

    a.   I only

    b.   III only

    c.   II and III only

    d.   II, III, and IV only

    e.   I, II, III, and IV

3. Which of the following tax items will be included when calculating the Andes' gross income this year?

   I.   Lolita's salary.

   II. The state tax refund from the previous year.

   III. The capital loss in United Motor Company.

   IV. Dividends earned, but not received, on the insurance policy.

   a. I and II only

   b. I and IV only

   c. II and III only

   d. I, II, and IV only

   e. I, III, and IV only

4. The Andes do not know whether they should take the standard deduction or itemize deductions this year. Which of the following statements is true in relation to this issue?

   a. It does not matter which deduction amount they choose because they are equal.

   b. They should claim itemized deductions because this amount is greater than the standard deduction.

   c. They should claim the standard deduction because this amount is greater than itemizing deductions.

   d. If they sell the United Motor Company stock, the loss will reduce their itemized deductions, making the standard deduction more attractive.

   e. Both c and d are correct.

5. Lolita and Larry are thinking about adding to their family next year. If they do have a child, Lolita plans to be a stay-at-home mom. Larry is concerned about what will happen to their tax situation when Lolita stops working. One issue, in particular, that they would like to discuss with their financial planner is whether they should sell the United Motor Company stock this year or wait until next year. What is the best recommendation in their situation?

   a. They should sell the stock this year while they are in the 25 percent marginal tax bracket because this will result in a larger deduction than waiting and selling when they are in a lower bracket.

   b. They should sell the stock next year, making the deduction more valuable as an offset to Lolita's lost income.

   c. They should sell the stock this year because the full value of the loss can be used this year to reduce their gross income level.

d.   They should sell the stock next year because they currently do not need a tax loss to reduce their reportable income.

6.   The Andes have considered moving to another state across the country so that Larry can work with his brother. Larry and his brother work in a similar business. If they do move, which of the following expenses will be an allowable moving expense deduction?

> I.   Payment of real estate expenses on the sale of their current home.
>
> II.   Any loss that they incur when selling their personal residence.
>
> III.   Cost of travel expenses, such as lodging, while in transit from one town to another.
>
> IV.   Cost of meals while in transit from one town to another.

a.   III only

b.   I and III only

c.   II and III only

d.   III and IV only

e.   II and IV only

7.   Which of the following tax planning strategies provides the greatest immediate tax benefit for the Andes?

a.   Contributing the maximum allowable to a Roth IRA.

b.   Making the maximum allowable deductible contribution to a traditional IRA.

c.   Establishing and contributing to an immediate fixed annuity.

d.   Purchasing additional whole-life insurance.

8.   Larry is considering changing jobs. A potential employer has offered him several employee benefits that make the job offer very attractive. Which of the following employee benefit alternatives will help reduce the Andes' reportable gross income for federal income tax purposes?

> I.   The immediate right to contribute to a 401(k) plan.
>
> II.   Employer-provided parking.
>
> III.   Group term life insurance equal to three times salary.
>
> IV.   The right to contribute to a § 125 plan.

a.   I only

b.   I and II only

    c.   I and IV only

    d.   II, III, and IV only

    e.   I, II, III, and IV

9.   One month ago Lolita's uncle gave Larry and Lolita a check for $25,000. He said that he had won some money while gambling in Reno. He wanted to share his good fortune with family. Larry is concerned about the tax ramifications of this transaction. Which statement(s) below is (are) true in this situation?

    I.   Larry and Lolita must pay state and federal income tax on the full $25,000.

    II.   Larry and Lolita must split the tax liability with Lolita's uncle.

    III.   Lolita's uncle must pay state and federal income taxes on the winnings.

    IV.   Lolita and Larry need not pay any tax because the $25,000 is a gift.

    a.   I only

    b.   II only

    c.   III only

    d.   II and III only

    e.   III and IV only

10.   If Larry and Lolita finalize a divorce this year and the court orders Larry to pay alimony in the amount of $700 per month for six months (through December), and then $700 per month for fifteen years or until Lolita dies, which of the following statements will be true?

    a.   Larry and Lolita may not file married filing jointly when completing this year's tax return.

    b.   Lolita must file as head of household when completing this year's tax return.

    c.   Larry may take a $4,200 deduction from gross income related to the alimony payments.

    d.   Lolita need not report the alimony paid, or any child support payments, when she files taxes in future years.

    e.   Both a and c are correct.

Case 3

The Roth Case

A TAX PLANNING MINI-CASE

Your clients, Ira and Flora Roth, have come to you for some basic tax-planning advice and guidance. Here are the facts you need to help them.

- Ira's earned income: $65,000.

- Flora's earned income: $52,000.

- They live in Kansas and own a municipal bond issued by the city of Wichita (not a private activity bond). The bond's face value is $100,000 and it has a 3.5 percent coupon.

- Ira paid $12,000 in alimony for the year to a former spouse.

- During the year they had the following transactions:

    o   Sold XXP stock for $11,000; originally purchased many years ago for $5,000.

    o   Purchased one-hundred shares of HHP stock for $3,000 in April of the year.

    o   Sold a KSU corporate bond originally purchased on February 6 of the year for $15,000 (basis); they received $11,000 for the bond on November 12.

    o   Redeemed $4,300 worth of EE savings bonds in July that they had held for twelve years; the bonds earned 6 percent interest and had doubled in value.

    o   Sold 1,000 shares of UNR stock at $7 per share that they had purchased earlier in the year for $13 per share.

- Flora (age sixty-one) received annuity distributions of $22,000 from a nonqualified annuity. At the beginning of the year, the annuity had a value of $300,000 and an after-tax basis of $100,000. Her remaining life expectancy is 13.64 years.

- Ira (age fifty-seven) terminated employment and took a distribution of $100,000 from his 401(k) plan with the intent of rolling the money over to a Fidelity IRA in thirty to forty-five days. His remaining life expectancy is 14.80 years.

- Ira and Flora paid $3,000 in housing expenses for their grandchild Chuck as a way to help offset some of his college expenses. They paid the $3,000 directly to Chuck.

- During the year, they paid the following items:

   o $12,600 in unreimbursed medical expenses

   o $7,000 in mortgage interest

   o $3,500 in property taxes

   o $3,000 in state income taxes

   o $2,800 in state and local sales taxes

   o $1,000 to the Salvation Army

   o $2,400 to their church

   o $750 to their alma mater

   o $500 in legal fees

   o $100 in safe deposit box fees

   o   They contributed $3,200 to a §529 plan to help pay for Chuck's college expenses.

Case Questions

1.   How much in long-term capital gains did the Roths have for the year?

   a.   -$3,000

   b. $0

   c. $1,000

   d. $6,000

2. Which of the following statements is true?

    a. The Roths had $1,000 in net short-term losses for the year.

    b. The Roths had $4,000 in net short-term losses for the year.

    c. The Roths had $10,000 in net short-term losses for the year.

    d. The Roths had $15,000 in net short-term losses for the year.

3. How much (rounded) of Flora's annuity distribution is taxable this year?

    a. 33 percent

    b. 67 percent

    c. 75 percent

    d. 100 percent

4. Which of the following statements is true?

    a. Ira's employer will withhold $20,000 in federal taxes from the 401(k) distribution.

    b. Ira will owe an immediate 10 percent penalty on the 401(k) distribution.

    c. Ira will need to contribute only $80,000 to the IRA rollover to avoid penalties.

    d. Ira needed to roll over the money to the IRA within thirty days to avoid taxes and penalties.

5. Had the Roths decided to give the XXP stock to a charity, they should have:

    I.   sold the stock first and then made the donation for a deduction.

    II. donated the stock first and then taken the deduction.

    III. donated cash to the charity then sold the stock.

    a. I only

    b. II only

    c. III only

    d. I, II, or III, because they result in the same tax outcome

6. Assuming they had decided to donate the KSU bond to a charity, they should have:

    I.   sold the bond first and then made the donation for a deduction.

    II. donated the bond first and then taken the deduction.

    III. donated the bond first and then deducted the loss.

  a. I only

  b. II only

  c. III only

  d. I, II, or III, because they result in the same tax outcome

7.   How much can the Roths deduct from their federal taxes for the § 529 plan contribution?

  a. $0

  b. $1,000

  c. $2,000

  d. $1,600

  e. $3,200

8.   In addition to the information already known about the Roths, you learn that Flora owns a vacant lot in Topeka that she purchased as an investment. She would like to exchange the lot so that she does not incur a tax liability. Which of the following properties can she take in trade to receive like-kind tax treatment?

  a. A duplex in Wichita.

  b. Collector coins owned by a coin dealer.

  c. A mortgage on a rental house in Topeka.

  d. A or c only.

9.   Instead of doing a straight exchange with someone, assume that Flora finds a person who is willing to provide her a combination of property and cash for her vacant lot. Flora will receive $5,000 cash and a vacant lot in town valued at $10,000 (basis of $8,000). If her original lot has a fair market value of $20,000 and a basis of $5,000, how much will Flora realize on this transaction?

  a. $0

  b. $5,000

  c. $8,000

  d. $10,000

  e. $15,000

10. Using the information in the previous question, how much gain must Flora recognize on the exchange for income tax purposes?

    a. $0

    b. $5,000

    c. $10,000

    d. $15,000

    e. $20,000

Case 4

The Shim Case

AN INSURANCE PLANNING MINI-CASE

Kevin and Sonya Shim are conducting an insurance review with their financial planner. Kevin and Sonya consider themselves middle-Americans—with a small but positive cash flow and a modest net worth. Kevin (age sixty-three) is just a few years away from retirement, whereas Sonya (age sixty-one) plans to work a few more years once Kevin officially retires. The following discussion provides a summary of the Shims' insurance planning situation.

Life Insurance

Kevin owns a $250,000 universal life insurance policy. Sonya is the insured and their son Wilbur (age thirty-seven) is the beneficiary. The policy has a cash value of $23,450 and a living benefits provision; all account earnings are used to offset premium expenses. Sonya owns a twenty-year $100,000 level-term life policy that she purchased five years ago. She pays approximately $450 per year in premium costs.

Property and Casualty Insurance

Kevin and Sonya own a home as JTWROS that has a market and replacement value of $245,000. The house is insured with a Standard HO-3 policy for $210,700. The policy requires that the Shims pay a $500 deductible per claim occurrence. Other provisions include the following:

- 10 percent coverage on detached structures.

- Coverage up to $250 for cash.

- Coverage up to $1,500 for collectibles, artwork, and similar assets.

- Personal property contents coverage equal to 20 percent of the insured dwelling.

- Living expense coverage for six months.

- Coverage up to $100,000 for personal liability.

- A replacement cost coverage endorsement is in place.

The Shims' two cars are insured under a personal automobile policy with split-limit coverage of $250,000/$500,000/$50,000. They also have a $1-million-dollar excess liability policy.

Health Insurance

The Shims are covered under Sonya's group health insurance plan. The traditional plan has a no lifetime maximum benefit, a $500-per-person deductible, and an 80 percent coinsurance clause, with a family stop-loss limit of $2,500.

Use the preceding case information to answer the questions that follow.

Case Questions

1. In preparation for retirement, Kevin is exploring his Social Security and Medicare insurance coverage. Which of the following is a benefit provided by Medicare?

    a. Hospice benefits for terminally ill persons.

    b. A stop-loss limit for annual medical expenses in excess of $2,500.

    c. Coverage for custodial care.

    d. Coverage for nonprescription drugs.

2. Kevin is considering purchasing a twelve-year-old pickup truck for use when he goes hunting. The truck that he has his eye on has 90,000 miles but is in generally good condition. Which of the following insurance coverage(s) should Kevin probably exclude when purchasing an insurance policy for this truck?

    I.   Part A—liability coverage.

    II.   Part B—medical payments coverage.

    III. Part C—uninsured motorist coverage.

    IV.   Part D—damage to insured's auto coverage.

    a. IV only

    b. II and IV only

    c. I, II, and III

    d.   I, III, and IV

    e.   II, III, and IV

3.   If Sonya were to die today, which of the following is true in relation to the $250,000 universal life insurance policy owned by Kevin?

    a.   Kevin will continue to own the policy for the benefit of Wilbur.

    b.   Kevin will make a taxable gift of life insurance proceeds to Wilbur.

    c.   Kevin will receive an amount equal to the cash value, and Wilbur will receive the remainder of the life insurance value as a tax-free gift.

    d.   Kevin will receive the proceeds of the policy.

    e.   Kevin must include the $250,000 face value of the policy as an asset when he calculates Sonya's taxable estate.

4.   What will be the result if Sonya decides to cancel her term life insurance policy?

    a.   She will incur a $2,250 tax liability based on the level of premium paid over the past five years.

    b.   She will receive $450 in premium paid for last year's coverage as a refund from the insurance company, and this amount will be fully taxable at the Federal level.

    c.   She will not have a tax liability associated with the cancellation.

    d.   She would incur a tax liability on the face amount received if she were to die after canceling the policy but before receiving refunded premiums.

5.   If the Shims sustain an $80,000 loss to their dwelling from a fire, how much will the insurance company pay (after the deductible) toward the dwelling loss claim?

    a. $64,000

    b. $68,000

    c. $79,500

    d. $80,000

6.   If a shed valued at $13,000 in the backyard is also destroyed in the fire, what is the maximum amount that the insurance company will pay, prior to the deductible, to replace the shed and any other detached dwellings?

    a. $225,000

    b. $25,000

    c. $21,070

   d. $13,000

   e. $1,300

7. Sonya believes that her husband is a reckless driver, and she worries about what will happen if he is ever in a serious car accident. If Kevin is involved in a car accident and causes physical harm to another motorist in the amount of $300,000, how much will be paid from the personal automobile policy (PAP) and how much from the excess liability policy?

   a. $300,000 PAP and $0 excess liability.

   b. $0 PAP and $300,000 excess liability.

   c. $150,000 PAP and $150,000 excess liability.

   d. $50,000 PAP and $250,000 excess liability.

   e. $250,000 PAP and $50,000 excess liability.

8. How much will the Shims' health insurance company pay if Sonya files a claim for a broken foot that cost $2,000 for emergency room treatment, $700 for bone setting, and $300 in rehabilitation services?

   a. $0

   b. $500

   c. $2,000

   d. $2,500

   e. $3,000

9. The Shims are curious about the alternatives available when planning for possible nursing home care costs in the future. Which of the following long-term care insurance strategies listed below is an appropriate financial planning alternative for the Shims?

     I. Use the living benefits provision within an accelerated death benefit rider available in the universal life insurance policy.

     II. Purchase a life insurance policy that has a long-term care insurance endorsement.

     III. Systematically save for future health care costs and use Medicare as the primary insurance coverage for long-term care expenses.

     IV. Use Medicaid coverage for long-term care expenses after age sixty-five.

   a. II only

   b. I and II only

   c. II and III only

    d.   III and IV only

    e.   I, II, and III only

10. Currently, neither Kevin nor Sonya has disability insurance coverage. Kevin and Sonya would like more information about disability insurance. Which of the following statements is (are) true in relation to disability insurance?

    I.   Shorter elimination periods result in lower premium costs.

    II.   Benefits paid from employer-provided group disability plans are received income tax free.

    III.   If a guaranteed renewable contract is used, the insurance company cannot increase premiums on individual policies but can raise premiums for all individuals covered by the policy.

    IV.   Disability policies are nearly always designed to provide lifetime benefits.

    a.   I only

    b.   I and II only

    c.   II and III only

    d.   III only

    e.   II, III, and IV only

The Butterfield Case

AN INSURANCE PLANNING MINI-CASE

John Butterfield, forty-nine, and his wife Haley Butterfield, forty-four, live in a relatively new home on the outskirts of Anycity, Anystate. They have been married for twenty-three years and have three children. Both John and Haley are in excellent health. Their son Troy, age twenty, is a baseball player on scholarship at the University of Anystate. Daughter Holly, age seventeen, hopes to attend State University next fall as a cadet to begin pursuing a career in the Marine Corps.

The choices of their first two children have allowed the Butterfields to concentrate their college saving goals on Naomi, the youngest, at age thirteen John and Haley have come to you for help in addressing several insurance planning questions and concerns. Use the following information to conduct a review of their financial situation and use your analyses to answer the questions that follow the case narrative.

Global Assumptions (Valid unless otherwise Specified in Certain Instances)

- Inflation: 3.5 percent

- All income and expense figures are given in today's dollars.

- Federal marginal tax bracket: 25 percent

- State marginal tax bracket: 5.75 percent

- Any qualified plan or IRA contribution growth rates are assumed to stop at the federally mandated limit unless otherwise restricted.

- All nominal rates of return are pretax returns.

Income Issues

John has worked for the last fourteen years as an engineer for CNS Design. He has an $81,000 salary. He would like to retire at age sixty-seven.

Haley has worked as a CPA for seventeen years, the last fourteen of which have been out of their home. She also does consulting work from home. Though her earnings vary from month to month, she estimates that she will earn $65,000 this year. She wants to retire at the same time as John.

They also assume that their salaries will increase, on average, by 3.5 percent per year over their working lives. This year they anticipate earning $600 in interest and non-qualified mutual fund dividend distributions, which will be reinvested.

Expense Issues

Figure VI.5 provides a summary of the Butterfields' fixed (non-discretionary) and variable (discretionary) expenses.

Figure VI.5 Summary of Expenses

Expenses	Amount	Frequency
Pretax health care premiums	$200	Monthly
401(k) contributions	$540	Monthly
Keogh contributions	$7,800	Annually
Mortgage	$1,600	Monthly
Home equity loan	$625	Monthly
Auto loan #1	$310	Monthly
Auto loan #2	$500	Monthly
Credit cards and installment debt	$2,100	Annual
Auto insurance	$1,100	Semiannual
Homeowner's insurance	$825	Annual
Disability insurance (pretax)	$200	Monthly
Life insurance	$400	Annual
IRA contributions (Haley)	$750	Quarterly
IRA contributions (John)	$750	Quarterly
Subscriptions	$650	Annual
Telephone	$1,560	Annual
Digital cable television	$125	Monthly
Hobbies	$750	Annual
Entertainment	$1,500	Annual
Education payments (spending money Troy)	$5,000	Annual
Travel costs for first child while in college	$1,200	Annual

Figure VI.5 Summary of Expenses (*cont'd*)

Expenses	Amount	Frequency
Groceries	$75	Weekly
Food away from home	$3,400	Annual
Real estate taxes	$1,300	Annual
Household maintenance	$2,700	Annual
Utilities	$175	Month
Clothing	$1,500	Annual
Dry cleaning	$50	Month
Personal care	$500	Annual
Furnishing	$1,000	Annual
Allowances	$2,000	Annual
Medical copayments	$700	Annual
Prescriptions	$250	Annual
Gas	$2,500	Annual
Personal property tax	$400	Semiannual
Banking fees	$75	Annual
IRA fees	$80	Annual
Travel	$100	Monthly
Contributions to church	$125	Monthly
Vacations	$3,000	Annual
Christmas gifts	$2,400	Annual

Home mortgage. They are eight years into a thirty-year 7.5 percent mortgage that had an original balance of $228,850, with a current outstanding balance of $206,602.

Home equity loan. The loan balance was used to pay off credit cards and purchase a vehicle for Troy to use at college. Since the loan was first taken, they have accumulated additional credit card debt. The monthly payment is approximately 2 percent of the outstanding balance. The credit line expires and will be due and payable in seven years. They have paid $3,000 in interest over the past year.

Auto Payments.

1. Auto 1: Balance is $8,500 with 2.5 years remaining.

2. Auto 2: Balance is $25,000 with fifty-seven months remaining.

Tax Issues

After reviewing their pay stubs, John and Haley calculated that their total annual federal withholdings and/or estimated tax payments totaled $20,250. Their state withholdings amounted to $8,000. Social Security withheld was $10,985. The Butterfields file taxes as "married filing jointly" and have $30,241 in itemized deductions for the year.

The Butterfields are eligible for a $5,000 state income tax deduction, and five $1,000-personal exemptions for John, Haley, and the children. The marginal tax bracket for their state is 5.75 percent.

Specific Client Goals

- Under any circumstance, they want to provide 50 percent of the cost of Holly's and Naomi's college education costs, and all of Troy's education costs that are not covered by scholarships.

- They want to maintain their current standard of living in retirement or in the event of either spouse's premature death.

- They want to protect their income and assets in the event of a catastrophic accident or illness, so that they can pass on their assets to their children.

- They both want to continue funding their IRAs to the current maximum limit.

See Figure VI.6 for information on the Butterfields' assets and liabilities.

Figure VI.6 The Butterfields' Assets and Liabilities

Asset	Amount	Ownership
Checking account	$950	Client
Large-cap mutual fund	$9,000	Client
Checking account	$1,200	Co-client
Small-cap mutual fund	$17,250	Co-client
Life insurance cash value	$3,800	Co-client
Checking account	$2,800	Joint
Savings account	$7,500	Joint
Money market account	$10,050	Joint
Mid-cap mutual fund	$40,000	Joint
Artwork	$25,000	Joint
401(k)	$62,000	Client
Keogh retirement plan	$125,000	Co-client
Individual retirement account (IRA)	$38,000	Client
Individual retirement account (IRA)	$41,500	Co-client
Home	$315,000	

Figure VI.6 The Butterfields' Assets and Liabilities (*cont'd*)

Asset	Amount	Ownership
Honda	$17,500	Joint
Toyota	$38,000	Joint
Collectibles	$13,000	Co-client
Furniture	$17,500	Client
Other assets	$69,000	Joint
Misc. assets	$39,000	Joint
Liabilities	**Amount**	**Ownership**
Visa credit card	$2,500	Co-client
MasterCard	$4,900	Joint
Mortgage	$206,602	Joint
Home equity loan	$32,000	Joint
Honda	$8,500	Joint
Toyota	$25,000	Joint
Short-term installment debt	$21,000	Client

Current Insurance Data

Property and Casualty

Auto: All vehicles

Liability: $300,000 single limit (including uninsured motorist)

Medical payments coverage: $1,000 limit per person

Deductible: $250 collision; $100 comprehensive

Premium: $1,100 every six months

Auto 1: 20XX Honda Accord LX Sedan

Mileage: 30,000

Color: light blue

Engine: six-cylinder

Transmission: manual

Payment: $310/month

Balance: $8,500 with 2.5 years remaining

Worth: $17,500

Auto 2: 20XX Toyota Sequoia Limited (4×4)

Mileage: 5,500

Color: silver

Engine: eight-cylinder

Transmission: automatic

Payment: $500/month

Balance: $25,000 with fifty-seven months remaining

Worth: $38,000

Home. Single-family dwelling

Insured value: $245,000

Replacement value: $315,000

Deductible: $500

Personal property: 50 percent of dwelling

Bodily injury: $100,000

Personal injury: $0

Other endorsements: None

Umbrella: None

Professional liability: None

Business: None

Life and Health

Life. Haley has a $50,000 universal life policy with XYZ Insurance Co. She pays the annual premium of $400. The policy has a current cash value of $3,800 (the cash value at the beginning of the period was $3,600). John is the primary beneficiary and Haley is the owner. At the time of purchase, policy projections were based on after-tax U.S. Treasury rates of 6 percent.

John has an employer-provided term policy that pays one times his annual salary. The face amount of the policy is reduced by 50 percent, regardless of his salary, at age sixty-five and terminates at age seventy.

Other life assumptions:

- For planning purposes, the Butterfields would like to use 80 percent of their combined incomes, before taxes, to represent their total household expenses in the event of a death.

- Final illness and burial expenses are estimated to be $15,000 each.

- Estate administration expenses are expected to be approximately $5,200 each.

- Child care expenses will be $10,000.

- Full retirement age, for insurance purposes, is assumed to be age sixty-seven.

- The Butterfields need $100,000 in annual income per year, before taxes, while retired. They would like to use this assumption for both insurance and retirement planning purposes.

- Social Security benefit while children are still at home is $32,000 if John dies, and $29,000 if Haley dies, in today's dollars.

- At age sixty, Haley is eligible for a $13,000 annual Social Security survivor benefit, while John is entitled to a $10,000 annual survivor benefit (in today's dollars).

- In the event of either spouse's death, the other spouse plans to stop working at age sixty and begin taking early retirement survivor benefits (if available).

- For conservative planning purposes, the Butterfields do not plan on using interest and/or dividends as an income source when planning insurance needs.

- At full retirement (i.e., at age sixty-seven) John will receive $18,000 per year in Social Security benefits; Haley will receive $16,500 in benefits (in today's dollars).

- Assumed ages at death for John and Haley are ninety and ninety-two, respectively.

- The assumed gross rate of return on insurance assets, in the event of death, is 9 percent.

Health. The Butterfields' health insurance is provided by Blue Cross/Blue Shield. Coverage currently includes everyone in the family. The monthly premium of $600 is paid 66 percent by John's employer, with the remainder paid out of pocket. The plan has a deductible of $250 per person and a family copayment of 20 percent. The out-of-pocket per-family cap on copayments is $1,000 per year.

Long-term care. None.

Disability. John's disability coverage is a group disability contract provided by his employer. It pays a $5,000 monthly benefit until age sixty-five. The contract has a liberal "own occupation" definition. The elimination period is 120 days. Haley does not have a disability policy. In the event of a disability, the Butterfields would like to continue saving for other goals; however, they do not want to rely on Social Security disability benefits when estimating disability income needs.

Vacation/medical leave. John has accumulated thirty sick days, which is the maximum he is allowed to carry. He could accrue one week per year if he fell below the maximum. He also is eligible for three weeks of vacation per year. He can carry over one week, but this has not previously been done.

Education Funding Goals

The Butterfields would like to assume that education expenses will increase 6.50 percent per year. They are comfortable assuming a growth rate of 9.00 percent per year for educational assets and savings in a tax-advantaged account before and after college begins (6.75 percent if assets are held in a taxable account). Each of the children is talented academically (GPA > 3.0) and in terms of extracurricular activities.

Troy is currently enrolled at University of Anystate. Current cost: $14,700/year (waiver).

- He is on a 3/4 baseball scholarship. His parents budget $5,000 per year in extra support; they pay tuition not covered in the scholarship and give Troy what is left from their $5,000 budget as a spending allowance.

- The Butterfields have also allocated $1,200 per year to help pay for Troy's travel expenses.

- He has completed one year of college.

- His health insurance is provided under his father's group health plan.

- Holly wants to attend State University; current cost: $10,500/year (possible tuition waiver).

- Holly wants to go to school on an ROTC scholarship and fund any additional expenses out of pocket from money earned during summers.

Naomi's college funding goals have not yet been formalized by the Butterfields, but John and Haley want to plan for college costs of $16,500 per year (in today's dollars).

- They prefer to use tax-advantaged savings plans to fund any expenses.

Retirement Information

The Butterfields would like to retire when John turns age sixty-seven. Based on today's dollars, they are willing to reduce their income by 80 percent of current income while retired. At full retirement (i.e., age sixty-seven) John will receive $18,000 per year in

Social Security benefits; Haley will receive $16,500 in benefits (in today's dollars) at age sixty-seven. When planning, they are comfortable assuming a 9.00 percent rate of return before retirement, and a 5.75 percent return after retirement. Contributions to their defined contribution plans are anticipated to increase 3 percent annually. They anticipate being in a combined 25 percent marginal tax bracket in retirement. Inflation before and after retirement will be 3.50 percent; their incomes should keep pace with inflation. John's employer matches 401(k) contributions $0.50 cents on the dollar. IRA assets are held in Roth accounts. Assumed age at death for John is age ninety and age ninety-two for Haley.

Estate Information

They both have simple wills. John leaves his estate to Haley and Haley leaves her estate to John. They believe that, on average, their estate will grow by 4 percent after the first spouse's death. Other assumptions include:

- Funeral expenses are expected to be approximately $12,000 each.

- Estate administrative expenses will be $5,200 each.

- The Butterfield do not expect to pay any executor fees.

Case Questions

1. Which of the following strategies can the Butterfields use to improve their cash flow situation?

   a. Pay off credit card balances with monetary assets.

   b. Decrease insurance deductibles.

   c. Reduce IRA contributions and use the proceeds to purchase a variable universal life insurance policy.

   d. All of the above.

2. The Butterfields' current ratio is (rounded):

   a. 0.62

   b. 0.79

   c. 1.68

   d. 3.00

3. The Butterfields' savings ratio, using gross earned income and including employer 401(k) matching but excluding reinvested interest and dividends, is (rounded):

   a. 4 percent

    b. 10 percent

    c. 16 percent

    d. 22 percent

4. John and Haley both have retirement account balances. They would like to know what their options will be when they reach retirement. Which of the following statements describes their IRA retirement situation?

    I.   John can roll over his 401(k) account balance into an IRA.

    II. Haley cannot roll over her account balance because her assets are held in a Keogh.

    III. Both John and Haley can roll over their account balances into an IRA and take a special five-year averaging tax technique on amounts withdrawn at that time.

    IV. Haley can roll over her Keogh account balance into an IRA.

    a. III only

    b. I and II only

    c. I and III only

    d. I and IV only

5. Which of the following is true if Haley closes her CPA practice to join a large consulting company this year?

    a. Because she will be changing jobs she will no longer be covered under her current health insurance plan; instead, she will need to continue coverage using COBRA provisions until she become eligible for coverage with the consulting company.

    b. She can remain on John's health insurance policy until she is eligible for benefits under her new employer's insurance plan.

    c. Because of her good health status, if she were to drop off of John's health insurance plan and move to a policy offered by the consulting company, John's health insurance premiums will increase.

    d. Both a and c are correct.

6. If John, Haley, and Naomi are involved in an accident that requires medical care, how much will their health insurance pay, including deductions and copayments, given the following expenses? Assume no annual limits have been met. John $1,800; Haley $3,700; Naomi $4,200.

    a. $1,750

    b. $7,160

    c. $7,950

d. $8,950

7. An HO-3 policy (Special Form) with no endorsements excludes which of the following perils?

a. Flood

b. Fire

c. Collapse caused by a covered peril

d. Weight of ice

e. Volcanic eruption

8. If the Butterfields suffer a $47,000 homeowner's loss due to fire, how much will the insurance company pay on the claim, accounting for any deductible and co-pay provisions?

a. $45,193

b. $45,693

c. $46,500

d. $47,000

9. The Butterfields recently lived through a major wind storm. The experts said it was not a tornado, but John and Haley would argue otherwise. Their home was terribly damaged. It has been estimated that it will cost $250,000 to fix the house. Excluding listed deductibles and copayments, how much must the Butterfields pay out of pocket toward the repairs?

a. $0

b. $500

c. $5,000

d. $7,500

10. The Butterfields might be able to reduce their automobile insurance premiums by taking which of the following discounts?

a. A good student discount.

b. A multicar discount.

c. A farm use discount.

d. Both a and b.

11. Which of the following statements is (are) true about the Butterfields' PAP?

I.   They are covered if injured while driving someone else's car.

II. They are covered while driving either the Honda or Toyota.

III. They are covered if they rent off-road motorcycles to tour the desert while on vacation.

a. I only

b. II only

c. I and II only

d. I, II, and III

12. During a recent thunderstorm, the Butterfields' Honda Accord received $2,300 in damage from hail. How much will their PAP pay for this claim?

a. $0

b. $2,050

c. $2,200

d. $2,300

13. Haley is worried that Troy will be without health insurance after he graduates from college with his B.S./B.A. degree in a few years. Her primary worry is that he may not immediately find employment or be eligible for employer-provided coverage for an extended period of time, such as ninety days. Given these concerns, which of the following are examples of appropriate insurance coverage recommendations for Troy once he graduates?

a. Purchase no coverage; Haley's concerns are not valid as the Affordable Care Act (ACA) of 2010 extends coverage under a parental policy until young adults reach the age of twenty-six.

b. Purchase no coverage; Haley's concerns are not valid as the Affordable Care Act (ACA) of 2010 extends coverage under a parental policy until the age of twenty-six as long as the young adult does not have coverage available through an employer plan. When available, he will have coverage.

c. Extend his current coverage through a COBRA extension.

d. Purchase insurance through an Affordable Care Act (ACA) of 2010 high-risk pool.

14. Which of the following risk management recommendations is (are) most appropriate to help the Butterfields manage their risk exposures?

I. Purchase an excess liability insurance policy.

II. Decrease their homeowner's coverage to 80 percent of the home's value.

III. Eliminate collision coverage on the Toyota.

IV. Purchase an endorsement to cover their art collection.

a. I and III only

b. II and IV only

c. II and III only

d. I and IV only

15. Which of the following strategies can the Butterfields use to increase their current discretionary cash flow situation?

a. Increase the deductible in their PAP policy.

b. Purchase an umbrella liability insurance policy.

c. Decrease the deductible in their HO policy.

d. All of the above.

16. The Butterfields are not sure whether they are paying an appropriate premium for their universal life insurance policy. Which statement below is true in relation to this concern?

a. The universal life policy is fairly priced according to the yearly-price-per -thousand formula.

b. Even though the yearly-price-per-thousand formula states that the policy is overpriced, given Haley's health status, she should hold the policy because she probably will not qualify for another policy.

c. Even though the universal policy is expensive, they should not replace it because the cost is less than two times the yearly-price-per-thousand formula benchmark price.

d. Haley should replace the universal policy because, according to the yearly-price-per-thousand formula, the cost is more than two times the benchmark price.

17. Haley would like to know the difference between variable life insurance and universal life insurance. Which of the following statements most accurately describes the difference?

a. Variable life insurance uses subcontracts that are invested to generate a guaranteed rate of return.

b. Universal life insurance uses a fixed mortality charge, and variable life insurance does not.

c. Variable life insurance has a death benefit that varies, and universal life insurance provides only a fixed death benefit.

d. Universal life insurance provides a crediting rate based on the insurance company's general account subject to a minimum guarantee, and variable life insurance uses subaccounts that can fluctuate based on market returns.

18. Which of the following is an advantage for John and Haley if they decide to fund their children's college expenses using a §529 plan?

a. The contribution will allow them to take a federal and state income-tax deduction, which will reduce their overall tax liability.

b. If a beneficiary of the §529 plan does not use the assets, John and Haley can name a new beneficiary of the account.

c. Because of the special tax structure of §529 plans, the assets held in the plan will not increase the expected family contribution for financial aid.

d. All of these answers are advantages.

19. Which of the following is an advantage associated with the Butterfields' current health insurance coverage?

a. John's employer pays two-thirds of the total premium, which makes the cost of the group health policy reasonably low.

b. The annual per person deductible and family co-payment associated with the policy is very reasonable, as compared to the maximum allowable family out-of-pocket limits set by the ACA of 2010 for a Health Insurance Marketplace plan.

c. Once Troy and Naomi graduate from college and obtain health insurance coverage through an employer, John and Haley should drop John's employer-provided health insurance coverage and purchase a plan through an Affordable Care Act of 2010 exchange because the costs will be lower and benefits higher.

d. All of the above are true.

e. Only a and b are correct.

20. Which of the following is true for John if he purchases additional life insurance through his employer?

a. Few exclusions are associated with these types of policies.

b. Because most group term policies have a conversion feature, he can be assured that upon termination of employment he can continue his coverage.

c. He can tailor the coverage to his own needs.

d. All of the above are true.

Supplemental Questions

Assume the following, given the facts of the case:

21. The Butterfields paid their ninety-sixth mortgage payment in March 20XX (they were "eight years in"). Based on your suggestion, they have decided to refinance their mortgage. They will make the April payment on April 15 and close on April 20.

a. What is the outstanding balance after the April payment? How much interest will be due on the mortgage at closing on April 20? In other words, what is the total payoff for mortgage one at the closing?

b. Assuming a high credit score and a low new mortgage rate of 4.0 percent for a twenty year mortgage, could they qualify to (1) refinance and (2) payoff the balance on the home equity loan? For simplicity, use the outstanding balance shown in the case for the home equity loan and ignore any reduction in the April balance.

c. If the answer is yes, what issues would you want to discuss with the Butterfields as a precaution.

d. If the answer is yes, is it possible to also pay off the short-term installment debt?

22. Given the increase in cash flow, what are the top three (no priority within those three, just top three) goals or identified needs toward which the money should be redirected?

Discussion Points and Questions

1. Briefly summarize the relevant facts of the case relating to insurance planning.

2. If the Butterfields were going to purchase additional life insurance, what type of policy, what face value, and what riders would be most appropriate given their ages and needs?

3. Explain the advantages and disadvantages of having John purchase additional life insurance through his employer.

4. Describe the 80 percent co-insurance rule and report to the Butterfields how this rule affects their homeowners coverage.

5. What actions can the Butterfields take to reduce their insurance premiums while maintaining adequate coverage in terms of liability and property coverage?

6. Explain why the Butterfields should consider purchasing an excess liability insurance policy.

7. Describe the purpose of long-term care insurance and indicate whether and when the Butterfields should consider purchasing this type of insurance.

8. Report on the advantages and disadvantages associated with the Butterfields' current health insurance policy.

Case 6

The Little Case

AN INVESTMENT SITUATION MINI-CASE

Lucas Little has been asked by his client to review the financial statements of Stuff Stores Company. Mr. Little's client is considering making a substantial purchase of Stuff Stores stock. Before doing so, the client would like to know a bit more about the financial stability of the company. The information in Figure VI.7 should be used to conduct a basic analysis of Stuff Stores' financial situation.

Figure VI.7 Annual Financial Data for Stuff Stores Company ($ millions)

Financial Attribute	Year 1	Year 2	Current
Market capitalization	200,000.5	212,234.0	249,926.5
Total sales	139,208.0	166,809.0	193,295.0
Net income (earnings)	4,430.0	5,377.0	6,295.0
Dividends per share	.16	.20	.24
Shares outstanding	4,474.8	4,443.8	4,464.5
Total assets	64,654.0	70,349.0	78,130.0
Debt	16,891.0	18,712.0	18,824.0
Shareholder's equity	19,136.0	24,216.0	31,343.0
Cash flow	7,580.0	8,194.0	9,604.0

Other relevant data include:

- Beta for Stuff Stores stock: .85

- Standard deviation for Stuff Stores stock: 14.5 percent

- Average return for Stuff Stores stock: 10.5 percent

- Risk-free rate of return: 4.0 percent

- Return on the market: 9.0 percent

Information on similar stocks is shown in Figure VI.8.

Figure VI.8 Data for Similar Stocks

Company	Stock Beta	Stock Standard Deviation	Average Stock Return
Wigwam Stores, Inc.	.90	15.5%	8.0%
Maryland Markets	.80	12.0%	9.0%
Pacific Mercantile, Inc.	.89	15.0%	11.0%

Please use this information to answer the following questions:

Case Questions

1. Based on current information, what is the net profit margin for Stuff Stores?

   a. 1.98 percent

   b. 2.97 percent

   c. 3.26 percent

   d. 3.56 percent

   e. 3.88 percent

2. Based on current information, the price to earnings ratio (P/E) for one share of Stuff Stores stock is:

   a. 1.29

   b. 7.97

   c. 20.08

   d. 26.02

   e. 39.70

3. When comparing Stuff Stores stock to similar stocks in the market, which has the highest required rate of return?

   a. Stuff Stores Company.

   b. Wigwam Stores, Inc.

c.   Marryland Markets.

d.   Pacific Mercantile, Inc.

e.   Stuff Stores Company and Pacific Mercantile, Inc. are the same.

4.   Based solely on past performance compared to the required rate of return, which stock should Mr. Little's client avoid?

a.   Stuff Stores Company.

b.   Wigwam Stores, Inc.

c.   Marryland Markets.

d.   Pacific Mercantile, Inc.

e.   Both Marryland Markets and Pacific Mercantile, Inc.

5.   Mr. Little would like to rank the four stocks in a standardized way before making a recommendation to his client. Using the average stock return data provided, rank the four stocks from highest to lowest using the Sharpe ratio.

   I.   Stuff Stores Company.

   II.   Wigwam Stores, Inc.

   III.   Maryland Markets.

   IV.   Pacific Mercantile, Inc.

a.   II, III, I, and IV

b.   IV, III , II, and I

c.   III, I, IV, and II

d.   IV, I, III, and II

e.   I, IV, III, and II

6.   Mr. Little's client has noticed that the price of Stuff Stores Company stock has remained steady during the past six months. He is convinced that the stock will continue to trade in a narrow range. He would like to make money on the stock, however. Which of the following strategies will cause Mr. Little's client to experience the greatest potential loss if Stuff Stores' stock price begins to fluctuate more widely?

a.   Selling a naked put option.

b.   Selling a naked call option.

c.   Selling a covered call option.

d.   Buying a call option.

e.   Buying shares in Stuff Stores Company directly.

7.   Assume that Mr. Little's client decides to purchase shares in Stuff Stores stock to add to his sizable portfolio. The client tells Mr. Little that he does not want to incur the cost of selling the stock or the entire portfolio. The client also does not want to risk mistiming the market should stock prices start to fall. One strategy for the client to protect against a possible decline in both Stuff Stores stock price and the value of the portfolio would be to:

a.   buy an index call option.

b.   sell an index call option.

c.   buy an index put option.

d.   sell an index put option.

e.   avoid all options strategies because the client cannot protect against the decline with these options.

8.   If the market risk premium were to increase, the value of common stock, including Stuff Stores Company stock, (holding all other factors constant) would:

a.   not change because this does not affect stock values.

b.   increase to compensate the investor for increased risk.

c.   increase because of higher risk-free rates.

d.   decrease to compensate the investor for increased risk.

e.   decrease because of lower risk-free rates.

9.   Mr. Little thinks that he has found an interesting bond investment for his client's portfolio. Mr. Little, when searching for investment ideas, focused on his client's goal of return maximization. The bond has a face value of $1,000 with a maturity date in seven years. The bond's coupon rate is 6.25 percent compounded annually. Today, the bond sells for $1,185.00. The indenture agreement states that the bond can be called for $1,100 after five years. Which of the following statements is (are) true?

a.   The current yield is greater than both the yield to maturity and yield to call.

b.   Given the client's investment objective, this bond should do particularly well if interest rates start to increase.

c.   Mr. Little can lock in a yield to maturity that is higher than the current yield by purchasing the bond today.

d.   The value of the bond today in comparison to the spread in the yield to maturity and the current yield indicates that this bond will not be called early.

10. According to the dividend growth model method of stock valuation, which of the following statements is true, assuming that Mr. Little's client has a required rate of return of 16 percent and that the dividend has grown from .16 to .24 in three years?

    I.   The current Stuff Stores stock price exceeds the calculated value.

    II.   The current Stuff Stores stock price is less than the calculated value.

    III.   Using the dividend growth model as the only measure, the Stuff Stores stock is undervalued.

    IV.   The market price and the calculated value for Stuff Stores match closely, as expected given the high degree of efficiency in the markets.

  a. I only

  b. III only

  c. II and III only

  d. III and IV only

Case 7

The Cantrell Case

AN INVESTMENT PLANNING MINI-CASE

Gabriel and Sarah Cantrell, both age twenty-six, were married four years ago. They have one daughter, Joyce, who is now age three. They also have a new son, Lee, who is age one. They live at 1315 Devonshire Drive in Anytown, Anystate, 78901.

Gabe works for TG Ag Services as a sales representative. He has been working since he turned age sixteen, and has spent the last five years with TG Ag Services. Gabe earns $45,000 per year.

Sarah started working when she was fifteen years old. Four years ago she took a clerk position at Dave's Discount Store in downtown Anytown. She makes $27,500 per year.

Use the following information to conduct a review of the Cantrell's financial situation.

Global Assumptions (Valid unless otherwise Specified in Certain Instances)

- Inflation: 3.5 percent

- Anystate has no state-imposed income tax.

- All income and expense figures are given in today's dollars.

- Planned retirement age: sixty-seven for both

- Federal marginal tax bracket: 15 percent

- State marginal tax bracket: No state income tax

- All nominal rates of return are pretax returns.

Income Issues

Currently Gabe earns $45,000 per year, and Sarah earns $27,500. Both Gabe and Sarah assume that their salaries will increase at the rate of inflation. They make approximately $60 (all of which is reinvested) in interest annually. They have no other sources of income.

Expense Summary

Before meeting with you, they summarized their expenses. These are shown in Figure VI.9. Their assets and liabilities are summarized in Figures VI.10 and VI.11, respectively.

Figure VI.9 The Cantrell's Dedicated and Discretionary Expenses

Expenses	Amount	Frequency
Health care expenses (Gabe)*	$300.00	Monthly
Health care expenses (Sarah)*	$50.00	Monthly
401(k) contribution (Gabe)*	$1,800.00	Annually
401(k) contribution (Sarah)*	$1,375.00	Annually
SS/Medicare (FICA) withholdings	$5,225.00	Annually
Federal tax withholdings	$4,500.00	Annually
Mortgage payments	$714.25	Monthly
Credit card payments	$20.00	Monthly
Auto insurance	$800.00	Semi-annually
Homeowner's insurance	$600.00	Annually
Subscriptions	$480.00	Annually
Telephone expense	$1,800.00	Annually
Home Internet	$90.00	Monthly
Hobbies (Sarah)	$1,450.00	Annually
Recreation/entertainment	$200.00	Monthly
Groceries	$400.00	Monthly
Food away from home	$3,000.00	Annually
Private mortgage insurance	$1,482.00	Annually
Household maintenance	$50.00	Monthly
Annually	$750.00	Annually
Utilities	$3,300.00	Annually
Clothing	$2,200.00	Annually
Laundry services	$300.00	Annually
Personal care	$50.00	Monthly
Furnishing	$750.00	Annually
Child care***	$600.00	Monthly

Figure VI.9 The Cantrell's Dedicated and Discretionary Expenses (*cont'd*)

Expenses	Amount	Frequency
Eye glasses	$300.00	Annually
Medical deductibles	$50.00	Monthly
Unreimbursed medical expenses	$100.00	Annually
Gasoline	$1,100.00	Annually
Car registrations	$575.00	Annually
Personal property tax	$450.00	Annually
Safe deposit box fee	$1.00	Monthly
Accounting fees	$150.00	Annually
Charitable contributions	$100.00	Monthly
Vacations	$2,800.00	Annually
Gifts to family members	$1,000.00	Annually
*Pretax § 125 plan expenses		
**Pretax expenses		
***The child care provider is licensed in Anystate.		
Note: Last year the Cantrells' paid $711 in Anystate sales taxes.		

Asset Summary

Figure VI.10 A Summary of the Cantrell's Assets

Asset	Amount	Ownership
Financial Assets		
Checking account	$350.00	Joint
Savings account	$500.00	Joint
EE savings bonds	$1,000.00	Joint
Retirement 401(k) Assets		
Large-cap funds	$5,000.00	Gabe
Mid-cap funds	$2,500.00	Gabe
Small-cap funds	$2,500.00	Gabe
Government bond funds	$1,000.00	Sarah
Mid-cap funds	$2,500.00	Sarah
Small-cap funds	$1,000.00	Sarah
Other Assets		
Primary residence	$124,000.00	Joint
Buick Regal	$12,000.00	Joint
GMC pickup	$9,800.00	Joint
Collectibles	$1,200.00	Joint
Golf clubs and equipment	$3,800.00	Joint
16-foot sailboat w/2-HP motor	$9,600.00	Joint
Furniture	$13,000.00	Joint
Other assets	$4,700.00	Joint

Liability Summary

Figure VI.11 A Summary of the Cantrell's Liabilities

Liability	Amount	Ownership
Visa credit card*	$2,400.00	Joint
MasterCard**	$500.00	Joint
Mortgage	Unknown	Joint
*17.95% APR		
** 14.25% APR		

Gabe and Sarah purchased a new home in town exactly two years ago today. The original mortgage was in the amount of $116,000 for thirty years at a 6.25 percent rate. They have made precisely twenty-four payments on the mortgage.

Life Insurance and Planning Issues

Gabe and Sarah would like you to analyze their life insurance situation using the following assumptions and facts:

- Upon the first death, household expenses will decrease to $55,000 per year.

- Final expenses are expected to be $9,500 each.

- Estate administration costs are anticipated to be $3,500 each.

- All outstanding liabilities will be paid at the first death.

- They would like to prefund $10,000 in child care expenses at the death of the first spouse.

- They would like to prefund college costs in the event of a spouse's death. They plan to invest any insurance proceeds for this goal in a tax-advantaged educational savings plan.

- They can earn 7 percent before taxes on any life insurance proceeds both pre- and postretirement.

- They anticipate that their marginal federal tax rate will increase to 25 percent in retirement.

- They would like to replace $58,000 in retirement income for the surviving spouse.

- They are willing to use all of their retirement savings to offset life insurance needs.

- In the event of either spouse's death, the other spouse plans to stop working at age sixty and begin taking early retirement survivor benefits (if available).

- For conservative planning purposes, the Cantrells' do not plan to use interest and/or dividends as an income source when determining insurance needs.

- Gabe's employer provides a term policy for two times his salary at no cost, which continues during periods of disability but terminates at retirement. Sarah is the beneficiary of the life insurance policy.

- Sarah's employer also provides two times her salary in term coverage at no cost, which continues during periods of disability but terminates at retirement. Gabe is the beneficiary of the life insurance policy.

- The surviving spouse's income is not expected to change after the death of the first spouse.

See Figure VI.12 for information on the Cantrell's Social Security and life insurance.

Figure VI.12 Social Security Survivor Benefit Information

Beneficiary	Amount (Monthly)*
Sarah and children (until last child turns age 18)	$2,582.50
Gabe and children (until last child turns age 18)	$1,843.10
Sarah (ages 60–67)	$1,048.00
Gabe (ages 60-67)	$1,118.00
Sarah (at age 67)	$1,466.00
Gabe (at age 67)	$1,563.00
* Income test limits could apply. See www.ssa.gov for more information.	

Additional Insurance Information and Planning Issues

Both TG Ag Services and Dave's Discount Store are large employers in the area; each employs more than twenty people at any given time. The Cantrells' do not currently have disability or long-term care insurance policies. Both are healthy, with both sets of parents still alive and well. Their home is currently covered by an HO-3 policy with an inflation rider and a $1,000 deductible. Both automobiles are insured with split-limit coverage of $25/$50/$10 and a $500 deductible.

Retirement Information and Planning Issues

The following information should be used when evaluating the Cantrell's current retirement planning situation:

- They anticipate being in the 25 percent federal marginal tax bracket after retirement.

- They are comfortable assuming that working with you, their financial planner, they can generate a 10.00 percent rate of return before retirement.

- When retired, they would prefer to maintain a conservative growth asset allocation that will generate an 8.25 percent rate of return.

- If retired today, they would like to replace 80 percent of their combined income.

- At retirement Gabe will be eligible to receive $1,563.00 in monthly Social Security benefits.

- At retirement Sarah will be eligible to receive $1,096.00 in monthly Social Security benefits.

- They are comfortable assuming a life expectancy of one-hundred years.

- Gabe currently contributes 4 percent of his salary to his company's 401(k) plan; his employer matches 50 percent on the first 6 percent contributed; his plan has a maximum deferral limit of 12 percent of salary.

- Sarah currently contributes 5 percent of her salary to her company's 401(k) plan; her employer matches 50 percent on the first 5 percent contributed, up to the maximum annual limit.

- Inflation before and after retirement is assumed to be 3.50 percent.

- Contributions to their 401(k) plans will increase by 3 percent even though their salaries are expected to increase by the rate of inflation.

Estate Information and Planning Issues

Both Gabe and Sarah have professionally prepared wills; Gabe's will leaves all of his assets to Sarah, and Sarah's will leaves all of her assets to Gabe. Their wills name their attorney as the estate executor, and in the event of a simultaneous death it is assumed that Gabe will predecease Sarah. Other estate planning facts include:

- Funeral and burial expenses will be $7,500 each.

- Estate and legal costs will be $2,000 each.

- Executor fees will be approximately 2 percent of the gross estate before the marital transfer.

- The net growth rate of the survivor's estate is estimated to be 4 percent annually.

- Both wills name Sarah's sister Lindsey as the guardian of their children.

- All individually owned assets that pass via property law or contract (e.g., IRAs, qualified plans, bank accounts, life insurance) name the surviving spouse as the primary beneficiary; no contingent beneficiaries have been named.

- No other estate planning documents are known to exist.

Figure VI.13 provides a summary of the current yield and rate information applicable to this case.

Figure VI.13 Yield and Rate Information for Use in the Cantrell Analysis

Investment Class	Yield
Checking account	0.00%
Savings account	3.00%
Taxable money market fund	3.50%
EE and I bonds	3.50%
Loan Rates	
30-year mortgage*	6.50%
15-year mortgage*	6.00%
Home equity line of credit*	7.25%
Home equity loan*	7.35%
5-year auto loan	7.90%
Personal loan	8.50%
*APR includes closing costs over life of loan.	

Goals and Objectives

The Cantrell's primary objective at this point is to fully fund four years of college for their two children. They have already been in contact with the universities that they hope their children will attend. Gabe and Sarah learned that the annual cost of college (including tuition, room, and board) in today's dollars is $18,000 at each school. College costs are estimated to increase by about 6 percent annually.

They would like to have the total amount needed to pay for a child's college costs available on the first day of college. Given their moderate level of risk tolerance, they are comfortable planning for these expenses using a 7 percent rate of return. They would also like to use a tax-advantaged investment to save for college.

Their second goal is to retire at age sixty-seven, using the assumptions already listed.

In preparation for a meeting with the Cantrells', you have been given a monitored list of mutual funds used by your firm. Your firm's investment committee will allow you to use any of the funds listed below when developing investment recommendations for the Cantrells' (see Figure VI.14).

Figure VI.14 Mutual Funds Approved for Cantrell Recommendations

Market Indexes		RoR*	SD	Corr (r) with Index	Yield
T-bills		4.00%	2.00%	1.00	4.00%
Equity market		12.00%	17.00%	1.00	2.00%
Bond market		8.00%	9.00%	1.00	4.70%
Fund	**Stated Equity Fund Objective** **Approved Mutual Funds**	**RoR***	**SD**	**Corr (r) with Stock Market**	**Yield**
Super Big Fund	Large-cap fund	13.00%	18.00%	0.95	2.00%
Maxi Fund	Large-cap fund	12.20%	17.40%	0.92	2.00%
Multivariate Fund	Mid-cap fund	14.00%	18.30%	0.90	1.00%
Germain Fund	Mid-cap fund	13.30%	16.90%	0.89	1.25%
Efficacy Fund	Small-cap fund	11.00%	19.00%	0.85	0.25%
Software Fund	Small-cap fund	12.00%	21.00%	0.70	0.00%
Clinical Fund	International fund	10.00%	13.00%	0.68	2.00%
Image Fund	International fund	9.80%	11.00%	0.63	1.00%
Measures Fund	Precious metals fund	6.00%	13.00%	0.40	0.50%
Thumb Fund	Real estate fund	11.00%	11.00%	0.99	4.00%
Factors Fund	Real estate fund	9.90%	12.00%	0.89	5.30%
Column Averages		**11.11%**	**15.51%**	**0.80**	**1.75%**
Fund	**Stated Bond Fund Objective**	**RoR***	**SD**	**Corr (r) with Bond Market**	**Yield**
Alumni Fund	Gov't bond fund	7.80%	8.00%	0.95	4.50%
Bush Fund	Gov't bond fund	8.20%	8.50%	0.90	5.00%
National Fund	Corporate bond fund	8.40%	9.00%	0.98	5.10%
CDR Fund	Corporate bond fund	7.56%	9.20%	0.85	5.40%
Fast Fund	High-yield bond fund	9.90%	13.00%	0.75	7.00%
Mobile Fund	High-yield bond fund	10.30%	12.80%	0.60	8.20%
Column Averages		**8.69%**	**10.08%**	**0.84**	**5.87%**

*Rates of return include yields.

Use the information provided in the case narrative to answer the questions that follow.

Case Questions

1. How much total § 79 income (rounded) for the year must the Cantrells' report for tax purposes?

    a. $0

    b. $6

    c. $29

    d. $32

    e. $35

2. Which of the following is true?

    a. Interest earned by the Cantrells' adds to their level of discretionary cash flow.

    b. § 79 income earned by the Cantrells' adds to their level of discretionary cash flow.

    c. Contributions to Gabe's 401(k) plan reduce discretionary cash flow.

    d. All of the above are true.

    e. A and b only are true.

3. The Cantrells' are eligible for which of the following tax credits?

    I.   income tax credit.

    II.   Child and dependent care tax credit.

    III. Earned Child tax credit.

    IV.   Low-income housing tax credit.

    a. I and II only

    b. II and III only

    c. III and IV only

    d. II, III, and IV only

4. The Cantrell's current net worth situation can best be described as:

    a. A positive $78,356

    b. A negative $2,900

    c. A positive $116,094

    d. A negative $113,194

    e. A positive $194,950

5.   When completing their tax return, the Cantrells' should:

    a. file married filing separately.

    b. claim a deduction from AGI for retirement plan contributions.

    c. use the sales tax deduction when calculating the amount they can claim for itemized deductions.

    d. claim Anystate income taxes as a tax credit.

6.   Which of the following strategies can the Cantrells' use to improve their discretionary cash flow situation?

    I.   Refinance their first mortgage using a fifteen-year loan.

    II.   Pay off some or all credit card debt with financial assets.

    III. Reduce the amount being withheld for federal taxes.

    IV. Increase the amount of reinvested interest earned on investments.

    a. I and III only

    b. II and III only

    c. II and IV only

    d. II, III, and IV only

7.   The Cantrell's current level of discretionary cash flow is enough to:

    a. fund this year's savings need for one child's college education.

    b. fund both children's savings need for college education this year.

    c. pay off credit card debts within one year.

    d. fund both a and c.

8.   Which of the following statements is true?

    a. The Cantrells' need to save an additional $3,700 per year to meet their retirement goal.

    b. The Cantrells' will fall short of their retirement goal by more than $1.5 million using their current retirement planning strategy.

    c. The Cantrells' must reduce their life expectancy in retirement to retire at age sixty-seven.

   d.   Both a and c.

   e.   None of the above.

9.   Which of the following is true regarding the Cantrell's estate situation?

     I.   The value of Gabe's group life insurance policy will be excluded from his gross estate.

     II.   The full value of jointly held liabilities can be deducted as an expense from the gross estate at the passing of the first spouse.

     III.   If Gabe and Sarah establish § 529 plans for their children by contributing $5,000, the assets held in the accounts will be excluded from Gabe and Sarah's gross estate.

     IV.   The Cantrells' should begin a gifting strategy to reduce their taxable estate.

   a.   I only

   b.   III only

   c.   I and II only

   d.   II and III only

   e.   I, III, and IV only

10.   All of the following are examples of tax-advantaged education savings alternatives appropriate for use by the Cantrells' except:

   a.   A § 529 plan.

   b.   A Coverdell savings plan.

   c.   EE savings bonds.

   d.   An immediate annuity.

11.   Sarah's grandmother has decided to gift Gabe and Sarah $150,000. Which of the following strategies can the Cantrells' fund with this gift?

     I.   Fully prefund their children's college education costs.

     II.   Earmark the gift as a source of emergency funds.

     III.   Use the gift to fully offset Gabe's need for additional life insurance.

   a.   I only

   b.   III only

   c.   I and II only

    d. II and III only

12. Rank the following funds in terms of their total portfolio risk (volatility), highest to lowest:

      I.   Maxi Fund

      II. Software Fund

      III. Image Fund

      IV. Clinical Fund

    a. I, II, IV, and III

    b. I, II, III, and IV

    c. II, I, IV, and III

    d. II, I, III, and IV

13. Which fund's expected rate of return, as measured by CAPM, is the lowest?

    a. Super Big Fund

    b. Efficacy Fund

    c. Image Fund

    d. Measures Fund

14. Rank the following funds based on the Sharpe ratio (highest to lowest):

      I.   Thumb Fund

      II. Germain Fund

      III. Multivariate Fund

      IV. Super Big Fund

    a. I, II, IV, and III

    b. I, II, III, and IV

    c. II, I, IV, and III

    d. II, I, III, and IV

15. Rank the following funds based on the Treynor index (highest to lowest):

      I.   Clinical Fund

    II.   Image Fund

    III. Measures Fund

    IV. Thumb Fund

  a. I, II, IV, and III

  b. I, II, III, and IV

  c. II, I, IV, and III

  d. II, I, III, and IV

16. Rank the following funds based on the Sharpe ratio (highest to lowest):

    I.   Germain Fund

    II.   Image Fund

    III. Multivariate Fund

    IV. Thumb Fund

  a. I, II, IV, and III

  b. I, II, III, and IV

  c. II, I, IV, and III

  d. IV, I, III, and II

17. Rank the following funds based on the Treynor index (highest to lowest):

    I.   Germain Fund

    II.   Image Fund

    III. Multivariate Fund

    IV. Thumb Fund

  a. I, II, IV, and III

  b. I, II, III, and IV

  c. II, IV, I, and III

  d. IV, I, III, and II

18. Which of the following funds has the highest alpha?

    a. Super Big Fund

    b. Thumb Fund

    c. Germain Fund

    d. Factors Fund

19. Assume that the correlation and standard deviation data for the bond funds are linked to the bond market index. Which bond fund has the highest alpha?

    a. Mobile Fund

    b. Fast Fund

    c. National Fund

    d. CDR Fund

20. Which of the following statements is correct?

    I.   High-yield bond funds are affected by both interest rate changes and changes in the economic performance of the company issuing the bonds.

    II.   Risk-adjusted performance can best be measured by beta.

    III. An investor who wanted to rank a list of diversified mutual funds could feel comfortable using the Treynor index.

    IV.   If an investor wanted to rank a list of sector funds, the Treynor index would be more appropriate than the Sharpe ratio.

    a. II only

    b. I and IV only

    c. I and III only

    d. II and IV only

Case 8

The Alpha Case

A RETIREMENT PLANNING MINI-CASE

Alpha Corporation is considering its alternatives in relation to establishing a retirement plan for its employees. Please help the CFO of Alpha Corporation answer the following questions:

Case Questions

1. Alpha Corporation has one-hundred full-time nonunion employees. What is the minimum number of employees that must be allowed to participate in the company's defined benefit plan?

    a. 40

    b. 50

    c. 75

    d. 100

2. The CFO would like to implement a 401(k)/profit sharing plan. If 75 percent of the firm's employees stay with the company for only two years (i.e., the firm has high turnover), and the remainder stay for an average of at least ten years, which vesting schedule should the CFO choose if she wants to minimize plan administration costs?

    a. 2-6 year graduated

    b. 3-year cliff

    c. 3-7 year graduated

    d. 5-year cliff

3.   Jana, age twenty-five, has worked for Alpha Corporation on a part-time basis (i.e., 900 hours per year) for four years. Is she eligible to participate in the firm's 401(k) plan?

    a.   Yes, because she is older than age twenty-one.

    b.   No, because she has not accumulated enough hours for the year.

    c.   Yes, because she has worked for more than two years.

    d.   No, because she has not worked for at least five years.

4.   The CFO's husband, Bud (age forty-three), also works at Alpha Corporation. He earns $28,000. He just contributed $3,000 to a Roth IRA. When must he begin taking distributions from the Roth IRA?

    a.   Never

    b.   At age 59½

    c.   At age 70½

    d.   At age 75

5.   The CFO would like to establish a deferred compensation plan for herself. She wants any money contributed to the plan to be protected from the firm's creditors. Which nonqualified deferred compensation plan should she choose?

    a.   A rabbi trust

    b.   A secular trust

    c.   A 457 plan

    d.   An unfunded promise-to-pay plan

6.   The CFO feels bad about having a plan for the exclusive benefit of key employees, including herself. She would like you to recommend a qualified plan that would allow her to restrict employee contributions but would permit the firm to make contributions as a tool to increase employee productivity. Which of the following three plans should she use?

    I.   A defined benefit plan

    II.   A stock bonus plan

    III.   An ESOP

    a.   I only

    b.   II only

    c.   II or III only

    d.   I, II, or III

7. Which type of plan should the CFO choose if she wants Alpha Corporation to absolutely guarantee benefits to eligible employees (i.e., employees will know exactly how much they will receive when they retire)?

    a.   A 401(k) plan

    b.   A profit-sharing plan

    c.   A target benefit plan

    d.   A defined benefit plan

8. Micala, an employee of Alpha Corporation, is fifty-three years old. She is considering divorcing her husband Jack. They have been married for nine years. If Micala gets a divorce, is she eligible to receive a spousal benefit from Jack's Social Security benefit?

    a.   No, because they have not been married for ten years.

    b.   Yes, because they have been married for at least five years.

    c.   No, because as someone with a job she can claim only her own Social Security benefit.

    d.   Yes, because she is younger than age sixty at the time of divorce.

9. Christina (age forty-one) terminates employment with Alpha Corporation, and she rolls over her 401(k) account balance to an IRA. Which of the following statements is true, assuming that she takes the money directly before rolling it over?

    I.   She must roll over the full amount of the distribution within sixty days to avoid taxation and penalties.

    II.   If she distributes $200,000 from the 401(k) plan, she must roll over $160,000 to avoid a penalty.

    III. If she fails to roll over the full distribution, she will incur a 10 percent penalty.

    a.   I only

    b.   III only

    c.   I and II only

    d.   I and III only

10. Which of the following health insurance options does Christina have as a result of quitting her job with Alpha Corporation?

    a.   She is ineligible for COBRA coverage because Alpha Corporation employs fewer than one-hundred employees.

    b.   She is eligible for COBRA coverage because Alpha Corporation employs more than twenty employees.

c.   COBRA coverage will cover expenses associated only with pre-existing conditions.

d.   Both b and c are correct.

Case 9

The Edwards Case

A RETIREMENT AND EMPLOYEE BENEFITS MINI-CASE

Nick Edwards owns a used car dealership. He is age sixty, has worked in the business for thirty years, and earns $110,000 per year. He has several employees with varying years of experience and tenure at the dealership. As the owner of the company, Nick has come to you for advice regarding the establishment of a retirement plan. He is also interested in learning more about employee benefits as a tool to help him recruit and retain good salespersons.

Over the course of several weeks of meetings with Nick you have compiled a list of attributes he would like to see in a retirement plan:

- He wants his employees to contribute to the plan.

- He is willing to match employee contributions if necessary.

- He wants the plan to be an incentive to increase productivity.

- He is willing to pay all of the plan's administrative costs.

- He would prefer not to assume any investment risk on the part of employees.

- He would be happy with a payroll deduction for his firm of 10 percent to 15 percent per year.

- Although he is willing to match contributions, he would prefer to maintain flexibility so that in low-profit years he could skip matching if needed.

- He does not want 100 percent immediate vesting for employees.

- He has no opinion regarding the ability of employees to make in-service withdrawals.

- He would like to maximize his own benefits, but not at the expense of running afoul of IRS highly compensated employee rules.

You have learned that, in addition to retirement benefits, Nick offers a mix of employee benefits, including life, health, and disability insurance for his employees. Information about these plans is summarized below:

- Group term life insurance equal to two times annual earnings.

    o Figure VI.15 shows the cost per $1,000 of life insurance protection offered through an employer on a monthly basis for tax purposes

- Group health insurance benefits

    o Traditional plan with a $500 annual deductible and 80/20 coinsurance provision

    o Out-of-pocket maximum equal to $5,000 annually

    o Benefit coverage includes employee and spouse only

    o Financed 100 percent through the dealership

- Group short-term disability insurance

    o Benefit equal to 50 percent of salary for six months

    o thirty-day waiting period

Figure VI.15 Cost per $1,000 of Employer-provided Life Insurance Protection

Attained Age on Last Day of Employee's Tax Year	Cost Per $1,000 of Protection for One-month Period
Under 25	$.05
25–29	.06
30–34	.08
35–39	.09
40–44	.10
45–49	.15
50–54	.23
55 – 59	.43
6 –64	.66
65–69	1.27
70 and above	2.06

Nick's best employee is Emily James. Emily has worked at the dealership full-time for seven years. She is fifty-six years old and makes $74,000 per year. Other employees' relevant data are shown in Figure VI.16.

Figure VI.16 Relevant Employee Data

Name	Salary	Years w/Firm	Age	Status
Kate	$36,000	6	28	Full-time employee
Mark	$32,000	4	47	Full-time employee
Joyce	$32,000	4	34	Full-time employee
Bill	$30,000	2	36	Full-time employee
Jack	$15,000	3	20	Part-time employee (< 1,000 hours/year)
Andy	$12,000	1	17	Part-time employee (< 1,000 hours/year)
Mary	$6,000	1	19	Part-time employee (< 1,000 hours/year)

Use this information to answer the following questions.

Case Questions

1. How much must Emily James report in yearly § 79 income (rounded) for tax purposes, assuming she stays employed for the year?

    a. $42

    b. $98

    c. $506

    d. $6,000

2. Nick purchased a $100,000 participating whole-life insurance policy on his life. To date, he has paid $50,000 in total premiums and received $10,000 in dividends. The policy currently has a net cash value of $15,000 and is subject to a $30,000 outstanding loan. If Nick decides to surrender the policy, he would realize a gain of:

    a. $0

    b. $5,000

    c. $10,000

    d. $15,000

3. Currently, Nick's brother Tommy owns an auto repair shop across town. Tommy owns the shop as a sole proprietorship. Nick has suggested that Tommy think about converting the shop to a corporation. Advantages for incorporating the repair shop into a C corporation include which of the following?

    I.   Allowing the flow-through of corporate profits to shareholders that could be taxed at each owner's marginal tax bracket.

    II. Withdrawing accumulated profits at capital gain rates.

    III. Providing tax-favored fringe benefits to employee shareholders.

    IV. Changing the form of business with ease once a corporation has been formed.

    a. II only

    b. III only

    c. I and III only

    d. I and IV only

4. Assuming that Nick is most interested in implementing a retirement plan that offers flexibility, low costs, and limited paperwork and regulation, he should consider establishing a:

    a. Cash balance plan

    b. 401(k) plan

    c. Roth 401(k) plan

    d. SIMPLE plan

    e. Stock bonus plan

5. Based on Nick's desires, as outlined in the list you developed, which of the following plans would meet his needs?

    I.   A 403(b) plan

    II. A profit sharing plan

    III. A stock bonus plan

    IV. A defined benefit plan

    a. I and IV only

    b. II and IV only

    c. II and III only

d. I, II, and III only

e. II, III, and IV only

6. Using the most restrictive vesting schedule and participation rules available, Nick can exclude which of the following employees from participating in a qualified defined contribution plan?

    I. Bill

    II. Jack

    III. Andy

    IV. Mary

a. I and II only

b. II and III only

c. I and IV only

d. I, II, and III only

e. II, III, and IV only

7. Nick is concerned about how he will fund contributions to a defined contribution plan. You recommend that he use a unit formula based on employee compensation and years of service. The formula is calculated using one unit of credit for each year of service and one unit of credit for each $10,000 in earnings. If Nick is willing to allocate $30,000 in total contributions in any given year, using a total allocation of 80 units (and disregarding any key employee or top-heavy restrictions), what is the maximum amount that will be contributed to Nick's account?

a. $9,675

b. $13,225

c. $15,375

d. $22,750

8. Nick's daughter, who is hoping one day to take over ownership of the dealership, is interested in your discussion with her father. She would like her father to receive the maximum plan benefit available before and after retirement. She would also like to establish a plan that guarantees her father a steady source of income during retirement. If you follow the daughter's desires, which of the following plans would be most appropriate?

a. A SIMPLE plan

b. A money purchase plan

c. A stock bonus plan

    d.   A defined benefit plan

    e.   A target benefit plan

9.   Nick is intrigued by his daughter's idea. However, he is still adamant about providing the best possible benefits to his employees, in addition to himself. The thought of maximizing tax deductions for contributions is something he would like to consider. Assuming that the dealership has steady to increasing levels of cash flow, which of the following plan(s) would be most appropriate?

       I.   A defined benefit plan

      II.   A target benefit plan

     III.   A 401(k) plan

     IV.   A stock bonus plan

      V.   A Roth 401(k) plan

    a.   I and V only

    b.   I and II only

    c.   IV and V only

    d.   II, III, and IV only

    e.   I, II, III, and V only

10. Joyce, one of Nick's employees, has come to you for advice. She would like guidance on choosing between contributing to a defined contribution plan and a Roth IRA. Assuming that Nick establishes a 401(k) plan, which of the following statements is true for Joyce?

    a.   If Nick's firm matches contributions to the 401(k) plan, she should contribute to the plan at least to the point of obtaining the match.

    b.   Under no circumstances will the 401(k) plan provide a better after-tax return than the Roth IRA.

    c.   If Joyce believes that tax rates in retirement will be higher than rates today, she should contribute to the 401(k) plan rather than the Roth IRA.

    d.   Regardless of employer matching, Joyce should maximize her contribution to the Roth IRA before contributing to the defined contribution plan.

Case 10

The Mayfield Case

A RETIREMENT PLANNING MINI-CASE

Peter and Ann Mayfield, both age fifty-two, recently sought your help in planning their financial future. Peter is the Anytown, Anystate, city manager. His wife is active in many civic organizations but not employed outside of the home. They live at 123 Maple Street, in Anytown. They have been married for slightly more than twenty-five years.

Their two children, Nick and Nedra, have both moved away from home and started their own families. In fact, Nick and his wife have two children, Lisa and Timmy, ages three and two, respectively. Figure VI.17 presents additional information about the Mayfields.

Additional Personal Information

Figure VI.17 The Mayfields' Personal Information

Occupation—Peter	City Manager
	123 Elm Street
	Anytown, Anystate 01010
	26 years of employment
Occupation—Ann	Homemaker
	26 years of employment

Global Assumptions (Valid unless otherwise Specified in Certain Instances)

- Inflation: 3 percent

- All income and expense figures are given in today's dollars.

- Federal marginal tax bracket: 25 percent

- State marginal tax bracket: 4.5 percent

- Any qualified plan or IRA contribution growth rates are assumed to stop at the federally mandated limit unless otherwise restricted.

- All nominal rates of return are pretax returns.

- They are currently qualified for Social Security benefits.

Income Issues

Peter currently earns $90,000 per year and expects his salary to increase at 3 percent per year until retirement. As shown in Figure VI.18, Peter contributes 10 percent of his salary to his employer-sponsored 403(b) plan. He receives a 33 percent match from the city. Ann and Peter are covered by an employer-sponsored health care plan, which has a premium of only $50 per month and is paid for directly out of Peter's paycheck on a pretax basis. The Mayfields currently use interest earned from their municipal bond holdings to supplement their income.

Dedicated and Discretionary Expenses

Figure VI.18 The Mayfields' Dedicated and Discretionary Expenses

Source of Expense	Amount	Frequency
Pretax medical premiums	$600	Annually
403(b) contributions	$750	Monthly
Social Security withholdings	$6,839	Annually
Federal tax withholdings	$10,000	Annually
State tax withholdings	$3,400	Annually
Mortgage payment (P&I)	$511.63	Monthly
Credit card payments	$450	Annually
Auto insurance	$550	Semi-Annually
Homeowner's insurance	$50	Monthly
Life insurance (private policy)	$780	Annually
Other insurance	Not calculated by client	
Umbrella policy	$150	Annually
Peter's traditional IRA contribution	$2,000	Annually
Ann's traditional IRA contribution	$2,000	Annually
Unallocated savings	$1,000	Quarterly
Subscriptions	$50	Monthly
Telephone charges	$1,560	Annually
Alarm system	$40	Monthly
Internet and cable	$90	Monthly
Hobbies	$100	Monthly
Recreation	$400	Monthly
Health club dues	$90	Monthly
Groceries	$3,900	Annually
Eating-out expenses	$4,900	Annually
Real estate taxes	$1,600	Annually
Household maintenance	$90	Monthly
Utilities	$2,160	Annually
Clothing	$1,700	Annually
Dry cleaning	$60	Monthly
Personal care	$100	Monthly
Stereo equipment	$800	Annually
Yard maintenance service	$900	Annually
Eye glasses	$725	Annually
Health insurance co-pays	$500	Annually
Prescriptions	$400	Annually
Other medical expenses	$350	Annually

Figure VI.18 The Mayfields' Dedicated and Discretionary Expenses (*cont'd*)

Source of Expense	Amount	Frequency
Gas and car maintenance	$800	Semi-annually
Car licenses (not tax deductible)	$250	Annually
Parking in city	$100	Annually
Trains and taxis in city	$300	Annually
Personal property tax	$750	Annually
Safe deposit fees	$40	Monthly
Bank fees	$4	Monthly
IRA fees	$45	Annually
Tax preparation fees	$450	Annually
Charitable contributions	$300	Monthly
Business travel*	$1,500	Annually
Vacations	$1,000	Quarterly
Business expenses*	$250	Annually
Alcohol expenses	$250	Semi-annually
Postage stamps	$125	Annually
Gifts to children/grandchildren	$1,300	Semi-annually
Other misc. expenses	$500	Annually
*Peter's employer does not reimburse these expenses.		

Asset and Liability Information

Figure VI.19 presents the Mayfields' asset and liability information.

Figure VI.19 The Mayfields' Assets and Liabilities

Asset/Liability	Value	Notes
Checking account	$13,000	No interest earned on asset
Municipal money market fund (general obligations)	$240,000	2.50% federal annual tax-free yield
I-bonds*	$42,000	Market value
Peter's 401(k)	$975,000	Invested in equities
Peter's traditional IRA	$52,000	Invested in equities
Ann's traditional IRA	$35,000	Invested in equities
Primary residence	$375,000	
Mazda	$6,700	5 years old
Honda	$5,200	6 years old
Household furnishings	$30,000	
Yard equipment	$7,500	
Other misc. assets	$14,000	
Visa credit card	$2,500	14.90% interest rate
MasterCard	$4,000	9.90% interest rate
Discover card	$1,000	18.90% interest rate
Macy's credit card	$500	21.00% interest rate
First mortgage	$25,685	Home purchased 25 years ago; $75,000 financed at 7.25% for 30 years; 300 payments made to date

Note: All nonretirement assets are jointly owned.

*The I bonds have been owned for 4 years.

Tax Information

The Mayfields' marginal state tax rate is 4.5 percent. The state income tax is tied to the federal AGI figure. The Mayfields are eligible for two state exemptions in the amount of $1,300 each and a state standard deduction of $10,000. The Mayfields are also eligible for $6,000 in state income tax adjustments. The municipal money market mutual fund is made up of general Anystate state obligations.

Insurance Information and Planning Issues

Life Insurance

Peter purchased a $250,000 ten-year term policy when he turned age fifty. Peter is the owner and insured. Ann is the beneficiary. In addition, Peter's employer provides him with a group term policy in the amount of one times his salary. When estimating life insurance needs, the Mayfields would like to make the following assumptions:

- Life expectancy: age ninety-five each

- Final expense needs: $12,000 each

- Estate administration needs: Peter: $36,500; Ann: $9,500

- Other immediate needs: $12,000 each

- They would like to pay off all debts at the first death.

- Anticipated expense needs at first death: $85,000 per year before and after retirement (in today's dollars).

- They believe they can earn 6 percent on any proceeds from insurance prior to retirement.

- They believe they can earn 5 percent on insurance proceeds after retirement.

- They anticipate being in a combined 25 percent federal and state marginal tax bracket after retirement.

- Projected inflation rate: 3 percent

- In the event of a spouse's death, Peter and Ann plan to stop working and collect early Social Security benefits at age sixty. They will receive $16,500 at that time.

- For conservative planning purposes, the Mayfields do not plan to use interest and/or dividends as an income source when planning insurance needs.

- Full retirement benefits, at age sixty-six, are $23,580.

- In addition to Peter's life insurance, they are willing to use all of their retirement, investments, and monetary assets to meet insurance needs.

Disability Insurance

Peter's employer provides both short- and long-term disability coverage. His short-term coverage pays 100 percent of his earned income for the first six months of disability. There is no wait period for this coverage. Peter's long-term coverage has a six-month wait period and pays a benefit equal to 60 percent of earned income until age sixty-five. All premiums, for both policies, are employer paid. If Peter were to become disabled, they would not continue to save for other goals. In case of disability:

- Total household expenses in the event of death or disability are $85,000.

- When calculating life insurance needs, the Mayfields are willing to use all their combined retirement savings to offset insurance needs.

- The Mayfields assume that in the event of a possible disability neither will be eligible for Social Security disability benefits.

- For life insurance planning purposes only, they would like to replace $85,000 per year, in today's dollars, for retirement.

Long-term Care Insurance

The Mayfields do not currently have long-term care insurance.

Retirement Information and Planning Issues

The following information should be used when evaluating the Mayfields' current retirement planning situation:

- Peter does not have a defined benefit plan at this time.

- Retirement age for reduced Social Security benefits is age sixty-two; they plan to retire and take benefits at the earliest possible date.

- Retirement age for full Social Security benefits is age sixty-six.

- Their individual life expectancies are ninety-five years of age.

- In the event of the death of one spouse, the surviving spouse is eligible to receive $16,500 per year starting at age sixty from Social Security.

- At age sixty-two, Peter's annual Social Security benefit will be $17,950 in today's dollars; Ann is eligible to receive a survivor benefit equal to $8,367.

- At age sixty-six, Peter's annual Social Security benefit will be $24,420 in today's dollars; Ann is eligible to receive one-half of this amount.

- At age seventy, Peter's annual Social Security benefit will be $32,900 in today's dollars; Ann is eligible to receive a survivor benefit.

- They would like to replace $90,000 in yearly income, in today's pretax dollars, on their first day of retirement. (Note that this figure is different from the assumption they want to use for insurance planning purposes.)

- Ann is the beneficiary of Peter's qualified retirement plan assets.

- For retirement planning purposes only, they believe that they can earn a 7.6 percent rate of return prior to retirement and a 5 percent rate of return after retirement.

- Inflation before and after retirement is expected to be 3 percent.

- Peter's salary will increase at the rate of inflation.

- All annual retirement savings will increase by the rate of inflation (3 percent) prior to retirement.

- The Mayfields are willing to assume that they will remain in the same marginal tax bracket after they retire.

- All nonretirement assets are owned as JTWROS at this time.

Estate Information and Planning Issues

- Final funeral, burial, and medical expenses for life insurance and estate planning purposes will be $12,000 each.

- Estate administration costs are anticipated to be $1,500, and executor fees will be approximately $35,000 for Peter and $8,000 for Ann.

- In the event of death, the Mayfields will need approximately $12,000 to cover immediate needs.

- They would like to leave a legacy for their grandchildren by fully funding both children's college education costs should Peter or Ann die.

- Assumed investment return on assets in the event that one spouse dies is 6.00 percent annually.

- The value of the surviving spouse's net estate is expected to grow by 4.00 percent annually.

Additional Planning Assumptions

The Mayfields would like to maintain their monetary assets as an emergency fund if possible, and use interest earned as a "slush fund" while in retirement.

Goals and Objectives

The Mayfields are very much looking forward to retirement. They hope to spend more time with their growing grandchildren. Given this goal, they plan to retire when Peter turns age sixty-two. They would like to know if they are currently on track to meet this goal.

Their second goal involves establishing an education funding plan to help their grandchildren pay for college expenses. They would like to fund one year of college tuition and room and board for each grandchild. Tuition plus expenses for colleges they have looked at average $18,000 per year. They believe that college costs will continue to rise at a 6 percent rate, but to offset some of this increase they are comfortable assuming an 8 percent rate of return in a tax-advantaged education savings account, which is roughly equivalent to a 5.5 percent after-tax rate of return.

Use the information provided in this narrative to answer the following case questions.

Case Questions

1. How much money market fund income did the Mayfields earn during the year?

    a. $0

    b. $6,000

    c. $6,325

    d. $7,200

2. Which of the following statements is true?

    I.   Peter must report $110 in § 79 income for tax purposes.

    II. Because Peter is over age fifty, he does not need to report § 79 income.

    III. § 79 income helps reduce a client's taxable income.

    IV. § 79 income should be accounted for as a taxable expense on the income and expense statement.

    II only

    I and II only

    I and IV only

    II and III only

    II, III, and IV only

3. How much of the Mayfields' gross income is considered total income for tax purposes on IRS Form 1040?

    a. $96,110

    b. $90,000

    c. $86,510

    d. $80,510

4. All of the following statements about the Mayfields' level of discretionary cash flow are *incorrect* except:

   a. After paying all dedicated and discretionary expenses, the Mayfields have a negative cash flow.

   b. Total dedicated expenses are greater than discretionary expenses.

   c. Savings expenses make up the largest dedicated/fixed expense item for the Mayfields.

   d. The Mayfields' savings ratio, including employer matching contributions, exceeds 10 percent.

5. Which of the following are strengths related to the Mayfields' financial situation?

   a. Their savings rate, as measured by the savings ratio, is acceptable at this time.

   b. Their debt as a percentage of net worth is low as measured by industry ratios.

   c. They could easily pay off all of their debt using monetary assets.

   d. All of the above.

6. Which of the following is true?

   a. The Mayfields should choose to itemize deductions on IRS Form Schedule A.

   b. Given their age, they will receive enhanced personal exemptions for this year's taxes.

   c. They can claim a tax credit for gifts made to their grandchild this year.

   d. The Mayfields' standard deduction is greater than their itemized deduction.

   e. Both a and b are correct.

7. During a benefits presentation for all city employees, the presenter talked about the need for those in attendance to think about long-term care needs. Peter was shocked to learn how much one year of nursing home care would cost. He is worried about depleting assets if he or his wife should need this type of care. He wants to know whether he and his wife should purchase long-term care insurance. Which of the following statements best represents the strategy that the Mayfields should consider?

   a. Purchase long-term care insurance because their net worth, exclusive of home value, is less than $1.5 million.

   b. They do not need long-term care insurance because they can afford to self-insure the costs of care.

   c. They should expect to spend down assets to a point where they will become eligible for Medicaid, and as such, they do not need long-term care insurance.

   d. They do not need long-term care insurance because they can use a combination of assets, Medicare funding, and Medicaid reimbursement to fund care needs.

8. Peter was recently approached by a financial adviser who wanted Peter to consider investing in a variable annuity for retirement. A few days later the adviser called Peter again and said that a variable universal life (VUL) insurance policy could also be used to fund retirement needs. Which of the following statement(s) is (are) true in relation to annuities and VULs?

  I.   Given their favorable tax treatment, variable annuities and VUL policies allow earnings to grow tax deferred until withdrawn.

  II.   Distributions from the annuity, after age 59½, will be taxed at the long-term capital gain rate if the annuity has been in existence for at least one year.

  III. Distributions from the VUL policy, if made in the form of a loan, will be taxed at the Mayfields' marginal tax rate.

  IV.   Distributions in the form of a VUL loan need not be reported on IRS Form 1040 for tax purposes.

  a. I and II only

  b. III and IV only

  c. I and IV only

  d. II, III, and IV only

9. Reducing a client's life expectancy assumption will have which of the following effects?

  a. Increase the amount of life insurance needed.

  b. Decrease the amount of retirement assets needed.

  c. Increase the amount of retirement assets needed.

  d. Both a and c are correct.

10. Which of the following disability insurance statements is true?

  a. All of the benefits received by Peter from his disability coverage will be taxable because his employer paid the premium.

  b. None of the benefits received by Peter from his disability coverage will be taxable because his employer paid the premium.

  c. If Ann becomes disabled, she is eligible for coverage under her state's workers' compensation program.

  d. Both a and c are correct.

  e. Both b and c are correct.

11. Peter and Ann have been discussing the possibility of retiring as early as age sixty. What do the Mayfields need to consider as factors that will impact the costs, risks, and benefits of this objective when conducting their planning?

   a. Distributions from their qualified retirement plans at that time will be subject to a 10 percent early withdrawal penalty.

   b. They can deal with the loss of health insurance by extending their current health insurance coverage using both COBRA and HIPAA benefits until age sixty-five, at which time they will be eligible to enroll in Medicare.

   c. The cost of Medicare will increase dramatically for each year that they postpone enrolling after age sixty.

   d. None of the above.

12. Which of the following strategies should the Mayfields consider to increase their level of discretionary cash flow?

   a. Pay off credit card debt with monetary assets.

   b. Open a home equity line of credit.

   c. Increase contributions to Peter's 403(b).

   d. Increase IRS W-4 withholdings on an annual basis.

   e. A and b only.

13. If Peter and Ann want to pay off their credit card debt, which of the following assets should they use first?

   a. Money market fund

   b. Proceeds from a 403(b) loan

   c. I-bonds

   d. Home equity

14. Suppose that the Mayfields decide to retire at age sixty. How much do they need in assets at that time to fund income needs from ages sixty–sixty-two, assuming that they still want $90,000 (in today's dollars) in annual income starting on their first day of retirement?

   a. $114,009

   b. $225,847

   c. $228,018

   d. $231,438

15. Peter and Ann are concerned about estate planning details. They have heard about income in respect of a decedent (IRD). They realize that their retirement plans could be subject to IRD taxation. Which of the following statements is true in relation to IRD property?

    I.   IRD property will be included in the Mayfields' estates at fair market value.

    II.   IRD property does not receive a step-up in basis.

    III. IRD property is subject to income taxation when the heir or estate collects income from the property.

    IV. IRD property will be included in the Mayfields' estates at a step-up in basis value.

    a.   I and III only

    b.   II and IV only

    c.   I, II, and III only

    d.   II, III, and IV only

16. Which of the following factors should help drive the Mayfields' decision to fund a capital preservation approach of retirement planning compared to a capital depletion method?

    a.   Their desire to leave a legacy at the death of the second spouse.

    b.   Their willingness to dedicate additional cash flow today to fund the higher retirement asset need in the future.

    c.   Their willingness to decrease their income replacement ratio assumption.

    d.   All of the above.

17. Calculating the future value of regular savings using a geometrically varying annuity assumption will tend to:

    a.   reduce the future value of the asset.

    b.   reduce the tax liability of the asset.

    c.   increase the future value of the asset.

    d.   increase the interest rate used to calculate future value.

18. Peter and Ann would like to establish a gifting program for their grandchildren. They have two desires. First, they want to implement a strategy that does not allow the grandchildren to access principal prior to age twenty-one, except to pay expenses for the welfare of the child. Second, they want to maintain the maximum flexibility in terms of the types of assets that they can gift. Which of the following alternatives meet(s) their desires?

    a.   A Uniform Gifts to Minors Act account

    b.   A § 2503(b) trust

    c.   A § 2503(c) trust

    d.   All of the above

    e.   B or c only

19. What is (are) the advantage(s) associated with suggesting prepaying the Mayfields' mortgage at this time?

    a.   The loss of the interest deduction will require them to claim the standard deduction.

    b.   Their annual level of discretionary cash flow will increase, which can be used to fund other financial goals and objectives.

    c.   They will have the satisfaction of knowing that they own their home outright.

    d.   All of the above.

    e.   B and c only.

20. The Mayfields should consider which of the following estate planning strategies to reduce the likelihood of owing federal estate taxes in the future?

    a.   Maximizing use of the marital deduction.

    b.   Gifting strategies to reduce the value of Peter's gross estate.

    c.   Using a credit equivalency or bypass trust arrangement.

    d.   A and b only.

    e.   B and c only.

Discussion Question

Describe how the Mayfields' asset allocation approach may need to change as they get closer to their retirement goal.

Case 11

The Dion Case

AN ESTATE PLANNING MINI-CASE

Marcel and Clio Dion are taking steps to begin evaluating their estate planning situation. Marcel is sixty years old. Clio is fifty-three years old. They have two children, ages thirteen and eighteen. Marcel is a successful executive with a Fortune 500 company, and Clio has achieved success as a cosmetics home sales trainer.

Currently, their wills state that if either Marcel or Clio were to pass away, the surviving spouse would inherit everything. Both Marcel and Clio value their privacy, but they have not established a trust at this time. They have an interest in providing charitable support to their church, but they have not made any sizable contributions. Figure VI.20 summarizes their asset, liability, and estate expense situation.

Figure VI.20 Asset, Liability, and Expense Situation for the Dion Family

Assets	Value	Ownership
Checking account	$26,000	JTWROS
Savings account	$20,000	JTWROS
Money market account	$90,000	JTWROS
Other monetary assets	$0	JTWROS
EE/I bonds	$100,000	JTWROS
Mutual funds (basis less than fair market value)	$1,720,000	JTWROS
Other investment assets	$250,000	JTWROS
Primary residence	$700,000	JTWROS
Other housing assets (vacation home)	$240,000	JTWROS
Vehicles	$86,000	JTWROS
Personal property	$134,000	JTWROS
Retirement assets (e.g., 401(k) and IRA)	$768,000	Marcel

Figure VI.20 Asset, Liability, and Expense Situation for the Dion Family (*cont'd*)

Assets	Value	Ownership
Retirement assets (e.g., 401(k) and IRA)	$345,000	Clio
Other assets	$48,000	Jointly held but not titled
Life insurance (variable universal life)*	$1,500,000	Marcel
Life insurance (universal life)	$250,000	Clio
Liabilities	**Value**	**Ownership**
Mortgage on vacation home	$112,000	Joint
Debts	$86,000	Joint
Expenses	**Costs**	
Funeral and final expenses assumed the same for both	$25,000	

*Clio is the beneficiary of Marcel's policy, and Marcel is the beneficiary of Clio's policy.

Use this information to answer the questions that follow:[1]

Case Questions

1. Identify the statement(s) below that correctly characterize(s) property interests held by Marcel that, at death, pass by operation of law.

    I.   If the property passes according to the operation of law, the property avoids probate.

    II. If the property passes according to the operation of law, it will not be included in the decedent's gross estate.

    III. Property that passes by operation of law cannot qualify for the marital deduction.

    IV. The titling on the instrument determines who shall receive the property.

    a. I only

    b. I, II, and III only

    c. I and IV only

    d. I, II, and IV only

    e. II and III only

---

2. As Marcel and Clio think about the value of their adjusted gross estate, they are unsure which assets and expenses might be deductible. Which of the following is a deduction from the gross estate used to calculate the adjusted gross estate?

    a. Costs associated with maintaining estate assets.

    b. Nontaxable gifts made within three years.

    c. Federal estate tax marital deduction.

    d. Property inherited from others.

3. Currently, the Dions own their personal residence as JTWROS. If instead they owned the property as a tenancy by the entirety, how could this form of ownership be terminated?

    I. Death, whereby the survivor takes the property.

    II. Mutual agreement.

    III. Divorce, which converts the estate into a tenancy in common or a joint tenancy.

    IV. Severance, whereby one spouse transfers his or her interest to a third party without the consent of the other spouse.

    a. IV only

    b. I and III only

    c. II and IV only

    d. I, II, and III only

    e. I, II, III, and IV

4. One of Marcel's primary financial planning goals includes making lifetime gifts to his children. He would like to do this to help his children and to reduce his potential estate tax liability. If he moves forward with his plan to maximize the value of the strategy, he should make gifts of property that:

    I. are expected to depreciate in the future.

    II. are expected to appreciate in the future.

    III. have already depreciated significantly.

    a. I only

    b. II only

    c. III only

    d.   I and III only

    e.   I, II, and III

5.   What is the value of Marcel's adjusted gross estate if he were to pass away today and before Clio?

    a. $2,475,000

    b. $3,225,000

    c. $3,851,000

    d. $3,975,000

6.   There are several weaknesses associated with the Dions' current estate plan. Which of the following are the significant weaknesses within their plan?

    I.   Failure to utilize the marital deduction.

    II.   Failure to maximize the unified credit.

    III.   Failure to utilize charitable gift strategies to reduce the taxable estate.

    IV.   Failure to avoid probate.

    a.   I and III only

    b.   II and IV only

    c.   I, II, and III only

    d.   II, III, and IV only

    e.   I, II, III, and IV

7.   In view of combined estate values for Marcel and Clio, and knowing that one of their planning objectives is the reduction of estate taxes, which of the following estate planning techniques might be appropriate?

    I.   Placing the life insurance policies in an irrevocable trust.

    II.   Establishing a revocable living trust and funding it by using the unlimited marital deduction and the full unified credit.

    III.   Making use of the gift tax annual exclusion.

    IV.   Establishing a qualified terminable interest property (QTIP) trust to pass property to their children.

    a.   II and III only

    b.   I and III only

   c.   II and IV only

   d.   II, III, and IV only

   e.   I, II, III, and IV

8.   Calculate Clio's taxable estate assuming that Marcel passes away first, followed closely by Clio's death.

   a. $6,029,000

   b. $6,484,000

   c. $7,860,000

   d. $7,736,000

   e. $7,984,000

9.   The Dions are considering making a sizable charitable gift to their local university using assets held in their mutual fund accounts. The primary purpose of their gift strategy is to reduce their taxable estate while providing a benefit for the university. Which of the following strategies will maximize the effectiveness of this estate planning strategy?

   a.   Give the mutual funds first to their oldest child, who can then sell them with a stepped-up basis and use the proceeds as a donation to the university.

   b.   Donate the mutual funds directly to the university and allow the university to sell the funds.

   c.   Sell the mutual funds first and then donate the cash proceeds to the university.

   d.   Transfer the mutual funds to a noncharitable irrevocable trust and then donate the trust income to the university.

10.   The local university has approached the Dions about making a charitable contribution. After discussing the possibility of making a donation, Marcel and Clio have decided that they would be willing to make the donation if they could receive an immediate tax deduction and income based on a fixed percentage of the amount donated (valued annually). They would also like to have the ability to increase their donation amount in future years. Which of the following charitable giving alternatives best serves the Dions' desires?

   a.   A charitable remainder unitrust.

   b.   A charitable remainder annuity trust.

   c.   A pooled income fund.

   d.   A grantor retained annuity trust.

Case 12

The Graham Case

A GENERAL PLANNING MINI-CASE

Onslo Graham is fifty-nine years of age. His wife, Daisy, is age fifty-eight. They have been married for nearly thirty years. The Grahams currently live at 3456 Speedway, Anycity, Anystate 01010. They have an adult child, Rose, who recently turned age twenty-eight. Rose also lives in Anycity.

Because of their strong relationship, they have tended to own all of their assets jointly even though Daisy has been a homemaker all of their married lives. Onslo does have one real estate asset that is not jointly owned.

Onslo is the general manager of Tarantula Industries, a closely held corporation, which owns a hockey team in an expanding southwestern minor league. The team is headquartered at 555 West Verity Road, Anycity, Anystate 01010. Onslo has been involved in professional sports management for nearly twenty-five years, and he currently earns $137,500 per year in income. Rose is also actively involved with the team. She works in the front office and manages day-to-day operations. Onslo and Daisy hope that Rose will eventually take over management of the team once Onslo retires.

Use the following information to conduct a review of the Grahams' financial situation.

Global Assumptions (Valid unless otherwise Specified in Certain Instances)

- Inflation: 4 percent

- All income and expense numbers are given in today's dollars.

- Planned retirement age: sixty-six for both

- Federal marginal tax bracket: 25 percent

- State marginal tax bracket: 4.72 percent

- Any qualified plan or IRA contribution growth rates are assumed to stop at the federally mandated limit unless otherwise restricted.

- All nominal rates of return are pretax returns.

- As of the date of the case, the Grahams are not subject to the alternative minimum tax (AMT).

- They are currently qualified for Social Security benefits.

Income Issues

Onslo currently earns $137,500 per year and expects his salary to increase at 5 percent per year until retirement. They also receive $15,403 in nonqualified dividends and interest from miscellaneous other investments, all of which are reinvested. Onslo and Daisy are covered by employer-sponsored health care. The premium, which is paid by Onslo directly, is $2,400 per year. Onslo also contributes $9,600 into a 401(k) plan. The plan provides matching at 33 cents on the dollar with no maximum beyond IRC statutory limitations. These expenses are paid for with pretax dollars.

Expense Summary

Based on his salary, Onslo had $27,000 withheld for federal, Social Security, and Medicare taxes. He also had $6,565 withheld for state taxes. Figure VI.21 summarizes other expenditures.

Figure VI.21 Other Dedicated and Discretionary Expenses for the Grahams

Expense	Amount	Frequency
Mortgage payments	$1,829.50	Monthly
Home equity loan payments	$286.67	Monthly
Auto payments	$483.33	Monthly
Credit card payments	$3,500.00	Annually
Auto insurance	$1,300.00	Semi-annually
Homeowners insurance	$450.00	Semi-annually
Life insurance	$3,200.00	Annually
Umbrella liability insurance	$125.00	Annually
Disability insurance	$2,250.00	Annually
IRA contributions (Daisy)	$2,000.00	Annually
IRA contributions (Onslo)	$2,000.00	Annually
Subscriptions	$500.00	Annually
Telephone expense	$91.67	Monthly
Home Internet	$50.00	Monthly
Hobbies (Daisy)	$500.00	Yearly

Figure VI.21 Other Dedicated and Discretionary Expenses for the Grahams (*cont'd*)

Expense	Amount	Frequency
Hobbies (Onslo)	$100.00	Yearly
Recreation/entertainment	$100.00	Monthly
Club dues	$500.00	Yearly
Groceries	$500.00	Monthly
Food away from home	$400.00	Monthly
Real estate taxes	$600.00	Semi-annually
Household maintenance	$200.00	Monthly
Utilities	$300.00	Monthly
Clothing (Daisy)	$300.00	Monthly
Clothing (Onslo)	$600.00	Semi-annually
Laundry services	$100.00	Monthly
Personal care	$100.00	Monthly
Furnishing	$1,000.00	Yearly
Yard maintenance	$100.00	Monthly
Medical copayments (Daisy)	$10.00	Monthly
Medical copayments (Onslo)	$10.00	Monthly
Prescriptions (Daisy)	$300.00	Yearly
Unreimbursed medical expenses	$10.00	Monthly
Gasoline	$100.00	Monthly
Car registrations	$320.00	Yearly
Parking and tolls	$400.00	Yearly
Personal property tax*	$450.00	Yearly
Safe deposit box fee	$100.00	Yearly
Monthly bank fees	$2.00	Monthly
IRA fees	$40.00	Yearly
Accounting fees	$400.00	Yearly
Charitable contributions	$400.00	Monthly
Travel expenses	$2,500.00	Yearly
Vacations	$2,500.00	Semi-annually
Alcohol expenses	$350.00	Annually
Gifts to family members (Daisy)	$500.00	Quarterly
Gifts to family members (Onslo)	$500.00	Annually
Other miscellaneous expenses	$500.00	Semi-annually

*Amount includes applicable car registration property tax.

Tax Issues

The Grahams complete their own tax returns using a nationally known tax preparation software package. Onslo pays his company's accountant to double-check his calculations. Onslo and Daisy file married filing jointly and they claim themselves as exemptions. They are currently in the Anystate 4.72 percent marginal tax bracket, where taxes are linked with the federal AGI figure. They are eligible for a $1,250 state standard deduction and a $275 exemption per person. Onslo is considered an employee of his firm and does not pay self-employment income taxes. The Grahams' assets are summarized in Figure VI.22. Their liabilities are summarized in Figure VI.23.

Asset Summary

Figure VI.22 Summary of the Grahams' Assets

Asset	Amount	Ownership
Financial Assets		
Checking account	$6,500	Joint
Savings account	$10,000	Joint
Taxable money market mutual fund	$230,000	Joint
I-bonds	$15,000	Joint
Government bond funds	$41,000	Joint
Corporate bond funds	$45,000	Joint
High-yield bond funds	$15,000	Joint
Large-cap funds	$151,600	Joint
Mid-cap funds	$70,600	Joint
Small-cap funds	$37,000	Joint
Rental real estate portfolio*	$2,100,000	Onslo
Retirement Assets		
Large-cap funds (401k)	$40,000	Onslo
Mid-cap funds (401k)	$35,000	Onslo
Small-cap funds (401k)	$15,000	Onslo
Corporate bond funds (401k)	$27,000	Onslo
International funds (IRA)	$19,000	Onslo
High-yield bond funds (IRA)	$17,500	Daisy

Figure VI.22 Summary of the Grahams' Assets (*cont'd*)

Asset	Amount	Ownership
Other Assets		
Primary residence	$375,000	Joint
Mazda MPV	$25,000	Joint
Ford Taurus	$7,800	Joint
Artwork	$2,500	Joint
Hockey collectibles	$1,500	Joint
Sporting/hobbies supplies	$3,500	Joint
14-foot aluminum boat	$7,000	Joint
Furniture	$28,000	Joint
Other assets	$6,500	Joint
*The rental real estate is income and tax neutral; the property does not generate income or losses for cash flow or tax purposes.		

Liability Summary

Figure VI.23 Summary of the Grahams' Liabilities

Liability	Amount	Ownership
Visa credit card	$12,000	Joint
MasterCard	$8,000	Joint
Discover card	$7,500	Joint
Garts sporting goods card	$5,000	Joint
Loan due in 45 days	$2,500	Onslo
Mortgage	$235,984	Joint
Home equity loan	$29,471	Joint
Mazda loan	$9,177	Joint

Loan Factors	Home Mortgage	Home Equity Loan	Mazda Loan
Original loan amount	$275,000	$30,000	$25,000
Interest rate	7.00%	8.00%	6.00%
Length of loan	30 Years	15 Years	5 Years
Number of payments made	120	6	40

Life Insurance Information and Planning Issues

Onslo and Daisy would like you to analyze their life insurance situation using the following assumptions and facts:

- In the event of a death, household expenses would drop to $105,000 per year.

- Final expenses (funeral and burial costs) will be $25,000 for each person.

- Estate and legal costs will be $69,930 for Onslo and $16,135 for Daisy.

- All outstanding liabilities will be paid at the first death.

- Other immediate needs should be funded with $10,000 each.

- They would like to plan conservatively in the event of a death by assuming a 6 percent before-tax rate of return on any insurance proceeds both pre- and post-retirement.

- They will be in a combined state and federal tax bracket of 30 percent before retirement.

- Full retirement age is sixty-six for both Onslo and Daisy.

- They would like to replace $90,000, before taxes, while in retirement for the surviving spouse.

- Daisy is eligible to receive $1,958 per month (in today's dollars) as a Social Security survivor benefit at age sixty-six (assumes that Onslo dies today).

- Onslo will receive $2,024 Social Security benefits per month (in today's dollars) in retirement at age sixty-six.

- They are eligible to receive survivor benefits equal to a 71.5 percent reduction in full benefits from age sixty to sixty-six.

- In the event of either spouse's death, the other spouse plans to stop working at age sixty and begin taking early retirement survivor benefits.

- For conservative planning purposes, the Grahams do not plan on using interest and/or dividends as an income source when determining insurance needs.

- They are willing to use all their retirement savings and $350,000 in other assets to offset life insurance needs.

- Onslo expects his salary to remain the same following Daisy's death.

- Daisy does not expect to work after Onslo's death.

Figure VI.24 summarizes life insurance policy information for Onslo and Daisy.

Figure VI.24 Life Insurance Policies

Policy Type	Face Value	Cash Value	Owner	Insured	Beneficiary	Premium
20-year term (12 years remaining)*	$250,000	NA	Onslo	Onslo	Daisy	Paid by Onslo and Daisy; $1,000 yearly
20-year term (20 years remaining)*	$150,000	NA	Onslo	Onslo	Daisy	Paid by Onslo and Daisy; $1,200 yearly
Group term	$50,000	NA	Onslo	Onslo	Daisy	Employer paid
Whole-life**	$100,000	$21,250	Onslo	Daisy	Rose	Paid by Onslo and Daisy; $1,000 yearly

*Both insurance companies are rated A by A.M. Best.

**Cash value at beginning of year was $21,250; current dividend is $100; an equivalent after-tax yield is 6 percent.

Disability Insurance Information and Planning Issues

The Grahams have not focused too heavily on disability planning issues. They do know that they do not want to account for Social Security benefits in the event of a disability. A few years ago Onslo purchased a long-term policy in the private market (not through a cafeteria plan at work). Information about the policy is summarized below:

- The policy is defined as own-occupation and is issued by an A.M. Best A-rated company.

- The policy has a six-month elimination period.

- The policy pays 50 percent of Onslo's current salary until age sixty-five.

- All premiums are paid with after-tax dollars.

- If disabled, they would like to continue to save for objectives.

Other Insurance Information and Planning Issues

The Grahams do not currently have a long-term care insurance policy. Both are healthy with both sets of parents still alive and well. In fact, Onslo and Daisy skate twice a week at the team's local indoor practice arena.

They have worked with the same property and casualty insurance agent for twenty-five years. Their agent encouraged them to purchase a $1-million umbrella policy four years ago. This required that the Grahams increase the split-limit coverage on their personal automobile policies to $100/$300/$100. Their current HO-3 homeowners policy provides 100 percent inflation protection coverage.

Current yield information for use when solving case questions is provided in Figure VI.25.

Current Yield Information

Figure VI.25

Investment Class	Yield
Checking account	0.00%
Savings account	2.00%
Taxable money market fund	3.00%
Anystate municipal money market fund	2.40%
EE savings bonds	3.50%
I bonds	4.50%
Government bonds	4.50%
Corporate bonds	5.00%
High-yield bonds	6.50%
Real estate	3.75%
Gold	0.00%
Large-cap stocks	2.00%
Mid-cap stocks	1.00%
Small-cap stocks	0.00%
Loan Rates	
30-year mortgage*	5.95%
15-year mortgage*	5.75%
Home equity line of credit*	5.85%
Home equity loan*	7.35%
5-year auto loan	6.10%
Personal loan	8.25%
*APR includes closing costs	

Retirement Information and Planning Issues

The following information should be used when evaluating the Grahams' current retirement planning situation:

- They would like to retire when Onslo reaches age sixty-six.

- They anticipate being in the 25 percent marginal tax bracket while in retirement.

- Prior to retirement, they are comfortable assuming that future rates of return will be 10.72 percent before taxes on their retirement assets and savings.

- If retired today, they would like to replace 90 percent of Onslo's salary.

- At retirement, Onslo will be eligible to receive $2,024 (in today's dollars) in Social Security benefits per month.

- Daisy has not yet earned forty quarters for Social Security benefits, but she does qualify for spousal benefits.

- They are comfortable assuming a life expectancy of ninety-five years.

- Contributions to Onslo's 401(k) will increase by 3 percent each year.

- Daisy is the primary beneficiary of Onslo's retirement assets.

- All qualified assets held outside of the 401(k) are in traditional IRAs.

- After retirement they plan to allocate retirement assets to generate a before-tax return of 8.7 percent.

Estate Information and Planning Issues

Onslo and Daisy have separate wills. Onslo's will leaves all his assets to Daisy. Daisy's will leaves all of her assets to Onslo. Their wills name their attorney as estate executors, and in the event of a simultaneous death it is assumed that Onslo predeceases Daisy. Other estate planning facts include:

- Funeral and burial expenses will be $25,000 each.

- Estate and legal costs will be $5,000 each.

- Executor fees will be approximately 2 percent of the gross estate before the marital transfer.

- The net growth rate of the survivor's estate is estimated to be, on average, 4 percent annually.

- Daisy is the sole beneficiary of Onslo's IRA and retirement plan assets.

- Onlso is the sole beneficiary of Daisy's IRA assets.

- Daisy has a strong allegiance to the University of Anystate. She would like to leave a legacy gift to the university, if possible.

- No other estate planning documents are known to exist.

Goals and Objectives

The Grahams have two primary goals. First, they would like to know whether they are on or off track to meet an age sixty-six retirement date. Second, they feel that a thorough review of their current estate situation is in order. Specifically, they would like to minimize any estate taxes paid in the event of death. Other planning objectives include reviewing their discretionary cash flow, net worth, and life insurance situation. They are looking for guidance on how to improve their general financial well-being.

Case Questions

1. Which of the following statements most accurately reflects the Grahams' current discretionary cash flow position?

   a. Their discretionary cash flow is greater than $0 but less than $1,000.

   b. Their discretionary cash flow is less than $0 but greater than -$1,000.

   c. Their discretionary cash flow is greater than $1,000 but less than $8,000.

   d. Their discretionary cash flow is less than -$1,000 but greater than -$8,000.

2. Which of the following statements is (are) true?

   I. Retirement plan assets make up approximately 5 percent of the Grahams' total assets.

   II. Given their age and income profile, one would expect the Grahams to have a substantially higher level of net worth.

   III. The Grahams' savings ratio, including reinvested dividends and interest, is below industry benchmark levels.

   IV. The Grahams' emergency fund ratio is adequate at this time.

   a. I and II only

   b. II and III only

   c. I and IV only

   d. I, III, and IV only

3. Which of the following strategies can the Grahams use to increase their discretionary cash flow situation?

   I. Refinance their first mortgage using a fifteen-year fixed-rate loan.

   II. Pay off outstanding credit card debt using money market mutual fund assets.

      III. Use a two-year home equity loan to refinance the Mazda car debt.

  a. II only

  b. I and II only

  c. II and III only

  d. I and III

4. According to your tax calculations, which of the following statements is (are) true?

  a. The Grahams should use the standard deduction rather than itemize expenses.

  b. Given their AGI, the Grahams can deduct Daisy's IRA contribution because she is not an active participant in a qualified plan.

  c. Even though Onslo is an active participant in a qualified plan, the Grahams can deduct his IRA contribution because he is over age fifty this year.

  d. Both a and b are correct.

5. Which of the following tax planning statements is true?

      I. The Grahams should, based on tax-equivalent investment calculations, transfer their money market mutual fund assets to an Anystate municipal money market fund.

      II. By paying off their home equity loan early, they will increase discretionary cash flow but lose a tax deduction.

      III. Using municipal bond investments will increase both the Grahams' level of discretionary cash flow and their taxable income.

      IV. Increasing 401(k) contributions will decrease the amount of taxes the Grahams will pay at the federal level.

  a. I and II only

  b. II and IV only

  c. I, II, and IV only

  d. II, III, and IV only

6. All of the following life insurance observations are true except?

  a. Based solely on the relative cost of the policy, Onslo should consider using a §1035 exchange procedure to replace the $100,000 whole-life insurance policy.

  b. The death benefit from Onslo's current life insurance policies is less than his calculated life insurance need.

c.   Term life insurance will provide the Grahams with the maximum amount of coverage for the lowest premium but leave them uninsured at some point in the future.

d.   Using the nonforfeiture provision in the whole-life insurance policy will result in a decrease in discretionary cash flow.

7.   Which of the following statements is true?

a.   The Grahams can afford to self-insure short-term disability needs by using a combination of cash flow and nonretirement assets.

b.   Because Onslo purchased his disability policy in the private market, if he receives benefits, then 100 percent of this income will be subject to federal income taxation.

c.   If the Grahams used all of their financial assets, excluding insurance cash values and Onslo's rental real estate interests, they would be able to self-insure Onslo's net long-term disability need.

d.   Both a and c are correct.

8.   Assume that long-term care costs in Anycity are currently $45,000 per year, and that these costs are increasing by 5 percent annually. If the Grahams anticipate that Daisy will enter a nursing home when she turns age seventy-one and stay for five years, and they can earn a 7 percent rate of return on investments, which of the following statements is true?

a.   The Grahams currently have enough financial assets to self-insure nursing home costs for Daisy.

b.   The Grahams do not need to worry because Daisy will qualify for Medicare benefits at that time.

c.   The cost of coverage for five years will exceed the Grahams' ability to self-insure the loss.

d.   Even if they wanted to purchase long-term care insurance, the cost to purchase this insurance today is prohibitively high.

9.   To retire at age sixty-six—based on the value of their current retirement assets—the Grahams need to consider which of the following?

a.   Be willing to reduce their income need in retirement.

b.   Increase the rate of return earned on retirement savings and assets.

c.   Increase the age-of-death assumption.

d.   All of the above.

e.   A and b only.

10. Given what they currently have saved, which of the following statements is (are) true in relation to their current retirement planning situation?

a. The Grahams currently have adequate cash flow to fund their age sixty-six retirement goal.

b. If Onslo can convert his rental real estate holdings to cash prior to age sixty-six, the Grahams can meet their retirement goal.

c. Postponing retirement by one year will allow them to reach their retirement goal without using any additional assets.

d. None of the above.

e. B and c only.

11. Which of the following assets would pass directly to Daisy if Onslo were to die today?

a. His 401(k) assets.

b. Proceeds from his group term life insurance policy.

c. His ownership interest in their house.

d. All of the above.

12. What is the approximate value of Onslo's gross estate today?

a. $1,000,000

b. $2,000,000

c. $3,000,000

d. $4,000,000

13. At Onslo's death, assuming Daisy is still alive:

a. if Anystate is a community property state, Daisy will receive a step-up in basis equal to 50 percent on all jointly owned taxable property.

b. if Anystate is a community property state, Daisy will receive a step-up in basis equal to 100 percent of all community property.

c. Daisy will retain the original basis in all property held jointly.

d. Daisy will be required to pay estate and gift taxes on all property received from Onslo.

14. What action(s) can Onslo take today to ensure a smooth transfer of his rental real estate holdings to either Daisy or Rose at his death?

I. Change the title from individual to trust ownership.

II. Consider a buy-sell agreement provision by funding the agreement with a life insurance provision so that the daughter can then buy the rental company from the mother (assume Daisy would be the owner because she is the beneficiary of the property).

      III. Use a grantor retained annuity or unitrust to pass these assets to Rose.

  a. I only

  b. III only

  c. I and II only

  d. I, II, and III

15. Which of the following estate planning tools generally allow Onslo Graham to maintain full control of his assets today while minimizing estate taxes at his death in the future?

      I. An A-B trust arrangement funded at his death.

      II. A QTIP trust arrangement.

      III. An irrevocable living trust arrangement.

      IV. A funded revocable living trust arrangement.

  a. I only

  b. I and II only

  c. I and III only

  d. III and IV only

16. Onslo and Daisy have indicated to you that they are considering adding Rose as a co-owner on their checking and savings accounts. They have heard that gift and/or income taxes could apply if they decide to move forward with the idea. Which of the following statements best describes the tax consequences of adding Rose to the account?

  a. Rose will owe a gift tax on one-third of the account balance when she is added to the account.

  b. Onslo and Daisy might owe a gift tax when Rose makes a withdrawal from the account.

  c. Rose will owe only federal income tax on her share of the account when either Onslo or Daisy dies.

  d. Onslo and Daisy will owe a gift tax when Rose is added to the account.

  e. Both a and d.

17. Daisy has been talking with a planned giving officer from the University of Anystate about funding a charitable trust that will also provide income during retirement. She and Onslo would like to begin funding the trust immediately and retain the right to add to the fund in future years. Which of the following gift alternatives will meet the Grahams' objective?

  a. A charitable remainder unitrust.

    b.   A charitable reminder annuity trust.

    c.   A pooled-income fund.

    d.   All of the above.

    e.   Both a and c.

18. Recently, Onslo indicated being concerned about the general strength of the stock market. As he and Daisy get closer to retirement, he is worried that the market will drop at just the moment they need to be drawing money from their equity fund holdings. Even so, he is reluctant to sell his stock funds at this time. Which of the following investing strategies could provide Onslo with a solution to his dilemma?

    a.   Periodically sell an index option put.

    b.   Periodically buy an index option put.

    c.   Periodically write a covered put.

    d.   Periodically buy an index option call.

19. Onslo has occasionally thought about buying municipal bond securities, but he never has because he does not have great faith that his local elected officials will make good on the bonds. Which of the following municipal bond alternatives would be most appropriate for Onslo, assuming that he wants to know that bond interest and principal will be paid from earnings on a project rather than tax revenues?

    a.   Debenture bonds.

    b.   General obligation bonds.

    c.   Revenue bonds.

    d.   Income bonds.

20. Before selling their taxable bond securities and purchasing municipal bond securities to reduce tax liabilities, Onslo and Daisy ought to consider which of the following factors as true in their situation?

    a.   Given their level and sources of income and deductions, there is the possibility that owning certain municipal bond securities that generate preference item interest will subject them to the AMT.

    b.   Anystate will tax all interest earned on bonds issued by another city in their state but not by Anycity, where Onslo and Daisy file taxes.

    c.   Although state income tax free, any municipal bond interest that they earn will still be taxable at the federal level.

    d.   Both a and c.

Discussion Points and Questions

1. Briefly summarize the relevant facts of the case.

2. Are there any areas in the Grahams' expense summary that can be reduced to improve their cash flow situation?

3. If the Grahams were going to purchase additional life insurance, what type of policy would be most appropriate given their age and needs?

4. What factors do the Grahams need to take into account regarding health insurance as they begin to think about retirement?

5. The Grahams' current retirement plan assumes the depletion of assets at the death of the surviving spouse. How much more do the Grahams need in assets on their first day of retirement to fully fund a capital preservation model of retirement if the following assumptions are used?

    a. They want to replace 90 percent of Onslo's salary in retirement.

    b. Onslo's salary is increasing by 5 percent annually.

    c. Social Security benefits are increasing by 4 percent annually.

    d. Inflation will remain at 4 percent throughout retirement.

    e. They can earn an 8.7 percent rate of return on investments in retirement.

    f. At retirement, they have a twenty-nine-year life expectancy.

6. Discuss property ownership and titling characteristics for the Grahams, assuming that they live in a community property state.

7. What can the Grahams do to avoid probate?

8. What action(s) can Onslo take today to ensure a smooth transfer of his rental real estate holdings to either Daisy or Rose at his death?

9. What type of gift strategies can be used by the Grahams to reduce their estate tax situation?

10. What other creative estate planning techniques can be used in this case?

Case 13

The Tun Case

A CASH FLOW AND EDUCATION PLANNING CASE

Maria and Jorge were married seven years ago when Jorge was thirty-five years old. He met Maria, who was also thirty-five years of age at the time, at a Caribbean resort. Jorge had flown down for the week with his golfing buddies. Maria was on the island taking a well-earned break from her hectic life. When they met, Maria was recently divorced, and although she had sworn off ever getting married again, when she got to know Jorge she knew that they were destined to be married.

Before meeting Jorge, Maria's life was chaotic. She married her high school sweetheart one week after they had walked through graduation. Maria reasoned that it was better to get married, pool resources, and grow old with a man she loved. It wasn't long before she and her husband had their first baby. Maria was nineteen years old. She felt blessed to hold her newborn son, whom they named Tony.

The realities of married life with children soon hit Maria and her husband with full force. He was working as a construction worker, while Maria held a job as a cashier at the local card shop. They were making a bit more than minimum wage, which was just enough to pay rent, cover car loan payments, pay for food, and cover baby expenses. There was nothing left at the end of the month. Maria knew that her family was in trouble. They were on a dead-end financial road.

At age twenty-one Maria made a life-changing decision. She quit her job and enrolled in a business program at a local community college. Her husband was skeptical, but he reluctantly agreed that Maria should go back to college, if for no other reason than to get a better paying job after graduation. In two years she completed an Associate's degree in Business Administration. Her instructors encouraged her to apply for a scholarship that would allow her to complete her Bachelor's degree from the local state university. Maria did not know if she would qualify, but with prompting by the community college faculty, she filled out the scholarship application. Maria was thrilled when she learned that the final two years of her college would be paid for from a special fund that was available to assist first generation mothers complete college. At age twenty-five, Maria completed her Bachelors of Science degree in Business Administration. Her graduation was a day of celebration.

Shortly after graduation Maria took a job as a teller at a local bank. Tony started kindergarten, while her husband continued to work as a tradesman. Maybe it was good fortune or just hard work, but it wasn't long before Maria was promoted to Head Teller. From there she moved into the loan department doing both personal and commercial loans. Time flew by, and Maria remained at the bank. Today, she is a loan manager and a highly valued employee of the bank.

During Maria's rise through the ranks at the bank, her husband's career remained basically unchanged. He was still working construction jobs with local contractors. During the summer months he made good money but was rarely home. During the winter months, when construction subsided, he stayed at home more often and tended to spend his days drinking. By her late twenties Maria had a feeling that her marriage was in trouble, but she continued to work at making the relationship function. Her primary thought was of Tony—making sure that Tony had a stable home environment. When Maria was thirty-four years she could no longer take her husband's drinking. She decided to end the marriage. It was not too long afterward that the divorce proceedings were finalized. The week after the divorce was final, she sent Tony to stay with his grandparents. She caught a plane for the Caribbean and it was there that she met Jorge.

Jorge grew up in a small Midwestern town. After graduation he worked at the local Co-Op. He started as a day worker in the grain elevator, but soon was promoted to work inside selling all sorts of farm and ranch supplies. Because he is an outgoing person, easily likeable, and a generally sincere person people immediately gravitate to him for advice and friendship. The problem, for both Maria and Jorge, was that life soon intruded on their budding relationship. Maria's life—her house, job, and son—were in one state. Jorge was living in another state. The romance would only work if Jorge were willing to move, which is exactly what he did. Jorge quit his job, loaded up his pick-up truck, sold what he could not take, and headed east to be with Maria. After a whirlwind time together they were married in a small church. That was seven years ago.

The Tun's Current Situation

Before marrying Jorge, Maria made it quite clear that they should work as a couple to achieve their financial goals. They agreed to pool their income to pay household expenses and to save for future goals. However, they were of the same opinion that some expenses should not be jointly paid. For example, Jorge agreed to fund his own health insurance premiums. This strategy helped reduce Maria's monthly expense by allowing her to provide coverage for herself and Tony.

Since their marriage, Maria's position at the bank has become even more secure. Last week, her manager pulled her aside and told her how valuable she was to the success of the branch. The manager also indicated that should she ever get a competing job offer, the bank would do everything possible to allow her to stay. This not only made her feel good, but it also helped her think about Jorge's situation.

Because of Jorge's good nature and skills, he was hired immediately by a regional hardware store when he arrived in Maria's hometown. He has been working at the store for seven years. He, like Maria, is considered a valuable employee. It is because of this that Jorge faces a life changing decision in relation to his job. Last week he learned that the store's owners are in the process of expanding. The owners hope to open five new branches over the next three years. They want to hire store managers from within the firm. There is just one problem. The firm has a policy of hiring only managers with a college degree. The preference has been to hire individuals with a marketing and accounting background. Of course, the owners know that hardware skills are critically important too, but in the final analysis they are looking to hire managers who have an understanding of the financial operations of each store.

Yesterday, Jorge met with the firm's regional manager. The regional manager made the following offer. If Jorge could complete a Bachelor's degree in Marketing within the next three years the firm would guarantee him a manager position at one of the new stores. If he chose to not pursue a college degree or did not finish in time, the firm would have no choice but to hire someone else for the position. The regional manager also made it quite clear that while Jorge is a valued employee, opportunities for management are restricted to those with a college degree.

The Tun's Questions, Dreams, and Goals

That night, Jorge went home in a rather excited, yet confused state. After dinner he sat down with Maria and explained the opportunity. Maria was excited for Jorge, but was concerned as well. Questions such as, "How will we pay for this?" and "Is it worth the expense?" came immediately to mind. Maria looked at Jorge and asked, "What would you like to do?" He knew his answer immediately. "I would love to be a store manager. I know that I can do the job. I love the company, and I can see great potential with the firm."

Maria replied, "Is this your dream job?"

Jorge was quick to reply, "I really think that this is my dream." He was quick to add, "If it makes financial sense to do it. Otherwise, I am happy being your husband and working at the store. I would only go to school if it was financially the smart thing to do."

Unfortunately, neither Maria nor Jorge knows if going back to college makes financial sense. This is the reason they have come to you as a financial planner. During your initial meeting with them, learn the following:

- Jorge's primary goal is to find a way to improve the family's financial situation. Together, the family income is just barely enough to make ends meet. Becoming a manager might help the Tun's overall financial situation, but Jorge wants to know if the investment, both time and money, will be worth the effort.

- The bottom line question for Jorge is this: Should he should stay in his current job and make do with what he and Maria live on, or should he return to school and work towards a marketing degree. While in your meeting, also note the following:

  o Jorge loves his job and would not be crushed if you recommend that he does not go back to school. In fact, he is a bit nervous about going to college. On the other hand, he knows that without a college degree his current job might be the best he can hope for, not only with the firm but in town as well.

- Neither Maria nor Jorge is willing or able to move so that Jorge can find a better job. Maria has deep ties in the community that would make moving unacceptable.

- Jorge does not want to earn a degree online; he performs better in a classroom situation.

- Given Jorge's work hours and variable work schedule, there is no way he can hold down a second job as a way to increase his income.

The Tun's Financial Position

When Maria and Jorge arrived at your office they had several folders containing financial records, tax returns, and other information they thought might be helpful in the planning process. Because Maria works at a bank, she had a good idea that you would need information about their incomes, expenses, assets, and liabilities. She and Jorge also brought information about their financial goals and objectives, time horizon for meeting objectives, expectations about their employment future, and their risk tolerance. The following discussion summarizes what you learned during your interview with Maria and Jorge.

Income and Expenses

When reviewing their financial documents you made a note of one thing immediately. The Tuns are very good at cutting costs and watching where they spend their money. Their annual cash flow statement is an example of frugality. When asked, Maria is quick to note her philosophy: it is important to live within one's means. While she is not opposed to debt, both she and Jorge are reluctant to go into more debt unless it makes financial sense to do so.

During your meeting, Maria disclosed that given their income and expense situation, they have been unable to save anything over the past several years. In fact, neither Maria nor Jorge have contributed to their 401(k) plans. (Maria began contributing to her company's 401(k) plan when she started as a teller, but she stopped contributing a few years ago.) There are several reasons for their lack of savings. First, their income is just not sufficient to meet daily needs, let alone fund their retirement objectives. Second, expenses associated with raising Tony have been higher than expected. Since her divorce, Maria has received nothing in terms of alimony or child support. Third, Tony is about to begin college, and Maria wants to help her son with some of those expenses (if possible), so she feels saving for retirement would only work against that goal. Maria estimates that it will take five years for Tony to finish college. Tony is now age twenty-three but he is considered a full-time student. Finally, when they were married neither had much in terms of assets. Maria's wealth was depleted during the divorce, while Jorge basically had very little in terms of financial assets. While they have been happily married, the one area of their life that has been somewhat stressed is their financial situation. The following table summarizes the Tun's income and expense situation:

Figure VI.26 Yearly Income and Expense Figures ($ rounded)

Income	Amount	Variable Expenses	Amount
Jorge's Wages	$27,900	Electricity	$2,400
Maria's Salary	$55,000	Other Utilities	$900
Interest	$2,000[1]	Telephone/Cell phone	$2,700
Other Income	???	Cable TV	$1,100
TOTAL	???	Home Repairs	$750
Fixed Expenses	**Amount**	Home Improvements	$1,500
Mortgage Principal and Interest[2]	$15,932	Food at Home and Eating Out	$5,800
Automobile Payments[3]	$5,366	Clothing	$2,750
Credit Card Payments[4]	???	Auto Gas and Oil	$3,000
Medical Insurance (Jorge)[5]	$1,170	Personal Care	$2,500
Medical Insurance (Maria)	$1,950	Entertainment	$2,300
Other Insurance	???	Travel	$1,700
Homeowner's Insurance	$1,200	Donations and Gifts	$4,800
Automobile Insurance	$1,500	Unreimbursed Medical Expenses	$700
Federal Income Taxes	$9,122[6]	Tony's Education	$1,000
State Income Taxes	$1,050	Other	$0
FICA	$6,108		
Real Estate Taxes	$2,450		
Personal Property Taxes	$600		
TOTAL FIXED	**???**	**TOTAL VARIABLE**	**???**
TOTAL INCOME			**???**
TOTAL EXPENSES			**???**
ANNUAL DISCRETIONARY CASH FLOW			**???**

Note: ??? indicates the need for a calculation by the financial planner.

1. Interest earned is based on receiving 2 percent interest on $100,000. The $100,000 was an inheritance received by Maria from her Aunt Haley.

2. Maria and Jorge live in Maria's home from her first marriage. Maria originally took out a $165,000 mortgage at 9.00 percent for thirty years. She and Jorge recently made the 120th payment on the mortgage.

3. Maria purchased a new car two weeks ago with a $22,000 zero down five year 7 percent APR loan.

4. The Tuns pay the minimum monthly payment, which is approximately 3 percent of the outstanding credit card balance. The balance has remained steady for several years.

5. Pre-tax contributions within the employer-sponsored health care plans.

6. Tax figures are based on 20XX actual liabilities.

Assets and Liabilities

Maria and Jorge are concerned that they will not be able to retire given the rate at which they are accumulating debt and saving money. Currently, every dollar in earnings that they make is spent on fixed (non-discretionary) and variable (discretionary) expenses. During the interview, Maria pointed out that they are not able to save money from the family's budget at the current time. The only savings the family has is shown on the balance sheet below. The Tuns have taken every step that they can think of to protect their assets. Maria is adamant about not wanting to spend down their assets to pay current bills if at all possible—after all, she reasons, this is their nest-egg. Also, they feel it would be difficult (you sense high reluctance when talking with Maria and Jorge) about efforts to slash their cash flow budget, especially in the areas of food, personal care, entertainment, and travel.

Figure VI. 27 Assets and Liabilities ($ rounded)

Assets	Amount	Liabilities	Amount
Cash	$250	Visa Credit Card[1]	$9,250
Checking Account	$500	MasterCard Credit Card[2]	$15,250
Savings Account[3]	$100,000	Mortgage	???
EE Savings Bonds[4]	$600	Automobile Loan[5]	$22,000
Primary Residence	$199,000	Other	$0
Automobile #1 (new car)	$22,000		
Automobile #2[6]	$9,000		
Furniture and Household Goods	$11,000		
Personal Property[7]	$5,000		
401(k) Plan Assets (Maria)	$160,000		
401(k) Plan Assets (Jorge)	$19,000		
TOTAL ASSETS	**???**	**TOTAL LIABILITIES**	**???**
NET WORTH			**???**

Note: ??? indicates the need for a calculation by the financial planner.

1. 18.50 percent annual interest rate.

2. 19.10 percent annual interest rate.

3. The savings account currently pays 2 percent on deposits greater than $5,000.

4. Purchased by Maria during the first few months of employment; Maria has not purchased savings bonds in over a year. The average annualized interest rate is 3.50 percent. She is willing to allocate these assets towards retirement.

5. They purchased a new car two weeks ago using a zero down five year 7 percent loan.

6. Second car is a four-year old Honda.

7. Family heirlooms primarily, including a silver bracelet with an estimated value of $3,000.

Other Information

During the course of the interview Maria and Jorge were able to provide information about other areas of their family financial situation. The key information is summarized below:

- All titled assets are jointly owned unless otherwise indicated.

- Tax information is based on their most recent 20XX tax return.

- For planning purposes, assume that their state income tax liability is approximately 11.50 percent of their federal tax liability. They pay a 3 percent marginal state tax with the following adjustments:

     o   one state deduction worth $14,750

     o   three state exemptions worth $4,700 each

     o   medical insurance of $3,120 can be used as a state adjustment

- They make a $400 monthly contribution to their church, which is the *minimum* that they want to provide as a charitable contribution.

- They currently use all of the interest earned on the savings account to help cover household expenses—i.e., interest is not reinvested.

- Their checking account is free of monthly charges but does not pay interest.

- Their homeowner's policy is an HO-3 policy with replacement coverage; the policy also has an inflation-adjustment rider.

     o   The house is insured for $141,000.

     o   The replacement value of the home equals the current market value.

     o   Liability coverage is equal to $100,000.

     o   Deductible information: 1 percent deductible.

- No personal property insurance endorsements are currently in place.

- Both Maria and Jorge are good drivers—no accidents in the past five years. They carry a $50/$150/$100 split limit PAP coverage on their automobiles (comprehensive coverage is included on both vehicles).

     o   Deductible information: $250 deductible.

- Maria's health situation is excellent (both are nonsmokers), and because she works at the bank, she is covered by an excellent PPO plan. When Tony graduates from college Maria's health insurance premium will drop by 33 percent.

o   Deductible information: $25 per visit with a $250 stop-loss limit.

- Jorge's health is also excellent. His insurance policy has a $2,500 annual deductible, with an 80/20 co-pay and $3,500 stop-loss provision.

- Maria's employer provides her with $100,000 group term life insurance coverage.

- Jorge's employer provides him with $35,000 in group term life insurance coverage.

- Maria's will is very basic; she has decided to leave all of her assets to Jorge with Tony as the secondary beneficiary. Jorge does not have a will.

- Neither Maria nor Jorge are worried about probate; in fact, Maria would like a full public disclosure of her final asset and liability position. Jorge has no opinion about probate issues.

- Besides Maria's will, they have no other estate planning documents.

- In the event of death, final administrative estate expenses are estimated to be 2 percent of each person's gross estate.

- Jorge has a relatively low level of financial risk tolerance, whereas Maria's risk tolerance is in the moderate range.

- Maria is willing to use her inheritance and the family's savings to help pay for Jorge's educational needs, but she is not comfortable investing the money outside of federally insured bank accounts or short-term certificates of deposit, if the money is to be used for college or as an emergency fund. This is not really an issue related to risk tolerance but rather a need to know that the money is safe and accessible if needed. It is reasonable to assume a 2.25 percent rate of return on these funds.

Research Findings[1]

The research process that was started as part of the data gathering phase of the client engagement revealed several areas where the Tuns could immediately improve their financial position. You plan on making recommendations in the areas of cash flow, net worth, insurance planning, and estate planning immediately. Addressing their second goal (question), within the context of education and retirement planning, has taken more research on the part of your planning staff. Here is what your para-planner uncovered during the additional background analyses:

- Inflation has been averaging 3.40 percent annually; you feel this rate of inflation will continue into the future.

---

1.   The assumptions shown should be used to solve the case. Note that the assumptions used are case specific. Data, rates, and other information may be different in your location; however, use the information provided in the case when conducting calculations. **Do not use any assumption or input other that what has been provided**.

- Maria's salary is expected to increase at the rate of inflation.

- Jorge's current wage is tied to the inflation rate and should increase over time. If he obtains a management position, the salary associated with the job will increase at the rate of inflation.

- Money market mutual funds and short-term certificates of deposit currently yield 2.25 percent.

- The thirty-year fixed rate mortgage interest rate is 7.00 percent.

- The twenty-year fixed rate mortgage interest rate is 6.25 percent.

- Closing costs for a refinanced mortgage are 2 percent of the amount borrowed.

- The current interest rate on home equity lines of credit is 7.25 percent. The typical draw period is ten years.

- The bank's 401(k) plan will match employee contributions $1 for $1 up to 3 percent of salary contributed to the plan.

  o The 401(k) plan does not currently allow for plan loans.

  o The hardware store's 401(k) plan does not provide matching contributions.

- A private college located forty-five miles away offers an accredited marketing degree program that can be completed in three years. The college's annual tuition fee is $14,000. This cost includes tuition, books, and all other college and program costs.

  o The degree is a full-time intensive academic program.

  o In order to complete the program in three years, Jorge must take a full load of classes fall, spring, and summer semesters. He plans to work ten hours per week at the hardware store (on weekends) while in school.

  o He can earn $13 per hour while working part-time.

  o The cost of tuition is increasing at a 4.00 percent annual rate.

  o Maria is willing to use their $100,000 savings to help fund Jorge's education goal, if you feel it is appropriate. Assume that these assets remain in the savings account until needed for education purposes.

  o Student loans (a combination of federal subsidized and institutional sources) can be obtained up to a maximum of $35,000 per year at a fixed 6.80 percent APR for ten years.

  o Loans may exceed the cost of college up to the maximum of $35,000 per year.

    o   Payments can be postponed until after graduation.

    o   Loans do not accrue interest during the payment deferral period.

    o   If Jorge returns to school they will need approximately $20,000 in additional income to offset his full-time income. (The figure is less than Jorge's current income because he will continue to work part-time on weekends, while reducing other work-related expenses. The $20,000 need is above what he can earn on the weekends.) They expect this income need while in school to increase at the inflation rate of 3.4 percent.

- Household expenses will increase at the rate of inflation.

- If Jorge leaves employment he will lose his health and life insurance benefits; however, he will be eligible for low-cost health benefits through the private college (or through a federal exchange). The monthly cost of the coverage is $45. The policy provides reasonable coverage for those in college. Adding Jorge to Maria's health insurance policy will cost $1,800 yearly.

- After talking with the Jorge, you believe that Jorge can earn *$43,500* (in three years) during his first year as a store manager, assuming he begins working after graduation from college.

- Life insurance planning assumptions:

    o   Burial expenses: $15,000.

    o   They will pay-off all outstanding debts at death.

    o   Total (anticipated) household expenses are defined as all expenses less savings.

    o   In order to help the family manage the transitional period, they would like to have $10,000 in cash available at death.

    o   *For life insurance planning purposes only*, assume a combined federal, state, and local marginal tax bracket of 18 percent.

    o   Before retirement, assume a 7.00 percent before-tax rate of return; after retirement, assume a 5.00 percent rate of return [these assumptions only apply for insurance planning purposes].

    o   Inflation is assumed to be 3.40 percent.

    o   In the event Maria or Jorge passes prior to retirement, the survivor plans to work until age sixty-seven.

    o   For life insurance planning purposes only, assume a survivor's annual retirement income need of $59,000.

o   They are willing to allocate Maria's $100,000 nest egg towards life insurance needs.

o   The income replacement ratio for the capital retention method is 90 percent.

o   They will make no charitable donations at death.

o   They do not wish to fund any additional educational expenses for Tony in the event of Maria or Jorge's death.

- Disability insurance planning assumptions:

o   Given their current income, assume a 100 percent income replacement in the event of disability.

o   If disabled, they plan to retire with full Social Security benefits at age sixty-seven but claim Medicare benefits at age sixty-five.

o   They are willing to allocate Maria's $100,000 in savings to help offset short- and long-term disability needs.

o   In the event of disability, they would be willing to reallocate assets to earn a slightly higher return (4.50 percent).

o   The bank provides a 180-day waiting period disability policy. If approved for long-term disability, employees receive 50 percent of their annual salary, payable in equal monthly installments, until age sixty-five. This income may be reduced by monies received from Workers' Compensation and/or the Social Security Administration.

o   They do not wish to plan for Social Security benefits in the event of disability.

o   The hardware store does not provide disability insurance for non-managers; however, managers receive a core disability benefit similar to the one offered to Maria.

- The regular retirement age for Maria and Jorge, for Social Security, is age sixty-seven.[1]

o   They would like to stop working at full retirement age, which is the end of the year of her sixty-seventh birthday (December 31st).

o   They would like to be debt free upon entering retirement.

o   At Maria's current salary, she will earn $1,800 per month in Social Security benefits at age sixty-seven.

---

1.   Assume that Maria and Jorge will retire sometime after Maria turns age sixty-seven but before age sixty-eight; that is, twenty-five years in the future.

- o At Jorge's current salary, he will earn $1,113 per month in Social Security benefits at age sixty-seven.

- o His Social Security benefit is expected to be larger than 50 percent of Maria's benefit.

- o If Jorge were to earn $43,500 per year and take Social Security benefits at age sixty-seven he would receive $1,471 per month.

- Even though they are earning 2.0 percent on their savings and 3.5 percent on the EE Savings Bonds, when calculating retirement savings needs, use the following assumptions:

  - o They are willing to allocate their savings bonds towards the retirement goal.

- The savings bonds have a fixed 3.50 percent yield

  - o Inflation pre- and post-retirement is/will be 3.40 percent.

  - o It is possible to receive a 5.90 percent annualized tax-adjusted rate of return using a diversified portfolio of mutual funds prior to retirement. This rate of return matches Maria's risk tolerance and their joint risk capacity. In other words, they are willing to have you invest the $100,000 (if available) and their 401(k) assets in a portfolio of mutual funds earning 5.90 percent for retirement purposes.[1]

  - o They can invest *after* retirement and earn 4.35 percent per year annualized (tax-adjusted).

  - o They will continue to be in the 15 percent federal marginal income tax bracket pre- and post-retirement.

  - o Maria believes that they can live comfortably on approximately 75 percent of *current* earned income, in today's dollars, when retired, regardless if Jorge takes a manager's position or not. (Note: the income replacement ratio is significantly less if Jorge goes back to school and earns a higher income as a store manager.)

- Maria is comfortable using her $100,000 inheritance for retirement (if available) or for education funding; if used for retirement, assume a 5.90 percent annualized tax-adjusted rate of return.

  - o If at all possible, she would like to leave a financial legacy for her son Tony and future grandchildren.

- Their joint life expectancy is age ninety-five.

Please use only the assumptions and data shown in the case when solving the client's situation. If you have specific questions or need additional assumption

---

1.   Their current 401(k) assets are earning an after-tax return of 5.90 percent annualized.

clarification please post your notes on the message board. Remember to only use Word and Excel when solving this case. You may use the Excel package that is bundled with your book, or you may create your own spreadsheets. Do not use professional software.

Case Questions

1. How much are the Tuns spending on PITI each month?

    a. $1,328

    b. $1,425

    c. $1,632

    d. $15,932

2. How much should Maria and Jorge list as the outstanding balance on their mortgage today?

    a. $165,000

    b. $147,338

    c. $147,559

    d. $150,286

3. Assume that you recommend that Maria and Jorge create a three month emergency savings fund with the fund based on total fixed and variable expenses. Which of the following statements is true?

    a. They have just enough in monetary assets to meet this need.

    b. Not only can they meet the need, they also have enough for a six month funding emergency fund.

    c. Monetary assets are insufficient to meet the three month need.

    d. Their financial situation today will allow them to fund only a two month emergency fund.

4. How are Maria and Jorge doing in relation to their current housing costs? Use the front- and back-end mortgage ratios to answer this question.

    a. They meet the 36 percent ratio but not the 28 percent ratio guidelines.

    b. They meet the 28 percent ratio but not the 36 percent ratio guidelines.

    c. They meet both the 28 percent and the 36 percent ratio guidelines.

    d. There is not enough information to answer this question.

5. Which of the following recommendations should be implemented by Maria and Jorge as soon as possible?

    Payoff the credit card debt using monetary assets.

    a. Refinance the mortgage.

    b. Begin contributions to a Roth IRA.

    c. All of the above.

    d. Only a and b.

6. Based on tuition and living expense estimates, what is the total cost of college over the three year time period, assuming he begins college this year (rounded)?

    a. $95,671

    b. $102,000

    c. $105,766

    d. $109,000

7. Assume that Maria is willing to allocate $50,000 of her savings to help fund Jorge's educational goal. How much in student loans will they need to take in order to fund tuition and expenses (rounded)?

    a. $43,702

    b. $61,383

    c. $67,415

    d. $74,744

8. Which of the following strategies can be used to (a) reduce the Tun's federal income tax liability this year, (b) increase saving for retirement, and (c) help increase the likelihood that Jorge might qualify for a need's based scholarship?

    a. Contribute the maximum yearly amount to a Roth IRA.

    b. Implement an income shifting strategy by having Maria max out her 401(k) contributions while using her $100,000 in savings to offset living expenses.

    c. Contribute fully to a qualified section 529 plan.

    d. Purchase a variable annuity using Maria's $100,000 in savings in order to defer taxes on distributions into the future, thereby decreasing assets available to fund Jorge's college costs.

9. How much do the Tuns need in retirement, on their first day of retirement, assuming no other recommendations have been implemented. In other words, taking into account current assets, liabilities, and assumptions, how much do they need as a lump sum when they retire (rounded)?

   a. $675,451

   b. $984,294

   c. $1,543,958

   d. $1,558,143

10. Assume the Tun's house catches on fire and they experience a $150,000 loss. How much will they be reimbursed?

   a. $139,500

   b. $141,000

   c. $148,500

   d. $150,000

11. Based on the human life value approach, what is the total amount of life insurance Maria needs today assuming that income from the insurance policy were to begin immediately for the beneficiary (rounded to the nearest thousand)?

   a. $557,000

   b. $686,000

   c. $757,000

   d. $915,000

12. Which of the following are client situational factors that need to be evaluated prior to making a financial planning recommendation?

   I.   The current level of interest rates in the marketplace.

   II. Both Maria's and Jorge's financial risk tolerance.

   III. Jorge's learning style preference.

   a. I only

   b. II and III only

   c. I and II only

   d. I, II, and III

13. After evaluating the Tun's financial situation, your paraplanner notices that interest rates have come down since Maria first purchased her home. Based on this observation and their current cash flow situation, which of the following recommendations is most appropriate in terms of increasing their current cash flow situation?

    a. Suggest that Maria and Jorge stick with the original mortgage in order to maintain the higher mortgage interest deduction.

    b. Suggest that they refinance the mortgage using a fifteen-year loan because this will reduce the amount of interest paid over time.

    c. Suggest that they refinance to a thirty-year fixed rate mortgage to lower the monthly payment.

    d. Refer the analysis and recommendation to a mortgage broker.

14. During the course of the initial client-planner meeting, the topic of retirement planning came up. Maria made a comment that they are probably not on track to meet their retirement objective. As their comprehensive financial planner you agree. How should you direct the discussion regarding retirement planning at this stage of the systematic financial planning process?

    a. Tell Maria and Jorge that they must increase their monthly retirement savings immediately.

    b. Recommend no changes because you anticipate an improvement in market conditions, which should get the Tuns back on track towards their retirement goal.

    c. Discuss alternatives currently available to increase the likelihood of success in the future.

    d. Suggest that they postpone retirement by at least three years.

15. Maria is still interested in helping Tony fund some of his college costs. Assuming that Maria and Jorge can improve their cash flow situation, which of the following strategies will ensure that the Tun's do not trigger the gift tax?

    a. Contribute funds to a UTMA account for Tony.

    b. Pay tuition and other expenses directly to the college or university.

    c. Contribute to a Section 529 qualified tuition plan.

    d. All of the above.

16. Maria was recently informed that she is eligible to receive stock options and restricted stock that is tied to her company's performance. Because of the tentative nature of the options and stock, Maria has requested that you do not include these assets in your planning calculations. Given this new information, in addition to what is in the case narrative, which of the following would you recommend that Tuns implement first?

    a. Exercise the stock options.

    b. Diversify their investment holdings.

    c. Draft new wills.

    d.   Create and fund an irrevocable life insurance trust.

17. Your paraplanner is concerned that the Tuns are living beyond their financial means. The paraplanner wants to recommend that Maria and Jorge reign in their spending immediately and stop using credit cards. The paraplanner is concerned that you will waste a lot of time and effort working with these clients. As their financial planner, which of the following is a reasonable financial planning strategy?

    a.   Terminate the client-planner relationship based on the insights of your paraplanner.

    b.   Ask the paraplanner to talk with Maria and Jorge about their poor spending habits and stress that unless they change their behavior the client-planner relationship will be terminated.

    c.   Review the Tun's current and potential income streams to identify ways to solve their immediate cash flow problem.

    d.   Recommend a reallocation of assets in Maria's 401(k) plan as a way to increase portfolio income that can be used to offset household expenditures.

18. Jorge has been approached by two friends who are interested in opening a new landscaping business. Jorge's friends are sure the economy is about to make a turn for the better, which should create demand for their services. They would like Jorge to invest $25,000 into the new venture. Which of the following is the most suitable recommendation for Jorge as he considers this possible business opportunity?

    a.   Borrow the $25,000 using a home equity line of credit (HELOC).

    b.   Cash out Maria's 401(k) plan.

    c.   Both a and b.

    d.   Given his financial risk tolerance and low risk capacity, walk away from the business opportunity.

19. Which of the following tax-efficient strategies can be used to fund Tony's or Jorge's college expenses, if necessary, while also providing retirement savings in case Tony and Jorge do not need additional school funding?

    a.   Fund a 529 plan for Jorge and transfer funds to Jorge if necessary.

    b.   Contribute the maximum amount to a Roth IRA.

    c.   Contribute the maximum amount to a tax-deductible IRA.

    d.   Both b and c.

20. Given an analysis of the Tun's financial situation and goals, which of the following conclusions is correct?

    a.   Jorge should go back to school because he will earn more income over the course of his working life.

b. Jorge should not go back to school because the standard student loan payment will exceed the extra income he can earn as a store manager.

c. Jorge should only go back to school if he can get a scholarship that will pay 100 percent of tuition expenses.

d. Jorge should postpone college for at least five years until the Tun's financial situation stabilizes and Tony is out of school.

Case 14

The Menjivar Case

A PROPERTY OWNERSHIP CASE

Your client Abed Menjivar is curious about the process of buying property—both autos and homes—as well as property insurance. Imagine that he comes to you with the following questions. Help him work out the math and details of his questions so that he gets a better understanding of the purchase and insurance aspects of financial planning.

Case Questions

1. Abed has determined that he needs a new car. By new he means either brand new or a relatively new "used" car. He has been going through his budget and he thinks he can afford $295 per month as an auto payment. He saw an advertisement on television stating that he can get a three year loan at a 3.9 percent annualized APR. Given this information, what is the maximum loan that he can afford?

   a. $8,202.08

   b. $10,006.95

   c. $11,246.87

   d. $22,421.80

2. Help Abed calculate his monthly PITI, based on the following facts:

   He currently earns $66,000 per year

   1. 4.5 percent annualized APR

   2. thirty year mortgage (fixed rate)

    3. $200,000 loan amount

    4. $150 monthly HO insurance premium

    5. $300 monthly HO tax

  a. $1,013

  b. $1,463

  c. $1,540

  d. $3,278

3.   Based on your answer to the last question, does Abed meet the front-end mortgage qualification rule?

  a. Yes, because his monthly PITI is less than 36 percent.

  b. No, because his monthly PITI is greater than 28 percent.

  c. Yes, because his monthly PITI is less than 28 percent.

  d. No, because his monthly PITI is greater than 36 percent.

4.   If Abed tells you that he also has a $100 furniture loan payment and that he pays $200 monthly on an outstanding credit card balance, do you think a bank will loan him money to buy a house with a $200,000 mortgage?

  a. Yes, because the combination of all his loan payments will be less than $1,980 monthly.

  b. No, because the passes neither the front-end or back-end mortgage qualification rules.

  c. Yes, because his monthly income is more than 2.5 time the actual loan amount.

  d. No, because while he passes the front-end mortgage qualification rule, he does not have enough income to meet the loan rule that states, "A borrower must not borrow more than 2.5 times his or her annual income."

5.   Based on the front-end mortgage qualification rule, and assuming the Abed goes to the maximum PITI level based on the rule, how much can he afford to borrow?

  a. $200,000

  b. $283,540

  c. $303,936

  d. $390,775

6.   Abed has obtained several loan offers from banks, credit unions, and mortgage brokers. Assuming he does not qualify for a VA or FHA loan at this time, which of the following borrowing strategies

will enable him to pay the least amount of interest over the course of the loan? Assume the purchase price of the home is $200,000?

   a. Obtain a thirty-year fixed rate 4.5 percent APR mortgage with a loan to value ratio of 80 percent.

   b. Obtain a thirty-year fixed rate 4.5 percent APR mortgage with a loan to value ratio of 50 percent.

   c. Obtain a fifteen-year fixed rate 3.9 percent APR mortgage with a loan to value ratio of 100 percent.

   d. Obtain a twenty-year fixed rate 4.0 percent APR mortgage with a loan to value ratio of 90 percent.

7.   Help Abed do some worst case planning. Assume that Abed purchases an HO policy with a maximum limit of $150,000 (remember his house has a replacement value of $200,000). If he has a $40,000 loss how much will he receive as a reimbursement (exclude the deductible for this problem)?

   a. $0

   b. $37,500

   c. $40,000

   d. $150,000

8.   In order for Abed to qualify for an excess liability insurance policy, which of the following statements is true?

   a. He must not have received a speeding ticket within the last year.

   b. He must own a house and car and bundle the insurance together.

   c. He must increase his liability coverage on his auto and home above the state required minimums.

   d. All of the above.

9.   Abed is a collector. Last week he estimated the following values on his collections:

   1. Stamps: $3,000

   2. Jewelry: $1,000

   3. Signed 1st Edition Books: $3,500

   4. Silver Coins: $800

Which of these collections needs a personal articles floater?

a. Only 3

b. 1 and 2

c. 2 and 4

d. 1 and 3

e. All of the items

10. Abed has the following split limit PAP: 100/300/50. If he is involved in an accident which of the following statement is true?

a. The maximum amount his insurance will pay to fix or repair damage to his car is $50,000.

b. The maximum his insurance will pay in medical expenses, per person, for himself, his family, and those in the other car is $100,000.

c. The maximum his insurance will pay, if he is liable in the accident, for medical expenses of those in the other car is $100,000.

d. Both a and b are correct.

The Case of the Good Gone Bad

A PLAY IN THREE SCENES[1]

To solve this case you must have access to Certified Financial Planner Board of Standards, Inc. (CFP Board) *Standards of Professional Conduct*, including the *Code of Ethics and Professional Responsibility, Rules of Conduct, Financial Planning Practice Standards, Disciplinary Rules and Procedures*, and *Candidate Fitness Standards*, which can be found at: www.cfp.net/Downloads/2010Standards.pdf. Information from the *Process of Financial Planning: Developing a Financial Plan*, Second Edition, the companion text to this book, can also be used to help answer questions..

Characters:

Ashley: A CFP® professional

Bill Jackson: Ashley's client and friend

Jane Jackson: Bill's wife and Ashley's friend

Phil Rheem: A prominent attorney in the area

Ben Pyles: Ashley's broker/dealer representative

Background

Ashley has been a Certified Financial Planner (CFP®) professional and registered representative for more than ten years. She prides herself on her excellent work and ethical standards. Ashley was recently ranked by her local newspaper as one of the top fifty planners in her region, and she was recently recognized at an awards banquet.

At 9:30 on a bright Thursday morning, Ashley received a phone call from a long-time client, Bill Jackson. Although Bill is married, Ashley manages only Bill's sizable

---

1.   This fictional (and lighthearted) play is intended to be acted out in class. The case takes approximately fifteen minutes to complete. A minimum of thirty minutes should be allocated to answer case questions.

investment portfolio. Bill is one of the wealthiest men in the area. He and Ashley have had a long client-planner relationship, and he considers her to be worthy of his full trust. Ashley and Bill have long been good friends, and dealing with Bill has always been a pleasure for her. When Ashley answers the phone, she is aware of Bill's altered mood and she immediately becomes concerned.

Bill: *(In a hushed tone.)* Ashley, I need to talk with you about asset protection.

Narrator: Ashley could sense that Bill was quite disturbed, and she wondered why this type of question might cause such panic in a person.

Ashley: Bill, your assets are fully protected. Your trust is fully secure, and your brokerage account has comprehensive SIPC coverage. Why the concern about asset protection all of a sudden?

Bill: *(More persistent.)* Listen Ashley, I just need to know how not to let anyone touch my investments or my property without my permission.

Narrator: Ashley was now getting annoyed; she could not figure out for the life of her what brought on this sudden panic about asset protection.

Ashley: Bill, are you in some sort of trouble? What is going on?

Narrator: There was silence on the other end of the line, and Ashley could sense the tension as she held the receiver. Finally, a long sigh came from Bill, and Ashley was temporarily relieved.

Bill: *(Pauses.)* Ashley, you and I have been friends for a long time. Our kids played with each other. For heaven's sake, I couldn't even count the number of barbecues our two families have had in my backyard.... Those were the easy times, Ashley—everything was so simple back then. Ashley, I don't know how to tell you this, *(long pause)* but I am leaving Jane. Another thing, she doesn't know yet.

Narrator: Ashley was shocked. She and Jane had been good friends for years—better friends than she was with Bill.

Ashley: Bill, what are you talking about? Why would you and Jane split up?

Narrator: Again, there was a long sigh on the other end of the line; then Ashley heard a voice—a female voice—but it wasn't Jane's. Ashley now knew why Bill wanted a divorce. He had met someone new. It wasn't a unique scenario for Ashley; she had seen it happen to a few of her other "fifty-something" friends. "After Jane had supported Bill for so long, he is going to trade her in for a newer model. What a creep!" Jane thought to herself. Well, there was no way she was going to let Bill leave Jane with nothing. In fact, Ashley thought to herself, "I'll fix it so that Jane is better off than she has ever been, and I'll make that slimeball pay!"

Ashley: Bill, you know I will do anything to help you out. I mean, after all, you have been so good to me over the years. Let me look into the situation, and I will call you back on Monday morning. Can you wait that long?

> **Narrator:** Ashley smiled on the other end of the line as she waited for Bill's response. She leaned back in her chair and began planning out her strategy. Bill's voice came back over the line a lot calmer than it had been at the beginning of their conversation.

Bill: Thanks Ashley, Monday will be fine.... I really didn't think you would understand, I mean … you know … since you and Jane have been such good friends.

Ashley: Well, Bill, you are my client, and what you do with your personal life is not a professional concern of mine. I'll call you on Monday. Have a good weekend.

Ashley: *(Talking to herself.)* Yeah, have a *great* weekend, you weasel—because it is the last good one you'll have after I get through with you.

> **Narrator:** As soon as she hung up the phone, Ashley immediately called Jane at the club. Ashley knew Jane always played tennis on Thursday mornings with a group of other "housies," as they liked to refer to themselves. When Jane finally got to the phone she sounded winded from the run up to the clubhouse.

Jane: *(In a cheerful voice.)* Hello Ashley, what in the world has given me the pleasure of hearing from you this morning?

Ashley: Jane, listen, I think there are some things we need to discuss; is there any way you can meet me for lunch this afternoon?

Jane: *(Suddenly serious.)* Well, normally I have lunch with my tennis group, but I'm sure they won't mind if I cancel. What is this about?

Ashley: Jane, I'll talk to you about it at lunch. Does *Le Marie* sound good to you … say 1:00?

Jane: Yes, that will be fine. I'll see you there at 1:00.

> **Narrator:** Later that afternoon when Ashley and Jane were at Le Marie for lunch, Ashley finally looked Jane in the eye and began to tell her the whole story.

Ashley: Listen, Jane, this is really hard for me to say. I don't even know where to begin. But, this morning I got a phone call from your husband. Can I just ask you one question?

Jane: *(Concerned.)* Ashley you know you can talk to me about anything. What is it?

Ashley: Jane, how is your marriage?

Jane: Ashley, what is this about? What do you mean how is my marriage?

Ashley: Bill is having an affair.

Jane: (*Suddenly angry.*) What are you talking about? Bill has always been faithful and for your information our marriage is fine. Now, if you have nothing else to say I will be leaving.

> **Narrator:** As Jane is getting up to leave, Ashley's voice softens and she touches Jane's arm.

Ashley: (*More softly.*) Jane, I know Bill is having an affair. Today when he called me I heard "her" voice in the background. And Bill was calling to figure out how he could protect his assets from someone—(*long pause*)—and that someone is you.

> **Narrator:** Jane sat down quietly and leaned her head in her hands. She was clearly shaken but didn't seem to be too surprised.

Jane: Oh, Ashley … if you only knew how hard it's been these last few years. Bill has been so distant. But, I never expected him to be unfaithful. I mean after all of this time. After everything I have given him. I mean I gave up my life and my career to be his perfect "trophy wife."

> **Narrator:** Jane was suddenly struck with anger. She didn't know what she could do, but there was no way she was going to let Bill leave her with nothing. After all she had sacrificed; she was not going to let him make her a poor little old lady without a penny to her name!

Jane: So, what can you do to help me? Would you act as my financial advisor?

Ashley: I thought you would never ask. First, I need some information. Who is your lawyer? You know you are going to need to hire a good divorce attorney—do you have someone in mind?

Jane: I have always worked with Phil Rheem. He was a dear friend of my father, and he was the one who handled my father's estate when he passed away; normally all he handles are divorce cases. I will stop by his office after I leave here.

Ashley: Also, I will be setting up a trust for your assets.

Jane: Are you qualified to do that sort of thing?

Ashley: Oh don't worry, I can take care of it—I've got a lot of experience with trusts and it will save us some time instead of having to worry about jumping through all the legal hoops.

Narrator: On the way back from lunch, Ashley was thinking about where to begin. She knew she wanted to leave Bill with nothing, but she also needed to make sure Jane was able to continue living the life she had become accustomed to.

Scene II

Narrator: Later that afternoon Ashley returned to her office. She knew that the day ahead was going to be a long one.

After she left her office she stopped by Phil Rheem's law practice. Even though Ashley only knew Phil on a casual basis, she had worked with him on a number of different occasions when she had clients with complicated estate matters. Ashley told Phil's secretary that the matter was urgent and she needed to see him immediately. When she entered Phil's office he was reviewing a case file that he placed to the side as he stood up to greet her.

Phil: Well ... Good afternoon, Ashley. What is it that gives me the good fortune to see your pretty face in my office today?

Narrator: Ashley had never really cared for Phil's charming style—she found it to be condescending and irritating. Nevertheless, he was the perfect type of attorney who had the power and connections to do what she needed him to do for her.

Ashley: (*Sounding charming herself.*) Good afternoon to you too, Phil. You know it is always *my* pleasure when I have a chance to work with you.

Narrator: Phil motioned for Ashley to sit down in one of the overstuffed leather chairs in front of his giant mahogany desk. As Ashley took a seat, she noticed the open file on Phil's desk. She glanced at it only briefly, but she noticed the name typed at the top of the papers. Ashley then realized that the file contained all of the legal documents for Bill Jackson's trusts. Of course, she also had a copy of them, but these were the originals, and the man who had signed and prepared them was sitting right in front of her. She silently crossed her fingers that Mr. Rheem would be as helpful as she was hoping.

Ashley: Phil, (*Pausing, then speaking in a direct tone.*) I am going to get right down to business here. (*Pausing again.*) I am here about Jane Jackson. Her husband has been a client of mine for more than ten years. I am sure you are acquainted with Bill?

Phil: Yes, I have worked with Bill on a few previous business matters.

Ashley: Well, this morning Bill contacted me. He was interested in protecting his assets. When I talked to him he seemed so frantic that I was concerned, of course. I could not understand where this sudden panic had come from, and it wasn't until I found out that he was going to leave his wife that it all made sense to me. Bill wants to make sure that his wife, Jane, will not be able to lay a finger on any of his wealth, which—if I may say say—Jane helped him to build. So, as you can see, this little situation has put me in quite a bind.

Phil: Yes, I can see where it would. Well, (pause) as Jane may have told you, I have been acquainted with her family for a long time. Her father and I used to play golf together out at the club. He was a great man. He helped me get my start in this profession. It saddened me greatly to see him pass away. (*Leaning back in his chair and sighing.*) I must tell you that I would have done anything for that man—I would be willing to do whatever it takes to protect Mrs. Jackson; she deserves at least that much.

Ashley: (*Leaning back in her chair.*) Thank you, Phil. I knew you would understand. Jane and I have talked, and she is willing to do whatever it takes also. I know she will be getting in touch with you soon about filing for divorce, but I felt like I needed to see you myself—I am sure you understand.

Phil: Of course I understand. (*Pause.*) Now don't you worry your pretty little head about a thing; I will make sure Jane is completely taken care of. Now, if you'll excuse me I'll make a few calls and see what I can do for you.

Ashley: Thank you, Phil. And you know that if you ever need anything, just give me a call. I will always be glad to return the favor.

Scene III

Narrator: Later that night, Ashley sat down in her still, dark office and pulled a file out of her briefcase. She switched on the desk lamp and opened the file containing Bill Jackson's original trust documents. Yesterday, when she was in Phil's office, she had secretly slipped them into her briefcase when he momentarily stepped out to talk with his secretary. She knew that she was treading in deep waters here, but it seemed so simple to her. Slowly, Ashley stood up and walked over to the shredding machine in the corner of the room, and one by one, she fed each sheet into the metal teeth that ground up the original documentation that Bill Jackson had ever established a trust.

The following morning she returned to her office. She picked up the phone and hit the speed dial. She was directly connected with Ben Pyles, her broker/dealer representative.

Ashley: Ben, yes, hello? And how are you this morning? Yes, it is early. Well, you know I wanted to get a jump on a few things before heading off for the weekend. Listen, I need to make a few trades for a client—his name is Bill Jackson. His account number is 9008765. (*Pausing, waiting for him to answer.*) Yes, that's right. I want to go ahead and liquidate the account. (*Pause.*) No, I do not want to reinvest the proceeds into a money market account. Just make a check out to Bill and Jane Jackson and send it to their home address. Secondly, I would like for you to liquidate Bill's second account and invest the proceeds in the following penny stocks.

Narrator: Ashley listed several penny stocks, directing Ben to split the assets evenly among the stocks she had given him. Ashley was fully aware that by moving the assets from the second account into penny stocks that Bill would almost certainly incur a loss. She also knew that this could hurt Jane by reducing the amount of assets available in the divorce, but she suspected that the account was nothing more than a place where Bill stashed money to pay for his own personal expenses. She felt justified in taking the action.

Ashley: *(Pausing and softly giggling.)* Now, Ben, you know I wouldn't do anything that wasn't in the best interest of my client. I tried to talk him out of these trades, but he was insistent. I guess he read some article in a personal investing magazine. It is all a bunch of bologna if you ask me, but I work for him so I have to do what he wants. You know…that's just the way the business goes. *(Pausing again.)* Well, I guess that will be all for me. You have a nice weekend. Tell your wife hello for me. Take care now. Goodbye to you, too.

Narrator: When the receiver finally clicked down, Ashley leaned back in her chair. She sighed to herself. She hated to see Bill and Jane's marriage end; it seemed like they were always so happy. But she wasn't going to allow Bill to make a mockery of all of Jane's sacrifice and devotion. No, Bill Jackson was going to be the sorry one in the end. By Monday morning, he wouldn't know what had hit him.

Case Questions

1. When asked later about her actions, Ashley affirmed that she did what she thought was right at the time because it served the interest of her friend. She argued that even though her actions might be wrong, the consequences for Jane were positive. Her view of the ethical situation was driven by which ethical outlook?

    a.   Normative ethics

    b.   Teleological ethics

    c.   Deontological ethics

    d.   Disclosure ethics

2. Which of the following statements is true?

    I.   Ashley is in violation of CFP Board *Practice Standards and Code of Ethics.*

    II.   Ashley is in violation of SEC financial adviser rules.

    III. Although some of Ashley's actions are questionable, nothing she did would fall under the rule making of the FINRA (NASD).

    a.   I only

    b.   III only

    c.   I and II only

    d.   I, II, and III

3. Which of the following will provide liability protection for Ashley in this case?

    a.   E&O insurance.

    b.   The arbitration clause in investment management contracts.

    c.   Disclaiming fiduciary status as a registered representative.

    d.   None of the above.

4. According to the definition of what constitutes a client, found in the terminology of financial planning practice standards section of CFP Board *Practice Standards and Code of Ethics*, who among the following is not considered Ashley's client?

    a.   Bill

    b.   Jane

    c.   Phil

    d.   Both a and b

    e.   Both b and c

5. Did Ashley break CFP Board *Practice Standards and Code of Ethics* confidentiality rules when she contacted Phil Rheem without the consent of Jane—even though Jane was most likely not going to be upset with Ashley?

    a.   Yes, because personal information was given without Jane's consent, a violation occurred.

    b.   No, because Jane could not be harmed by the use of her personal information.

    c.   No, because Ashley is allowed to share client information with other professional advisors.

    d.   Because Jane is only a friend of Ashley's, the CFP Board *Practice Standards and Code of Ethics* do not apply.

6. Would Jane's attorney, Phil Rheem, need to follow the CFP Board *Practice Standards and Code of Ethics*?

    a.   Yes, because any professional who deals with a CFP® professional must also follow the standards.

    b.   No, because Phil is not a CFP® professional.

    c.   Yes, because as an attorney, he must abide by all applicable and published ethical standards.

    d.   Attorneys have no ethical standards, so he does not have to follow CFP Board rules—or any other rules, for that matter.

7. The Principle of Integrity states that "A CFP® professional shall offer and provide professional services with integrity." Which of the following statements is true in relation to this principle?

    I.   This principle allows for honest mistakes and innocent errors.

    II.   This principle allows a client who is dissatisfied with his or her planner to sue for lack of disclosure.

    III.   This principle requires CFP® professionals to provide fee-only services whenever a client requests an initial planning review.

  a. I only

  b. II only

  c. III only

  d. I and II only

  e. II and III only

8. Prior to her trouble with the Jacksons, Ashley prospected for clients using seminars. She advertised herself as Ashley Smith, CFP®, RIA. Is this permissible?

  a. Yes, so long as she describes what the certifications mean during her seminar.

  b. No, because the SEC does not allow the use of RIA in marketing materials.

  c. Yes, as long as she tells the audience that she is not also a registered representative.

  d. It depends on the size of the seminar and whether or not she is promoting the sale of securities.

9. CFP Board *Practice Standards and Code of Ethics* indicate that a CFP® professional may not solicit clients using false or misleading advertisements. Which of the following statements is *not* an example of a misleading statement/advertisement?

  a. "Our mutual fund portfolios have averaged over 18 percent returns during the last three years."

  b. "We guarantee a 100 percent improvement on your portfolio's annual return."

  c. "Our firm offers fee-based services, but also receives commissions from the investment products sold."

  d. "I practice as a fee-only planner, but I receive a commission on the insurance products I sell."

10. About a year ago Ashley was dealing with a client, Bob Hernandez, who was trying to minimize estate taxes. Ashley was not clear on all of the estate laws, so she called an attorney friend who deals primarily with criminal cases to help resolve a few of Bob's questions. Did Ashley violate rules related to planning competence within CFP Board *Practice Standards and Code of Ethics*?

  a. No; she called a qualified person for help.

  b. Yes; she should not be dealing with estate planning issues at all as a CFP® professional.

    c.   Yes; she should have contacted a qualified estate attorney.

    d.   No; she acted in the best interest of her client.

11. Which of the following statements is true?

    I.   If a CFP® professional must earn continuing education credits from a licensing board other than CFP® Board, he/she does not have to meet CFP continuing education credits.

    II. A CFP® professional shall not engage in any conduct that reflects adversely on his or her integrity or fitness as a CFP® professional.

    III. All CFP® professionals are prohibited from actively practicing other professions and offering services in related fields, regardless of license and practice standards.

    a.   I only

    b.   II only

    c.   III only

    d.   II and III only

    e.   I, II, and III

12. A CFP® professional must have and use a written disclosure form that includes which of the following?

    a.   A statement of philosophy the professional adopts when working with clients.

    b.   A statement identifying conflicts of interest.

    c.   A statement disclosing how the professional receives compensation.

    d.   All of the above.

13. CFP Board *Practice Standards and Code of Ethics* state that a CFP® professional must always make timely disclosures of all material information to clients. Which of the following forms will meet this requirement?

    a.   SEC Form ADV, Part II.

    b.   Form FPD—Disclosure Form—provided by CFP Board.

    c.   A statement of the planners' life and business philosophy.

    d.   All of the above.

    e.   Only a and b.

14. In which of the following situations is it impermissible to reveal personal information about a client?

    a. To establish a brokerage account for a client.

    b. While the planner is being audited for his or her own tax return.

    c. To defend the CFP® professional against charges of wrongdoing.

    d. In a civil dispute between the CFP® professional and the client.

15. After finding out what Ashley had done, Bill terminated his working relationship with her and requested that she return all documents about his account immediately. Is Ashley in violation of any rule under the Principle of Professionalism if one year goes by and she fails to return Bill's original documents used in the financial planning process?

    a. Yes, because she is not allowed under the rules to hold original client documents.

    b. No, CFP Board gives planners at least two years to return files to terminated clients.

    c. Yes, because principles and rules require that she return the documents in a timely fashion.

    e. No, a CFP® professional is under no legal, moral, or ethical responsibility to return client data. In fact, this information must be retained by the planner in case of an audit.

16. Which of the following statements is true?

    I. According to the Principle of Professionalism, a CFP® professional is not allowed to practice any profession unless a license is required by law.

    II. The Principle of Confidentiality states that the same standards of confidentiality must be held between the CFP® professional, employers, and clients.

    III. The Principle of Diligence states that a planner must make only recommendations that are suitable for each client.

    a. I only

    b. II only

    c. II and III only

    d. I, II, and III

17. Ashley, as a CFP® professional, is required to properly supervise subordinates when dealing with the subordinate's delivery of financial planning services. Which of the following would be considered properly supervised?

    a. An intern makes recommendations that have not been reviewed by Ashley to a client.

    b. Ashley's office manager, Marge, who is not licensed, is asked to research and suggest stocks to be included in a client's portfolio.

   c. A licensed intern, before making a client recommendation, reviews the recommendation with Ashley.

   d. An intern, who is not licensed, makes a trade, with Ashley's permission, in a client's account while Ashley is at lunch.

18. Which of the following statements is true?

   a. When Ashley contacted Jane about Bill's divorce plans, she was also required by CFP Board *Practice Standards and Code of Ethics* to disclose conflicts of interest in writing.

   b. Instructing the broker to purchase penny stocks was a violation of the CFP Board *Practice Standards and Code of Ethics*, which require implementing strategies suitable for the client.

   c. Sharing information about Bill and Jane with Phil Rheem is a direct violation of CFP Board *Practice Standards and Code of Ethics*.

   d. All of the above are true.

   e. Only a and c are true.

19. Which of the following statements is true in relation to Ashley's reallocation of Bill Jackson's investment assets?

   a. FINRA would find that these investments were unsuitable for Bill.

   b. Ashley would be held harmless against a claim of unsuitability because she, in fact, conducted some research on the stocks before making the purchases.

   c. Her actions are a prime example of churning.

   d. If Ashley had discretion over Bill's account, she was entirely within her rights to make the penny stock purchases.

20. CFP Board *Practice Standards and Code of Ethics* rules state that a CFP® professional must offer advice only in the areas in which he or she is competent to do so. Ashley has obviously broken rules related to Principle 3. Why? Choose the best possible answer.

   a. Ashley did not gain enough information from Bill before entering into the relationship with Jane.

   b. Jane should have recognized Ashley's conflict of interest.

   c. Ashley was unable to meet Bill's needs and objectives adequately.

   d. Ashley was unable to provide competent services because of the conflict of interest concerning her friendship with Jane.

Index

Key words are in **bold.**